*To
Daniel Charles Sager,
James Jeffrey Sager,
Shannon Lynne Sager*

The Elgar Dictionary of Economic Quotations

The Elgar Dictionary of Economic Quotations

Edited by
Charles Robert McCann Jr.
*Research Associate, Department of Economics,
University of Pittsburgh, USA*

Edward Elgar
Cheltenham, UK • Northampton, MA, USA

© Charles Robert McCann Jr. 2003

All rights reserved. No part of this publication may be reproduced, stored in a retrieval system or transmitted in any form or by any means, electronic, mechanical or photocopying, recording, or otherwise without the prior permission of the publisher.

Published by
Edward Elgar Publishing Limited
Glensanda House
Montpellier Parade
Cheltenham
Glos GL50 1UA
UK

Edward Elgar Publishing, Inc.
136 West Street
Suite 202
Northampton
Massachusetts 01060
USA

A catalogue record for this book
is available from the British Library

Library of Congress Cataloguing in Publication Data

The Elgar dictionary of economic quotations/edited by Charles Robert McCann Jr.
   p.cm.
   'This collection . . . was initiated by a suggestion of Edward Elgar at the January 2001 meeting of the American Economic Association in New Orleans'—P.
   Includes bibliographical references and index.
   1. Economics—Quotations, maxims, etc. 2. Economists—Quotations. I. Title: Dictionary of economic quotations. II. McCann, Charles R. (Charles Robert), 1956– III. Edward Elgar Publishing.

PN6084.E36E44 2004
330—dc21
                                                                                    2003049103

ISBN 1 84064 820 1 (cased)

Typeset by Cambrian Typesetters, Frimley, Surrey
Printed and bound in Great Britain by MPG Books Ltd, Bodmin, Cornwall

Contents

Preface	vii
Notes on Appearance	ix
Acknowledgements	xi
Dictionary of Economic Quotations	1
References	223
Index	249

Preface

Very often, economists and other social scientists, as well as public officials, journalists, pamphleteers, and others in the business of public persuasion, require in their writings, speeches, and pronouncements some rhetorical device beyond that of the argument itself. Typically this device is a resort to quotations from those great and near-great authorities of the past. Many an argument that may be otherwise unsustainable on the merits seems to take on legitimacy and purpose when dressed in the words of a distinguished intellectual, beloved social or cultural figure, or esteemed wit.

At times it appears as though every writer and critic thinks himself qualified to offer opinions on the state of the economy, whether or not he actually has any knowledge of or expertise in the area, and seeks to justify his contributions to the debates through reference to the great works of the past, to which he of course establishes agreement. One problem that frequently arises, however, is that the quotations employed to this end are either misstated, erroneously attributed, incomplete, or taken out of the context in which they were originally presented. This is especially so in regard to ruminations on the state of the economy and to matters economic. What is needed is a sourcebook of passages relating to matters of economic import, a guide through which references can be checked. Thus the need for a dictionary of economic quotations.

This collection of quotations is by economists and others on topics of specific interest to *economists* – although one may hope it has an appeal to social scientists in general and to others interested in the areas covered under the rubric of economics as well. There have of course been other efforts at collecting in encapsulated form the economic wit and wisdom of the past – especially notable are *A Dictionary of Economic Quotations*, edited by Simon James (London: Croom Helm, 1981, 1984), and *The Macmillan Book of Social Science Quotations: Who Said What, When, and Where*, edited by David L. Sills and Robert K. Merton (New York: Macmillan, 1991) – but the present work is designed to be different. First, while the arrangement is alphabetical by author, within each such heading the quotations are categorized by topic. This allows the reader greater ease in searching – one need not peruse an entire list of material of a favorite author to discover a quote of interest on a specific topic, for each topic is clearly identified within each author heading.

Second, the extent of the coverage is different. More often than not, a dictionary of quotations will present some pithy phrase in isolation from its context, as though the expression itself holds the key to understanding a complex philosophical position. One seems to find support on some such issue, while in reality the actual context of the passage is suggestive of quite another meaning altogether. This is not the method employed here, for this is not primarily a dictionary of *phrases*. The context is at least as significant as the phraseology. Adam Smith's two statements of the invisible hand cannot be appreciated apart from the contexts in which they occur; one would be the poorer if the imageries of Thomas Robert Malthus, David Ricardo, and John Stuart Mill were reduced to trite passages devoid of the elegance which has largely been responsible for their continued appeal; the literary stylings of George Bernard Shaw and Robert Southey would hold little interest or meaning to social scientists divorced from their settings. Here the decision was made to include as much material as necessary for the reader to appreciate the *argument* presented, as well as the phrases which have come to such importance.

Third, while the selection of writers is somewhat eclectic, it is not without a purpose. The book is designed not so much as a survey of the ideas presented within the dominant economic texts as it is a compendium of ideas on topics of interest to economists and writers on economic subjects. Among those included here are many non-economists – scientists, sociologists, politicians, political agitators, jurists, essayists, theologians, poets, philosophers, religious figures are among those who have contributed to an understanding of economic problems, and who have provided some of the more interesting observations of economic phenomena, broadly defined. After all, it was the essayist Thomas Carlyle who dubbed political economy 'the Dismal Science,' the philosopher Francis Bacon who observed that 'Money is like Muck,' and the United States Supreme Court Chief Justice John Marshall who declared that 'An unlimited power to tax involves, necessarily, a power to destroy.'

One may object that the many non-economists have been accorded more space than those typically recognized as economists. The American clergyman Francis Wayland has ten entries, the British critic and writer John Ruskin fourteen, and Pope Leo XIII five, while Nobel Prize winners Lawrence Klein, Gerard Debreu, and Robert Lucas have, respectively, but three, two, and one. This is not to imply that the non-economists were and are more influential than the economists, or even that, as they have often appealed to a greater audience, they are somehow deserving of more acclaim. It is simply to argue that what they have written is so more interesting, more pointed, more directed to the issues of interest, and that their positions have a greater immediacy and even a more dramatic quality, style, and wit missing from the more technical jargon of the professional economist.

Finally, it is abundantly clear that some may have difficulties with the selections, both with the choice of authors and with the range, depth, and scope of quotations. Undoubtedly some favorite author has been ignored or appears to have been given short shrift, or a particularly sanguine quote did not make the cut and so has upset the reader. So be it. All I have to say is, this is the reason for second editions.

Notes on Appearance

(1). To the greatest extent possible, quotations are from the earliest editions available of a work. Where the earliest editions were not available, 'standard editions' have been used, and the dates given reflect this. For example, the standard edition of Adam Smith's *Wealth of Nations*, initially published in 1776, is the edition edited by Edwin Cannan in 1937, which follows the text of the fifth edition of 1789. In the case of a non-English work, the year given is that of the edition translated, so that, for example, Léon Walras' *Élements de Économie Pure – Elements of Pure Economics* – is dated 1926, while the original French edition appeared in 1871.

(2). There has been no attempt made to correct for misspellings or otherwise to alter passages, except (1) when extraneous material is excised, where no loss of meaning is thought to occur, (2) where a passage is to begin in the middle of a sentence, and (3) when additional material is deemed essential to understanding. In each case, the appropriate marks – ellipses, square brackets – are employed. With respect to modern works, [sic] is inserted to denote a typographical error or misspelling as it appeared in the original work, while for those early works – typically of the seventeenth and eighteenth centuries, but extending as well into the nineteenth — as the spelling had yet to be standardized and so is frequently inconsistent, the text was left as it appears.

(3). All italics are as they appear in the original. Should an entire quotation be presented in italics, this is retained.

Acknowledgements

This collection of quotations was initiated by a suggestion of Edward Elgar at the January 2001 meeting of the American Economic Association in New Orleans. To him I am profoundly grateful for the opportunity.

In putting together this compendium, extensive use was made of the resources of Hillman Library of the University of Pittsburgh, the Hunt Library of Carnegie-Mellon University, and the Carnegie Library of Pittsburgh. In addition, the Darlington Library of the University of Pittsburgh made available an 1848 first American edition of John Stuart Mill's *Principles of Political Economy*, from which the quotations herein were selected. (Readers will undoubtedly notice differences between these passages and the material in the Ashley edition of the same work. One will also note the Americanized spellings of certain words.) The databases of the Making of America websites – at Cornell University and the University of Michigan – were invaluable sources of scarce and otherwise unavailable material, as was the Early English Books Online site. Where possible, these sources were checked against actual (hard) copies of the same works. Lastly, essays appearing in British periodicals of the Victorian period – especially the *Edinburgh Review* and *Westminster Review* – characteristically had no assigned author. These essays, which provide many of the more interesting and colorful quotations, are listed and the authors identified in the *Wellesley Index of Victorian Periodicals* (Toronto: University of Toronto Press), which proved to be an invaluable source of information.

Although virtually all the material presented here was researched by me, and so I alone am responsible for any disagreements readers may have as to inclusion and exclusion, I would like to thank Robert Dimand, Andrea Micocci, Mark Perlman, and Alex Viskavotoff for providing favorite quotes and even suggesting favorite writers whose work, I was to discover, simply could not have been excluded. While I could not take all their suggestions into consideration, I am nonetheless appreciative of the interest shown. I also wish to thank Dymphna Evans and Bob Pickens of Edward Elgar Publishing for handling the task of shepherding the manuscript through production.

A

Henry Jacob Aaron (1936–)

economics and economists:

1 Behind most economic analysis meant to influence policy lies an explicit view of government. Although most economists proclaim skepticism regarding the efficiency of government action or of the goodwill of politicians, the view implicit in most of their work is of an efficient and beneficent state.

'Politics and the Professors Revisited' (1989), Sec.III: 12

Henry Carter Adams (1851–1921)

laissez-faire:

1 A tyranny which springs from the unregulated workings of self-interest is as pernicious in its results, and presses as hardly upon the individual, as a tyranny which rests upon political privilege. . . . [T]he science of industrial society has not rendered to humanity the highest service of which it is capable, until its analysis of social relations discovers some principle for the guidance of legislation in directing or limiting competitive action.

'Relation of the State to Industrial Action' (1887) – 'The Test of Conservatism': 82

wealth distribution:

2 Wealth will not perform its true ministry until it is so distributed that the necessity of excessive toil shall disappear. Then, and not till then, will the thought that labor and pain are bound together in the constitution of things be remembered among the superstitions of the past. Then, and not till then, will man have entered into the possession of that liberty which is his by nature of his manhood and rendered possible by the service of inventions.

'The Social Ministry of Wealth' (1894): 182

George Arthur Akerlof (1940–)

economics and economists:

1 [E]conomic theorists, like French chefs in regard to food, have developed stylized models whose ingredients are limited by some unwritten rules. Just as traditional French cooking does not use seaweed or raw fish, so neoclassical models do not make assumptions derived from psychology, anthropology, or sociology. I disagree with any rules that limit the nature of the ingredients in economic models.

An Economic Theorist's Book of Tales (1984), Introduction: 2–3

Johan Henrik Åkerman (1896–1982)

economics and economists:

1 A review of recent contributions to economic theory tends to show – if attention is concentrated on the setting of the central problem, that in economics the time has not come to speak of many things, the time has come to speak of fundamental things.

'Annual Survey of Economic Theory: The Setting of the Central Problem' (1936), Sec.6: 122

methodology:

2 In the social sciences and especially in economics the real problem often coincides with the methodological problem. The result of the analysis is more or less a function of the setting of the inquiry. 'What do you want to know?' is intimately correlated with the question: 'What is your form of reasoning?'

Theory of Industrialism (1960), Ch.I, Sec.1: 11

Armen Albert Alchian (1914–)

property:

1 It seems to be a fact that individuals will not stand by idly while some other person's property is stolen. It seems to be a fact that

private property rights are rights not merely because the state formally makes them so but because individuals want such rights to be enforced, at least for a vast, overwhelming majority of people. And yet if I recognize the number of socialist states, I must admit to some confusion (I appeal for edification).
'Some Economics of Property Rights' (1965), Sec.3: 817

2   In essence, economics is the study of property rights. Without scarce resources property rights are pointless. The allocation of scarce resources in a society is the assignment of rights to uses of resources. So the question of economics, or of how prices should be determined, is the question of how property rights should be defined and exchanged, and on what terms.
Pricing and Society (1967): 6

Sir Roy George Douglas Allen
(1906–1983)

mathematics in economics:

1   [T]here can be no doubt that mathematical methods are *possible* in economics and that economic relations are expressible by means of mathematical functions. Whether it is *helpful* to introduce the mathematical technique is another question and it is not proposed to devote any space here to a discussion of this purely methodological matter. It is sufficient that mathematical analysis is applicable and can be called into service when convenient.
Mathematical Analysis for Economists (1938), Ch.V: 107

2   There is no longer any doubt that mathematical methods are appropriately and usefully employed in the development of economic theory. The question, rather, is whether the mathematics should be discarded in the final exposition or whether they should take their place in the main argument. Do mathematics form the scaffolding or the steel framework of the structure?
'The Mathematical Foundations of Economic Theory' (1949), Sec.I: 111; cf. Edgeworth 6

St. Thomas Aquinas (1225–1274)

property:

1   Community of goods is said to be part of the natural law not because the natural law decrees that all things are to be possessed in common and nothing held privately, but because the distribution of property is not a matter of natural law but of human agreement which pertains to the positive law. . . . Therefore private property is not against natural law but it has been added to natural law by the inventiveness of human reason.
Summa Theologiae II–II(1271–1272), Question 66, Sec.2

usury:

2   To receive interest (usury) for lending money is unjust in itself for something is sold that does not exist, and this obviously results in an inequality which is contrary to justice.
Summa Theologiae II–II(1271–1272), Question 78, Sec.1

3   Human laws leave some sins unpunished because of the imperfection of men who would lack many things that are useful to them if all sins were strictly prohibited by the application of legal penalties. Therefore human law allows usury not because it considers it just but to avoid interference with the useful activities of many people.
Summa Theologiae II–II(1271–1272), Question 78, Sec.1

George Christopher Archibald
(1926–)

economics and economists:

1   Accepting non-testable conclusions is a simple act of faith; if the conclusions of welfare economics were non-testable, the whole subject would be metaphysics.
'Welfare Economics, Ethics, and Essentialism' (1959): 326–327

Aristotle (384–322 BC)

exchange:

1   There are two sorts of wealth-getting . . .; one is a part of household management, the

other is retail trade: the former is necessary and honourable, while that which consists in exchange is justly censured; for it is unnatural, and a mode by which men gain from one another.
Politics, Bk.I, Sec.10 (1258a39–1258b3)

poverty:

2   One would have thought that it was even more necessary to limit population than property; and that the limit should be fixed by calculating the chances of mortality in the children, and of sterility in married persons. The neglect of this subject, which in existing states is so common, is a never–failing cause of poverty among the citizens; and poverty is the parent of revolution and crime.
Politics, Bk.II, Sec.6 (1265b5–1265b12)

property:

3   Property should be in a certain sense common, but, as a general rule, private; for, when everyone has a distinct interest, men will not complain of one another, and they will make more progress, because everyone will be attending to his own business.
Politics, Bk.II, Sec.5 (1263a25–29)

4   I do not think that property ought to be common, as some maintain, but only that by friendly consent there should be a common use of it; and that no citizen should be in want of subsistence.
Politics, Bk.VII, Sec.10 (1329b41–1330a2)

usury:

5   The most hated sort [of wealth-getting], and with the greatest reason, is usury, which makes a gain out of money itself, and not from the natural object of it. For money was intended to be used in exchange, but not to increase at interest. And this term interest, which means the birth of money from money, is applied to the breeding of money because the offspring resembles the parent. That is why of all modes of getting wealth this is the most unnatural.
Politics, Bk.I, Sec.10 (1258b3–8)

Kenneth Joseph Arrow (1921–)

economics and economists:

1   An economist by training thinks of himself as the guardian of rationality, the ascriber of rationality to others, and the prescriber of rationality to the social world.
The Limits of Organization (1974): 16

Sir William James Ashley (1860–1927)

economics and economists:

1   When one looks back on a century of economic teaching and writing, the chief lesson should, I feel, be one of caution and modesty, and especially when we approach the burning issues of our own day. We economists – for, whether we like it or not, we of to-day have to bear the sins of our predecessors – we economists have been so often in the wrong! On so very much that had to do with the condition of the great body of the people we were for half a century either so glaringly mistaken or so annoyingly unsympathetic that even to-day a man is ashamed to avow himself an economist in the face of an English working-class audience.
'The Present Position of Political Economy' (1907): 487–488

trade:

2   Among serious economists there is hardly one left who would maintain that theory is capable of furnishing a conclusive proof either of the wisdom or the unwisdom of free trade under all circumstances. Nothing is easier than to adduce a number of theoretic arguments on either side. The right decision in each case must be reached, not by abstract reasoning, but by estimating the concrete facts and probabilities which give the several arguments their due weight.
'The Present Position of Political Economy' (1907): 488

Edward Atkinson (1827–1905)
American businessman and pamphleteer

poverty and poor relief:

1   The remedy for poverty must . . . be sought in great measure by reform from within

rather than from without; from individual development rather than from the collective action either of State or of nation.
'A Single Tax Upon Land' (1890): 385

taxation:

2 Those who expect so much benefit from a mere change in the method of collecting taxes overlook the fact that *taxation* and *work* are synonymous terms.
'A Single Tax Upon Land' (1890): 386; cf. Henry George 8

3 Taxes will not stay where they are put; if they would, the tax question could be solved with very little difficulty.
'A Single Tax Upon Land' (1890): 388

Lyman Hotchkiss Atwater
(1813–1883)
American philosopher, social scientist

economics and economists:

1 The definitions given of political economy by its great expounders are no more numerous or conflicting than those of logic, a science of apodictic certainty, and one to which everything truly scientific must conform; nay, they are less so than those given of science itself by the leading authorities. All definitions of any science in its immature state are necessarily provisional.
'Political Economy a Science – Of What?' (1880): 425

Clarence Edwin Ayres (1891–1972)

capitalism:

1 [T]he socialists have perennially insisted that economic 'science' is a conscious partisan defense of capitalism. But this implies that economists have been the defenders of capitalists, and such is certainly not the case. From Adam Smith to the latest of his followers economists have been virtually unanimous in deploring the character and behavior which unfortunately seem to be typical of the capitalist. If they have nevertheless accepted him, that is not because they feel moved to approve and defend him, but because they regard him, disagreeable as he is, as the human vehicle of capital accumulation, and because they consider capital accumulation the essential economic function.
The Problem of Economic Order (1938), Ch.III, Sec.20: 54

2 Societies make mistakes. They also make discoveries. The discoveries mean progress. But the discoveries get mixed up with the mistakes, and this retards the progress. That is what happened in the case of capitalism.
The Divine Right of Capital (1946), Part I, Ch.2: 7

economics and economists:

3 Economics is the study of the activities in which men engage in getting a living.
The Problem of Economic Order (1938), Ch.I, Sec.1: 3

4 The classical economists quite properly endeavored to be scientists. They had read Newton and respected his achievements, and they tried to approach the analysis of the economic order in his spirit. This could not be done mathematically, of course. The mathematical laws of gravitation and the rest have no application to economics.
The Problem of Economic Order (1938), Ch.III, Sec.15: 38

5 Price theory is all things to all men.
The Theory of Economic Progress (1944), Ch.I

6 So long as economics has remained by common consent the science of price, any particular aspersion upon any particular principle could only be followed by the elaboration of other principles to substantially the same effect.
The Theory of Economic Progress (1944), Ch.I

7 Economists are members of a highly skilled profession. By long practice and by use of a multitude of adroit literary devices they have been able to bring the art of double-vision and double-talk to a high degree of perfection.
The Divine Right of Capital (1946), Part I, Ch.1: 4

8 Economists have done only what professional thinkers always do: they have organized and

systematized the ideas of the community. If the basic ideas are right, the system will be right; if they are wrong, the system will be wrong.
> *The Divine Right of Capital* (1946), Part I, Ch.1: 4

9   Economics seeks to break down the whole congeries of social organization so as to distinguish the economic system and the forces at work in it from the other systems, which together comprise organized society, and the forces at work in them. In doing so, economics necessarily makes considerable use of the term, 'institutions,' since this is one of the basic categories, if not the basic category, of all social analysis.
> *The Industrial Economy* (1952), Ch.2, Sec.4: 42

money:

10 In our society money is power. Money makes the mare go. When any one of us allows himself to daydream, what does he imagine? How do we symbolize success and happiness? Everybody knows! We dream of being rich.
> *The Divine Right of Capital* (1946), Part I, Ch.1: 5

William Edmonstoune Aytoun
(1813–1865)
Scottish poet

economics and economists:

1   [T]he whole race of political economists are cast into dismay by the aspect of the apparition which they have evoked, so widely differing from that which they really expected to appear.
> 'Latter Days of the Free-Trade Ministry' (1851): 506

trade:

2   [W]hat is to become of our people, whom free trade is reducing to pauperism? The political economist, whose heart is as hard as the machinery he drives, will scarcely pause for a moment to answer so trivial a question. His *ultimatum* is, the factory, the workhouse, or emigration.
> 'Our Currency, Our Trade, and Our Tariff' (1847): 765

3   We have tried free trade, and it has failed.
> 'Our Currency, Our Trade, and Our Tariff' (1847): 765

B

Charles Babbage (1791–1871)

manufacturing:

1 The first object of every person who attempts to make any article of consumption, is, or ought to be, to produce it in a perfect form; but in order to secure to himself the greatest and most permanent profit, he must endeavour, by every means in his power, to render the new luxury or want which he has created, cheap to those who consume it.
   The Economy of Machinery and Manufactures (1835; 4th edn), Ch.XIII, Sec. 163: 85

taxation:

2 As soon as a tax is put upon any article, the ingenuity of those who make, and of those who use it, is directed to the means of evading as large a part of the tax as they can; and this may often be accomplished in ways which are perfectly fair and legal.
   The Economy of Machinery and Manufactures (1835; 4th edn), Ch.XXXIII, Sec. 414: 236

Roger Ward Babson (1875–1967)

government:

1 The purpose of every *worthwhile* government, institution, and other organization is to make people more truly happy. Moreover, a really happy nation must be prosperous.
   The Future of Nations (1914), First Section: 11

Francis Bacon, Baron Verulam of Verulam, Viscount St. Albans (1561–1626)

concentration of wealth:

1 Above all things, good Policie is to be used, that the Treasure and Moneyes, in a State, be not gathered into few Hands. For otherwise, a State may have a great Stock, and yet starve. And Money is like Muck, not good except it be spread. This is done, chiefly, by suppressing, or at the least, keeping a strait Hand, upon the Devouring Trades of *Usurie*, *Ingrossing*, great *Pasturages*, and the like.
   The Essays (1625), Essay XV, 'Of Seditions and Troubles'

entrepreneurship:

2 The *Fortune*, in being the First in an *Invention*, or in a *Priviledge*, doth cause sometimes a wonderfull Overgrowth in *Riches*; As it was with the first Sugar Man, in the *Canaries*: Therefore, if a Man can play the true *Logician*, to have as well Judgement, as Invention, he may do great Matters; especially if the Times be fit. He that resteth upon *Gaines Certain*, shall hardly grow to great *Riches*: And he that puts all upon *Adventures*, doth often times breake, and come to Poverty: It is good therefore, to guard *Adventures* with *Certainties*, that may uphold losses.
   The Essays (1625), Essay XXXIV, 'Of Riches'

innovation:

3 As the Births of Living Creatures, at first, are ill shapen: So are all *Innovations*, which are the Births of Time.
   The Essays (1625), Essay XXIV, 'Of Innovations'

taxation:

4 Neither will it be, that a People over laid with *Taxes*, should ever become Valiant, and Martiall. It is true, that *Taxes* levied by Consent of the Estate, doe abate Mens Courage lesse. . . . For you must note, that we speake now, of the Heart, and not of the Purse. So that, although the same *Tribute* and *Tax*, laid by Consent, or by Imposing, be all one to the Purse, yet it workes diversly upon the Courage. So that you may conclude; *That no People, over-charged with Tribute, it fit for Empire*.
   The Essays (1625), Essay XXIX, 'Of the True Greatnesse of Kingdomes and Estates'

usury:

5 I say this onely, that *Usury* is a *Concessum propter Duritiem Cordis*: For Since there must be Borrowing and Lending, and Men are so hard of Heart, as they will not lend freely, *Usury* must be permitted.
The Essays (1625), Essay XLI, 'Of Usurie'

Walter Bagehot (1826–1877)

banking:

1 A system of credit which has slowly grown up as years went on, which has suited itself to the course of business, which has forced itself on the habits of men, will not be altered because theorists disapprove of it, or because books are written against it.
Lombard Street (1873), Ch.XIII: 160

business:

2 Business is really more agreeable than pleasure; it interests the whole mind, the aggregate nature of man more continuously, and more deeply. But it does not *look* as if it did.
The English Constitution (1872; 2nd edn), Ch.(No.)IV ('The House of Lords'): 117–118

capital:

3 Complete freedom of capital presupposes complete freedom of labour, and can only be attained when and where this exists.
'The Postulates of English Political Economy: II' (1876): 729

4 If capital is to be tempted from trade to trade by the prospect of high profits, it must be allowed to keep those profits when they have been made.
'The Postulates of English Political Economy: II' (1876): 736

economics and economists:

5 [N]o real English gentleman, in his secret soul, was ever sorry for the death of a political economist: he is much more likely to be sorry for his life.
'The First Edinburgh Reviewers' (1855): 164

6 [Political economy] assumes that every man who makes anything, makes it for money, that he always makes that which brings him in most at least cost, and that he will make it in the way that will produce most and spend least; it assumes that every man who buys, buys with his whole heart, and that he who sells, sells with his whole heart, each wanting to gain all possible advantage. Of course we know that this is not so, that men are not like this; but we assume it for simplicity's sake, as an hypothesis. And this deceives many excellent people, for from deficient education they have very indistinct ideas what an abstract science is.
'The Postulates of English Political Economy: I' (1876), Sec.I: 218

7 [P]olitical economy is in no sense the highest study of mind – there are others which are much higher, for they are concerned with things much nobler than wealth or money. . . .
'The Postulates of English Political Economy: I' (1876), Sec.I: 218

8 [Political economy] is an abstract science which labours under a special hardship. Those who are conversant with its abstractions are usually without a true contact with its facts; those who are in contact with its facts have usually little sympathy with and little cognizance of its abstractions.
'The Postulates of English Political Economy: I' (1876), Sec.I: 219

9 And here we come across another of the inevitable verbal difficulties of Political Economy. Taking its words from common life, it finds that at times and for particular discussions it must twist them in a way which common people would never think of. . . . Political Economy (like most moral sciences) requires not only to change its definitions as it moves from problem to problem, but also for some problems to use definitions which, unless we see the motive, seem most strange. . . .
'The Postulates of English Political Economy: II' (1876): 726–727

government:

10 All Governments like to interfere; it elevates their position to make out that they can cure the evils of mankind.
'The Postulates of English Political Economy: I' (1876), Sec.I: 217

money:

11 No nation which was not clever enough to invent a money, was ever able to conceive so thin and hard an idea as 'exchangeable value.'
'The Postulates of English Political Economy: II' (1876): 721

12 But money is never 'second-hand'; it will always fetch itself, and it loses nothing by keeping.
'The Postulates of English Political Economy: II' (1876): 722

taxation:

13 [T]he primitive notion of taxation is that when a government sees much money it should take some of it, and that if it sees more money it should take more of it.
'The Postulates of English Political Economy: II' (1876): 736

Samuel Bailey (1791–1870)

economics and economists:

1 The object of Political Economy is not to ascertain all the laws by which wealth is produced and distributed, but only one class of them, namely, the moral or mental laws, or, in other words, those laws of human nature on which the economical condition of nations depends. It has nothing to do with investigating the comparative merits of systems of husbandry, or of road-making, or the superiority of one machine for making cloth over another – circumstances which may greatly affect the production and distribution of wealth, yet do not enter at all, or only incidentally, into the inquiries of this science. While these circumstances would fall respectively within the province of the agriculturist, the engineer, and the manufacturer, the political economist would be concerned only with investigating the motives or the principles of human nature which are brought into play in all these cases, together with their effects on the wealth of the community.
'On the Science of Political Economy' (1852): 109

2 Multifarious in its facts, and requiring great closeness in its deductions, it [political economy] must necessarily have erred in the past, and must still be imperfect for ages to come; but, in the mean time, it comprehends a large body of truths which cannot be neglected without individual detriment and national suffering.
'On the Science of Political Economy' (1852): 128

Thomas Balogh, Baron Balogh of Hampstead (1905–1985)

economics and economists:

1 The orthodox economists seem to use words not to elucidate but to distort their meaning.
The Dollar Crisis (1949), Ch.6: 195

Paul Alexander Baran (1910–1964)

Marxism:

1 Contrary to widespread opinion, Marxism is not and never was intended to be a 'positive science,' an assortment of statements about past and present facts, or a set of predictions about the shape or timing of future events. It was always an intellectual attitude, a way of thought, a philosophical position the fundamental principle of which is continuous, systematic, and comprehensive *confrontation of reality with reason*.
'On the Nature of Marxism' (1958), Sec.I: 259

Nicholas Barbon (c.1640–1698)

interest:

1 Interest is the Rule that the Merchant Trades by; And Time, the Artificer, By which they cast up Profit, and Loss; for if the Price of their Wares, so alter either by Plenty, or by Change of the Use, that they do not pay the Merchant Interest, nor the Artificer for his Time, they both reckon they lose by their Trade.
A Discourse of Trade (1690), 'Of the Value and Price of Wares': 19–20

2 Interest is commonly reckoned for Mony; because the Mony Borrowed at Interest, is to be repayed in Mony; but this is a mistake; For the Interest is paid for Stock: for the Mony borrowed, is laid out to buy Goods, or

pay for them before bought: No Man takes up Mony at Interest, to lay it by him, and lose the Interest of it.

    A Discourse of Trade (1690), 'Of Mony, Credit and Interest': 31–32

markets:

3 [T]he Market is the best Judge of Value; for by the Concourse of Buyers and Sellers, the Quantity of Wares, and the Occasion for them are Best known: Things are just worth so much, as they can be sold for, according to the Old Rule, *Valet Quantum Vendi potest.*

    A Discourse of Trade (1690), 'Of the Value and Price of Wares': 20

money and credit:

4 Mony is a Value made by a Law. . . .

    A Discourse of Trade (1690), 'Of Mony, Credit and Interest': 20

5 Credit is a Value raised by Opinion. . . .

    A Discourse of Trade (1690), 'Of Mony, Credit and Interest': 27

trade:

6 Prodigality is a Vice that is prejudicial to the Man, but not to *Trade*; It is living a pace, and spending that in a Year, that should last all his Life: Covetousness is a Vice, prejudicial both to Man & *Trade*; It starves the Man, and breaks the Trader; and by the same way the Covetous Man thinks he grows rich, he grows poor; for by not consuming the Goods that are provided for Man's Use, there ariseth a dead Stock, called Plenty, and the Value of those Goods fall, and the Covetous Man's Estates, whether in Land, or Mony, become less worth:. . . .

    A Discourse of Trade (1690), 'Of the Chief Causes That Promote Trade': 62–63

7 The common Argument for the Prohibiting Foreign Commodities, is, That the Bringing in, and Consuming such Foreign Wares, hinders the Making and Consuming the like sort of Goods of our own Native Make and Growth; . . . But this is a mistaken Reason, and ariseth by not considering what it is that Occasions *Trade*. It is not Necessity that causeth the Consumption, Nature may be Satisfied with little; but it is the wants of the Mind, Fashion, and desire of Novelties and things scarce, that causeth *Trade*. A Person may have *English*-Lace, Gloves, or Silk, as much as he wants, and will Buy no more such; and yet, lay out his Mony on a Point of *Venice*, *Jessimine*-Gloves, or *French*-Silks; he may desire to Eat *Westphalia* Bacon, when he will not *English*; so that, the Prohibition of Forreign Wares, does not necessarily cause a greater Consumption of the like sort of *English*.

    A Discourse of Trade (1690), 'Of the Chief Causes of the Decay of Trade in England, and Fall of the Rents of Land': 72–73

8 If the Suppressing or Prohibiting of some sorts of Goods, should prove an Advantage to the *Trader*, and Increase the Consumption of the same sort of our Native Commodity: Yet it may prove a Loss to the Nation. For the Advantage to the Nation from *Trade*, is, from the Customs, and from those Goods that Imploys most Hands. So that, tho' the Prohibition may Increase, as the Consumption of the like sort of the Native; yet if it should Obstruct the Transporting of other Goods which were Exchanged for them, that Paid more Custom, Freight, or Imployed more Hands in making; The Nation will be a loser by the Prohibition.

    A Discourse of Trade (1690), 'Of the Chief Causes of the Decay of Trade in England, and Fall of the Rents of Land': 75–76

value:

9 The Value of all Wares arise from their Use; Things of no Use, have no Value, as the *English* Phrase is, *They are good for nothing*.

    A Discourse of Trade (1690), 'Of the Value and Price of Wares': 13

wants:

10 The Wants of the Mind are infinite, Man naturally Aspires, and as his Mind is elevated, his Senses grow more refined, and more capable of Delight; his Desires are inlarged, and his Wants increase with his Wishes, which is for every thing that is rare, can gratifie his Senses, adorn his Body, and

promote the Ease, Pleasure, and Pomp of Life.
A Discourse of Trade (1690), 'Of the Value and Price of Wares': 15

Robert J. Barro (1944–)

economics and economists:

1 The panel of economists also considered briefly an award for the least efficient monopoly in America. This choice was easy. It goes to the American Economic Association, which has been a dismal failure at establishing licensing requirements or other restrictions on entry into the economics profession. It is a sad state of affairs when almost anyone can assume the title of economist.
Getting It Right (1996), Ch.4: 131

taxation:

2 [T]he problem with a good (efficient) tax is that it makes it too easy for the government to grow.
Getting It Right (1996), Ch.3: 126

Robert Leon Basmann (1926–)

econometrics:

1 The recommendations put forward by economists and econometricians are by no means uniquely or even narrowly determined by the empirical evidence and scientific economic hypotheses that are available, but also by the philosophic attitudes of the economists and econometricians towards the conduct of scientific investigation in economics.
'Argument and Evidence in the Brookings–S.S.R.C. Philosophy of Econometrics' (1972), Sec.1: 63

Charles Francis Bastable (1855–1945)

taxation:

1 There is no pure *a priori* system of taxation. Each state requires what is fitted for its special circumstances. The place of general principles is not to assist the financier in laying down hard and fast rules, but in indicating the forces that are likely to operate in all cases, but with varying intensity in each separate instance.
'Taxation Through Monopoly' (1891): 325

Claude Frédéric Bastiat (1801–1850)

economics and economists:

1 So here I am, discredited forever; and it is now an accepted fact that I am a *heartless, pitiless* man, a dry philosopher, an individualist, a bourgeois – in a word, an economist of the English or American school.
'The State' (1848): 142

2 Political economy takes priority over political science. The former determines whether human interests are naturally harmonious or antagonistic. The latter must know this before establishing the prerogatives of government.
'The Law' (1850), note 7: 327

3 There is only one difference between a bad economist and a good one: the bad economist confines himself to the *visible* effect; the good economist takes into account both the effect that can be seen and those effects that must be *foreseen*.
'What Is Seen and What Is Not Seen' (1850): 1

government:

4 Today, when it is an accepted principle that the function of the state is to distribute wealth to everybody, it is natural that the state is held accountable for this commitment. To keep it, it multiplies taxes and produces more poverty than it cures. With new demands on the part of the public and new taxes on the part of the state, we cannot but go from one revolution to another. But if it were well understood that the state can take from the workers only what is strictly indispensable to guarantee them against all fraud and all violence, I cannot perceive from what side disorder would come.
'Justice and Fraternity' (1848): 125–126

5 The *state*! What is it? Where is it? What does it do? What should it do?
All that we know about it is that it is a mysterious personage, and certainly the

most solicited, the most tormented, the busiest, the most advised, the most blamed, the most invoked, and the most provoked in the world.
'The State' (1848): 140

6 *The state is the great fictitious entity by which everyone seeks to live at the expense of everyone else.*
'The State' (1848): 144

7 The state understands ... very quickly the use it can make of the role the public entrusts to it. It will be the arbiter, the master, of all destinies. It will take a great deal; hence, a great deal will remain for itself. It will multiply the number of its agents; it will enlarge the scope of its prerogatives; it will end by acquiring overwhelming proportions.
'The State' (1848): 144

socialism:

8 [L]egal plunder can be committed in an infinite number of ways; hence, there are an infinite number of plans for organizing it: tariffs, protection, bonuses, subsidies, incentives, the progressive income tax, free education, the right to employment, the right to profit, the right to wages, the right to relief, the right to the tools of production, interest-free credit, etc., etc. And it is the aggregate of all these plans, in respect to what they have in common, legal plunder, that goes under the name of *socialism*.
'The Law' (1850): 61–62

9 Socialism, like the ancient political ideology from which it emanates, confuses government with society. That is why, every time that we do not want a thing to be done by the government, the socialists conclude that we do not want that thing to be done at all. We are opposed to state education; hence, we are opposed to all education. We object to a state religion; hence, we do not want any religion at all. We are against an equality imposed by the state; hence, we are opposed to equality; etc., etc. It is as if they accused us of not wanting men to eat, because we oppose the cultivation of grain by the state.
'The Law' (1850): 68

10 In fact, they [the socialists] begin by supposing that men are endowed with neither motivation nor discernment; that they are devoid of initiative; that they are constituted of inert matter, of passive particles, of atoms without spontaneity, at the most a form of vegetation indifferent to its own mode of existence, susceptible of receiving from an external will and hand an infinite number of more or less symmetrical, artistic, and perfected forms.
'The Law' (1850): 68–69

taxation:

11 You compare the nation to a parched piece of land and the tax to a life-giving rain. So be it. But you should also ask yourself where this rain comes from, and whether it is not precisely the tax that draws the moisture from the soil and dries it up.
'What Is Seen and What Is Not Seen' (1850), Sec.3: 8

12 When it is a question of taxes, gentlemen, prove their usefulness by reasons with some foundation, but not with that lamentable assertion: 'Public spending keeps the working class alive.' It makes the mistake of covering up a fact that it is essential to know: namely, that *public spending* is *always* a substitute for *private spending*, and that consequently it may well support one worker in place of another but adds nothing to the lot of the working class taken as a whole. Your argument is fashionable, but it is quite absurd, for the reasoning is not correct.
'What Is Seen and What Is Not Seen' (1850), Sec.4: 16

Peter Thomas (Pieter Tamas) Bauer, Baron Bauer of Market Ward in the City of Cambridge
(1915–2002)

economics and economists:

1 The exposure of economics to political influences and to intellectual fashion is likely to ensure the persistence of its confused state, in which there will continue to flourish side by side genuine advances of knowledge, meretricious displays of technique, and crude lapses which acquire a life of their own.
Equality, the Third World, and Economic Delusion (1981), Ch.15, Sec.8: 266

foreign aid:

2 Foreign aid is central to the economic relations between the West and the Third World. It will remain so long as there is a Third World. The Third World and its antecedents and synonyms, such as the underdeveloped world, the less developed world and the developing world (all still used) and now also the South, are for all practical purposes the collection of countries whose governments, with the odd exception, demand and receive official aid from the West. The concept of the Third World or the South and the policy of official aid are inseparable. They are two sides of the same coin. The Third World is the creation of foreign aid: without foreign aid there is no Third World.
Equality, the Third World, and Economic Delusion (1981), Ch.5, Sec.2: 87

mathematics in economics:

3 An uncritical attitude to mathematical methods has inhibited understanding, and obscured or confused basic issues. It has thereby contributed to the survival or spread of simple transgressions. As a result substantial areas of economics have become less informative than they were before this burgeoning of mathematical methods. Such an untoward and unexpected outcome is not a consequence of the adoption of mathematical methods but only of their inappropriate employment.
Equality, the Third World, and Economic Delusion (1981), Ch.15, Sec.6: 262–263

poverty and the poor laws:

4 Relief of poverty, especially the improvement in the position of the very poor, has nothing to do with the pursuit of equality. The policies of egalitarianism often ignore the poor, especially those who are self-reliant and enterprising.
Equality, the Third World, and Economic Delusion (1981), Ch.1, Sec.10: 23

5 [T]he pursuit of economic equality is more likely to harm than to benefit the living standards of the very poor by politicizing life, by restricting the accumulation and effective deployment of capital, by obstructing social and economic mobility at all levels, and by inhibiting enterprise in many different ways. Continued poverty, whether resulting from soi-disant egalitarian measures or from other causes, then serves as plausible argument or rationalization for further and more stringent egalitarianism. These repercussions are necessarily ignored when the promotion of equality and the alleviation of poverty are regarded as identical.
Equality, the Third World, and Economic Delusion (1981), Ch.1, Sec.10: 23–24

Peter Thomas (Pieter Tamas) Bauer, Baron Bauer of Market Ward in the City of Cambridge (1915–2002) and Alan Arthur Walters (1926–)

econometrics:

1 The prestige of econometrics has probably contributed to the widespread tendency to forget that in social study quantification is often, perhaps even generally, meaningless without going behind the figures.
'The State of Economics' (1975), Sec.4: 19

economics and economists:

2 The familiar difficulties of laymen in coming to grips with certain simple and fundamental ideas of economics have come to afflict the practitioners themselves.
'The State of Economics' (1975), Sec.1: 4

mathematics in economics:

3 The prestige of mathematical methods has drawn many practitioners into areas in which they were not at home. This has induced a sense of insecurity in many economists which in turn has not only placed them at the mercy of intellectual fashion, but has even loosened their grip on fundamentals and blinded them to the pertinence and use of established knowledge and readily available evidence. This influence operates in two directions. Some economists with modest analytical ability or competence in mathematics are drawn into mathematical or quasi-mathematical economics; and some mathematical economists address themselves to practical problems where they ignore many of the basic pertinent issues. Both forms of false position induce intellectual insecurity.
'The State of Economics' (1975), Sec.3: 16

William Jack Baumol (1922–)

mathematics in economics:

1. Programming, both linear and nonlinear, is entirely a mathematical technique. Its economic content is therefore nil.
   'Activity Analysis in One Lesson' (1958), Sec.I: 837

methodology:

2. There surely is no philosopher's stone in economic method – no one approach whose unqualified success and power mean that it deserves to replace all (or even any) of its rivals. *Every* method used in the social sciences has its glaring shortcomings which one can only hope to ameliorate by recourse, as a supplement, to other approaches. Here, if anywhere, there is need to let a thousand flowers bloom, and there is, consequently, no reason to impede or discourage the work of even the most abstraction-minded and esoteric of mathematical economists.
   'Toward a Newer Economics: The Future Lies Ahead!' (1991), Sec.I.A: 2

Gary Stanley Becker (1930–)

altruism:

1. I believe that altruism is less common in market transactions and more common in families because altruism is less 'efficient' in the marketplace and more 'efficient' in families.
   A Treatise on the Family (1981), Ch.8: 194

family:

2. [I]f a head [of a household] exists, *other members also are motivated to maximize family income and consumption, even if their welfare depends on their own consumption alone.* ...
   In other words, when one member cares sufficiently about other members to be the head, all members have the same motivation as the head to maximize family opportunities and to internalize fully all within-family 'externalities,' regardless of how selfish (or, indeed, how envious) these members are.
   'A Theory of Social Interactions' (1974), Sec.3.A: 1080

This, an early version of the Rotten Kid Theorem, was later reformulated as:

3. Rotten Kid Theorem. Each beneficiary, no matter how selfish, maximizes the family income of his benefactor and thereby internalizes all effects of his actions on other beneficiaries.
   A Treatise on the Family (1981), Ch.8: 183

rationality:

4. My work may have sometimes assumed too much rationality, but I believe it has been an antidote to the extensive research that does not credit people with enough rationality.
   Accounting for Tastes (1996), Part II, Ch.7, Sec.6: 155–156

Daniel Bell (1919–)
American sociologist

capitalism:

1. The cultural, if not moral, justification of capitalism has become hedonism, the idea of pleasure as a way of life. And in the liberal ethos that now prevails, the model for a cultural imago has become the modernist impulse, with its ideological rationale of the impulse quest as a mode of conduct. It is this which is the cultural contradiction of capitalism. It is this which has resulted in the double bind of modernity.
   The Cultural Contradictions of Capitalism (1976), Introduction: 21–22

Jeremy Bentham (1748–1832)

economics and economists:

1. Political economy may be considered as a science or as an art. But in this instance, as in others, it is only as a guide to the art that the science is of use.
   Manual of Political Economy (1793–95), Part I, Sec.1: 223

2. Political economy is at once a science and an art. The value of the science has for its efficient cause and measure its subserviency to the art.
   Institute of Political Economy (1801–4), 'The Science,' Sec.1: 318

government:

3 The great object, the great *desideratum*, is to know what ought and what ought not to be done by government. It is in this view, and in this view only, that the knowledge of what is done and takes place without the interference of government can be of any practical use.
Manual of Political Economy (1793–95), Part I, Sec.1: 224

4 Eating is as indubitably beneficial as trade, and more immediately so: it is a wonder that no politician in his wisdom ever thought of giving bounties upon eating.
Manual of Political Economy (1793–95), Part I, Sec.4: 233–234

taxation:

5 The natural and only original object of taxation is *revenue*....
Manual of Political Economy (1793–95), Part II, Sec.15: 257

6 A tax, in as far as the thing taxed is abstained from, operates as a prohibition: as a discouragement to that branch of trade or production to which the thing belongs, and as an encouragement to rival branches, that is more or less to all other branches.
Institute of Political Economy (1801–4), 'The Art,' Part III, Sec.2: 363

usury:

7 [N]o man of ripe years and of sound mind, acting freely, and with his eyes open, ought to be hindered, with a view to his advantage, from making such bargain, in the way of obtaining money, as he thinks fit: nor, (what is a necessary consequence) *any body hindered from supplying him, upon any terms he thinks proper to accede to*.
Defence of Usury (1787), Letter I: 129

utility:

8 Nature has placed mankind under the governance of two sovereign masters, *pain* and *pleasure*. It is for them alone to point out what we ought to do, as well as to determine what we shall do. On the one hand the standard of right and wrong, on the other the chain of causes and effects, are fastened to their throne. They govern us in all we do, in all we say, in all we think: every effort we can make to throw off our subjection, will serve but to demonstrate and confirm it. In words a man may pretend to abjure their empire: but in reality he will remain subject to it all the while The *principle of utility* recognises this subjection, and assumes it for the foundation of that system, the object of which is to rear the fabric of felicity by the hands of reason and of law. Systems which attempt to question it, deal in sounds instead of sense, in caprice instead of reason, in darkness instead of light.
The Principles of Morals and Legislation (1781), Ch.I, Sec.I: 1–2

9 By utility is meant that property in any object, whereby it tends to produce benefit, advantage, pleasure, good, or happiness, (all this in the present case comes to the same thing) or (what comes again to the same thing) to prevent the happening of mischief, pain, evil, or unhappiness to the party whose interest is considered: if that party be the community in general, then the happiness of the community: if a particular individual, then the happiness of that individual.
The Principles of Morals and Legislation (1781), Ch.I, Sec.III: 2

10 All value is founded on utility, on the use which can be made of the object. Where there is no use, there cannot be any value.
The True Alarm (1801), Book I, Ch.5: 83

George Berkeley, Bishop of Cloyne
(1685–1753)

government:

1 A private family in difficult circumstance, all men agree, ought to melt down their plate, walk on foot, retrench the number of their servants, wear neither jewels nor rich clothes, and deny themselves expensive diversions; and why not the public? Had anything like this been done, our taxes had been less, or, which is the same thing, we should have felt them less.
'An Essay Towards Preventing the Ruin of Great Britain' (1721): 76

money and credit:

2 Money is so far useful to the public as it promoteth industry, and credit having the

same effect is of the same value with money; but money or credit circulating through a nation from hand to hand without producing labour and industry in the inhabitants, is direct gaming.

'An Essay Towards Preventing the Ruin of Great Britain' (1721): 71

prosperity:

3   Men are apt to measure national prosperity by riches. It would be righter to measure it by the use that is made of them. Where they promote an honest commerce among men, and are motives to industry and virtue, they are, without doubt, of great advantage; but where they are made (as too often happens) an instrument to luxury, they enervate and dispirit the bravest people.

'An Essay Towards Preventing the Ruin of Great Britain' (1721): 74–75

wealth-creation:

4   The more methods there are in a State for acquiring riches without industry or merit, the less there will be of either in that State: this is as evident as the ruin that attends it. Besides, when money is shifted from hand to hand in such a blind, fortuitous manner that some men shall from nothing in an instant acquire vast estates without the least desert, while others are as suddenly stripped of plentiful fortunes, and left on the parish by their own avarice and credulity, what can be hoped for, on the one hand, but abandoned luxury and wantonness, or, on the other, but extreme madness and despair?

'An Essay Towards Preventing the Ruin of Great Britain' (1721): 71

5   It is an easy matter to contrive projects for the encouragement of industry: I wish it were as easy to persuade men to put them in practice.

'An Essay Towards Preventing the Ruin of Great Britain' (1721): 72

Adolf Augustus Berle, Jr.
(1895–1971)

capitalism and communism:

1   '[C]apitalism,' as that word is classically understood, and 'Communism,' meaning Marxism in any of its current organized forms, are both obsolete. They belong in museums of nineteenth-century thought and culture.

The American Economic Republic (1963), Introduction, Sec.3: 16

Adolf Augustus Berle, Jr. (1895–1971) and Gardiner Coit Means (1896–1988)

corporations:

1   It is an odd paradox that a corporate board of directors and a communist committee of commissars should so nearly meet in a common contention. The communist thinks of the community in terms of a state; the corporation director thinks of it in terms of an enterprise; and though this difference between the two may well lead to a radical divergence in results, it still remains true that the corporation director who would subordinate the interests of the individual stockholder to those of the group more nearly resembles the communist in mode of thought than he does the protagonist of private property.

The Modern Corporation and Private Property (1932), Book II, Ch.VIII: 278

Eduard Bernstein (1850–1932)
German social democrat

socialism:

1   *The prospects of socialism depend not on the decrease but on the increase of social wealth.* Socialism, or the socialist movement of modern times, has already outlived many superstitions; it will also outlive the superstition that its future depends on the concentration of property or, if one prefers, on the absorption of surplus value by a diminishing group of capitalist mammoths.

The Preconditions of Socialism (1899), Ch.3, Sec.(b): 61–62

value theory:

2   The theory of value no more provides a criterion for the justice or injustice of the distribution of the produce of labour than

does atomic theory for the beauty or ugliness of a piece of sculpture.
The Preconditions of Socialism (1899), Ch.3, Sec.(a): 55

William Henry Beveridge, 1st Baron Beveridge of Tuggal
(1879–1963)

private property:

1 [F]ull employment is in fact attainable while leaving the conduct of industry in the main to private enterprise. . . . But if, contrary to this view, it should be shown by experience or by argument that abolition of private property in the means of production was necessary for full employment, this abolition would have to be undertaken.
Full Employment in a Free Society (1945), Part I, Introduction and Summary, Para.18: 23

social security:

2 [S]ocial security must be achieved by cooperation between the State and the individual. The State should offer security for service and contribution. The State in organising security should not stifle incentive, opportunity, responsibility; in establishing a national minimum, it should leave room and encouragement for voluntary action by each individual to provide more than that minimum for himself and his family.
Social Insurance and Allied Services (1942), Part I, Para.9: 6–7

unemployment:

3 Unemployment is like a headache or a high temperature – unpleasant and exhausting but not carrying in itself any explanation of its cause. A high temperature may be got by catching malaria or by breaking one's leg or by eating too much; it may mean that one has something wrong with one's appendix or lungs or teeth, that one is in the thick of a bad cold or is sickening for cholera. Until one finds out which of these and many other possible causes is at work, one will not have gone far in finding a cure simply by knowing how many degrees of fever one has. The clinical thermometer is an indispensable but limited instrument.
Causes and Cures of Unemployment (1931), Ch.I: 1

Mark Blaug (1927–)

methodology:

1 [T]he central weakness of modern economics is in fact the reluctance to produce theories which yield unambiguously refutable implications.
'Kuhn versus Lakatos *or* Paradigms versus Research Programmes in the History of Economics' (1976), Sec.4: 172

2 Someone has said: 'Methodology is like medicine. We tolerate it because it is supposed to be good for us, but we secretly despise it.' But despising methodology as they do, all economists nevertheless have their favourite home remedy for every theoretical illness; unfortunately, they rarely make it clear either to themselves or to others why they believe that these remedies will work.
'Economic Methodology in One Easy Lesson' (1986): 265

Alan Stuart Blinder (1945–)

economic policy:

1 Murphy's Law of Economic Policy:
Economists have the least influence on policy where they know the most and are most agreed; they have the most influence on policy where they know the least and disagree most vehemently.
Hard Heads, Soft Hearts (1987), Introduction: 1

Eugen von Böhm-Bawerk
(1851–1914)

value:

1 What then is the 'ultimate standard' for the determination of the value of goods, in the search for which, men have been as indefatigable during the last one hundred years, as they formerly were in their endeavors to square the circle. If we wish to answer this

question in a single phrase, then we cannot choose any less general expression than 'human well-being.' The ultimate standard for the value of all goods is the degree of well-being which is dependent upon goods in general.
'The Ultimate Standard of Value' (1894): 59–60

Lawrence Arthur Boland (1939–)

methodology:

1 Before we can examine the theoretical issues of the appropriate conception of the decision-maker's methodology, we need to develop a clear idea about the mainstream methodology embodied in neoclassical economics. But first, we have to do a little detective work because the embodied methodology is not very visible. On the one hand, few economists discuss methodology while they are using it because they take it for granted; and on the other hand, when it is discussed, few neoclassical economists practice what they preach.
The Foundations of Economic Method (1982), Introduction: 3

James Bonar (1852–1941)

economics and economists:

1 In science honesty is not the best policy merely; it is the only policy; without honesty there is no science. We should have no right or title to be a Section of the British Association for the Advancement of Science if we were not prepared to accept any conclusion to which the facts might lead us, in scorn of consequence; and we cannot be grateful to those who tempt us to do otherwise. Only, like our brethren in the senior branches of this Association, we must make sure of our conclusions before we proclaim them proved, and we must not cling to a theory simply because it is our own.
'Old Lights and New in Economic Study' (1898): 453

economic motives:

2 Economists have probably been right in considering that it is, on the whole, more easy to discover uniformity in human action proceeding from economic motives, whether to make a living or a fortune, than to trace it elsewhere; but this is a long way from the assertion that it does not exist elsewhere, or that the economic motives are over all persons and in all causes supreme.
'Old Lights and New in Economic Study' (1898): 449

Robert Heron Bork (1927–)
American legal scholar, jurist

antitrust:

1 The life of the antitrust law – meaning by that its areas of policy growth – is, in contrast to Holmes's dictum about the common law, neither logic nor experience but bad economics and worse jurisprudence. The economics consists of a woefully unsophisticated theory of the means by which firms can gain monopolies, or at any rate injure the competitive process and so injure consumers, by attacking or foreclosing their rivals. The jurisprudence . . . consists of the notion that under existing antitrust statutes the courts may properly implement a variety of mutually inconsistent goals, most notably the goals of consumer welfare and small business welfare. Together, these ideas are creating a broad trend of policy directed less to the interest of consumers in free markets than to the interest of inefficient producers in safe markets. The question is whether this trend is either necessary or proper. I think it is neither.
'Antitrust and Monopoly: The Goals of Antitrust Policy' (1967): 242

economics and economists:

2 Economics may be a science best confined to analysis and shunning the normative.
'Antitrust and Monopoly: The Goals of Antitrust Policy' (1967): 243

Kenneth Ewert Boulding
(1910–1993)

decision theory:

1 Decision theory is a large mathematical apparatus resting like an inverted cone on the delicate point that everybody does what he thinks is best at the time; and it is astonishing

that a principle apparently so empty could produce such an enormous mass of mathematical content.

'The Basis of Value Judgments in Economics' (1967): 64

2   If we once admit that it is possible to die for anything, nicely calculated less or more seems to go out the window. The economist can retort, of course, that even if utility functions have discontinuities and infinite rates of substitution, they are still utility functions, and the formal theory applies. However, this makes the theory so formal as to be virtually without any content.

'The Basis of Value Judgments in Economics' (1967): 66

economic man:

3   The economist has a certain sneaking suspicion that economic man has perfect mental health, having no delusions of grandeur, no Freudian complexes, no heroic attitudinizing, and at least an Olympian neutrality toward his exchange mates. Superman is only a costume, and Batman a mask; and after all their heroic exploits they will have to go back to economic Mama and count their costs, ask their rewards, pay the bills, and face the inexorable consequences of real scarcities, which their heroic antics have actually increased. There is unquestionably a demand for the heroic, a lot of which perhaps rises out of a subconscious protest against the disgreeable [sic] fact of scarcity itself. There is more to it than this, however. The demand for the heroic cannot merely be dismissed as irrational, for without it human life would be deprived of a great deal that makes it worth living. What we have to achieve, however, is a creative tension between heroic man and, dare we say it, economic woman. Economics, if we remember, in Greek is the science of householdry, and the demands of domesticity are perhaps the best check on the excesses of the heroic.

'The Basis of Value Judgments in Economics' (1967): 67

4   No one is his senses would want his daughter to marry an economic man, one who counted every cost and asked for every reward, was never afflicted with mad generosity or uncalculating love, and who never acted out of a sense of inner identity and indeed had no inner identity even if he was occasionally affected by carefully calculated considerations of benevolence or malevolence. The attack on economics is an attack on calculatedness and the very fact that we think of the calculating as cold suggests how exposed economists are to romantic and heroic criticism.

'Economics as a Moral Science' (1969): 10

economics and economists:

5   The economist, in his better moments, is aware that it is not commodities that behave, but men; that commodities move not of themselves, like the planets, but are moved by men; and that every exchange involves two people or groups of people as well as two commodities. He rightly bears this information at the back of his mind, however, rather than at the front, because his very skill as an economist depends on his ability to abstract from the complexity of human behavior those aspects which concern commodities and to summarize these aspects in fairly simple functional relationships among commodity variables. Thus he is somewhat in the position of the astronomer who can neglect the problem of whether angels move the planets, because whether they do or not their behavior toward the planets is perfectly regular, and therefore predictable, and hence any other quirks of motive or character which they possess can be neglected.

'Collective Bargaining and Fiscal Policy' (1950): 308

6   In the face of the wonder and beauty of economics, it is somewhat of a shock to the economist to be brought up against the proposition, to enlarge the quotation from Wordsworth, that high heaven rejects the lore of nicely calculated less or more. Here we have economics confronted with what I suppose might be called theonomics. In this rejection of the whole kit and kaboodle of the economic ethic, economic behavior, rational choice, maximizing utility, and this whole apparatus of nice calculation of gain and loss, the poet is joined by the preachers, prophets, lovers, and military men, who unite with high heaven against the economist, insisting on

fine frenzy, unconfined joy, giving without cost, and not reasoning why. When this united blast has swept all the papers off his desk, the economist may pick them up again and argue that he can still reduce these objections to rational mathematics.

'The Basis of Value Judgments in Economics' (1967): 65

7 Economics, as such, does not contribute very much to the formal study of human learning. ... Our main contribution as economists is in the description of what is learned; the preference functions which embody what is learned in regard to values, and the production functions which describe the results of the learning of technology. We may not have thought much about the genetics of knowledge, but we have thought about its description, and this is a contribution not to be despised.

'Economics as a Moral Science' (1969): 4

labor:

8 [T]he labor movement is a slight embarrassment, not because of its impact on the distribution of income, which over the long pull is almost negligible, but because of its impact on the flexibility of the whole price structure. With a strong labor movement we cannot afford to have deflations; and this may mean that we cannot escape a secular inflation.

'Collective Bargaining and Fiscal Policy' (1950): 320

mathematics in economics:

9 [I]t is a question of acute importance for economics as to why the macroeconomic predictions of the mathematical economists have been on the whole less successful than the hunches of the mathematically unwashed.

'Samuelson's *Foundations*: The Role of Mathematics in Economics' (1948), Sec.I: 189

10 If economics becomes a preserve of the higher mathematicians, it will lose its essentially humanistic and empirical quality. There is not time, in the average life, to acquire *both* the higher mathematics and the critical judgment. For the exceptional mind this may be possible; for the general run it is not.

'Samuelson's *Foundations*: The Role of Mathematics in Economics' (1948), Sec.II: 199

Francis Bowen (1811–1890)

communism:

1 Little reasoning is needed to confute the theory of the Communists, who propose an equal division of goods as a remedy for nearly all the evils with which society is afflicted. They are not aware, or do not reflect, that the sight of the two extremes of opulence and poverty, – the hope of rising to the one and the fear of falling into the other, – is the constant stimulus which keeps up that energy and activity of the human race, through which alone these goods are created. Make men secure of a provision for all their wants, take away from them all objects of ambition, destroy both anxiety and emulation, – and these are the certain results of an enforced equality of property and condition, – and after a few years, even if there remained anything to be divided among them, (which there would not, for their wastefulness under such circumstances would equal their indolence,) they would become useless and discontented drones, devoured by ennui, or eager for wrangling and fighting with each other, as the only means of relieving their otherwise stagnant existence.

The Principles of Political Economy (1856), Ch.XXV: 499

economics and economists:

2 There is a general science of Human Nature, of which the special sciences of Ethics, Psychology, Æsthetics, Politics, and Political Economy are so many departments, all founded upon the essential unity of the human mind and character, and the consequent similarity of its manifestations under similar circumstances.

The Principles of Political Economy (1856), Preface

3 Political Economy begins with the supposition, that man is disposed to accumulate wealth beyond what is necessary for the immediate gratification of his wants, and

that this disposition, in the great majority of cases, is in fact unbounded; that man's inclination to labor is mainly controlled by this desire; that he is constantly competing with his fellows in this attempt to gain wealth; and that he is sagacious enough to see what branches of industry are most profitable, and eager enough to engage in them, so that competition regularly tends to bring wages, profits, and prices to a level. The science, then, is more closely allied with the Philosophy of Mind, than with Natural History, or the physical sciences. It has been called *Catallactics*, or 'the Science of Exchanges'; and, agreeably to this notion, man himself has been defined to be, *an animal* that makes exchanges. . . .
The Principles of Political Economy (1856), Ch.I: 3

4 Political Economy is not, as many suppose, the art of money-making, any more than meteorology is the art of predicting the weather. It is no *art* at all, but a *science*; for its immediate end is knowledge, not action, or the guidance of conduct.
The Principles of Political Economy (1856), Ch.II: 13

laissez-faire:

5 The attempts of legislators to turn the industry of society in one direction or another, out of its natural and self-chosen channels, – here to encourage it by bounties, and there to load it with penalties, to increase or diminish the supply of the market, to establish a *maximum* of price, to keep specie in the country, – are almost invariably productive of harm. *Laissez-faire*; 'these things regulate themselves,' in common phrase; which means, of course, that God regulates them by his general laws, which always, in the long run, work to good. In these modern days, the ruler or governor who is most to be dreaded is, not the tyrant, but the busybody. Let the course of trade and the condition of society alone, is the best advice which can be given to the legislator, the projector, and the reformer. Busy yourselves, if you must be busy, with *individual cases* of wrong, hardship, or suffering; but do not meddle with the general laws of the universe.
The Principles of Political Economy (1856), Ch.II: 23

money:

6 Money is the universal form or garb which all the items or commodities that constitute wealth occasionally assume. At any one time and place, it is a universal measure of the comparative value of those commodities, and a common denomination, to which, when we wish to ascertain their aggregate or sum total, they are all reduced.
The Principles of Political Economy (1856), Ch.XVIII: 279

7 Money is even now only a hypothetical or abstract medium of exchange in all the larger transactions of commerce. I almost anticipate the time, in the progress of invention and the discovery of new expedients and facilities in commerce, when it will become so universally; when, at any rate, so costly and useless a realization of the idea as gold and silver coin will be entirely done away. Only practical difficulties, or what may be called difficulties of detail, even now obstruct this desirable consummation.
The Principles of Political Economy (1856), Ch.XIX: 334

wealth:

8 Thus, it is a natural law, that wealth favors the growth of wealth, and poverty tends to generate poverty.
The Principles of Political Economy (1856), Ch.XXV: 538

Louis Dembitz Brandeis (1856–1941)
Associate Justice, US Supreme Court

oligopoly:

1 The practice of interlocking directorates is the root of many evils.
Other People's Money (1914), Ch.III: 51

2 We must break the Money Trust or the Money Trust will break us.
Other People's Money (1914), Ch.X: 201

Martin Bronfenbrenner (1914–1997)

econometrics:

1 It is not enough to charge 'the other fellow' with 'misspecification,' a common dodge,

merely because his specifications differed from one's own. One must also explain why his own specifications are more nearly correct. Nor does it suffice to cast aspersions for 'data-mining' when one's adversary presents variant 606 of his model, whereas your own model worked the first time. (But for the Grace of God, the variant which worked for you might have been number 607!).
'Sensitivity Analysis for Econometricians' (1972): 66

economics and economists:

2   The Economic Adviser should be at once a philosopher and a salesman. When his philosophy is deficient, his advice is dismissed as special pleading and he is included among the 'kept economists.' When his salesman's foot is not in the door – when too wide an institutional gap opens up between what is and what he proposes – his counsel is dismissed as subversive dreaming. The customer wants prospects and policies for the year or the biennium ahead, and not for 'comes the revolution.'
'Changing Fashions in Philosopher-Salesmen' (1954): 262

Henry Peter Brougham, 1st Baron Brougham and Vaux (1778–1868)
British lawyer and politician

money:

1   Money is a part of the capital of every nation. It is that part which is required for the distribution of the other portions.
'Wheatley on Currency and Finance' (1803): 233–234

usury:

2   It is evident, that if the protection of indigence were really the object of these laws [respecting usury], they stop short of their mark; – they prevent a poor man, no doubt, from borrowing at a high rate; but they take no means of compelling the rich to lend him at a lower rate.
'Defence of Usury' (1816): 342

Orestes Augustus Brownson
(1803–1876)

government:

1   But what shall government do? Its first doing must be an *un*doing. There has been thus far quite too much government, as well as government of the wrong kind. The first act of government we want, is a still further limitation of itself. It must begin by circumscribing within narrower limits its powers. And then it must proceed to repeal all laws which bear against the laboring classes, and then to enact such laws as are necessary to enable them to maintain their equality. We have no faith in those systems of elevating the working classes, which propose to elevate them without calling in the aid of government. We must have government, and legislation expressly directed to this end.
The Laboring Classes (1840): 23

Karl Brunner (1916–1989)

government:

1   The state is not a producer of wealth. It shapes *conditions* which encourage the creation of wealth. But it also frequently represents political institutions which impede expanding welfare. The state can, and frequently does, obstruct the wealth creating process and contributes to sustained poverty. Its wealth impeding activities yield an economic rent to a small group with access to the socio-political institutions. The emerging social organization of western societies will thus determine whether a nation *accumulates* wealth or *persists* in poverty.
'The Poverty of Nations' (1985): 11

William Jennings Bryan (1860–1925)
American politician

monopoly:

1   A man cannot long be a monopolist and remain a believer in the doctrines of a republic, because a monopoly rests upon arbitrary power; and, as it ignores inalienable rights, it

cannot consistently recognize the people as the source of power.
  'Concentration of Wealth: A Menace to Government and Civilization' (1902): 1069

2 [A] private monopoly, due as it is to a perversion of government, and defying as it does every moral principle, hardens those who possess it, embitters those who suffer from it, breeds hatred between citizens, materializes religion, jeopardizes the Government and arrests the progress of civilization.
  'Concentration of Wealth: A Menace to Government and Civilization' (1902): 1069

James McGill Buchanan, Jr. (1919–)

economics and economists:

1 Economists should, I think, face up to their basic responsibility; they should at least try to know their subject matter.
  'What Should Economists Do?' (1964): 213

2 Economists crossed the bridge from individual to social maximization because they wanted to be able to say something about policy alternatives. They desperately needed some instrument which would allow them to play the social engineer even if they eschewed the explicit intrusion of their own values in the process. With the social welfare function construction, they could then talk as if their policy statements were operationally meaningful, and this ability provided them with a certain inner satisfaction.
  'A Contractarian Paradigm for Applying Economic Theory' (1975): 226

3 *The* principle that exposure to economics *should* convey is that of the spontaneous coordination which the market achieves. The central principle of economics is not the economizing process; it is not the maximization of objective functions subject to constraints. Once we become methodologically trapped in the maximization paradigm, economics becomes applied mathematics or engineering.
  What Should Economists Do? (1979), Ch.4: 81

4 Macroeconomic theory, in both its lower and its higher reaches, need not have been born at all, along with the whole industry that designs, constructs and operates the large macroeconomic models.
  The State of Economic Science (W. Sichel, ed., 1989, Ch.5, Sec.III): 86; cf. Solow 2

methodology:

5 In my opinion, the economist should not retreat ever further into technical and terminological obscurity while refusing to accept the obvious conclusions of very simply analysis.
  'Confessions of a Burden Monger' (1964): 488

socialism:

6 Once any thought at all is given to the actual processes of collective decision-making, the claims for efficiency-generating properties of the socialist alternative collapse of their own weight.
  What Should Economists Do? (1979), Ch.15: 272

Nikolai Ivanovich Bukharin
(1888–1938)

capitalism:

1 The convulsions of the present-day capitalist world that is drenched in blood and is agonised in mortal pain, are the expression of those contradictions in the capitalist system, which in the long run will cause it to explode.
  Imperialism and World Economy (1930), Part IV, Ch.XV: 169

2 Thus capitalism, driving the concentration of production to extraordinary heights, and having created a centralised production apparatus, has therewith prepared the immense ranks of its own grave-diggers. In the great clash of classes, the dictatorship of finance capital is being replaced by the dictatorship of the revolutionary proletariat. 'The hour of capitalist property has struck. The expropriators are being expropriated.'
  Imperialism and World Economy (1930), Part IV, Ch.XV: 170

Marxism:

3 The historian or economist who places under one denominator the structure of modern capitalism, *i.e.*, modern production relations, and the numerous types of production relations that formerly led to wars of conquest, will understand nothing in the development of modern world economy. One must single out the specific elements which characterise our time, and analyse them. This was *Marx's* method, and this is how a Marxist must approach the analysis of imperialism.
   Imperialism and World Economy (1930), Part III, Ch.IX: 114

Edmund Burke (1729–1797)

economics and economists:

1 But the age of chivalry is gone. – That of sophisters, oeconomists, and calculators, has succeeded; and the glory of Europe is extinguished for ever.
   Reflections on the Revolution in France (1790): 113 [238]

taxation:

2 To mortgage the public revenue implies the sovereign dominion, in the fullest sense, over the public purse. It goes far beyond the trust even of a temporary and occasional taxation.
   Reflections on the Revolution in France (1790): 162 [273]

Arthur Frank Burns (1904–1987)

economics and economists:

1 I look forward to the day when economists will not rest content until they have at least specified the observable conditions that would contradict their theories, when the conformity of a theory to facts is respected no less than its logical consistency, and when carefully formulated theories are tested promptly and thoroughly in a score of research centers.
   'Keynesian Economics Once Again' (1947), Sec.IV: 263

C

John Elliott Cairnes (1823–1875)

economics and economists:

1 That Political Economy – assuming that it fulfils its limited purpose of unfolding the natural laws of wealth – is capable of throwing light on the evolutions of history, will scarcely be denied, if only it be considered how large a proportion of all human existence is absorbed in the mere pursuit of physical well-being, how extensively the material interests of men prevail in determining their political opinions and conduct, and in how many subtle ways worldly considerations gain an entrance into the heart and conscience, and help to give the cue to moral and religious ideas. It is scarcely possible, I say, to reflect on this, and not perceive that to the right interpretation and correct exposition of the conduct of men in past times – that conduct which makes history – a knowledge of the laws of wealth, a knowledge of the direction in which, in a given epoch, material interests draw the men who live in it, forms an indispensable qualification. Obvious, however, as this reflection is, the truth (except in a few eminent instances) has been all but wholly ignored. Speaking generally, it is not yet supposed ... that a knowledge of Political Economy is any necessary part of the equipment of an historian. It is impossible to doubt that the consequences of this view of things to historic study have been very serious; that many precious indications, which to a student furnished with the economic key would have opened light through not a few of the dark, but important crises of history, have been wholly lost to us – thrown away upon investigators who, however rich in erudition, perhaps embarrassed with their riches, were unprovided with this potent instrument. Our historians have but rarely been economists, and I fear it must be acknowledged that our economists have quite as rarely been profound students of history; and it has thus come to pass that this important field of economic research has yet produced but scanty fruit.
'M. Comte and Political Economy' (1870): 602; cf. Allyn Young 1

laissez-faire:

2 [T]he maxim of *laissez-faire* has no scientific basis whatever, but is at best a mere handy rule of practice, useful, perhaps, as a reminder to statesmen on which side the presumption lies in questions of industrial legislation, but totally destitute of all scientific authority.
'Political Economy and Laissez-Faire' (1871): 86

3 It is one thing to repudiate the scientific authority of *laissez-faire*, freedom of contract, and so forth; it is a totally different thing to set up the opposite principle of State control, the doctrine of paternal government. For my part I accept neither one doctrine nor the other; and, as a practical rule, I hold *laissez-faire* to be incomparably the safer guide. Only let us remember that it is a *practical rule*, and not a doctrine of science; a rule in the main sound, but like most other sound practical rules, liable to numerous exceptions; above all, a rule which must never for a moment be allowed to stand in the way of the candid consideration of any promising proposal of social or industrial reform.
'Political Economy and Laissez-Faire' (1871): 90

mathematics in economics:

4 [W]hile not denying that some of the doctrines of political economy may be exhibited mathematically, and may possibly thus be made clearer to some minds, my own belief is that this mode of presenting economic truths admits of but very limited application. When mathematics are carried further than this in the moral or social sciences, and used for conducting processes of reasoning, without constant reference to the concrete meaning of the terms for which the mathematical symbols are employed, I own I regard the practice with profound distrust.
'New Theories in Political Economy' (1872): 76

methodology:

5   *The economist starts with a knowledge of ultimate causes.* He is already, at the outset of his enterprise, in the position which the physicist only attains after ages of laborious research.
    The Character and Logical Method of Political Economy (1888; 2nd edn), Lecture III, Sec.3: 87

socialism:

6   Where I take issue with the Socialists is as to the present feasibility of their schemes, and as to the means by which the ends they desire are to be promoted. I altogether deny that in the actual circumstances of mankind the distribution of wealth on the principles they contend for is feasible; and I believe that the attempt to carry those principles into effect by invoking for this purpose the powers of the State – which I take to be the essential characteristic of Socialism, and that which broadly distinguishes it from other modes of social speculation – could only issue in disaster and ruin.
    Some Leading Principles of Political Economy, Newly Expounded (1874), Part II, Ch.V, Sec.2: 265

Edwin Cannan (1861–1935)

economics and economists:

1   The practice of those who have been believed by themselves and others to be writing about and teaching economics has been sufficiently uniform to make it possible for 'economic' to become a useful word in the everyday conversation of educated people. Such people commonly talk of 'economic questions,' 'economic interests,' and 'the economic point of view.' They separate economic questions from religious questions, from literary questions, from historical questions, and from hundreds of other questions. They inquire whether in some particular case the economic interests of some persons are opposed to their political or their religious interests. They regard some things as desirable from an economic point of view which for some non-economic reasons they reject as on the whole undesirable.
    Wealth (1930; 3rd edn), Ch.I, Sec.1: 1–2

2   For ordinary purposes economic things can best be described as economic, just as blue things can best be described as blue.
    Wealth (1930; 3rd edn), Ch.I, Sec.1: 4

laissez-faire:

3   The whole of civilized society is based on the principle that people should be allowed to do what they like until good reason is shown to the contrary, and this implies a presumption that profitable specialization is good. To justify interference with it some positive argument must be brought forward, showing that it, or the part of it which is attacked, is bad. A bare proof that complete *laisser-faire* is bad, impossible, and inconceivable does not carry with it a corollary that every proposal for preventing people from doing what they want to do is right.
    Wealth (1930; 3rd edn), Ch.XIV, Sec.3: 249–250

Richard Cantillon (1680–1734?)

markets:

1   It often happens that Sellers who are too obstinate in keeping up their price in the Market, miss the opportunity of selling their Produce or Merchandise to advantage and are losers thereby. It also happens that by sticking to their prices they may be able to sell more profitably another day.
    Essay on the Nature of Commerce in General (1755), Part Two, Ch.II: 51

value:

2   [T]he Price or intrinsic value of a thing is the measure of the quantity of Land and of Labour entering into its production, having regard to the fertility or produce of the Land and to the quality of the Labour.
    But it often happens that many things which have actually this intrinsic value are not sold in the Market according to that value: that will depend on the Humours and Fancies of men and on their consumption.
    Essay on the Nature of Commerce in General (1755), Part One, Ch.X: 16

wealth:

3   The Land is the Source or Matter from whence all Wealth is produced. The Labour of man is the Form which produces it: and Wealth in

itself is nothing but the Maintenance, Conveniencies, and Superfluities of Life.
Essay on the Nature of Commerce in General (1755), Part One, Ch.I: 5

Henry Charles Carey (1793–1879)

economics and economists:

1   [I]t may now, we think, be hoped, that at no distant day it will come to be admitted that, in common with all other organized bodies, science develops from within and never from without; that the tree of science grows from the roots upward; and, that its various branches are all co-operating for accomplishment of one great object, to wit: that of giving to man increased power for control of the great natural forces, and for development of those faculties, mental and moral, whose germs have been incorporated into the system of every individual of the race. When it shall have come, the world will cease to be mystified by economic 'assumptions' that are wholly without a base on which to stand; and so little comprehended by even their very teachers, that these latter fail totally when seeking to make them comprehensible by those who would be taught.
The Unity of Law (1872), Preface: xxi

financial markets:

2   A money market always in perfect health and soundness would imply infallible wisdom in those who conduct its operations.
Financial Crises (1864), Letter First: 3

mathematics in economics:

3   Mathematics must be used in social science, as it is now in every other branch of inquiry, and the more the former is used, the more the latter takes the form of real science, and the more intimate are shown to be its relations with other departments of knowledge.
Principles of Social Science (1858), Vol.I, Ch.I, Sec.6: 33

value:

4   *Value is the measure of the resistance to be overcome in obtaining those commodities or things required for our purposes – of the power of nature over man.*
Principles of Social Science (1858), Vol.I, Ch.VI, Sec.5: 158

wealth:

5   Wealth grows with the growth of the power of man to satisfy that first and greatest want of his nature – the desire for association with his fellow-men. The more rapid its growth, the greater is the tendency towards the disappearance of 'indigence,' on the one hand, and 'profusion and avarice,' on the other – towards the termination of existing 'abuses,' tending to limit the exercise of the power of association, to restrain the development of individuality, and to impair the feeling of strict responsibility towards God and man – and towards having society assume that form which is most calculated for facilitating the progress of the latter towards the high position for which he was originally intended; and therefore the form most calculated to inspire respect and 'reverence.'
Principles of Social Science (1858), Vol.I, Ch.VII, Sec.5: 197

Thomas Carlyle (1795–1881)
British essayist, historian, and social critic

economics and economists:

1   Truly, my philanthropic friends, Exeter Hall Philanthropy is wonderful; and the Social Science – not a 'gay science,' but a rueful – which finds the secret of this universe in 'supply-and-demand,' and reduces the duty of human governors to that of letting men alone, is also wonderful. Not a 'gay science,' I should say, like some we have heard of; no, a dreary, desolate, and indeed quite abject and distressing one; what we might call, by way of eminence, the *dismal science*. These two, Exeter Hall Philanthropy and the Dismal Science, led by any sacred cause of Black Emancipation, or the like, to fall in love and make a wedding of it, – will give birth to progenies and prodigies; dark extensive mooncalves, unnameable abortions, widecoiled monstrosities, such as the world has not seen hitherto!
'Occasional Discourse on the Negro Question' (1849): 672–73; cf. Ludwig von Mises 8, Robert Nathan 2, Rexford Tugwell 1

poverty and the poor laws:

2   The New Poor-Law is an announcement, sufficiently distinct, that whosoever will not

work ought not to live. Can the poor man that is willing to work, always find work, and live by his work? Statistic Inquiry . . . has no answer to give. Legislation presupposes the answer – to be in the affirmative. A large postulate; which should have been made a proposition of; which should have been demonstrated, made indubitable to all persons! A man willing to work, and unable to find work, is perhaps the saddest sight that Fortune's inequality exhibits under this sun.
Chartism (1839), Ch.IV: 135

Andrew Carnegie (1835–1919)
Scottish–American industrialist and philanthropist

charity:

1 There is really no true charity except that which will help others to help themselves, and which does not place within the reach of the aspiring the means to climb.
'The Advantages of Poverty' (1891): 378

inheritance:

2 [L]et us state the proposition thus: that wealth left to young men, as a rule, is disadvantageous; that lives of poverty and struggle are advantageous.
'The Advantages of Poverty' (1891): 371

3 The transmission of wealth and rank, without regard to merit or qualifications, may pass from one peer to another not without much, but without serious injury, since the duties are matter of routine and seldom involve the welfare or means of others, but the management of business, never.
'The Advantages of Poverty' (1891): 372

poverty and the poor laws:

4 Common humanity impels us to provide for the actual wants of human beings to see through our poor laws, that none die of starvation, to provide comfortable shelter, clothing, and instruction which should, however, always be dependent upon work performed; but, in doing this, our thoughts should also turn to the benefits that are to accrue to those who are yet sound and industrious, and seeking through labour the means of betterment, by removing from their midst and placing under care of the State in workhouses the social lepers. Every drunken vagabond or lazy idler supported by alms bestowed by wealthy people is a source of moral infection to a neighbourhood. It will not do to teach the hardworking industrious man that there is an easier path by which his wants can be supplied. The earnest reformer will think as much, if not more, of the preservation of the sound and valuable members among the poor, as of any real change which can be effected in those who seem hopelessly lost to temperance, industry, and thrift. He will labour more to prevent than to cure, feeling that it is necessary to remove the spoiled grape from the bunch, the spoiled apple from the barrel, mainly for the sake of the sound fruit that remains. He who would plunge the knife into the social cancer, if any good is to be effected thereby, must needs be a skilled surgeon with steady hand and calm judgment, with the feelings as much under control as possible, the less emotion the better.
'The Advantages of Poverty' (1891): 379

social welfare:

5 In a country where the millionaire exists there is little excuse for pauperism; the condition of the masses is satisfactory just in proportion as a country is blessed with millionaires.
'The Advantages of Poverty' (1891): 370

Thomas Nixon Carver (1865–1961)

economic man:

1 A new kind of an economic man has been, or is in process of being, constructed by what is known as the behavioristic school of economists. He is the result of an over-emphasis upon the non-pecuniary and the neglect or under-emphasis upon the pecuniary motives, as the old economic man was the result of the opposite tendencies.
'The Behavioristic Man' (1918): 195

economics and economists:

2 [E]conomic activities, rather than economic goods, form the subject-matter of the science [of economics].
The Distribution of Wealth (1904), Introduction: xi

3 If economic sense had been preached half as effectively as economic nonsense, we should be very near a practical and rational solution of our difficulties.
Essays in Social Justice (1915), Ch.IX: 242–243

4 The destinies of civilization are safer when entrusted to the general common sense of the people, – which is a kind of empiric wisdom, based upon ages of accumulated experience – than when placed in the hands of half-baked economists, who have studied just enough to lose their common sense and not enough to get it back again.
Essays in Social Justice (1915), Ch.IX: 259

labor:

5 There is no such thing as human labor in the abstract. There are various kinds of labor in the concrete. One does not hire labor in the abstract any more than one buys bread in the abstract. One buys concrete loaves of bread. One hires individual men to do specific kinds of work.
Essays in Social Justice (1915), Ch.IX: 249–250

6 He who has consciously and intelligently done something to increase the demand for labor, or to reduce the supply of it, has a right to speak on the labor problem. All others who exercise their verbosity in this field are mere charlatans.
Essays in Social Justice (1915), Ch.XV: 383

socialism:

7 Socialism as a movement is merely a development of class spirit among propertyless workers, and of class antagonism against the owners of capital. This movement does not depend in the least upon justice or injustice, or upon economic soundness or unsoundness. It is wholly a matter of class consciousness and class antagonism. It will succeed, whether its views be just or not, whenever its class consciousness becomes strong enough, and its class antagonism bitter enough to sweep away the present social order. It will fail, whether its views be sound or unsound, if this class consciousness fails to include the majority of the people, or if their class hatred does not become bitter enough to make them revolutionists.
Essays in Social Justice (1915), Ch.IX: 257–258

taxation:

8 Since taxation must affect distribution, if we accept the principle of the 'greatest good to the greatest number' as the criterion of justice in distribution, it ought to follow that the least evil to the least number is the criterion of justice in taxation.
'The Ethical Basis of Distribution and Its Bearings on Taxation' (1895): 97

9 If taxes were voluntary contributions for the support of the state, it would be important that we should recognize some principle by which to determine how much each individual ought to give. Since the payment of such a tax and its amount would be matters for the individual conscience, it would be pertinent to ask what principle of obligation the individual ought to adopt as his rule of action. But since taxes are not voluntary contributions but forced payments, we need not so much to know what the duty of the individual is as what the duty of the state is: not how much the individual ought in conscience to give, but how much the state ought in justice to take from him, and under what conditions the state ought to take it.
'The Minimum Sacrifice Theory of Taxation' (1904): 66

Karl Gustav Cassel (1866–1945)

forecasting:

1 It has become a fashion among economists, or rather among statisticians without a thoro economic training, to look upon everything that happens in economic life as subordinate to statistical curves and subject to being predicted by a mathematical analysis of these curves. . . . [I]t is plain enough that our future is not determined by mathematical curves but by our own intelligence and will. But if this is so, the whole so-called science of business-forecasting inevitably becomes very much discredited. What the economist can do is to examine present facts and proposed lines of action, and to show how they are likely to influence the development

of economic life. But he can never make a prediction of our future independent of our own actions. And we should never lose sight of the fact that the future is influenced by coming events about which we know nothing, and the prediction of which in any case does not belong to economic science.

'The Rate of Interest, The Bank Rate, and the Stabilization of Prices' (1928): 528–529

interest:

2   No part of economic theory has suffered more than the theory of interest from the idea that it should be obligatory first to explain the whole economic system in an imagined moneyless society before daring to approach our actual economic life, so essentially based upon the conception of money. Such horrible formulas as 'the general overvaluation of present goods in relation to future ones,' which were invented by advocates of a separate theory of value for explaining the phenomenon of interest, were as deficient in scientific stringency as they were unnecessarily difficult for the student to grasp.

'The Rate of Interest, The Bank Rate, and the Stabilization of Prices' (1928): 512–513

money:

3   The only quality demanded of a monetary system which is of any importance for promoting the trade and general welfare of the world, is stability.

Money and Foreign Exchange After 1914 (1923), 'The Problem of Stabilisation': 254

price controls:

4   [It] has always been the natural thing to try and prevent all troubles and nuisances in the life of the community by forbidding them to occur. . . . A rise in price was an evil thing, and consequently should be simply prohibited by legislation. Thus 'maximum price' legislation came into being. In vain did scientists point out the unreasonableness of this arbitrary attack on the most vital factor governing the economic life of the community, the natural formation of prices. In vain did they foretell the series of grave consequences which such attacks were bound to involve. The modern community must, ever to its shame and hurt, go through that stern system of education in the first principles of social economics and finance which so many peoples have had to undergo during periods of inflation ever since the days of ancient Egypt, and that without having learned one single jot from all the wealth of experience gathered during these thousands of years.

Money and Foreign Exchange After 1914 (1923), 'The Rise in Prices': 23–24

usury:

5   [U]sury is only one variety of that more general form of robbery which consists in taking advantage of the defects of the organisation of the market.

The Nature and Necessity of Interest (1903), Ch.VII: 180–181

Sir Edwin Chadwick (1800–1890)

poverty:

1   [Poverty] is the natural, the primitive, the general, and the unchangeable state of man; and that as labour is the source of wealth, so is poverty of labour. Banish poverty, you banish wealth. Indigence, therefore, and not poverty, is the evil, the removal of which is the proper object of Poor Laws. Indigence may be provided for – mendicity may be extirpated; but all attempts to extirpate poverty can have no effects but bad ones.

'The New Poor Law' (1836): 501

Thomas Chalmers (1780–1847)
Scottish Presbyterian minister

poverty and the poor laws:

1   It is evident, that every levy upon property for the support of the indigent, trenches on the means of its owners for the employment and maintenance of the disposable population. There is no new provision created under such an economy. A part of the old provision is simply transferred, or withdrawn, from the sustenance of one class to the sustenance of another class. Every additional impost that is laid upon

me in the shape of poor's rate, lessens my ability to support those industrious who are remunerated for their services by my expenditure.
    On Political Economy (1832), Ch.XIV, Sec.2: 399–400

taxation:

2 There is not a more popular topic of declamation than the oppressiveness of taxes, and, more especially, their injurious effect on the condition of the working classes in society. The imagination is, that, when laid on the necessaries of life, they trench directly on the comfort and sufficiency of the labourer; and that, when laid on profit, or laid on commodities in general, they trench upon capital, and so upon that power which exists in the country for the remuneration of labour. It is thus that the distresses of the poor, and the straitened condition of the lower orders generally, stand associated in many a mind with the exactions of government.
    On Political Economy (1832), Ch.VIII, Sec.1: 241

Joseph Chamberlain (1836–1914)
British politician

government:

1 There is no need to abase the rich in order to raise the poor, and it is neither possible nor expedient to drag everything down to one dead level. We cannot, if we would, equalize the conditions and the capacities of men. The idler, the drunkard, the criminal, and the fool must bear the brunt of their defects. The strong, the prudent, the temperate, and the wise will always be first in the race. But it is desirable that the government, which no longer represents a clique or a privileged class, but which is the organized expression of the wants and wishes of the whole nation, should rise to a true conception of its duties, and should use the resources, the experience, and the talent at its disposal to promote the greater happiness of the masses of the people.
    'Favorable Aspects of State Socialism' (1891): 548

David Gawen Champernowne
(1912–2000)

mathematics in economics:

1 The cautious economic theorist, whose over-riding ambition is never to appear wrong and yet to appear in print at all, has little scope beyond the discussion of economic models.
    'On the Use and Misuse of Mathematics in Presenting Economic Theory' (1954): 369

2 The ability to judge the relevance of an economic theory and its conclusions to the real world is but rarely associated with the ability to understand advanced mathematics.
    'On the Use and Misuse of Mathematics in Presenting Economic Theory' (1954): 369

Sir Josiah Child, 1st Baronet
(1630–1699)

poverty and the poor laws:

1 *He that gives to any in Want does well, but he that gives to Employ and Educate the Poor, so as to render them useful to the Kingdom, in my judgement does better.*
    A Method Concerning the Relief and Employment of the Poor (1699): 6

trade:

2 *Live and let Live*, is an honest and usual Saying in Trade; And if the unconscionable Usurers, insatiable Thirst after ungodly Gain, will not permit him to say so. The Law may with great Justice compel him to do so; For wherever common Convenience or Necessity requires any thing to be done for the Publick Welfare, every Man owes a conformity thereto, and many be restrained by Law from doing otherwise.
    A Discourse of the Nature, Use and Advantages of Trade (1694): 23

Carl Finley Christ (1923–)

economics and economists:

1 Some people think that economists care only about money. I have heard an unkind critic

say that an economist is someone who would sell his grandmother to the highest bidder. This is quite wrong. An economist, or at least a good economist, would not sell his grandmother to the highest bidder unless the highest bid was enough to compensate him for the loss of his grandmother.
'Economics and Public Policy' (1991): 15

Cicero (Marcus Tullius) (106–43 BC)
Roman politician, lawyer, and philosopher

money:

1 [F]or there is nothing so characteristic of narrowness and littleness of soul as the love of riches; and there is nothing more honourable and noble than to be indifferent to money, if one does not possess it, and to devote it to beneficence and liberality, if one does possess it.
On Duties, Book I, Sec.XX: 71

Sir John Harold Clapham
(1873–1946)

constant returns:

1 Constant returns, it may be observed in passing, must always remain a mathematical point, their box an empty one. It is inconceivable that a method can ever be devised for so measuring these real but infinitely subtle and imponderable tendencies towards diminishing and increasing returns that someone will be able to say, Lo, here a perfect balance. If this is so, constant returns industries may be relegated finally to the limbo of the categories, in company for the present with such still disembodied phantoms as the 'commodity whose elasticity of demand is unity.'
'Of Empty Economic Boxes' (1922): 310

Colin Grant Clark (1905–1989)

economics and economists:

1 There is room for two or three economic theorists in each generation, not more. Only men of transcendental powers of reasoning can be candidates for these positions. Restatements of economic theory, of which we are offered so many, are only occasionally needed, as factual knowledge advances and institutions change.
The rest of us should be economic scientists, content steadily to lay stone on stone in building the structure of ordered knowledge. Instead, it seems to be the ambition of nearly every teacher of economics to put his name to a new formulation of economic theory. The result is a vast output of literature of which, it is safe to say, scarcely a syllable will be read in fifty years' time. But the discovery of new facts, and of generalizations based on them, is work for all time.
The Conditions of Economic Progress (1940), Preface

2 Economics ... must take its place in the hierarchy of arts and sciences. Economics should dominate and coordinate the activities of engineering, agricultural science, industrial chemistry, accountancy and all sciences whose main object is the production and exchange of useful goods and services.
The Conditions of Economic Progress (1951; 2nd edn), Ch.I: 1

John Bates Clark (1847–1938)

communism:

1 Communism, in its more lawless form, proposes to reform society by methods of violence; if we are to deal with this movement successfully, we must first endeavor to accomplish the needed reformation by methods of peace.
'How to Deal with Communism' (1878): 542

competition:

2 Competition, pure and simple, implies the exclusive action of selfish motives, and would be a savage and ignoble strife, in which every man's hand would be for himself and against his neighbor. Fowls in a barnyard running together for a handful of corn, apes in a cage greedily snatching pieces of bread from each other, present but an imperfect picture of what would result from the exclusive action of selfish motives among men. Competition unrestricted is a monster as completely antiquated as the saurians, of which the geologists tell us.
'Business Ethics, Past and Present' (1879): 158

economics and economists:

3 Economic laws depend on the voluntary action of men, and the science therefore professes, in effect, to teach how men will act under given circumstances. The motives of human action are the ultimate determining forces, and a misconception as to the nature of these motives is liable to vitiate any conclusion thus attained. The accuracy of the conclusions of Political Economy depends on the correctness of its assumptions with regard to the nature of man. If man is not the being he is assumed to be, there is no certainty that the conclusions will be even approximately correct.
  'Unrecognized Forces in Political Economy' (1877): 710

4 Inaccuracies in the science which result from inadequate conceptions of man are not to be rectified, as has been asserted, by a proper allowance for 'disturbing forces.' The actual course of a cannon ball may be determined by a mathematical computation followed by the proper allowance for atmospheric resistance; but the social activities of men can not be accurately determined by assuming that man is a being of a certain kind, elaborating the conclusions with nicety, and then endeavoring to introduce subsequent allowance for the fact that man is, after all, a being of quite a different kind.
  'Unrecognized Forces in Political Economy' (1877): 711

5 The ideal of Political Economy is not unrestricted competition, but competition that is truly free, because controlled by justice and by law. The distinction between freedom and license needs to be preserved in this department of political philosophy. With that distinction clearly maintained, we may still retain, in economics as in politics, our beautiful watchword, liberty. It is the function of moral influence to separate true liberty from false, by imposing restraints on competition.
  'Business Ethics, Past and Present' (1879): 167

6 The new economic science, as statesmen come to apprehend it, will have some effect on law-making, and as the people ultimately come to apprehend it, will have more. Some conception of the laws of progress will of necessity take form in the popular mind. Inevitably will each thinking man try to perceive what forces are impelling us, whither we are moving, and whether we can control the movement. The invitation which the age extends to its economic students is to exercise such control and to show in what direction the movement should be turned. The age needs principles for its practical guidance. To fail to furnish them would bring economists into merited discredit; to succeed in this task will require a great extension of economic theory.
  'The Field of Economic Dynamics' (1905): 255–256

7 It is entirely possible to strip of technicalities a very large number of economic principles and make them simpler than the problems of mathematics with which a child of ten years is expected to grapple.
  'Economics for Children' (1910): 434

socialism:

8 I mean by socialism, not a doctrine, but a practical movement, tending not to abolish the right of property, but to vest the ownership of it in social organizations, rather than in individuals. The organizations may be private corporations, village-communities, cities, states, or nations, provided only that working men be represented in them. The object of the movement is to secure a distribution of wealth founded on justice, instead of one determined by the actual results of the struggle of competition. Wherever numbers of men unite in the owning of capital, as they already do in the performing of labor, and determine the division of the proceeds by some appeal to a principle of justice, rather than by a general scramble, we have a form of socialism.
  'The Nature and Progress of True Socialism' (1879): 566

9 The most intelligent socialist will be the most zealous opponent of what commonly terms itself socialism. Facts sustain this inference; ... Were theoretical socialism to be inaugurated in practice, practical socialism would be put backward a hundred years.
  'The Nature and Progress of True Socialism' (1879): 577

10 There are two ways in which a socialistic plan of industrial life might come, by successive steps, to completion. The state might assume one industry after another, till none should be left in private hands. The new system would thus spread by local accretion. On the other hand the state might, at first, interfere with all industries in a slight degree, and gradually increase the measure of its control. Socialism would thus begin everywhere at once, and would grow from weakness to strength. It would be by intensive progress, rather than by extensive, that it would come, in the end, to fully possess the field. It is the beginnings of this movement that need to be carefully distinguished.
'The Modern Appeal to Legal Forces in Economic Life' (1894): 10

11 The essence of socialism consists in a new mode of making the power of society felt; and a crude and imperfect way it is, to be thought of as a last resort in case the present system shall work hopelessly ill.
'Concentration of Wealth: A Modified Individualism' (1902): 1066

value:

12 A diamond accidentally discovered does not owe its value to any labor actually expended in its production, but it does owe the measure of its value to a calculation in the mind of the purchaser as to how much labor would be necessary in order to obtain another like it.
'The New Philosophy of Wealth' (1877): 181

13 Value is quantitative measure of utility. Always and everywhere there is present to the mind that makes a valuation, whether for use or exchange, the conception of a concrete thing, of a quality of that thing and of the quantitative measure of that quality.
'The Philosophy of Value' (1881): 459

John Maurice Clark (1884–1963)

competition:

1 Competition is our main safeguard against exploitation. In our sophisticated civilization we dare not trust the terms of exchange to tribal custom and sense of honor, as some primitive peoples can. Under self-interest, people of our advanced stage of culture would naturally incline to give as little and get as much as possible; they would increase their gains by reducing their services, by producing less to sell for more. But competition works the simple miracle whereby each one increases his individual gains by increasing his services rather than reducing them: he makes more by producing more to sell for less.
Alternative to Serfdom (1948), Ch.III, Sec.1: 62

economics and economists:

2 [H]umanity will derive answers to its practical problems from the work of the economists, whether the work of the economists is intended for that purpose or not.
Preface to Social Economics (1936), Part I, Ch.I, Sec.2: 5

3 The economist may attempt to ignore psychology, but it is a sheer impossibility for him to ignore human nature, for his science is a science of human behavior. Any conception of human nature that he may adopt is a matter of psychology, and any conception of human behavior that he may adopt involves psychological assumptions, whether these be explicit or no. If the economist borrows his conception of man from the psychologist, his constructive work may have some chance of remaining purely economic in character. But if he does not he will not thereby avoid psychology. Rather he will force himself to make his own, and it will be bad psychology.
'Economics and Modern Psychology' (1918), Part I, Sec.II: 4

4 Economic theory should be actively relevant to the issues of its time and it should be based on a foundation of terms, conceptions, standards of measurement, and assumptions which is sufficiently realistic, comprehensive, and unbiased to furnish a common meeting ground for argument between advocates of all shades of conviction on practical issues. This is not an ideal of scholarly detachment, for that may lead to studies that are inconsequential or irrelevant to the issues of the day. It is an ideal of scientific impartiality, which is a very different thing.
'Economic Theory in an Era of Social Readjustment' (1919), Sec.I: 280

5 The place of economic generalization lies in the realm of things useful, somewhere between a futility and an impossibility. It is impossible to tell the whole truth about the world and if we insist on summing it up under a simple formula, the only ones that can be one hundred per cent true are in the form: 'Whatever is, is,' a proposition whose futility may be camouflaged but not cured.
'Economic Theory in an Era of Social Readjustment' (1919), Sec.II: 282

social reform:

6 One of the besetting fallacies of reformers is the delusion that their plans will be carried out by people who think precisely as they do.
Guideposts in Time of Change (1949), Ch.VII, Sec.7: 202

social welfare:

7 It is socially safe for individuals to concede the supremacy of the community only if the community is the kind that finds its life and welfare in those of its members and in their sound relations to one another. And it is safe for the community to regard its welfare as consisting in that of its members, and accordingly to give their individual purposes large scope, only if they are social animals and not self-seeking monsters or machines – if they take one another's purposes and needs into account and regard themselves as basically responsible for behaving as members of a community.
Alternative to Serfdom (1948), Ch.I, Sec.5: 20–21

socialism:

8 It is often raised as a conclusive objection to Socialism that it relies on altruism, while the present system harnesses to our service the more reliable force of self-interest. The fact is that in this respect the contrast between the two systems is a matter of degree only. Socialistic industry would find many ways of enlisting and utilizing selfish motives, and we cannot say how great its demands on altruism would be without more extensive experiments than have yet been tried. But we do know that the present system also calls for a great deal of public spirit to make it run properly, and this fact is daily becoming more prominent, and is driven home afresh by every reading of the morning paper.
'The Changing Basis of Economic Responsibility' (1916), Sec.V: 226

Henry Clay (1777–1852)
American politician

trade:

1 Free trade! Free trade! The call for free trade is as unavailing, as the cry of a spoiled child in its nurse's arms, for the moon, or the stars that glitter in the firmament of heaven. It never has existed, it never will exist.
'On the American System' (Speech before the US Senate, 2 February 1832)

Robert Wayne Clower (1926–)

economics and economists:

1 If successful prediction were the sole criterion of the merit of a science, economics should long since have ceased to exist as a serious intellectual pursuit.
'Monetary History and Positive Economics' (1964): 364

2 [E]conomists tend to proceed on the supposition that those they presume to instruct have a good general background knowledge about economic phenomena, as well as a clear appreciation of the nature of scientific inquiry. . . .
In these circumstances, most people would think it perverse if economists insisted on treating their discipline as anything more than systematized common sense.
'How Economists Think' (1989): 9

3 I should no more think of burdening the economics profession with the sins of its practitioners than of burdening the medical profession with the sins of its quacks.
'How Economists Think' (1989): 16

4 For the immediate future . . . it seems to me that the proper business of economists is to advance their own understanding of how the economic system works. It will be time enough for economists to bring light to the world when they are able to

convince themselves that they are no longer groping in the dark.
'How Economists Think' (1989): 17

5 [F]rom a non-normative point of view, economics is just Social Astronomy. Its purported aim is to enhance understanding of the working of the economic universe. If we are ever to be taken seriously as scientists we would be well advised to proceed with this task as most practitioners of other inductive sciences have proceeded – by taking a hard look at the world around us in a serious effort to lend intellectual order to the 'chaos' that strikes our eyes at first sight.
'Economics as an Inductive Science' (1994): 807

6 I won't waste time drawing obvious parallels between 'rational' hydrodynamics and most of what passes for 'serious' theory in contemporary economics. Suffice it to say that, in my opinion, what we presently possess by way of so-called pure economic theory is objectively indistinguishable from what the physicist Richard Feynman, in an unflattering sketch of nonsense 'science,' called 'cargo cult science.'
'Economics as an Inductive Science' (1994): 809

Ronald Henry Coase (1910–)

economics and economists:

1 The problem is that economists seem willing to give advice or [sic] questions about which we know very little and on which our judgments are likely to be fallible while what we have to say which is important and true is quite simple – so simple indeed that little or no economics is required to understand it. What is discouraging is that it is these simple truths which are so commonly ignored in the discussion of economic policy.
'Economists and Public Policy' (1974): 171

2 If we look at the work that economists are doing at the present time, there can be little doubt that economics is expanding its boundaries or, at any rate, that economists are moving more and more into other disciplines. . . . The reason for this movement of economists into neighbouring fields is certainly not that we have solved the problems of the economic system; it would perhaps be more plausible to argue that economists are looking for fields in which they can have some success.
'Economics and Contiguous Disciplines' (1977): 483–484

Arthur William (Bob) Coats (1924–)

economics and economists:

1 Economics may be disintegrating into an increasing number of partially segregated compartments, but it is unlikely to disappear in the foreseeable future. Given the power of professional inertia, as revealed in recent lively discussions of the education of economists, it will not be easy to reform the *status quo* radically.
'The Past, Present and Future of Economics' (1994): 18

Roger Coke (fl.1696)

man and society:

1 That though God made all things for the use of Man, yet few things are useful to Man, but as they are prepared and made so by Human Art and Industry, God never without Man made an House, Ship, Cloth, &c.
Treatise Concerning the Regulation of the Coyn of England (1696), Ch.I

2 No man lives out of Society, *viz.*, out of mutual Conversation with other Men.
Treatise Concerning the Regulation of the Coyn of England (1696), Ch.I

trade:

3 *Trade is now become the Lady, which in this present Age is more Courted and Celebrated than in any former by all the Princes and Potentates of the World, and that deservedly too; For she acquires not her Dominion by the Horrid and Rueful face of Warr, whose footsteps leave ever behind them deep impressions of misery, devastation, and poverty, but with the pleasant aspect of wealth and plenty of all things conducing to the benefit of Humane life and Society, accompanied with strength to defend her, in*

case any shall attempt to Ravish or Invade her.
  A Discourse of Trade (1670), Preface

4 Trade is an Art of Getting, Preparing, and Exchanging things Commodious for Humane Necessities and Convenience.
  A Discourse of Trade (1670), Part I

John Rogers Commons (1862–1945)

concentration of wealth:

1 [I]t is only when it possesses special privileges that concentration of wealth is economically dangerous. Special privileges are always supported by law, or they spring from defects in the law, and the danger of concentration is the danger of perpetuation through law of special privileges.
  'Concentration of Wealth: Its Dangers' (1902): 1040

economics and economists:

2 Economics is a department of Social Philosophy.
  'Twentieth Century Economics' (1939): 29

3 Economics deals with the problems of mankind as they go about trying to make a living or get rich.
  The Economics of Collective Action (1951), Part I, Introduction: 21

Institutionalism:

4 In fact, it is from the field of corporation finance, with its changeable assets and liabilities, rather than from the field of wants and labor, or pains and pleasures, or wealth and happiness, or utility and disutility, that institutional economics derives a large part of its data and methodology. Institutional economics is the assets and liabilities of concerns. . . .
  'Institutional Economics' (1931): 650

5 The classic and hedonic economists, with their communistic and anarchistic offshoots, founded their theories on the relation of man to nature, but institutionalism is a relation of man to man.
  'Institutional Economics' (1931): 652

institutions:

6 If we endeavor to find a universal circumstance, common to all behavior known as institutional, we may define an institution as collective action in control, liberation and expansion of individual action.
  'Institutional Economics' (1931): 649

John Rogers Commons (1862–1945) and John Bertram Andrews (1880–1943)

taxation:

1 The taxing power is an authorization under which government takes private property for public purposes without compensation.
  Principles of Labor Legislation (1916; 2nd edn), Ch.I, Sec.3(1)(b): 11

trade unions:

2 Unions of labor are just as likely to abuse their power as are unions of manufacturers. No organization can be trusted with unlimited power.
  Principles of Labor Legislation (1916; 2nd edn), Ch.III, Sec.1(5): 118

3 It is to the interest of the public, not only that labor shall be free to bargain collectively, but that the employers should also be allowed to combine. Without organization upon both sides there is only one-sided or *pseudo-collective* bargaining.
  Principles of Labor Legislation (1916; 2nd edn), Ch.III, Sec.1(5): 118–119

4 Restrictions in the law upon collective action upon either side are inconsistent with collective bargaining. Complete freedom to combine should be given to both employers and employees.
  Principles of Labor Legislation (1916; 2nd edn), Ch.III, Sec.1(5): 120

Benedetto Croce (1866–1952)
Italian philosopher/historian

economics and economists:

1 Do you wish for the simplest and clearest proof of the non-mechanical nature of the economic principle? Note, then, that in the

data of economics a quality appears which is on the contrary repugnant to that of mechanics. *To an economic fact words can be applied which express approval or disapproval.* Man behaves economically *well* or *ill*, with *gain* or *loss*, *suitably* or *unsuitably*: he behaves, in short, *economically* or *uneconomically*. A fact in economics is, therefore, capable of *appraisement* (positive or negative); whilst a fact in mechanics is a mere fact, to which praise or blame can only be attached metaphorically.
Historical Materialism and the Economics of Karl Marx (1914), Ch.VI, Letter I: 162–163

mathematics in economics:

2 The mathematicians who have a quick feeling for scientific procedure, have done much for economic science by reviving in it the dignity of abstract analysis, darkened and overwhelmed by the mass of anecdotes of the historical school. But, as it happens, they have also introduced into it the prejudice of their profession, and, being themselves students of the general conditions of the physical world, the particular prejudice that mathematics can take up in relation to economics – which is the science of *man*, of a form of the conscious activity of man – the same attitude which it rightly takes up in relation to the empirical natural sciences.
Historical Materialism and the Economics of Karl Marx (1914), Ch.VI, Letter II: 186

Charles Anthony Raven Crosland
(1918–1977)

socialism:

1 Socialists have no desire to penalise small savings, or enterprise and initiative; their aims are social justice and genuine equality of opportunity. Once these are achieved, and the dead hand of inheritance removed, we shall more easily be able to lighten the load of taxation on incomes from work, and restore to individual effort and enterprise some of the rewards which the unequal distribution of property now forces us to tax away.
The Future of Socialism (1956), Part Four, Ch.XV, Sec.V: 332

William Cunningham (1849–1919)

economics and economists:

1 When a case is argued fully, as that of Political Economy has been during the last century, and the listeners remain unconvinced, there seem to be only two possible alternatives – either that the statements are untrue, or that they have been badly expressed. The latter appears to me to be the true explanation . . . .
'Political Economy as a Moral Science' (1878), Introduction: 369

2 Political Economy has been a science of *things*, and discoursed of intrinsic value; it has been a science of *mechanism*, and explained the interaction of competing interest; may we not treat it as a moral science which considers *the resources of human nature for the satisfying of human wants?*
'Political Economy as a Moral Science' (1878), Sec.I: 373

3 If there is one thing from which Political Economy has suffered more than another it is from the fact that the public have formed an undue estimate of what it could really do, and have then been disappointed because it failed to come up to their expectations.
'The Relativity of Economic Doctrine' (1892), Introduction: 1

4 Political Economy cannot lay down laws which hold good of all times and all places. If economic phenomena were similar to physical phenomena and preserved the same general character uniformly for the whole period of human existence on the globe, it might be possible to detect the laws which describe their regular sequences. But economic phenomena are not characterized by this uniformity; there are no regular and unchanging movements for us to detect.
'The Relativity of Economic Doctrine' (1892), Sec.III: 14

5 If Political Economy cannot give us the limits of possible human action and human responsibility, it certainly cannot set forth positive rules of duty. All it can do, as a practical doctrine, is to prescribe means to a given end. If a nation desires glory it may

give suggestions as to the best means of maintaining armaments and of quarrelling to advantage; if it desire [sic] solid comfort and industrial success it may show how this too is to be obtained. But it cannot lay down any criterion as to the end that ought to be pursued; it cannot speak with authority. Religion or Ethics may give us some ideal for human society which we desire to realize, and then Political Economy may be able to point out some of the means for accomplishing this end, or some of the obstacles that stand in its way. But as a practical doctrine too, it is relative – relative to the ethical aims and objects we set before us; it cannot point out the duty we ought to do, but it can only help us to see ways of accomplishing something that we believe it is our duty to try to accomplish. It has no authority to dictate a course of action; but in subservience to Ethics or Religion – to ideals which they furnish and relatively to them – it may help us to take a wise course for accomplishing a right object.

'The Relativity of Economic Doctrine' (1892), Sec.III: 15

6 The ordinary economist, who assumes free competition and the laws of supply and demand, has awakened to realize that there is a vast field of industry and enterprise of which he ought to take account. He professes himself extremely interested in History, and like a French king of whom one has heard, expresses a wish to do anything he can for it. To this polite desire it is surely not discourteous to reply, *Laissez faire, laissez aller*. Economists will not leave it alone; they do not pursue it seriously, but try to incorporate some of its results into that curious amalgam, the main body of economic tradition; and the result is the perversion of Economic History.

'The Perversion of Economic History' (1892), Introduction: 491

7 The misunderstanding of the sphere and scope of the science [of political economy] is common enough, and it is one for which economists are partly to blame, even while they deplore it; but though common and excusable, it is none the less complete. The so-called laws of political economy – in so far as they are universal in form – are hypothetical principles which it is convenient to use as instruments for investigating the complicated phenomena of society; but it is absurd to treat mere instruments of investigation, assumed for convenience' sake, as principles for practical guidance. Some of the so-called laws of political economy have a different character, since they are generalisations from experience; they tell us what has happened, and so enable us to forecast what will happen under any similar conditions. They formulate what has occurred in the past, but do not tell us what ought to occur in the future; they neither condemn nor approve what is yet untried.

'A Living Wage' (1894), Sec.I: 17

8 Political economy does not approve or condemn; it gives us the best available means of forecasting the probable result of some change in its effects on the material prosperity of the country; the science then leaves it to politicians and moralists to approve or disapprove of the project.

'A Living Wage' (1894), Sec.I: 17

9 Political Economists, in trying to pass beyond the old limitations of the science, have lost their bearings; their reasoning loses touch with actuality, and fails to throw light on the course of affairs. Elaborate calculations, illustrated by complicated diagrams, may only end in a re-statement of the data from which the argument started. Economic Science is at its best in analysing the phenomena of the past and of the present, but it cannot give a sufficiently authoritative forecast of the future to supply definite guidance in the perplexities of practical life. Enquiries which are devoted to the examination of states of consciousness in the present can give us little guidance in regard to the possibilities of the future, – either as to the conditions on which increased material prosperity depends, or as to the anticipated progress of improvement in human capacity and character. Economists appear to be nonplussed from the difficulty of finding formulæ which take adequate account of the means of life on the one hand, and of human habits and temperaments on the other, as elements in personal welfare; and it is misleading to take individual happiness as a unit from which the good of mankind can be built up. To insist that the national wealth consists of the aggregate of the wealth of

individuals is plausible; but the welfare of the community is something more than the aggregate sum of the satisfaction enjoyed by separate individuals.
Christianity and Economic Science (1914), Ch.VI: 92–93

mathematics in economics:

10 If economic science is little regarded by practical men, it is partly because economists have been so much inclined to cast it in such a form that they can employ mathematical methods. Such reasonings have high and transcendent validity, but no direct relation to actual life.
'Political Economy and Practical Life' (1893), Sec.II: 191

Sir Henry Hardinge Samuel Cunynghame (1848–1935)

taxation:

1 Nothing is more difficult than to fix the true incidence of taxation when its secondary effects are considered. In a healthy community as in a healthy body, the parts are so co-related that what hurts one hurts all. In taxation injustice is more often produced by sudden changes than by any other cause.
'Some Improvements in Simple Geometrical Methods of Treating Exchange Value, Monopoly, and Rent' (1892), Sec.8: 52

D

Bernardo Davanzati (1529–1606)

money:

1 Some maintain that *Money* was a very ill Invention, for this reason, *viz*. That the Desire of other things could not be so great, nor the cause of so many Evils as is the Thrist of Gold; because so much of those could not be laid up and preserv'd, as there may be treasur'd of this. . . . Money was an excellent Invention, and an Instrument of doing infinite good; if any makes an ill use of it, 'tis not the Thing but the Person that is to be blam'd and punish'd.
A Discourse Upon Coins (1588), Sec.16

Charles D'Avenant (1656–1714)

credit:

1 Of all Beings that have Existence only in the Minds of Men, nothing is more fantastical and nice than Credit; 'tis never to be forc'd; it hangs upon Opinion; it depends upon our Passions of Hope and Fear; it comes many times unfought for, and often goes away without Reason; and when once lost, is hardly to be quite recover'd.
Discourses on the Publick Revenues, and on the Trade of England (1698), Part I, Discourse II: 38

trade:

2 Trade is in its Nature Free, finds it own Channel, and best directeth its own Course: and all Laws to give it Rules, and Directions, and to Limit, and Circumscribe it, may serve the Particular Ends of Private Men, but are seldom Advantagious to the publick.
An Essay on the East-India-Trade (1696): 25

Herbert Joseph Davenport (1861–1931)

economics and economists:

1 It may not be too much to say that the next line of advance in economic theory will be distinctly psychological in character, and that further progress awaits its new impulse at the hands of the psychologist.
'Proposed Modifications in Austrian Theory and Terminology' (1902), Sec.I: 355

2 Economics must keep itself abreast of modern thought or, at the worst, must more or less belatedly follow after.
'Proposed Modifications in Austrian Theory and Terminology' (1902), Sec.I: 355

3 It is probably true that the last word in economics will be said only after the last work has been done in philosophy or in psychology or in both. . . . It seems indeed certain that, if there can be no political economy till all the issues of psychology are settled, there can never be any political economy at all.
'Scope, Method, and Psychology in Economics' (1917): 617

Phyllis Mary Deane (1918–)

economics and economists:

1 If economics is a science – and it is not as clear as it used to be what *that* is – it is evidently a science whose powers of prediction and control are limited, largely because the phenomena it seeks to explain are subject to persistent change and often for reasons that may lie outside the traditional boundaries of the discipline.
'The Scope and Method of Economic Science' (1983): 11–12

Gerard Debreu (1921–)

mathematics in economics:

1 Mathematics provides him [the economist] with a language and a method that permit an effective study of economic systems of forbidding complexity; but it is a demanding master. It ceaselessly asks for weaker as-

sumptions, for stronger conclusions, for greater generality. In taking a mathematical form, economic theory is driven to submit to those demands.
'The Mathematization of Economic Theory' (1991), Sec.II: 4

2   The spread of mathematized economic theory was helped even by its esoteric character. Since its messages cannot be deciphered by economists who do not have the proper key, their evaluation is entrusted to those who have access to the code. But acceptance of their technical expertise also implies acceptance of their values. Our profession may take pride in its exceptional intellectual diversity.... Yet that diversity is strained by the increasing impenetrability to the overwhelming majority of our Association of the work done by its most mathematical members.
'The Mathematization of Economic Theory' (1991), Sec.III: 6

Daniel De Leon (1852–1914)
American socialist

trade unionism:

1   The mission of unionism is not to act as rearguard to an army defeated, seasoned in defeat, habituated to defeat, and fit only for defeat. The mission of unionism is to organize and drill the working class for final victory – to 'take and hold' the machinery of production, which means the administration of the country.
'The Preamble of the IWW' (1905): 36

2   Capitalist economics is at home, capitalist economics is tolerated, capitalist economics is safeguarded, aye, capitalist economics is fought for in craft unionism – who would dare gainsay that politics *is* a palpitating fact in the union?
'The Preamble of the IWW' (1905): 48

3   Industrial Unionism is the Socialist Republic in the making; and the goal once reached, the Industrial Union is the Socialist Republic in operation.
Accordingly, the Industrial Union is at once the battering ram with which to pound down the fortress of Capitalism, and the successor of the capitalist social structure itself.
'Industrial Unionism' (1913): 65

Thomas De Quincey (1785–1859)

economics and economists:

1   Political Economy does not advance.... It has always been my own conviction that the reason lies not in any material defect of facts (except as to the single question of money), but in the laxity of some amongst the distinctions which are elementary to the science.... Let us judge by analogy from mathematics. If it were possible that but three elementary definitions, or axioms, or postulates in geometry should be liable to controversy and to a *precarious* use (a use dependent upon petition and momentary consent), what would follow? Simply this, – that the whole vastaerial synthesis of that science, at present towering upwards towards infinity, would exhibit an eclipse eternally, perhaps, renewing itself by parts, but eternally tottering in some parts, and in other parts mouldering eternally into ruins. That science, which now holds 'acquaintance with the stars' by means of its inevitable and imperishable truth, would become as treacherous as Shakespeare's 'stairs of sand'; or, like the fantastic architecture which the winds are everlastingly pursuing in the Arabian desert, would exhibit phantom arrays of fleeting columns and fluctuating edifices, which, under the very breath that had created them, would be for ever collapsing into dust. Such, even to this moment, as regards its *practical* applications, is the science of Political Economy. Nothing can be postulated – nothing can be demonstrated; for anarchy, even as to the earliest principles, is predominant.
The Logic of Political Economy (1844): 118–119

value:

2   The question from which all Political Economy will be found to move – the question to which all its difficulties will be found reducible – is this: *What is the ground of exchangeable value?*
'Dialogues of Three Templars on Political Economy' (1824), Dialogue the First: 54

Antoine-Louis-Claude Destutt, Comte de Tracy (1754–1836)
French philosopher and soldier

government:

1. A first thing very certain is, that government cannot be ranked amongst the consumers of the industrious class. The expenditure it makes does not return into its hands with an increase of value. It does not support itself on the profits it makes. I conclude, then, that its consumption is very real and definitive; that nothing remains from the labour which it pays; and that the riches which it employs, and which were existing, are consumed and destroyed when it has availed itself of them.
    A Treatise on Political Economy – First Part of the Treatise on the Will and Its Effects: Of Our Actions (1817), Ch.XII: 197

Thomas Roderick Dew (1802–1846)

economics and economists:

1. [W]hen men arise in deliberative bodies, and thank their God they are no *political economists, no theorists*, they in a short time shew by their unwarrantable generalizations, how much they stand in need of that sound theory against which their philippics are directed.
    Lectures on the Restrictive System (1829), Lecture X: 194

government:

2. The great object of government is to hold the aegis of its power over the individual, while he is left unassailed and unannoyed, to accomplish the great objects of his creation. Its advantages are rather negative, than positive; rather calculated to ward off the evils by which we are beset, than procure for us any positive good.
    Lectures on the Restrictive System (1829), Lecture I, Part I: 8

Maurice Herbert Dobb (1900–1976)

capitalism:

1. In a planless economy ruled by the market individual *entrepreneurs* can have no assurance that such a level of investment in expanding the capital goods sector will continue. Any expectation that it will do so can only be an act of faith – a triumph of irrationality in a system that economists and economic historians claim has exalted rationality to be the sovereign rule of business life!
    An Essay on Economic Growth and Planning (1960), Ch.V: 75

economics and economists:

2. If all that is postulated is simply that men *choose*, without anything being stated even as to how they choose or what governs their choice, it would seem impossible for economics to provide us with any more than a sort of algebra of human choice, indicating certain rather obvious forms of inter-relationship between choices, but telling us little as to the way in which any actual situation will behave.
    Political Economy and Capitalism (1945; revised edition), Ch.V: 171

3. If truth is to be gleaned from practice as well as inspire it, the economist can as little stand aloof *qua* economist as *qua* citizen of the world from such issues. To breathe life into the bones of abstract notions, he must, it would seem, not only descend from his cloister to walk in the market-places of the world, but must take part in their battles, since only then can he be of the world as well as in it. This is not to sell his birthright: it is to march in the best tradition of Political Economy. At any rate, if he does not, the world, and his cloister with it, may soon start tumbling about his ears.
    Political Economy and Capitalism (1945; revised edition), Ch.VIII: 337–338

mathematics in economics:

4. [S]o long as mathematical technique retains its servitude to a particular mode of thought, the concepts which it fashions are calculated to veil rather than to reveal reality. For this mode of thought, which is enshrined in the subjective theory of value, first creates for us a realm where disembodied minds hold communion with etherealized objects of choice, and then, unmindful of the distance between this abstract world and reality,

seeks to represent the relations which it finds in this realm as governing the relations which hold in actual economic society and as controlling the shape which events must have under any and every system of social institutions. This is to confuse thought and to distort reality. It is to have everything standing on its head. To emancipate economic thought from this heritage is a task that is long overdue.
Political Economy and Capitalism (1945; revised edition), Ch.V: 183–184

Robert Dorfman (1916–2002)

mathematics in economics:

1 Practitioners of mathematical economics already have their hands full coping with some of the toughest problems which the science offers and it is unfair to impose on them the special problems of literary lucidity. Mathematical and literary talents do not always dwell in the same man.
'A Catechism: Mathematics in Social Science' (1954): 376

Clifford Hugh Douglas (1879–1952)

money:

1 *The proper function of a money system is to furnish the information necessary to direct the production and distribution of goods and services.* It is, or should be, an 'order' system, not a 'reward' system. It is essentially a mechanism of administration, subservient to policy, and it is because it is superior to all other mechanisms of administration, that the money control of the world is so immensely important.
Social Credit (1933; revised edn), Part I, Ch.VII: 62

James Stemble Duesenberry (1918–)

mathematics in economics:

1 Criticisms of mathematical methods may be a bit childish, but after all it was a child who saw that the king had no clothes.
'The Methodological Basis of Economic Theory' (1954): 363

monetary policy:

2 The more we use monetary policy, the less satisfactory it seems.
'Alternatives to Monetary Policy' (1974): 105

Charles Franklin Dunbar
(1830–1900)

economics and economists:

1 When the economist restricts his discussion to something less than the sum of all the considerations of right and expediency which must weigh in questions of political action, his contribution toward the final decision may indeed be pronounced important or the reverse, according to the judgment of the critic; but there is as little ground for the moral condemnation sometimes fulminated, as when one investigator declares his field to be physiology and not therapeutics, or another devotes himself to the mechanical and chemical properties of the rocks, and not to their geological relations. It is only when the economist undertakes to apply his conclusions in disregard of other aspects of the political or social questions before him, and treats these questions as problems in political economy only, that there is room for the reprobation of his neglect of ethical considerations; and, in this case, he is sinning against the law implied in his own method. Much confusion and misplaced censure, however, upon other points as well as this, might easily be avoided, by keeping in mind more carefully the necessary distinction between a science and its applications.
'The Reaction in Political Economy' (1886): 8–9

2 It is only by extending the definition of political economy itself, so as to include a vast region of politics and ethics, and thus destroying the possibility of all scientific precision, that we can describe as economic questions a great mass of those which commonly pass for such. This confusion of boundaries is no doubt often ventured upon, and with the eager student the temptation to it must always exist.
'The Academic Study of Political Economy' (1891): 412

Arsène Jules Etienne Juvenal Dupuit (1804–1866)

mathematics in economics:

1 [T]he less complete and accurate are the available data in problems of political economy, the more needful is it that the rigour of fundamental scientific principles be applied to them if they are to be handled skilfully and effectively in practice.
    'On the Measurement of the Utility of Public Works' (1844): 106

2 So soon as it is realized ... that political economy is concerned with quantities susceptible of a more or a less, it must also be recognized that it is in the realm of mathematics. If one has gone astray in political economy every time one has relied on mathematical calculations, it is because there are mathematicians who make false calculations, just as there are logicians who produce false arguments: the former no more invalidate mathematics than the latter invalidate logic, which alone is sometimes regarded as a science.
    'On the Measurement of the Utility of Public Works' (1844), Note: 109–110

Evan Frank Mottram Durbin (1906–1948)

economics and economists:

1 Economists, like mathematicians, have no choice but to agree, in the long run, about economic theory.
    'Economists and the Future Functions of the State' (1943), Sec.3: 257

2 Economists are the paid 'remembrancers' of the public conscience. It is their duty to denounce the specious pleas of monopolist and trade unionist and to summon the lazy citizen to repentance. We are uncomfortable folk, professional prophets, unless we shirk our obligations.
    'Economists and the Future Functions of the State' (1943), Sec.8: 267

E

John L. Eatwell, Baron Eatwell of Stratton St. Margaret (1945–)

economics and economists:

1 Economists' ideas do not lead events, they follow them. Brilliant political fashions are often economically old-hat. Ideas are picked up, dropped, revived, given more attractive covering (mathematics being the fashionable top-dressing at the moment) and presented as penetrating and new. Nothing is quite so powerful as an idea whose time has come.
Whatever Happened to Britain? (1982), Ch.2: 33

2 Although economists are often the intellectual hired guns of political interests, this does not mean that they don't sometimes identify some elements of the process by which the market mechanism actually works. But it does mean that we should always be aware of just where ideas come from. For even the most abstract bit of theorising is erected round the skeleton of its ideological origins.
Whatever Happened to Britain? (1982), Ch.2: 33

3 In economics there is always a temptation to choose assumptions that are convenient rather than realistic – a vice that afflicts all economists, though some more than others.
Whatever Happened to Britain? (1982), Ch.2: 36

monetarism:

4 Monetarism is the most bizarre form taken by devotion to the market, for as well as relying on a mechanism that does not work, cuts in government expenditure, designed to lower the growth of the money supply, reduce demand and worsen unemployment.
Whatever Happened to Britain? (1982), Ch.8: 148

Sir Frederic Morton Eden, Baronet (1766–1809)

poor relief:

1 That it is the duty of every man, according to his abilities and opportunities, to relieve his fellow creatures in distress, will no doubt be readily and generally admitted. It is the never-failing theme of the moralist and the Divine, and the politician is no less persuaded that the *Infant Poor* should be relieved from beggary and want, the *Sick Poor* restored to health, and that a bare subsistence for the *Aged Poor* is no more than the fair right of those, who have spent their best days, and exhausted their strength, in the service of the public.
The State of the Poor (1797), Bk.II, Ch.I: 85

Francis Ysidro Edgeworth (1845–1926)

economics and economists:

1 The first principle of Economics is that every agent is actuated only by self-interest. The workings of this principle may be viewed under two aspects, according as the agent acts *without*, or *with*, the consent of others affected by his actions. In wide senses, the first species of action may be called *war*; the second, *contract*.
Mathematical Psychics (1881), Part II: 16–17

2 It is in economics only, when we have excepted the mathematical physics, that there is realized with some perfection that type of science to which Greek thought aspired, which Aristotle taught if he did not practise: the leading up to general principles and leading down to particular conclusions. The logical methods, which are studied in the School of *literæ humaniores* may be exemplified in political economy without

going beyond the range of subjects conterminous to that school.
'An Introductory Lecture on Political Economy' (1891): 626

3 Economic controversy is generally a thankless task. You cannot hope to make any impression on your opponent. Yet he is the only reader on whose interest you can count.
'Professor Graziani on the Mathematical Theory of Monopoly' (1898): 234

institutions:

4 Milton, when, galled by the yoke of an ill-assorted marriage, he proposed as a remedy for marital troubles freedom of divorce, thus reflected complacently on that proposal: 'I doubt not but with one gentle stroking to wipe away ten thousand tears out of the life of man.' But the economist, remembering how often the appearance of easy remedies for human ills, in his sphere at least, has proved deceptive, will not expect much from a stroke, gentle or violent, intended to revolutionise established institutions which have worked well for the production of wealth and economic welfare. The only reforms of such institutions which the economist can approve are tentative and gradual.
'Women's Wages in Relation to Economic Welfare' (1923): 495

mathematics in economics:

5 He that will not verify his conclusions as far as possible by mathematics, as it were bringing the ingots of common sense to be assayed and coined at the mint of the sovereign science, will hardly realize the full value of what he holds, will want a measure of what it will be worth in however slightly altered circumstances, a means of conveying and making it current.
Mathematical Psychics (1881), Part I: 3

6 The parsimony of symbols, which is often an elegance in the physicist, is a necessity for the economist. Indeed, it is tenable that our mathematical constructions should be treated as a sort of scaffolding, to be removed when the edifice of science is completed.
'Points at which mathematical reasoning is applicable to political economy' (1889): 500; cf. R.G.D. Allen 2

Thomas Rowe Edmonds
(1803–1889)

taxation:

1 The proper object of taxation is, to increase the national power, – by diminishing the labour employed on luxuries, and adding to the labour engaged in the production of necessaries, or wealth.
Practical Moral and Political Economy (1833), Book II, Ch.X: 153

2 Taxation, when applied to the purpose of repressing useless, and encouraging useful labour, is the best and most powerful engine of government.
Practical Moral and Political Economy (1833), Book II, Ch.X: 160

Albert Einstein (1879–1955)
German–American physicist

socialism:

1 Since the real purpose of socialism is precisely to overcome and advance beyond the predatory phase of human development, economic science in its present state can throw little light on the socialist society of the future.
'Why Socialism?' (1949): 9

William Ellis (1800–1881)

poverty:

1 Destitution unrelieved is intolerable to a humane people. Where it has not been prevented, it must be relieved.
'Relief Measures' (1850): 85

2 In relieving the destitute, it must never be forgotten that the means of relief are procured from the labour and self-denial of others who are struggling to support themselves.
'Relief Measures' (1850): 85

Jon Elster (1940–)

economics and economists:

1 [N]eoclassical economics will be dethroned if and when satisficing theory and psychology

join forces to produce a simple and robust explanation of aspiration levels, or sociological theory comes up with a simple and robust theory of the relation between social norms and instrumental rationality. Until this happens, the continued dominance of neoclassical theory is ensured by the fact that one can't beat something with nothing.
Introduction to *Rational Choice* (1986), Sec.V

Richard Theodore Ely (1854–1943)

collectivism:

1 It is prejudice which exists against many of our great industries which stands in the way of our profiting by what they have to teach us in regard to national prosperity. Why should we not learn from Germany what Germany has to teach, even if the last Kaiser were as bad as some think he is? Why should we not learn what the Standard Oil has to teach us in regard to integration and wise management in the utilization of natural resources, even if the Standard Oil Company in its past history may have been guilty of anti-social practices? Into this past it is not necessary to enter either pro or con. From the point of view of conservation and wise employment of labor and capital, it is scarcely too much to say that the Standard Oil Company, as a whole, affords suggestions for improvement that have greater value for the country than all the benefactions of the Rockefellers.
Hard Times – The Way In and the Way Out (1931), Ch.VI: 61

competition:

2 When we come to speak of the disadvantages of the modern system of freedom, that is to say, of competition, it occurs to us that the moral atmosphere of a race-course is not a wholesome one. Competition tends to force the level of economic life down to the moral standard of the worst men who can sustain themselves in the business community.
An Introduction to Political Economy (1889), Part I, Ch.IX: 83

economics and economists:

3 'Orthodox' and 'heterodox' must be as completely driven out of economic discussion as out of biology and mineralogy. Those who use these phrases must necessarily look back to the past to discover the belief of others, whereas science should ever keep its glance directed to the future and press on to the discovery of new truth.
'Political Economy in America' (1887): 114–115

4 The true economist is a guide who always keeps in advance, who marks out new paths of social progress. This explains why the 'heterodox' economist of one age becomes the 'orthodox' economist of a succeeding one.
'Political Economy in America' (1887): 115

5 [Economists] are not concerned merely with the material life of men in its narrow sense, for there can scarcely be a phase of the life of society which does not come within the province of the economist.
An Introduction to Political Economy (1889), Part I, Ch.II: 25

government:

6 How any one who believes in the fatherhood of God and in paternalism in the family is able to sneer at paternalism and reject every element of it in government as a bad thing, I am unable to conceive. I must confess that I am too much of a conservative in my views and sentiments to do this.
'Fraternalism vs. Paternalism in Government' (1898): 781

socialism:

7 Socialism seeks such a reconstruction of society that the entire products of labor shall accrue to the laborer. It would extend the application of St. Paul's injunction – 'If a man will not work neither shall he eat' – to all men impartially. Socialism aims, then, not to abolish capital – a folly which no sane man ever contemplated – but it desires to do away forever with a distinct class of capitalists.
'Socialism in America' (1886): 519

8 There are, as a matter of fact, two kinds of socialism – paternal and fraternal; but the popular socialism of the day is altogether fraternal in character. I am inclined to urge,

taxation:

9 It is first of all to be remembered that taxation in itself is not an evil; it is a blessing. This sounds paradoxical; does it not? Nevertheless, it is true, as it will be found on an examination of the historical development of constitutional governments that taxation was the instrumentality whereby the common people obtained their liberties. Monarchs needed revenues, and were obliged to ask for them; as a matter of fact, they could not secure sufficient and regular revenues otherwise. These revenues have been granted conditionally. 'Yes,' the people said to their sovereigns, 'we will grant you the revenues if you will grant us our demands.' Thus step by step popular rights have been secured. The total abolition of taxation would undoubtedly be one of the most effective and most dangerous blows to popular government which it could well receive.
An Introduction to Political Economy (1889), Part VI, Ch.II: 301

10 Very generally increased freedom is accompanied by increased taxation.
An Introduction to Political Economy (1889), Part VI, Ch.II: 301

truth:

11 People are learning, both in political economy and natural science, that truth alone can make them free; that truth alone has in it the power of life; that truth – not error – is able to conserve the good, and that to fear it is unworthy of an enlightened people.
'Political Economy in America' (1887): 118

Friedrich Engels (1820–1895)

protectionism:

1 Protection is a plan for artificially manufacturing manufacturers, and therefore also a plan for artificially manufacturing wage-laborers.
'Protection and Free Trade' (1888): 536

socialism:

2 Insofar as modern socialism, no matter of what tendency, starts out from bourgeois political economy, it almost without exception takes up the Ricardian theory of value.
'Marx and Rodbertus' (1884): 279

3 To make a science of Socialism, it had first to be placed upon a real basis.
Socialism, Utopian and Scientific (1901), Ch.I: 17

4 These two great discoveries, the materialist conception of history and the revelation of the secret of capitalist production through surplus value, we owe to Marx. With these discoveries Socialism became a science. The next thing was to work out all its details and relations.
Socialism, Utopian and Scientific (1901), Ch.II: 28

Desiderius Erasmus (1469–1536)

money:

1 In the coinage of money the good prince will display the trustworthiness he owes both to God and to the people, and will not allow himself to do things for which he punishes other people most harshly.
The Education of a Christian Prince (1516), Sec.4: 262

public finance:

2 The most welcome way of increasing revenue would be for the prince to abolish superfluous expenditure, to disband redundant offices, to avoid wars and foreign tours (which are very like wars), to check the acquisitiveness of officialdom, and to pay more attention to the just administration of his territory than to its expansion.
The Education of a Christian Prince (1516), Sec.4: 260

taxation:

3 [I]f necessity requires some taxation of the people, then it is the good prince's job

to do it in such a way that the least possible hardship falls on the poor. For it is perhaps politic to summon the rich to austerity, but to reduce poor people to hunger and servitude is both very cruel and very risky.
The Education of a Christian Prince (1516), Sec.4: 261

4   [I]t is impossible for a measure ever to be abolished, once it has been introduced to meet some temporary situation, if it seems to be to the financial advantage of the prince or the nobility. When the need for a tax has passed, not only should the people's burden be lifted but as far as possible their expenditure during that previous period should be reimbursed in compensation.
The Education of a Christian Prince (1516), Sec.4: 261

5   The good prince will therefore impose as little tax as possible on those things whose use is shared also by the poorest ranks of the people, such as corn, bread, beer, wine, clothes, and all the other things without which human life cannot be carried on. But these things at present carry a very heavy burden, and in more than one way: first by the very heavy taxes which the revenue agents extort . . ., then by import duties, which even have their own agents to themselves, and lastly by the monopolies. In order that a very little income may get back to the prince from these sources, the poorer people are milked dry by this expenditure.
The Education of a Christian Prince (1516), Sec.4: 262

Walter Eucken (1891–1950)

economics and economists:

1   Definitions and questions about definitions can have no place at the outset of the study of economics, and they are usually no longer put at the beginning of other sciences. A science is quite unable at the beginning of its investigations to provide scientific definitions. There is no basis on which to define the concept 'economising' before investigating the facts. A definition which is attempted without such investigation can only be founded on popular usage and this leads to hazy and uncertain constructions being built up on terms defined in this way. It is hardly surprising that different students of the subject, according to their preferences, have different definitions of the basic concepts to offer, and thus start controversies as to what 'economising' is – controversies as violent as they are valueless from the point of view of advancing our knowledge of economic reality.
The Foundations of Economics (1950), Part I, Ch.I, Sec.I,4: 24–25

2   The first task of the economist is to get a grasp of economic reality. This may be a requirement which, however justified and necessary, may not be *possible*. The economist has to see economic events as part of a particular individual-historical situation if he is to do justice to the real world. He must see them also as presenting general-theoretical problems if the relationships of the real world are not to escape him. How can he combine these two views? If he does only the one or only the other, he is out of touch with the real world.
The Foundations of Economics (1950), Part I, Ch.II, Sec.III: 41

3   The economist resembles a traveller starting off on a journey from which he promises himself striking and spacious vistas. But already after the first step he finds himself surrounded by what seems to be an impenetrable jungle.
The Foundations of Economics (1950), Part I, Ch.II, Sec.III: 44

4   Economics must maintain its independence of all other sciences, for they have different problems to solve. It will fail in its task if it is dominated by methods of investigation taken over from the history of the natural sciences which have not arisen out of the problem of the great antinomy in economics. As no other science has the same conflicting problems to overcome, any simple transfer to economics of methods derived from other sciences would be inapposite and misleading.
The Foundations of Economics (1950), Part III, Ch.VI: 311

5 Economic thought is a political force. It determines and orientates economic and political action.
This Unsuccessful Age (1951), Ch.V: 83

6 Economic science must proceed from the individual and historical manifold nature of its subject matter, otherwise the ground is cut away from under its feet.
This Unsuccessful Age (1951), Ch.V: 87

Alexander Hill Everett (1790–1847)
American diplomat and author

poor laws:

1 [T]he supposition that the sight of the almshouse will tempt the poor to be improvident and idle, is about as reasonable as it would be to imagine that the view of the gallows would seduce them to the commission of highway robbery.
New Ideas on Population (1826; 2nd edn), Ch.X: 105

F

Henry Fawcett (1833–1884)

economics and economists:

1 Whenever political economy is applied to any practical question, it is most important to remember that this science frequently only investigates and affirms tendencies.
   'Strikes: Their Tendencies and Remedies' (1860): 4

2 Political economy if kept within its proper limits does not provide a code of social ethics which will enable us to decide what is right or wrong, and what is just or unjust. It is the business of political economy to explain the effect which any circumstance such as the imposition of a tax, or the enforcement of a particular landed tenure, will exert upon the production, the distribution, and the exchange of wealth; and it is therefore manifest that political economy cannot take account of various other consequences which may be independent of any considerations concerning wealth.
   Manual of Political Economy (1863), Book I, Ch.I: 6

methodology:

3 It is a fundamental error to direct attention only to the effects of social phenomena, and not to investigate the causes from which these effects flow as natural results. The consideration of the visible effects of any social movement cannot afford sufficient data to decide whether its tendency is good or bad, and as long as the causes of a social movement remain unexplained, its tendency cannot be directed, and such a direction and not resistance is generally all that can be done either by the politician or by the philanthropist.
   'Strikes: Their Tendencies and Remedies' (1860): 3

protectionism:

4 People who are perpetually told that the degree of prosperity which an industry enjoys, depends upon the amount of protection which it receives from the State, are really nurtured in the belief that the State can remedy all that is unsatisfactory in their own condition.
   'The Recent Development of Socialism in Germany and the United States' (1878): 611

socialism:

5 Between the Socialism of former days, and the Socialism of the present time, there is this distinction: the schemes of the earlier Socialists were voluntary organizations, and however much individual liberty had to be sacrificed by those who joined a Socialistic community, no attempt was made to coerce any one to join it. The Socialists, however, of the present day, propose to use the power of the State to fashion the entire community to a prescribed economic model. Modern Socialism therefore possesses an importance which is incalculably greater than can be attributed to any of the various communistic schemes which have been carried out simply by individual effort.
   'The Recent Development of Socialism in Germany and the United States' (1878): 605

6 Each fresh encroachment that the State is permitted to make on individual liberty, prepares a community more willingly to accept the principles of modern Socialism, by teaching them to rely less upon themselves and more upon the State.
   'The Recent Development of Socialism in Germany and the United States' (1878): 614

Dame Millicent [Garrett] Fawcett (1847–1929)

equality of wages:

1 I have always regarded it as an error, both in principle and in tactics, to advise women under all circumstances to demand the same wages for the same work as men.... The cry 'the same wages for the same work' is very

plausible, but it is proved to be impossible of achievement when the economic conditions of the two sexes are so widely different.
'Mr. Sidney Webb's Article on Women's Wages' (1892): 176

Adam Ferguson (1723–1815)

undirected order:

1 Mankind, in following the present sense of their minds, in striving to remove inconveniencies, or to gain apparent and contiguous advantages, arrive at ends which even their imagination could not anticipate, and pass on, like other animals, in the track of their nature, without perceiving its end.
An Essay on the History of Civil Society (1767), Part Third, Sec.II: 119

2 Men, in general, are sufficiently disposed to occupy themselves in forming projects and schemes: but he who would scheme and project for others, will find an opponent in every person who is disposed to scheme for himself. Like the winds, that come we know not whence, and blow whithersoever they list, the forms of society are derived from an obscure and distant origin; they arise, long before the date of philosophy, from the instincts, not from the speculations, of men. The croud [sic] of mankind, are directed in their establishments and measures, by the circumstances in which they are placed; and seldom are turned from their way, to follow the plan of any single projector.

Every step and every movement of the multitude, even in what are termed enlightened ages, are made with equal blindness to the future; and nations stumble upon establishments, which are indeed the result of human action, but not the execution of any human design.
An Essay on the History of Civil Society (1767), Part Third, Sec.II: 119

Frank Albert Fetter (1863–1949)

economics and economists:

1 *Economics, or political economy, may be defined, briefly, as the study of men earning a living; or, more fully, as the study of the material world and of the activities and mutual relations of men so far as all these are the objective conditions to gratifying desires.*
The Principles of Economics (1904), Part I, Division A, Ch.1, Sec.I,1: 3

2 *The ideal of political economy here set forth is that it should be a science, a search for truth, a systematized body of knowledge, arriving at a statement of the laws to which economic actions conform.* It is not the advocacy of any particular policy or idea, but if it arrives at any conclusions, any truths, these cannot fail to affect the practical action of men.
The Principles of Economics (1904), Part I, Division A, Ch.1, Sec.III,1: 7

3 *[T]he study of political economy is a social study for social ends and not a selfish study for individual advantage.*
The Principles of Economics (1904), Part I, Division A, Ch.1, Sec.III,2: 7

taxation:

4 *Provision for the expense of organized government is the fundamental purpose of taxation.*
The Principles of Economics (1904), Part III, Division B, Ch.49, Sec.I,1: 471

5 By taxation the government interferes with the individual's free choice and with the impersonal economic forces. It expends income in different ways from those which would be chosen by the individual.
The Principles of Economics (1904), Part III, Division B, Ch.49, Sec.I,1: 471

6 Taxation that is variable, shifting, dependent on personal whim and favoritism, is despotism.
The Principles of Economics (1904), Part III, Division B, Ch.49, Sec.III,2: 478

7 The [tax] assessor is as near a despot as any agent of popular government to-day. Not infrequently it is to men incapable of earning two dollars a day in any private business that the power is given of passing judgment on the value of millions of dollars' worth of property.
The Principles of Economics (1904), Part III, Division B, Ch.49, Sec.III,2: 479

Irving Fisher (1867–1947)

business cycles:

1 I am open to conviction, if and when evidence shall be presented of self-starting and self-perpetuating economic rhythms, but thus far I have been able to see only a tangle of coincidence and contradiction, which may be illustrated by a rocking chair, or a sea craft, in surroundings which furnish both rhythmic and erratic influences. The chair, when tipped, certainly has a tendency to keep rocking – but not forever. And perhaps it is either restarted or put out of rhythm by a new jolt from the dusting housewife.

The seacraft, when tipped by a wave, tends to return upon itself and to rock on regularly; but its rhythm is constantly put out by the buffeting of additional waves. The waves themselves act under laws of rhythm which are unfailing; yet the actual rhythm will fail, through the buffeting of cross winds. Imagine, then, a rocking chair on the deck of a rocking ship, on a rolling sea. The ultimate chair is subjected to so many influences that its motion will not conform with any simple rhythm. The net motion will be made up of many rhythms and non-rhythms, and will, therefore, appear sometimes rhythmic and sometimes completely unrhythmic. At all events, no one would think of referring to it as '*the* rocking chair cycle.'
Booms and Depressions (1932), Part I, Ch.V: 57

capital:

2 Man is the most versatile of all forms of capital. . . .
The Theory of Interest (1930), Part II, Ch.VIII, Sec.8: 200

capitalism:

3 The capitalist is, in a sense, always living on the product of *past* labor.
The Theory of Interest (1930), Part I, Ch.III, Sec.2: 50

depressions:

4 A depression is a condition in which business becomes unprofitable. It might well be called The Private Profits disease. Its worst consequences are business failures and wide-spread unemployment. But almost no one escapes a degree of impoverishment. Some of the mightiest and best managed enterprises, such as railroads, are among the worst sufferers. If they do not break, it is often only because they are saved by their reserves. Many rich stockholders, too, are compelled to live on reserves; while many persons who had lived modestly are compelled to live from hand to mouth; and many who already lived from hand to mouth become jobless and live on charity, or die, or become thieves. In a word, a depression is a form of almost universal poverty, relative or absolute. And though this poverty is transient for society as a whole, it is, for countless individuals, tragically permanent.
Booms and Depressions (1932), Part I, Ch.I: 3

economics and economists:

5 I am one of those who believe that when the usage of academic economics conflicts with the ordinary usage of business, the latter is generally the better guide. This is not only because business usage has a thousand times the currency of academic usage, but also because in general it comes closer to the needs of economic analysis.
Elementary Principles of Economics (1912; 3rd edn), Preface: xiv

6 The purpose of economics is to treat the nature of wealth; the human wants served by wealth; the satisfaction of those wants and the efforts required to satisfy them; the forms of the ownership of wealth; the modes of its accumulation and dissipation; the reasons that some people have so much of it and others so little; and the principles that regulate its exchange and the prices which result from exchange. In a word, everything which concerns wealth in its general sense comes within the scope of economics.
Elementary Principles of Economics (1912; 3rd edn), Ch.I, Sec.1: 1

7 Academic economists, from their very open-mindedness, are apt to be carried off, unawares, by the bias of the community in which they live.

Economists whose social world is Wall Street are very apt to take the Wall Street point of view, while economists at state universities situated in farming districts are

apt to be partisans of the agricultural interests.
'Economists in Public Service' (1919): 10

8   In economics it is difficult to prove originality; for the germ of every new idea will surely be found over and over again in earlier writers. For myself, I would be satisfied to have my conclusions accepted as *true* even if their origin should be credited by the critics wholly to earlier writers.
The Theory of Interest (1930), Preface: ix

inflation:

9   Inflation might almost be called legal counterfeiting.
Stabilizing the Dollar (1920)

mathematics in economics:

10   For good or for ill the mathematical method has finally taken root, and is flourishing with a vigor of which both its friends and enemies little dreamed.
'Cournot and Mathematical Economics' (1898): 119

11   Mathematical economists are sometimes accused of forming an exclusive guild and withdrawing themselves from the practical world of commerce and labor. We are told that economists ought not to be recluses, but men of affairs, especially in these days of social upheaval. Mathematical economics is useless in a political mass meeting.
'Cournot and Mathematical Economics' (1898): 137–138

poverty:

12   While it is true that *waste begets poverty*, it is equally true that *poverty begets waste*.
The Theory of Interest (1930), Part IV, Ch.XV, Sec.6: 339

socialism:

13   Socialism especially has enlisted under its banner a motley group of theorists eager for some realization of their humanitarian intentions. In a sense, of course, 'we are all socialists nowadays.' But what should give us pause before enrolling under that banner is that, in reality, it is the red flag of class war. Whatever we may say of theoretical socialism of various types, and however much we may and ought, in my opinion, to favor in some form an increase of socialized industry, the great fact remains that the socialist group derives its real strength from class antagonism.
'Economists in Public Service' (1919): 10

Philip Sargant Florence
(1890–1982)

economics and economists:

1   The function of economics and political science is to advance knowledge on matters of direct importance to human welfare; the function of statistics and the statistical approach is to make sure that this knowledge, and the minds growing into this knowledge, are objective, realistic, and precise.
The Statistical Method in Economics and Political Science (1929), Part I, Ch.I: 8

2   Definitions of the scope of economics frequently fail to suggest that economics is a science of human behaviour. 'The study of wealth' does not mention, and scarcely implies, the existence of human beings at all. And other definitions where wealth is taken not as a material good but as some state of consciousness, a form of happiness or welfare to correspond as well as to rhyme with health, fail to give the idea of objective *activity* and reaction.
The Statistical Method in Economics and Political Science (1929), Part I, Ch.III, Sec.2: 16–17

taxation:

3   The essential condition of taxation is not the voluntary exchange of goods and services, but the fact that governments compel payments from individuals without necessarily giving them personally any utility in exchange.
The Statistical Method in Economics and Political Science (1929), Part I, Ch.III, Sec.3: 23

Herbert Somerton Foxwell
(1849–1936)

socialism:

1 Socialists make merry at any differences of opinion or treatment which exist among economists; but we shall hunt in vain through expositions of socialism to find one which even remotely approaches in detail and consistency, or in general acceptance, the ordinarily received *corpus* of economic science. Hence the critic of socialism has no definite objective. He has to reply to a desultory, guerilla attack: the socialists have the advantage of *franc-tireurs*, their position is constantly shifting and always obscure. So many socialists, so many social philosophies.
   Introduction to Anton Menger, *The Right to the Whole Produce of Labour* (1899), Sec.2: xxiii

Benjamin Franklin (1706–1790)
American inventor and statesman

money:

1 Upon the Whole it may be observed, That it is the highest Interest of a Trading Country in general to make Money plentiful; and that it can be a Disadvantage to none that have honest Designs.
   A Modest Enquiry into the Nature and Necessity of a PaperCurrency (1729): 153

Milton Friedman (1912–)

capitalism:

1 It is the mark of the political freedom of a capitalist society that men can openly advocate and work for socialism. Equally, political freedom in a socialist society would require that men be free to advocate the introduction of capitalism.
   Capitalism and Freedom (1962), Ch.I: 16

distribution:

2 The ethical principle that would directly justify the distribution of income in a free market society is, 'To each according to what he and the instruments he owns produces.' The operation of even this principle implicitly depends on state action.
   Capitalism and Freedom (1962), Ch.X: 161–162

economics and economists:

3 The role of the economist in discussions of public policy seems to me to be to prescribe what should be done in the light of what can be done, politics aside, and not to predict what is 'politically feasible' and then to recommend it.
   'Comments on Monetary Policy' (1951), Sec.II: 187

4 Economists may not know much. But we do know one thing very well: how to produce shortages and surpluses.
   The Balance of Payments: Free Versus Fixed Exchange Rates (1967), First Lecture: 1

5 A 'wert-frei' economics is an ideal and like most ideals often honored in the breach. The economist's value judgments doubtless influence the subjects he works on and perhaps also at times the conclusions he reaches. And ... his conclusions react on his value judgments. Yet this does not alter the fundamental point that, in principle, there are no value judgments in economics. ...
   'Value Judgments in Economics' (1967): 86

6 We have been driven into a widespread system of arbitrary and tyrannical control over our economic life, not because 'economic laws are not working the way they used to,' not because the classical medicine cannot, if properly applied, halt inflation, but because the public at large has been led to expect standards of performance that as economists we do not know how to achieve. Perhaps, as our knowledge advances, we can come closer to specifying policies that would achieve these high standards. Perhaps, the random perturbations inherent in the economic system make it impossible to achieve such standards. And perhaps, even if there are policies that would attain them, considerations of political economy will make it impossible for these policies to be adopted.
   'Have Monetary Policies Failed?' (1972): 17

7 I believe that we economists in recent years have done vast harm – to society at large and to our profession in particular – by claiming more than we can deliver. We have thereby encouraged politicians to make extravagant promises, inculcate unrealistic expectations in the public at large, and promote discontent with reasonably satisfactory results because they fall short of the economists' promised land.
  'Have Monetary Policies Failed?' (1972): 17–18

8 Certainly for economists, there is nothing that produces jobs for economists like government controls and government intervention. And all economists are therefore schizophrenic: their discipline, derived from Adam Smith, leads them to favour the market; their self-interest leads them to favour intervention. And in large part the profession has been led to reconcile these two opposing forces by being in favour of the market in general but opposed to it in particular. We are very clever at finding 'special cases' – there are external effects, there are monopolies, there are imperfections in the market; therefore we can have our cake and eat it. We can be in favour of the free market and we can at the same time promote those separate interventions that promote our private interest by providing jobs for economists.
  From Galbraith to Economic Freedom (1977), Part I, Sec.IV: 41–42

government:

9 A government which maintained law and order, defined property rights, served as a means whereby we could modify property rights and other rules of the economic game, adjudicated disputes about the interpretation of the rules, enforced contracts, promoted competition, provided a monetary framework, engaged in activities to counter technical monopolies and to overcome neighborhood effects widely regarded as sufficiently important to justify government intervention, and which supplemented private charity and the private family in protecting the irresponsible, whether madman or child – such a government would clearly have important functions to perform. The consistent liberal is not an anarchist.
  Capitalism and Freedom (1962), Ch.II: 34

inflation:

10 Inflation is always and everywhere a monetary phenomenon, resulting from and accompanied by a rise in the quantity of money relative to output. . . . It follows that the only effective way to stop inflation is to restrain the rate of growth of the quantity of money.
  'What Price Guideposts?' (1966): 18

11 The greatest difficulty in curtailing inflation is that, after a while, people begin to think they'd rather have the sickness than the cure.
  Playboy Interview (1973): 52

12 Perhaps the single most important and most thoroughly documented yet obstinately rejected proposition is that 'inflation is always and everywhere a monetary phenomenon.' That proposition has been known by some scholars and men of affairs for hundreds, if not thousands, of years. Yet it has not prevented governmental authorities from yielding to the temptation to mulct their subjects by debasing their money – taxation without representation – while vigorously denying that they are doing anything of the kind and attributing the resulting inflation to all sorts of other devils incarnate.
  Money Mischief (1994), Ch.11: 262

minimum wage:

13 A minimum-wage law is, in reality, a law that makes it illegal for an employer to hire a person with limited skills.
  Playboy Interview (1973): 54

monetary policy:

14 Policy does not always have a close relation to theory. The world of the academic halls and the world of policy makers often seem to move on two wholly different levels with little contact between them.
  'Post-War Trends in Monetary Theory and Policy' (1964), Sec.III

15 Monetary theory is like a Japanese garden. It has esthetic unity born of variety; an apparent simplicity that conceals a sophisticated reality; a surface view that dissolves in ever deeper perspectives. Both can be fully appreciated only if examined from many different angles, only if studied leisurely but

in depth. Both have elements that can be enjoyed independently of the whole, yet attain their full realization only as part of the whole.
The Optimum Quantity of Money, and Other Essays (1969), Preface: v

16 Monetary policy had not been tried [during the Great Depression] and found wanting. It had not been tried. Or, alternatively, it had been tried perversely.
The Counter-Revolution in Monetary Theory (1970), Sec.III: 17

17 In one sense, monetary policy has clearly failed. It has not produced nirvana. It has not stopped inflation without a recession. From a scientific point of view, this is a trivial and uninteresting answer. It is equivalent to saying, medicine has failed because men still die. From a political point of view, it is not at all a trivial answer. A major problem of our time is that people have come to expect policies to produce results that they are incapable of producing.
'Have Monetary Policies Failed?' (1972): 12

18 I dislike the term *monetarist*. The theory that now goes by that label has a perfectly respectable ancient name, namely the quantity theory of money. However, the usage has become established, so I shall simply conform.
'Monetarism in Rhetoric and in Practice' (1985): 15

monopoly:

19 Exchange is truly voluntary only when nearly equivalent alternatives exist. Monopoly implies the absence of alternatives and thereby inhibits effective freedom of exchange.
Capitalism and Freedom (1962), Ch.II: 28

morality:

20 No society can be stable unless there is a basic core of value judgments that are unthinkingly accepted by the great bulk of its members. Some key institutions must be accepted as 'absolutes,' not simply as instrumental.
Capitalism and Freedom (1962), Ch.X: 167

socialism:

21 There are still intellectuals who believe that concentrated power is a force for good as long as it's in the hands of men of good will. I'm waiting for the day when they reject socialism, communism and all other varieties of collectivism; when they realize that a security blanket isn't worth the surrender of our individual freedom even if it *can* be provided by government. There are faint stirrings and hopeful signs. Even some of the intellectuals who were most strongly drawn to the New Deal in the Thirties are rethinking their positions, dabbling just a little with free-market principles. They're moving slowly and taking each step as though they were exploring a virgin continent. But it's not dangerous. Some of us have lived here quite comfortably all along.
Playboy Interview (1973): 74

taxation:

22 I find it hard, as a liberal, to see any justification for graduated taxation solely to redistribute income. This seems a clear case of using coercion to take from some in order to give to others and thus to conflict head-on with individual freedom.
Capitalism and Freedom (1962), Ch.X: 174

23 I favor a negative income tax not because I believe anyone has a 'right' to be fed, clothed and housed at someone else's expense but because I want to join my fellow taxpayers in relieving distress and feel a special compulsion to do so because governmental policies have been responsible for putting so many of our fellow citizens in the demeaning position in which they now find themselves.
'Is Welfare a Basic Human Right?' (1972): 90

Ragnar Anton Kittil Frisch
(1895–1973)

econometrics:

1 Intermediate between mathematics, statistics, and economics, we find a new discipline which, for lack of a better name, may be called *econometrics*.

Econometrics has as its aim to subject abstract laws of theoretical political economy or 'pure' economics to experimental and numerical verification, and thus to turn pure economics, as far as is possible, into a science in the strict sense of the word.

'On a Problem in Pure Economics' (1926): 386; purportedly the first use of the term 'econometrics'

economic planning:

2   My purpose is to make economic planning at a high aspiration level one of the pillars of a living democracy. I want a society which is a living democracy, not only a formal one with free elections, socalled freedom of speech, a socalled free press and so on, but a democracy that is living in the sense of actually engaging as many as possible of the citizens to take an active part in the affairs of the small community where they are living, and also to take an active part in the affairs of the nation as a whole.

'From Utopian Theory to Practical Applications: The Case of Econometrics' (1970), Sec.6: 234

economics and economists:

3   Indeed, at the global level the goal of economic theory is to lay bare the way in which the different economic factors act and interact *on each other* in a highly complex system, and to do this in such a way that the results may be used *in practice* to carry out in the most effective way specific desiderata in the steering of the economy.

'From Utopian Theory to Practical Applications: The Case of Econometrics' (1970), Sec.3: 221

G

John Kenneth Galbraith (1908–)

affluence:

1 An affluent society, that is also both compassionate and rational, would, no doubt, secure to all who needed it the minimum income essential for decency and comfort. The corrupting effect on the human spirit of a small amount of unearned revenue has unquestionably been exaggerated as, indeed, have the character-building values of hunger and privation.
   The Affluent Society (1958), Ch.XXIII, Sec.V: 329

economics and economists:

2 Professional economists, like members of city gangs, religious congregations, public schools, aboriginal tribes, fashionable regiments, craft unions, clubs, learned disciplines, holders of diplomatic passports, and, one is told, the intellectually more demanding criminal pursuits, have the natural desire of all such groups to delineate and safeguard the boundary between those who belong and those who do not. This has variously been called the tribal, gang, club, guild, union, or aristocratic instinct.
   'The Language of Economics' (1962): 169

inequality:

3 [T]he concern for inequality had vitality only so long as the many suffered privation while a few had much. It did not survive as a burning issue in a time when the many had much even though others had much more. It is our misfortune that when inequality declined as an issue, the slate was not left clean. A residual and in some ways rather more hopeless problem remained.
   The Affluent Society (1958), Ch.XXIII, Sec.IV: 329

inflation:

4 Inflation does lubricate trade but by rescuing traders from their errors of optimism or stupidity.
   Money: Whence It Came, Where It Went (1975), Ch.II: 13

mathematics in economics:

5 There can be no question . . . that excessive and prolonged commitment to mathematical exercises in economics is damaging. It leads to the atrophy of judgment and intuition, which are indispensable for real solutions, and on occasion also to the habit of mind that simply excludes the mathematically inconvenient factors from consideration.
   'The Language of Economics' (1962): 171

money:

6 When money is bad, people want it to be better. When it is good, they think of other things.
   Money: Whence It Came, Where It Went (1975), Ch.I: 3

poverty:

7 People are poverty-stricken when their income, even if adequate for survival, falls markedly behind that of the community. Then they cannot have what the larger community regards as the minimum necessary for decency; and they cannot wholly escape, therefore, the judgment of the larger community that they are indecent.
   The Affluent Society (1958), Ch.XXIII, Sec.II: 323–324

taxation:

8 The finest tax authority goes to waste if the minister does not believe in collecting taxes, does not want to do so, or has an overly developed feeling for his friends.
   Economic Development in Perspective (1962), Ch.I, Sec.4: 8

David Peter Gauthier (1932–)
Canadian philosopher

economic man:

1 Economic man is a radical contractarian in that all of his free or non-coercive interpersonal relationships are contractual. For him, voluntary social relationships require a

rationale; contract provides it. The idea underlying contract, that persons who take no interest in one another's interests may nevertheless be able to interact in a mutually advantageous and therefore voluntarily acceptable manner, is ... one of the great liberating ideas in human history, freeing persons from the requirement that they be affectively dependent on their fellows. But economic man carries this liberation to its full extreme; his exclusively asocial motivation precludes voluntary non-contractual interpersonal relationships. He is not only freed from compulsory affective dependence; he is incapable of voluntary affection.
Morals By Agreement (1986), Ch.X, Sec.2.2: 319

market:

2   The market exemplifies an ideal of interaction among persons who, taking no interest in each other's interests, need only follow the dictates of their own individual interests to participate effectively in a venture for mutual advantage. We do not speak of a *co-operative* venture, reserving that label for enterprises that lack the natural harmony of each with all assured by the structure of market interaction.
Morals By Agreement (1986), Ch.I, Sec.3.3: 13

Henry George (1839–1897)

economics and economists:

1   The progress of civilization requires that more and more intelligence be devoted to social affairs, and this not the intelligence of the few, but that of the many. We cannot safely leave politics to politicians, or political economy to college professors. The people themselves must think, because the people alone can act.
Social Problems (1883), Ch.I: 9

labor:

2   What more unnatural than that alms should be asked, not for the maimed, the halt and the blind, the helpless widow and the tender orphan, but for grown men, strong men, skilful men, men able to work and anxious to work! What more unnatural than that labor – the producer of all food, all clothing, all shelter – should not be exchangeable for its full equivalent in food, clothing, and shelter; that while the things it produces have value, labor, the giver of all value, should seem valueless!
'How to Help the Unemployed' (1894): 177

3   What keeps any of us at work are our desires and hopes – our wants and our pride. Kill hope and lessen desire by crucifying the feeling of personal independence and accustoming your man to a life maintained by alms, and you will make of the most industrious a tramp. For the law of our being is that we seek the gratification of our desires with the least exertion.
'How to Help the Unemployed' (1894): 178

poverty:

4   Poverty is the Slough of Despond which Bunyan saw in his dream, and into which good books may be tossed forever without result. To make people industrious, prudent, skillful, and intelligent, they must be relieved from want. If you would have the slave show the virtues of the freeman, you must first make him free.
Progress and Poverty (1880; 4th edn), Book VI, Ch.I, Sec.II: 310

5   There is in nature no reason for poverty – not even for the poverty of the crippled or the decrepit. For man is by nature a social animal, and the family affections and the social sympathies would, where chronic poverty did not distort and embrute, amply provide for those who could not provide for themselves.
Social Problems (1883), Ch.VIII: 78

6   The cause of poverty is not in human nature; it is not in the constitution of the physical world; it is not in the natural laws of social growth. It is in the injustice which denies to men their natural rights; in the stupidity which diverts from its proper use the value which attaches to land with social growth, and then imposes on industry and thrift taxes which restrain production and put premiums on greed and dishonesty; injustice and stupidity which ignore the true rights of property and turn governments into

machines by which the unscrupulous may rob their neighbors.
'A Single Tax on Land Values' (1890): 403

socialism:

7   As in the development of species, the power of conscious, coördinated action of the whole being must assume greater and greater relative importance to the automatic action of parts, so is it in the development of society. This is the truth in socialism, which, although it is being forced upon us by industrial progress and social development, we are so slow to recognize.
Social Problems (1883), Ch.XVII: 177

taxation:

8   Taxation and work are no more synonymous than addition and subtraction. But it *is* true that taxation can be paid only in the products of work.
'A Single Tax on Land Values' (1890): 396; cf. Edward Atkinson 2

9   Taxes on incomes are unjust in nature and cannot be collected fairly; taxes on bequests and inheritances are also unjust in nature, and would soon be evaded where large amounts were involved. But the tax on land values has preëminently the element of justice. It takes from the individual not in proportion to his needs, or to his energy, industry, or thrift, but in proportion to the value of the special privilege he enjoys. It can be collected with the maximum of ease and certainty and the minimum of cost.
'A Single Tax on Land Values' (1890): 399

10 Tax anything of human production, and in a little while there will be less of it in existence.
'A Single Tax on Land Values' (1890): 399

11 Taxes on the products of labor, taxes which take the earnings of industry and the savings of thrift, always have begotten, and always must beget, fraud, corruption, and evasion. All the penalties of the law – imprisonment, fines, torture, and death – have failed to secure their honest and equal collection. They are unjust and unequal in their very nature, always falling on the poor with greater severity than on the rich. Their collection always entails great waste and cost, increases the number of office holders and the complexity of government, and compels interference with individual affairs; always checks production, lessens general wealth, and takes from labor and capital their due reward – the stimulus to productive exertion. Men naturally evade and resist them, and with the sanction of the moral sense even where their duller intellectual faculties are convinced that such taxes are right and beneficial in themselves.
'A Single Tax on Land Values' (1890): 401

trade unions:

12 The methods by which a trade union can alone act are necessarily destructive; its organization is necessarily tyrannical.
Progress and Poverty (1880; 4th edn), Book VI, Ch.I, Sec.III: 315

Nicholas Georgescu-Roegen
(1906–1994)

capitalism:

1   [C]apitalism, like all other economic systems that preceded it and that will be produced by the continuous evolution of human society, is a form of life. Some aspects of its functioning lend themselves perfectly to mathematical analysis. Yet, when we come to the problem of its *evolution*, of its mutation into another form, mathematics proves to be too rigid and hence too simple a tool for handling it.
'Mathematical Proofs of the Breakdown of Capitalism' (1960), Sec.4: 243

Arthur Stanley Goldberger (1930–)

econometrics:

1   [I]t should be clear that the quantification of economic theory is not a mechanical task. In particular, it is not simply a matter of fitting curves to data, of 'measurement without theory.'
Econometric Theory (1964), Ch.1, Sec.2: 4

Emma Goldman (1869–1940)
American anarchist

syndicalism:

1 Syndicalism is, in essence, the economic expression of Anarchism.
   Syndicalism: The Modern Menace to Capitalism (1913)

Sir James Goldsmith (1933–1997)
Anglo-French financier

government:

1 Those who wish to destroy the conditions which allow for a strong democratic nation can do little better than to reduce the self-reliance of citizens and of their families by converting them into dependants of the state. Inevitably the result is the strengthening of state bureaucracy and the weakening of civil society.
   The Trap (1994), Ch.4: 89

Carter Goodrich (1897–1971)

mathematics in economics:

1 Economic historians have always rested heavily on economic arithmetic. They will doubtless learn, perhaps with some lag, to make use of economic algebra and economic calculus. But I trust they will also continue to use their wits . . . when they need answers that the quantitative methods do not supply.
   'Economic History: One Field or Two?' (1960): 535

Frank Dunstone Graham
(1890–1949)

monetary systems:

1 The existing monetary system could scarcely work more effectively to frustrate men's efforts if it had been deliberately designed, by some malevolent genius, to that end.
   Social Goals and Economic Institutions (1942), Part II, Ch.V: 118

socialism:

2 Individualism and socialism, properly construed, are not antithetical but complementary and even identical things. No true comradeship is possible except on the basis of the fullest feasible recognition of individual personality. On the other hand, equality of opportunity, for the fullest feasible exertion of individual powers, is possible only through large concessions to the social entity.
   Social Goals and Economic Institutions (1942), Part I, Ch.II: 27

Horace Greeley (1811–1872)
American journalist

protectionism:

1 The Free-Traders are accustomed to assure the people that they, too, are in favor of a Tariff, not, indeed, for Protection, but for Revenue alone. Assuming that they are sincere in this assertion, they seem to me the most inconsistent of mortals.
   Essays Designed to Elucidate the Science of Political Economy (1870), Ch.XXIV: 349

Alan Greenspan (1926–)

antitrust:

1 The world of antitrust is reminiscent of Alice's Wonderland: everything seemingly is, yet apparently isn't, simultaneously. It is a world in which competition is lauded as the basic axiom and guiding principle, yet 'too much' competition is condemned as 'cutthroat.' It is a world in which actions designed to limit competition are branded as criminal when taken by businessmen, yet praised as 'enlightened' when initiated by the government. It is a world in which the law is so vague that businessmen have no way of knowing whether specific actions will be declared illegal until they hear the judge's verdict – after the fact.
   'Antitrust' (1961): 63

capitalism:

2 Capitalism is based on self-interest and self-esteem; it holds integrity and trustworthiness as cardinal ·virtues and makes them pay off in the market place, thus demanding that men survive by means of virtues, not of vices. It is this superlatively moral system that the welfare statists propose to improve

upon by means of preventive law, snooping bureaucrats and the chronic goad of fear.
'The Assault on Integrity' (1963): 32

government regulation:

3 Government regulation is not an alternative means of protecting the consumer. It does not build quality into goods, nor accuracy into information. Its sole 'contribution' is to substitute force and fear for incentive as the 'protector' of the consumer. The euphemisms of government press releases to the contrary notwithstanding, the basis of regulation is armed force. At the bottom of the endless pile of paper work which characterizes all regulation lies a gun. What are the results?
'The Assault on Integrity' (1963): 31

profit motive:

4 [I]t is precisely the 'greed' of the businessman or, more appropriately, his profit-seeking, which is the unexcelled protector of the consumer.
'The Assault on Integrity' (1963): 31

supply and demand:

5 The law of supply and demand is not to be conned.
'Gold and Economic Freedom' (1966): 15

welfare state:

6 Stripped if its academic jargon, the welfare state is nothing more than a mechanism by which governments confiscate the wealth of the productive members of a society to support a wide variety of welfare schemes. A substantial part of the confiscation is effected by taxation. But the welfare statists were quick to recognize that if they wished to retain political power, the amount of taxation had to be limited and they had to resort to programs of massive deficit spending, i.e., they had to borrow money, by issuing government bonds, to finance welfare expenditures on a large scale.
'Gold and Economic Freedom' (1966): 15

H

Gottfried von Haberler (1900–1995)

Marxism:

1 The Marxist economic system has slowly lost its influence and has no future. But the 'close of the Marxian system' does not mean the end of socialism, and Marxian economics will always maintain a prominent place in the history of the social sciences and the intellectual history of the 19th and 20th centuries. The historian of economic thought will never cease rummaging in the voluminous writings of Marx and the specialist will find flashes of insight and even genuine analytical discoveries, bits and pieces of usable scrap. People will always marvel . . . at the boldness of the whole lofty construction, but Marxism as an economic system is closed and will not be reopened.
  'Marxian Economics in Retrospect and Prospect' (1966): 82

Frank Horace Hahn (1925–)

economics and economists:

1 Economists do not grow bitter gracefully. Many of them came to the subject hoping to do good and to be useful and find that they can do far less than they had expected. Many others with a theoretical bent find that they cannot now understand what the best minds in their subject are saying. Others again came to paint a great canvas and find themselves in the studio of miniaturists.
  'The Winter of Our Discontent' (1973): 322

2 One of the dangers of a philosophy of economics, and I suspect of other such endeavours, is that it takes the subject far too seriously as something complete and secure.
  'Rerum Cognoscere Causas' (1996), Sec.III: 192

expectations:

3 [P]eople who base policies for real economies on the belief that citizens form their expectations rationally and that the invisible hand, if left to its own devices, will guide us to a rational expectations equilibrium with not much delay cannot, I think, be taken seriously. By this I mean that I consider the direct evidence overwhelmingly against this view and I regard the 'as if' evidence from such econometric models as there are, as I do evidence for miracles: the story is simply too much at variance with experience.
  'Reflections on the Invisible Hand' (1982): 11–12

methodology:

4 It is at this point that I must pause, with some reluctance, to face a number of methodological questions. I must do so because they keep coming up in discussions even with the wise and good and because if I don't get them out of the way now some of you will go away unenlightened by the substantive points to come.
  'Why I am Not a Monetarist' (1984), Sec.I: 309

monetarism:

5 [Monetarism] represents the triumph of artifact over plain and direct thinking. It is sensational in its conclusion that the market always yields the best of all possible worlds. It is sensational in its contention that there are no social phenomena relevant to economic life which are not captured by prices. It is sensational in the sheer bravado of reducing the beautiful structure of general equilibrium theory to one or two log-linear equations and in its neglect of every subtlety. It is sensational in its ignorance of both the scope and limit of economic theory. Above all it is sensational in its confidence in conclusions which are neither proven nor plausible. For all these reasons I am not a monetarist.
  'Why I am Not a Monetarist' (1984), Sec.III: 326

socialism:

6 [T]he history of socialist countries suggests that the dislike of bourgeois greed has

frequently had to give way to the necessity of providing coherent and appealing motives for people to do what is wanted.
'Reflections on the Invisible Hand' (1982): 17–18

theory:

7   A good theory has powerful antibodies which soon destroy the carping which comes from incomprehension and hostility.
'The Winter of Our Discontent' (1973): 322

8   I am pretty certain that the following prediction will prove to be correct: theorising of the 'pure' sort will become both less enjoyable and less and less possible.
'The Next Hundred Years' (1991): 47

Sir Matthew Hale (1609–1676)
English jurist

poverty and the poor laws:

1   The prevention of poverty, idleness, and a loose and disorderly Education, even of poor Children, would do more good to this Kingdom than all the Gibbets, and Cauterizations, and Whipping Posts, and Jayls in this Kingdom, and would render these kinds of Disciplines less necessary and less frequent.
A Discourse Touching Provision for the Poor (1683), Preface

Robert Hamilton (1743–1829)

economics and economists:

1   The amelioration of the condition of mankind, and the increase of human happiness, ought to be the leading objects of every political institution, and the aim of every individual, according to the measure of his power, in the situation he occupies.
The Progress of Society (1830), Ch.I: 8

government:

2   The statesman too often considers the public wealth not as a means of increasing the happiness of the people, but as a fund from which he may draw additional taxes to be employed in pursuing his objects of ambition and aggrandizement.
The Progress of Society (1830), Ch.I: 9

property:

3   There is a limit beyond which equalization of property ceases to be desirable. A state of complete equality is unsuitable to human nature, and would detract from those energies, the exercise of which, under due regulation, promotes the improvement of our intellectual and active powers, and extends the sphere of our higher enjoyments.
The Progress of Society (1830), Ch.XII: 178

Alvin Harvey Hansen (1887–1975)

economics and economists:

1   Unhappily the history of economic theory and empirical research suggests that ours is a field of study in which we shall never be able to reach perfectly *definitive* conclusions. As economists, we have to be content with something less than that.
'Dr. Burns on Keynesian Economics' (1947): 247

2   I am not interested in classifying economists in Schools. Labels are misleading and had better be avoided.
'Dr. Burns on Keynesian Economics' (1947): 251

James Harrington (1611–1677)
English political philosopher

laws:

1   *Fundamentall Lawes* are such as state what it is that a man may call his own, that is to say, Proprietie; and what the meanes be whereby a man may enjoy his own, that is to say Protection: the first is also called Dominion, and second Empire or Soveraigne power, whereof this (as hath been shewn) is the naturall product of the former, for such as is the Ballance of the Dominion in a Nation, such is the nature of her Empire.
The Commonwealth of Oceana (1656), 'The Modell of the Common-Wealth of Oceana'

riches and poverty:

2   There is a mean in things; as exorbitant riches overthrow the ballance of a Common-wealth,

so Extream poverty cannot hold it, nor is by any means to be trusted with it.
The Commonwealth of Oceana (1656), 'The Modell of the Common-Wealth of Oceana': 59

taxation:

3 It is true, that the *Provincial Ballance* being in Nature quite contrary unto the *National*, you are no wayes to plant a *Provinciall Army upon Dominion*. But then you must have a native *Territory* in strength, *Situation*, or *Government* able to *overballance* the forreign, or you can never hold it. That an *Army* should in any other case be long supported by a meer Tax, is a meer Phansie as void of all reason and Experience, as if a man should think to maintain such an one by robbing of Orchards: for *a meer Tax is but pulling of Plumbtrees, the roots whereof are in other mens grounds*, who suffering perpetuall violence, come to hate the Author of it: And it is a *Maxime*, that *no Prince that is hated by his people can be Safe*. Arms planted upon Dominion extirpate enemies, and make friends; but maintained by a meer *Tax*, have enemies that have roots, and friends that have none.
The Commonwealth of Oceana (1656), Preliminaries, Part II

Sir Roy Forbes Harrod (1900–1978)

econometrics:

1 I am convinced that economic theory will only make good progress to the extent that it can transform itself into econometrics.
Towards a Dynamic Economics (1948), Lecture One: 14

methodology:

2 Exposed as a bore, the methodologist cannot take refuge behind a cloak of modesty. On the contrary, he stands forward ready by his own claim to give advice to all and sundry, to criticise the work of others, which, whether valuable or not, at least attempts to be constructive; he sets himself up as the final interpreter of the past and dictator of future efforts.
'Scope and Method of Economics' (1938): 383

money:

3 Money is a social phenomenon, and many of its current features depend on what people think it is or ought to be.
Money (1969), Preface: x

4 It is a strange fact that after so many centuries of experience in so many countries man has not yet succeeded in providing for himself a money with a stable value. It may be laid down that a primary objective of the science of money should be to yield such practical maxims as might serve to make it possible for a society so desiring to have a money of stable value. It is a mistake to think that failures have been due only to the perversities or mischief of the governmental authorities.
Money (1969), Part I, Ch.1: 4

social security:

5 Increased benefits under social security may bring many scrimshankers on to the Register who have hitherto preferred a life of independent poverty.
Towards a Dynamic Economics (1948), Lecture Five: 138

Friedrich August von Hayek
(1899–1992)

capitalism:

1 The more complicated the whole, the more dependent we become on that division of knowledge between individuals whose separate efforts are co-ordinated by the impersonal mechanism for transmitting the relevant information known by us as the price system.
The Road to Serfdom (1944), Ch.4: 56

communal action:

2 Wherever communal action can mitigate disasters against which the individual can neither attempt to guard himself nor make provision for the consequences, such communal action should undoubtedly be taken.
The Road to Serfdom (1944), Ch.9: 134

competition:

3 [O]ne of the main arguments in favor of competition is that it dispenses with the need

for 'conscious social control' and that it gives the individuals a chance to decide whether the prospects of a particular occupation are sufficient to compensate for the disadvantages and risks connected with it.
The Road to Serfdom (1944), Ch.3: 41–42

economic planning:

4   'Planning' owes its popularity largely to the fact that everybody desires, of course, that we should handle our common problems as rationally as possible and that, in so doing, we should use as much foresight as we can command. In this sense everybody who is not a complete fatalist is a planner, every political act is (or ought to be) an act of planning, and there can be differences only between good and bad, between wise and foresighted and foolish and shortsighted planning.
The Road to Serfdom (1944), Ch.3: 39–40

5   The idea of complete centralization of the direction of economic activity still appalls most people, not only because of the stupendous difficulty of the task, but even more because of the horror inspired by the idea of everything being directed from a single center.
The Road to Serfdom (1944), Ch.3: 47

6   It is indisputable that if we want to secure a distribution of wealth which conforms to some predetermined standard, if we want consciously to decide who is to have what, we must plan the whole economic system. But the question remains whether the price we should have to pay for the realization of somebody's ideal of justice is not bound to be more discontent and more oppression than was ever caused by the much-abused free play of economic forces.
The Road to Serfdom (1944), Ch.7: 109

economics and economists:

7   The position of the economist in the intellectual life of our time is unlike that of the practitioners of any other branch of knowledge. Questions for whose solution his special knowledge is relevant are probably more frequently encountered than questions relating to any other science. Yet, in large measure, this knowledge is disregarded and in many respects public opinion even seems to move in a contrary direction. Thus the economist appears to be hopelessly out of tune with his time, giving unpractical advice to which the public is not disposed to listen and having no influence upon contemporary events.
'The Trend of Economic Thinking' (1933), Sec.I: 121

8   It is true that economics was contemptuously dubbed a mere utilitarian science because it did not pursue knowledge for its own sake. But nothing would have aroused more resentment than if economists had tried to do so. Even to-day it is regarded almost as a sign of moral depravity if the economist finds anything to marvel at in his science; i.e. if he finds an unsuspected order in things, which arouses his wonder. And he is bitterly reproached if he does not emphasise, at every stage of his analysis, how much he regrets that his insight into the order of things makes it less easy to change them whenever we please.
'The Trend of Economic Thinking' (1933), Sec.V: 124

9   I am certain there are many who regard with impatience and distrust the whole tendency, which is inherent in all modern equilibrium analysis, to turn economics into a branch of pure logic, a set of self-evident propositions which, like mathematics or geometry, are subject to no other test but internal consistency. But it seems that if only this process is carried far enough it carries its own remedy with it. In distilling from our reasoning about the facts of economic life those parts which are truly *a priori*, we not only isolate one element of our reasoning as a sort of Pure Logic of Choice in all its purity, but we also isolate, and emphasise the importance of, another element which has been too much neglected. My criticism of the recent tendencies to make economic theory more and more formal is not that they have gone too far, but that they have not yet been carried far enough to complete the isolation of this branch of logic and to restore to its rightful place the investigation of causal processes, using formal economic theory as a tool in the same way as mathematics.
'Economics and Knowledge' (1937), Sec.1: 35

10 If conscious action can be 'explained,' this is a task for psychology but not for economics or linguistics, jurisprudence or any other social science. What we do is merely to classify types of individual behavior which we can understand, to develop their classification – in short, to provide an orderly arrangement of the material which we have to use in our further task. Economists, and the same is probably also true in the other social sciences, are usually a little ashamed to admit that this part of their task is 'only' a kind of special logic. I think they would be wise frankly to recognize and to face this fact.
'The Facts of the Social Sciences' (1943), Sec.II: 8

11 On the one hand the still recent establishment of the Nobel Memorial Prize in Economic Science marks a significant step in the process by which, in the opinion of the general public, economics has been conceded some of the dignity and prestige of the physical sciences. On the other hand, the economists are at this moment called upon to say how to extricate the free world from the serious threat of accelerating inflation which, it must be admitted, has been brought about by policies which the majority of economists recommended and even urged governments to pursue. We have indeed at the moment little cause for pride: as a profession we have made a mess of things.
'The Pretence of Knowledge' (1975): 433

individualism:

12 The chief concern of the great individualist writers was indeed to find a set of institutions by which man could be induced, by his own choice and from the motives which determined his ordinary conduct, to contribute as much as possible to the need of all others. . . .
'Individualism: True and False' (1945), Sec.3: 12–13; as published in *Individualism and Economic Order* (1948)

13 [T]he fundamental attitude of true individualism is one of humility toward the processes by which mankind has achieved things which have not been designed or understood by any individual and are indeed greater than individual minds.
'Individualism: True and False' (1945), Sec.11: 32; as published in *Individualism and Economic Order* (1948)

laissez-faire:

14 Probably nothing has done so much harm to the liberal cause as the wooden insistence of some liberals on certain rough rules of thumb, above all the principle of laissez faire.
The Road to Serfdom (1944), Ch.1: 21

monetary policy:

15 One of our chief problems will be to protect our money against those economists who will continue to offer their quack remedies, the short-term effectiveness of which will continue to ensure them popularity.
Choice in Currency (1976), Sec.II: 13

16 Without the conviction of the public at large that certain immediately painful measures are occasionally necessary to preserve reasonable stability, we cannot hope that any authority which has power to determine the quantity of money will long resist the pressure for, or the seduction of, cheap money.
Choice in Currency (1976), Sec.III: 15

17 The politician, acting on a modified Keynesian maxim that in the long run we are all out of office, does not care if his successful cure of unemployment is bound to produce more unemployment in the future. The politicians who will be blamed for it will not be those who created the inflation but those who stopped it. No worse trap could have been set for a democratic system in which the government is forced to act on the beliefs that the people think to be true. Our only hope for a stable money is indeed now to find a way to protect money from politics.
Choice in Currency (1976), Sec.III: 16

18 I have no objection to governments issuing money, but I believe their claim to a *monopoly*, or their power to *limit* the kinds of money in which contracts may be concluded within their territory, or to determine the *rates* at which monies can be exchanged, to be wholly harmful.
Choice in Currency (1976), Sec.IV: 17

private property:

19 What our generation has forgotten is that the system of private property is the most important guaranty of freedom, not only for those who own property, but scarcely less for those who do not. It is only because the control of the means of production is divided among many people acting independently that nobody has complete power over us, that we as individuals can decide what to do with ourselves. If all the means of production were vested in a single hand, whether it be nominally that of 'society' as a whole or that of a dictator, whoever exercises this control has complete power over us.
The Road to Serfdom (1944), Ch.8: 115

20 A system based on private property and control of the means of production presupposes that such property and control can be acquired by any successful man. If this is made impossible, even the men who otherwise would have been the most eminent capitalists of the new generation are bound to become the enemies of the established rich.
The Constitution of Liberty (1960), Ch.Twenty, Sec.7: 321

profit:

21 The disdain of profit is due to ignorance, and to an attitude that we may if we wish admire in the ascetic who has chosen to be content with a small share of the riches of this world, but which, when actualised in the form of restrictions on profits of others, is selfish to the extent that it imposes asceticism, and indeed deprivations of all sorts, on others.
The Fatal Conceit (1988), Ch.Six: 105

social insurance:

22 Though a redistribution of incomes was never the avowed initial purpose of the apparatus of social security, it has now become the actual and admitted aim everywhere. No system of monopolistic compulsory insurance has resisted this transformation into something quite different, an instrument for the compulsory redistribution of income.
The Constitution of Liberty (1960), Ch.Nineteen, Sec.2: 289

23 [A] compulsory scheme of so-called unemployment insurance will always be used to 'correct' the relative remunerations of different groups, to subsidize the unstable trades at the expense of the stable, and to support wage demands that are irreconcilable with a high level of employment. It is therefore likely in the long run to aggravate the evil it is meant to cure.
The Constitution of Liberty (1960), Ch.Nineteen, Sec.8: 302

social justice:

24 The desire to eliminate the effects of accident, which lies at the root of the demand for 'social justice,' can be satisfied in the field of education, as elsewhere, only by eliminating all those opportunities which are not subject to deliberate control. But the growth of civilization rests largely on the individuals' making the best use of whatever accidents they encounter, of the essentially unpredictable advantages that one kind of knowledge will in new circumstances confer on one individual over others.
The Constitution of Liberty (1960), Ch.Twenty-four, Sec.5: 385

25 As primitive thinking usually does when first noticing some regular processes, the results of the spontaneous ordering of the market were interpreted as if some thinking being deliberately directed them, or as if the particular benefits or harm different persons derived from them were determined by deliberate acts of will, and could therefore be guided by moral rules. This conception of 'social' justice is thus a direct consequence of that anthropomorphism or personification by which naive thinking tries to account for all self-ordering processes. It is a sign of the immaturity of our minds that we have not yet outgrown these primitive concepts and still demand from an impersonal process which brings about a greater satisfaction of human desires than any deliberate human organization could achieve, that it conforms to the moral precepts men have evolved for the guidance of their individual actions.
Law, Legislation, and Liberty, vol. II (1976), Ch.Nine: 62–63

social welfare:

26 The welfare and the happiness of millions cannot be measured on a single scale of less

and more. The welfare of a people, like the happiness of a man, depends on a great many things that can be provided in an infinite variety of combinations. It cannot be adequately expressed as a single end, but only as a hierarchy of ends, a comprehensive scale of values in which every need of every person is given its place.
The Road to Serfdom (1944), Ch.5: 64

27 The common welfare or the public good has to the present time remained a concept most recalcitrant to any precise definition and therefore capable of being given almost any content suggested by the interests of the ruling group.
Law, Legislation, and Liberty, vol. II (1976), Ch.Seven: 1

socialism:

28 The economic freedom which is the prerequisite of any other freedom cannot be the freedom from economic care which the socialists promise us and which can be obtained only by relieving the individual at the same time of the necessity and of the power of choice; it must be the freedom of our economic activity which, with the right of choice, inevitably also carries the risk and the responsibility of that right.
The Road to Serfdom (1944), Ch.7: 110–111

taxation:

29 Individual taxes, and especially the income tax, may be graduated for a good reason – that is, so as to compensate for the tendency of many indirect taxes to place a proportionally heavier burden on the smaller incomes. This is the only valid argument in favor of progression.
The Constitution of Liberty (1960), Ch.Twenty, Sec.1: 307

30 I doubt whether a society consisting mainly of 'self-employed' individuals would ever have come to take the concept of income so much for granted as we do or would ever have thought of taxing the earnings from a certain service according to the rate at which they accrued in time.
The Constitution of Liberty (1960), Ch.Twenty, Sec.7: 319

James Joseph Heckman (1944–)

economic history:

1 Only if economics turns its back on the major social policy issues of the day, and economic historians fail to address them, will economic history cease to contribute useful knowledge to the mainstream of the economics profession.
'The Value of Quantitative Evidence on the Effect of the Past on the Present' (1997), Sec.IV: 407

economics and economists:

2 Any branch of economics is worth preserving only if it contributes useful knowledge.
'The Value of Quantitative Evidence on the Effect of the Past on the Present' (1997), Sec.III: 405

Georg Wilhelm Friedrich Hegel (1770–1831)
German philosopher

abstraction:

1 [T]o make abstractions hold good in actuality means to destroy actuality.
Lectures on the History of Philosophy (1840; 2nd 'amended' edition), vol. III: 425

money:

2 Money is, in fact, not a special kind of wealth, but the universal element in all kinds, in so far as they in production are given such an external reality as can be apprehended as an object. Only at this external point of view is it possible and just to estimate performances quantitatively.
Philosophy of Right (1821), Third Part, Third Section, A (I,c), para.299 note

poverty:

3 [P]overty causes men to lose more or less the advantage of society, the opportunity to acquire skill or education, the benefit of the administration of justice, the care for health, even the consolation of religion. Amongst the poor the public power takes the place of the family in regard to their immediate need, dislike of work, bad disposition, and other

vices, which spring out of poverty and the sense of wrong.
Philosophy of Right (1821), Third Part, Second Section, C(a), para.241

4   When a large number of people sink below the standard of living regarded as essential for the members of society, and lose that sense of right, rectitude, and honour which is derived from self-support, a pauper class arises, and wealth accumulates disproportionately in the hands of a few.
Philosophy of Right (1821), Third Part, Second Section, C(a), para.244

wealth:

5   [P]articular wealth, or the possibility of sharing in the general wealth, is based partly on skill, partly on something which is directly the individual's own, namely, capital. Skill in turn depends on capital, and on many accidental circumstances. These also in their manifold variety make more pronounced the differences in the development of natural endowments, physical and mental, which were unequal to begin with. These differences are conspicuous everywhere in the sphere of particularity. They, along with other elements of chance and accident, necessarily produce inequalities of wealth of skill.
Philosophy of Right (1821), Third Part, Second Section, A(c), para.200

Robert Louis Heilbroner (1919–)

capitalism:

1   Capitalism, let us keep in mind, is a social arrangement – the product more of historical forces than purely ideological ones. Until the groundwork had been laid in politics, law, technology and a dozen other social areas, the business enterprise as we know it could not evolve.
The Quest for Wealth (1956), Ch.VI: 140

2   Capitalism and business are ... virtually synonymous – *capitalism* being the historian's term for the system abstractly conceived, *business* the common word for the system in its daily operation.
The Limits of American Capitalism (1965), Part I, Sec.1: 5

3   [T]he history of capitalism can be conceived in large part as a continuing struggle to find an acceptable balance between the hyperactive business sector that is the dynamo of the system and the sometimes more passive, but still indispensable, nonbusiness structures that shape and define life outside the economic realm.
The Limits of American Capitalism (1965), Part I, Sec.1: 6

4   The persistent breakdowns of the capitalist economy, whatever their immediate precipitating factors, can all be traced to a single underlying cause. This is the anarchic or planless character of capitalist production.
The Limits of American Capitalism (1965), Part II, Sec.4: 88

5   The world of science, as it is applied by society, is committed to the idea of man as a being who shapes his collective destiny; the world of capitalism to an idea of man as one who permits his common social destination to take care if itself. The essential idea of a society built on scientific engineering is to impose human will on the social universe; that of capitalism to allow the social universe to unfold as if it were beyond human interference.
The Limits of American Capitalism (1965), Part II, Sec.6: 132

David Forbes Hendry (1944–)

econometrics:

1   Unfortunately, I must now try to explain what 'econometrics' comprises. Do not confuse the word with 'econo-mystics' or with 'economic-tricks,' nor yet with 'iconometrics.' While we may indulge in all of these activities, they are not central to the discipline. Nor are econometricians primarily engaged in measuring the heights of economists.
'Econometrics – Alchemy or Science?' (1980), Sec.II: 388

2   [E]conometrics may be the sole beneficiary from government manipulation of the economy.
'Econometrics – Alchemy or Science?' (1980), Sec.IV: 397

3 Econometricians may well tend to look too much where the light is and too little where the key might be found. Nevertheless, they are a positive help in trying to dispel the poor public image of economics (quantitative or otherwise) as a subject in which empty boxes are opened by assuming the existence of can-openers to reveal contents which any 10 economists will interpret in 11 ways.
'Econometrics – Alchemy or Science?' (1980), Sec.VI: 403

Sir John Richard Hicks (1904–1989)

economics and economists:

1 Pure economics has a remarkable way of producing rabbits out of a hat – apparently *a priori* propositions which apparently refer to reality.
Value and Capital (1946; 2nd edn), Part I, Ch.I, Sec.8: 23

2 Economics, surely, is a social science. It is concerned with the operations of human beings, who are not omniscient, and not wholly rational; who (perhaps because they are not wholly rational) have diverse, and not wholly consistent, ends. As such, it cannot be reduced to a pure technics, and may benefit by being distinguished from a pure technics; for we can then say that its concern is with the use that can be made of pure technics by man in society. And that looks like being a distinctly different matter.
'Linear Theory' (1960), Sec.VII: 707–708

3 Economics is more like art or philosophy than science, in the use that it can make of its own history.
' "Revolutions" in Economics' (1976): 207

Rudolf Hilferding (1877–1941)

credit:

1 In credit transactions the material, business relationship is always accompanied by a personal relationship, which appears as a direct relationship between members of society in contrast to the material social relations which characterize other economic categories such as money; namely, what is commonly called 'trust.' In this sense a fully developed credit system is the antithesis of capitalism, and represents organization and control as opposed to anarchy. It has its source in socialism, but has been adapted to capitalist society; it is a fraudulent kind of socialism, modified to suit the needs of capitalism. It socializes other people's money for use by the few. At the outset it suddenly opens up for the knights of credit prodigious vistas: the barriers to capitalist production – private property – seem to have fallen, and the entire productive power of society appears to be placed at the disposal of the individual. The prospect intoxicates him, and in turn he intoxicates and swindles others.
Finance Capital (1910), Part II, Ch.10: 180

Thomas Hobbes (1588–1679)

poverty and the poor laws:

1 And whereas many men, by accident inevitable, become unable to maintain themselves by their labour; they ought not to be left to the Charity of private persons; but to be provided for, (as farforth as the necessities of Nature require,) by the Lawes of the Common-wealth. For as it is Uncharitablenesse in any man, to neglect the impotent; so it is in the Soveraign of a Common-wealth, to expose them to the hazard of such uncertain Charity.
Leviathan (1651), Part II, Ch.XXX: 387

taxation:

2 To Equall Justice, appertaineth also the Equall imposition of Taxes; the Equality whereof dependeth not on the Equality of riches, but on the Equality of the debt, that every man oweth to the Common-wealth for his defence. It is not enough, for a man to labour for the maintenance of his life; but also to fight, (if need be,) for the securing of his labour. ... For the Impositions that are layd on the People by the Sovereign Power, are nothing else but the Wages, due to them that hold the publique Sword, to defend private men in the exercise of severall Trades, and Callings. Seeing then the benefit

that every one receiveth thereby, is the enjoyment of life, which is equally dear to poor, and rich; the debt which a poor man oweth them that defend his life, is the same which a rich man oweth for the defence of his; saving that the rich, who have the service of the poor, may be debtors not onely for their own persons, but for many more. Which considered, the Equality of Imposition, consisteth rather in the Equality of that which is consumed, than of the riches of the persons that consume the same. For what reason is there, that he which laboureth much, and sparing the fruits of his labour, consumeth little, should be more charged, then he that living idley, getteth little, and spendeth all he gets; seeing the one hath no more protection from the Common-wealth, then the other? But when the Impositions, are layd upon those things which men consume, every man payeth Equally for what he useth: Nor is the Common-wealth defrauded, by the luxurious waste of private men.
Leviathan (1651), Part II, Ch.XXX: 386

John Atkinson Hobson (1858–1940)

collectivism:

1 So soon as the idea of a social industrial organism is grasped, the question of State interference in, or State assumption of, an industry becomes a question of social expediency – that is, of the just interpretation of the facts relating to the particular case. In large measure this social control is to be regarded, not as a necessary protection against the monopolic power of individuals, but as necessary for the security of individual property within the limits prescribed by social welfare.
The Evolution of Modern Capitalism (1917; New edn), Ch.XVII, Sec.6: 409–410

2 The evolution in the structure of capitalist enterprise, while it breeds and aggravates the diseases of trade depression, sweating, etc., likewise prepares the way and facilitates the work of social control. It is easier to inspect a few large factories than many small ones, easier to arbitrate where capital and labour stands organised in large masses, easier to municipalise big joint-stock businesses in gas, water, or conveyance. Every legislative interference, in the way of inspection or minor control, quickens the evolution of an industry, and hastens the time when it acquires the position of monopoly which demands a fuller measure of control, and finally passes into the ranks of public industry.
The Evolution of Modern Capitalism (1917; New edn), Ch.XVII, Sec.7: 410

communism:

3 A morally sound communism, indeed any securely practicable communism, implies a conscious and continuous desire for the good of the community far stronger than appears to exist in any civilized people.
Economics and Ethics (1929), Part IV, Ch.I, §3: 222

4 The communist principle 'From each according to his ability, to each according to his needs,' might be generally accepted as the right rule for an economic society, if it could be made to work.
Confessions of an Economic Heretic (1938), Ch.XVI: 189

economic behavior:

5 [W]hereas good private conduct involves the constant suppression of personal selfish aims, good economic conduct involves the fullest and keenest expression of these aims under the protecting cloak of a theory that such selfishness contributes to a final harmony of human welfare.
Free-Thought in the Social Sciences (1926), Part I, Ch.III: 33

economics and economists:

6 Objective costs and utilities must be reduced to terms of subjectivity and the relation between the law of the distribution of the objective surplus and of the subjective surplus clearly formulated before we can have a science of political economy bearing any assignable reference to human happiness. Until this is done we have ideas of wealth and work which have no human significance; we have a study as far removed from any practical interest as geometry of the fourth dimension. Such a political economy can have no art attached to it. The purely objective treatment of political economists has been, in fact,

responsible for nearly all the clumsy errors which its exponents have made when invited to display their art in advice or prophecy. Until the science is thus subjectivised it can be brought into no true relations either with ethics or politics and is not properly a branch of sociology at all, but what Ruskin called it, a branch of 'mental gymnastics.'
'The Subjective and the Objective View of Distribution' (1893): 54–55

7   Economics, politics, ethics, sociology, handle, at close quarters, material so full of vital interest and so inflammable that it is very difficult for students to preserve an attitude of scientific impartiality.
Free-Thought in the Social Sciences (1926), Part I, Ch.III: 34

8   So plain, immediate, and powerful, are the reactions upon economic practice of thought and feeling embodied in economic theory, that business practitioners must constantly desire that certain economic theories shall prevail, and must be disposed to use their influence upon the organs of public information and opinion to make them prevail.
Free-Thought in the Social Sciences (1926), Part II, Ch.I: 78

poverty:

9   Real poverty is a subjective condition; it consists in or is measured by the number of felt wholesome needs which cannot be satisfied. When our means of attainment are inadequate to our desires we feel the pain of dissatisfaction. If our desires are rightly adjusted to legitimate objects of human satisfaction, to the attainment of a higher life, while the barriers of external environment and the influences they exercise upon the efficiency of effort disable us from any reasonable prospect of success, that disability constitutes poverty alike from the individual and the social standpoint.
'Is Poverty Diminishing?' (1896): 498

property:

10 Unless property, in origin and utilisation, is set upon a basis of recognised equity, riches may be as injurious as poverty to human personality and to community.
Economics and Ethics (1929), Part III, Ch.I, §10: 163

saving:

11 The real sacrifice of 'saving,' once clearly conceived from the standpoint of the marginal saver as a continuous painful self-restraint, obliges us to admit it as a pain commensurable with other painful efforts of production.
'The Subjective and the Objective View of Distribution' (1893): 48

utopia:

12 It is easier for uneducated people to accept Utopias, panaceas and sudden revolutions, than for persons with some training in history.
Free-Thought in the Social Sciences (1926), Part II, Ch.V: 159

13 [U]topias have always been wrecked upon the rocks of a human nature, envisaged as essentially immutable, or, at any rate, unadaptable to utopian requirements. The validity of modern socialistic and communistic principles and schemes turns upon the same critical consideration, the nature and amount of the adaptability of human nature.
Economics and Ethics (1929), Part IV, Ch,I, §1: 218

wealth:

14 Economic wealth is diminished when a millionaire donates his private grounds for a public park, or his pictures to a public gallery.
Economics and Ethics (1929), Part II, Ch.II, §9: 105

Thomas Hodgskin (1787–1869)

public good:

1   The public good is not cognizable by human faculties; and he who pretends that his actions are guided by a view to that, is an imposter, who looks only to his own interest and ambition. To make that the pretended motive for action, is so obviously a mere pretext, as to need no further refutation.
The Natural and Artificial Right of Property Contrasted (1832), Letter the Fifth: 77

Geoffrey Martin Hodgson (1946–)

theory of the firm:

1 The firm has to compete not simply for profit but for our confidence and trust. To achieve this, it has to abandon profit-maximisation, or even shareholder satisfaction, as the exclusive objectives of the organisation. Its explicit mission has to lie elsewhere: in product quality, customer satisfaction, ethical business practices and environmentally friendly policies, for example. Mission statements, and other such moral window dressing, are not enough: the efficient functionaries of the firm have to *believe* in its higher and fuller aims.

Economics and Utopia (1999), Part III, Ch.11: 256

Jacob Henry Hollander (1871–1940)

economics and economists:

1 The state of mind wherein the economist as teacher finds it essential, as evidence of intellectual autonomy, to prepare a textbook of his own composition, ... is of course unfortunate. But at worst this is prodigal waste of a scholar's energy. Far more serious in its scientific consequence is it for the textbook to be exploited in the exposition of scientifically incomplete theories. With the manual become in so far treatise, demanding that every new element undergo the hard rigorous test of scientific method, that gaps be neither evaded nor glossed but remain gaps until properly bridged, – substitution of hypotheses for theories, of assumption for proof, is a mischievous, because a masked, lapse.

'Economic Theorizing and Scientific Progress' (1916): 135

2 If the economist, tutored by his past, maintain his full scientific stature, toiling laboriously in the assembly of data, formulating trial hypotheses with caution, abstaining religiously from armchair theorizing, subjecting tentative uniformitives to rigid verification, fearless in the knowledge that is power – he will preserve his scientific vantage with widening range and profounder impress. By the sheer virtue of his scholarship, he will prevail upon affairs.

'The Economist's Spiral' (1922), Sec.V: 20

James Martin Hollis (1938–1998)
British philosopher

economics and economists:

1 Economics is finally no more a self-contained discipline than the economy is an isolable realm of social life.

'Penny Pinching and Backward Induction' (1991): 488

Oliver Wendell Holmes, Jr.
(1841–1935)
Associate Justice, US Supreme Court

economics and the law:

1 This case is decided upon an economic theory which a large part of the country does not entertain. If it were a question whether I agreed with that theory, I should desire to study it further and long before making up my mind. But I do not conceive that to be my duty, because I strongly believe that my agreement or disagreement has nothing to do with the right of a majority to embody their opinions in law. It is settled by various decisions of this court that state constitutions and state laws may in many ways which we as legislators might think as injudicious, or if you like as tyrannical, as this, and which, equally with this, interfere with the liberty to contract. Sunday laws and usury laws are ancient examples. A more modern one is the prohibition of lotteries. The liberty of the citizen to do as he likes so long as he does not interfere with the liberty of others to do the same, which has been a shibboleth for some well-known writers, is interfered with by school laws, by the Postoffice, by every state or municipal institution which takes his money for purposes thought desirable, whether he likes it or not. The 14th Amendment does not enact Mr. Herbert Spencer's Social Statics.

Lochner v. People of the State of New York, 198 U.S. 45, 75 (1905); dissenting opinion

2 [A] Constitution is not intended to embody a particular economic theory, whether of

paternalism and the organic relation of the citizen to the state or of *laissez faire*.
> *Lochner v. People of the State of New York*, 198 U.S. 45, 75 (1905); dissenting opinion

property:

3 When this seemingly absolute protection [of the right of property] is found to be qualified by the police power, the natural tendency of human nature is to extend the qualification more and more until at last private property disappears. But that cannot be accomplished in this way under the Constitution of the United States.
   The general rule at least is that while property may be regulated to a certain extent, if regulation goes too far it will be recognized as a taking.
> *Pennsylvania Coal Co. v. Mahon*, 260 U.S. 393, 415 (1922)

social change:

4 We are in danger of forgetting that a strong public desire to improve the public condition is not enough to warrant achieving the desire by a shorter cut than the constitutional way of paying for the change.
> *Pennsylvania Coal Co. v. Mahon*, 260 U.S. 393, 416 (1922)

taxation:

5 [E]very exaction of money for an act is a discouragement to the extent of the payment required, but that which in its immediacy is a discouragement may be part of an encouragement when seen in its organic connection with the whole. Taxes are what we pay for civilized society. . . .
> *Compañia General de Tabacos de Filipinas v. Collector of Internal Revenue*, 275 U.S. 87, 100 (1927); dissenting opinion

6 The power to tax is not the power to destroy while this court sits. The power to fix rates is the power to destroy if unlimited, but this court while it endeavors to prevent confiscation does not prevent the fixing of rates. A tax is not an unconstitutional regulation in every case where an absolute prohibition of sales would be one.
> *Panhandle Oil Co. v. State of Mississippi Ex Rel. Knox*, 277 U.S. 218, 223 (1928); dissenting opinion

Francis Horner (1778–1817)
Scottish politician

mathematics in economics:

1 In its own province, the peculiar language of algebra will never fail to gratify those who can appreciate the admirable structure of the most perfect instrument that has yet been invented by man. But that injudicious and unskilful pedantry ought most severely to be censured, which diverts an instrument from its proper use, and attempts to remove those landmarks by which the sciences are bounded from each other. The peculiar forms of expression, which have been introduced into the modern analysis, are sanctioned by the facilities which they afford, both of perspicuous abridgement, and of prosecuting a train of investigation to new and remote results. . . . We will not deny that some branches of political economy, especially those which relate to circulation, money, and the analysis of price, admit of being treated with a precision, which almost approaches to mathematical exactness. But a subject may possess this precision, without requiring, or even admitting, the symbolic representations of algebra. We would not even exclude altogether the use of analogies borrowed from mathematical learning: they afford much delight to those minds which are habituated to pass occasionally from the vague conclusions of moral induction to the full assurance of knowledge in the stricter sciences. Both as illustrations, and as ornaments, such analogies may be introduced with the happiest effect.
> 'M. Canard, *Principes d'Economie Politique*' (1803): 439–440

Robert Franklin Hoxie (1868–1914)

economics and economists:

1 Few men of intelligence fail to recognize in the abstract the importance of economic science or the great educational and practical value of its study. However, it must be admitted that economics in the concrete does not command a full measure of interest or respect. Distrust is, in fact, more or less characteristic of the attitude toward economics taken alike by scientists, students,

and practical men of affairs. To formulate completely the causes of this distrust would be a difficult and laborious task. Much of it is doubtless due, as economists have been wont to assume, to prejudice and misconception. But it is equally certain that a greater portion rests upon a valid basis and that among the valid causes of the disesteem of economics stands inadequate economic teaching.

'On the Empirical Method of Economic Instruction' (1901), Sec.I: 481

labor:

2 Labor, using the term in the generally accepted sense as including all those who work for hire, is not a true, functional, social group possessing a single, distinctive and consistent moral code, but is a group of groups representing, ethically speaking, common humanity in all its heights and depths, manifold diversity and contradictoriness. In other words, those who work for hire constitute a single and distinctive social group only in a mechanical or statistical sense of the term.

Trade Unionism in the United States (1917), Ch.XIV: 354

rational man:

3 [T]he perfectly rational man, preceding action, always weighs and balances utilities against disutilities, and always acts in the direction of the greatest net surplus of utility. This implies deliberate calculation before action, an entire absence of emotion, or else a complete disregard of emotion or feeling. If emotion is ever present in the rational human being it is never allowed to enter as a disturbing factor into his calculation or to influence his subsequent action. The rational man is never moved directly by fear, hate, anger, revenge, love of wife, home, country, love of approbation, desire for power or prestige. These things move him, if at all, only after being translated into terms of utilities and disutilities. He is never moved by any of these things to act impulsively or thoughtlessly. If you strike him, he always calculates the consequences before he strikes back.

Trade Unionism in the United States (1917), Ch.XIV: 362

David Hume (1711–1776)

commerce:

1 The greatness of a state, and the happiness of its subjects, how independent soever they may be supposed in some respects, are commonly allowed to be inseparable with regard to commerce; and as private men receive greater security, in the possession of their trade and riches, from the power of the public, so the public becomes powerful in proportion to the opulence and extensive commerce of private men. This maxim is true in general; though I cannot forbear thinking, that it may possibly admit of exceptions, and that we often establish it with too little reserve and limitation.

Essays, Moral, Political, and Literary (1777), vol. I, Part II, Essay I 'Of Commerce': 288–289

income equality:

2 A too great disproportion among the citizens weakens any state. Every person, if possible, ought to enjoy the fruits of his labour, in a full possession of all the necessaries, and many of the conveniencies of life. No one can doubt, but such an equality is most suitable to human nature, and diminishes much less from the *happiness* of the rich than it adds to that of the poor. It also augments the *power of the state*, and makes any extraordinary taxes or impositions be paid with more chearfulness. Where the riches are engrossed by a few, these must contribute very largely to the supplying of the public necessities. But when the riches are dispersed among multitudes, the burthen feels light on every shoulder, and the taxes make not a very sensible difference on any one's way of living.

Add to this, that, where the riches are in few hands, these must enjoy all the power, and will readily conspire to lay the whole burthen on the poor, and oppress them still farther, to the discouragement of all industry.

Essays, Moral, Political, and Literary (1777), vol. I, Part II, Essay I 'Of Commerce': 296–297

interest:

3   Nothing is esteemed a more certain sign of the flourishing condition of any nation than the lowness of interest.
    Essays, Moral, Political, and Literary (1777), vol. I, Part II, Essay IV 'Of Interest': 320

money:

4   Money is not, properly speaking, one of the subjects of commerce; but only the instrument which men have agreed upon to facilitate the exchange of one commodity for another. It is none of the wheels of trade: It is the oil which renders the motion of the wheels more smooth and easy.
    Essays, Moral, Political, and Literary (1777), vol. I, Part II, Essay III 'Of Money': 309

5   It is indeed evident, that money is nothing but the representation of labour and commodities, and serves only as a method of rating or estimating them.
    Essays, Moral, Political, and Literary (1777), vol. I, Part II, Essay III 'Of Money': 312

public debt:

6   We have always found, where a government has mortgaged all its revenues, that it necessarily sinks into a state of languor, inactivity, and impotence.
    Essays, Moral, Political, and Literary (1777), vol. I, Part II, Essay IX 'Of Public Credit': 369

taxation:

7   There is a prevailing maxim, among some reasoners, *that every new tax creates a new ability in the subject to bear it, and that each encrease of public burdens encreases proportionably the industry of the people*. This maxim is of such a nature as is most likely to be abused; and is so much the more dangerous, as its truth cannot be altogether denied: but it must be owned, when kept within certain bounds, to have some foundation in reason and experience.
    Essays, Moral, Political, and Literary (1777), vol. I, Part II, Essay VIII 'Of Taxes': 356

8   The best taxes are such as are levied upon consumptions, especially those of luxury; because such taxes are least felt by the people. They seem, in some measure, voluntary; since a man may chuse how far he will use the commodity which is taxed: They are paid gradually, and insensibly: They naturally produce sobriety and frugality, if judiciously imposed: And being confounded with the natural price of the commodity, they are scarcely perceived by the consumers. Their only disadvantage is, that they are expensive in the levying.
    Essays, Moral, Political, and Literary (1777), vol. I, Part II, Essay VIII 'Of Taxes': 358

9   [T]he most pernicious of all taxes are the arbitrary. They are commonly converted, by their management, into punishments on industry; and also, by their unavoidable inequality, are more grievous, than by the real burden which they impose. It is surprising, therefore, to see them have place among any civilized people.
    Essays, Moral, Political, and Literary (1777), vol. I, Part II, Essay VIII 'Of Taxes': 358

William Huskisson (1770–1830)
English statesman and financier

money:

1   *Money*, or a given quantity of gold or silver, is not only the *common measure*, and *common representative* of all other commodities; but also the *common and universal equivalent*.
    The Question Concerning the Depreciation of Our Currency (1810; 3rd edn): 579

Francis Hutcheson (1694–1746)

utilitarianism:

1   In comparing the *moral Qualitys* of Actions, in order to regulate our Election among various Actions propos'd, or to find which of them has the greatest *moral Excellency*, we are led by *our moral Sense* of *Virtue* thus to judge, that in *equal Degrees* of Happiness, expected to proceed from the Action, the

Virtue is in proportion to the *Number* of Persons to whom the Happiness shall extend: And here the *Dignity*, or *moral Importance* of Persons, may compensate Numbers; and in equal *Numbers*, the *Virtue* is as the *Quantity* of the Happiness, or natural Good; or that the *Virtue* is in a *compound Ratio* of the *Quantity* of Good, and *Number* of Enjoyers: And in the same manner, the *moral Evil*, or *Vice*, is as the *Degree* of Misery, and *Number* of Sufferers; so that, *that Action* is *best*, which accomplishes the *greatest Happiness* for the *greatest Numbers*; and *that, worst*, which, in *like manner*, occasions *Misery*.
An Inquiry Into the Original of Our Ideas of Beauty and Virtue (1725), Treatise II, Sec.III, Subject VIII: 163–164

Terence Wilmot Hutchison (1912–)

economics and economists:

1 We suggest that the economic scientist is transgressing the frontiers of his subject whenever he resorts to, or advances as possessing some empirical content, propositions which, whatever emotional associations they may arouse, can never conceivably be brought to an intersubjective empirical test, and of which one can never conceivably say that they are confirmed or falsified, or which cannot be deduced from propositions of which that can conceivably be said.
The Significance and Basic Postulates of Economic Theory (1938), Introduction, Sec.3: 10

2 Perhaps a majority of economists – but not all – would agree that improved predictions of economic behaviour or events is the main or primary task of the economist.
Knowledge and Ignorance in Economics (1977), Ch. Two, Sec.I: 8

3 [O]ne feels bound to record the impression that what economists actually do and decide (and have done and decided) is not, and has not been, invariably what, according to tenable methodological or scientific criteria, they *ought* to have done or decided.
Knowledge and Ignorance in Economics (1977), Ch. Three, Sec.I: 35

4 [I]t may well be that it is even more difficult for economists to predict their colleagues' views on controversial issues than it is to predict many or most kinds of economic behaviour.
Knowledge and Ignorance in Economics (1977), Ch. Five, Sec.VII: 140

methodology:

5 [T]the kind of 'methodology' which many economists want and value is one that boosts up their prestige – vital for raising funds – as 'Scientists' with a capital 'S', while being flexibly permissive, barring no holds, or even letting 'anything go', when it comes to throwing one's weight around in the political arena as a professional 'expert' on behalf of one's particular favourite policies.
'On the History and Philosophy of Science and Economics' (1976), Sec.VI: 200

6 [P]hilosophers of science and methodological critics should be suspicious of methodological claims and prescriptions which are popular with economists.
'On the History and Philosophy of Science and Economics' (1976), Sec.VI: 201

William Harold Hutt (1899–1988)

economics and economists:

1 [W]hilst there are few intelligent members of the public who would dare to argue with a professor of mathematics about *his* subject, there are few who would *not* be prepared to question the validity of an economist's teachings.
Economists and the Public (1936), Ch.I: 36

I

John Kells Ingram (1823–1907)

economics and economists:

1 Economic science is something far larger than the Catallactics to which some have wished to reduce it. . . . Teleology and optimism on the one hand, and the jargon of 'natural liberty' and 'indefeasible rights' on the other, must be finally abandoned.
   A History of Political Economy (1915; revised edition), Ch.VIII: 295–296

2 The laws of wealth . . . must be inferred from the facts of wealth, not from the postulate of human selfishness. We must bend ourselves to a serious direct study of the way in which society has actually addressed itself and now addresses itself to its own conservation and evolution through the supply of its material wants.
   A History of Political Economy (1915; revised edition), Ch.VIII: 296

J

William Jaffé (1898–1980)

laissez-faire:

1 Free competition often exists only by virtue of the fact that the state does not 'let alone and get out of the way,' whereas monopoly not infrequently comes into existence because of laissez faire. Only in so far as trusts and cartels result from or invoke the aid of the state, is it justifiable by definition, to see in them signs of the decline of laissez faire.
    Round Table Conference: Economic History – The Decline of Laissez Faire (1931): 8

Thomas Jefferson (1743–1826)
3rd President of the United States

economics and economists:

1 [I]n so complicated a science as political economy, no one axiom can be laid down as wise and expedient for all times and circumstances, and for their contraries.
    Letter to Benjamin Austin (9 January 1816)

intellectual property:

2 Stable ownership is the gift of social law, and is given late in the progress of society. It would be curious then, if an idea, the fugitive fermentation of an individual brain, could, of natural right, be claimed in exclusive and stable property. If nature has made any one thing less susceptible than all others of exclusive property, it is the action of the thinking power called an idea, which an individual may exclusively possess as long as he keeps it to himself; but the moment it is divulged, it forces itself into the possession of every one, and the receiver cannot dispossess himself of it. Its peculiar character, too, is that no one possesses the less, because every other possesses the whole of it. He who receives an idea from me, receives instruction himself without lessening mine; as he who lights his taper at mine, receives light without darkening me. That ideas should freely spread from one to another over the globe, for the moral and mutual instruction of man, and improvement of his condition, seems to have been peculiarly and benevolently designed by nature, when she made them, like fire, expansible over all space, without lessening their density in any point, and like the air in which we breathe, move, and have our physical being, incapable of confinement or exclusive appropriation. Inventions then cannot, in nature, be a subject of property. Society may give an exclusive right to the profits arising from them, as an encouragement to men to pursue ideas which may produce utility, but this may or may not be done, according to the will and convenience of the society, without claim or complaint from anybody.
    Letter to Isaac McPherson (13 August 1813)

property:

3 I am conscious that an equal division of property is impracticable. But the consequences of this enormous inequality producing so much misery to the bulk of mankind, legislators cannot invent too many devices for subdividing property, only taking care to let their subdivisions go hand in hand with the natural affections of the human mind. The descent of property of every kind therefore to all the children, or to all the brothers and sisters, or other relations in equal degree is a politic measure, and a practicable one.
    Letter to James Madison (28 October 1785)

public debt:

4 I ... place economy among the first and most important of republican virtues, and public debt as the greatest of the dangers to be feared.
    Letter to Governor William Plumer (21 July 1816)

William Stanley Jevons (1835–1882)

economic and economists:

1 I come to the conclusion ... that the first principles of political economy are so widely true and applicable, that they may be considered universally true as regards human nature. Historical political economy, so far from displacing the theory of economy, will only exhibit and verify the long-continued action of its laws in most widely different states of society.

'The Future of Political Economy' (1876): 624

2 The fact is it will no longer be possible to treat political economy as if it were a single undivided and indivisible science. The advantages of the division of labour are as great and indispensable in the pursuit of knowledge as in manual industry; and it is out of the question that political economy alone should fail to avail itself of these advantages.

'The Future of Political Economy' (1876): 624

3 Pleasure and pain are undoubtedly the ultimate objects of the Calculus of Economics. To satisfy our wants to the utmost with the least effort – to procure the greatest amount of what is desirable at the expense of the least that is undesirable – in other words, *to maximise pleasure*, is the problem of Economics.

The Theory of Political Economy (1911; 4th edn), Ch.III: 37

4 I protest against deference for any man, whether John Stuart Mill, or Adam Smith, or Aristotle, being allowed to check inquiry. Our science has become far too much a stagnant one, in which opinions rather than experience and reason are appealed to.

The Theory of Political Economy (1911; 4th edn), Ch.VIII: 276–277

labor value:

5 *[L]abour once spent has no influence on the future value of any article*: it is gone and lost for ever. In commerce bygones are for ever bygones; and we are always starting clear at each moment, judging the values of things with a view to future utility.

The Theory of Political Economy (1911; 4th edn), Ch.IV: 164

mathematics in economics:

6 To me it seems that *our science must be mathematical, simply because it deals with quantities*. Wherever the things treated are capable of being *greater or less*, there the laws and relations must be mathematical in nature. The ordinary laws of supply and demand treat entirely of quantities of commodity demanded or supplied, and express the manner in which the quantities vary in connection with the price. In consequence of this fact the laws *are* mathematical. Economists cannot alter their nature by denying them the name; they might as well try to alter red light by calling it blue.

The Theory of Political Economy (1911; 4th edn), Ch.I: 3–4

trade unions:

7 [A]ll classes of society are trades unionists at heart, and differ chiefly in the boldness, ability, and secrecy with which they push their respective interests.

The State in Relation to Labour (1882), Preface: viii

value:

8 There are, doubtless, qualities inherent in such a substance as gold or iron which influence its value; but the word Value, so far as it can be correctly used, merely expresses *the circumstance of its exchanging in a certain ratio for some other substance*.

The Theory of Political Economy (1911; 4th edn), Ch.IV: 77

Pope John XXIII (1881–1963) (Angelo Giuseppe Roncalli)

property:

1 Our predecessors have insisted time and again on the social function inherent in the right of private ownership, for it cannot be denied that in the plan of the Creator all of this world's goods are primarily intended for the worthy support of the entire human race.

Mater et Magistra (15 May 1961), Sec.119

social justice:

2 [I]f the whole structure and organization of an economic system is such as to compromise

human dignity, to lessen a man's sense of responsibility or rob him of opportunity for exercising personal initiative, then such a system, We maintain, is altogether unjust – no matter how much wealth it produces, or how justly and equitably such wealth is distributed.
Mater et Magistra (15 May 1961), Sec.83

Harry Gordon Johnson (1923–1977)

economics and economists:

1 The basic problems of economics are simple; the hard part is to recognize simplicity when you see it. The next hardest part is to present simplicity as common sense rather than ivory tower insensitivity. Theory needs to teach more of both.
'The State of Theory' (1974): 324

Richard Jones (1790–1855)

economics and economists:

1 Political economy has been distrusted. The facts on which its conclusions must be founded, have been thought too multitudinous, too variable, and too capricious in their combinations, to admit of their being accurately observed or truly analyzed; or, consequently, of their yielding any safe permanent general principles: and men have been inclined to shrink from the task of even examining opinions, which they have thought doomed only to startle without convincing, and then to disappear, and give place to another crop of paradoxes.
An Essay on the Distribution of Wealth and on the Sources of Taxation (1831), Preface: xviii–xix

methodology:

2 The principles which determine the position and progress, and govern the conduct, of large bodies of the human race, placed under different circumstances, can be learnt only by an appeal to experience. He must, indeed, be a shallow reasoner, who by mere efforts of consciousness, by consulting his own views, feelings and motives, and the narrow sphere of his personal observation, and reasoning *a priori*, from them expects that he shall be able to anticipate the conduct, progress and fortunes of large bodies of men, differing from himself in moral or physical temperament, and influenced by differences, varying in extent and variously combined, in climate, soil, religion, education and government.
An Essay on the Distribution of Wealth and on the Sources of Taxation (1831), Preface: xv

Thomas Joplin (1790–1847)

money:

1 All wise Governments observe a due Proportion in the Plenty and Scarcity of their Money, according to the Commodities of the Country: Which when observed, their Money, whatever it is made of, is of as much Use for Commerce there, as Bullion is in the World.
An Essay on Money & Bullion (1718), Ch.II

trade:

2 You often hear of the Circulation of Money: As that ought to circulate in a Nation, so ought Bullion to circulate in the World; and our Coin, as long as it keeps a Proportion of Value with it. You may as well expect to keep Life in the Body, by stopping up the Arteries, and leaving the Veins open, and so filling the Heart with Blood, as to keep the Life in Trade, by leaving those Ports open at which bullion enters, and stopping up those at which it goes out. As the Blood by running preserves Life in the Body, and conveys a proper Increase to every Part, though it self be neither; so bullion, by running about the World, preserves the Life of Trade, and brings Riches whereever it comes, tho' in it self it be neither. Those Nations who prohibit the Exportation of it, seem to me like that Clown, who observing the Overflowing of the River made his Meadow fruitful; the next Flood damm'd the Water all in, and so turned it into a Bogg, which for a long time after bore nothing but Sedge: Whereas it was not the Water it self that enriched his Soil; but those Particles of Earth it brought, and left behind it.
An Essay on Money & Bullion (1718), Ch.II

value:

3   Value is an Affection of the Mind, and signifies the Liking we have to any Thing, from a Principle of Reason: Love is an Affection like it, and sometimes accompanies it, but that generally proceeds from Passion. There are many Things we Love without Reason, but nothing we Value without, tho' very often with a wrong one.
An Essay on Money & Bullion (1718), Ch.I

K

Nicholas Kaldor, Baron Kaldor of Newnham (1908–1986)

economics and economists:

1 [T]he powerful attraction of the habits of thought engendered by 'equilibrium economics' has become a major obstacle to the development of economics as a *science* – meaning by the term 'science' a body of theorems based on assumptions that are *empirically* derived (from observations) and which embody hypotheses that are capable of verification both in regard to the assumptions and the predictions.
   'The Irrelevance of Equilibrium Economics' (1972), Introduction: 1237

2 [E]quilibrium theory has reached the stage where the pure theorist has successfully (though perhaps inadvertently) demonstrated that the main implications of this theory cannot possibly hold in reality, but has not yet managed to pass his message down the line to the textbook writer and to the classroom.
   'The Irrelevance of Equilibrium Economics' (1972), Sec.I: 1240

Michal Kalecki (1899–1970)

capitalism:

1 The fundamentals of capitalist ethics require that 'You shall earn your bread in sweat' – unless you happen to have private means.
   'Political Aspects of Full Employment' (1943), Sec.II, 3: 326

2 If capitalism can adjust itself to full employment a fundamental reform will have been incorporated in it. If not, it will show itself an outmoded system which must be scrapped.
   'Political Aspects of Full Employment' (1943), Sec.V, 2: 331

Leonid Vitaliyevich Kantorovich (1912–1986)

planning:

1 Planning of the national economy and of individual branches within the framework of the state is only possible when private ownership of the means of production is replaced by common socialist ownership. Such planning becomes possible only when capitalist relations of production have been eliminated and replaced by socialist ones.
   The Best Use of Economic Resources (1965), Introduction: xxi

Karl Johann Kautsky (1854–1938)
German–Austrian socialist

money:

1 Socialism is called upon to remove the degrading effects of money. They arise from private property in the source of life and in the socially created wealth, which has hitherto been closely bound up with money. The abolition of this private property will make an end of the curse which has hitherto attached to money.
   The Labour Revolution (1925), Ch.XI: 280

socialism:

2 If indeed the socialist commonwealth were an impossibility, then mankind would be cut off from all further economic development. In that event modern society would decay, as did the Roman empire nearly two thousand years ago, and finally relapse into barbarism.
   The Class Struggle (1910), Ch.IV, Sec.6: 118

3 Should socialist society ever decide to decree equality of incomes, and should the effect of such a measure threaten to be the dire one prophesied, the natural result would be, not that socialist production, but that the principle of equality of incomes, would be thrown overboard.
   The Class Struggle (1910), Ch.IV, Sec.9: 142

4   The difference between Socialism and capitalism does not consist in the fact that the one makes a profit, and the other not, but in the fact that the one makes a profit for individuals, while the other makes a profit for the community.
    The Labour Revolution (1925), Ch.VIII, Sec.f: 212

John Maynard Keynes, Baron Keynes of Tilton (1883–1946)

capitalism:

1   For my part, I think that capitalism, wisely managed, can probably be made more efficient for attaining economic ends than any alternative system yet in sight, but that in itself it is in many ways extremely objectionable. Our problem is to work out a social organization which shall be as efficient as possible without offending our notions of a satisfactory way of life.
    'The End of Laissez-Faire' (1926), Part II, Sec.III: 41

2   When the accumulation of wealth is no longer of high social importance, there will be great changes in the code of morals. We shall be able to rid ourselves of many of the pseudo-moral principles which have hagridden us for two hundred years, by which we have exalted some of the most distasteful of human qualities into the position of the highest virtues. We shall be able to afford to dare to assess the money-motive at its true value. The love of money as a possession – as distinguished from the love of money as a means to the enjoyments and realities of life – will be recognized for what it is, a somewhat disgusting morbidity, one of those semi-criminal, semi-pathological propensities which one hands over with a shudder to the specialists in mental disease. All kinds of social customs and economic practices, affecting the distribution of wealth and of economic rewards and penalties, which we now maintain at all costs, however distasteful and unjust they may be in themselves, because they are tremendously useful in promoting the accumulation of capital, we shall then be free, at last, to discard.
    'Economic Possibilities for Our Grandchildren' (1930), Part II: 97

consumption:

3   The fundamental psychological law, upon which we are entitled to depend with great confidence both *a priori* from our knowledge of human nature and from the detailed facts of experience, is that men are disposed, as a rule and on the average, to increase their consumption as their income increases, but not by as much as the increase in their income.
    The General Theory of Employment, Interest, and Money (1936), Book III, Ch.8, Sec.III: 96

economics and economists:

4   The study of economics does not seem to require any specialised gifts of an unusually high order. Is it not, intellectually regarded, a very easy subject compared with the higher branches of philosophy and pure science? Yet good, or even competent, economists are the rarest of birds. An easy subject, at which very few excel! The paradox finds its explanation, perhaps, in that the master-economist must possess a rare *combination* of gifts. He must reach a high standard in several different directions and must combine talents not often found together. He must be mathematician, historian, statesman, philosopher – in some degree. He must understand symbols and speak in words. He must contemplate the particular in terms of the general, and touch abstract and concrete in the same flight of thought. He must study the present in the light of the past for the purposes of the future. No part of man's nature or his institutions must lie entirely outside his regard. He must be purposeful and disinterested in a simultaneous mood; as aloof and incorruptible as an artist, yet sometimes as near the earth as a politician.
    'Alfred Marshall, 1842–1924' (1924), Sec.II: 321–322

5   If economists could manage to get themselves thought of as humble, competent people, on a level with dentists, that would be splendid!
    'Economic Possibilities for Our Grandchildren' (1930), Part II: 98

6   For the next twenty-five years in my belief, economists, at present the most incompetent, will be nevertheless the most important, group of scientists in the world. And it is to

be hoped – if they are successful – that after that they will never be important again.
'The Dilemma of Modern Socialism' (1932): 159

7 [I]n writing economics one is not writing either a mathematical proof or a legal document. One is trying to arouse and appeal to the reader's intuitions; and, if he has worked himself into a state when he has none, one is helpless!
Letter to R.B. Bryce (10 July 1935)

8 [T]he ideas of economists and political philosophers, both when they are right and when they are wrong, are more powerful than is commonly understood. Indeed the world is ruled by little else. Practical men, who believe themselves to be quite exempt from any intellectual influences, are usually the slaves of some defunct economist. Madmen in authority, who hear voices in the air, are distilling their frenzy from some academic scribbler of a few years back.
The General Theory of Employment, Interest, and Money (1936), Book VI, Ch.24, Sec.V: 383

government intervention:

9 The important thing for government is not to do things which individuals are doing already, and to do them a little better or a little worse; but to do things which at present are not done at all.
'The End of Laissez-Faire' (1926), Part II, Sec.II: 40

10 If the Treasury were to fill old bottles with banknotes, bury them at suitable depths in disused coalmines which are then filled up to the surface with town rubbish, and leave it to private enterprise on well-tried principles of *laissez-faire* to dig the notes up again . . ., there need be no more unemployment and, with the help of the repercussions, the real income of the community, and its capital wealth also, would probably become a good deal greater than it actually is. It would, indeed, be more sensible to build houses and the like; but if there are political and practical difficulties in the way of this, the above would be better than nothing.
The General Theory of Employment, Interest, and Money (1936), Bk.III, Ch.10, Sec.VI: 129

individualism:

11 It is *not* true that individuals possess a prescriptive 'natural liberty' in their economic activities. There is *no* 'compact' conferring perpetual rights on those who have or on those who acquire. The world is *not* so governed from above that private and social interest always coincide. It is *not* so managed here below that in practice they coincide. It is *not* a correct deduction from the principles of economics that enlightened self-interest always operates in the public interest. Nor is it true that self-interest generally *is* enlightened; more often individuals acting separately to promote their own ends are too ignorant or too weak to attain even these. Experience does *not* show that individuals, when they make up a social unit, are always less clear-sighted than when they act separately.
'The End of Laissez-Faire' (1926), Part II, Sec.II: 39

inflation:

12 Lenin is said to have declared that the best way to destroy the Capitalist System was to debauch the currency. By a continuing process of inflation, governments can confiscate, secretly and unobserved, an important part of the wealth of their citizens. By this method they not only confiscate, but they confiscate *arbitrarily*; and, while the process impoverishes many, it actually enriches some. The sight of this arbitrary rearrangement of riches strikes not only at security, but at confidence in the equity of the existing distribution of wealth. Those to whom the system brings windfalls, beyond their deserts and even beyond their expectations or desires, become 'profiteers,' who are the object of the hatred of the bourgeoisie, whom the inflationism has impoverished, not less than of the proletariat. As the inflation proceeds and the real value of the currency fluctuates wildly from month to month, all permanent relations between debtors and creditors, which form the ultimate foundation of capitalism, become so utterly disordered as to be almost meaningless; and the process of wealth-getting degenerates into a gamble and a lottery.
  Lenin was certainly right. There is no subtler, no surer means of overturning the existing basis of society than to debauch the

currency. The process engages all the hidden forces of economic law on the side of destruction, and does it in a manner which not one man in a million is able to diagnose.
The Economic Consequences of the Peace (1920), Ch.VI: 235–236

13 The power of taxation by currency depreciation is one which has been inherent in the State since Rome discovered it. The creation of legal-tender has been and is a Government's ultimate reserve; and no State or Government is likely to decree its own bankruptcy or its own downfall, so long as this instrument still lies at hand unused.
A Tract on Monetary Reform (1923), Ch.I, Sec.I: 9

14 A Government can live for a long time ... by printing paper money. That is to say, it can by this means secure the command over real resources, – resources just as real as those obtained by taxation. The method is condemned, but its efficacy, up to a point, must be admitted. A Government can live by this means when it can live by no other. It is the form of taxation which the public finds hardest to evade and even the weakest Government can enforce, when it can enforce nothing else.
A Tract on Monetary Reform (1923), Ch.II, Sec.I: 41

justice:

15 The policy of reducing Germany to servitude for a generation, of degrading the lives of millions of human beings, and of depriving a whole nation of happiness should be abhorrent and detestable, – abhorrent and detestable, even if it were possible, even if it enriched ourselves, even if it did not sow the decay of the whole civilized life of Europe. Some preach it in the name of Justice. In the great events of man's history, in the unwinding of the complex fates of nations Justice is not so simple. And if it were, nations are not authorized, by religion or by natural morals, to visit on the children of their enemies the misdoings of parents or of rulers.
The Economic Consequences of the Peace (1920), Ch.V: 225

'long run':

16 But this *long run* is a misleading guide to current affairs. *In the long run* we are all dead. Economists set themselves too easy, too useless a task if in tempestuous seasons they can only tell us that when the storm is long past the ocean is flat again.
A Tract on Monetary Reform (1923), Ch.III, Sec.I: 80

mathematics in economics:

17 The object of our analysis is, not to provide a machine, or method of blind manipulation, which will furnish an infallible answer, but to provide ourselves with an organised and orderly method of thinking out particular problems; and, after we have reached a provisional conclusion by isolating the complicating factors one by one, we then have to go back on ourselves and allow, as well as we can, for the probable interactions of the factors amongst themselves. This is the nature of economic thinking. Any other way of applying our formal principles of thought (without which, however, we shall be lost in the wood) will lead us into error. It is a great fault of symbolic pseudo-mathematical methods of formalising a system of economic analysis ... that they expressly assume strict independence between the factors involved and lose all their cogency and authority if this hypothesis is disallowed; whereas, in ordinary discourse, where we are not blindly manipulating but know all the time what we are doing and what the words mean, we can keep 'at the back of our heads' the necessary reserves and qualifications and the adjustments which we shall have to make later on, in a way in which we cannot keep complicated partial differentials 'at the back' of several pages of algebra which assume that they all vanish. Too large a proportion of recent 'mathematical' economics are mere concoctions, as imprecise as the initial assumptions they rest on, which allow the author to lose sight of the complexities and interdependencies of the real world in a maze of pretentious and unhelpful symbols.
The General Theory of Employment, Interest, and Money (1936), Book V, Ch.21, Sec.III: 297–298

money:

18 Money is only important for what it will procure.
A Tract on Monetary Reform (1923), Ch.I: 1

19 *[T]he importance of money essentially flows from its being a link between the present and the future.*
    The General Theory of Employment, Interest, and Money (1936), Book V, Ch.21, Sec.I: 293

money-making:

20 There are valuable human activities which require the motive of money-making and the environment of private wealth-ownership for their full fruition. Moreover, dangerous human proclivities can be canalised into comparatively harmless channels by the existence of opportunities for money-making and private wealth, which, if they cannot be satisfied in this way, may find their outlet in cruelty, the reckless pursuit of personal power and authority, and other forms of self-aggrandisement. It is better that a man should tyrannise over his bank balance than over his fellow-citizens; and whilst the former is sometimes denounced as being but a means to the latter, sometimes at least it is an alternative.
    The General Theory of Employment, Interest, and Money (1936), Book VI, Ch.24, Sec.I: 374

'political problem':

21 The political problem of mankind is to combine three things: Economic Efficiency, Social Justice, and Individual Liberty. The first needs criticism, precaution, and technical knowledge; the second, an unselfish and enthusiastic spirit, which loves the ordinary man; the third, tolerance, breadth, appreciation of the excellencies of variety and independence, which prefers, above everything, to give unhindered opportunity to the exceptional and to the inspiring.
    'Liberalism and Labour' (1926): 708

poverty:

22 Whatever may be the best remedy for poverty in plenty, we must reject all those alleged remedies which consist, in substance, of getting rid of the plenty.
    'Poverty in Plenty: Is the Economic System Self-Adjusting?' (1934): 486

socialism:

23 Marxian socialism must always remain a portent to the historians of opinion – how a doctrine so illogical and so dull can have exercised so powerful and enduring an influence over the minds of men, and, through them, the events of history.
    'The End of Laissez-Faire' (1926), Part II, Sec.I: 38

24 I criticize doctrinaire state socialism, not because it seeks to engage men's altruistic impulses in the service of society, or because it departs from laissez-faire, or because it takes away from man's natural liberty to make a million, or because it has courage for bold experiments. All these things I applaud. I criticize it because it misses the significance of what is actually happening; because it is, in fact, little better than a dusty survival of a plan to meet the problems of fifty years ago, based on a misunderstanding of what someone said a hundred years ago.
    'The End of Laissez-Faire' (1926), Part II, Sec.II: 40

25 Besides two arms and two legs for oratory, gesticulation and movement, Socialism has two heads and two hearts which are always at war with one another. The one is ardent to do things because they are economically sound. The other is no less ardent to do things which are admitted to be economically unsound.
    'The Dilemma of Modern Socialism' (1932): 155

26 I conceive, therefore, that a somewhat comprehensive socialisation of investment will prove the only means of securing an approximation to full employment; though this need not exclude all manner of compromises and of devices by which public authority will co-operate with private initiative. But beyond this no obvious case is made out for a system of State Socialism which would embrace most of the economic life of the community. It is not the ownership of the instruments of production which it is important for the State to assume. If the State is able to determine the aggregate amount of resources devoted to augmenting the instruments and the basic rate of reward to those who own them, it will have accomplished all that is necessary.
    The General Theory of Employment, Interest, and Money (1936), Book VI, Ch.24, Sec.III: 378

State:

27 I believe that in many cases the ideal size for the unit of control and organization lies somewhere between the individual and the modern state. I suggest, therefore, that progress lies in the growth and the recognition of semi-autonomous bodies within the state – bodies whose criterion of action within their own field is solely the public good as they understand it, and from whose deliberations motives of private advantage are excluded. . . .
   'The End of Laissez-Faire' (1926), Part II, Sec.II: 39

John Neville Keynes (1852–1949)

economics and economists:

1 The attempt to combine theoretical and practical enquiries tends to confirm the popular confusion as to the nature of many economic truths. What are laid down as theorems of pure science are constantly interpreted as if they were maxims for practical guidance. In spite of repeated protests from economists themselves, there is an inveterate disposition on the part of the public to regard the principles of political economy as essentially rules of conduct, even when the sole intention of those who formulate them is to determine what is, and not to prescribe what ought to be.
   The Scope and Method of Political Economy (1904; 3rd edn), Ch.II, Sec.3: 50

2 If political economy regarded from the theoretical standpoint is to make good progress, it is essential that all extrinsic or premature sources of controversy should be eliminated; and we may be sure that the more its principles are discussed independently of ethical and practical considerations, the sooner will the science emerge from the controversial stage.
   The Scope and Method of Political Economy (1904; 3rd edn), Ch.II, Sec.3: 52

3 [W]hen we pass . . . to problems of taxation, or to problems that concern the relations of the State with trade and industry, or to the general discussion of communistic and socialistic schemes – it is far from being the case that economic considerations hold the field exclusively. Account must also be taken of ethical, social, and political considerations that lie outside the sphere of political economy regarded as a science.
   The Scope and Method of Political Economy (1904; 3rd edn), Ch.II, Sec.4: 56–57

4 [Political economy] is not primarily concerned with either physical or psychological or political phenomena as such, but with phenomena that originate in the activity of human beings in their social relations one with another.
   The Scope and Method of Political Economy (1904; 3rd edn), Ch.III, Sec.5: 100–101

Israel M. Kirzner (1930–)

entrepreneurship:

1 The incentive [of the entrepreneur] is to try to get something for nothing, if only one can see what it is that can be done.
   Perception, Opportunity, and Profit (1979), Ch.1: 11

ignorance:

2 Ignorance of knowledge or information that might be known through deliberate search or learning can be explained and accounted for. Such ignorance is in fact to be defended as justified by the high cost of search or learning. Such ignorance has, then, been deliberately accepted; in a sense it is *optimal*.
   Perception, Opportunity, and Profit (1979), Ch.9: 144–145

Lawrence Robert Klein (1920–)

econometrics:

1 The provision of a large public data bank is no panacea for econometric researchers. There will always be the need for specialized data not in the file. What is more significant, however, is the fact that a large public file cannot plausibly serve the specialized needs of econometrics in fine detail. It will always be necessary for the research econometrician to adjust, manipulate and rework public data

in order to build statistical series that suit the concepts of economic analysis.
'Whither Econometrics?' (1971), Sec.3: 417

2   It is narrow and surely wrong to think that quantitative numerical data available to us as econometricians contain the full secrets of the true undisclosed economic process. We are pitifully short of information and must make use of whatever we can put our hands on.
'Whither Econometrics?' (1971), Sec.3.7: 420

mathematics in economics:

3   Non-mathematical contributions to economic analysis often tend to be fat, sloppy, and vague. There is a real merit in condensing wordy volumes or manuscripts into a few understandable pages. I have come to like compact, elegant arguments and hazard the guess that many others would like this feature also if they would participate in the development of the mathematical approach to economics. In fact 'reading with tears' has come to mean, for me, reading verbose treatises in literary economics.
'The Contributions of Mathematics in Economics' (1954): 360

Frank Hyneman Knight (1885–1972)

choice:

1   The whole theory of conduct may now be summed up, as far as it is relevant for our purposes, in a comprehensive 'Law of Choice': *When confronted with alternative, quantitatively variable lines of action or experience, we tend to combine them in such proportions that the physically correlated amounts or degrees of each are of equal utility to the person choosing.*
Risk, Uncertainty, and Profit (1921), Part Two, Ch.III: 64

communism:

2   The plea of Communism, like that of Christianity, is justice, under absolute authority, ignoring freedom. (The former does extol progress, and progress through science, both of which Christianity despised; by the same argument, Communism is overtly less devoted to law and tradition, more openly claims the right to ignore or break the law.)
'The Role of Principles in Economics and Politics' (1951): 25

economic activity:

3   Economic activity is *at the same time* a means of want-satisfaction, an agency for want- and character-formation, a field of creative self-expression, and a competitive sport. While men are 'playing the game' of business, they are also molding their own and other personalities, and creating a civilization whose worthiness to endure cannot be a matter of indifference.
'The Ethics of Competition' (1923), Introduction: 587

economic man:

4   A society made up of economic men, even as consumers, would be a fantastic monstrosity and a physical impossibility.
Intelligence and Democratic Action (1960), Ch.IV: 107

economics and economists:

5   Economists who pretend to eschew ethical problems, to confine themselves to 'price economics,' or contrast price economics and welfare economics, or pecuniary and social efficiency, have in general merely worked in terms of unformulated, unconscious ethical standards, and hence, in the literal sense, unintelligently.
Round Table Conference on the Relation Between Economics and Ethics (1922): 193

6   We must know when we are stating facts and when we are passing judgment, and must make it unmistakably clear in our exposition which we are doing. Only through such an understanding and such a separation can economic theory come into its own.
Round Table Conference on the Relation Between Economics and Ethics (1922): 193

7   One of the most serious defects of economics as an interpretation of reality is the assumption that men produce in order to consume. Except for those very low in the economic scale the opposite is as near the

truth, and the motives of a large part of even 'lower-class' consumption are social in their nature.

'Ethics and the Economic Interpretation' (1922): 463 note 7.

8 It is an accident of the way in which economic science has developed, and especially of the peculiar relation between science and practice in this field, that so little serious effort has been made to state with rigor and exactitude the assumptions involved in the notion of perfect competition, the premises of pure economics. Literary writers on economics have been interested in administrative problems, for which the results of any exact treatment of principles are too abstract to be of direct application, and have not generally been trained to use or appreciate rigorous methods. The mathematical economists have commonly been mathematicians first and economists afterward, disposed to oversimplify the data and underestimate the divergence between their premises and the facts of life. In consequence they have not been successful in getting their presentation into such a form that it could be understood, and its relation to real problems recognized, by practical economists.

'The Ethics of Competition' (1923), Sec.I: 589

9 There is no more important prerequisite to clear thinking in regard to economics itself than is recognition of its limited place among human interests at large.

The Economic Organization (1951), 'Social Economic Organization': 3

10 Economics deals with the *social organization* of economic activity. In practice its scope is much narrower still; there are many ways in which economic activity may be socially organized, but the predominant method in modern nations is the price system, or free enterprise. Consequently it is the structure and working of the system of free enterprise which constitutes the principal topic of discussion is a treatise on economics.

The Economic Organization (1951), 'Social Economic Organization': 6

11 If we could write economics as observed from some other planet and if we never published the results on earth, economics would come nearer to being a natural science.

Intelligence and Democratic Action (1960), Ch.III: 73

Keynes' General Theory:

12 I must confess that the labour I have spent on *The General Theory of Employment, Interest, and Money* leaves me with a feeling of keen disappointment. The chief value of the book has seemed to lie in the hard labour involved in reading it, which enforces intensive grappling with the problems.

'Unemployment: And Mr. Keynes's Revolution in Economic Theory' (1937), Sec.VI: 123

money:

13 Money serves only to get valuable things away from other people. . . .

Intelligence and Democratic Action (1960), Ch.I: 7

prediction:

14 The assumption of a stable satisfaction function is of course highly unreliable, but it has predictive value, in the absence of any discoverable reason for believing that it has changed. The point is important particularly because of the difference between predicting human behavior and predicting the behavior of physical objects under changed conditions, in that the latter neither behave irrationally or sentimentally, nor make mistakes, nor 'change their minds' (and more or less correspondingly their reaction patterns), as human beings are notoriously liable to do. This trait of human beings, in contrast with physical things, whose responses reflect an inner nature which is either invariant or changes only for objectively discoverable reasons, is admittedly embarrassing to the economist as a scientist, but there does not seem to be anything that he can do about it.

' "What Is Truth" in Economics?' (1940): 29

property:

15 Private property is a social institution; society has the unquestionable right to change or abolish it at will, and will maintain the

institution only so long as property-owners serve the social interest better than some other form of social agency promises to do.
Risk, Uncertainty, and Profit (1921), Part Three, Ch.XII: 359–360

rationality:

16 If one behaves with perfect economic rationality he does not behave rationally as a human being.
Intelligence and Democratic Action (1960), Ch.III: 72

society:

17 Man is as completely social as a termite in being unable to live at all outside a group of considerable size and of complex yet fairly stable structure (even a Crusoe is no real exception). . . .
'Free Society: Its Basic Nature and Problem' (1948): 39

Tjalling Charles Koopmans
(1910–1985)

econometrics:

1 Econometricians are bound to be frustrated individuals as long as performance in accurately forecasting the future paths of economic variables for an extended period ahead is regarded as the main criterion of success, by themselves or by others.
'Toward Partial Redirection of Econometrics: Comment' (1952), Sec.I: 201

2 The main purpose of econometric model construction is to determine which dials and levers are sufficiently fast and predictable in their effects so that the policy-maker, by adjusting these dials continually in prompt response to the observed path of economic variables, has a more than even chance to steer a more stable, efficient, and growth-enabling course than the economy would take if other or fewer conscious policies were applied.
'Toward Partial Redirection of Econometrics: Comment' (1952), Sec.I: 201

methodology:

3 If methods of scaling are ever applied to measure the relative prestige of various topics in economic research, methodological discussion will undoubtedly be found to rank near the low end of the scale.
Three Essays on the State of Economic Science (1957), Essay II, Sec.I: 129

Paul R. Krugman (1953–)

economics and economists:

1 Even if the ultimate aim of economic theory is better policy, one does not best serve that aim by trying to make every journal article into a policy proposal. The immediate policy implications of a new idea are in the end less important than its intellectual contribution. There are plenty of people out there trying to change the world in various ways; the point of economic research is to understand it.
'The Narrow and Broad Arguments for Free Trade' (1993), Sec.IV: 366

trade:

2 Why are economists free-traders? It is hard not to suspect that our professional commitment to free trade is a sociological phenomenon as well as an intellectual conviction, that it, that there is more to it than our altruistic desire to persuade society to avoid deadweight losses. After all, if social welfare were all that were at stake, we should as a profession be equally committed to, say, the use of the price mechanism to limit pollution and congestion. However, support for free trade is a badge of professional integrity in a way that support for other, equally worthy causes is not. By emphasizing the virtues of free trade, we also emphasize our intellectual superiority over the unenlightened who do not understand comparative advantage. In other words, the idea of free trade takes on special meaning precisely because it is someplace where the ideas of economists clash particularly strongly with popular perceptions.
'The Narrow and Broad Arguments for Free Trade' (1993): 362

L

Kelvin John Lancaster (1924–1999)

economics and economists:

1 Like Tweedledum and Tweedledee, comparative statics and qualitative economics are rarely found apart.
'The Scope of Qualitative Economics' (1962), Sec.I: 100

Oskar Lange (1904–1965)

capitalism:

1 That capitalism has been the carrier of the greatest economic progress ever witnessed in the history of the human race the socialists are the last to deny. Indeed, there has scarcely ever been a more enthusiastic eulogy of the revolutionising achievements of the capitalist system than that contained in the Communist Manifesto.
'On the Economic Theory of Socialism, Part II' (1937), Sec.5: 128

2 An economic system based on private enterprise and private property of the means of production can work only as long as the security of private property and of income derived from property and from enterprise is maintained. The very existence of a government bent on introducing socialism is a constant threat to this security. Therefore, the capitalist economy cannot function under a socialist government unless the government is socialist in name only.
'On the Economic Theory of Socialism, Part II' (1937), Sec.6: 134

competition:

3 The system of free competition is a rather peculiar one. Its mechanism is one of *fooling* entrepreneurs. It requires the pursuit of maximum profit in order to function, but it destroys profits when they are actually pursued by a larger number of people.
'On the Economic Theory of Socialism, Part II' (1937), Sec.5: 131

economic planning:

4 Planning is the means of subjecting the operation of economic laws and the economic development of society to the direction of human will.
'Role of Planning in Socialist Economy' (1962): 16

5 The capitalist economy may be compared to an old fashioned balloon which is moved by the current of air in the direction in which the wind pushes it. Man has no control whatever over the direction in which the balloon is moving. The socialist economy in the period of realisation of plan by administrative measures can be compared to an old fashioned airplane, where the pilot with his hands moves the steering rod. By sitting always by the steering rod the pilot directs the plane in the direction he chooses, whenever the current of the air changes he moves the rod in such a way as to keep his chosen direction.
I would compare planning in which the realisation is based on economic means to a modern plane which has an automatic steering mechanism. The pilot sets the mechanism in the direction in which he wants the plane to go and the automatic mechanism keeps the plane in the desired direction. The pilot can read a book or a newspaper in the meantime, and the plane by itself keeps the desired course. But it is not the direction where the wind pushes the plane but the direction which the pilot has chosen, consciously chosen. It is the pilot who determines the direction of the plane, if he wishes he can change the direction by setting the automatic mechanism in a different direction.
'Role of Planning in Socialist Economy' (1962): 25

socialism:

6 Only a socialist economy can fully satisfy the claim made by many economists with regard to the achievements of free competition.
'On the Economic Theory of Socialism, Part II' (1937), Sec.5: 127

7 A socialist government really intent upon socialism has to decide to carry out its socialisation programme *at one stroke*, or to give it up altogether. The very coming into power of such a government must cause a financial panic and economic collapse. Therefore, the socialist government must either guarantee the immunity of private property and private enterprise in order to enable the capitalist economy to function normally, in doing which it gives up its socialist aims, or it must go through resolutely with its socialisation programme at maximum speed. Any hesitation, any vacillation and indecision provokes the inevitable economic catastrophe. Socialism is not an economic policy for the timid.
'On the Economic Theory of Socialism, Part II' (1937), Sec.6: 134–135

James Laurence Laughlin
(1850–1933)

economics and economists:

1 Economics deals not only with psychological, but also with physiological and physical phenomena, – that is, with mental operations as well as with bodily and physical facts; and it aims at the discovery and exposition of causes and effects in regard to this subject-matter. Preëminently concerned as it is with every-day life, it demands careful investigation into the accuracy of data, and a keen sense to note their relations to existing science. The field of economics is, fortunately, quite definite, but it includes different orders of things. It does not deal solely with physical nature, as do the natural sciences; nor solely with ethical or psychic data, as do the moral sciences. It deals with conclusions taken from both these groups of sciences. Therefore its field is somewhat peculiar, although its aim, common to other sciences, is the discovery and verification of a body of principles.
'Teaching of Economics' (1896): 682–683

2 [T]he economic student, who has been taught merely the facts of a certain period or subject, and who has not been trained primarily in using principles to explain these facts, has been given the counterfeit of an education, and not the real thing. If he has been plunged at once into figures and facts before he has received a careful preliminary training in principles, he is cheated by his instructor into a false belief that he is being educated, when he is not. Such a student is like a traveler in the dark, who has a lantern, but, when an emergency arises, finds, to his chagrin, that it contains no light.
'Teaching of Economics' (1896): 683

3 A student of economics, however loaded his mind may be with information, if untrained in the power to trace the operation of cause and effect in his facts, is distinctly not an economist.
'Teaching of Economics' (1896): 686

4 As matters stand now, there is no reason for pride in the mental power of the general body of thinkers in economics. With obvious exceptions, there is a great deal of mediocre work. Men in political economy are, of course, human beings, and exhibit the peculiarities of human nature that exist the world over; but it is a question whether the scientific frame of mind is not too generally sacrificed to the demands of personal feeling, or to the assumptions of self-constituted groups.
Industrial America (1912), Ch.VII, Sec.III: 230

5 In spite of the intellectual ferment among economic students, in spite of much admirable writing intended for popular consumption, it remains true that the professional economists have very little influence upon the convictions of the great body of our people.
Industrial America (1912), Ch.VII, Sec.V: 240

equality:

6 Is it injustice that the stupid and the incapable should get less in this system than the clever and the gifted? On what principle of justice is the universe founded, if men of unequal powers be given equal rewards?
'Economics and Socialism' (1899): 254

7 Equality of reward without equality of results would make a desert of a rich and populous land.
'Economics and Socialism' (1899): 255

socialism:

8   The socialist can not assure us that, so long as men remain what they are, there would be no bad activity of selfish and criminal persons in his collective system. There is no reason to suppose that human perfection will be produced merely by changing the external forms of government and industrial production.
    'Economics and Socialism' (1899): 255

Carl Friedrich Wilhelm Launhardt (1832–1918)

mathematics in economics:

1   That indeed mathematics cannot explain in a satisfactory manner all aspects of economic problems, some of which lead into moral and political realms, must not be allowed to be a reason for condemning its application altogether or for sacrificing the help it alone has to offer.
    Mathematical Principles of Economics (1885), Preface: 15

Emile Louis Victor de Laveleye (1822–1892)

socialism:

1   The Socialist is a pessimist. He paints in bold relief the worst side of social conditions, and shows the strong oppressing the weak, the rich crushing the poor, inequality becoming harder and more abominable. He sighs for an ideal in which well-being will be portioned out according to the deserts of each, and as a reward for services rendered.
    The Economist is an optimist. He thinks that the man who pursues his personal interest contributes as much as possible to the general interest; and that social order must be the result of free play being allowed to individual selfishness. In his opinion, the only thing therefore to be done is to do away with all obstacles, to reduce to a minimum the power of the State, to govern as little as possible. The world can get on of itself. Socialism takes its stand on justice enforced by law: the Economist counts only on personal interest individually pursued.
    'The Progress of Socialism' (1883): 563

2   It was at one time imagined that the teaching of political economy would serve to combat Socialism. But, on the contrary, this science has provided contemporary Socialists with its most formidable weapons. Instead of rejecting economic conclusions, after the example of their predecessors, they accept them without reserve, and bring them forward in proof of their statement that present social conditions are opposed to the principles of right and justice. Economists have proved that all value and all property is derived from labour. Then, add the Socialists, it evidently follows that wealth ought to belong to those whose labour creates it, and that all value – *i.e.*, all the produce – should be the remuneration of its producer. . . . Political economy has thus furnished Socialism with a scientific basis, and has been the means of its quitting the region of Communistic aspirations and Utopian schemes.
    'The Progress of Socialism' (1883): 575

3   The great error of the majority of Socialists is, that they do not sufficiently take into consideration the fact that the great incentive to labour and economy is individual interest. True, minds under the influence of the elevated sentiments of religion or of philosophy will obey impulses of charity, devotedness, and honour; but the stimulant of personal interest and responsibility is necessary to the regular production of wealth.
    'The Progress of Socialism' (1883): 581

John Law (1671–1729)

money:

1   Money is the Measure by which Goods are Valued, the Value by which goods are Exchanged, and in which Contracts are made payable.
    Money is not a pledge, as some call it. It's a Value payed, or Contracted to be payed, with which 'tis supposed, the Receiver may, as his occasions require, Buy an equal Quantity of the same Goods he has Sold, or other Goods equal in Value to them: And that Money is the most secure Value, either to Receive, to Contract for, or to Value Goods by; which is least lyable to a change in its Value.
    Money and Trade Considered With a Proposal for Supplying the Nation with Money (1705), Ch.V: 61

value:

2   Goods have a Value from the Uses they are apply'd to; And their Value is Greater or Lesser, not so much from their more or less valuable, or necessary Uses: As from the greater or lesser Quantity of them in proportion to the Demand for them. *Example.* Water is of great use, yet of little Value; Because the Quantity of Water is much greater than the Demand for it. Diamonds are of little use, yet of great Value, because the Demand for Diamonds is much greater, than the Quantity of them.
    Money and Trade Considered With a Proposal for Supplying the Nation with Money (1705), Ch.I: 4

Tony Lawson (1950–)

choice:

1   A dilemma often noted by economists is that the widely accepted intuition that people have real choice appears inconsistent with the widely pursued objective of continually increasing the explanatory power of economic theory; that the more successful economic explanation becomes, the more human choice is, and must be, recognized as illusory.
    'Critical Realism and the Analysis of Choice, Explanation, and Change' (1994), Sec.I

Edward Emery Leamer (1944–)

econometrics:

1   Hardly anyone takes data analyses seriously. Or perhaps more accurately, hardly anyone takes anyone else's data analyses seriously. Like elaborately plumed birds who have long since lost the ability to procreate but not the desire, we preen and strut and display our *t*-values.
    'Let's Take the Con Out of Econometrics' (1983), Sec.IV: 37

2   As I see it, the fundamental problem facing econometrics is how adequately to control the whimsical character of inference, how sensibly to base inferences on opinions when facts are unavailable.
    'Let's Take the Con Out of Econometrics' (1983), Sec.IV: 38

economics and economists:

3   Economists have inherited from the physical sciences the myth that scientific inference is objective, and free of personal prejudice. This is utter nonsense. All knowledge is human belief; more accurately, human opinion.
    'Let's Take the Con Out of Econometrics' (1983), Sec.IV: 36

Gustave Le Bon (1841–1931)
French psychologist and sociologist

socialism:

1   If we would comprehend the profound influence of modern Socialism we need only to examine its doctrines. When we come to investigate the causes of its success we find that this success is altogether alien to the theories proposed, and the negations imposed by these doctrines. Like religions (and Socialism is tending more and more to put on the guise of a religion) it propagates itself in any manner rather than by reason. Feeble in the extreme when it attempts to reason, and to support itself by economic arguments, it becomes on the contrary extremely powerful when it remains in the region of dreams, affirmations, and chimerical promises, and if it were never to issue thence it would become even more redoubtable.
    The Psychology of Socialism (1899), Preface: ix

2   Modern Socialism is far more of a mental state than a doctrine.
    The Psychology of Socialism (1899), Book VI, Ch.II, Sec.2: 399

3   As the experiment of Socialism must be made in some country or another, since only such an experience can cure the nations of their illusions, all our efforts should be directed to secure the accomplishment of the experiment in any country but our own. It is the duty of the writer, however small his influence may be, to do his best to avert such a disaster in his own country. He must give fight to Socialism, and retard the hour of its triumph – and in such a manner that this triumph may realise itself abroad. For this he must know the secrets of its strength and

weakness, and he must also know the psychology of its disciples.
The Psychology of Socialism (1899), Book VI, Ch.II, Sec.5: 411

Emil Lederer (1882–1939)

socialism:

1 Socialism is one of the intellectual's ways of solving the age-old problem of how to save the individual.
State of the Masses (1940), Ch.7: 203

Harvey Leibenstein (1922–1994)

economics and economists:

1 The mind set of most economists in approaching new problems is determined to a great extent by the mode of analysis derived from the competitive model. Even in cases where it is not clear initially which model may apply, the mode of thinking that underlies the competitive model is likely to be used, at least in part, simply because of the absence of alternatives.
General X-Efficiency Theory and Economic Development (1978), Ch.1: 4

Vladimir Ilyich Lenin (V.I. Ulyanov) (1870–1924)
Russian revolutionary

communism:

1 We give the name of communism to the system under which people form the habit of performing their social duties without any special apparatus for coercion, and when unpaid work for the public good becomes a general phenomenon.
'Report on Subbotniks' (December 1919): 284–285

competition:

2 Among the absurdities which the bourgeoisie are fond of spreading about socialism is the allegation that socialists deny the importance of competition. In fact, it is only socialism which, by abolishing classes, and, consequently, by abolishing the enslavement of the people, for the first time opens the way for competition on a really mass scale.
'The Immediate Tasks of the Soviet Government' (1918): 259

socialism:

3 When people here say that socialism can be won without learning from the bourgeoisie, I know this is the psychology of an inhabitant of Central Africa. The only socialism we can imagine is one based on all the lessons learned through large-scale capitalist culture. Socialism without postal and telegraph services, without machines is the emptiest of phrases.
'Session of the All-Russia C. E. C.' (1918), Sec.2: 310

taxation:

4 It is sometimes said that indirect taxation is the fairest form of taxation: you pay according to the amount you buy. But this is not true. Indirect taxation is the most unfair form of taxation, because it is harder for the poor to pay indirect taxes than it is for the rich. ... The richer the man, the *smaller* is the share of his income that he pays in indirect taxes. That is why indirect taxation is *the most unfair* form of taxation. Indirect taxes are taxes on the poor.
'To the Rural Poor' (1903), Sec.5: 402–403

Pope Leo XIII (Gioacchino Vincenzo Raffaele Luigi Pecci) (1810–1903)

property:

1 [W]hile the socialists would destroy the 'right' of property, alleging it to be a human invention altogether opposed to the inborn equality of man, and, claiming a community of goods, argue that poverty should not be peaceably endured, and that the property and privileges of the rich may be rightly invaded, the Church, with much greater wisdom and good sense, recognizes the inequality among men, who are born with different powers of body and mind, inequality in actual possession, also, and holds that the right of property and of ownership, which springs from nature itself, must not be touched and stands

inviolate. For she knows that stealing and robbery were forbidden in so special a manner by God, the Author and Defender of right, that He would not allow man even to desire what belonged to another, and that thieves and despoilers, no less than adulterers and idolaters, are shut out from the Kingdom of Heaven.
Quod Apostolici Muneris (28 December 1878), Sec.9

2   It is the mind, or reason, which is the predominant element in us who are human creatures; it is this which renders a human being human, and distinguishes him essentially from the brute. And on this very account – that man alone among the animal creation is endowed with reason – it must be within his right to possess things not merely for temporary and momentary use, as other living things do, but to have and to hold them in stable and permanent possession; he must have not only things that perish in the use, but those also which, though they have been reduced into use, continue for further use in after time.
Rerum Novarum (15 May 1891), Sec.6

3   The fact that God has given the earth for the use and enjoyment of the whole human race can in no way be a bar to the owning of private property. For God has granted the earth to mankind in general, not in the sense that all without distinction can deal with it as they like, but rather that no part of it was assigned to any one in particular, and that the limits of private possession have been left to be fixed by man's own industry, and by the laws of individual races. Moreover, the earth, even though apportioned among private owners, ceases not thereby to minister to the needs of all, inasmuch as there is not one who does not sustain life from what the land produces. Those who do not possess the soil contribute their labor; hence, it may truly be said that all human subsistence is derived either from labor on one's own land, or from some toil, some calling, which is paid for either in the produce of the land itself, or in that which is exchanged for what the land brings forth.
Rerum Novarum (15 May 1891), Sec.8

socialism:

4   Socialists, therefore, by endeavoring to transfer the possessions of individuals to the community at large, strike at the interests of every wageearner, since they would deprive him of the liberty of disposing of his wages, and thereby of all hope and possibility of increasing his resources and of bettering his condition in life.
Rerum Novarum (15 May 1891), Sec.5

5   [T]he main tenet of socialism, community of goods, must be utterly rejected, since it only injures those whom it would seem meant to benefit, is directly contrary to the natural rights of mankind, and would introduce confusion and disorder into the commonweal. The first and most fundamental principle, therefore, if one would undertake to alleviate the condition of the masses, must be the inviolability of private property. This being established, we proceed to show where the remedy sought for must be found.
Rerum Novarum (15 May 1891), Sec.15

Bruno Leoni (1913–1967)

economics and economists:

1   Economics as an empirical science has not yet, unfortunately, attained the ability to offer indubitable conclusions, and the attempts so frequently made in our time by economists to play the role of physicists are probably much more damaging than useful in inducing people to make their choices according to the results of that science.
Freedom and the Law (1961), Ch.8: 160

Footnote to the above: 195:

2   Perhaps one should also take account of the damage resulting from physicists' playing the role of economists!

Wassily Wassilyovich Leontief
(1906–1999)

economics and economists:

1   The methods used to maintain intellectual discipline in this country's most influential economics departments can occasionally remind one of those employed by the

Marines to maintain discipline on Parris Island.
'Academic Economics' (1982): 107

mathematics in economics:

2 Economics, mathematical economics, in particular, acquired very early in its development the attitudes and manners of the exact empirical sciences without really having gone through the hard school of direct, detailed factual inquiry. Possibly it will do us good to be sent down in order that we may catch up with the experience we have missed.
'Mathematics in Economics' (1954), Sec.9: 232

3 Some of the most advanced applications of mathematical methods in economics are found in the fields of general equilibrium analysis and business-cycle theory – both recognized as quasi-mechanical, automatic phenomena formed and operating to a large extent beyond the calculations, outside the control of, and mostly against the wills of, the millions of individuals whom they affect.
'The Problem of Quality and Quantity in Economics' (1959), Sec.I: 623

4 Much is being made of the widespread, nearly mandatory use by modern economic theorists of mathematics. To the extent to which the economic phenomena possess observable quantitative dimensions, this is indisputably a major forward step. Unfortunately, any one capable of learning elementary, or preferably advanced calculus and algebra, and acquiring acquaintance with the specialized terminology of economics can set himself up as a theorist. Uncritical enthusiasm for mathematical formulation tends often to conceal the ephemeral substantive content of the argument behind the formidable front of algebraic signs.
'Theoretical Assumptions and Nonobserved Facts' (1971): 1–2

5 Page after page of professional economic journals are filled with mathematical formulas leading the reader from sets of more or less plausible but entirely arbitrary assumptions to precisely stated but irrelevant theoretical conclusions.
'Academic Economics' (1982): 104

Abba Ptachya Lerner (1903–1982)

economics and economists:

1 Economics could with more justice be accused, not of pessimism, but of over-optimism. Usually it is the economist who comes up with projects for making the world better and happier; and the political scientists, psychologists, sociologists and politicians are the ones who maintain, often with good reason, that the economist's optimistic projects are impracticable because of the ignorance, obstinacy, and laziness of the people who have to carry them out.
Everybody's Business (1961), Ch.I: 3

inequality:

2 A much more effective and more useful way to reduce inequality is to eliminate the *causes* of inequality by removing the restrictions which prevent poor people from becoming richer, that is, from competing with those in privileged positions. The greatest equalizer is competition, competition of all kinds: competition for jobs as well as competition in business.
Everybody's Business (1961), Ch.XII: 99

taxation:

3 [H]igh tax rates can more properly be said to *be* socialism than to *threaten* it.
Everybody's Business (1961), Ch.XIV: 125

wealth:

4 People who earn millions of dollars don't usually consume millions of dollars; they wouldn't know how to. Instead they save it and invest it or give it away. They are, in fact, acting as agents for society. It is as if the wealth belonged to society at large, and they were merely looking after it on behalf of the rest of us.
Everybody's Business (1961), Ch.XII: 98

Thomas Edward Cliffe Leslie (1825–1882)

economic man:

1 The family finds no place in a system which takes cognizance only of individuals, and of

no motive save personal gain. Yet without the family and the altruistic as well as self-regarding motives that maintain it, the work of the world would come almost to a standstill; saving for a remote future would cease; there would be no durable wealth; men would not seek to leave anything behind them; the houses of the wealthiest, if there were any houses at all, would be built to last only for their own time.
  'Political Economy and Sociology' (1879): 29

2 If you know all a man's inclinations and motives, and their relative force, you may foretell how he will act under given conditions. But if you set aside all save the desire of pecuniary gain and aversion from labour, you will to a certainty go wrong about human conduct in general; you will not be right about even the miser, for he has sometimes some human affections, and on the other hand thinks nothing of trouble.
  'Political Economy and Sociology' (1879): 29

economics and economists:

3 It is a curious characteristic of the deductive political economy, that in spite of its show of logic, its followers have never firmly grasped either their own premises or their conclusions.
  'The Known and the Unknown in the Economic World' (1879): 938

4 Political economy, he [the deductivist economist] tells you, with an air of offended dignity, is a science of tendencies in the long run, and in the absence of disturbing causes; it does not predict in individual cases. A great general used to say that a man who was good at excuses was never good for anything else, and nearly as much may be said of a theory.
  'The Known and the Unknown in the Economic World' (1879): 939–940

5 By assuming that the laws determining profits, prices, and the division of employment are fully understood, and pursuing the method of deduction from arbitrary assumptions to the neglect of the investigation of facts, he [the deductivist economist] has left us in darkness with respect to many matters as to which the economic world might be less unknown that it is.
  'The Known and the Unknown in the Economic World' (1879): 945

6 To imagine that a clever man with his eyes shut can think out the laws of the economic world, is as reasonable as to suppose that he could in the same manner discover the laws of the physical world.
  'The Known and the Unknown in the Economic World' (1879): 946

prediction:

7 The desire of wealth, or of its representative money, instead of enabling the economist to foretell values and prices, destroys the power of prediction that formerly existed, because it is the mainspring of industrial and commercial activity and progress, of infinite variety and incessant alteration in the structure and operations of the economic world.
  'The Known and the Unknown in the Economic World' (1879): 935

Sir William Arthur Lewis
(1915–1991)

economic development:

1 In an economy depending mainly on public enterprise, the Government has no difficulty in seeing the close connection between the share of profits and the rate of growth, and in the early stages of its development programme, always throws its weight on the side of keeping down real wages. In a private enterprise economy dominated politically by capitalists, the same philosophy is effective. In a private enterprise economy whose Government is hostile to capitalists, the conflict between growth and distribution comes to a head.
  Development Planning (1966), Part II, Sec.6: 93

government:

2 Governments have first to learn to control the public sector before they can hope usefully to control the private sector.
  'A Review of Economic Development' (1965), Sec.II: 5

3 Economists in the twentieth century usually call upon governments to redress the imperfections of the market, just as their forebears in the nineteenth century looked to the market to replace the imperfections of the government. The last fifteen years have lengthened the list of things which governments can usefully do and improved the statistical and theoretical tools for making decisions, but only a handful of governments show promise of rising to their opportunities. Here the economist must hand the development problem over to his colleagues in the other social sciences.
   'A Review of Economic Development' (1965), Sec.V: 15

Assar Lindbeck (1930–)

economics and economists:

1 The only subjective element in *positive* economics is, in principle, the choice of topic; in this respect the social sciences hardly differ from the natural sciences, however. The same type of subjectivism in choosing topics obviously is involved when a physicist chooses to study some topic on atoms or a zoologist decides to study the eyes of fishes.
   The Political Economy of the New Left (1971), Part One: 26

2 Economics without a theory of information, incentives, allocation, and coordination is not like Hamlet without the Prince. It is not Hamlet at all.
   The Political Economy of the New Left (1977; 2nd edn), Part Four: Polemics: Rejoinder: 166

laissez-faire:

3 If a market system is added to the anarchistic model, we are in the world of laissez faire economics.
   The Political Economy of the New Left (1971), Part Three: 94

Charles Edward Lindblom (1917–)

trade unions:

1 The union is a monopoly because it can and does raise the price of labor to levels which will in a competitive price system inevitably cause waste, unemployment, inflation, or all combined. And union monopoly destroys the price system because it produces these consequences to a degree which the economy cannot survive.
   Unions and Capitalism (1949), Ch.II: 22

Friedrich List (1789–1846)

economics and economists:

1 In the science of economics, theory and practice are virtually divorced from one another – to the detriment of both. Economists condemn practical men as mere followers of routine who fail to appreciate either the truth or the grandeur of the doctrines enunciated by economists. Practical men, on the other hand, regard economists as mere doctrinaires who ignore the facts of life and inhabit a dream world of economic theories that exists only in their imagination.
   The Natural System of Political Economy (1837), Introduction: 17

tariffs:

2 The policy of protection confers no privilege on one citizen at the expense of another. The privilege is one enjoyed by a whole nation at the expense of another nation.
   The Natural System of Political Economy (1837), Ch.Fifteen: 81

3 Tariffs are doubtless a very great nuisance but they should be regarded as the lesser of two evils, just as the maintenance of a standing army, the construction of fortresses and war itself are lesser evils when compared with the loss of a people's sovereignty and nationhood.
   The Natural System of Political Economy (1837), Ch.Twenty One: 107

Ian Malcolm David Little (1918–)

economic policy:

1 When discussing a good economic policy, we tried to aim at general acceptability; but that does not, of course, imply that what is generally acceptable is good. We only aim at general acceptability in order that the

analysis should be of interest to as many people as possible.
A Critique of Welfare Economics (1957; 2nd edn), Ch.VI: 115

methodology:

2 The men whom some economists . . . tend to despise they call 'methodologists.' Perhaps they should be despised. What is the use of the man who studies scientific method? He may explain to students how scientists reached their new theories; but this is unlikely to help the students reach new theories of their own. He may try to generalize, and lay down canons of inquiry. But there is no technique for forming good hypotheses which can be taught. Discussions of scientific method are often trite, and seldom helpful.
A Critique of Welfare Economics (1957; 2nd edn), Introduction: 1

utility maximization:

3 [T]he interpretation of the postulate that 'utility is maximized' is simply *that the man must behave in the way in which he said he would behave. Roughly speaking, maximizing utility means telling the truth – or, less paradoxically, being able correctly to predict one's own behaviour.*
A Critique of Welfare Economics (1957; 2nd edn), Ch.II: 25

welfare:

4 [W]elfare conclusions are important and influential, especially among economists, although few economists are clear as to what the word means, or what the theory is about.
A Critique of Welfare Economics (1957; 2nd edn), Introduction: 3

John Locke (1632–1704)

interest:

1 The first thing to be consider'd, is, Whether the Price of the Hire of Money can be regulated by *Law*. And to that I think, generally speaking, one may say, 'tis manifest it cannot. For since it is impossible to make a Law that shall hinder a Man from giving away his Money or Estate to whom he pleases, it will be impossible, by any Contrivance of Law, to hinder Men, skill'd in the Power they have over their own Goods, and the ways of Conveying them to others, to purchase Money to be Lent them at what Rate soever their Occasions shall make it necessary for them to have it. For it is to be Remembred, That no Man borrows Money, or pays *Use*, out of mere Pleasure; 'tis the want of Money drives Men to that Trouble and Charge of Borrowing: And proportionably to this Want, so will every one have it, whatever Price it cost him. Wherein the Skilful, I say, will always so manage it, as to avoid the Prohibition of your Law, and keep out of its Penalty, do what you can.
Some Considerations of the Consequences of the Lowering of Interest, and Raising the Value of Money (1692): 1–2

labor:

2 [T]he Property of labour should be able to overballance the Community of Land. For 'tis labour indeed that puts the difference of value on every thing; and let any one consider, what the difference is between an Acre of Land planted with Tabaco, or Sugar, sown with Wheat or Barley; and an Acre of the same Land lying in common, without any Husbandry upon it; and he will find, that the improvement of labour makes the far greater part of the value. I think it will be but a very modest Computation to say, that of the Products of the Earth useful to the Life of Man 9/10 are the effects of labour: nay, if we will rightly estimate things as they come to our use, and cast up the several expences about them, what in them is purely owing to Nature, and what to labour, we shall find, that in most of them 99/100 are wholly to be put on the account of labour.
Two Treatises of Government (1690), Second Treatise, Ch.V, Sec.40: 258–259

money:

3 For Money being an universal Commodity, and as necessary to Trade, as Food is to Life, every body must have it at what Rate they can get it, and unavoidably pay dear when it is scarce, and Debts, no less than Trade, have made Borrowing in Fashion.
Some Considerations of the Consequences of the Lowering of Interest, and Raising the Value of Money (1692): 6

property:

4 Though the Earth, and all inferior Creatures be common to all Men, yet every Man has a *Property* in his own *Person*. This no Body has any Right to but himself. The *Labour* of his Body, and the *Work* of his Hands, we may say, are properly his. Whatsoever then he removes out of the State that Nature hath provided, and left it in, he hath mixed his Labour with it, and joined to it something that is his own, and thereby makes it his Property. It being by him removed from the common state Nature placed it in, it hath by this labour something annexed to it, that excludes the common right of other Men. For this *labour* being the unquestionable Property of the Labourer, no Man but he can have a right to what that is once joined to, at least where there is enough, and as good left in common for others.
Two Treatises of Government (1690), Second Treatise, Ch.V, Sec.27: 245–246

5 *God has given us all things richly*, 1 Tim. vi. 12. Is the Voice of Reason confirmed by Inspiration. But how far has he given it us, *to enjoy*? As much as any one can make use of to any advantage of life before it spoils; so much he may by his labour fix a Property in. Whatever is beyond this, is more than his share, and belongs to others. Nothing was made by God for Man to spoil or destroy. And thus considering the plenty of natural Provisions there was a long time in the World, and the few spenders, and to how small a part of that provision the industry of one Man could extend it self, and ingross it to the prejudice of others; especially keeping within the bounds set by reason of what might serve for his use; there could be then little room for quarrels or contentions about Property so establish'd.
Two Treatises of Government (1690), Second Treatise, Ch.V, Sec.31: 249

6 God gave the World to Men in Common, but since he gave it them for their benefit, and the greatest Conveniencies of Life they were capable to draw from it; it cannot be supposed he meant it should always remain common and uncultivated. He gave it to the use of the industrious and rational, (and labour was to be his title to it;) not to the phancy or covetousness of the quarrelsome and contentious. He that had as good left for his improvement, as was already taken up, needed not complain, ought not to meddle with what was already improved by another's labour: if he did, 'tis plain he desired the benefit of anothers pains which he had no right to, and not the ground which God had given him in common with others to labour on, and whereof there was as good left as that already possessed; and more than he knew what to do with, or his industry could reach to.
Two Treatises of Government (1690), Second Treatise, Ch.V, Sec.34: 251–252

7 Land that is left wholly to Nature, that hath no improvement of Pasturage, Tillage, or Planting, is called, as indeed it is, wast; and we shall find the benefit of it amount to little more than nothing.
Two Treatises of Government (1690), Second Treatise, Ch.V, Sec.42: 260–261

Samuel Mountifort Longfield
(1802–1884)

economics and economists:

1 Political-Economy must be studied, to teach nations the method of avoiding wealth, if it be an evil, or of creating it and distributing it judiciously, if it be a good.
Lectures on Political Economy (1834), Lecture I: 3

2 It is universally allowed that Political-Economists are not too apt to follow in each other's track. On the contrary, the difference of opinion which exists among them on some important points is frequently brought forward unjustly as an argument against the science.
Lectures on Political Economy (1834), Lecture I: 9

3 The study of definitions is a dry uninteresting task in every science, and in none more so than in Political-Economy. Its terms are those employed in common life, and he who learns them appears at first to have acquired no reward for his labour. He does not carry away any of those new and sonorous words which in other sciences serve to display the lately acquired information.
Lectures on Political Economy (1834), Lecture II: 24–25

Robert Emerson Lucas, Jr. (1937–)

economics and economists:

1 Macroeconomics receives a great deal of attention in the newspapers, but this is not the level at which progress is made or continuity is to be discovered.
   Models of Business Cycles (1987), Ch.II: 6

Martin Luther (1483–1546)

money:

1 You cannot make money just with money.
   Trade and Usury (1524), Usury, Part Two: 299

taxation:

2 [T]he people cannot tolerate it very long if their rulers set confiscatory tax rates and tax them out of their very skins. What good would it do a peasant if his field bore as many gulden as stalks of wheat if the rulers only taxed him all the more and then wasted it as though it were chaff to increase their luxury, and squandered his money on their own clothes, food, drink, and buildings? Would not the luxury and the extravagant spending have to be checked so that a poor man could keep something for himself?
   Admonition to Peace (1525), To the Princes and Lords: 23

trade:

3 [F]oreign trade, which brings from Calcutta and India and such places wares like costly silks, articles of gold, and spices – which minister only to ostentation but serve no useful purpose, and which drain away the money of land and people – would not be permitted if we had [proper] government and princes.
   Trade and Usury (1524): 246 (brackets in original presentation)

Rosa Luxemburg (1871–1919)

capitalism:

1 Capitalism is the first mode of economy with the weapon of propaganda, a mode which tends to engulf the entire globe and to stamp out all other economies, tolerating no rival at its side. Yet at the same time it is also the first mode of economy which is unable to exist by itself, which needs other economic systems as a medium and soil. Although it strives to become universal, and, indeed, on account of this its tendency, it must break down – because it is immanently incapable of becoming a universal form of production.
   The Accumulation of Capital (1913), Sec.III, Ch.XXXII: 467

economics and economists:

2 It appears incredible, and yet it is true, that most professors of Economics have a very nebulous idea of the actual subject matter of their erudition.
   What Is Economics? (1968), Sec.I: 7

socialism:

3 The aim of socialism is not accumulation but the satisfaction of toiling humanity's wants by developing the productive forces of the entire globe. And so we find that socialism is by its very nature an harmonious and universal system of economy.
   The Accumulation of Capital (1913), Sec.III, Ch.XXXII: 467

4 One cannot realise socialism with lazy, frivolous, egoistic, thoughtless and indifferent human beings. A socialist society needs human beings from whom each one in his place, is full of passion and enthusiasm for the general well-being, full of self-sacrifice and sympathy for his fellow human beings, full of courage and tenacity in order to dare to attempt the most difficult.
   The Socialisation of Society (1918)

M

Fritz Machlup (1902–1983)

econometrics:

1 Let us remember the unfortunate econometrician who, in one of the major functions of his system, had to use a proxy for risk and a dummy for sex.
 'Proxies and Dummies' (1974)

economics and economists:

2 The terms micro-theory and macro-theory are now so widely used among economists that one should think it is clear what they mean. Unfortunately, it is not.
 'Micro- and Macro-economics' (1960), Sec.I: 97

methodology:

3 The antipathy to methodology among a good many economists originated in the times when such discussions consisted mainly in advertising the writers' and maligning others' methods.
 'Why Bother With Methodology?' (1936): 39

4 I wonder whether it is necessary to write on methodology in a form so forbidding that it is likely to drive away the reader from any attention to methodological problems. It can be shown, I believe, that profound philosophy is not essential to expounding methodological thought and, moreover, that certain methodological questions are directly relevant for discussions of immediate practical interest to any economist.
 'Why Bother With Methodology?' (1936): 39

Thomas Mackay (1849–1912)

poverty and the poor laws:

1 No instructed Socialist, so far as we are aware, has ever desired to attain the particular form of legislative communism which he favours, by advancing on it through an expansion of the Poor Law. The Poor Law is, in a sense, a socialistic experiment, but it would be unfair to the theoretic Socialist to hold him or his system responsible for its failure to make pauperism an honourable and happy condition.
 A History of the English Poor Law (1900), Part the First, Ch.I: 5

2 Poor Law legislation has unfortunately, from the very nature of the case, a greater permanence than any other form of legislation, and error once committed quickly creates a party so deeply interested in its continuance that it becomes almost impossible to eradicate it.
 A History of the English Poor Law (1900), Part the First, Ch.I: 19–20

3 The necessity of relief is evidence of stunted growth or social disorder.
 Public Relief of the Poor (1901), Introductory

4 Too often the problem of poverty has been presented to us as one requiring an explanation of how the poor have fallen away from some original condition of comfort which existed in an earlier golden age. This view does not appear to rest on any solid foundation of fact or theory.
 Public Relief of the Poor (1901), Introductory

Henry Dunning Macleod (1821–1902)

economics and economists:

1 There is nothing, apparently, in the name Political Economy to suggest either that it is the science of the production, distribution, and consumption of wealth, or that it is the science of exchanges; and in such a very young science as this, in which there is such a conflict of opinion, writers should give some historical account of the mode by which they arrive at the conclusion that it is either the one or the other.
 'What is Political Economy?' (1875): 871–872

2 *Economics is the science which treats of the laws which govern the relations of exchangeable quantities.*
'What is Political Economy?' (1875): 893

James Maitland, 8th Earl of Lauderdale (1759–1839)

division of labor:

1 Nothing has a more powerful effect in misleading even the best and most accurate understandings, than an anxious desire to maintain a favourite opinion, or to support a favourite theory; and there is perhaps no stronger illustration of this unfortunate tendency, than what is to be derived from the strained manner in which it has been attempted to establish the opinion, that the division of labour is the cause of that universal opulence which fortunately prevails in many civilized societies.
An Inquiry Into the Nature and Origin of Public Wealth (1804), Ch.V: 291

economics and economists:

2 Public Oeconomy, which professes to teach the means of increasing the wealth of a State, and of applying it to the most useful purposes, is of necessity, in all stages of society, a subject of discussion, even amongst the most vulgar and illiterate, whose rude and erroneous conceptions must naturally lead to expressions founded on inaccuracy, and pregnant with error.
An Inquiry Into the Nature and Origin of Public Wealth (1804), Introduction: 3–4

inequality:

3 In general, ... it may be observed, that great inequality of fortune, by impoverishing the lower orders, has every where been the principal impediment to the increase of public wealth.
An Inquiry Into the Nature and Origin of Public Wealth (1804), Ch.V: 345

wealth distribution:

4 It seems ... an undeniable inference, (if demand proceeds from the desire of possessing, combined with the means of acquiring), that the distribution of wealth, which at once furnishes the means of acquiring, and instils the desire of possessing, must imperiously regulate the nature and extent of demand.
An Inquiry Into the Nature and Origin of Public Wealth (1804), Ch.V: 315

Edmond Malinvaud (1923–)

economics and economists:

1 [A]ny model user who advises the authorities in charge of economic policy must avoid dogmatism and must remain modest about those of his recommendations that are thus affected by the choice of model. All we can hope for is to see future progress reducing progressively the number of cases in which econometricians are thus uncertain of their conclusions.
'Econometrics Faced With the Needs of Macroeconomic Policy' (1981), Sec.2: 1370

Thomas Robert Malthus
(1766–1834)

economics and economists:

1 The differences of opinion among political economists have of late been a frequent subject of complaint; and it must be allowed, that one of the principal causes of them may be traced to the different meanings in which the same terms have been used by different writers.
Definitions in Political Economy (1827), Preface: vii

2 It has sometimes been said of political economy, that it approaches to the strict science of mathematics. But I fear it must be acknowledged, particularly since the great deviations which have lately taken place from the definitions and doctrines of Adam Smith, that it approaches more nearly to the sciences of morals and politics.
Definitions in Political Economy (1827), Ch.I: 2

perfectability of man:

3 I have read some of the speculations on the perfectibility of man and of society, with great pleasure. I have been warmed and delighted with the enchanting picture which they hold forth. I ardently wish for such

happy improvements. But I see great, and, to my understanding, unconquerable difficulties in the way to them. These difficulties it is my present purpose to state; declaring, at the same time, that so far from exulting in them, as a cause of triumph over the friends of innovation, nothing would give me greater pleasure than to see them completely removed.
An Essay on the Principle of Population (1798), Ch.I: 7

poverty and the poor laws:

4 That population cannot increase without the means of subsistence, is a proposition so evident, that it needs no illustration.

That population does invariably increase, where there are the means of subsistence, the history of every people that have ever existed will abundantly prove.

And, that the superior power of population cannot be checked, without producing misery or vice, the ample portion of these too bitter ingredients in the cup of human life, and the continuance of the physical causes that seem to have produced them, bear too convincing a testimony.
An Essay on the Principle of Population (1798), Ch.II: 37–38

5 To remedy the frequent distresses of the common people, the poor laws of England have been instituted; but it is to be feared, that though they may have alleviated a little the intensity of individual misfortune, they have spread the general evil over a much larger surface. It is a subject often started in conversation, and mentioned always as a matter of great surprise, that notwithstanding the immense sum that is annually collected for the poor in England, there is still so much distress among them. Some think that the money must be embezzled; others that the church wardens and overseers consume the greater part of it in dinners. All agree that some how or other it must be very ill-managed. In short the fact, that nearly three millions are collected annually for the poor, and yet that their distresses are not removed, is the subject of continual astonishment. But a man who sees a little below the surface of things, would be very much more astonished, if the fact were otherwise than it is observed to be, or even if a collection universally of eighteen shillings in the pound instead of four, were materially to alter it.
An Essay on the Principle of Population (1798), Ch.V: 74–75

6 The poor-laws of England tend to depress the general condition of the poor in these two ways. Their first obvious tendency is to increase population without increasing the food for its support. A poor man may marry with little or no prospect of being able to support a family in independence. They may be said therefore in some measure to create the poor which they maintain; and as the provisions of the country must, in consequence of the increased population, be distributed to every man in smaller proportions, it is evident that the labour of those who are not supported by parish assistance, will purchase a smaller quantity of provisions than before, and consequently, more of them must be driven to ask for support.

Secondly, the quantity of provisions consumed in workhouses upon a part of the society, that cannot in general be considered as the most valuable part, diminishes the shares that would otherwise belong to more industrious, and more worthy members; and thus in the same manner forces more to become dependent. If the poor in the workhouses were to live better than they now do, this new distribution of the money of the society would tend more conspicuously to depress the condition of those out of the workhouses, by occasioning a rise in the price of provisions.
An Essay on the Principle of Population (1798), Ch.V: 83–84

7 Hard as it may appear in individual instances, dependent poverty ought to be held disgraceful. Such a stimulus seems to be absolutely necessary to promote the happiness of the great mass of mankind; and every general attempt to weaken this stimulus, however benevolent its apparent intention, will always defeat its own purpose. If men are induced to marry from a prospect of parish provision, with little or no chance of maintaining their families in independence, they are not only unjustly tempted to bring unhappiness and dependence upon themselves and children; but they are tempted, without knowing it, to injure all in the same class with themselves. A labourer who

marries without being able to support a family, may in some respects be considered as an enemy to all his fellow-labourers.
An Essay on the Principle of Population (1789), Ch.V: 85–86

8 I feel no doubt whatever, that the parish laws of England have contributed to raise the price of provisions, and to lower the real price of labour. They have therefore contributed to impoverish that class of people whose only possession is their labour. It is also difficult to suppose that they have not powerfully contributed to generate that carelessness, and want of frugality observable among the poor, so contrary to the disposition frequently to be remarked among petty tradesmen and small farmers. The labouring poor, to use a vulgar expression, seem always to live from hand to mouth. Their present wants employ their whole attention, and they seldom think of the future. Even when they have an opportunity of saving they seldom exercise it; but all that is beyond their present necessities goes, generally speaking, to the ale-house. The poor-laws of England may therefore be said to diminish both the power and the will to save, among the common people, and thus to weaken one of the strongest incentives to sobriety and industry, and consequently to happiness.
An Essay on the Principle of Population (1798), Ch.V: 86–87

9 The evil is perhaps gone too far to be remedied; but I feel little doubt in my own mind, that if the poor-laws had never existed, though there might have been a few more instances of very severe distress, yet that the aggregate mass of happiness among the common people would have been much greater than it is at present.
An Essay on the Principle of Population (1798), Ch.V: 94

10 To prevent the recurrence of misery, is, alas! beyond the power of man. In the vain endeavour to attain what in the nature of things is impossible, we now sacrifice not only possible, but certain benefits. We tell the common people, that if they will submit to a code of tyrannical regulations, they shall never be in want. They do submit to these regulations. They perform their part of the contract: but we do not, nay cannot, perform ours: and thus the poor sacrifice the valuable blessing of liberty, and receive nothing that can be called an equivalent in return.
An Essay on the Principle of Population (1798), Ch.V: 98–99

rationality:

11 I am willing to allow that every voluntary act is preceded by a decision of the mind; but it is strangely opposite to what I should conceive to be the just theory upon the subject, and a palpable contradiction to all experience, to say, that the corporal propensities of man do not act very powerfully, as disturbing forces, in these decisions. The question, therefore, does not merely depend, upon whether a man may be made to understand a distinct proposition, or be convinced by an unanswerable argument. A truth may be brought home to his conviction as a rational being, though he may determine to act contrary to it, as a compound being. The cravings of hunger, the love of liquor, the desire of possessing a beautiful woman, will urge men to actions, of the fatal consequences of which, to the general interests of society, they are perfectly well convinced, even at the very time they commit them. Remove their bodily cravings, and they would not hesitate a moment in determining against such actions. Ask them their opinion of the same conduct in another person, and they would immediately reprobate it. But in their own case, and under all the circumstances of their situation with these bodily cravings, the decision of the compound being is different from the conviction of the rational being.
An Essay on the Principle of Population (1798), Ch.XIII: 254–255

society:

12 And thus it appears, that a society constituted according to the most beautiful form that imagination can conceive, with benevolence for its moving principle, instead of self-love, and with every evil disposition in all its members corrected by reason and not force, would, from the inevitable laws of nature, and not from any original depravity of man, in a very short period, degenerate into a society, constructed upon a plan not essentially different from that which prevails

in every known State at present; I mean, a society divided into a class of proprietors, and a class of labourers, and with self-love for the main-spring of the great machine.
An Essay on the Principle of Population (1798), Ch.X: 206–207

universal laws of nature:

13 I think I may fairly make two postulata.
First, That food is necessary to the existence of man.
Secondly, That the passion between the sexes is necessary, and will remain nearly in its present state.
These two laws ever since we have had any knowledge of mankind, appear to have been fixed laws of our nature; and, as we have not hitherto seen any alteration in them, we have no right to conclude that they will ever cease to be what they now are, without an immediate act of power in that Being who first arranged the system of the universe; and for the advantage of his creatures, still executes, according to fixed laws, all its various operations.
An Essay on the Principle of Population (1798), Ch.I: 11–12

14 Through the animal and vegetable kingdoms, nature has scattered the seeds of life abroad with the most profuse and liberal hand. She has been comparatively sparing in the room, and the nourishment necessary to rear them. The germs of existence contained in this spot of earth, with ample food, and ample room to expand in, would fill millions of worlds in the course of a few thousand years. Necessity, that imperious all pervading law of nature, restrains them within the prescribed bounds. The race of plants, and the race of animals shrink under this great restrictive law. And the race of man cannot, by any efforts of reason, escape from it. Among plants and animals its effects are waste of seed, sickness, and premature death. Among mankind, misery and vice. The former, misery, is an absolutely necessary consequence of it. Vice is a highly probable consequence, and we therefore see it abundantly prevail; but it ought not, perhaps, to be called an absolutely necessary consequence. The ordeal of virtue is to resist all temptation to evil.
An Essay on the Principle of Population (1798), Ch.I: 14–16

15 It has appeared, that from the inevitable laws of our nature, some human beings must suffer from want. These are the unhappy persons who, in the great lottery of life, have drawn a blank.
An Essay on the Principles of Population (1798), Ch.X: 204

Bernard de Mandeville (1670–1733)

conspicuous consumption:

1   Those who would too nearly imitate others of Superior Fortune must thank themselves if they are ruin'd. This is nothing against Luxury; for whoever can subsist and lives above his Income is a Fool.
The Fable of the Bees (1732), Vol. I, Remark Y: 249

money:

2   [I]t would be easier, where Property was well secured, to live without Money than without Poor; for who would do the Work?
The Fable of the Bees (1732), Vol. I, Remark Q: 193

3   The only thing ... that can render the labouring Man industrious, is a moderate quantity of Money; for as too little will, according as his Temper is, either dispirit or make him Desperate, so too much will make him Insolent and Lazy.
The Fable of the Bees (1732), Vol. I, Remark Q: 194

4   There is no Intrinsick Worth in Money but what is alterable with the Times, and whether a Guinea goes for Twenty Pounds or for a Shilling, it is ... the Labour of the Poor, and not the high and low value that is set on Gold or Silver, which all the Comforts of Life must arise from.
The Fable of the Bees (1732), Vol. I, 'An Essay on Charity and Charity-Schools': 301

5   Which way shall I persuade a Man to serve me, when the Service, I can repay him in, is such as he does not want or care for? No Body, who is at Peace, and has no Contention with any of the Society, will do any thing for a Lawyer; and a Physician can purchase nothing of a Man, whose whole

Family is in perfect Health. Money obviates and takes away all those Difficulties, by being an acceptable Reward for all the Services Men can do to one another.
The Fable of the Bees (1732), Vol. II, Sixth Dialogue: 349

Mao Tse-tung (1893–1976)
Chinese revolutionary

capitalism:

1 There is a serious tendency towards capitalism among the well-to-do peasants. This tendency will become rampant if we in the slightest way neglect political work among the peasants during the co-operative movement and for a very long period after.
Introductory note to 'A Resolute Struggle Must Be Waged Against the Tendency Towards Capitalism' (1955), *The Socialist Upsurge in China's Countryside*. (Reprinted in *Quotations from Chairman Mao Tse-tung*, Part III.)

Alfred Marshall (1842–1924)

competition:

1 Hope and ambition, and some scope for the play of free competition, are conditions – necessary conditions so far as we can tell – of human progress. But the great evil of our present system, which it is one chief aim of cooperation – as I take it – to remove, lies in the fact that the hope and ambition by which men's exertions are stimulated have in them too much that is selfish and too little that is unselfish.
'Co-operation' (1889): 238

2 If competition is contrasted with energetic co-operation in unselfish work for the public good, then even the best forms of competition are relatively evil; while its harsher and meaner forms are hateful. And in a world in which all men were perfectly virtuous, competition would be out of place; but so also would be private property and every form of private right. Men would think only of their duties; and no one would desire to have a larger share of the comforts and luxuries of life than his neighbours. Strong producers could easily bear a touch of hardship; so they would wish that their weaker neighbours, while producing less should consume more. Happy in this thought, they would work for the general good with all the energy, the inventiveness, and the eager initiative that belonged to them; and mankind would be victorious in contests with nature at every turn. Such is the Golden Age to which poets and dreamers may look forward. But in the responsible conduct of affairs, it is worse than folly to ignore the imperfections which still cling to human nature.
Principles of Economics (1920; 8th edn), Bk.I, Ch.I, Sec.4: 8–9

economics and economists:

3 Those writers who have most furthered the science [of economics] have not in general been those for whom its chief attractions were in the athletic exercise which its reasonings offer to the vigorous intellect, or in the entertainment which its results provide for the curious inquirer. Rather they have been men whose eager interest in the great problems of social life and well-being rendered it intolerable to them that one of the constituent elements of the solution of these problems should needlessly remain in a condition of vague uncertainty.
'The Province of Political Economy' (1874): 3

4 Political economy will have wider opportunities of aiding each man to judge his own conduct by analysing it, and by putting before him, as Nathan did before David, the likeness between it and other conduct on which he is able to give an unbiased judgment. In this indirect mode will she contribute to the clearness of men's notions about duty; direct decisions on questions of moral principle she must leave to her sister, the Science of Ethics.
'The Province of Political Economy' (1874): 4

5 [T]hat part of economic doctrine, which alone can claim universality, has no dogmas. It is not a body of concrete truth, but an engine for the discovery of concrete truth, similar to, say, the theory of mechanics.
'The Present Position of Economics' (1885): 159

6 The economic organon brings to bear the accumulated strength of much of the best genius of many generations of men. It shows how to analyse the motives at work, how to group them, how to trace their mutual relations. And thus by introducing systematic and organized methods of reasoning, it enables us to deal with this one side of the problem with greater force and certainty than almost any other side; although it would have probably been the most unmanageable side of all without such aid. Having done its work it retires and leaves to common sense the responsibility of the ultimate decision; not standing in the way of, or pushing out any other kind of knowledge, not hampering common sense in the use to which it is able to put any other available knowledge, nor in any way hindering; helping where it could help, and for the rest keeping silence.
'The Present Position of Economics' (1885): 164–165

7 It is true that an economist, like any other citizen, may give his own judgment as to the best solution of various practical problems, just as an engineer may give his opinion as to the right method of financing the Panama canal. But in such cases the counsel bears only the authority of the individual who gives it: he does not speak with the voice of his science. And the economist has to be specially careful to make this clear; because there is much misunderstanding as to the scope of his science, and undue claims to authority on practical matters have often been put forward on its behalf.
'The Present Position of Economics' (1885): 165

8 *Political Economy*, or *Economics*, is a study of man's actions in the ordinary business of life; it inquires how he gets his income and how he uses it.
Principles of Economics (1890), Book I, Ch.I, Sec.1; cf. A.C. Pigou 2

9 The fact is I am the dull mean man, who holds Economics to be an organic whole, & has as little respect for pure theory (otherwise than as a branch of mathematics or the science of numbers), as for that crude collection & interpretation of facts without the aid of high analysis which sometimes claims to be a part of economic history.
Letter to W.A.S. Hewins (12 October 1899)

10 Why should the economist be ashamed to admit that the more he studies 'the mystery of evil' on its economic side, the more he is convinced that the key to the mystery is not in human hands; and that ill-considered remedies for evil . . . are likely to do in the future, as in the past, much harm below the surface, with a little good above it.
Letter to Bishop Westcott (24 January 1900)

11 Political Economy or Economics is a study of mankind in the ordinary business of life; it examines that part of individual and social action which is most closely connected with the attainment and with the use of the material requisites of wellbeing.
Principles of Economics (1920; 8th edn), Book I, Ch.I, Sec.1: 1; cf. A.C. Pigou 2

12 It might have been expected that a science, which deals with questions so vital for the wellbeing of mankind, would have engaged the attention of many of the ablest thinkers of every age, and be now well advanced towards maturity. But the fact is that the number of scientific economists has always been small relatively to the difficulty of the work to be done; so that the science is still almost in its infancy. One cause of this is that the bearing of economics on the higher wellbeing of man has been overlooked. Indeed, a science which has wealth for its subject-matter, is often repugnant at first sight to many students; for those who do most to advance the boundaries of knowledge, seldom care much about the possession of wealth for its own sake.
Principles of Economics (1920; 8th edn), Bk.I, Ch.I, Sec.3: 4

13 The laws of economics are to be compared with the laws of the tides, rather than with the simple and exact law of gravitation. For the actions of men are so various and uncertain, that the best statement of tendencies, which we can make in a science of human conduct, must needs be inexact and faulty. This might be urged as a reason against making any statements at all on the subject;

but that would be almost to abandon life. Life is human conduct, and the thoughts and emotions that grow up around it. By the fundamental impulses of our nature we all – high and low, learned and unlearned – are in our several degrees constantly striving to understand the courses of human action, and to shape them for our purposes, whether selfish or unselfish, whether noble or ignoble. And since we *must* form to ourselves some notions of the tendencies of human action, our choice is between forming those notions carelessly and forming them carefully. The harder the task, the greater the need for steady patient inquiry; for turning to account the experience, that has been reaped by the more advanced physical sciences; and for framing as best we can well thought-out estimates, or provisional laws, of the tendencies of human action.
Principles of Economics (1920; 8th edn), Bk.I, Ch.III, Sec.3: 32–33

14 The *raison d'etre* of economics as a separate science is that it deals chiefly with that part of man's action which is most under the control of measurable motives; and which therefore lends itself better than any other to systematic reasoning and analysis. We cannot indeed measure motives of any kind, whether high or low, as they are in themselves: we can measure only their moving force.
Principles of Economics (1920; 8th edn), Bk.I, Ch.IV, Sec.1: 38–39

15 The economist needs the three great intellectual faculties, perception, imagination and reason: and most of all he needs imagination, to put him on the track of those causes of visible events which are remote or lie below the surface, and of those effects of visible causes which are remote or lie below the surface.
Principles of Economics (1920; 8th edn), Bk.I, Ch.IV, Sec.5: 43

16 The economist needs imagination especially in order that he may develop his ideals. But most of all he needs caution and reserve in order that his advocacy of ideals may not outrun his grasp of the future.
Principles of Economics (1920; 8th edn), Bk.I, Ch.IV, Sec.6: 46

government:

17 Governmental intrusion into businesses which require ceaseless invention and fertility of resource is a danger to social progress the more to be feared because it is insidious. It is notorious that, though departments of central and municipal government employ many thousands of highly-paid servants in engineering and other progressive industries, very few inventions of any importance are made by them: and of those few nearly all are the work of men ... who had been thoroughly trained in free enterprise before they entered Government service. Government creates scarcely anything.
'The Social Possibilities of Economic Chivalry' (1907), Sec.9: 21; cf. Herbert Spencer 3

18 A Government could print a good edition of Shakespeare's works, but it could not get them written.
'The Social Possibilities of Economic Chivalry' (1907), Sec.9: 22

19 Foolish ostentatious expenditure by the State, like the similar expenditure of private persons, is, no doubt, an enemy to good employment: because the funds used up in it do not create, as they pass away, fresh sources of future production, and therefore future income; as they would if they were spent on building up improved iron works or human beings.
Letter to Lord Reay (12 November 1909)

mathematics in economics:

20 When a man has cleared up his mind about a difficult economic question by mathematical reasoning, he generally finds it best to throw aside his mathematics and express what he has to say in language that is understood [sic] of the people.
Review of *Mathematical Psychics* (1881): 457

21 In my view every economic fact, whether or not it is of such a nature as to be expressed in numbers, stands in relation as cause & effect to many other facts: and since it *never* happens that all of these can be expressed in numbers, the application of exact mathematical methods to those wh[ich] can is nearly always waste of time: while in the large

majority of cases it is positively misleading; & the world would have been further on its way forward if the work had never been done at all.
Letter to Arthur Bowley (3 March 1901)

22 I know I had a growing feeling in the later years of my work at the subject that a good mathematical theorem dealing with economic hypotheses was very unlikely to be good economics: and I went more and more on the rules – (1) Use mathematics as a shorthand language, rather than as an engine of inquiry. (2) Keep to them till you have done. (3) Translate into English. (4) Then illustrate by examples that are important in real life. (5) Burn the mathematics. (6) If you can't succeed in 4, burn 3. This last I did often.
Letter to Arthur Bowley (27 February 1906)

money:

23 [T]though it is true that 'money' or 'general purchasing power' or 'command over material wealth,' is the centre around which economic science clusters; this is so, not because money or material wealth is regarded as the main aim of human effort, nor even as affording the main subject-matter for the study of the economist, but because in this world of ours it is the one convenient means of measuring human motive on a large scale. If the older economists had made this clear, they would have escaped many grievous misrepresentations; and the splendid teachings of Carlyle and Ruskin as to the right aims of human endeavour and the right uses of wealth, would not then have been marred by bitter attacks on economics, based on the mistaken belief that that science had no concern with any motive except the selfish desire for wealth, or even that it inculcated a policy of sordid selfishness.
Principles of Economics (1920; 8th edn), Book I, Ch.II, Sec.4: 22

poverty and the poor laws:

24 Nearly all the schemes for enabling the poor to live better in London tend to raise their self-respect as well as to make them more comfortable, and by so doing help them indirectly to live out of London. But such schemes, admirable as they are, require to be worked in conjunction with other schemes for directly helping the poor to move out.
'The Housing of the London Poor' (1884): 229

25 If people do not get help when they really need it, they and their children are apt to become weak in body and character, and unable to contribute much to the production of material wealth; but they are sure to become even more degraded if they frequently get help when they do not need it, and so drift into the habit of laying themselves out to get it.
'The Poor Law in Relation to State-Aided Pensions' (1892): 186

26 [M]aterial relief does not bring happiness; it is but one of the conditions necessary for the removal of misery.
'Poor-Law Reform' (1892): 377

27 I believe that our first step towards finding out what is needed to be done, and what can safely be done by the State for the relief of distress, is the appointment of a Commission, which shall include among its members and its witnesses not only 'experts in the art of raising the poor,' but also men and women who have seen the working of the Poor Law and of Charity Organization Societies from below. A Commission to inquire whether the people are well shod should add to the counsel of experts in shoe-making that of people who wear shoes and know where they pinch.
'Poor-Law Reform' (1892): 379

28 There is only one effective remedy that I know of [for the alleviation of poverty], and that is *not* short in its working. It needs patience for the ills of others as well as our own. It is to remove the sources of industrial weakness: to improve the education of home life, and the opportunities for fresh-air joyous play of the young; to keep them longer at school; and to look after them, when their parents are making default, much more paternally than we do.

Then the Residuum should be attacked in its strongholds. We ought to expend more money, and with it more force, moral and physical, in cutting off the supply of people

unable to do good work, and therefore unable to earn good wages.
Letter to Bishop Westcott (24 January 1900)

socialism:

29 I think that the chief dangers of Socialism lie not in its tendency towards a more equal distribution of incomes, for I can see no harm in that, but in its sterilising influence on those mental activities which have gradually raised the world from barbarism. . . .
'The Post Office and Private Enterprise' (24 March 1891): 11

30 I cordially agree . . . that the true danger of socialism lies in its tendency to destroy the constructive force of variation & selection: & that in the permanent interests of the race we cannot afford to diminish suffering by means that appreciably choke up the springs of vigour.
Letter to Benjamin Kidd (6 June 1894)

31 My own notion of Socialism is that it is a movement for taking the responsibility for a man's life and work, as far as possible, off his shoulders and putting it on to the State.
Letter to Lord Reay (12 November 1909)

trade:

32 Every cheapening of the means of communication, every new facility for the free interchange of ideas between distant places alters the action of the forces which tend to localize industries.
Principles of Economics (1920; 8th edn) Bk.IV, Ch.X, Sec.4: 273

utility:

33 Freedom and hope increase not only man's willingness but also his power for work; physiologists tell us that a given exertion consumes less of the store of nervous energy if done under the stimulus of pleasure than of pain: and without hope there is no enterprise. Security of person and property are two conditions of this hopefulness and freedom; but security always involves restraints on freedom, and it is one of the most difficult problems of civilization to discover how to obtain the security which is a condition of freedom without too great a sacrifice of freedom itself.
Principles of Economics (1920; 8th edn), Bk.IV, Ch.V, Sec.4: 197, note 1

value:

34 We might as reasonably dispute whether it is the upper or the under blade of a pair of scissors that cuts a piece of paper, as whether value is governed by utility or cost of production. It is true that when one blade is held still, and the cutting is effected by moving the other, we may say with careless brevity that the cutting is done by the second; but the statement is not strictly accurate, and is to be excused only so long as it claims to be merely a popular and not a strictly scientific account of what happens.
Principles of Economics (1920; 8th edn), Bk.V, Ch.III, Sec.7: 348

John Marshall (1755–1835)
4th Chief Justice, US Supreme Court

corporations:

1 A corporation is an artificial being, invisible, intangible, and existing only in contemplation of law. Being the mere creature of law, it possesses only those properties which the charter of its creation confers upon it, either expressly or as incidental to its very existence. These are such as are supposed best calculated to effect the object for which it was created. Among the most important are immortality, and, if the expression may be allowed, individuality; properties by which a perpetual succession of many persons are considered as the same, and may act as a single individual. They enable a corporation to manage its own affairs, and to hold property without the perplexing intricacies, the hazardous and endless necessity, of perpetual conveyances for the purpose of transmitting it from hand to hand. It is chiefly for the purpose of clothing bodies of men, in succession, with these qualities and capacities, that corporations were invented, and are in use. By these means, a perpetual succession of individuals are capable of acting for the promotion of the particular object, like one immortal being. But this being does not share in the civil government of the country, unless that be the purpose for which it was created. Its immortality no more confers on it political power, or a political character, than immortality would confer such power or character on a natural person. It is no more a state instrument than a natural

person exercising the same powers would be.
>   *Trustees of Dartmouth College v. Woodward* (17 U.S. 518, 636; February Term, 1819)

taxation:

2 An unlimited power to tax involves, necessarily, a power to destroy; because there is a limit beyond which no institution and no property can bear taxation. A question of constitutional power can hardly be made to depend on a question of more or less.
>   *McCulloch v. State of Maryland et al.* (17 U.S. 316, 327; February Term, 1819)

3 Taxation, it is said, does not necessarily and unavoidably destroy. To carry it to the excess of destruction would be an abuse, to presume which, would banish that confidence which is essential to all government.
>   *McCulloch v. State of Maryland et al.* (17 U.S. 316, 431; February Term, 1819)

Karl Heinrich Marx (1818–1883)

alienation:

1 The laws of political economy express the estrangement of the worker in his object thus: the more the worker produces, the less he has to consume; the more values he creates, the more valueless, the more unworthy he becomes; the better formed his product, the more deformed becomes the worker; the more civilized his object, the more barbarous becomes the worker; the more powerful labor becomes, the more powerless becomes the worker; the more ingenious labor becomes, the less ingenious becomes the worker and the more he becomes nature's bondsman.
>   *The Economic and Philosophic Manuscripts of 1844* ('Estranged Labor'): 109

capitalism:

2 To be a capitalist, is to have not only a purely personal, but a social *status* in production. Capital is a collective product, and only by the united action of many members, nay, in the last resort, only by the united action of all members of society, can it be set in motion. Capital is, therefore, not a personal, it is a social power.
>   *The Communist Manifesto* (1848), Sec.II: 68

3 The contest between the capitalist and the wage labourer dates back to the very origin of capital. It raged on throughout the whole manufacturing period. But only since the introduction of machinery has the workman fought against the instrument of labour itself, the material embodiment of capital. He revolts against this particular form of the means of production, as being the material basis of the capitalist mode of production.
>   *Capital* (1887; first English edn), Vol. I, Part IV, Ch.XV, Sec.5: 430

4 Capitalist production is not merely the production of commodities, it is essentially the production of surplus value. The labourer produces, not for himself, but for capital. It no longer suffices, therefore, that he should simply produce. He must produce surplus value. That labourer alone is productive, who produces surplus value for the capitalist, and thus works for the self-expansion of capital.
>   *Capital* (1887; first English edn), Vol. I, Part V, Ch.XVI: 510

5 The law of capitalist production, that is at the bottom of the pretended 'natural law of population,' reduces itself simply to this: The correlation between accumulation of capital and rate of wages is nothing else than the correlation between the unpaid labour transformed into capital, and the additional paid labour necessary for the setting in motion of this additional capital. It is therefore in no way a relation between two magnitudes, independent one of the other: on the one hand, the magnitude of the capital; on the other, the number of the labouring population; it is rather, at bottom, only the relation between the unpaid and the paid labour of the same labouring population.
>   *Capital* (1887; first English edn), Vol. I, Part VII, Ch.XXV, Sec.1: 615–616

6 The law of capitalistic accumulation, metamorphosed by economists into pretended law of Nature, in reality merely states that the very nature of accumulation excludes every diminution in the degree of exploitation of

labour, and every rise in the price of labour, which could seriously imperil the continual reproduction, on an ever-enlarging scale, of the capitalistic relation. It cannot be otherwise in a mode of production in which the labourer exists to satisfy the needs of self-expansion of existing values, instead of, on the contrary, material wealth existing to satisfy the needs of development on the part of the labourer. As, in religion, man is governed by the products of his own brain, so in capitalistic production, he is governed by the products of his own hand.
   Capital (1887; first English edn), Vol. I, Part VII, Ch.XXV, Sec.1: 616

communism:

7   *Communism* as the *positive* transcendence of *private property*, as *human self-estrangement*, and therefore as the real *appropriation of the human* essence by and for man; communism therefore as the complete return of man to himself as a *social* (i.e., human) being – a return become conscious, and accomplished within the entire wealth of previous development. This communism, as fully developed naturalism, equals humanism, and as fully developed humanism equals naturalism; it is the *genuine* resolution of the conflict between man and nature and between man and man – the true resolution of the strife between existence and essence, between objectification and self-confirmation, between freedom and necessity, between the individual and the species. Communism is the riddle of history solved, and it knows itself to be this solution.
   The Economic and Philosophic Manuscripts of 1844 ('Private Property and Communism'): 135

8   Socialism is man's *positive self-consciousness*, no longer mediated through the annulment of religion, just as *real life* is man's positive reality, no longer mediated through the annulment of private property, through *communism*. Communism is the position as the negation of the negation, and is hence the *actual* phase necessary for the next stage of historical development in the process of human emancipation and rehabilitation. *Communism* is the necessary pattern and the dynamic principle of the immediate future, but communism as such is not the goal of human development – which goal is the structure of human society.
   The Economic and Philosophic Manuscripts of 1844 ('Private Property and Communism'): 146

9   Communism deprives no man of the power to appropriate the products of society; all that it does is to deprive him of the power to subjugate the labour of others by means of such appropriation.
   The Communist Manifesto (1848), Sec.II: 70

economics and economists:

10 Economists have a singular method of procedure. There are only two kinds of institutions for them, artificial and natural. The institutions of feudalism are artificial institutions, those of the bourgeoisie are natural institutions. In this they resemble the theologians, who likewise establish two kinds of religion. Every religion which is not theirs is an invention of men, while their own is an emanation from God.
   The Poverty of Philosophy (1847), Ch.II, Sec.1, Seventh observation: 120–121

11 All political economists of any standing admit that the introduction of new machinery has a baneful effect on the workmen in the old handicrafts and manufactures with which this machinery at first competes. Almost all of them bemoan the slavery of the factory operative. And what is the great trump-card that they play? That machinery, after the horrors of the period of introduction and development have subsided, instead of diminishing, in the long run increases the number of the slaves of labour! Yes, political economy revels in the hideous theory, hideous to every 'philanthropist' who believes in the eternal Nature-ordained necessity for capitalist production, that after a period of growth and transition, even its crowning success, the factory system based on machinery, grinds down more workpeople than on its first introduction it throws on the streets.
   Capital (1887; first English edn), Vol. I, Part IV, Ch.XV, Sec.7: 450

family:

12 On what foundation is the present family, the bourgeois family, based? On capital, on

private gain. In its completely developed form this family exists only among the bourgeoisie. But this state of things finds its complement in the practical absence of the family among proletarians, and in public prostitution.

The bourgeois family will vanish as a matter of course when its complement vanishes, and both will vanish with the vanishing of capital.
The Communist Manifesto (1848), Sec.II: 71

13 However terrible and disgusting the dissolution, under the capitalist system, of the old family ties may appear, nevertheless, modern industry, by assigning as it does an important part in the process of production, outside the domestic sphere, to women, to young persons, and to children of both sexes, creates a new economic foundation for a higher form of the family and of the relations between the sexes.
Capital (1887; first English edn), Vol. I, Part IV, Ch.XV, Sec.9: 492

individualism:

14 The solitary and isolated hunter or fisherman, who serves Adam Smith and Ricardo as a starting point, is one of the unimaginative fantasies of eighteenth-century romances *à la* Robinson Crusoe; ...
A Contribution to the Critique of Political Economy (1859), Appendix, Part I, Sec.1: 188

15 The prophets of the eighteenth century, on whose shoulders Adam Smith and Ricardo were still wholly standing, envisaged this 18th-century individual – a product of the dissolution of feudal society on the one hand and of the new productive forces evolved since the sixteenth century on the other – as an ideal whose existence belonged to the past. They saw this individual not as an historical result, but as the starting point of history; not as something evolving in the course of history, but posited by nature, because for them this individual was in conformity with nature, in keeping with their idea of human nature.
A Contribution to the Critique of Political Economy (1859), Appendix, Part I, Sec.1: 188

16 Man is a *Zoon politikon* in the most literal sense: he is not only a social animal, but an animal that can be individualised only within society.
A Contribution to the Critique of Political Economy (1859), Appendix, Part I, Sec.1: 189

money:

17 Money degrades all the gods of man – and turns them into commodities. Money is the universal self-established *value* of all things. It has therefore robbed the whole world – both the world of men and nature – of its specific value. Money is the estranged essence of man's work and man's existence, and this alien essence dominates him, and he worships it.
'On the Jewish Question' (1843), Part II: 172

18 Money is a crystal formed of necessity in the course of the exchanges, whereby different products of labour are practically equated to one another and thus by practice converted into commodities.
Capital (1887; first English edn), Vol. I, Part I, Ch.II: 97

19 Money, like every other commodity, cannot express the magnitude of its value except relatively in other commodities.
Capital (1887; first English edn), Vol. I, Part I, Ch.II: 102

20 One sum of money is distinguishable from another only by its amount.
Capital (1887; first English edn), Vol. I, Part II, Ch.IV: 161

private property:

21 Private property has made us so stupid and one-sided that an object is only *ours* when we have it – when it exists for us as capital, or when it is directly possessed, eaten, drunk, worn, inhabited, etc., – in short, when it is *used* by us. Although private property itself again conceives all these direct realizations of possession only as *means of life*, and the life which they serve as means is the *life of private property* – labor and conversion into capital.
The Economic and Philosophic Manuscripts of 1844 ('Private Property and Communism'): 139

22 The distinguishing feature of Communism is not the abolition of property generally, but the abolition of bourgeois property. But modern bourgeois private property is the final and most complete expression of the system of producing and appropriating products, that is based on class antagonisms, on the exploitation of the many by the few.
   In this sense, the theory of the Communists may be summed up in the single sentence: Abolition of private property.
   The Communist Manifesto (1848), Sec.II: 68

utility:

23 A use value, or useful article, therefore, has value only because human labour in the abstract has been embodied or materialised in it.
   Capital (1887; first English edn), Vol. I, Part I, Ch.I, Sec.1: 48

24 Lastly nothing can have value, without being an object of utility. If the thing is useless, so is the labour contained in it; the labour does not count as labour, and therefore creates no value.
   Capital (1887; first English edn), Vol. I, Part I, Ch.I, Sec.1: 51

25 So far no chemist has ever discovered exchange value either in a pearl or a diamond.
   Capital (1887; first English edn), Vol. I, Part I, Ch.I, Sec.4: 94

Thomas Mayer (1927–)

econometrics:

1 The most advanced methods do little good, if in transcribing the results a decimal point is allowed to slip one digit.
   'Economics as a Hard Science: Realistic Goal or Wishful Thinking?' (1980), Sec.III: 170

2 [M]y own attitude towards econometrics is like that of the person who upon being told that the craps game he was about to participate in is crooked; replied, 'Sure, I know that, but it is the only game in town.'
   'Economics as a Hard Science: Realistic Goal or Wishful Thinking?' (1980), Sec.IV: 173

economics and economists:

3 Academic economists claim to produce knowledge that society wants, but actually are each others' main customers.
   Doing Economic Research (1995), Ch.3: 17

4 [A]nyone who claims that what practicing economists actually do, not what they say, must be the right way to do economics, ignores one of the great teachings of economics: only agents themselves act, so we must look at the incentives faced by the individual agent. Producers of economic research have an incentive to seem like scientists by preaching high standards, while themselves putting shoddy intellectual goods on the market. Thus, at least in this case, what is preached may be a better guide to what should be done than is what is actually done.
   Doing Economic Research (1995), Ch.3: 18

mathematics in economics:

5 [I]t would be hard to argue that mathematics has helped to purge economics of irrelevance.
   'Economics as a Hard Science: Realistic Goal or Wishful Thinking?' (1980): 165 note 2

methodology:

6 Methodologists should model themselves less on the missionary who preaches to the natives the commandments of an alien god (epistemology), and more on the peace corps worker who shows them how to plant better crops.
   Doing Economic Research (1995), Ch.2: 8

Donald Nansen (now Deirdre N.) McCloskey (1942–)

economics and economists:

1 An economist hopping along without a historical leg, unless he is a decathalon [sic] athlete, has a narrow perspective on the present, shallow economic ideas, little appreciation for the strengths and weaknesses of economic data, and small ability to

apply economics to large issues. If we interrogate our students, we will find that they believe economic research to consist chiefly of a passing acquaintance with the latest pronouncement of the Council of Economic Advisors, the latest assumption relaxed in an economic model, and the latest revision in the local canned regression program. One does not have to look beyond their teachers to find where they acquired this peculiar set of notions.
'Does the Past Have Useful Economics?' (1976), Sec.II(E): 454–455

2   Economics should come back into the conversation of mankind. It is an extraordinarily clever way of speaking, and can do a lot of good. The way to bring it back is to persuade economists that they are not so very different from poets and novelists. For a long time now they have been standing aside, believing they have only the mathematical sciences as models, and practising a physics-worship that misunderstands both physics and themselves. Economists could get their gods from poetry or history or philology and still do much the same job of work, with a better temper.
'Storytelling in Economics' (1990): 73

John Ramsay McCulloch
(1789–1864)

economics and economists:

1   Political Economy may be defined to be the science of the laws which regulate the production, accumulation, distribution, and consumption of those articles or products that are necessary, useful, or agreeable to man, and which at the same time possess exchangeable value.
The Principles of Political Economy (1849; 4th edn), Introduction: 1

government:

2   Restrictions and prohibitions are uniformly productive of uncertainty and fluctuation. Every artificial stimulus, whatever may be its momentary effect on the department of industry to which it is applied, is immediately disadvantageous to others, and ultimately injurious even to that which it was intended to promote. No arbitrary regulation, no act of the legislature, can add any thing to the capital of the country; it can only force it into artificial channels.
The Principles of Political Economy (1849; 4th edn), Part I, Ch.VII: 226

poverty and the poor laws:

3   The real use of a workhouse is to be an asylum for the able-bodied poor – for the maimed and impotent poor, may, speaking generally, be more advantageously provided for elsewhere: But it ought to be such an asylum as will not be resorted to except by those who have no other resource, and who are wholly without the means of supporting themselves. The workhouses of England, though there have been some exceptions, have, in most instances, been too comfortable. Every possible precaution should be adopted to preserve the health of the inmates, and efforts should be made, by a proper classification or otherwise, to amend their morals, or at least to prevent them from becoming worse. But this is all that ought to be attempted. The able-bodied tenant of a workhouse should be made to feel that his situation is decidedly less comfortable than that of the industrious labourer who supports himself; and that a life of unremitting toil, supported on coarse and scanty fare, is to be his portion so long as he continues in this dependent and degraded state. The humanity of those who would turn workhouses into respectable inns, who would place paupers and beggars on the same level, in point of comfort, with the honest labourer who provides for his own wants, is spurious and mischievous in the last degree. The intentions of such persons may be good; but their mistaken bounty encourages those who receive it to continue in their idle and vicious courses, and weakens all the motives to exertion in others.
'Poor Laws' (1828): 308–309

4   It is proper, speaking generally, to do nothing that may weaken the spirit of industry; but if, in order to strengthen it, all relief were refused to the maimed and impotent poor, the habits and feelings of the people would be degraded and brutalised by familiarity with the most abject wretchedness; at the same time that, by driving the victims of poverty to despair, a foundation would be

laid for the most dreadful crimes, and such a shock given to the security of property and of life, as would very much overbalance whatever additional spur the refusal of support might give to industry and economy.
The Principles of Political Economy (1849; 4th edn), Part III, Ch.III: 446

5   The labourer who has saved some little property by contributing to a savings bank or a friendly society, and who perhaps has acquired a cottage and garden, has nothing in common with a pauper. He is elevated by the consciousness that he has not neglected the opportunities afforded him of improving his condition; that he is not indebted for his subsistence to the grudging charity of others; and he enjoys a much larger share of comfort and respectability than those in higher situations will readily imagine.
A Treatise on the Circumstances Which Determine the Rate of Wages (1854), Ch.X: 111

property:

6   The right of property has not made poverty, but it has powerfully contributed to make wealth.
The Principles of Political Economy (1849; 4th edn), Part I, Ch.II, Sec.I: 89

taxation:

7   We must not suppose that there is any thing productive in taxation – any thing advantageous to the productive classes. It cannot indeed be altogether dispense with; but the lower it is reduced the better.
'Effects of Machinery and Accumulation' (1821): 122

8   Taxation in every form is an evil. . . .
'Effects of Machinery and Accumulation' (1821): 123

9   The true way to put down smuggling, is to render it unprofitable – to diminish the temptation to engage in it; and this is to be done, not be surrounding the coasts with cordons of troops, by the multiplication of oaths and bonds, and making the country the theatre of ferocious and bloody contests in the field, or of perjury and chicanery in the courts of law, but simply and exclusively by *reducing the duties on the smuggled commodities!* It is this, and only this, that will put an end to smuggling.
'Comparative Productiveness of High and Low Taxes' (1822): 536

10 An increase of taxation, provided it be not carried to an excess – for then it is productive only of despair and misery – has the same effect upon a nation that an increase of his family, or of his necessary expenses, has upon a private individual. It stimulates every one to make greater efforts to preserve his place in society; and is often, in this way, the cause of a much greater amount of wealth being produced than is swallowed up by the tax. A diminution of taxation has necessarily an opposite effect. It enables individuals to preserve their place in society with less industry and economy, and they are, therefore, less practised.
'Progress of the National Debt – Best Method of Funding' (1828): 82

11 A moderate increase of taxation has the same effect on the habits and industry of a nation, that an increase of his family, or of his necessary and unavoidable expenses, has upon a private individual. Man is not influenced solely by hope; he is also powerfully operated upon by fear. Taxation brings the latter principle into the field. To the desire of rising in the world, inherent in the breast of every individual, an increase of taxation superadds the fear of being cast down to a lower station, of being deprived of conveniencies and gratifications which habit has rendered almost indispensable; and the combined influence of the two principles produces efforts that could not be produced by the unassisted agency of either. They stimulate individuals to endeavour, by increased industry and economy, to repair the breach taxation has made in their fortunes; and it not unfrequently happens that their efforts do more than this, and that, consequently, the national wealth is increased through the increase of taxation. But we must be on our guard against the abuse of this doctrine. To render an increase of taxation productive of greater exertion, economy, and invention, it should be slowly and gradually brought about; and it should never be carried to such a height as to incapacitate individuals from meeting the sacrifices it imposes, by such an increase of

industry and economy as it may be in their power to make without requiring any very violent change of their habits. The increase of taxation must not be such as to make it impracticable to overcome its influence, or to induce the belief that it is impracticable. Difficulties that are seen to be surmountable sharpen the inventive powers, and are readily grappled with; but an apparently insurmountable difficulty, or such an excessive weight of taxation as it was deemed impossible to meet, would not stimulate but destroy exertion. Instead of producing new efforts of ingenuity and economy, it would produce only despair. Whenever taxation becomes so heavy that the produce it takes from individuals can no longer be replaced by fresh efforts, they uniformly cease to be made; the population becomes dispirited; industry is paralyzed; and the country rapidly declines.
The Principles of Political Economy (1849; 4th edn), Part I, Ch.II, Sec.III: 116–117

12 A Tax is a portion, or the value of a portion, of the property or labour of individuals taken from them and disposed of by government.
A Treatise on the Principles and Practical Influence of Taxation and the Funding System (1863; 3rd edn), Introduction: 15

13 The produce of taxes is to the body politic what food is to the human body; and if they be imposed for necessary and legitimate purposes, judiciously assessed, and collected in the way least likely to be injurious, their payment cannot reasonably be objected to.
A Treatise on the Principles and Practical Influence of Taxation and the Funding System (1863; 3rd edn), Introduction: 16

14 [W]henever the sums taken by taxation are not fully compensated by increased production or increased saving, it encroaches on the means of future production, and the country begins to retrograde. When carried to this extent, taxation is one of the severest scourges to which a people can be subjected.
A Treatise on the Principles and Practical Influence of Taxation and the Funding System (1863; 3rd edn), Introduction: 19

The Reverend John McVickar
(1787–1868)

economics and economists:

1 Political Economy is not a science of speculation, but of fact and experiment.
Outlines of Political Economy (1825), Part I ('Principles of the Science – Nature of its Evidence'): 15

2 It must always be kept in mind that it is no part of the business of the economist to inquire into the means by which individual fortunes may have been increased or diminished, except to ascertain their general operation and effect. The *public interests* ought always to form the exclusive objects of his attention. He is not to frame systems, and devise schemes, for increasing the wealth and enjoyments of *particular classes*; but to apply himself to discover the sources of *national wealth*, and *universal prosperity*, and the means by which they may be rendered most productive.
Outlines of Political Economy (1825), Part I ('Principles of the Science – Nature of its Evidence'): 17

government:

3 [Governments] consume the produce of the labour of *others*, not of their own; and this circumstance prevents them from being so much interested in its profitable expenditure, and so much alive to the injurious consequences of extravagant and wasteful expenditure as their subjects.
Outlines of Political Economy (1825), Part IV ('Consumption of Government'): 174

Ronald Lindley Meek (1917–1978)

socialism:

1 In the socialist world commonwealth of the future, there may well be more statues of Pigou than of Keynes or even of Marx. Socialism, after all, almost by definition, has no Keynesian slumps; Marxism ... cannot teach us much about running a central bank; but socialism does have a Pigouvian problem of allocating scarce resources among alternative employments in a rational manner.
Smith, Marx, and After (1977), Ch.X: 183

2   It may raise the morale of Soviet economists to maintain that their economy is subject to bigger and better laws than ours, but many of their so-called 'economic laws of socialism' seem to me to consist either of elementary platitudes about certain aggregates which have to be kept in balance, or of mere definitions.
    Smith, Marx, and After (1977), Ch.X: 184

Carl Menger (1840–1921)

economics and economists:

1   Economic theory is related to the practical activities of economizing men in much the same way that chemistry is related to the operations of the practical chemist. Although reference to freedom of the human will may well be legitimate as an objection to the complete predictability of economic activity, it can never have force as a denial of the conformity to definite laws of phenomena that condition the outcome of the economic activity of men and are entirely independent of the human will. It is precisely phenomena of this description, however, which are the objects of study in our science.
    Principles of Economics (1871), Preface: 48–49

Herman Merivale (1806–1874)

economics and economists:

1   Let it be allowed that we employ an incorrect and misleading denomination for our science. Its derivation, we readily concede, points out rather an art than a science – the art of managing the resources of a nation. But that, we contend, is an art founded on the maxims of several sciences, – of moral philosophy, of political philosophy, and, finally, of the abstract science of national wealth. This last it is, to which English authors have given the name of Political Economy. They may have adopted an inconvenient title. We are quite ready to change it, provided the world can agree on a new one. Let it be *Chrematistics* or *Catallactics*, or *Chrysology*, or any other hard word which its inventor may succeed in making popular. But let it be conceded that there is such a science, by whatever name it may be called. Let it be acknowledged that it is a science which neither recommends to do, or to abstain from doing; which does not direct legislation; which regards Man in the abstract, and, simply as a wealth-creating animal, laying aside for the occasion all the other tendencies of his complicated nature. Sufficient for the economist to establish sound principles, any departure from which can only be justified by proving the interference of disturbing causes to render their practical application impossible.
    'Definitions and Systems of Political Economy' (1837): 83

James Mill (1773–1836)

economics and economists:

1   The great difficulty with which the salutary doctrines of political economy are propagated in this country, is, in truth, a very serious object of curiosity, as well as of regret. So long have the leading principles been demonstrated, and so industriously have they been inculcated, that nothing short of direct experience could convince us of the extent to which ignorance prevails.
    'Smith *on Money and Exchange*' (1808): 35

government:

2   All governments constantly spend as much as ever the people will let them. An expensive government is a curse. Every farthing which is spent upon it, beyond the expence necessary for maintaining law and order, is so much dead loss to the nation, contributes so far to keep down the annual produce, and to diminish the happiness of the people.
    Commerce Defended (1808; 2nd edn), Ch.VIII: 157

3   No good government can ever want more than two things for its support: 1*st*, Its own excellence; and, 2*dly*, a people sufficiently instructed, to be aware of that excellence. Every other pretended support must ultimately tend to its subversion, by lessening its dependence upon these, – and consequently lessening the inducement to promote good government and general instruction.
    'Education of the Poor' (1813): 217–218

money:

4 Money is so remarkable an agent in that class of transactions about which political economy is conversant, that vague and confused ideas on that subject almost necessarily infect our modes of thinking in regard to the whole science.
'Smith *on Money and Exchange*' (1808): 35

public goods:

5 We are not perfectly sure that we ought to be sorry at the obstacles which oppose the transfer of education into public hands. It is not agreeable to experience, that what is managed by public functionaries is the best managed part of a nation's concerns. It is now a maxim of politics, which philosophy has extracted from experience, that wherever private interests are competent to the provision and application of their own instruments and means, such provision and application ought to be left to themselves.
'Education of the Poor' (1813): 211

John Stuart Mill (1806–1873)

economics and economists:

1 [O]nly through the principle of competition has political economy any pretension to the character of a science. So far as rents, profits, wages, prices, are determined by competition, laws may be assigned for them. Assume competition to be their exclusive regulator, and principles of broad generality and scientific precision may be laid down, according to which they will be regulated. The political economist justly deems this his proper business; and as an abstract or hypothetical science, political economy cannot be required to do anything more.
Principles of Political Economy (1848), Vol. I, Bk.II, Ch.IV, Sec.1: 286

government:

2 [I]n all the more advanced communities, the great majority of things are worse done by the intervention of government, than the individuals most interested in the matter would do them, or cause them to be done, if left to themselves. The grounds of this truth are expressed with tolerable exactness in the popular dictum, that people understand their own business and their own interests better, and care for them more, than the government does, or can be expected to do. This maxim holds true throughout the greatest part of the business of life, and wherever it is true we ought to condemn every kind of government intervention that conflicts with it.
Principles of Political Economy (1848), Vol. II, Bk.V, Ch.XI, Sec.5: 520

3 It must be remembered . . . that even if a government were superior in intelligence and knowledge to any single individual in the nation, it must be inferior to all the individuals of the nation taken together. It can neither possess in itself, nor enlist in its service, more than a portion of the acquirements and capacities which the country contains, applicable to any given purpose.
Principles of Political Economy (1848), Vol. II, Bk.V, Ch.XI, Sec.5: 520

human development:

4 It is scarcely necessary to remark that a stationary condition of capital and population implies no stationary state of human improvement. There would be as much scope as ever for all kinds of mental culture, and moral and social progress; as much room for improving the Art of Living, and much more likelihood of its being improved, when minds ceased to be engrossed by the art of getting on. Even the industrial arts might be as earnestly and as successfully cultivated, with this sole difference, that instead of serving no purpose but the increase of wealth, industrial improvements would produce their legitimate effect, that of abridging labor.
Principles of Political Economy (1848), Vol. II, Bk.IV, Ch.VI, Sec.2: 317

money:

5 [Money] is a machinery for doing quickly and commodiously, what would be done, though less quickly and commodiously, without it; and like many other kinds of machinery, it only exerts a distinct and independent influence of its own when it gets out of order.
Principles of Political Economy (1848), Vol. II, Bk.III, Ch.VII, Sec.3: 8

poverty and poor relief:

6   Apart from any metaphysical considerations respecting the foundation of morals or of the social union, it will be admitted to be right that human beings should help one another; and the more so, in proportion to the urgency of the need; and none needs help so urgently as one who is starving. The claim to help, therefore, created by destitution is one of the strongest which can exist; and there is *prima facie* the amplest reason for making the relief of so extreme an exigency as certain to those who require it, as by any arrangements of society it can be made.
    Principles of Political Economy (1848), Vol. II, Bk.V, Ch.XI, Sec.13: 545–546

7   There are few things for which it is more mischievous that people should rely on the habitual aid of others, than for the means of subsistence, and unhappily there is no lesson which they more easily learn. The problem to be solved is therefore one of peculiar nicety as well as importance; how to give the greatest amount of needful help, with the smallest encouragement to undue reliance on it.
    Principles of Political Economy (1848), Vol. II, Bk.V, Ch.XI, Sec.13: 546

8   If the condition of a person receiving relief is made as eligible as that of the laborer who supports himself by his own exertions, the system strikes at the root of all individual industry and self-government; and, if fully acted up to, would require as its supplement an organized system of compulsion, for governing and setting to work like cattle, those who had been removed from the influence of the motives that act on human beings. But if, consistently with guaranteeing all persons against absolute want, the condition of those who are supported by legal charity can be kept considerably less desirable than the condition of those who find support for themselves, none but beneficial consequences can arise from a law which renders it impossible for any person, except by his own choice, to die from insufficiency of food.
    Principles of Political Economy (1848), Vol. II, Bk.V, Ch.XI, Sec.13: 547

9   Poverty, in any sense implying suffering, may be completely extinguished by the wisdom of society, combined with the good sense and providence of individuals.
    'Utilitarianism' (1861), Ch.II: 399

property:

10 If the land derived its productive power wholly from nature, and not all from industry, or if there were any means of discriminating what is derived from each source, it not only would not be necessary, but it would be the height of injustice, to let the gift of nature be engrossed by a few. The use of the land in agriculture must indeed, for the time being, be of necessity exclusive; the same person who has ploughed and sown must be permitted to reap. . . .
    Principles of Political Economy (1848), Vol. I, Bk.II, Ch.II, Sec.5: 271–272

11 In no sound theory of private property was it ever contemplated that the proprietor of land should be merely a sinecurist quartered on it.
    Principles of Political Economy (1848), Vol. I, Bk.II, Ch.II, Sec.6: 273

12 No man made the land. It is the original inheritance of the whole species. Public reasons exist for its being appropriated. But if those reasons lost their force, the thing would be unjust.
    Principles of Political Economy (1848), Vol. I, Bk.II, Ch.II, Sec.6: 275

socialism:

13 With moral conceptions in many respects far ahead of the existing arrangements of society, they [Socialist writers] have in general very confused and erroneous notions of its actual working; and one of their greatest errors, as I conceive, is to charge upon competition all the economical evils which at present exist. They forget that wherever competition is not, monopoly is; and that monopoly, in all its forms, is the taxation of the industrious for the support of indolence, if not of plunder. They forget, too, that with the exception of competition among labourers, all other competition is for the benefit of the labourers, by cheapening the articles they consume; that competition even in the labour market is a source not of low but of high wages, wherever the competition *for* labour exceeds the competition *of* labour, as in America, in the colonies, and in the

skilled trades; and never could be a cause of low wages, save by the overstocking of the labour market through the too great numbers of the labourers' families; while, if the supply of labourers is excessive, not even Socialism can prevent their remuneration from being low. . . .

It is the common error of Socialists to overlook the natural indolence of mankind; their tendency to be passive, to be the slaves of habit, to persist indefinitely in a course once chosen. Let them once attain any state of existence which they consider tolerable, and the danger to be apprehended is that they will thenceforth stagnate; will not exert themselves to improve, and by letting their faculties rust, will lose even the energy required to preserve them from deterioration. Competition may not be the best conceivable stimulus, but it is at present a necessary one, and no one can foresee the time when it will not be indispensable to progress. . . .

Instead of looking upon competition as the baneful and anti-social principle which it is held to be by the generality of Socialists, I conceive that, even in the present state of society and industry, every restriction of it is an evil, and every extension of it, even if for the time injuriously affecting some class of labourers, is always an ultimate good. To be protected against competition is to be protected in idleness, in mental dulness; to be saved the necessity of being as active and as intelligent as other people; and if it is also to be protected against being underbid for employment by a less highly paid class of labourers, this is only where old custom, or local and partial monopoly, has placed some particular class of artisans in a privileged position as compared with the rest; and the time has come when the interest of universal improvement is no longer promoted by prolonging the privileges of a few.

Principles of Political Economy (1871; 7th edn), Bk.IV, Ch.VII, Sec.7: 792–794

14 Though much of their allegations is unanswerable, not a little is the result of errors in political economy; by which, let me say once and for all, I do not mean the rejection of any practical rules of policy which have been laid down by political economists, I mean ignorance of economic facts, and of the causes by which the economic phenomena of society as it is, are actually determined.

'Chapters on Socialism' (1879), Part II: 373

15 In truth, when competition is perfectly free on both sides, its tendency is not specially either to raise or to lower the price of articles, but to equalise it; to level inequalities of remuneration, and to reduce all to a general average, a result which, in so far as realised (no doubt very imperfectly), is, on Socialistic principles, desirable.

'Chapters on Socialism' (1879), Part II: 375

16 The distinctive feature of Socialism is not that all things are in common, but that production is only carried on upon the common account, and that the instruments of production are held as common property. The *practicability* then of Socialism, on the scale of Mr. Owen's or M. Fourier's villages, admits of no dispute.

'Chapters on Socialism' (1879), Part III: 515

17 Communistic management would thus be, in all probability, less favourable than private management to that striking out of new paths and making immediate sacrifices for distant and uncertain advantages, which, though seldom unattended with risk, is generally indispensable to great improvements in the economic condition of mankind, and even to keeping up the existing state in the face of a continual increase of the number of mouths to be fed.

'Chapters on Socialism' (1879), Part III: 518

18 The one certainty is, that Communism, to be successful, requires a high standard of both moral and intellectual education in all the members of the community – moral, to qualify them for doing their part honestly and energetically in the labour of life under no inducement but their share in the general interest of the association, and their feelings of duty and sympathy towards it; intellectual, to make them capable of estimating distant interests and entering into complex considerations, sufficiently at least to be able to discriminate, in these matters, good counsel from bad.

'Chapters on Socialism' (1879), Part III: 522–523

19 If Communist associations show that they can be durable and prosperous, they will multiply, and will probably be adopted by successive portions of the population of the more advanced countries as they become morally fitted for that mode of life. But to force unprepared populations into Communist societies, even if a political revolution gave the power to make such an attempt, would end in disappointment.
'Chapters on Socialism' (1879), Part III: 523

taxation:

20 For what reason ought equality to be the rule in matters of taxation? For the reason that it ought to be so in all affairs of government. As a government ought to make no distinction of persons or classes in the strength of their claims on it, whatever sacrifices it requires from them should be made to bear as nearly as possible with the same pressure upon all, which, it must be observed, is the mode by which least sacrifice is occasioned on the whole. If any one bears less than his fair share of the burden, some other person must suffer more than his share, and the alleviation to the one is not, *cæteris paribus*, so great a good to him, as the increased pressure upon the other is an evil. Equality of taxation, therefore, as a maxim of politics, means equality of sacrifice. It means, apportioning the contribution of each person towards the expenses of government, so that he shall feel neither more nor less inconvenience from his share of the payment than every other person experiences from his. This standard, like other standards of perfection, cannot be completely realized; but the first object in every practical discussion should be, to know what perfection is.
Principles of Political Economy (1848), Vol. II, Bk.V, Ch.II, Sec.2: 352

21 Government ought to set an example of rating all things at their true value, and riches, therefore, at the worth, for comfort or pleasure, of the things which they will buy; and ought not to sanction the vulgarity of prizing them for the pitiful vanity of being known to possess them, or the still more paltry shame of being suspected to be without them, the presiding motives of three fourths of the expenditure of the middle classes. The sacrifices of real comfort or indulgence which government requires, it is bound to apportion among all persons with as much equality as possible; but their sacrifices of the imaginary dignity dependent on expense, it may spare itself the trouble of estimating.
Principles of Political Economy (1848), Vol. II, Bk.V, Ch.II, Sec.3: 356–357

22 To tax the larger incomes at a higher per centage than the smaller, is to lay a tax on industry and economy; to impose a penalty on people for having worked harder and saved more than their neighbors. It is partial taxation, which is a mild form of robbery. A just and wise legislation would scrupulously abstain from opposing obstacles to the acquisition of even the largest fortune by honest exertion. Its impartiality between competitors would consist in endeavoring that they should all start fair, and not that, whether they were swift or slow, all should reach the goal at once. Many, indeed, fail with greater efforts than those with which others succeed, not from difference of merits, but difference of opportunities; and it is the part of a good government to provide, that, as far as more paramount considerations permit, the inequality of opportunities shall be remedied.
Principles of Political Economy (1848), Vol. II, Bk.V, Ch.II, Sec.3: 357

23 Over-taxation, carried to a sufficient extent, is quite capable of ruining the most industrious community, especially when it is in any degree arbitrary, so that the payer is never certain how much or how little he shall be allowed to keep; or when it is so laid on as to render industry and economy a bad calculation.
Principles of Political Economy (1848), Vol. II, Bk.V, Ch.II, Sec.7: 369

24 Simple over-taxation by government, though a great evil, is not comparable in the economical part of its mischiefs to exactions much more moderate in amount, but which either subject the contributor to the arbitrary mandate of government officers, or are so laid on as to place skill, industry, and frugality at a disadvantage.
Principles of Political Economy (1848), Vol. II, Bk.V, Ch.VIII, Sec.2: 446

25 No tax is in itself absolutely just; the justice or injustice of taxes can only be comparative: if just in the conception, they are never completely so in the application. . . .
Critical Notice of L'Avere et l'Imposta (1873): 398

value:

26 In a state of society . . . in which the industrial system is entirely founded on purchase and sale, each individual, for the most part, living not on things in the production of which he himself bears a part, but on things obtained by a double exchange, a sale followed by a purchase, the question of Value is fundamental. Almost every speculation respecting the economical interests of a society thus constituted, implies some theory of Value; the smallest error on that subject infects with corresponding error all our other conclusions; and anything vague or misty in our conception of it, creates confusion and uncertainty in everything else. Happily, there is nothing in the laws of Value which remains for the present or any future writer to clear up; the theory of the subject is complete; the only difficulty to be overcome is that of so stating it as to solve by anticipation the chief perplexities which occur in applying it; and to do this, some minuteness of exposition, and considerable demands on the patience of the reader, are unavoidable. He will be amply repaid, however, (if a stranger to these inquiries,) by the ease and rapidity with which a thorough understanding of this subject will enable him to fathom most of the remaining questions of political economy.
Principles of Political Economy (1848), Vol. I, Bk.III, Ch.I, Sec.1: 520–521

John Stuart Mill (1806–1873) and William Ellis (1800–1881)

economics and economists:

1 If there is one sign of the times upon which more than any other we should be justified in resting our hopes of the future progression of the human race in the career of improvement, that sign undoubtedly is, the demand which is now manifesting itself on the part of the public for instruction in the science of Political Economy.
'M'Culloch's *Discourse on Political Economy*' (1825)

Hyman Philip Minsky (1919–1996)

economics and economists:

1 Economists as advisers have failed to teach legislators and administrators that although government may propose, it is the economy that disposes.
Stabilizing an Unstable Economy (1986), Part IV, Ch.12: 287

Ludwig Edler von Mises (1881–1973)

capitalism:

1 The market economy is a man-made mode of acting under the division of labor. But this does not imply that it is something accidental or artificial and could be replaced by another mode. The market economy is the product of a long evolutionary process. It is the outcome of man's endeavors to adjust his action in the best possible way to the given conditions of his environment that he cannot alter. It is the strategy, as it were, by the application of which man has triumphantly progressed from savagery to civilization.
Human Action (1949), Part IV, Ch.XV, Sec.3: 266

2 There is no kind of freedom and liberty other than the kind which the market economy brings about. In a totalitarian hegemonic society the only freedom that is left to the individual, because it cannot be denied to him, is the freedom to commit suicide.
Human Action (1949), Part IV, Ch.XV, Sec.6: 280

3 The market economy becomes a chaotic muddle if this predominance of private property which the reformers disparage as selfishness is eliminated. In urging people to listen to the voice of their conscience and to substitute considerations of public welfare for those of private profit, one does not create a working and satisfactory social order. It is not enough to tell a man *not* to buy on the cheapest market and *not* to sell on the dearest market. It is not enough to tell him *not* to strive after profit and *not* to avoid losses. One must establish unambiguous

rules for the guidance of conduct in each concrete situation.
Human Action (1949), Part VI, Ch. XXVII, Sec.4: 721

4 The truth is that capitalism has not only multiplied population figures but at the same time improved the people's standard of living in an unprecedented way. Neither economic thinking nor historical experience suggest that any other social system could be more beneficial to the masses than capitalism. The results speak for themselves. The market economy needs no apologists and propagandists. It can apply to itself the words of Sir Christopher Wren's epitaph in St. Paul's: *Si monumentum requiris, circumspice.*
Human Action (1949), Part VI, Ch. XXXV, Sec.5: 850

5 The much talked about sternness of capitalism consists in the fact that it handles everybody according to his contribution to the well-being of his fellow men. The sway of the principle, *to each according to his accomplishments*, does not allow of any excuse for personal shortcomings. Everybody knows very well that there are people like himself who succeeded where he himself failed. Everybody knows that many of those whom he envies are self-made men who started from the same point from which he himself started. And, much worse, he knows that all other people know it too.
The Anti-Capitalistic Mentality (1956), Ch.I, Sec.4: 12

collective bargaining:

6 [Collective bargaining] is bargaining at the point of a gun. It is bargaining between an armed party, ready to use its weapons, and an unarmed party under duress. It is not a market transaction. It is a dictate forced upon the employer. And its effects do not differ from those of a government decree for the enforcement of which the police power and the penal courts are used. It produces institutional unemployment.
Human Action (1949), Part VI, Ch.XXX, Sec.3: 773

economics and economists:

7 Economics does not deal with an imaginary *homo oeconomicus* as ineradicable fables reproach it with doing, but with *homo agens* as he really is, often weak, stupid, inconsiderate, and badly instructed. It does not matter whether his motives and emotions are to be qualified as noble or as mean. It does not contend that man strives only after more material wealth for himself and for his kin. Its theorems are neutral with regard to ultimate judgments of value, and are valid for all actions irrespective of their expediency.
'The Treatment of "Irrationality" in the Social Sciences' (1944), Sec.IV: 534

8 Economics is not a 'dismal science,' because it starts from the acknowledgment of the fact, that the means for the attainment of ends are scarce. (With regard to human concerns which can be fully satisfied because they do not depend on scarce factors, man does not act, and praxeology, the science of human action, does not have to deal with them.) As far as there is scarcity of means, man behaves rationally, i.e., he acts. So far there is no room left for 'irrationality.'
'The Treatment of "Irrationality" in the Social Sciences' (1944), Sec.VIII: 544; cf. Thomas Carlyle 1, Robert Nathan 2, Rexford Tugwell 1

9 It is true that economics is a theoretical science and as such abstains from any judgment of value. It is not its task to tell people what ends they should aim at. It is a science of the means to be applied for the attainment of ends chosen, not, to be sure, a science of the choosing of ends. Ultimate decisions, the valuations and the choosing of ends, are beyond the scope of any science. Science never tells a man how he should act; it merely shows how a man must act if he wants to attain definite ends.
Human Action (1949), Introduction, Sec.3: 10

10 Economics is, of course, not a branch of history or of any other historical science. It is the theory of all human action, the general science of the immutable categories of action and of their operation under all thinkable special conditions under which man acts.
Human Action (1949), Part IV, Ch.XV, Sec.3: 266

11 Economics deals with the real actions of real men. Its theorems refer neither to ideal nor to perfect men, neither to the phantom of a fabulous economic man (homo oeconomicus) nor to the statistical notion of an average man (homme moyen). Man with all his weaknesses and limitations, every man as he lives and acts, is the subject matter of catallactics. Every human action is a theme of praxeology.
Human Action (1949), Part IV, Ch.XXIII, Sec.4: 646–647

12 The development of a profession of economists is an offshoot of interventionism. The professional economist is the specialist who is instrumental in designing various measures of government interference with business. He is an expert in the field of economic legislation, which today invariably aims at hindering the operation of the unhampered market economy.
Human Action (1949), Part VII, Ch. XXXVIII, Sec.2: 865

13 Economics, as a branch of the more general theory of human action, deals with all human action, i.e., with man's purposive aiming at the attainment of ends chosen, whatever these ends may be. To apply the concept *rational* or *irrational* to the ultimate ends chosen is nonsensical. We may call irrational the ultimate given, viz., those things that our thinking can neither analyze nor reduce to other ultimately given things. Then every ultimate end chosen by any man is irrational. It is neither more nor less rational to aim at riches like Croesus than to aim at poverty like a Buddhist monk.
Human Action (1949), Part VII, Ch. XXXIX, Sec.2: 880

14 A man who publicly talks or writes about the opposition between capitalism and socialism without having fully familiarized himself with all that economics has to say about these issues is an irresponsible babbler.
The Anti-Capitalistic Mentality (1956), Ch.II, Sec.2: 47

inflation:

15 Inflation is the true opium of the people and it is administered to them by anticapitalist governments and parties.
The Theory of Money and Credit (1953), Part Four, Ch.23, Sec.2: 485

innovation:

16 To illustrate the difference between the innovator and the dull crowd of routinists who cannot even imagine that any improvement is possible, we need only refer to a passage in Engels' most famous book. Here, in 1878, Engels apodictically announced that military weapons are 'now so perfected that no further progress of any revolutionizing influence is any longer possible.' Henceforth 'all further [technological] progress is by and large indifferent for land warfare. The age of evolution is in this regard essentially closed.' This complacent conclusion shows in what the achievement of the innovator consists: he accomplishes what other people believe to be unthinkable and unfeasible.
Theory and History (1957), Part III, Ch.9, Sec.3: 193–194

laissez-faire:

17 Laissez faire does not mean: Let soulless mechanical forces operate. It means: Let each individual choose how he wants to cooperate in the social division of labor; let the consumers determine what the entrepreneurs should produce. Planning means: Let the government alone choose and enforce its rulings by the apparatus of coercion and compulsion.
Human Action (1949), Part VI, Ch. XXVII, Sec.5: 726

18 Laissez faire means: Let the common man choose and act; do not force him to yield to a dictator.
Human Action (1949), Part VI, Ch. XXVII, Sec.5: 727

measurement:

19 There cannot be any such thing as measurement in the field of economics. All statistical figures available have importance only for economic history; they are data of history like the figures concerning the battle of Waterloo; they tell us what happened in an unique and non repeatable historical case. The only way to utilize them is to interpret them by *Verstehen*.
'The Treatment of "Irrationality" in the Social Sciences' (1944), Sec.VI: 538

money:

20 All the processes of our economic life appear in a monetary guise; and those who do not see beneath the surface of things are only aware of monetary phenomena and remain unconscious of deeper relationships. Money is regarded as the cause of theft and murder, of deception and betrayal. Money is blamed when the prostitute sells her body and when the bribed judge perverts the law. It is money against which the moralist declaims when he wishes to oppose excessive materialism. Significantly enough avarice is called the love of money; and all evil is attributed to it.
The Theory of Money and Credit (1953), Part One, Ch.6, Sec.2: 111

morality:

21 Moral behaviour is the name we give to the temporary sacrifices made in the interests of social co-operation, which is the chief means by which human wants and human life generally may be supplied. All ethics are social ethics.... To behave morally, means to sacrifice the less important to the more important by making social co-operation possible.
Socialism (1981), Part IV, Ch.32, Sec.2: 408

poverty and poor relief:

22 No civilized community has callously allowed the incapacitated to perish. But the substitution of a legally enforceable claim to support or sustenance for charitable relief does not seem to agree with human nature as it is. Not metaphysical prepossessions, but considerations of practical expediency make it inadvisable to promulgate an actionable right to sustenance.
Human Action (1949), Part VI, Ch. XXXV, Sec.2: 835–836

23 Nobody is needy in the market economy because of the fact that some people are rich. The riches of the rich are not the cause of the poverty of anybody.
The Anti-Capitalistic Mentality (1956), Ch.II, Sec.1: 43

rationality:

24 Human action is necessarily always rational. The term 'rational action' is therefore pleonastic and must be rejected as such. When applied to the ultimate ends of action, the terms rational and irrational are inappropriate and meaningless. The ultimate end of action is always the satisfaction of some desires of the acting man.
Human Action (1949), Part I, Ch.I, Sec.4: 18

rule of law:

25 The contractual order of society is an order of right and law. It is a government under the rule of law (*Rechtsstaat*) as differentiated from the welfare state (*Wohlfahrtsstaat*) or paternal state. Right or law is the complex of rules determining the orbit in which individuals are free to act. No such orbit is left to wards of a hegemonic society. In the hegemonic state there is neither right nor law; there are only directives and regulations which the director may change daily and apply with what discrimination he pleases and which the wards must obey. The wards have one freedom only: to obey without asking questions.
Human Action (1949), Part II, Ch.X, Sec.2: 199

social insurance:

26 By weakening or completely destroying the will to be well and able to work, social insurance creates illness and inability to work; it produces the habit of complaining – which is in itself a neurosis – and neuroses of other kinds. In short, it is an institution which tends to encourage disease, not to say accidents, and to intensify considerably the physical and psychic results of accidents and illnesses. As a social institution it makes a people sick bodily and mentally or at least helps to multiply, lengthen, and intensify disease.
Socialism (1981), Part V, Ch.34, Sec.3: 432

socialism:

27 A society that chooses between capitalism and socialism does not choose between two social systems; it chooses between social cooperation and the disintegration of society. Socialism is not an alternative to capitalism; it is an alternative to any system under which men can live as *human* beings. To stress this point is the task of economics

as it is the task of biology and chemistry to teach that potassium cyanide is not a nutriment but a deadly poison.
Human Action (1949), Part IV, Ch.XXIV, Sec.3: 676

28 The essential mark of socialism is that *one will* alone acts. It is immaterial whose will it is. The director may be an anointed king or a dictator, ruling by virtue of his *charisma*, he may be a Führer or a board of Führers appointed by the vote of the people. The main thing is that the employment of all factors of production is directed by one agency only. One will alone chooses, decides, directs, acts, gives orders. All the rest simply obey orders and instructions.
Human Action (1949), Part V, Ch.XXV, Sec.3: 691–692

29 What pushes the masses into the camp of socialism is, even more than the illusion that socialism will make them richer, the expectation that it will curb all those who are better than they themselves are. The characteristic feature of all utopian plans from that of Plato down to that of Marx is the rigid petrification of all human conditions. Once the 'perfect' state of social affairs is attained, no further changes ought to be tolerated. There will no longer be any room left for innovators and reformers.
The Ultimate Foundation of Economic Science (1962), Ch.7, Sec.5: 123

30 The impracticability of Socialism is the result of intellectual, not moral, incapacity. Socialism could not achieve its end, because a socialist economy could not calculate value. Even angels, if they were endowed only with human reason, could not form a socialistic community.
Socialism (1981), Part IV, Ch.32, Sec.1: 407

society:

31 Society is concerted action, cooperation.
Society is the outcome of conscious and purposeful behavior. This does not mean that individuals have concluded contracts by virtue of which they have founded human society. The actions which have brought about social cooperation and daily bring it about anew do not aim at anything else than cooperation and coadjuvancy with others for the attainment of definite singular ends. The total complex of the mutual relations created by such concerted actions is called society. It substitutes collaboration for the – at least conceivable – isolated life of individuals. Society is division of labor and combination of labor. In his capacity as an acting animal man becomes a social animal.
Human Action (1949), Part II, Ch.VIII, Sec.1: 143

32 In a daily repeated plebiscite in which every penny gives a right to vote the consumers determine who should own and run the plants, shops and farms. The control of the material means of production is a social function, subject to the confirmation or revocation by the sovereign consumers.
The Anti-Capitalistic Mentality (1956), Ch.I, Sec.1: 2

33 Social cooperation under the division of labor is the ultimate and sole source of man's success in his struggle for survival and his endeavors to improve as much as possible the material conditions of his well-being.
The Anti-Capitalistic Mentality (1956), Ch.IV, Sec.4: 90

taxation:

34 If taxes grow beyond a moderate limit, they cease to be taxes and turn into devices for the destruction of the market economy.
Human Action (1949), Part VI, Ch. XXVIII, Sec.3: 734

Wesley Clair Mitchell (1874–1948)

money:

1 [Money] is the foundation of that complex system of prices to which the individual must adjust his behavior in getting a living. Since it molds his objective behavior, it becomes part of his subjective life, giving him a method and an instrument for the difficult task of assessing the relative importance of dissimilar goods in varying quantities, and affecting the interests in terms of which he makes his valuations. Because it thus rationalizes economic life itself, the use of money lays the foundation for a rational

theory of that life. Money may not be the root of *all* evil, but it is the root of economic science.
'The Rôle of Money in Economic Theory' (1916), Sec.VI: 156–157

social science:

2 It is not the business of the social sciences to say what is good and what bad; all they can do is to trace functional relationships among social processes, and so elucidate the most effective means of attaining whatever ends we set ourselves.
'Intelligence and the Guidance of Economic Evolution' (1936), Sec.VII: 461

statistics:

3 A biologist or anthropologist working upon statistical problems is often able to collect his own data by measuring material in his laboratory. Such measurements can be made to fit the requirements of the problem, and their accuracy can be controlled within assignable limits. A meteorologist is dependent upon data collected mainly by other observers; but these observers are men with at least a modicum of training, using scientific apparatus, and working under scientific direction. The quantitative worker upon economic problems is less fortunate in respect to his raw materials. Seldom can he make in his statistical laboratory a significant collection of measurements. He deals not with 'material,' but with the behavior of men, and that behavior must be observed and recorded 'in the field.' Because his phenomena are highly variable, he usually needs a large array of cases, more than he can collect by himself or through the trained assistants at his disposal. Forced to rely upon observations made by others, he must often adapt his problem to the data, when he wishes to adapt his data to the problem.
Business Cycles (1927), Vol.I, Ch.III, Sec.III, 1: 202–203

Gustave de Molinari (1819–1912)

socialism:

1 Socialism pretends that society is compelled to guarantee the life and well-being of the individual, but it ignores the inevitable consequence – that government, having this duty to perform, must be invested with the means – a sovereign power over the life and all possessions of that individual. If government is under an obligation to forthwith reduce social misery, the members of society should invest it with authority to regulate their consumption and reproduction, as the master regulated that of his slaves. The panacea for all evils, the last step on the road of progress, would thus be nothing else than a return to the first and barbarous stage of slavery.
The Society of To-morrow: A Forecast of Its Political and Economic Organization (1904), Part II, Ch.13

Henry Ludwell Moore (1869–1958)

methodology:

1 In the case of every science it is wise economy to make an appraisement, from time to time, of dominant conceptions and prevailing methods. Like the relative values of material commodities the relative values of ideas and processes shift with the passing of time, and the appearance of new problems amid the pressing exigencies of practical life requires that we frequently take stock of our scientific capital, if the expenditure of energy is to yield its proper return. The economist particularly should attend to the changing efficiency of his scientific machinery, for he himself has taught that the value of capital is proportional to its yield, and that the maximum yield is in the direction of greatest social service.
'The Statistical Complement of Pure Economics' (1908), Introduction: 1–2

St., Sir Thomas More (1478–1535)

communal ownership:

1 It seems to me that men cannot possibly live well where all things are in common. How can there be plenty of commodities where every man stops working? If the hope of gain does not spur him on, won't he rely on others, and become lazy? If men are impelled by need, and yet no man can legally protect what he has obtained, what can follow but continual bloodshed and turmoil,

especially when respect for magistrates and their authority has been lost? I for one cannot conceive of authority existing among men who are equal to one another in every respect.
Utopia (1516), Book I: 40

Oskar Morgenstern (1902–1977)

mathematics in economics:

1   The purpose of mathematical economics is, of course, primarily to advance economics, not to apply mathematics merely because some mathematics exists and one has learned that science to some extent. Nor is it to find new mathematics theorems per se. But it may, and most assuredly will, happen that economics cannot be advanced decisively without proving fundamentally new mathematical theorems.
'Limits to the Uses of Mathematics in Economics' (1963): 18

2   As far as the use of mathematics in economics is concerned, there is an abundance of formulas where such are not needed. They are frequently introduced, one fears, in order to show off. The more difficult the mathematical theorem, the more esoteric the name of the mathematician quoted, the better. Then one is 'in.' So it happens that statements are proved – laudable by itself and correctly done – by means of complicated reasoning and use of elaborate machinery, though they can also be proved by elementary means.
'Limits to the Uses of Mathematics in Economics' (1963): 18

Glenn Raymond Morrow
(1895–1973)

economics and economists:

1   If the economist chooses to consider only one aspect of human activity with the purpose of contributing to the interpretation of the whole of concrete experience, there can be no logical objection. It must be recognized, however, that the mechanics of social life which the economic analysis exhibits is not all there is in social experience. For the economist, wealth is the end of activity, but in concrete experience it is only one of many ends. For the economist, every action is merely individual; but human activity is also universal as well as particular. Because of these two initial assumptions, which belong to the very nature of his science, the economist – *qua* economist – can never grasp the full meaning of social experience.
The Ethical and Economic Theories of Adam Smith (1923), Ch.V: 90–91

Smith's *Wealth of Nations*:

2   Once upon a time there was a man who read the *Wealth of Nations*; not a summary, nor a volume of selected passages, but the *Wealth of Nations* itself. He began with the Introduction, he read the famous first chapter on the division of labor, the chapters on the origin and use of money, the prices of commodities, the wages of labor, the profits of stock, the rent of land, and all the other well-known economic portions of the first book, not omitting the long digression on the fluctuation in the value of silver during the last four centuries, and the statistical tables at the end. Having completed the first book he went on to the second, not deterred by the fact that it is supposed to contain an erroneous theory of capital and an untenable distinction between productive and unproductive labor. In Book III he found an account of the economic development of Europe since the fall of the Roman Empire, with digressions upon various phases of medieval life and civilization. In the fourth book he came upon extended analyses and criticisms of the commercial and colonial policies of European nations, and a whole battery of free-trade arguments. Finally he attacked the long concluding book on the revenue of the sovereign. Here he found even more varied and unexpected matters: an account of the different methods of defense and of administering justice in primitive societies, and of the origin and growth of standing armies in Europe; a history of education in the Middle Ages and a criticism of eighteenth-century universities; a history of the temporal power of the church, of the growth of public debts in modern nations, of the mode of electing bishops in the ancient church; reflections upon the disadvantages of the division of labor, and – what is the

main purpose of the book – an examination of principles of taxation and of systems of public revenue. Time is too short to enumerate all that he found here before he finally came to the concluding paragraphs, written during the opening events of the American Revolution, concerning the duty of colonies to contribute toward the expenses of the mother-country.

Now of course I may have exaggerated somewhat. There probably never was any such man.
'Adam Smith: Moralist and Philosopher' (1928): 156–157

Gaetano Mosca (1858–1941)

economics and economists:

1 Political economy studies the constant laws or tendencies that govern the production and distribution of wealth in human societies; but that science is by no means the same as the art of amassing wealth and keeping it. A very competent economist may be incapable of making a fortune; and a banker or a businessman may acquire some understanding from knowledge of economic laws but does not need to master them, and may, in fact, get along very well in his business even in utter ignorance of them.
The Ruling Class (1939), Ch.I, Sec.1: 1

2 Among the political or social sciences one branch, so far, has attained such scientific maturity that through the abundance and the accuracy of its results it has left all the others far behind. We are thinking of political economy.
The Ruling Class (1939), Ch.I, Sec.2: 2

3 The study of economics is an excellent thing, but it is not in itself sufficient to cleanse the public mind of the chimerical fancies alluded to. Economic science has penetratingly investigated the laws that regulate the production and distribution of wealth. It has as yet done little with the relations of those laws to other laws that operate in the political organization of human societies. Economists have not concerned themselves with those beliefs, those collective illusions, which sometimes become general in given societies, and which form so large a part of the history of the world – as has been well said, man does not live by bread alone.
The Ruling Class (1939), Ch.XI, Sec.11: 327–328

Thomas Mun (1571–1641)

money:

1 For we must know, that mony is not only the true measure of all our other means in the Kingdom, but also of our forraign commerce with strangers, which therefore ought to be kept just and constant to avoid those confusions which ever accompany such alterations.
England's Treasure by Forraign Trade (1664), Ch.VIII: 71–72

taxation:

2 I will add this as a necessary rule to be observed, that when more treasure must be raised than can be received by the ordinary taxes, it ought ever to be done with equality to avoid the hate of the people, who are never pleased except their contributions be granted by general consent. . . .
England's Treasure by Forraign Trade (1664), Ch.XVII: 165–166

trade:

3 The ordinary means therefore to encrease our wealth and treasure is by *Forraign Trade*, wherein wee must ever observe this rule; to sell more to strangers yearly than wee consume of theirs in value.
England's Treasure by Forraign Trade (1664), Ch.II: 11

4 Behold then the true form and worth of forraign Trade, which is, *The great Revenue of the King, The honour of the Kingdom, The Noble profession of the Merchant, The School of our Arts, The supply of our wants, The employment of our poor, The improvement of our Lands, The Nurcery of our Mariners, The walls of the Kingdoms, The means of our Treasure, The Sinnews of our wars, The terror of our Enemies*.
England's Treasure by Forraign Trade (1664), Ch.XXI: 219–220

usury:

5   How can we well say, That as *Usury encreaseth*, so *Trade decreaseth*? For although it is true that some men give over trading, and buy Lands, or put out their Money to use when they are grown rich, or old, or for some other the like occasions; yet for all this it doth not follow, that the quantity of the trade must lessen; for this course in the rich giveth opportunity presently to the *younger & poorer* Merchants to rise in the world, and to enlarge their dealings; to the performance whereof, if they want means of their own, they may, and do, take it up at interest: so that our money lies not dead, it is still traded.
    England's Treasure by Forraign Trade (1664), Ch.XV: 143–144

Richard Abel Musgrave (1910–)

economics and economists:

1   Indeed, the conduct of government is the testing ground of social ethics and civilized living. Intelligent conduct of government requires an understanding of the economic relations involved; and the economist, by aiding in this understanding, may hope to contribute to a better society. This is why the field of public finance has seemed of particular interest to me; and this is why my interest in the field has been motivated by a search for the good society, no less than by scientific curiosity. The form of this good society involves value judgment, and value judgment may enter into the issues that the economist chooses to examine. From there on, however, the economist's function is to aim at a scientific and thus objective answer.
    The Theory of Public Finance (1959), Preface: v–vi

Gunnar Myrdal (1898–1987)

economics and economists:

1   Economics, like other sciences, consists of a number of quite different problems thrown together partly by tradition and partly by considerations of what is convenient for research and teaching. Attempts to define its precise scope are bound to be artificial. They are often motivated by the metaphysical intention, not just to give a definition, but to give a definition in such a way that a normative content can be smuggled into apparently scientific propositions.
    The Political Element in the Development of Economic Theory (1953), Ch.6: 154–155

2   Modern establishment economists have retained the welfare theory from the earliest neo-classical authors, but have done their best to conceal and forget its foundation upon a particular and now obsolete moral philosophy. They have thus succeeded in presenting what appears to be an amoral economic theory, and they are often proud of stressing this as 'professionalism.'
    Against the Stream (1972), Preface: vii

3   Economists have a duty to be ahead of their time and not only to adjust – with a nagging and less deep-boring criticism – to the ongoing development.
    Against the Stream (1972), Ch.2, Sec.7: 31

4   What economists and also other social scientists have commonly done is to conceal the valuations that underlie their analytical structures – and, indeed, the very terminology they use – so deeply that they can happily remain unaware of them in their researches and trust that the latter are merely factual. Very generally, social scientists are unsophisticated 'positivists.'
    Against the Stream (1972), Ch.7, Sec.10: 149

taxation:

5   Taxation is a most flexible and effective but also a dangerous instrument of social reform. One has to know precisely what one is doing lest the results diverge greatly from one's intentions. The worst is that one may not even notice what is happening.
    The Political Element in the Development of Economic Theory (1953), Ch.7: 188

N

Robert Roy Nathan (1908–2001)

economics and economists:

1 It will not be very helpful if the teachers of economics who resent adverse appraisals counter by citing the biases of the critics. It may be a valid defense but it is hardly conducive to constructive solutions to say that most criticisms come from those who do not like what economists conclude or propose.

'Economic Analysis and Public Policy: The Growing Hiatus' (1964): 610

2 [W]e must do far better in the future than in the past and make economics the happy science instead of the dismal science.

'Economic Analysis and Public Policy: The Growing Hiatus' (1964): 622; cf. Thomas Carlyle 1, Ludwig von Mises 8, Rexford Tugwell 1

Simon Newcomb (1835–1909)

competition:

1 The practice of competition continually tends to reduce to a minimum the equivalent which men can charge for their services. This also is in perfect accord with equity, since, as the number of persons who can render any services increases, the relative importance of each person diminishes. Thus, even from an idealistic point of view, nothing can be said against the general equity of the existing system of free competition.

Principles of Political Economy (1886), Bk.V, Ch.VI, Sec.45: 517–518

economics and economists:

2 [R]ejecting the conclusions of political economy on the ground that, being uncertain, they can be of no practical value is like rejecting all the rules about seed-time and harvest because meteorology can never tell us what kind of weather we shall have on any particular day. We must do in economics just as we would do in the scientific investigation of all other general causes. We must frame hypotheses which shall come as nearly as possible to the general average of things as they exist in the world.

Principles of Political Economy (1886), Bk.I, Ch.V, Sec.30: 38

3 An *economic question* is one whose issue concerns only wealth and its enjoyment, including the power of each individual to gain the maximum amount of gratification from his labor. When other subjects are involved in the question, it ceases to be a purely economic one, and therefore an answer founded solely on economic considerations may not be conclusive.

Principles of Political Economy (1886), Bk.V, Ch.I, Sec.2: 445

interest:

4 As a general rule, the most charitable purpose to which a man can put his money is to find for it the best paying investment he can. The interest which it pays him is an index of the amount of good his money is doing to his fellow men, and the more he receives the greater the good to others.

'Principles of Taxation' (1880): 155

socialism:

5 Socialism is a general term applied to a number of systems which propose that society, by organized action, shall force the individual to surrender his liberty, or, what amounts to the same thing, his right to the unconditional acquisition and use of property, for the general good.

Principles of Political Economy (1886), Bk.V, Ch.VI, Sec.43: 512

6 A little consideration will show us that no system of socialism is possible without such an abridgement of individual liberty as no class of men would for a moment tolerate. If society is to guarantee an individual a living, it is quite certain that it must prescribe some conditions. To say that every man shall be entitled to a living, and yet retain the right to seek work where he pleases and to prescribe

his own condition of labor, would be little short of an absurdity. What society now does is to offer him the best living it can, on the best conditions he can command, leaving him free to accept or decline them. Better than this it cannot do. When society prescribed the conditions to which he must submit, a rebellion would begin.
Principles of Political Economy (1886), Bk.V, Ch.VI, Sec.50: 525

taxation:

7 [I]t is not at all to the point to prove that any special form of taxation is bad: we may admit at the outset that every possible form is objectionable, without doing away with the necessity of making a 'choice of evils.'
'Principles of Taxation' (1880): 142; cf. Robert Owen 7, David Ricardo 11, Erasmus Smith 4

8 The first thing to be said of the income-tax is, that it is, in its aims, the most equitable tax of all. In fact, the very problem which the statesman has in view when he seeks to levy a tax is, to levy according to the wealth-producing power of the individual. This power is measured by the individual income, and thus a tax on income is really what should be, in most cases, aimed at. . . .

But when we consider the practical working of an income-tax, we find it to be the most unfair and demoralizing one that can be levied. It is one of the first requirements of a proper system of taxation that the amount which each man has to pay must be determined, so far as possible, independently of his own judgment. When the individual is called upon to communicate to the collector the data for assessing his taxes, a premium is offered for a failure to perform this duty. Every one knows that a not inconsiderable portion of the community will therefore fail to pay the tax. This knowledge will lead others not entirely devoid of conscience to fail also, because they know that if they make their returns they will really pay more than their share. The very fact that the tax requires a statement in which the individual is to be truthful at his own expense, renders it an unfair tax in the present state of society, and leads many who, in a better state of society, would scorn a delinquency in this respect, to consider that they are not bound to be any better than their neighbors. We may look forward to a stage in human progress in which every man will send the tax-collector semi-annually a check for the amount of his contribution, as determined by law, without the necessity of any assessment whatever. But we do nothing but mischief by assuming that we have reached this stage and acting accordingly.
'Principles of Taxation' (1880): 149–150

usury:

9 The usury law is a relic of barbarism, the continued existence of which in this age of civilization is extraordinary. It is in direct conflict with the plainest dictates, not only of natural right, but of common honesty. If A lends B money at any rate of interest which the latter is willing to give, it must be for the advantage of the latter to pay that rate of interest; else he would not be a borrower. Moreover, A does what he is under no obligation to do, and he does it on terms more favorable to B than any other person can be found to do it, for otherwise B would borrow from this other person. Moreover, the transaction does no harm to anybody else. It therefore fulfils all the conditions of a valid and rightful contract, and government does a great wrong in stepping in to release B from his obligation. It increases the absurdity of the law, that, if A had refused to assist his neighbor on any terms or conditions, had allowed him to suffer financial ruin or whatever other calamity might have been the result of his failure to obtain the money he wanted, the law would have had no punishment for A, who would likewise have saved his money. It is like a statute making it lawful for any one to see his neighbor drown, without moving a finger to save him, but providing that if he should pull him out, but charge him for his loss of time, he should be punished.
'The Let-alone Principle' (1870): 8

John Shield Nicholson (1850–1927)

economics and economists:

1 In my view one of the greatest merits of the orthodox economists was the careful distinction they drew between economic and other social sciences. They refused to merge it in

the misty regions of general sociology, and they excluded from its borders the rocks and quicksands, as well as the green pastures, of ethics and religion. This specialization, they argued, was necessary if any real advance was to be made beyond the expression of platitudes and sentiments. They allowed that in practical social problems there were in general other considerations besides the purely economic; but these they left to the jurist, the moralist, or the politician.

Address to the Economic Science and Statistics Section of the British Association (1893): 124

2 Political economy has a vast literature, and you will not find all the good concentrated in the last marginal increment; you must master the old before you can appreciate the new; a portion of truth just rediscovered for the hundredth time by some amateur is not of such value as a body of doctrines that have been developed for more than a century by economists of repute.

Address to the Economic Science and Statistics Section of the British Association (1893): 131

3 Let those who think they have discovered, unaided by the researches of others, some truly original idea in economics – let them calculate the probability that their discovery has not been anticipated. The recorded discussions of economic problems began with Plato and Aristotle, and the actual discussion began as soon as men could speak. The cave dwellers and the dwellers in lake villages had their problems of production and distribution and no doubt talked about them, and I have no doubt some of them expressed, though not in the lofty language now popular, the first approximations to the ideas of the uncultured socialists. And the chances are not only that those supposed original opinions or ideas have already been discovered – possibly a thousand times over – but also that some government or body of enthusiasts has already tried to put them in practice.

Inaugural Address to the Scottish Society of Economists (1897): 546–547

taxation:

4 [I]f there is one position that has been firmly established in theory and confirmed by the abundant experience of many nations, it is that excessive taxation is ruinous to a country.

Address to the Economic Science and Statistics Section of the British Association (1893): 130

Douglass Cecil North (1920–)

economic history:

1 If economists were to apply the same critical standards to economic history that they apply to the rest of the field of economics, very little of today's economic history would be recognized as high-quality research.

'The State of Economic History' (1965): 86

Sir Dudley North (1641–1691)

interest:

1 I do not believe, but the Usurer, according to the saying, will take half a Loaf, rather than no Bread: But I averr, that high Interest will bring Money out from Hoards, Plate, &c. into Trade, when low Interest will keep it back.

Discourses Upon Trade (1691), 'A Discourse Concerning the Abatement of Interest': 6

2 It is probable that when Laws restrain Interest of Money, below the Price, which the Reason of Trade settles, and Traders cannot (as we will suppose) evade the Law, or not without great difficulty, or hazard, and have not Credit to borrow at Legal Interest, to make, or increase their Stock; so much of Trade is lopt off; and there cannot be well a greater obstruction to diminish Trade then that would be. The consideration of all these Matters, makes out an universal Maxime, That as more Buyers than Sellers raiseth the price of a Commodity, so more Borrowers than Lenders, will raise Interest.

Discourses Upon Trade (1691), 'A Discourse Concerning the Abatement of Interest': 8

self-interest:

3 For whenever Men consult for the Publick Good, as for the advancement of Trade,

wherein all are concerned, they usually esteem the immediate Interest of their own to be the common Measure of Good and Evil. And there are many, who to gain a little in their own Trades, care not how much others suffer; and each Man strives, that all others may be forc'd, in their dealings, to act subserviently for his Profit, but under the covert of the Publick.

Discourses Upon Trade (1691), Preface: vii

4   The main spur to Trade, or rather to Industry and Ingenuity, is the exorbitant Appetites of Men, which they will take pains to gratifie, and so be disposed to work, when nothing else will incline them to it; for did Men content themselves with bare Necessaries, we should have a poor World.

Discourses Upon Trade (1691), 'A Discourse of Coyned Money': 14

trade:

5   [T]here can be no Trade unprofitable to the Publick; for if any prove so, men leave it off; and whereever the Traders thrive, the Publick, of which they are a part, thrives also.

Discourses Upon Trade (1691), Preface: viii

6   Trade is nothing else but a Commutation of Superfluities; for instance: I give of mine, what I can spare, for somewhat of yours, which I want, and you can spare.

Discourses Upon Trade (1691), 'A Discourse Concerning the Abatement of Interest': 2

wealth:

7   No Man is richer for having his Estate all in Money, Plate, &c. lying by him, but on the contrary, he is for that reason the poorer. That man is richest, whose Estate is in a growing condition, either in Land at Farm, Money at Interest, or Goods in Trade: If any man, out of an humour, should turn all his Estate into Money, and keep it dead, he would soon be sensible of Poverty growing upon him, whilst he is eating out of the quick stock.

Discourses Upon Trade (1691), 'A Discourse of Coyned Money': 11

O

Mancur Lloyd Olson (1932–1998)

taxation:

1 Almost any government is economically beneficial to its citizens, in that the law and order it provides is a prerequisite of all civilized economic activity. But despite the force of patriotism, the appeal of the national ideology, the bond of a common culture, and the indispensability of the system of law and order, no major state in modern history has been able to support itself through voluntary dues or contributions. Philanthropic contributions are not even a significant source of revenue for most countries. Taxes, *compulsory* payments by definition, are needed. Indeed, as the old saying indicates, their necessity is as certain as death itself.
   The Logic of Collective Action (1965), Ch.I, Sec.B: 13

Robert Owen (1771–1858)

government:

1 The end of government is to make the governed and the governors happy.
   That government, then, is the best, which in practice produces the greatest happiness to the greatest number; including those who govern, and those who obey.
   A New View of Society (1813–16), Fourth Essay: 62

inequality:

2 All parties who have occupied themselves in studying human nature, have uniformly come to the conclusion, that without equality of condition, there can be no permanent virtue or stability in society. . . .
   Manifesto of Robert Owen (1840; 5th edn); 'On Private Property': 361

3 There can be nothing deserving the name of virtue, of justice, or of real knowledge in society, as long as private property and inequality in rank and condition shall constitute component parts of it; but the present system of the world cannot be supported without private property and inequality of condition; consequently it is irrational to expect to find real virtue, justice, or knowledge, in the present system, in any part of the world.
   Manifesto of Robert Owen (1840; 5th edn); 'On Private Property': 364

poverty and the poor laws:

4 Benevolence says, that the destitute must not starve; and to this declaration political wisdom readily assents. Yet can that system be right, which compels the industrious, temperate, and comparatively virtuous, to support the ignorant, the idle, and comparatively vicious? Such, however, is the effect of the present British Poor Laws; for they publicly proclaim greater encouragement to idleness, ignorance, extravagance, and intemperance, than to industry and good conduct: and the evils which arise from a system so irrational are hourly experienced, and hourly increasing.
   A New View of Society (1813–16), Fourth Essay: 69

5 Either give the poor a rational and useful training, or mock not their ignorance, their poverty, and their misery, by merely instructing them to become conscious of the extent of the degradation under which they exist. And, therefore, in pity to suffering humanity, either keep the poor, if you now can, in the state of the most abject ignorance, as near as possible to animal life, or at once determine to form them into rational beings, into useful and effective members of the state.
   A New View of Society (1813–16), Fourth Essay: 75

6 Poverty and ignorance existing amidst an excess of wealth and exclusive privileges, will necessarily create envy, jealousy, and a desire to possess, by any means in their power, what their rich neighbours appear to enjoy in superfluity and to waste; and poverty and ignorance are sure to create

ignoble and inferior characters in the great majority who are trained under those unfavourable and demoralizing circumstances.

   Manifesto of Robert Owen (1840; 5th edn); 'On Private Property': 361

taxation:

7   Law and taxation, as these are now necessarily administered, are evils of the greatest magnitude. They are a curse to every part of society. *But while man remains individualized they must continue*, and both must unavoidably still increase in magnitude of evil.

   'Address Delivered at the City of London Tavern,' 21 August 1817: 201; cf. Simon Newcomb 7, David Ricardo 11, Erasmus Smith 4

P

Sir Robert Harry Inglis Palgrave
(1827–1919)

taxation:

1   The place which taxation takes either in ordinary history or in general literature, is disproportionately small to the influence exerted by a good or a bad system of finance over both the happiness and the habits of mankind. A force which, among other results, has excited dangerous revolts, has split and severed mighty empires, has brought about the decline of kingdoms, has moulded the forms of the dwelling-places, has modified the clothes, and at times even excited the diseases of nations, must be admitted to be amongst one of the most powerful, as well as one of the most all-pervading of the influences which sway the shifting currents of human life.
    'Taxes and Taxation' (1885): 382

2   Direct taxation, the readiest method of raising a revenue from a fiscal point of view, is open, among others, to one serious objection, by which the extreme severity of its application is fortunately checked. The method . . . is so ready and so easy to put in practice by those who have to raise the revenue, that the draughts on those who have to find the money are apt to be prolonged and redoubled till they will bear it no longer.
    'Taxes and Taxation' (1885): 385

3   [T]he imposing a tax does not create the power to bear it.
    'Taxes and Taxation' (1885): 410

Maffeo Pantaleoni (1857–1924)

economics and economists:

1   Economic science consists of the laws of wealth systematically deduced from the hypothesis that men are actuated exclusively by the desire to realise the fullest possible satisfaction of their wants, with the least possible individual sacrifice. This hypothesis is appropriately termed the hedonic premiss of economics, inasmuch as every economic theorem may be expressed in the form of the conclusion of a syllogism, having for its major or minor premiss the hedonic hypothesis, and for its other premiss some matter of fact, which may be a truth borrowed from some other science, or ascertained inductively by the economist himself.
    Pure Economics (1898), Part I, Ch.I

labor:

2   For the person engaged in it, labour is an evil, *i.e.* a negative commodity, and can only possess a *negative value*; the labour of *others*, on the contrary, is a direct, or an instrumental commodity, *i.e.* a positive commodity susceptible of various uses.
    Pure Economics (1898), Part III, Ch.V: 284

The Marquis Vilfredo Federico Damaso Pareto (1848–1923)

economics and economists:

1   Theories have only a very limited effect in the determination of man's actions; self-interest and passions play a much greater role, and some obliging theory is always found in the nick of time to justify them.
    Manual of Political Economy (1927), Ch.IX, Sec.20: 342

2   Let Q stand for the theory of political economy. A concrete situation O presents not only an economic aspect, e, but the further aspects c, g . . . of a sociological character. It is a mistake to include, as many have included, the sociological elements c, g . . . under political economy. The only sound conclusion to be drawn from the facts is that the economic theory which accounts for e must be supplemented (*supplemented*, not replaced) by other theories which account for c, g. . . .
    The Mind and Society (1935), Vol. I, Ch.I, §34: 20

3   Straightway one of those numberless unfortunates who are cursed with the mania for

talking about things they do not understand comes forward with the discovery – lo the wonders of genius! – that pure economics is not applied economics, and concludes, not that something must be added to pure economics if we are to understand concrete phenomena, but that pure economics must be replaced by his gabble. Alas, good soul, mathematical economics helps, at least, to a rough understanding of the effects of the interdependence of economic phenomena, while your gabble shows absolutely nothing!

And lo, another prodigious genius, who holds that because many economic phenomena depend on the human will, economics must be replaced by psychology. But why stop at psychology? Why not geography, or even astronomy? For after all the economic factor is influenced by seas, continents, rivers, and above all by the Sun, fecundator general of 'this fair family of flowers and trees and all earthly creatures.' Such prattle has been called *positive* economics, and for that our best gratitude, for it provokes a laugh, and laughter, good digestion!

The Mind and Society (1935), Vol. I, Ch.I, §§36, 37: 20–21

mathematics in economics:

4   To try to state economic phenomena in the shape of mathematical formulæ would be very much like the physicist trying to apply without modification his mathematical formula for the descent of falling bodies in a vacuum to the movement of a feather floating on the wind.

'The New Theories of Economics' (1897): 489

5   The problem of pure economics bears a striking likeness to that of rational mechanics. Now, in point of empirical fact, men have as yet not succeeded in treating the latter problem without the aid of mathematics. It therefore appears quite legitimate to appeal also to mathematics for assistance in the solution of the economic problem.

'The New Theories of Economics' (1897): 490

methodology:

6   Rational mechanics, when it reduces bodies to simple physical points, and pure economics, when it reduces real men to the *homo oeconomicus*, make use of completely similar abstractions, imposed by similar necessities.

Manual of Political Economy (1927), Ch.I, Sec.21: 12

7   One is grossly mistaken . . . when he accuses a person who studies economic actions – or *homo oeconomicus* – of neglecting, or even of scorning moral, religious, etc., actions – that is the *homo ethicus*, the *homo religiosus*, etc. –; it would be the same as saying that geometry neglects and scorns the chemical properties of substances, their physical properties, etc. The same error is committed when political economy is accused of not taking morality into account. It is like accusing a theory of the game of chess of not taking culinary art into account.

Manual of Political Economy (1927), Ch.I, Sec.24: 13

8   Disputes about the 'method' of political economy are useless. The goal of the science is to know the uniformities of phenomena. Consequently, it is necessary to employ all procedures and utilize all methods which lead us toward that goal. The good and bad methods are discovered by trial. One which leads us to the goal is good – at least as long as a better one has not been found. History is useful in that it extends the experience of the past into the present and supplies experiments which we are unable to make; hence the historical method is good. But the deductive method, or the inductive method, which is applied to present facts, is no less worthy. Where ordinary logic is adequate in deductions, we are satisfied with it; where it is not we replace it, without any qualms, by the mathematical method. In short, if an author prefers such or such a method, we will not quibble about it. We will simply ask him to show us the scientific laws, without caring too much about how he came to know them.

Manual of Political Economy (1927), Ch.I, Sec.35: 18–19

Simon Nelson Patten (1852–1922)

economic man:

1   The primitive man associates pleasure with the present, and retribution with the future. The economic man thinks of the future as

the place where he can realize the pleasure for which he is now preparing. The first man enjoys to-day and suffers to-morrow, while the other works to-day and enjoys tomorrow; his capital, the future goods of today, will then be his present goods, and ready for consumption. The imagination of the one will fill the future with horrid pictures of suffering which face him as a retribution of his past deeds; the imagination of the other creates an economic paradise where he will be exempt from present woes.
  'The Economic Causes of Moral Progress' (1892): 17–18

economics and economists:

2   There is probably no science that has so great a need of additional terms to denote new meanings as economics. During the past generation it has been thoroughly transformed, and new ideas by the score have been introduced; yet scarcely a new word, through which these ideas can be expressed, has found its way into general use. Every writer has been compelled to use old words with a new meaning, and thus endless confusion and needless misunderstandings are introduced into economic discussion. The slow progress towards agreement in economic theory is largely due to this cause, nor does there seem to be any hope of relief so long as the number of words are so few that they must be used to express a variety of meanings.
  'The Need of New Economic Terms' (1891): 372

3   The popular speaker and writer are quoted everywhere, and thus gain a name on which position and income depend. The theorist, however, finds few readers, and his contrasts when fresh and striking are appropriated by popular writers without credit.
  'The Making of Economic Literature' (1909): 3

4   Every economist should seek for journalistic experience and have his standing measured by his success. No economist is an economist until he has said to himself, 'I wish I were an editor.'
  'The Making of Economic Literature' (1909): 13

5   Economists are by education and tradition revolutionists. The Lord made the world in seven days; we want to remake it in one. So we join hands with anarchists, socialists, and other advocates of violent change, and cry ourselves hoarse in advancing their measures. Economics is like a South American republic; no one is satisfied unless there is a revolution once a decade.
  'The Making of Economic Literature' (1909): 13

6   It is a weakness of economics that the social ideas upon which its theories rest have been neglected.
  'The Background of Economic Theories' (1913): 689

Charles Sanders Peirce (1839–1914)
American philosopher

economics and economists:

1   [The nineteenth century] will be called, I guess, the Economical Century; for political economy has more direct relations with all the branches of its activity than has any other science. Well, political economy has its formula of redemption, too. It is this: Intelligence in the service of greed ensures the justest prices, the fairest contracts, the most enlightened conduct of all the dealings between men, and leads to the *summum bonum*, food in plenty and perfect comfort. Food for whom? Why, for the greedy master of intelligence. I do not mean to say that this is one of the legitimate conclusions of political economy, the scientific character of which I fully acknowledge. But the study of doctrines, themselves true, will often temporarily encourage generalisations extremely false, as the study of physics has encouraged necessitarianism. What I say, then, is that the great attention paid to economical questions during our century has induced an exaggeration of the beneficial effects of greed and of the unfortunate results of sentiment, until there has resulted a philosophy which comes unwittingly to this, that greed is the great agent in the elevation of the human race and in the evolution of the universe.
  'Evolutionary Love' (1893): 178–179

mathematics in economics:

2   The idea that there can be any vigorous and productive thought upon any great subject without reasoning like that of the differential calculus is a futile and pernicious idea. Some newspapers maintain that all doctrines involving such reasoning ought to be struck out of political economy because that science is of no service unless everybody, or the great majority of voters, individually comprehend it and assent to its reasonings. I do not observe that it is a fact that voters are such asses as to insist upon thinking they personally comprehend the effects of tariff-laws, etc. But whether they be so or not, it is certain that the ratio of the circumference to the diameter is 3.14159265358979323846264338327950288 41971694 . . . whether the reasoning that proves it is hard or easy. That I feel sure of, although I personally have not verified the above figures; and if I had, I should not feel perceptibly more sure of the matter than I am. Certainly, if on attempting to verify them I got a slightly different result, I should feel pretty sure it was I who had committed an error. But whether people be wise or foolish, it remains that there is no possible way of establishing the true doctrines of political economy except by reasonings about *limits*, that is, reasoning essentially the same as that of the differential calculus.
    'The Logic of Quantity' (1893), §5: 86

Edith Tilton Penrose (1914–1996)

economics and economists:

1   The appeal of . . . biological analogies to the social scientist plainly springs from a persistent yearning to discover 'laws' that determine the outcome of human actions, probably because the discovery of such laws would rid the social sciences of the uncertainties and complexities that arise from the apparent 'free will' of man and would endow them with that more reliable power of prediction which for some is the essence of 'science.'
    'Biological Analogies in the Theory of the Firm' (1952): 818

Mark Perlman (1923–)

economics and economists:

1   There is no doubt in my mind that if Molière were alive today and were aware of what is going on in economics that he would observe that the language of abstraction is the passion of the trained economist.
    Editor's Note, *Journal of Economic Literature* (1981): 2

2   [Abstraction] tends to make the expression of thoughts terse. If a picture is supposed to replace a thousand words, it is quite likely that five good difference equations could replace a thousand pictures.
    Editor's Note, *Journal of Economic Literature* (1981): 2

3   The body of economic knowledge as we know it, I propose, should be imagined as a tapestry, or, better yet, considering our propensity for wiping our feet on the past, as an oriental rug. It is a rug woven by different generations of thinkers and doers, each working within the framework of the facts and ideas of his or her time, and each hoping that from observation and/or excogitation some immutables could be distilled and put to permanent use.
    'The Fabric of Economics and the Golden Threads of G. L. S. Shackle' (1990): 9

4   For economists, the theory of demand should not 'start' with an examination of what transactions reveal about market-place agreements; rather, it actually starts with choices within the mind between a spectrum of imagined possibilities. Or, to put the matter in its harshest form, settling for the final step (revealed preference) just because it is 'quantitatively' measurable is akin to looking for one's keys not where one suspects they have fallen (in the middle of a block in a dark street), but looking for them under the nearest lamp-post because there one can easily see. Relying upon revealed preference may be settling for unnecessarily cold potatoes.
    'The Fabric of Economics and the Golden Threads of G. L. S. Shackle' (1990): 17

markets:

5   Economists sell themselves short intellectually, and underestimate their analytical abilities, if all they see in an economic market is a venue for exchange. The market serves a variety of other, typically neglected functions, not all of which are economic, a great deal being moral, social and political functions.
    'Hayek, the Purpose of the Market, and American Economic Institutionalism' (1997): 222

Selig Perlman (1888–1959)

class warfare:

1   No one who knows the American business class will even dream that it would under any circumstances surrender to a revolution perpetrated by a minority, or that it would wait for foreign intervention before starting hostilities. A Bolshevist *coup d'état* in America would mean a civil war to a bitter end, and a war in which the numerous class of farmers would join the capitalists in the defense of the institution of private property.
    A History of Trade Unionism in the United States (1923), Ch.15: 302

trade unionism:

2   Withal, then, trade unionism, despite an occasional revolutionary facet and despite a revolutionary clamor especially on its fringes, is a conservative social force. Trade unionism seems to have the same moderating effect upon society as a wide diffusion of private property. In fact the gains of trade unionism are to the worker on a par with private property to its owner.
    A History of Trade Unionism in the United States (1923), Ch.15: 303; cf. Henry C. Simons 7

Sir William Petty (1623–1687)

inflation:

1   Sometimes it hath hapned, that States (I know not by what raw advice) have raised or embased their money, hoping thereby, as it were, to multiply it, and make it pass for more then it did before; that is, to purchase more commodity or labour with it: All which indeed and in truth, amounts to no more then a Tax, upon such People unto whom the State is indebted, or a defalkation of what is due; as also the like burthen upon all that live upon Pensions, established Rents, Annuities, Fees, Gratuities, &c.
    A Treatise of Taxes and Contributions (1662), Ch.XIV: 84

2   [R]aising or embasing of Moneys is a very pittiful and unequal way of Taxing the people; and 'tis a sign that the State sinketh, which catcheth hold on such Weeds as are accompanied with the dishonour of impressing a Princes Effigies to justifie Adulterate Commodities, and the breach of Publick Faith, such as is the calling a thing what it really is not.
    A Treatise of Taxes and Contributions (1662), Ch.XIV: 90–91

labor:

3   [B]etter to burn a thousand mens labours for a time, then to let those thousand men by non-employment lose their faculty of labouring.
    A Treatise of Taxes and Contributions (1662), Ch.VI: 60

lotteries:

4   Now in the way of Lottery men do also tax themselves in the general, though out of hopes of Advantage in particular: A Lottery therefore is properly a Tax upon unfortunate self conceited fools; men that have good opinion of their own luckiness, or that have believed some Fortune-teller or Astrologer, who had promised them great success about the time and place of the Lottery, lying Southwest perhaps from the place where the destiny was read.
    A Treatise of Taxes and Contributions (1662), Ch.VIII: 64

methodology:

5   The Method I take to do this, is not yet very usual; for instead of using only comparative and superlative Words, and intellectual Arguments, I have taken the course (as a Specimen of the Political Arithmetick I have long aimed at) to express my self in Terms of *Number*, *Weight*, or *Measure*; to use only

Arguments of Sense, and to consider only such Causes, as have visible Foundations in Nature; leaving those that depend upon the mutable Minds, Opinions, Appetites, and Passions of particular Men, to the Consideration of others: Really professing my self as unable to speak satisfactorily upon those Grounds (if they may be call'd Grounds), as to foretel the cast of a Dye; to play well at Tennis, Billiards, or Bowles, (without long practice,) by virtue of the most elaborate Conceptions that ever have been written *De Projectilibus & Missilibus*, or of the Angles of Incidence and Reflection.
Political Arithmetick (1676), Preface: 244

money:

6   For Money is but the Fat of the Body-politick, whereof too much doth as often hinder its Agility, as too little makes it sick.
Verbum Sapienti (1664), Ch.V: 113

monopoly:

7   Monopoly (as the word signifies) is the sole selling power, which whosoever hath can vend the commodity whereupon he hath this power, either qualified as himself pleases, or at what price he pleaseth, or both, within the limits of his Commission.
A Treatise of Taxes and Contributions (1662), Ch.XI: 74

taxation:

8   Now that which angers men most, is to be taxed above their Neighbours.
A Treatise of Taxes and Contributions (1662), Ch.III: 32

9   When the people are weary of any one sort of Tax, presently some Projector propounds another, and gets himself audience, by affirming he can propound a way how all the publick charge may be born without the way that is. As for example, if a Land-tax be the present distasted way, and the people weary of it, then he offers to do the business without such a Land-tax, and propound either a Poll-money, Excize, or the institution of some new Office or Monopoly; and hereby draws some or other to hearken to him; which is readily enough done by those who are not in the places of profit relating to the way of Levies in use, but hope to make themselves Offices in the new Institution.
A Treatise of Taxes and Contributions (1662), Ch.XIII: 82

10 It is generally allowed by all, that men should contribute to the Publick Charge but according to the share and interest they have in the Publick Peace; that is, according to their Estates or Riches. . . .
A Treatise of Taxes and Contributions (1662), Ch.XV: 91

usury:

11 What reason there is for taking or giving Interest or Usury for any thing which we may certainly have again whensoever we call for it, I see not; nor why Usury should be scrupled, where money or other necessaries valued by it, is lent to be paid at such a time and place as the Borrower chuseth, so as the Lender cannot have his money paid him back where and when himself pleaseth, I also see not. Wherefore when a man giveth out his money upon condition that he may not demand it back until a certain time to come, whatsoever his own necessities shall be in the mean time, he certainly may take a compensation for this inconvenience which he admits against himself: And this allowance is that we commonly call Usury.
A Treatise of Taxes and Contributions (1662), Ch.V: 47

Edmund S. Phelps (1933–)

taxation:

1   Cicero said that man plants trees for future generations. Had he rather remarked that man levies taxes for future generations, he would have founded fiscal theory (instead of capital theory).
'Justice in the Theory of Public Finance' (1979), Sec.I: 681

2   To tax at all the highest earner's last dollar of earnings is to impose a spiteful penalty on that earner at no gain, at even a loss, of tax revenue.
'Justice in the Theory of Public Finance' (1979), Sec.II: 689

Willard Phillips (1784–1873)

trade:

1 The free-trade creed assumes and asserts, that, as to matters of industry and trade, the whole world is one community, and that legislation and the administration of law ought to proceed upon this supposition of universal fraternity; and that, whenever any country acts upon the notion that its commercial or industrial interest is in competition with that of any other, and endeavors to favor and protect its own, it commits a great blunder. This doctrine is necessarily included in the comprehensive, negative, one idea of '*let alone.*' We are only to study 'the greater increase of the aggregate produce of the world.' What avails addressing arguments to persons who, in practical affairs of business, and, in fact, of life and death to poor laborers, talk about '*increasing the aggregate produce of the world*?' This theory of national communism is inculcated with as solemn gravity and confidence as religious enthusiasts assume, when they announce the millennium.
Propositions Concerning Protection and Free Trade (1850), Proposition XI: 25

Arthur Cecil Pigou (1877–1959)

economic welfare:

1 The goal sought is to make more easy practical measures to promote welfare – practical measures which statesmen may build upon the work of the economist, just as Marconi, the inventor, built upon the discoveries of Hertz. Welfare, however, is a thing of very wide range. There is no need here to enter upon a general discussion of its content. It will be sufficient to lay down more or less dogmatically two propositions; first, that welfare includes states of consciousness only, and not material things; secondly, that welfare can be brought under the category of greater and less. A general investigation of all the various groups of causes by which welfare thus conceived may be affected would constitute a task so enormous and complicated as to be quite impracticable. It is, therefore, necessary to limit our subject-matter. In doing this we are naturally attracted towards that portion of the field in which the methods of science seem likely to work at best advantage. This they can clearly do when there is present something measurable on which analytical machinery can get a firm grip. The one obvious instrument of measurement available in social life is money. Hence, the range of our inquiry becomes restricted to that part of social welfare that can be brought directly or indirectly into relation with the measuring-rod of money.
The Economics of Welfare (1920), Part I, Ch.I, §5: 10–11

economics and economists:

2 If it were not for the hope that a scientific study of men's social actions may lead, not necessarily directly or immediately, but at some time and in some way, to practical results in social improvement, not a few students of these actions would regard the time devoted to their study as time misspent. That is true of all social sciences, but especially true of Economics. For Economics 'is a study of mankind in the ordinary business of life'; and it is not in the ordinary business of life that mankind is most interesting or inspiring.
The Economics of Welfare (1920), Part I, Ch.I, §1: 4; cf. Alfred Marshall 8, 11

3 Wonder, Carlyle declared, is the beginning of philosophy. It is not wonder, but rather the social enthusiasm which revolts from the sordidness of mean streets and the joylessness of withered lives, that is the beginning of economic science.
The Economics of Welfare (1920), Part I, Ch.I, §1: 5

minimum wage:

4 The establishment of a national minimum time-wage would really accomplish very little more than could be accomplished without it. If there is not a well-organised system of care for the poor, there is no reason to suppose that any of the persons expelled from private industry by the operation of the minimum will be trained and rehabilitated; and, even if there is such a system, only those persons will come in contact with it and so secure its benefit who do not belong to families able and willing to support them without State help. But, if there were no

national minimum, most of the people, whom the minimum expels from private industry, would, since the minimum itself will presumably be a low one based on a consideration of what is essential for subsistence, be earning so little that they would be nearly sure, in one way or another, to come into contact with the State organisation for looking after poor persons. This organisation, therefore, will have much the same opportunity for withdrawing from private industry those suitable for training or those needing treatment for sickness as it would have if there were no national minimum wage.
The Economics of Welfare (1920), Part III, Ch.XVII, §5: 557

taxation:

5 Here it is enough to observe generally that the expectation of indirect taxes tends to divert resources from more to less productive channels, and the expectation of direct taxes to lessen the inducement people have to work and save.
The Economics of Welfare (1920), Part V, Ch.VIII, §5: 751

6 Economic advance in the past has owed a great deal to adventurous enterprise, where people have been prepared to take risks for the sake of a possible large success rather than play for safety. Special State levies from large incomes by means, for example, of a steeply graduated income tax, hits successful and unsuccessful adventurers together much more hardly than players for safety, and so discourages daring enterprise. There is a danger here that ought not to be ignored.
Income: An Introduction to Economics (1948), Ch.VII: 116

Pope Pius XI (1857–1939) (Ambrogio Damiano Achille Ratti)

socialism:

1 If Socialism, like all errors, contains some truth (which, moreover, the Supreme Pontiffs have never denied), it is based nevertheless on a theory of human society peculiar to itself and irreconcilable with true Christianity. Religious socialism, Christian socialism, are contradictory terms; no one can be at the same time a good Catholic and a true socialist.
Quadragesimo Anno (15 May 1931), Sec.120

Karl Polanyi (1886–1964)

division of labor:

1 Division of labor, a phenomenon as old as society, springs from differences inherent in the facts of sex, geography, and individual endowment; and the alleged propensity of man to barter, truck, and exchange is almost entirely apocryphal.
The Great Transformation (1944), Part II, Ch.4: 44; cf. Adam Smith 7

socialism:

2 Socialism is, essentially, the tendency inherent in an industrial civilization to transcend the self-regulating market by consciously subordinating it to a democratic society. It is the solution natural to the industrial workers who see no reason why production should not be regulated directly and why markets should be more than a useful but subordinate trait in a free society.
The Great Transformation (1944), Part III, Ch.19: 234

Michael Polanyi (1891–1976)

planning:

1 General planning is wholesale destruction of freedom; cultural planning would be the end of all inspired enquiry, of every creative effort, and planned economy would make life into something between a universal monastery and a forced labour camp. Our aim must be not to destroy the mechanism of liberty but to amend it by renewing the rules and principles on which individuals are called upon to act. Common sense will not admit that the only alternative to unemployment, to unjust gains, and to undeserved poverty is to bind ourselves hand and foot, to gag our mouths and blindfold our eyes. But common sense will not be heard until we rid ourselves of magic beliefs. We must realize that planning, as applied to social affairs, does not in general mean

order and intelligent foresight; and at the same time we have to reduce the market in our minds to its proper position of an element of social machinery, subordinate to our will, so long as it is used in conformity with its inherent mechanism.
  'Collectivist Planning' (1940): 60

2 Consider how ingeniously the knobs of each potato fit into the hollows of a neighbour. Weeks of careful planning by a team of engineers equipped with a complete set of cross-sections for each potato would not reduce the total volume filled by the potatoes in the sack so effectively as a good shaking and a few kicks will do.
  'Towards a Theory of Conspicuous Consumption' (1960): 91

Richard Allen Posner (1939–)
American legal scholar, jurist

economics and economists:

1 One cannot say that economics is what economists do, because many noneconomists do economics.
  'The Law and Economics Movement' (1987): 1

2 Economics does not have a predestined mission to dispel all the mysteries of the market.
  'The Law and Economics Movement' (1987): 2

Bonamy Price (1807–1888)

economics and economists:

1 Every science in turn has cruelly suffered from the loose habit of attaching many ill-digested, and often conflicting, senses to the same word; but none, I believe, has been so great a victim in this respect as political economy. It borrows its language from common life; it is compelled, as a science, to assign to it a sharply determined meaning; but it is most difficult to impress that meaning on the common understanding of men. The every-day world uses language after its own fashion, with little reflection and no science; it is ever transferring the same term to different objects, often from a fancied similarity which has no foundation in fact. Political economy is thus exposed to perpetual misinterpretation. The mischief, however, would be comparatively slight if it were confined to its hearers; but it spreads even to its teachers, and the ravages which it then commits are disastrous. The loose expressions of common talk are made the foundation of scientific exposition; they are taken as the primary elements of the science; and the inaccuracy they involve becomes the more mischievous precisely in proportion as the deductions are drawn with severe and skilful logic. It thus behoves the political economist, beyond all other men of science, to be jealous of the language which he is forced to procure from common life, and to be careful of the exact nature of the first principles which he derives from it.
  'What Is Money? And Has It Any Effect on the Rate of Discount?' (1870): 236–237

minimum wage:

2 If Trade-Union orators were challenged to explain to their followers what they propose to do with the workmen for whom no work at the fixed rate of wages can be found, and what measures they mean to adopt to prevent the continuance of such an excess of labourers, the pleasant dream of a minimum of wages would speedily vanish from their speech.
  'Trade-Unions' (1870), Part II: 746

protectionism:

3 The loss entailed by protection must not be measured solely by the difference of price of the article protected; it greatly exceeds that limit. ... Protection cripples industry on every side, for the sake of the relatively small advantage which it confers on the protected trades. The diminution of the national wealth which is its direct and necessary offspring impedes the progress of the nation; and besides this positive and immediate loss, it renders many operations of industry, with their attendant profits, impossible. Free trade not only bestows on the nation the products of many additional hours of work, without any increase of time, or effort, or labour, or cost of maintenance, but also enables the intelligence and the energy of the whole people to apply their industry to

those fields in which the largest returns may be obtained. Free trade gives more wealth, and infinitely more profit to the application of that wealth, as capital for the support of industry. The crippling effect of protection must never be left out of view for an instant, in the consideration of this most national question.
'Free Trade and Reciprocity' (1870): 330

trade unions:

4   Men of great intellectual ability have tried to grapple with the phenomenon [of trade unions]; economical and social science has brought its light to bear on the examination of its character; and still no final judgment has been pronounced on the great question, whether its existence is compatible with the welfare of society.
'Trade-Unions' (1870), Part I: 554

5   The Unions appeal to political economy. They profess to act in obedience to its laws and to seek the execution of its suggestions. They put forward in their defence a body of doctrine, and thereby raise an issue of which economical science must be the judge. ... The Unions themselves, by the profession of certain doctrines, admit the necessity of establishing the position of masters and men on scientific grounds.
'Trade-Unions' (1870), Part II: 744

Pierre-Joseph Proudhon
(1809–1864)

communism:

1   The inconveniences of communism are so obvious that its critics never had to employ much eloquence to arouse disgust with it.
What Is Property? (1840), Ch.Five, Second Part, Sec.2: 195

2   Communism is inequality, but in a sense opposite to that of property. Property is the exploitation of the weak by the strong; communism is the exploitation of the strong by the weak. In property the inequality of conditions is the result of force, under whatever name it is disguised – physical and mental force, force of events, chance, fortune, force of accumulated property, etc. In communism the inequality comes from making mediocrity of talent and achievement equal to excellence. This damaging equation repels conscience and causes merit to complain; for while it may be the duty of the strong to aid the weak, they prefer to do it out of generosity, and they never will endure a comparison. Let them be equal in conditions of labour and wages, equal opportunities of labour and equal in wages, but never let a mental suspicion of infidelity to the common task arouse their jealousy.
    Communism is oppression and slavery. Man is very willing to submit to the law of duty, to serve his country, and to oblige his friends; but he wants to labour how, when, and as much as he pleases. He wants to dispose of his own time, to be ruled only by necessity, to choose his friendships, his recreations, and his discipline; to serve as a result of reason, not command, and to sacrifice himself through egoism, not slavish obligation. Communism is essentially opposed to the free exercise of our faculties, noblest inclinations, and deepest feelings. Any plan that could be devised for reconciling it with the demands of individual reason and free will would result only in changing the thing itself while preserving the name. Now, if we seek the truth in good faith, we must avoid such quibbles over words.
What Is Property? (1840), Ch.Five, Second Part, Sec.2: 197

competition:

3   Competition is the vital force which animates the collective being: to destroy it, if such a supposition were possible, would be to kill society.
System of Economical Contradictions: Or, the Philosophy of Misery (1888), Ch.6

economics and economists:

4   Political economy, at the point to which it has now arrived, resembles ontology: discussing effects and causes, it knows nothing, explains nothing, concludes nothing. What people adorn with the name of economic laws are reduced to a few trifling generalities, to which the economists thought to give an appearance of depth by clothing them in fancy jargon. As for the attempts made by the economists to solve social problems, all that can be said of them

is that if their lucubrations sometimes show good sense, they immediately fall back into absurdity.
What Is Property? (1840), Ch.Three, Sec.7: 106

monopoly:

5   Monopoly is at bottom simply the autocracy of man over himself: it is the dictatorial right accorded by nature to every producer of using his faculties as he pleases, of giving free play to his thought in whatever direction it prefers, of speculating, in such specialty as he may please to choose, with all the power of his resources, of disposing sovereignly of the instruments which he has created and of the capital accumulated by his economy for any enterprise the risks of which he may see fit to accept on the express condition of enjoying alone the fruits of his discovery and the profits of his venture.
System of Economical Contradictions: Or, the Philosophy of Misery (1888), Ch.6

property:

6   Property is theft!
What Is Property? (1840), Ch.One: 13

R

John Rae (1796–1872)

government regulation:

1 [E]very restraint is a hindrance to a man's acquiring wealth, and he always gains by evading it. As, therefore, all interference on the part of the legislator, operates as a restraint, he never in any case ought to interfere.
New Principles on the Subject of Political Economy (1834), Book I, Introduction: 7

2 The community adds to its wealth by creating wealth, and if we understand by the legislator the power acting for the community, it seems not absurd or unreasonable that he should direct part of the energies of the community towards the furtherance of this power of invention, this necessary element in the production of the wealth of nations.
New Principles on the Subject of Political Economy (1834), Book I, Ch.I: 15

invention:

3 Invention is the only power on earth, that can be said to create.
New Principles on the Subject of Political Economy (1834), Book I, Ch.I: 15

motivations:

4 The ends which individuals and nations pursue, are different. The object of the one is to acquire, of the other to create. . . . Though each member of a community may be desirous of the good of all, yet in gaining wealth, as he seeks only his own good, and as he may gain it by acquiring a portion of the wealth already in existence, it follows not that he creates wealth.
New Principles on the Subject of Political Economy (1834), Book I, Ch.I: 15

Ayn Rand (*born* Alice Rosenbaum) (1905–1982)

capitalism:

1 Laissez-faire capitalism is the only social system based on the recognition of individual rights and, therefore, the only system that bans force from social relationships. By the nature of its basic principles and interests, it is the only system fundamentally opposed to war.
'The Roots of War' (1966): 3

2 No social system can stand for long without a moral base. Project a magnificent skyscraper being built on quicksands: while men are struggling upward to add the hundredth and two-hundredth stories, the tenth and twentieth are vanishing, sucked under by the muck. That is the history of capitalism, of its swaying, tottering attempt to stand erect on the foundation of the altruist morality.
'Requiem for Man' (1967), Part III: 4

government:

3 The role of government in a private enterprise system is that of a policeman who protects man's individual rights (including property rights) by protecting men from physical force; in a free economy, the government does not control, regulate, coerce or interfere with men's economic activities.
'The New Fascism: Rule by Consensus,' Part II (1965): 23

wealth distribution:

4 It is morally obscene to regard wealth as an anonymous, tribal product and to talk about 'redistributing' it. The view that wealth is the result of some undifferentiated, collective process, that we all did something and it's impossible to tell who did what, therefore some sort of equalitarian 'distribution' is necessary – might have been appropriate in a primordial jungle with a savage horde moving boulders by crude physical labor (though even there someone had to initiate and organize the moving). To hold that view in an industrial society – where individual achievements are a matter of public record – is so crass an evasion that even to give it the benefit of the doubt is an obscenity.
'What Is Capitalism?' (1965): 30

Albert Everett Rees (1921–)

economics and economists:

1 Economists do a good job of teaching the agreed parts of economic theory to college students, particularly those who take more than one course in economics, although students who pass their final exams may later forget what they have learned. However, economists do a very bad job of communicating the principles on which we agree to the general public through trade books, newspapers, and television.
'The Marketplace of Economic Ideas' (1986): 138

2 Agreement among economists is simply not news.
'The Marketplace of Economic Ideas' (1986): 139

Nicholas Rescher (1928–)
American philosopher

Pareto principle:

1 There is little that economists of different schools and persuasions agree on almost universally, but the Pareto principle seems to be among the few exceptions to this rule. Virtually without exception, economists, decision theorists, social-choice theoreticians, and the like, are inclined to espouse it as a well-nigh self-evident truth. It is viewed as so secure in itself as to qualify as a touchstone by which the adequacy of social-choice mechanisms can be assessed. Accordingly, it has become established dogma in the field that, when a Pareto optimal alternative exists, then only a social decision process that leads to this alternative can possibly qualify as 'rational' (appropriate, justified, or what have you).
Unpopular Essays on Technological Progress (1980), Ch.6: 69–70

David Ricardo (1772–1823)

capitalists:

1 A capitalist, in seeking profitable employment for his funds, will naturally take into consideration all the advantages which one occupation possesses over another. He may therefore be willing to forego a part of his money profit, in consideration of the security, cleanliness, ease, or any other real or fancied advantage which one employment may possess over another.
On the Principles of Political Economy and Taxation (1821; 3rd edn), Ch.IV: 90

comparative advantage:

2 Under a system of perfectly free commerce, each country naturally devotes its capital and labour to such employments as are most beneficial to each. This pursuit of individual advantage is admirably connected with the universal good of the whole. By stimulating industry, by rewarding ingenuity, and by using most efficaciously the peculiar powers bestowed by nature, it distributes labour most effectively and most economically: while, by increasing the general mass of productions, it diffuses general benefit, and binds together by one common tie of interest and intercourse, the universal society of nations throughout the civilized world. It is this principle which determines that wine shall be made in France and Portugal, that corn shall be grown in America and Poland, and that hardware and other goods shall be manufactured in England.
On the Principles of Political Economy and Taxation (1821; 3rd edn), Ch.VII: 133–134

economics and economists:

3 Political Economy, when the simple principles of it are once understood, is only useful, as it directs Governments to right measures in taxation.
Letter to Hutches Trower (12 November 1819)

4 Political Economy you think is an enquiry into the nature and causes of wealth – I think it should rather be called an enquiry into the laws which determine the division of the produce of industry amongst the classes who concur in its formation.
Letter to T.R. Malthus (9 October 1820)

poverty and the poor laws:

5 I would gladly compound for such a change in the Poor Laws as should restore them to what appears to have been the original

intention in framing them; namely, the relieving only the aged and infirm and under some circumstances, children. Any change would be an improvement which had not a tendency to increase the evil which it proposes to remedy.

Letter to Hutches Trower (26 January 1818)

6 Like all other contracts, wages should be left to the fair and free competition of the market, and should never be controlled by the interference of the legislature.

The clear and direct tendency of the poor laws, is in direct opposition to these obvious principles: it is not, as the legislature benevolently intended, to amend the condition of the poor, but to deteriorate the condition of both poor and rich; instead of making the poor rich, they are calculated to make the rich poor; and whilst the present laws are in force, it is quite in the natural order of things that the fund for the maintenance of the poor should progressively increase, till it has absorbed all the net revenue of the country, or at least so much of it as the state shall leave to us, after satisfying its own never failing demands for the public expenditure.

On the Principles of Political Economy and Taxation (1821; 3rd edn), Ch.V: 105–106

7 It is a truth which admits not a doubt, that the comforts and well-being of the poor cannot be permanently secured without some regard on their part, or some effort on the part of the legislature, to regulate the increase of their numbers, and to render less frequent among them early and improvident marriages. The operation of the system of poor laws has been directly contrary to this. They have rendered restraint superfluous, and have invited imprudence, by offering it a portion of the wages of prudence and industry.

The nature of the evil points out the remedy. By gradually contracting the sphere of the poor laws; by impressing on the poor the value of independence, by teaching them that they must look not to systematic or casual charity, but to their own exertions for support, that prudence and forethought are neither unnecessary nor unprofitable virtues, we shall by degrees approach a sounder and more healthful state.

On the Principles of Political Economy and Taxation (1821; 3rd edn), Ch.V: 106–107

8 If by law every human being wanting support could be sure to obtain it, and obtain it in such a degree as to make life tolerably comfortable, theory would lead us to expect that all other taxes together would be light compared with the single one of poor rates. The principle of gravitation is not more certain than the tendency of such laws to change wealth and power into misery and weakness; to call away the exertions of labour from every object, except that of providing mere subsistence; to confound all intellectual distinction; to busy the mind continually in supplying the body's wants; until at last all classes should be infected with the plague of universal poverty.

On the Principles of Political Economy and Taxation (1821; 3rd edn), Ch.V: 108

taxation:

9 There are no taxes which have not a tendency to lessen the power to accumulate. All taxes must either fall on capital or revenue. If they encroach on capital, they must proportionably diminish that fund by whose extent the extent of the productive industry of the country must always be regulated; and if they fall on revenue, they must either lessen accumulation, or force the contributors to save the amount of the tax, by making a corresponding diminution of their former unproductive consumption of the necessaries and luxuries of life. Some taxes will produce these effects in a much greater degree than others; but the great evil of taxation is to be found, not so much in any selection of its objects, as in the general amount of its effects taken collectively.

On the Principles of Political Economy and Taxation (1821; 3rd edn), Ch.VIII: 152

10 The desire which every man has to keep his station in life, and to maintain his wealth at the height which it has once attained, occasions most taxes, whether laid on capital or on income, to be paid from income; and therefore as taxation proceeds, or as government

increases its expenditure, the annual enjoyments of the people must be diminished, unless they are enabled proportionally to increase their capitals and income. It should be the policy of governments to encourage a disposition to do this in the people, and never to lay such taxes as will inevitably fall on capital; since by so doing, they impair the funds for the maintenance of labour, and thereby diminish the future production of the country.
On the Principles of Political Economy and Taxation (1821; 3rd edn), Ch.VIII: 153

11 Taxation under every form presents but a choice of evils; if it do not act on profit, or other sources of income, it must act on expenditure; and provided the burthen be equally borne, and do not repress reproduction, it is indifferent on which it is laid. Taxes on production, or on the profits of stock, whether applied immediately to profits, or indirectly, by taxing the land or its produce, have this advantage over other taxes; that provided all other income be taxed, no class of the community can escape them, and each contributes according to his means.
On the Principles of Political Economy and Taxation (1821; 3rd edn), Ch.IX: 167; cf. Simon Newcomb 7, Robert Owen 7, Erasmus Smith 4

12 It is not to be inferred from this view of tithes, and taxes on the land and its produce, that they do not discourage cultivation. Every thing which raises the exchangeable value of commodities of any kind, which are in very general demand, tends to discourage both cultivation and production; but this is an evil inseparable from all taxation....
On the Principles of Political Economy and Taxation (1821; 3rd edn), Ch.XII: 184–185

13 Every new tax becomes a new charge on production, and raises natural price. A portion of the labour of the country which was before at the disposal of the contributor to the tax, is placed at the disposal of the State, and cannot therefore be employed productively. This portion may become so large, that sufficient surplus may not be left to stimulate the exertions of those who usually augment by their savings the capital of the State. Taxation has happily never yet in any free country been carried so far as constantly from year to year to diminish its capital. Such a state of taxation could not be long endured; or if endured, it would be constantly absorbing so much of the annual produce of the country as to occasion the most extensive scene of misery, famine, and depopulation.
On the Principles of Political Economy and Taxation (1821; 3rd edn), Ch.XII: 185

14 There are no circumstances under which taxation does not abridge the enjoyments of those on whom the taxes ultimately fall, and no means by which those enjoyments can again be extended, but the accumulation of new revenue.
On the Principles of Political Economy and Taxation (1821; 3rd edn), Ch.XVI: 239

Lionel Charles Robbins, Baron Robbins of Clare Market
(1898–1984)

economics and economists:

1 The rational scrutiny of economic phenomena is an inquiry so repellent to many that there are always those who will seize upon the least dispute among economists as a sign that economic science as a whole is worthless, and that economists themselves cannot agree on the simplest propositions of their science. I do not wish to give any countenance to that attitude, and I do not know any economist who would.
'The Present Position of Economic Science' (1930), Sec.II: 15

2 The sort of Economics which the Press and the public would like is an Economics which is bound either to be wrong or to be misapprehended.
'The Present Position of Economic Science' (1930), Sec.V: 23–24

3 That the object of economics is to understand reality is not a proposition which is likely to be questioned by any economist. Indeed, if this had not actually been questioned by

others, an apology would be necessary for stating anything so obvious.
> 'Live and Dead Issues in the Methodology of Economics' (1938), Sec.II: 342

government:

4   The creation of state-aided restriction is the creation of privilege. It is the creation of closed groups, the creation of a syndicalist society.
> *The Economic Basis of Class Conflict* (1939), Part I, Ch.II, Sec.8: 43

methodology:

5   The passive observation of facts, unassisted by theoretical hypothesis, must of necessity be sterile. It is not the scientist, it is the village idiot who is content to approach the world in this manner.
> 'The Present Position of Economic Science' (1930), Sec.IV: 20–21

taxation:

6   We may wish to increase taxation to *maintain* expenditure. In such a case there is room for much difference of opinion concerning the right taxes to choose. But to increase taxation to *increase* expenditure is not likely to be recommended by many as a cure for the pessimism of investors.
> *The Economic Basis of Class Conflict* (1939), Part II, Ch.I, Sec.2: 216

Sir Dennis Holme Robertson
(1890–1963)

econometrics:

1   As soon as I could safely toddle
My parents handed me a Model.
My brisk and energetic pater
Provided the accelerator.
My mother, with her kindly gumption,
The function guiding my consumption;
And every week I had from her
A lovely new parameter,
With lots of little leads and lags
In pretty parabolic bags.

With optimistic expectations
I started on my explorations,
And swore to move without a swerve
Along my sinusoidal curve.
Alas! I knew how it would end:
I've mixed the cycle with the trend,
And fear that, growing daily skinnier,
I have at length become non-linear.
I wander glumly round the house
As though I were exogenous,
And hardly capable of feeling
The difference 'tween floor and ceiling.
I scarcely now, a pallid ghost,
Can tell *ex ante* from *ex post*:
My thoughts are sadly inelastic,
My acts invariably stochastic.
> 'The Non-Econometrician's Lament' (1955)

Joan Violet [Maurice] Robinson
(1903–1983)

capitalism:

1   There is a strong propensity in human nature – perhaps rooted in the instincts which give social cohesion to a company of apes – to develop loyalty to whatever institution an individual finds himself in. Managerial capitalism requires a high degree of attachment of the staff to a corporation. Self-interest, of course, is involved but pure self-interest would lead to great mobility between businesses and the disclosure of the secrets of one to another. Loyalty which invests the ego of the individual in his corporation is an essential feature of the system.
> *Freedom and Necessity* (1970), Ch.8: 83

economic growth:

2   A universal paean was raised in praise of *growth*. Growth was going to solve all problems. No need to bother about poverty. Growth will lift up the bottom and poverty will disappear without any need to pay attention to it.
> 'The Second Crisis of Economic Theory' (1972): 7

economics and economists:

3   Heaven help us if posterity is to pore over all the backs of old envelopes on which economists have jotted down numerical examples in working out a piece of analysis.
> 'Introduction' to *The Accumulation of Capital*, by Rosa Luxemburg (1951): 13

4 The purpose of studying economics is not to acquire a set of ready-made answers to economic questions, but to learn how to avoid being deceived by economists.
Marx, Marshall, and Keynes (1955): 17

5 The rate of accumulation that a family undertakes is an effect of its general character, expressing its foresight, self-discipline, sense of duty to the future, and appetite for economic improvement, playing against its love of leisure, self-indulgence or contempt for worldly goods.

If some bright spark amongst them sets up as an economist, he cannot tell the rest of the family what they ought to do. He may, however, influence their attitudes by making them conscious of what they are doing and helping them to be aware of what benefits would follow from what efforts. At the same time he may distort their natural good sense by overweighting the measurable aspects of the problem (which he likes talking about) at the expense of imponderables that are actually more important. But the economic effects of economics is too subtle a subject to take up in these exercises.
Exercises in Economic Analysis (1960), Part I, Ch.I, Sec.12: 21

6 [E]conomics limps along with one foot in untested hypotheses and the other in untestable slogans. Here our task is to sort out as best we may this mixture of ideology and science. We shall find no neat answers to the questions that it raises. The leading characteristic of the ideology that dominates our society today is its extreme confusion. To understand it means only to reveal its contradictions.
Economic Philosophy (1962), Ch.I, Sec.3: 25

7 In economics, arguments are largely devoted, as in theology, to supporting doctrines rather than testing hypotheses.
'What Are the Questions?' (1977), Sec.I: 1318

8 The present state of affairs in theoretical economics is very distressing. There are deep and prolonged controversies going on about purely logical points. Differences of opinion there will always be where political issues are involved; these are differences of judgment and of moral values. They should not affect logical analysis. In economics, unfortunately, logic is corrupted by opinions. Arguments are judged by their conclusions, not by their consistency. Terms are used without definitions, so that propositions containing them are merely incantations. Economics is a branch of theology.
'Economics Today' (1980): 122

Marxists and Marxism:

9 *Marxism is the opium of the Marxists.*
On Re-Reading Marx (1953), Title page

10 I understand Marx far and away better than you do. . . .

When I say I understand Marx better than you, I don't mean to say that I know the text better than you do. If you start throwing quotations at me you will have me baffled in no time. In fact, I refuse to play before you begin.

What I mean is that I have Marx in my bones and you have him in your mouth. To take an example – the idea that constant capital is an embodiment of labour power expended in the past. To you this is something that has to be proved with a lot of Hegelian stuff and nonsense. Whereas I say (though I do not use such pompous terminology): 'Naturally – what else did you think it could be?'
On Re-Reading Marx (1953), Ch.3: 20

11 Why are the academic economists always nagging away at Marx's system of analysis? If, as they maintain, it is all a tissue of fallacies, why do they not leave it to moulder away with other antiquated doctrines instead of feeling obliged to combat it as though it were a modern heresy, freshly produced by some young contemporary?
'Economic Versus Political Economy' (1968): 57

12 Marx did not have very much to say about the economics of socialism. As Kalecki once remarked, it was not his business to write science fiction.
'Economic Versus Political Economy' (1968): 60

mathematics in economics:

13 Of course mathematics can be very useful. But good mathematicians avoid fudging. If

you want to prevent yourself from being bamboozled, I can offer a very simple tip – never allow your professors to write K on the blackboard without asking in what units it is expressed. Perhaps it will make them cross – but if they get cross instead of giving an answer you will know that you are on the right track.

'Economics Today' (1980): 127

normality:

14 There is no such thing as a normal period of history. Normality is a fiction of economic textbooks.

'The Second Crisis of Economic Theory' (1971): 2

social science and social scientists:

15 The objective of an engineering programme is given to the engineer; for the social scientist the objective of the programme is precisely what he has to discuss. It is of no use to explain people to themselves as though they were automata. 'Every man hath business and desire.' The scientist cannot set himself up as a superior being who is exempt from the operation of the laws that he is expounding. The readers can retort to the writer – if we are automata, what are you?

Freedom and Necessity (1970), Ch.14: 120

16 The task of social science now is to raise self-consciousness to the second degree, to find out the causes, the mode of functioning and the consequences of the adoption of ideologies, so as to submit them to rational criticism. Only too often would-be scientists are still operating at the first degree, propagating some ideology which serves some particular interest, as the economists' doctrine of laissez faire served the particular interest of capitalist business.

Freedom and Necessity (1970), Ch.14: 122

17 But to eliminate value judgments from the subject-matter of social science is to eliminate the subject itself, for since it concerns human behaviour it must be concerned with the value judgments that people make. The social scientist (whatever he may privately believe) has no right to pretend to know any better than his neighbours what ends society should serve. His business is to show them why they believe what they purport to believe (as far as he can make it out) and what influence beliefs have on behaviour.

Freedom and Necessity (1970), Ch.14: 122

John E. Roemer (1945–)

socialism:

1 I am not one to cheer the inglorious end of the Soviet Union, despite what that state had become. Its demise marks a setback for socialism, because, for many hundreds of millions, its existence continued to support the belief that one could more than dream about founding a society based on a norm of equality. And holding that belief is a precondition for struggling to create such a society.

Egalitarian Perspectives (1994), Part IV, Essay 15: 332

James Edwin Thorold Rogers (1823–1890)

socialism:

1 The word 'Socialism' is in the last degree ambiguous, or, if my reader pleases elastic. In one sense it includes not only all critical investigations into the progress, the arrest, and the retrogression of civilization, but any effort which individuals, governments, or communities make in the direction of detecting social mischief, and in providing remedies against that which they discover. It is possible to include under the socialist hypothesis any religious movement which has intended to benefit humanity generally, any theory of the philosopher, from Plato to Herbert Spencer, which disputes the excellence of present arrangements, and propounds more or less drastic remedies for discovered and reputed evils, and any effort which Governments and Legislatures have attempted and carried out with a view to controlling and modifying individual action. In short, all that people call Altruism may be called Socialist action.

'Contemporary Socialism' (1885): 52

Wilhelm Georg Friedrich Roscher
(1817–1894)

communism:

1 Communism is the logically not inconsistent exaggeration of the principle of equality.
Principles of Political Economy (1878), Book I, Ch.V, Sec.LXXVIII, D: 239

2 We thus see, that the attempts made by socialism and communism are, by no means, phenomena unheard of in the past, and peculiar to modern times, as the blind adherents and opponents of them would have us believe. They are rather diseases of the body social, which have affected every highly civilized nation at certain periods of its existence. If the body be too weak to react healthily and curatively . . ., the evil is very apt to lead to the decline of all true freedom and order.
Principles of Political Economy (1878), Book I, Ch.V, Sec.LXXX: 241–245

economics and economists:

3 It would seem . . . that political economists, especially in Germany, have attached too much importance to putting formal bounds to their special science. Why not rather follow the example of the students of nature who care little whether this or that discovery belongs to physics or chemistry, to astronomy or mathematics, provided, only, very many and important discoveries are made.
Principles of Political Economy (1878), Introduction, Ch.II, Sec.XX: 98–99

mathematics in economics:

4 That which is general in Political Economy has, it must be acknowledged, much that is analogous to the mathematical sciences. Like the latter, it swarms with abstractions. Just as there are, strictly speaking, no mathematical lines or points in nature, and no mathematical lever, there is nowhere such a thing as production or rent, entirely pure and simple. The mathematical laws of motion operate in a hypothetical vacuum, and, where applied, are subjected to important modifications, in consequence of atmospheric resistence. Something similar is true of most of the laws of our science; as, for instance, those in accordance with which the price of commodities is fixed by the buyer and seller. It also, always supposes the parties to the contract to be guided only by a sense of their own best interest, and not to be influenced by secondary considerations. It is not, therefore, to be wondered at, that many authors have endeavored to clothe the laws of Political Economy in algebraic formulæ. And, indeed, wherever magnitudes and the relations of magnitudes to one another are treated of, it must be possible to subject them to calculation. . . . But the advantages of the mathematical mode of expression diminish as the facts to which it is applied become more complicated. This is true even in the ordinary psychology of the individual. How much more, therefore, in the portraying of national life! Here the algebraic formulæ would soon become so complicated, as to make all further progress in the operation next to impossible. Their employment, especially in a science whose sphere it is, at present, to increase the number of the facts observed, to make them the object of exhaustive investigation, and vary the combinations into which they may be made to enter, is a matter of great difficulty, if not entirely impossible. For, most assuredly, as our science has to do with men, it must take them and treat them as they actually are, moved at once by very different and non-economic motives, belonging to an entirely definite people, state, age etc. The abstraction according to which all men are by nature the same, different only in consequence of a difference in education, position in life etc., all equally well equipped, skillful and free in the matter of economic production and consumption, is one which . . . must pass as an indispensable stage in the preparatory labors of political economists. It would be especially well, when an economic fact is produced by the cooperation of many different factors, for the investigator to mentally isolate the factor of which, for the time being, he wishes to examine the peculiar nature. All other factors should, for a time, be considered as not operating, and as unchangeable, and then the question asked, What would be the effect of a change in the factor to be examined, whether the change be occasioned by enlarging or diminishing it? But it should

never be lost sight of, that such a one is only an abstraction after all, for which, not only in the transition to practice, but even in finished theory, we must turn to the infinite variety of real life.
Principles of Political Economy (1878), Introduction, Ch.III, Sec.XXII: 103–105

Edward Alsworth Ross (1866–1951)

economics and economists:

1 The student of economics cannot remain unaware that his is a realm bordered by other realms. He pushes his inquiries as to the rôle of nature in production, and lands in economic botany or zoölogy. He goes deeply into the subject of labor, and finds himself studying physiology. He undertakes to reach the basis of rent, and, ere he knows it, is poring over the bulletins of the experiment stations. The principle of division of labor takes him into technology. Transportation drives him to the law of carriers. The study of property involves him in jurisprudence. International trade or monopoly conducts him to political science. Consumption, with its study of wants and choices, is a short cut to ethics. Now I wish to raise the question, 'Is there not a field of investigation lying up against economics which, although social, is yet not jurisprudence or political science or ethics?'
'The Sociological Frontier of Economics' (1899): 386

2 The empire of the Czar is bounded on its western frontier by the clearly defined and well-explored territories of highly organized governments like Austria and Germany. On its eastern side, until recently at least, it melted vaguely into the little-known lands disputed among the khanates of Central Asia. Economics likewise is bounded for the most part by regions that have been well defined and thoroughly explored by highly organized sciences. But on one side it is embarrassed by an uncertain and disputed frontier with a little-known territory, subject to the contradictory and unreasonable claims of rival chieftains. Sociology is its Central Asia.
'The Sociological Frontier of Economics' (1899): 394–395

Walt Whitman Rostow (1916–2003)

communism:

1 Even Communist totalitarianism cannot afford enough policemen to follow the peasant about in his daily round and make him produce what economic growth requires. The devices of a police state, which work with tragic efficiency in urban areas, adapt with difficulty to the countryside.
'Marx Was a City Boy, or, Why Communism May Fail' (1955): 30

individualism:

2 As Myrdal and Robbins have pointed out in this generation, the individualist-utilitarian creed did, indeed, make the case for free competitive markets and for private property; but it also contained within its presuppositions the case for free elections, on a one-man-one-vote basis; for destroying or controlling monopolies; for social legislation which would set considerations of human welfare off against profit incentives; and, above all, for the progressive income tax.
    In wrestling loyally with the dilemmas posed by the individualist-utilitarian creed, in finding balances that respected its conflicting imperatives, the societies of the West have thus made their way to the brink of communism without succumbing to Marx's prognosis.
'The Stages of Economic Growth' (1959): 16

Murray Newton Rothbard (1926–1995)

government:

1 Statistics are the bureaucrat's only form of economic knowledge, replacing the intuitive, 'qualitative' knowledge of the entrepreneur, guided only by the quantitative profit-and-loss test. Accordingly, the drive for government intervention, and the drive for more statistics, have gone hand in hand.
'The Politics of Political Economists: Comment' (1960): 659

2 Statistics ... are the eyes and ears of the interventionists: of the intellectual reformer,

the politician, and the government bureaucrat. Cut off those eyes and ears, destroy those crucial guidelines to knowledge, and the whole threat of government intervention is almost completely eliminated.
'Statistics: Achilles' Heel of Government' (1961): 43

3   The State provides a legal, orderly, systematic channel for predation on the property of the producers; it makes certain, secure, and relatively 'peaceful' the lifeline of the parasitic caste in society.
For a New Liberty (1973) Part I, Ch.3: 54

mathematics in economics:

4   Simply to develop economics verbally, then to translate into logistic symbols, and finally to retranslate the propositions back into English, makes no sense and violates the fundamental scientific principle of Occam's razor, which calls for the greatest possible simplicity in science and the avoidance of unnecessary multiplication of entities or processes.
Man, Economy, and State (1962), Vol. I, Ch.1, Appendix A: 65

market economy:

5   On the market all is harmony.
Man, Economy, and State (1962), Vol. II, Ch.12, Sec.3: 769

minimum wage:

6   Minimum wage laws tragically generate unemployment, especially so among the poorest and least skilled or educated workers. . . . Because a minimum wage, of course, does not guarantee any worker's employment; it only prohibits, by force of law, anyone from being employed at the wage which would pay his employer to hire him. It therefore compels unemployment.
For a New Liberty (1973), Part II, Ch.8: 178

poverty and poor relief:

7   State poor relief is clearly a *subsidization of poverty*, for men are now automatically entitled to money from the State because of their poverty.
Man, Economy, and State (1962), Vol. II, Ch.12, Sec.9.B: 818

8   What, then, *can* the government do to help the poor? The only correct answer is also the libertarian answer: Get out of the way. Let the government get out of the way of the productive energies of all groups in the population, rich, middle class, and poor alike, and the result will be an enormous increase in the welfare and the standard of living of everyone, and most particularly of the poor who are the ones supposedly helped by the miscalled 'welfare state.'
For a New Liberty (1973), Part II, Ch.8: 184

socialism:

9   Socialism . . . is the violent abolition of the market, the compulsory monopolization of the entire productive sphere by the State.
Man, Economy, and State (1962), Vol. II, Ch.12, Sec.9.I: 830

taxation:

10   *Only* the government obtains its income by coercion and violence – i.e., by the direct threat of confiscation or imprisonment if payment is not forthcoming. This coerced levy is 'taxation.'
For a New Liberty (1973), Part I, Ch.3: 49

11   In a sense, the entire system of taxation is a form of involuntary servitude. . . . Part of the essence of slavery, after all, is forced work for someone at little or no pay. But the income tax means that we sweat and earn income, only to see the government extract a large chunk of it by coercion for its own purposes. What is this but forced labor at no pay?
For a New Liberty (1973), Part II, Ch.5: 93–94

12   The State is the only legal institution in society that acquires its revenue by the use of coercion, by using enough violence and threat of violence on its victims to ensure their paying the desired tribute. The State benefits itself at the expense of its robbed victims. The State is, therefore, a centralized, regularized organization of theft. Its payments extracted by coercion are called 'taxation' instead of tribute, but their nature is the same.
'The Myth of Neutral Taxation' (1981)

13 Taxation is theft, purely and simply, even though it is theft on a grand and colossal scale which no acknowledged criminals could hope to match. It is a compulsory seizure of the property of the State's inhabitants, or subjects.
The Ethics of Liberty (1982), Part III, Ch.22: 162–163

Jean-Jacques Rousseau (1712–1778)
French philosopher

government:

1 What is most necessary, and perhaps most difficult, in government, is rigid integrity in doing strict justice to all, and above all in protecting the poor against the tyranny of the rich. The greatest evil has already come about, when there are poor men to be defended, and rich men to be restrained. It is on the middle classes alone that the whole force of the law is exerted; they are equally powerless against the treasures of the rich and the penury of the poor. The first mocks them, the second escapes them. The one breaks the meshes, the other passes through them.

It is therefore one of the most important functions of government to prevent extreme inequality of fortunes; not by taking away wealth from its possessors, but by depriving all men of means to accumulate it; not by building hospitals for the poor, but by securing the citizens from becoming poor. The unequal distribution of inhabitants over the territory, when men are crowded together in one place, while other places are depopulated; the encouragement of the arts that minister to luxury and of purely superfluous arts at the expense of useful and laborious crafts; the sacrifice of agriculture to commerce; the necessitation of the tax-farmer by the maladministration of the funds of the State; and in short, venality pushed to such an extreme that even public esteem is reckoned at a cash value, and virtue rated at a market price: these are the most obvious causes of opulence and of poverty, of public interest, of mutual hatred among citizens, of indifference to the common cause, of the corruption of the people, and of the weakening of all the springs of government. Such are the evils, which are with difficulty cured when they make themselves felt, but which a wise administration ought to prevent, if it is to maintain, along with good morals, respect for the laws, patriotism, and the influence of the general will.
A Discourse on Political Economy (1755): 146–147

property:

2 The first man who, having enclosed a piece of ground, bethought himself of saying 'This is mine', and found people simple enough to believe him, was the real founder of civil society. From how many crimes, wars, and murders, from how many horrors and misfortunes might not any one have saved mankind, by pulling up the stakes, or filling up the ditch, and crying to his fellows: 'Beware of listening to this impostor; you are undone if you once forget that the fruits of the earth belong to us all, and the earth itself to nobody.'
A Discourse on the Origins and Foundations of Inequality Among Men (1755), Second Part: 84

3 It is certain that the right of property is the most sacred of all the rights of citizenship, and even more important in some respects than liberty itself; either because it more nearly affects the preservation of life, or because, property being more easily usurped and more difficult to defend than life, the law ought to pay a greater attention to what is most easily taken away; or finally, because property is the true foundation of civil society, and the real guarantee of the undertakings of citizens: for if property were not answerable for personal actions, nothing would be easier than to evade duties and laugh at the laws. On the other hand, it is no less certain that the maintenance of the State and the government involves costs and outgoings; and as every one who agrees to the end must acquiesce in the means, it follows that the members of a society ought to contribute from their property to its support. Besides, it is difficult to secure the property of individuals on one side, without attacking it on another; and it is impossible that all the regulations which govern the order of succession, will, contracts, etc., should not lay individuals under some constraint as to the disposition of their

goods, and should not consequently restrict the right of property.
A Discourse on Political Economy (1755): 151–152

taxation:

4   He who possesses only the common necessaries of life should pay nothing at all [in taxes], while the tax on him who is in possession of superfluities may justly be extended to everything he has over and above necessaries.
A Discourse on Political Economy (1755): 160

5   Putting all these considerations carefully together, we shall find that, in order to levy taxes in a truly equitable and proportionate manner, the imposition ought not to be in simple ratio to the property of the contributors, but in compound ratio to the difference of their conditions and the superfluity of their possessions.
A Discourse on Political Economy (1755): 162

John Ruskin (1819–1900)
British art and social critic

economics and economists:

1   Among the delusions which at different periods have possessed themselves of the minds of large masses of the human race, perhaps the most curious – certainly the least creditable – is the modern *soi disant* science of political economy, based on the idea that an advantageous code of social action may be determined irrespectively of the influence of social affection.
'Unto This Last' (1860), Part I: 'The Roots of Honour': 155

2   'The social affections,' says the economist, 'are accidental and disturbing elements in human nature; but avarice and the desire of progress are constant elements. Let us eliminate the inconstants, and, considering the human being merely as a covetous machine, examine by what laws of labour, purchase, and sale, the greatest accumulative result in wealth is obtainable. Those laws once determined, it will be for each individual afterwards to introduce as much of the disturbing affectionate element as he chooses, and to determine for himself the result on the new conditions supposed.'
'Unto This Last' (1860), Part I: 'The Roots of Honour': 155

3   The real science of political economy, which has yet to be distinguished from the bastard science, as medicine from witchcraft, and astronomy from astrology, is that which teaches nations to desire and labour for the things that lead to life; and which teaches them to scorn and destroy the things that lead to destruction.
'Unto This Last' (1860), Part IV: 'Ad Valorem': 547

4   Political economy is neither an art nor a science, but a system of conduct and legislature, founded on the sciences, directing the arts, and impossible, except under certain conditions of moral culture.
'Essays on Political Economy' (1862), Part I: 784

inequality:

5   Inequalities of wealth, unjustly established, have assuredly injured the nation in which they exist during their establishment; and, unjustly directed, they injure it yet more during their existence. But inequalities of wealth justly established, benefit the nation in the course of their establishment; and, nobly used, aid it yet more by their existence.
'Unto This Last' (1860), Part II: 'The Veins of Wealth': 280

just exchange:

6   The general law, then, respecting just or economical exchange, is simply this – There must be advantage on both sides (or if only advantage on one, at least no disadvantage on the other) to the persons exchanging; and just payment for his time, intelligence, and labour, to any intermediate person effecting the transaction (commonly called a merchant): and whatever advantage there is on either side, and whatever pay is given to the intermediate person, should be thoroughly known to all concerned. All attempt at concealment implies some practice of the

opposite, or undivine science, founded on nescience.

'Unto This Last' (1860), Part IV: 'Ad Valorem': 552

money:

7 Money has been inaccurately spoken of as merely a means of circulation. It is, on the contrary, an expression of right. It is not wealth, but a documentary claim to wealth, being the sign of the relative quantities of it, or of the labour producing it, to which, at a given time, persons or societies are entitled.

'Essays on Political Economy' (1862), Part I, Sec.II: 790

8 Only a few can understand, none measure, superiorities in other things; but everybody can understand money, and count it.

'Essays on Political Economy' (1862), Part III: 748

property:

9 [W]hereas it has long been known and declared that the poor have no right to the property of the rich, I wish it also to be known and declared that the rich have no right to the property of the poor.

'Unto This Last' (1860), Part III: 'Qui Judicatis Terram': 418

10 The first necessity of all economical government is to secure the unquestioned and unquestionable working of the great law of Property – that a man who works for a thing shall be allowed to get it, keep it, and consume it, in peace; and that he who does not eat his cake to-day, shall be seen, without grudging, to have his cake tomorrow. This, I say, is the first point to be secured by social law; without this, no political advance, nay, no political existence, is in any sort possible. Whatever evil, luxury, iniquity, may seem to result from it, this is nevertheless the first of all Equities; and to the enforcement of this, by law and by police-truncheon, the nation must always primarily set its mind – that the cupboard door may have a firm lock to it, and no man's dinner be carried off by the mob, on its way home from the baker's.

'Essays on Political Economy' (1862), Part II: 280

riches:

11 Men nearly always speak and write as if riches were absolute, and it were possible, by following certain scientific precepts, for everybody to be rich. Whereas riches are a power like that of electricity, acting only through inequalities or negations of itself. The force of the guinea you have in your pocket depends wholly on the default of a guinea in your neighbour's pocket. If he did not want it, it would be of no use to you; the degree of power it possesses depends accurately upon the need or desire he has for it – and the art of making yourself rich, in the ordinary mercantile economist's sense, is therefore equally and necessarily the art of keeping your neighbour poor.

'Unto This Last' (1860), Part II: 'The Veins of Wealth': 278

utility:

12 [T]he economical usefulness of a thing depends not merely on its own nature, but on the number of people who can and will use it. A horse is useless, and therefore unsaleable, if no one can ride – a sword if no one can strike, and meat, if no one can eat. Thus every material utility depends on its relative human capacity.

'Unto This Last' (1860), Part IV: 'Ad Valorem': 545

value:

13 The value of a thing, therefore, is independent of opinion, and of quantity. Think what you will of it, gain how much you may of it, the value of the thing itself is neither greater nor less. For ever it avails, or avails not; no estimate can raise, no disdain depress, the power which it holds from the Maker of things and of men.

'Unto This Last' (1860), Part IV: 'Ad Valorem': 547

14 The reader must, by anticipation, be warned against confusing value with cost, or with price. Value is the life-giving power of anything; cost, the quantity of labour required to produce it; price, the quantity of labour which its possessor will take in exchange for it. Cost and price are commercial conditions, to be studied under the head of money.

'Essays on Political Economy' (1862), Part I, Sec.I: 787–788

S

Paul Anthony Samuelson (1915–)

economics and economists:

1   The first lesson in economics is: things are often not what they seem.
    Economics: An Introductory Analysis (1951; 2nd edn), Part One, Ch.1: 9

2   It is an ethical rather than a scientific question as to just how large each person's final income ought to be. As a science, economics can concern itself only with the best means of attaining given ends; it cannot prescribe the ends themselves.
    Economics: An Introductory Analysis (1951; 2nd edn), Part Six, Ch.35, Sec.B: 736

3   Economists use terribly complicated jargon: long words, fine definitions, cabalistic mathematical symbols and graphs, complicated statistical techniques. Yet, if they have done their job well, they end up with what is simple common sense.
    'What Economists Know' (1959): 185

4   I will tell you a secret. Economists are supposed to be dry as dust, dismal fellows. This is quite wrong, the reverse of the truth. Scratch a hard-boiled economist of the libertarian persuasion and you find a Don Quixote underneath. No lovesick maiden ever pined for the days of medieval chivalry with such sentimental impracticality as some economists long for the return to a Victorian marketplace that is completely free. Completely free? Well, almost so. There must, of course, be the constable to ensure that voluntary contracts are enforced and to protect the property rights of each molecule which is an island unto itself.
    'Modern Economic Realities and Individualism' (1963): 129

5   Economists are like pedants (a redundancy!) in wanting to save the face of their principles even when naught is at stake.
    'Personal Freedoms and Economic Freedoms in the Mixed Economy' (1964): 616

6   I must confess to the belief that truth is not merely in the eye of the beholder, and that certain regularities of economic life are as valid for a Marxist as for a classicist, for a post-Keynesian as for a monetarist.
    In short, economics is neither astrology nor theology.
    'Economics in a Golden Age: A Personal Memoir' (1972): 168

imperfect competition:

7   Years ago, economists used to regard perfect competition as the ideal; any deviation from it was regarded as a 'bad thing.' Today, we realize that all the world is an exception to perfect competition. Were we to chop off the head of everyone who is an imperfect competitor, there would be few heads left.
    Economics: An Introductory Analysis (1951; 2nd edn), Part Three, Ch.25: 526

mathematics in economics:

8   The laborious literary working over of essentially simple mathematical concepts such as is characteristic of much of modern economic theory is not only unrewarding from the standpoint of advancing the science, but involves as well mental gymnastics of a peculiarly depraved type.
    Foundations of Economic Analysis (1947), Part I, Ch.I: 6

9   On the title page of my *Foundations of Economic Analysis*, I quoted the only speech that the great Willard Gibbs was supposed ever to have made before the Yale Faculty. As professors do at such meetings, they were hotly arguing the question of required subjects: Should certain students be required to take languages or mathematics? Each man had his opinion of the relative worth of these disparate subjects. Finally Gibbs, who was not a loquacious man, got up and made a four-word speech: 'Mathematics is a language.'
    I have only one objection to that statement. I wish he had made it 25 per cent shorter – so as to read as follows: 'Mathematics *is* language.' Now I mean this

entirely literally. In principle, mathematics cannot be worse than prose in economic theory; in principle, it certainly cannot be better than prose. For in deepest logic – and leaving out all tactical and pedagogical questions – the two media are strictly identical.
'Economic Theory and Mathematics – An Appraisal' (1952): 56

10 [M]athematics is neither a necessary nor a sufficient condition for a fruitful career in economic theory. It can be a help. It can certainly be a hindrance, since it is only too easy to convert a good literary economist into a mediocre mathematical economist.
'Economic Theory and Mathematics – An Appraisal' (1952): 65

utility:

11 Literally hundreds of learned papers have been written on the subject of utility. Take a little bad psychology, add a dash of bad philosophy and ethics, and liberal quantities of bad logic, and any economist can prove that the demand curve for a commodity is negatively inclined.
Foundations of Economic Analysis (1947), Part I, Ch.I: 4

Thomas J. Sargent (1943–)

laissez-faire:

1 A football team is an example of a system for which complete decentralization or 'laissez faire' is not a good idea.
' "Reaganomics" and Credibility' (1985): 235

Jean-Baptiste Say (1767–1832)

economics and economists:

1 The study of statistics may gratify curiosity, but it can never be productive of advantage when it does not indicate the origin and consequences of the facts it has collected; and by indicating their origin and consequences, it at once becomes the science of political economy.
A Treatise on Political Economy (1880; New American edition), Book I, Introduction: xiv

government:

2 The whole skill of government . . . consists in the continual and judicious comparison of the sacrifice about to be incurred, with the expected benefit to the community; for I have no hesitation in pronouncing every instance, where the benefit is not equivalent to the loss, to be an instance of folly, or of criminality, in the government.
A Treatise on Political Economy (1880; New American edition), Book III, Ch.VI: 416

property:

3 The poor man, that can call nothing his own, is equally interested with the rich in upholding the inviolability of property. His personal services would not be available, without the aid of accumulations previously made and protected. Every obstruction to, or dissipation of these accumulations, is a material injury to his means of gaining a livelihood; and the ruin and spoliation of the higher is as certainly followed by the misery and degradation of the lower classes.
A Treatise on Political Economy (1880; New American edition), Book I, Ch.XIV: 132

taxation:

4 Taxation, pushed to the extreme, has the lamentable effect of impoverishing the individual, without enriching the state.
A Treatise on Political Economy (1880; New American edition), Book III, Ch. VIII: 449

5 Taxation is the taking a portion of the general product of the community, which never returns to the community in the channel of consumption.
A Treatise on Political Economy (1880; New American edition), Book III, Ch. VIII: 471

Gustav von Schmoller (1838–1917)

economic reform:

1 No great social or economic reform can conquer the sluggish resistance which opposes it by merely showing its utility. Only when it can be made to appear that

what is demanded is the demand of justice, does it inflame and move the masses.
'The Idea of Justice in Political Economy' (1894), Introduction: 2

socialism:

2   The error of socialism was simply that it overlooked the difference between material and formal justice, as well as the significance of other equally justified social ideal conceptions; that it imagined the individual conceptions of certain idealists of what is just, would suffice to overthrow suddenly and immediately primeval institutions. With its crude excrescences it returned to standards of justice which perhaps correspond to the first stages of civilization, certainly to rough views, but not to refined conceptions of higher morality.
'The Idea of Justice in Political Economy' (1894), Sec.IV: 32–33

Henry Schultz (1893–1938)

economics and economists:

1   No disciple of any school of economics can afford to close his eyes to a new discovery, obtained from another point of view, which will not fit in with his own ideas, nor must he treat it as unimportant, if not incorrect.
'Mathematical Economics and the Quantitative Method' (1927): 706

2   [P]ure theory is only a part, a small part, of economic science.
'Rational Economics' (1928): 648

mathematics in economics:

3   Just as a sailor needs a compass, so the quantitative worker, if he is to have a deep understanding of his own work, needs an economic theory. It may not be a perfect theory, it may need a good deal of overhauling, but a theory he must have.
'Mathematical Economics and the Quantitative Method' (1927): 702

4   Without stretching the metaphor, it may be affirmed that the pure (mathematical) theory of economics stands in the same relation to the literary theories as the Sperry gyroscopic compass does to the ordinary variety of mariner's compasses.
'Mathematical Economics and the Quantitative Method' (1927): 703

Theodore William Schultz
(1902–1998)

economics and economists:

1   The scientific prestige of physics rests in large part on knowledge that has been verified by means of controlled experiments. Astronomers, however, have accumulated an impressive body of knowledge not by running experiments but mainly by analyzing the differences in the history of various celestial bodies. Although economists may hanker to do what the physicists do, it is a will-o'-the-wisp. Our analytical opportunities in advancing knowledge about economic behavior are akin to those of astronomers. *Herein lie the importance and necessity of economic history.*
'On Economic History in Extending Economics' (1977): 245–246

2   Most economists are born with a strong urge to sell their wares to policymakers; economic historians have an extra gene, which accounts for their desire to reform the historians.
'On Economic History in Extending Economics' (1977): 246

3   Economic behavior is more complex than our thoughts about it. Our thoughts, however, are more comprehensive than our economic language, our language is more comprehensive than standard theory, and standard theory is more comprehensive than mathematical economics.
'On Economic History in Extending Economics' (1977): 247

Ernst Friedrich Schumacher
(1911–1977)

materialism:

1   In the excitement over the unfolding of his scientific and technical powers, modern man has built a system of production that ravishes nature and a type of society that mutilates

man. If only there were more and more wealth, everything else, it is thought, would fall into place. Money is considered to be all-powerful; if it could not actually buy non-material values, such as justice, harmony, beauty or even health, it could circumvent the need for them or compensate for their loss. The development of production and the acquisition of wealth have thus become the highest goals of the modern world in relation to which all other goals, no matter how much lip-service may still be paid to them, have come to take second place. The highest goals require no justification; all secondary goals have finally to justify themselves in terms of the service their attainment renders to the attainment of the highest.
This is the philosophy of materialism. . . .
Small is Beautiful (1973), Epilogue: 277

nationalization:

2   If the purpose of nationalisation is primarily to achieve faster economic growth, higher efficiency, better planning, and so forth, there is bound to be disappointment. The idea of conducting the entire economy on the basis of private greed, as Marx well recognised, has shown an extraordinary power to transform the world.
Small is Beautiful (1973), Part IV, Ch.III: 239

Joseph Alois Schumpeter
(1883–1950)

business cycles:

1   Analyzing business cycles means neither more nor less than analyzing the economic process of the capitalist era. Most of us discover this truth which at once reveals the nature of the task and also its formidable dimensions. Cycles are not, like tonsils, separable things that might be treated by themselves, but are, like the beat of the heart, of the essence of the organism that displays them.
Business Cycles (1939), Vol. I, Preface: v

capitalism:

2   It is the cheap cloth, the cheap cotton and rayon fabric, boots, motorcars and so on that are the typical achievements of capitalist production, and not as a rule improvements that would mean much to the rich man. Queen Elizabeth owned silk stockings. The capitalist achievement does not typically consist in providing more silk stockings for queens but in bringing them within the reach of factory girls in return for steadily decreasing amounts of effort.
Capitalism, Socialism, and Democracy (1950; 3rd edn), Part II, Ch.V: 67

3   Capitalism . . . is by nature a form or method of economic change and not only never is but never can be stationary.
Capitalism, Socialism, and Democracy (1950; 3rd edn), Part II, Ch.VII: 82

4   [C]apitalist civilization is rationalistic 'and anti-heroic.' The two go together of course. Success in industry and commerce requires a lot of stamina, yet industrial and commercial activity is essentially unheroic in the knight's sense – no flourishing of swords about it, not much physical prowess, no chance to gallop the armored horse into the enemy, preferably a heretic or heathen – and the ideology that glorifies the idea of fighting for fighting's sake and of victory for victory's sake understandably withers in the office among all the columns of figures. Therefore, owning assets that are apt to attract the robber or the tax gatherer and not sharing or even disliking warrior ideology that conflicts with its 'rational' utilitarianism, the industrial and commercial bourgeoisie is fundamentally pacifist and inclined to insist on the application of the moral precepts of private life to international relations. It is true that, unlike most but like some other features of capitalist civilization, pacifism and international morality have also been espoused in non-capitalist environments and by pre-capitalist agencies, in the Middle Ages by the Roman Church for instance. Modern pacifism and modern international morality are nonetheless products of capitalism.
Capitalism, Socialism, and Democracy (1950; 3rd edn), Part II, Ch.XI: 127–128

economics and economists:

5   Those economists who really count do not differ so much as most people believe; they start from much the same premises; problems

present themselves to them in much the same light; they attack them with much the same tools; and, although some of them have a way of laying more stress on points of difference than of points of agreement, their results mostly point towards common goals. This is not only true of fundamentals of fact and machinery, but also of what is going on within the precincts of every one of our time-honoured problems.

'The Explanation of the Business Cycle' (1927), Sec.I, §1: 286

6 As a doctor at the bedside sees and understands more than he would be able to prove by exact test, so every economist who is at all worthy of this name acquires by lifelong familiarity with contemporaneous and historical fact a vision or an understanding of the intimate necessities in the life of the organism he deals with which carries him much further than the exact tools at his command and may count for more in remedial advice than provable theorems.

Business Cycles (1939), Vol. I, Ch.I.A: 6

Marxism:

7 In one important sense, Marxism *is* a religion. To the believer it presents, first, a system of ultimate ends that embody the meaning of life and are absolute standards by which to judge events and actions; and, secondly, a guide to those ends which implies a plan of salvation and the indication of the evil from which mankind, or a chosen section of mankind, is to be saved. We may specify still further: Marxist socialism also belongs to that subgroup which promises paradise on this side of the grave.

Capitalism, Socialism, and Democracy (1950; 3rd edn), Part I, Ch.I: 5

8 To him [the Marxist], as to any believer in a Faith, the opponent is not merely in error but in sin. Dissent is disapproved of not only intellectually but also morally. There cannot be any excuse for it once the Message has been revealed.

Capitalism, Socialism, and Democracy (1950; 3rd edn), Part I, Ch.I: 5, note 1

mathematics in economics:

9 There is . . . one sense in which economics is the most quantitative, not only of 'social' or 'moral' sciences, but of *all* sciences, physics not excluded. For mass, velocity, current, and the like *can* undoubtedly be measured, but in order to do so we must always invent a distinct process of measurement. This must be done before we can deal with these phenomena *numerically*. Some of the most fundamental economic facts, on the contrary, already present themselves to our observation as quantities made numerical by life itself. They carry meaning only by virtue of their numerical character. There would be movement even if we were unable to turn it into measurable quantity, but there cannot be prices independent of the numerical expression of every one of them, and of definite numerical relations among all of them.

'The Common Sense of Econometrics' (1933): 5–6

10 The only way to a position in which our science might give positive advice on a large scale to politicians and business men, leads through quantitative work. For as long as we are unable to put our arguments into figures, the voice of our science, although occasionally it may help to dispel gross errors, will never be heard by practical men. They are, by instinct, econometricians all of them, in their distrust of anything not amenable to exact proof.

'The Common Sense of Econometrics' (1933): 12

socialism:

11 [W]e have to face what I shall refer to as the Cultural Indeterminateness of Socialism. In fact, according to our definition as well as to most others, a society may be fully and truly socialist and yet be led by an absolute ruler or be organized in the most democratic of all possible ways; it may be aristocratic or proletarian; it may be a theocracy and hierarchic or atheist or indifferent as to religion; it may be much more strictly disciplined than men are in a modern army or completely lacking in discipline; it may be ascetic or eudemonist in spirit; energetic or slack; thinking only of the future or only of the day; warlike and nationalistic or peaceful and internationalist; equalitarian or the opposite; it may have the ethics of lords or the ethics of slaves; its art may be subjective or objective; its forms of life individualistic

or standardized; and – what for some of us would by itself suffice to command our allegiance or to arouse our contempt – it may breed from its supernormal or from its subnormal stock and produce supermen or submen accordingly.
Capitalism, Socialism, and Democracy (1950; 3rd edn), Part III, Ch.XV: 170

Tibor de Scitovsky (1910–2002)

capitalism:

1 Capitalism, when you think of it, is not an attractive form of social organization; but it is, or at any rate has been, redeemed by two great merits: the impersonal nature of its constraints; and its unequalled flexibility – flexibility in exploiting opportunities, absorbing shocks, adapting to changed circumstances.
'Can Capitalism Survive? – An Old Question in a New Setting' (1980): 1

economics and economists:

2 In our society ... the economist must make a choice. If he wants to maintain strict objectivity, he becomes a technician; if he wants to advise on policy, he must in most cases relinquish his claim to the objectivity of a natural scientist.
'The State of Welfare Economics' (1951): 315

3 Not surprisingly, perhaps, economists are human. They sometimes do and sometimes do not find what they are looking for; but very seldom do they find what they are *not* looking for.
'Are Men Rational or Economists Wrong?' (1974), Introduction: 224

George Julius Duncombe Poulett [Thomson] Scrope (1797–1876)
British geologist

economics and economists:

1 It must, we fear, be conceded by all who are acquainted with the most recent works on political economy, that whatever the degree to which the science was advanced by Dr. Smith, it has received few or no substantial improvements since his time, in spite of the volumes that have issued from the press on the subject, and the tribes of authors that have successively lectured upon it *ex cathedrâ*. Professor after Professor has brought forward his special doctrine with no small flourish of trumpets, as a newly discovered truth: but, each having for his new erection uniformly destroyed the productions of his predecessor, and occasionally his own, the sum total of our acquisitions during this period, even in the estimation of the most enthusiastic devotees of the science, is but small.
'The Political Economists' (1831): 1

2 [W]e think it will appear that the principal writers on political economy, within the present century, have had but a very indistinct notion of the nature and limits of their subject; that they have habitually employed the same terms in contradictory senses, and so rendered their writings, in a great measure, unintelligible, not only to their readers, but even to themselves; that there is scarcely one of the numerous topics handled by them, such as the laws regarding value, labour, wages, profits, rent, and free trade, which they have not left in a worse condition than they found it; and finally, that the whole science, as hitherto understood and carried on, has been founded on an entirely false assumption, which must infallibly either vitiate the whole superstructure, or render it, in its present condition, anything but the trusty and unerring guide in legislation, for which it has been ostentatiously put forward by its cultivators.
'The Political Economists' (1831): 2

3 Political Economy teaches the art of managing the resources of a society to the best advantage of its members. It does not, however, ... embrace the moral and religious education, the political constitution, or the personal protection of a people, but concerns itself solely with the artificial means of enjoyment, composing the necessaries, comforts, and luxuries of life – things which are the result of labour and the objects of exchange; and which, when accumulated to any considerable extent, are ordinarily spoken of as *wealth*.
Principles of Political Economy (1833), Ch.I: 40

4 [T]he principles of Political Economy will amount only to moral probability, and must fall far short of the accuracy that characterizes the laws of the physical sciences. This consideration should have prevented the attempts which have been made by many writers on Political Economy to attribute the force of mathematical demonstration to its conclusions.
Principles of Political Economy (1833), Ch.I: 41

government interference:

5 Interference of any kind ... in the spontaneous direction of industry, and the free employment by their owners of the great agents in production, labour, land, and capital, has the certain effect of benumbing their powers and lessening the sum of production, and consequently the shares, of the producing parties; as well as of needlessly, and therefore unjustly, curtailing their freedom of action.
Principles of Political Economy (1833), Ch.IX: 231

poverty and the poor laws:

6 The principle of the poor-law is the maintenance of the peace and security of society by the suppression of mendicancy, vagrancy, and petty plunder, which no other course can by possibility prevent. It is not to be looked upon as a measure of charity, so much as one of *police*.
Principles of Political Economy (1833), Ch.XII: 304

7 It is the very first duty of a government to secure the means of subsistence to every well-disposed and well-conducted member of the community over whose welfare it presides.
Principles of Political Economy (1833), Ch.XII: 305

taxation:

8 [T]he only real limit at any time existing to the amount of taxation imposed upon the people has been that of their patience under the infliction.
Principles of Political Economy (1833), Ch.XVIII: 433

9 We need scarcely observe on the injustice and impolicy of taxing a nation beyond the fair value of the services rendered by its government. Whatever sums are needed to defray the necessary expenses of the state for the due administration of justice, the defence of the country against foreign foes, and the protection of persons and property – are expended productively, and in a manner highly conducive to the national welfare. But all beyond this is so much taken from productive to be expended in unproductive channels of employment – so much abstracted from the industrious and economical to be wasted by the idle and extravagant. If left in the pockets of the people, that sum would have germinated and borne a crop of future wealth. When given to sinecurists, undeserving pensioners, or overpaid placemen, it is consumed by them in a way which leaves nothing behind, but an increased appetency for further plunder of the public.
Principles of Political Economy (1833), Ch.XVIII: 434–435

10 The only true justice in taxation is that every one be made to pay in exact proportion to his means; – and this is to be more accurately effected by a tax on *income* than any other.
Principles of Political Economy (1833), Ch.XVIII: 444

Theodore Sedgwick (1780–1839)

money and banking:

1 One of the greatest scourges that has fallen upon poor people in modern times is that of irresponsible paper money, which, by some bad management or other, cannot be converted into gold or silver. This inconvertible paper money is one of the great causes to many, not of *nominal* only, but of *real* dearness in those necessary things which the poor must have, which dearness is scarcity with them, and often little better than a famine. Those who are allowed to make any portion of the currency, which becomes a *debt* due from individuals or companies to the people at large, ought to be compelled to give the public the greatest security possible for its redemption; and this will be best done through a proper system of *free private banking*.
Public and Private Economy, Part II (1838), Ch.III, Sec.78: 94–95

poverty:

2 Fashion, fashion, this is the only tyrant left to exercise an uncontrolled sway over the labour of the people of the United States. It is a prodigious passion for finery and fashion, that makes poor and keeps poor very many among us.
Public and Private Economy, Part I (1836), Ch.XII, Sec.203: 186

property:

3 Property is our *Power*, or a great portion of it; it is the power to do good, or to do evil; if then there be property in the oppressor to do evil, there should be property in the virtuous and the oppressed to counteract it, and to do good.
Public and Private Economy, Part I (1836), Ch.I, Sec.2: 14

4 [P]roperty is not only power, it is happiness, or the cause of happiness, unless it be abused.
Public and Private Economy, Part I (1836), Ch.I, Sec.2: 15

5 Those who desire a wise and fair distribution of property must conspire to be economical; to save their wages; to produce the most useful kinds of property; to create something that will last, and may be beneficially distributed; instead of working for trash, and where no work is wanted; being servants where no servants are required; grinding where there is nothing to grind; drawing for water, where there is no water. They must cease to produce or use that immense amount of trinkets, finery, gewgaws, fashionable trifles, dainties, and poisonous drink ... with which our persons are decorated, our groceries, stores, cellars, kitchens, pantries, and houses, are now too often crammed. This is not the kind of property that wise people wish to see distributed; nor is it property at all in their eyes. So far as this kind of property is imported from foreign nations, and paid for by our products, it is certain, that we may substitute the more useful productions of those nations, for this trash.
Public and Private Economy, Part I (1836), Ch.XV, Sec.279: 243–244

Edwin Robert Anderson Seligman
(1861–1939)

economics and economists:

1 Economic science is an outgrowth of economic conditions. It is a product of social unrest.
'Economics and Social Progress' (1903): 52

2 If economics is to be of any real service, it must deal with the important phenomena of economic life.
'Economics and Social Progress' (1903): 53

3 The economist, if he is worthy of his calling, will proceed without fear or favor; he will be tabooed as a socialist by some, as a minion of capital by others, as a theorist by more; but if he preserves his clearness of vision, his openness of mind, his devotion to truth, and his sanity of judgment, the deference paid to his views, which is even now beginning to be apparent in this country, will become more and more pronounced.
'Economics and Social Progress' (1903): 69

4 Economics is ... both the creature and the creator. It is the creature of the past; it is the creator of the future. Correctly conceived, adequately outlined, fearlessly developed, it is the prop of ethical upbuilding, it is the basis of social progress.
'Economics and Social Progress' (1903): 70

5 Nothing is harder than to construct a true theory. For a true theory must fit into every fact; otherwise it is not the correct theory. The hasty and untrue generalizations of those that set themselves up as 'theorists' are really responsible for the seeming antagonism. There can be as little divergence between true economic theory and actual economic life as between the theory of chemistry and chemical phenomena. It is the theory which must be made to fit the facts, and not the facts which must be twisted to suit the theory.
Principle of Economics (1921; 9th edn), Ch.II, §10: 28

socialism:

6 The difficulty of defining Socialism is that while Capitalism is an institution, Socialism is only a theory. . . . There are all manner of forms of Socialism and Socialistic theory. There is the Communistic Socialism. There is the Anarchistic Socialism. There is the State Socialism. There is the sentimental and scientific Socialism. And finally there is the Guild Socialism. What is worse, the Socialists themselves are by no means in agreement. The scientific Socialist, the Marxist, scorns the sentimental Socialist. The Marxian Socialism is supposed to be interpreted by the Menshevik Socialist, but the Menshevik is put by the Bolshevik Socialist in the ranks of the bourgeois. So that you have your choice of the different brands of Socialism as a theory.
A Debate on Capitalism vs. Socialism (1921), Presentation: 9

7 Socialism is bringing about a situation, the most horrible, the most frightful, the most hideous that the world has ever seen – the disappearance of culture, the disappearance of cities, the disappearance of civilization, and the rapid progression of universal starvation among the workers themselves. That is socialism in practice.
A Debate on Capitalism vs. Socialism (1921), Summary: 41

taxation:

8 It is notorious . . . that of all taxes the income tax is perhaps the most difficult to assess with scrupulous justice and accuracy; so that what is conceived in justice often results in crass injustice.
The Income Tax (1911), Introduction, Sec.4: 18

9 It is notorious that the ascertainment of individual income is exceedingly difficult. If the attempt to reach the income of the individual rests upon the declaration of the taxpayer himself, we are putting upon him a strain which, in the present state of the relations of the individual to the government, may be characterized as exceedingly severe. It presumes a condition of integrity, a readiness to support one's share, and a complete absence of any desire to benefit oneself at the expense of one's neighbor, which is unfortunately still too rare at the present time.
The Income Tax (1911), Introduction, Sec.9: 34

Nassau William Senior (1790–1864)

economics and economists:

1 [The economists'] conclusions, whatever be their generality and their truth, do not authorize him in adding a single syllable of advice. That privilege belongs to the writer or the statesman who has considered all the causes which may promote or impede the general welfare of those whom he addresses, not to the theorist who has considered only one, though among the most important, of those causes. The business of a Political Economist is neither to recommend nor to dissuade, but to state general principles, which it is fatal to neglect, but neither advisable, nor perhaps practicable, to use as the sole, or even the principal, guides in the actual conduct of affairs.
An Outline of the Science of Political Economy (1836), Introduction: 3

2 Political Economy does not deal with particular facts but with general tendencies. . . .
An Outline of the Science of Political Economy (1836), Distribution of Wealth: Exchange: 102

3 One of the great obstacles to the progress of the Moral Sciences is the tendency of doctrines, supposed to have been refuted, to reappear. In the Pure and in the Physical Sciences, each generation inherits the conquests made by its predecessors. No mathematician has to redemonstrate the problems of Euclid; no physiologist has to sustain a controversy as to the circulation of the blood; no astronomer is met by a denial of the principle of gravitation. But in the Moral Sciences the ground seems never to be incontestably won; and this is peculiarly the case with respect to the sciences which are subsidiary to the arts of administration and legislation. Opinions prevail and are acted on. The evils which appear to result from their practical application lead to enquiry. Their erroneousness is proved by philosophers, is acknowledged by the educated public, and at length is admitted

even by statesmen. The policy founded on the refuted error is relaxed, and the evils which it inflicted, so far as they are capable of remedy, are removed or mitigated. After a time new theorists arise, who are seduced or impelled by some moral or intellectual defect or error to reassert the exploded doctrine. They have become entangled by some logical fallacy, or deceived by some inaccurate or incomplete assumption of facts, or think that they see the means of acquiring reputation, or of promoting their interests, or of gratifying their political or their private resentments, by attacking the altered policy. All popular errors are plausible; indeed, if they were not so they would not be popular. The plausibility to which the revived doctrine owed its original currency, makes it acceptable to those to whom the subject is new; and even among those to whom it is familiar, probably ninety-nine out of every hundred are accustomed to take their opinions on such matters on trust. They hear with surprise that what they supposed to be settled is questioned, and often avoid the trouble of enquiring, by endeavouring to believe that the truth is not to be ascertained. And thus the cause has again to be pleaded before judges, some of whom are prejudiced, and others will not readily attend to reasoning founded on premises which they think unsusceptible of proof.
'Free Trade and Retaliation' (1843): 1–2

poverty and the poor laws:

4 There is so much pain in witnessing distress, and so much pleasure in procuring its relief; there is so much sympathy with unmerited misfortune, and with the sufferings to which the wife and children are exposed through the misconduct of the husband and father; misery and destitution are so severe a punishment for idleness or improvidence; the niggardliness of those whose refusal throws the whole burden of charity on the benevolent is so disgusting; and we must add, the assessment and distribution of a poor rate, give so many opportunities of undue profit, and so many means of gratifying the love of power and of popularity, that nothing but the strictest rules, vigilantly superintended and severely enforced, can restrain those whom the law enables to create and to manage a fund for charitable purposes – to decide how much shall be raised, and to whom and on what grounds and in what proportions it shall be awarded.
'Poor Law Reform' (1841): 11

5 We now know that to attempt to provide by legislative interference, that, in all the vicissitudes of commerce and of the seasons, all the labouring classes, whatever be the value of their services, shall enjoy a considerable subsistence, is an attempt which would in time ruin the industry of the most diligent, and the wealth of the most opulent community.
'Poor Law Reform' (1841): 15

George Lennox Sharman Shackle
(1903–1992)

economics and economists:

1 In natural science, what is thought is built upon what is seen: but in economics, what is seen is built upon what is thought.
Epistemics and Economics (1972), Bk.I, Ch.5, Sec.8: 66

2 By its insistence on measuring the unmeasurable, economics bludgeons the face of reality, the detail and vitality of human concerns are flattened to an unrecognizable tedium.
Epistemics and Economics (1972), Bk.II, Ch.10, Sec.4: 111

3 Economics has veritably turned imprecision itself into a science: economics, the science of the quantification of the unquantifiable and the aggregation of the incompatible. It has followed this road at so violent a gallop, that much which is of significance and influence has been trampled on, much territory has been claimed which cannot be held.
Epistemics and Economics (1972), Bk. VI, Ch.33: 360

exchange:

4 Does it take two people to make an exchange? Not when one and the same person has before him a choice of this or that. If he takes *this*, he will in effect be giving *that* in exchange for it. He will be giving up one thing, in order to have another. Exchange is choice, and choice is the act of

a particular person. What he chooses may be such that he needs another person's agreement, another person's choice. But we can look at the action of exchange through the eyes of one person at a time. It involves preference and sacrifice. It is deliberate. It gives advantage.
An Economic Querist (1973), Ch.I: 1

government:

5   Government policy is in its basic nature *statistical*, whether or not it has supplied itself with data. It cannot itself directly care for the individual but only for the mass and the average of society. The individual soldier must take his chance, so long as the army wins the battle. This is the necessary, irremediable philosophy of government.
Epistemics and Economics (1972), Bk. VI, Ch.33: 362

George Bernard Shaw (1856–1950)
Irish playwright

capitalism:

1   Capitalism ... means that the only duty of the Government is to maintain private property in land and capital, and to keep on foot an efficient police force and magistracy to enforce all private contracts made by individuals in pursuance of their own interests, besides, of course, keeping civil order and providing for naval and military defence or adventure.
The Intelligent Woman's Guide to Socialism and Capitalism (1928), Ch.28: 101

2   Capitalism, in its ceaseless search for investment, its absolute necessity for finding hungry men to eat its spare bread before it goes stale, breaks through every barrier, rushes every frontier, swallows every religion, levels every institution that obstructs it, and sets up any code of morals that facilitates it, as soullessly as it sets up banks and lays cables. And you must approve and conform, or be ruined, and perhaps imprisoned or executed.
The Intelligent Woman's Guide to Socialism and Capitalism (1928), Ch.67: 314

communism:

3   This need for pocket money (change) is greatly reduced by Communism.
The Intelligent Woman's Guide to Socialism and Capitalism (1928), Ch.55: 262

money:

4   [T]he most sacred economic duty of a Government is to keep the value of money steady; and it is because Governments can play tricks with the value of money that it is of such vital importance that they should consist of men who are honest, and who understand money thoroughly.
The Intelligent Woman's Guide to Socialism and Capitalism (1928), Ch.55: 256

socialism:

5   The first and last commandment of Socialism is 'Thou shalt not have a greater or less income than thy neighbor'....
The Intelligent Woman's Guide to Socialism and Capitalism (1928), Ch.27: 97

6   In opposition to Capitalism, Socialism insists that the first duty of the Government is to maintain equality of income, and absolutely denies any private right of property whatever.
The Intelligent Woman's Guide to Socialism and Capitalism (1928), Ch.28: 101

7   Socialism may be preached, not as a far-reaching economic reform, but as a new Church founded on a new revelation of the will of God made by a new prophet. It actually is so preached at present. Do not be misled by the fact that the missionaries of Church Socialism do not use the word God, nor call their organization a Church, nor decorate their meeting-places with steeples. They preach an inevitable, final, supreme category in the order of the universe in which all the contradictions of the earlier and lower categories will be reconciled. They do not speak, except in derision, of the Holy Ghost or the Paraclete; but they preach the Hegelian Dialectic. Their prophet is named neither Jesus nor Mahomet nor Luther nor Augustine nor Dominic nor

Joseph Smith, Junior, nor Mary Baker Glover Eddy, but Karl Marx. They call themselves, not the Catholic Church, but the Third International. Their metaphysical literature begins with the German philosophers Hegel and Feuerbach, and culminates in Das Kapital, the literary masterpiece of Marx, described as 'The Bible of the working classes', inspired, infallible, omniscient. Two of their tenets contradict oneanother [sic] as flatly as the first two paragraphs of Article 27 of the Church of England. One is that the evolution of Capitalism into Socialism is predestined, implying that we have nothing to do but sit down and wait for it to occur. This is their version of Salvation by Faith. The other is that it must be effected by a revolution establishing a dictatorship of the proletariat. This is their version of Salvation by Works.
The Intelligent Woman's Guide to Socialism and Capitalism (1928), Ch.82: 441

Henry Sidgwick (1838–1900)

methodology:

1 There seem to be two conditions which it is on different grounds desirable that a definition should satisfy as far as possible; but we should bear in mind that we frequently cannot satisfy either completely – still less both together. In the first place, we should keep as closely as we can to the common use of language: otherwise we are not only exposed to the danger of being misunderstood by others, through the force of habitual usage overcoming the impression produced by express definition; but we further run serious risk of being inconsistent with ourselves, on account of the similar effect of habit on our own minds. Secondly, our definitions should be carefully adapted to the doctrine that we have to expound; so that we may avoid as far as possible the continual use of qualifying epithets and phrases. In aiming at the first of these results, we should not forget that common usage may be inconsistent; on the other hand, we should not hastily assume that this is the case. Economists have sometimes missed the useful lessons which common thought has to teach, by deciding prematurely that a word is used in two or more distinct senses, and thus omitting to notice the common link of meaning that connects them.
'Economic Method' (1879): 310

2 [S]ome of the most eminent of them [economists] have not always seen that it is impossible to think definitely of the quantity of any aggregate of diverse elements, except so far as these elements admit of being reduced to a common quantitative standard; and that unless this is done, when we speak of such an aggregate as having increased or decreased in amount, or of something else as 'varying in proportion to' it, we are using words to which there are necessarily no definite thoughts corresponding.
'Economic Method' (1879): 311

socialism:

3 I object to socialism not because it would divide the produce of industry badly, but because it would have so much less to divide.
Principles of Political Economy (1901; 3rd edn), Bk.III, Ch.VI, Sec.6: 516

Georg Simmel (1858–1918)
German sociologist and philosopher

money:

1 Money is a specific realization of what is common to economic objects ... and the general misery of human life is most fully reflected by this symbol, namely by the constant shortage of money under which most people suffer.
The Philosophy of Money (1900), Ch.1, Sec.III: 120

2 Money is measured by the goods against which it is exchanged and also by money itself. For not only is money paid for by money, as the money market and interest-bearing loans show, but the money of one country becomes the measure of value for the money of another country, as is illustrated by foreign exchange transactions. Money is therefore one of those normative ideas that obey the norms that they themselves represent.
The Philosophy of Money (1900), Ch.1, Sec.III: 122

3   The inner polarity of the essence of money lies in its being the absolute means and thereby becoming psychologically the absolute purpose for most people, which makes it, in a strange way, a symbol in which the major regulators of practical life are frozen.
    The Philosophy of Money (1900), Ch.3, Sec.II: 232

4   Money, more than any other form of value, makes possible the secrecy, invisibility and silence of exchange. By compressing money into a piece of paper, by letting it glide into a person's hand, one can make him a wealthy person. Money's formlessness and abstractness makes it possible to invest it in the most varied and most remote values and thereby to remove it completely from the gaze of neighbours. Its anonymity and colourlessness does not reveal the source from which it came to the present owner: it does not have a certificate of origin in the way in which, more or less disguised, many concrete objects of possession do.
    The Philosophy of Money (1900), Ch.5, Sec.I: 385

5   The tendency of money to converge and to accumulate, if not in the hands of individuals then in fixed local centres; to bring together the interests of and thereby individuals themselves; to establish contact between them on a common ground and thus, as determined by the form of value that money represents, to concentrate the most diverse elements in the smallest possible space – in short, this tendency and capacity of money has the psychological effect of enhancing the variety and richness of life, that is of increasing the pace of life.
    The Philosophy of Money (1900), Ch.6, Sec.III: 505

Herbert Alexander Simon
(1916–2001)

decision-making:

1   Decision processes, like all other aspects of economic institutions, exist inside human heads. They are subject to change with every change in what human beings know, and with every change in their means of calculation. For this reason the attempt to predict and prescribe human economic behavior by deductive inference from a small set of unchallengeable premises must fail and has failed.
    'From Substantive to Procedural Rationality' (1976), Sec.4: 146

economic man:

2   The reluctance of economic theory to relinquish its classical model of economic man is understandable. When even a small concession has been made in the direction of admitting the fallibility of economic man, his psychological properties are no longer irrelevant. Deductive reasoning then no longer suffices for the unique prediction of his behavior without constant assistance from empirical observation.
    Models of Man (1957), Part IV, Introduction: 198

economics and economists:

3   Economics is one of the sciences of the artificial. It is a description and explanation of human institutions, whose theory is no more likely to remain invariant over time than the theory of bridge design.
    'From Substantive to Procedural Rationality' (1976), Sec.4: 146

4   In economics, hypotheses are certainly what we lack the least.
    The State of Economic Science (W. Sichel, ed., 1989, Ch.6): 105

5   What distinguishes science from every other form of human intellectual activity is that it disciplines speculation with facts. Theory and data are the two blades of the scissors. But the metaphor is not quite right, for the blades are not symmetric. When theories and facts are in conflict, the theories must yield. Economics has strayed from that simple principle, and it must return to it.
    The State of Economic Science (W. Sichel, ed., 1989, Ch.6): 110

rationality:

6   It is only a slight exaggeration to say that what an economist or statistical theorist regards as a 'rational decision process' is

what a psychologist might regard as 'habitual behavior'; while what a psychologists [sic] regards as 'rational choice,' an economists [sic] would refuse to regard as 'rational' at all.

'The Role of Expectations in an Adaptive or Behavioristic Model' (1958)

7 Economics, like chess, is inevitably culture-bound and history-bound. A business firm equipped with the tools of operations research does not make the same decisions as it did before it possessed those tools. The substantial secular decline over recent years of inventories held by American firms is probably due in considerable part to this enhancement of rationality by new theory and new computational tools.

'From Substantive to Procedural Rationality' (1976), Sec.4: 146

Julian Lincoln Simon (1932–1998)

population growth:

1 It is your mind that matters economically, as much or more than your mouth or hands. In the long run, the most important economic effect of population size and growth is the contribution of additional people to our stock of useful knowledge. And this contribution is large enough in the long run to overcome all the costs of population growth.

The Ultimate Resource (1981), Part Two, Ch.14: 196

shortages:

2 Greater consumption due to an increase in population and growth of income heightens scarcity and induces price run-ups. A higher price represents an opportunity that leads inventors and businesspeople to seek new ways to satisfy the shortages. Some fail, at cost to themselves. A few succeed, and the final result is that we end up better off than if the original shortage problems had never arisen. That is, we need our problems, though this does not imply that we should purposely create additional problems for ourselves.

The Ultimate Resource 2 (1996), Introduction: 12

Jean-Charles-Léonard Simonde de Sismondi (1773–1842)

economics and economists:

1 The physical well-being of man, so far as it can be produced by his government, is the object of Political Economy.

Political Economy (1815), Ch.I: 1

exploitation:

2 The advantage of an employer of labor is often nothing else than the plunder of the worker he hired; he does not profit because his enterprise produced much more than its costs, but because he does not pay all the costs, because he does not grant to the worker sufficient compensation for his work. Such an industry is a social evil since it reduces to ultimate penury those who perform the work, while it secures only an ordinary profit of capital to him who manages it.

New Principles of Political Economy (1827; 2nd edn), Bk.2, Ch.4: 83

government:

3 When government means to protect commerce, it often acts with precipitation, in complete ignorance of its true interests; almost always with despotic violence, which tramples under foot the greater part of private arrangements; and almost always with an absolute forgetfulness of the advantage of consumers, who, as they form by far the most numerous class, have more right than any other to confound their wellbeing with that of the nation. Yet it must not be inferred, that government never does good to trade. It is government which can give habits of dissipation or economy; which can attach honour or discredit to industry and activity; which can turn the attention of scientific men to apply their discoveries to the arts: government is the richest of all consumers; it encourages manufactures by the mere circumstance of giving them its custom. If to this indirect influence it join the care of rendering all communications easy; of preparing roads, canals, bridges; of protecting property, of securing a fair administration of justice; if it do not overload its subjects with taxation; if, in levying the taxes, it adopt no disastrous system, – it will effectually have served

commerce, and its beneficial influence will counterbalance many false measures, many prohibitory laws, in spite of which, and not by reason of which, commerce will continue to increase under it.
Political Economy (1815), Ch.IV: 78

public debt:

4   A government which borrows, after having dissipated its capital, makes posterity perpetually debtor in the clearest part of the profit arising from its work. An overwhelming burden is cast upon it, to bow down one generation after another. Public calamities may occur, trade may take a new direction, rivals may supplant us. The reproduction which is sold beforehand may never reappear; yet notwithstanding we are loaded with a debt above our strength, with a debt of hypothecating our future labour, which we shall not perhaps be able to accomplish.
Political Economy (1815), Ch.VI: 108

taxation:

5   Taxation, of itself always an object of repugnance to the subject, has become a nearly intolerable burden; the question is no longer how to make it easy; it is not to do good, but to do the least possible evil, that all the efforts of governments in this respect are limited.
Political Economy (1815), Ch.VI: 94

6   Governments have not been contented with taxing revenues and expenditure; they have gone forth to seek out all the acts of civil life which might afford them an opportunity of asking money.
Political Economy (1815), Ch.VI: 105

7   Every taxpayer, through his money, ought to obtain more enjoyments from roads, canals, public fountains, the security of his person, the education he received, than if he would have sought to provide all these things at his own cost. The money the tax takes from him will then be well used if, on the one hand, all that is taken in the name of social happiness is really devoted to social benefits, and not to satisfy or pamper the passions of the rulers; if, on the other hand, those to whom such benefits are to be secured are capable of purchasing them with their incomes.
New Principles of Political Economy (1827; 2nd edn), Bk.6, Ch.1: 447

Henry Calvert Simons (1899–1946)

capitalism:

1   [T]he so-called failure of capitalism (of the free-enterprise system, of competition) may reasonably be interpreted as primarily a failure of the political state in the discharge of its minimum responsibilities under capitalism.
Economic Policy for a Free Society (1948), Ch.II: 43

2   It seems clear, at all events, that there is an intimate connection between freedom of enterprise and freedom of discussion and that political liberty can survive only within an effectively competitive economic system. Thus, *the great enemy of democracy is monopoly, in all its forms*: gigantic corporations, trade associations and other agencies for price control, trade-unions – or, in general, organization and concentration of power within functional classes.
Economic Policy for a Free Society (1948), Ch.II: 43

collectivism:

3   Collectivism is a name for an extreme form of governmental centralization or power concentration. To the student of society, it must seem wholly unnatural and utterly unstable. It may serve useful purposes for a time; but it is not itself a viable social or political order. Its order is synthetic and fragile; its order is imposed from above, while real social order is a growth or building-upward. A highly centralized world government is nearly unthinkable – save as a hysterical imputation of evil purpose in an enemy power. It could be the imposition only of a predominant, militarized nation and, in the modern world, would be the most precarious basis of peace – if it is not the antithesis of peace – in any discerning apprehension of meanings.
Economic Policy for a Free Society (1948), Ch.I: 22

socialism:

4   Socialism, of necessity, has been deeply corrupted by liberalism and conversely, for they have been contemporaries in a world of free discussion and have been catalyzed by

the same evils and guided by much the same aspirations. Indeed, it is now hard to see how socialists and libertarians can long sustain substantial differences, save by avoiding all discussion.
Economic Policy for a Free Society (1948), Ch.I: 30

trade unions:

5   Questioning the virtues of the organized labor movement is like attacking religion, monogamy, motherhood, or the home.
'Some Reflections on Syndicalism' (1944): 1

6   For my part, I simply cannot conceive of any tolerable or enduring order in which there exists widespread organization of workers along occupational, industrial, functional lines.
'Some Reflections on Syndicalism' (1944): 1

7   Unionists are much like our communist friends. They are good fighters and like fighting for its own sake. They are extremely effective at undermining the political and economic system which we have but are surprisingly unconcerned and inarticulate about the nature of the world which they would create afterward. In neither case is there much constructive thought. Communists are out to destroy capitalism; unionists are out to destroy competition in labor markets. The former talk a lot about the evils of capitalism but never tell us much descriptively about the good life. Unionists, on the other hand, have never bothered to draw us a picture of their utopia. In other words, they have taken unions for granted as necessary elements in the good society but have not bothered about the nature of the good society within which unions would be good.
'Some Reflections on Syndicalism' (1944): 19–20; cf. Selig Perlman 2

Christopher Albert Sims (1942–)

economics and economists:

1   The fact that economics is not physics does not mean that we should not aim to apply the same fundamental standards for what constitutes legitimate argument; we can insist that the ultimate criterion for judging economic ideas is the degree to which they help us order and summarize data, that it is not legitimate to try to protect attractive theories from the data.
'Macroeconomics and Methodology' (1996): 111

William T. Smart (1853–1915)

wealth:

1   What most stirs the imagination of the economist is the possibility of material wealth now within man's grasp. What most perplexes him is that, with it all, the majority of our people are yet poor, and that the drift of the time seems to be towards keeping them poor.
'The Place of Industry in the Social Organism' (1893): 437

Adam Smith (1723–1790)

bankruptcy:

1   Bankruptcy is perhaps the greatest and most humiliating calamity which can befal an innocent man. The greater part of men, therefore, are sufficiently careful to avoid it. Some, indeed, do not avoid it; as some do not avoid the gallows.
Wealth of Nations (1789; 5th edn), Bk.II, Ch.III: 325

benevolence:

2   It is not from the benevolence of the butcher, the brewer, or the baker, that we expect our dinner, but from their regard to their own interest. We address ourselves, not to their humanity but to their self-love, and never talk to them of our necessities but of their advantages.
Wealth of Nations (1789; 5th edn), Bk.I, Ch.II: 14

3   No benevolent man ever lost altogether the fruits of his benevolence.
Theory of Moral Sentiments (1790; 6th edn), Part VI, Sec.II, Ch.I: 225

consumption:

4   Consumption is the sole end and purpose of all production; and the interest of the

producer ought to be attended to, only so far as it may be necessary for promoting that of the consumer.
Wealth of Nations (1789; 5th edn), Bk.IV, Ch.VIII: 625

division of labor:

5   The greatest improvement in the productive powers of labour, and the greater part of the skill, dexterity, and judgement with which it is any where directed, or applied, seem to have been the effects of the division of labour.
Wealth of Nations (1789; 5th edn), Bk.I, Ch.I: 3

6   It is the great multiplication of the productions of all the different arts, in consequence of the division of labour, which occasions, in a well-governed society, that universal opulence which extends itself to the lowest ranks of the people.
Wealth of Nations (1789; 5th edn), Bk.I, Ch.I: 11

7   The division of labour, from which so many advantages are derived, is not originally the effect of any human wisdom, which foresees and intends that general opulence to which it gives occasion. It is the necessary, though very slow and gradual, consequence of a certain propensity in human nature which has in view no such extensive utility; the propensity to truck, barter, and exchange one thing for another.
Wealth of Nations (1789; 5th edn), Bk.I, Ch.II: 13; cf. Karl Polanyi 1

8   The difference of natural talents in different men is, in reality, much less than we are aware of; and the very different genius which appears to distinguish men of different professions, when grown up to maturity, is not upon many occasions so much the cause, as the effect of the division of labour. The difference between the most dissimilar characters, between a philosopher and a common street porter, for example, seems to arise not so much from nature, as from habit, custom, and education.
Wealth of Nations (1789; 5th edn), Bk.I, Ch.II: 15

government:

9   [T]hough the profusion of government must, undoubtedly, have retarded the natural progress of England towards wealth and improvement, it has not been able to stop it.
Wealth of Nations (1789; 5th edn), Bk.II, Ch.III: 328

10 The statesman, who should attempt to direct private people in what manner they ought to employ their capitals, would not only load himself with a most unnecessary attention, but assume an authority which could safely be trusted, not only to no single person, but to no council or senate whatever, and which would nowhere be so dangerous as in the hands of a man who had folly and presumption enough to fancy himself fit to exercise it.
Wealth of Nations (1789; 5th edn), Bk.IV, Ch.II: 423

11 The sovereign is completely discharged from a duty, in the attempting to perform which he must always be exposed to innumerable delusions, and for the proper performance of which no human wisdom or knowledge could ever be sufficient; the duty of superintending the industry of private people, and of directing it towards the employments most suitable to the interest of the society. According to the system of natural liberty, the sovereign has only three duties to attend to . . .: first, the duty of protecting the society from the violence and invasion of other independent societies; secondly, the duty of protecting, as far as possible, every member of the society from the injustice or oppression of every other member of it, or the duty of establishing an exact administration of justice; and, thirdly, the duty of erecting and maintaining certain public works and certain public institutions, which it can never be for the interest of any individual, or small number of individuals, to erect and maintain. . . .
Wealth of Nations (1789; 5th edn), Bk.IV, Ch.IX: 651

12 There is no art which one government sooner learns of another, than that of draining money from the pockets of the people.
Wealth of Nations (1789; 5th edn), Bk.V, Ch.II, Appendix to Articles I and II: 813

'invisible hand':

13 The rich . . . divide with the poor the produce of all their improvements. They are led by an invisible hand to make nearly the same distribution of the necessaries of life, which would have been made, had the earth been divided into equal portions among all its inhabitants . . .
The Theory of Moral Sentiments (1790; 6th edn), Part IV Ch.1: 184–185; cf. Adam Smith 21

monopoly:

14 The price of monopoly is upon every occasion the highest which can be got.
Wealth of Nations (1789; 5th edn), Bk.I, Ch.VII: 61

15 Monopoly . . . is a great enemy to good management . . .
Wealth of Nations (1789; 5th edn), Bk.I, Ch.XI, Part I: 147

16 [E]very system which endeavours, either, by extraordinary encouragements, to draw towards a particular species of industry a greater share of the capital of the society than what would naturally go to it; or, by extraordinary restraints, to force from a particular species of industry some share of the capital which would otherwise be employed in it; is in reality subversive of the great purpose which it means to promote. It retards, instead of accelerating, the progress of the society towards real wealth and greatness; and diminishes, instead of increasing, the real value of the annual produce of its land and labour.

All systems either of preference or of restraint, therefore, being thus completely taken away, the obvious and simple system of natural liberty establishes itself of its own accord. Every man, as long as he does not violate the laws of justice, is left perfectly free to pursue his own interest his own way, and to bring both his industry and capital into competition with those of any other man, or order of men.
Wealth of Nations (1789; 5th edn), Bk.IV, Ch.IX: 650–651

poverty:

17 [W]hat improves the circumstances of the greater part can never be regarded as an inconveniency to the whole. No society can surely be flourishing and happy, of which the far greater part of the members are poor and miserable.
Wealth of Nations (1789; 5th edn), Bk.I, Ch.VIII: 78–79

privatization:

18 In every great monarchy of Europe the sale of the crown lands would produce a very large sum of money, which, if applied to the payment of the public debts, would deliver from mortgage a much greater revenue than any which those lands have ever afforded to the crown. . . . When the crown lands had become private property, they would, in the course of a few years, become well-improved and well-cultivated. The increase of their produce would increase the population of the country, by augmenting the revenue and consumption of the people. But the revenue which the crown derives from the duties of customs and excise, would necessarily increase with the revenue and consumption of the people.
Wealth of Nations (1789; 5th edn), Bk.V, Ch.II, Part I: 776

regulation:

19 To widen the market and to narrow the competition, is always the interest of the dealers. To widen the market may frequently be agreeable enough to the interest of the public; but to narrow the competition must always be against it, and can serve only to enable the dealers, by raising their profits above what they naturally would be, to levy, for their own benefit, an absurd tax upon the rest of their fellow-citizens. The proposal of any new law or regulation of commerce which comes from this order, ought always to be listened to with great precaution, and ought never to be adopted till after having been long and carefully examined, not only with the most scrupulous, but with the most suspicious attention. It comes from an order of men, whose interest is never exactly the same with that of the public, who have generally an interest to deceive and even to oppress the public, and who accordingly have, upon many occasions, both deceived and oppressed it.
Wealth of Nations (1789; 5th edn), Bk.I, Ch.XI, Conclusion: 250

self-interest:

20 The uniform, constant, and uninterrupted effort of every man to better his condition, the principle from which public and national, as well as private opulence is originally derived, is frequently powerful enough to maintain the natural progress of things toward improvement, in spite both of the extravagance of government, and of the greatest errors of administration. Like the unknown principle of animal life, it frequently restores health and vigour to the constitution, in spite, not only of the disease, but of the absurd prescriptions of the doctor.
Wealth of Nations (1789; 5th edn), Bk.II, Ch.III: 326

21 As every individual, therefore, endeavours as much as he can both to employ his capital in the support of domestic industry, and so to direct that industry that its produce may be of the greatest value; every individual necessarily labours to render the annual revenue of the society as great as he can. He generally, indeed, neither intends to promote the public interest, nor knows how much he is promoting it. By preferring the support of domestic to that of foreign industry, he intends only his own security; and by directing that industry in such a manner as its produce may be of the greatest value, he intends only his own gain, and he is in this, as in many other cases, led by an invisible hand to promote an end which was no part of his intention. Nor is it always the worse for the society that it was no part of it. By pursuing his own interest he frequently promotes that of the society more effectually than when he really intends to promote it. I have never known much good done by those who affected to trade for the public good. It is an affectation, indeed, not very common among merchants, and very few words need be employed in dissuading them from it.
Wealth of Nations (1789; 5th edn), Bk.IV, Ch.II: 423; cf. Adam Smith 13

22 How selfish soever man may be supposed, there are evidently some principles in his nature, which interest him in the fortune of others, and render their happiness necessary to him, though he derives nothing from it except the pleasure of seeing it.
The Theory of Moral Sentiments (1790; 6th edn), Part I, Sec.I, Ch.I: 9

taxation:

23 The proprietor of stock is properly a citizen of the world, and is not necessarily attached to any particular country. He would be apt to abandon the country in which he was exposed to a vexatious inquisition, in order to be assessed to a burdensome tax, and would remove his stock to some other country where he could either carry on his business, or enjoy his fortune more at his ease. By removing his stock he would put an end to all the industry which it had maintained in the country which he left. Stock cultivates land; stock employs labour. A tax which tended to drive away stock from any particular country, would so far tend to dry up every source of revenue, both to the sovereign and to the society. Not only the profits of stock, but the rent of land and the wages of labour, would necessarily be more or less diminished by its removal.
Wealth of Nations (1789; 5th edn), Bk.V, Ch.II, Part II, Article II: 800

value:

24 [Value] is adjusted ... not by any accurate measure, but by the higgling and bargaining of the market, according to that sort of rough equality which, though not exact, is sufficient for carrying on the business of common life.
Wealth of Nations (1789; 5th edn), Book I, Ch.V: 31

wants:

25 A very poor man may be said in some sense to have a demand for a coach and six; he might like to have it; but his demand is not an effectual demand, as the commodity can never be brought to market in order to satisfy it.
Wealth of Nations (1789; 5th edn), Bk.I, Ch.VII: 56

26 The desire of food is limited in every man by the narrow capacity of the human stomach; but the desire of the conveniencies and ornaments of building, dress, equipage, and household furniture, seems to have no limit or certain boundary.
Wealth of Nations (1789; 5th edn), Bk.I, Ch.XI, Part II: 164

Erasmus Peshine Smith (1814–1882)

economics and economists:

1 To investigate the laws which explain man's attainment, through association, of enlarged power over matter in all its forms, and the development of his intellectual and moral faculties, in virtue of that power, is the object of Political Economy.
A Manual of Political Economy (1853), Introduction: 12

taxation:

2 In one thing all governments agree. All require taxes in some shape or another.
A Manual of Political Economy (1853), Ch.IX: 264

3 The principle of equality demands that all taxes for the sake of revenue should be imposed directly, because such is the only mode in which the contribution of each individual can be adjusted in proportion to his means.
A Manual of Political Economy (1853), Ch.IX: 265

4 [T]axes should be levied in such a form as to promote the general purposes for which government is instituted, to diminish the evils it is designed to avert, and thus decrease the necessity for future taxation.
A Manual of Political Economy (1853), Ch.IX: 265; cf. Simon Newcomb 7, Robert Owen 7, David Ricardo 11

Vernon Lomax Smith (1927–)

economics and economists:

1 The critics of economic theory charge that, while theorists fiddle, the empire burns. We are urged to abandon what we have considered to be economic science and rise to an attack upon the agonizing social problems of the day. Ultimately, I believe, there is only one way to change the course of economic analysis, and that is for its disheartened critics, or others, to chart and pursue a new direction. If it leads to something insightful, it will command a respectable following. But generally the critics have not chosen to change the course of economics in this manner. Instead, they have paid us the high compliment of attacking what we have done and urging us to turn our efforts to the ends they seek. Unfortunately, most of us have remained stonily silent about what they have said.
'Economic Theory and Its Discontents' (1974): 320

William Henry Smith (1808–1872)
British philosopher

economics and economists:

1 In the old feud between the man of experience and the man of theory, it sometimes happens that the former obtains a triumph by the mere activity of the latter. Cases have been known where the theorist, in the clarifying and perfecting his own theory, has argued himself round to those very truths which his empirical antagonist had held to with a firm though less reasoning faith. He stood to his post; the stream of knowledge seemed to be flowing past him, and those who floated on it laughed at his stationary figure as they left him behind. Nevertheless he stood still; and by-and-by this meandering stream, with the busy crew that navigated it, after many a turn and many a curve, have returned to the very spot where he had made his obstinate halt.
This has been illustrated, and we venture to say will be illustrated still further, in the progress of the science of political economy. The man of experience has been taunted for his obstinacy and blindness in adhering to something which he called common sense and matter of fact; and behold! the scientific economist, in the course of his own theorizing, is returning to those very positions from which he has been endeavouring to drive his opponent.
'Political Economy, by J.S. Mill' (1848): 407

2 Our main quarrel – though we have many – with the political economists is on this ground – that, having constructed a theory explanatory of the *wealth* of nations, they have wished to enforce this upon our legislature, as if it had embraced all the causes which conspire to the *well-being* of nations; as if wealth and well-being were synonimous [sic]. Having determined the state of

things best fitted to procure, in general, the greatest aggregate amount of riches, they have proceeded to deal with a people as if it were a corporate body, whose sole object was to increase the total amount of its possessions. They have overlooked the equally vital questions concerning the distribution of these possessions, and of the *various employments* of mankind. Full of their leading idea, and accustomed to abstractions and generalities, they forget the *individual*, and appear to treat their subject as if the aggregate wealth of a community were to be enjoyed in some aggregate manner, and a sum-total of possessions would represent the comforts and enjoyments of its several members. To know what measures tend to increase the national wealth is undoubtedly of great importance, but it is not *all*; the theory of riches or of commerce, is not the theory of society.
'Political Economy, by J.S. Mill' (1848): 408

3 Political economists have some of them wasted much time, and produced no little ennui, by unprofitable discussions on the definitions of terms.
'Political Economy, by J.S. Mill' (1848): 415

trade:

4 What if England, by carrying out, without pause or exception, the doctrine of free-trade, should aggravate the most alarming symptoms of her present social condition – must this *law* of the political economist be still, with unmitigated strictness, urged upon her! She pleads for exception, for delay; but the political economist will not see the grounds of her plea – will not recognise her reasons for exception: full of his partial science, which has been made to occupy too large a portion of his field of vision, he *cannot* see them.
'Political Economy, by J.S. Mill' (1848): 409

Robert Merton Solow (1924–)

econometrics:

1 I am trying to express an attitude towards the building of very simple models. I don't think that models like this lead directly to prescription for policy or even to detailed diagnosis. But neither are they a game. They are more like reconnaissance exercises. If you want to know what it's like out there, it's all right to send two or three fellows in sneakers to find out the lay of the land and whether it will support human life. If it turns out to be worth settling, then that requires an altogether bigger operation. The job of building usable larger-scale econometric models on the basis of whatever analytical insights come from simple models is much more difficult and less glamorous. But it may be what God made graduate students for. Presumably he had something in mind.
Growth Theory: An Exposition (1970), Conclusion: 105

economics and economists:

2 Distinguished and clever economists have been heard to remark knowingly that they understand microeconomics perfectly well and know what they think about this or that, but do not understand macroeconomics at all and find it a mystery. I have no patience with that ploy. Macroeconomics is what it is all about. If you do not understand the business cycle, unemployment, inflation, the real exchange rate, well, you do not understand economics at all. Microeconomics is easier, of course; it does not set itself such hard problems or aim at passing such hard tests.
The State of Economic Science (W. Sichel, ed., 1989, Ch.2): 25; cf. Buchanan 4

3 The funny thing is that the sophisticated economist sometimes errs by assuming that every observed transaction marks the intersection of a demand curve and a supply curve, while the economically unsophisticated noneconomist forgets that most observed transactions *are* at the intersection of a demand curve and a supply curve.
'It Ain't the Things You Don't Know That Hurt You, It's the Things You Know That Ain't So' (1997): 108

4 Maybe the main function of economics in general is not, as we usually think, the systematic building of theories and models,

or their empirical estimation. Maybe we are intellectual sanitation workers. The world is full of nonsense, full of things people and institutions know that 'ain't so.' Maybe the higher function of economics is to hold out against nonsense. . . .
    'It Ain't the Things You Don't Know That Hurt You, It's the Things You Know That Ain't So' (1997): 108

mathematics in economics:

5 One often sees the question: 'Have economists gone too far in the use of mathematics?' as if mathematics were the gin in the martini of economics. The only test is the flavor and potency of the result, its *economic* content, not the weighing of ingredients. On this the profession (or Natural Selection or Supply and Demand) will judge.
    'The Survival of Mathematical Economics' (1954): 374

theory:

6 [A] theory capable of explaining anything that might possibly be observed is hardly a theory at all.
    Growth Theory: An Exposition (1970), Ch.1: 5

Werner Sombart (1863–1941)

economic history:

1 The inadequate equipment of economic historians is responsible for those innumerable, almost valueless, compilations which constitute the bulk of the contributions to the subject. Even as compilations these works cannot be commended, for their authors are deficient in the understanding of principles. Without such an understanding, which only a theoretical training can impart, it is impossible to produce even a good compilation. Facts are like beads: they require a string to hold then together, to connect them. But if there is no string, if there is no unifying idea, then even the most distinguished authorities cannot help producing unsatisfactory work.
    'Economic Theory and Economic History' (1929), Sec.III: 4–5

Robert Southey (1774–1843)
British poet, rhetorician, miscellaneous writer

economics and economists:

1 A science they call it [political economy], though they cannot yet agree among themselves upon their definitions, and differ as widely in most of their conclusions. Yet it is a science forsooth! one for which professorships have been founded, and in conformity to which, government was called upon to regulate its fiscal and financial measures. . . . Practical men raised their warning voices in vain, the ministers were flattered into an acquiescence with the schemes of these theorists, and they were then insulted, as they deserved, for having so acquiesced. None but a weak man will suppose, that national affairs can be conducted wisely without philosophy; but the philosophy must be of a very different kind from that which is taught by our political economists; it must look farther and wider, rise higher and go deeper, have a better foundation to rest on, and a nobler end in view.
    'Moral and Political State of the British Empire' (1831): 278

public works:

2 If stagnant manufactures, and languishing agriculture, and a population suddenly turned loose from the military or naval services of the country, produce a supply of hands for which there is no work, a partial and temporary remedy might perhaps have been found in undertakings of public utility and magnificence – in the improvement of roads, the completion of canals, the erection of our National Monuments for Waterloo and Trafalgar – undertakings which government might have supplied, if the means had been at their disposal. To attempt to raise money for such a purpose in the present state of the country would be, indeed, an adventurous policy.
    'Parliamentary Reform' (1816): 277

Thomas Sowell (1930–)

morality:

1 Morality as an input into the social process is subject to diminishing returns, and ultimately

to negative returns. With no morality at all, force would be more prevelant [sic] – a loss both to those subject to it and to the efficiency of the social processes. A modicum of honesty and decency greatly reduces the incessant and desperate efforts otherwise necessary to protect life and belongings from every other human being. Beyond some point, social morality becomes irksome to individual autonomy. Finally, if each individual were to become absolutely committed to moral behavior as he saw it, no society would be possible among diverse individuals or groups.
Knowledge and Decisions (1980), Part I, Ch.4: 107

social justice:

2   Envy was once considered to be one of the seven deadly sins before it became one of the most admired virtues under its new name, 'social justice.'
The Quest for Cosmic Justice (1999), Ch.II: 77

Herbert Spencer (1820–1903)
British social theorist

government:

1   Indeed, the more numerous public instrumentalities become, the more is there generated in citizens the notion that everything is to be done for them, and nothing by them. Each generation is made less familiar with the attainment of desired ends by individual actions or private combinations, and more familiar with the attainment of them by governmental agencies; until, eventually, governmental agencies come to be thought of as the only available agencies.
'The Coming Slavery' (1884): 471

2   See then the many concurrent causes which threaten continually to accelerate the transformation now going on. There is that spread of regulation caused by following precedents, which become the more authoritative the further the policy is carried. There is that increasing need for administrative compulsions and restraints which results from the unforeseen evils and shortcomings of preceding compulsions and restraints. Moreover, every additional State-interference strengthens the tacit assumption that it is the duty of the State to deal with all evils and secure all benefits. Increasing power of a growing administrative organization is accompanied by decreasing power of the rest of the society to resist its further growth and control.
'The Coming Slavery' (1884): 473–473

3   It is not to the State that we owe the multitudinous useful inventions from the plough to the telephone; it is not the State which made possible extended navigation by a developed astronomy; it is not the State which made the discoveries in physics, chemistry and the rest, which guide modern manufacturers; it is not the State which devised the machinery for producing fabrics of every kind, for transferring men and things from place to place, and for ministering in a thousand ways to our comforts. The world-wide transactions conducted in merchants' offices, the rush of traffic filling our streets, the retail distributing system which brings everything within easy reach and delivers the necessaries of life daily at our doors, are not of governmental origin. All these are the results of the spontaneous activities of citizens, separate or grouped.
'The Sins of Legislators,' Part II (1884): 764; cf. Alfred Marshall 17

poverty and poor relief:

4   There is a notion, always more or less prevalent and just now vociferously expressed, that all social suffering is removable, and that it is the duty of somebody or other to remove it. Both these beliefs are false. To separate pain from ill-doing is to fight against the constitution of things, and will be followed by far more pain. Saving men from the natural penalties of dissolute living, eventually necessitates the infliction of artificial penalties in solitary cells, on treadwheels, and by the lash.
'The Coming Slavery' (1884): 462

socialism:

5   All socialism involves slavery.
'The Coming Slavery' (1884): 474

Piero Sraffa (1898–1983)

money:

1 [M]oney is not only the medium of exchange, but also a store of value, and the standard in terms of which debts, and other legal obligations, habits, opinions, conventions, in short all kinds of relations between men, are more or less rigidly fixed.
    'Dr. Hayek on Money and Capital' (1932): 43; cf. F.A. Walker 3

Josiah Charles Stamp, 1st Baron Stamp of Shortlands (1880–1941)

economics and economists:

1 Most economists find enough work to do in taking aims for granted, and working upon the remaining factors, unconfused by values and valuations, just as an engineer does not much want to ponder on the direction in which his bridge leads, and the people that will use it. Its uses may be an inspiration for his work, but no guidance in it.
    Christianity and Economics (1938), Ch.7, Sec.I: 164

Herbert Stein (1916–1999)

economics and economists:

1 Even though we are economists we like to think that we have not only a price, but also a value, which is presumably greater.
    'The Washington Economics Industry' (1986): 9

Sir James Steuart-Denham, 4th Baronet (1712–1780)

credit:

1 Credit is the *reasonable expectation entertained by him who fulfils his side of any contract, that the other contracting party will reciprocally make good his engagements.*
    An Inquiry Into the Principles of Political Œconomy (1767) Book IV, Part I, Ch.I: 141

economics and economists:

2 The great art ... of political œconomy is, first to adapt the different operations of it to the spirit, manners, habits, and customs of the people; and afterwards to model these circumstances so, as to be able to introduce a set of new and more useful institutions.
    The principal object of this science is to secure a certain fund of subsistence for all the inhabitants, to obviate every circumstance which may render it precarious; to provide every thing necessary for supplying the wants of the society, and to employ the inhabitants (supposing them to be free-men) in such a manner as naturally to create reciprocal relations and dependencies between them, so as to make their several interests lead them to supply one another with their reciprocal wants.
    An Inquiry Into the Principles of Political Œconomy (1767) Book I, Introduction: 3

interest:

3 I shall leave it to divines and casuists to determine how far the exacting of interest for money is lawful, according to the principles of our religion.
    An Inquiry Into the Principles of Political Œconomy (1767) Book IV, Part I, Ch.III: 151

money:

4 Money, which I call of account, is no more than *an arbitrary scale of equal parts, invented for measuring the respective value of things vendible.*
    An Inquiry Into the Principles of Political Œconomy (1767) Book III, Part I, Ch.I: 270

taxation:

5 The net produce alone of the earth is to be considered as a fund liable to taxation; and every contribution which bears not a just proportion to this quantity, is wrong imposed....
    An Inquiry Into the Principles of Political Œconomy (1767), Book V, Ch.II: 179

6 Raising money by taxes must always be burdensome, less or more, to those who pay it; and the advantages resulting from taxes

can proceed only from the right application of the money when it is raised.
An Inquiry Into the Principles of Political Œconomy (1767), Book V, Ch.VII: 227

William Stevenson (1772–1829)
British journalist

economics and economists:

1   [I]f we can succeed in proving – which we flatter ourselves we shall be able to do – that Political Economy – professing to develope [sic] and explain the sources and causes of social wealth, and the means by which it is distributed – must have its foundation in facts and experience; and, therefore, can be reduced to general laws, which, as drawn from these facts, must be such as will explain all other facts and events that may occur, relative to social wealth; we shall then have, in a great measure, destroyed one of the principal strongholds of those who deny to Political Economy the name and dignity of a science.
'The Political Economist' (1824), Essay First: 527

2   Rash and unwarranted conclusions are perhaps in no investigations more frequent and dangerous, than in those which relate to Political Economy. Against their occurrence and influence, therefore, we ought to be most carefully and continually on our guard, especially as they often steal upon us unawares, or insinuate themselves into our opinions or reasonings, under the guise of well-founded and indisputable truths.
'The Political Economist' (1824), Essay III, Part I: 202–203

mathematics in economics:

3   The application of algebra, or the fluctional calculus, to reasoning in Political Economy, is another instance of the improper mixing of sciences, as well as a proof that this science resembles others with respect to the causes which have impeded its progress, or obscured its real nature and limits. The application to which we have just alluded, has another indirect evil consequence, for we are so much the creatures of habit, and under the influence of associations and first impressions – that a student of Political Economy, on perceiving the principles or reasonings of this branch of knowledge thrown into a mathematical form, with what bears all the appearance of a strict analytical proof, is insensibly led into the belief, that they are not only true, but true to a mathematical certainty; whereas they may really be without foundation, and undoubtedly cannot rest on the same basis of certainty as the mathematics.
'The Political Economist' (1824), Essay First: 530

Dugald Stewart (1753–1828)

economics and economists:

1   [I]t is the business of the Political Economist to watch over the *concerns of all*, and to point out to the Legislator the danger of listening exclusively to claims founded in local or in partial advantages. . . .
Lectures on Political Economy (1855), Volume I, Introduction, Ch.I: 12

2   [W]hat I would chiefly rest my hopes upon, in looking forward to the future condition of mankind, is the influence which the science of *Political Economy* (a science in a great measure of modern origin) must necessarily have, in directing the rulers of nations to just principles of administration, by shewing them how intimately the interests of government are connected with those of the people, and the authority which this science must gradually acquire over the minds both of the governors and the governed, in proportion as its fundamental principles are generally diffused and understood.
Lectures on Political Economy (1856), Volume II, Part Second, Ch.I, Sec.II, Subsection III: 399–400

George Joseph Stigler (1911–1991)

economics and economists:

1   Some economists are fond of repeating that we are all dead in the long run; they appear not to have noticed that this is true only with special and uninteresting meanings of 'we' and 'long run.'
'A Survey of Contemporary Economics' (1949), Sec.II: 103

2   Because our views have been guided by casual observation, ours has become a flabby science. A single contrary investigation causes consternation, for the whole edifice may tumble – indeed, it will tumble if a few sufficiently prominent economists capitulate. This would be impossible if economics had been accumulating carefully tested regularities of economic behavior; then we could be sure that most of what we knew would continue to be true, no matter how breath-takingly original the ideas advanced in the next numbers of the journals, no matter how disconcerting the replies of several dozen entrepreneurs to a questionnaire.
   'A Survey of Contemporary Economics' (1949), Sec.II: 104

3   Economists are subject to the coercion of the ruling ideologies of their times, and if they wholly resist them they would lose all rapport with their societies – the expression would become, the visitor from economics, not from Mars.
   'The Politics of Political Economists' (1959), Sec.II: 524

4   In general there is no position ... which cannot be reached by a competent use of respectable economic theory.
   'The Politics of Political Economists' (1959), Sec.IV: 531

5   We [economists] shall no doubt continue to bend before a strong wind, but I consider it a remarkable effect of our professional discipline that we shall not be contributing to the wind.
   'The Politics of Political Economists' (1959), Sec.V: 532

6   Why has it been fashionable to abuse economists (even granting the possibility that they may deserve it)? The main reason is easily named – economists have been the premier 'pourers of cold water' on proposals for social improvement, to the despair of the reformers and philanthropists who support these proposals.
   Memoirs of an Unregulated Economist (1988), Prologue: 4

7   Expert testimony to Congress by academic economists is usually objective in one narrow sense: No one pays the economist to do it. I must confess to my annoyance at the importance assigned to this fact by almost everyone.
   Memoirs of an Unregulated Economist (1988), Ch.8: 123

government:

8   The modern state is a myopic Robin Hood: stealing from almost everyone but giving to many people, not only the poor, the fraction of the booty which survives the substantial administrative costs.
   The Pleasures and Pains of Modern Capitalism (1982), Sec.II: 16

9   Any group receiving the state treasury's largesse which tempers its demands for favours has no way of preventing other beneficiaries from simply scaling up their requests. A pound saved on public housing is a pound available for eyeglasses.
   The Pleasures and Pains of Modern Capitalism (1982), Sec.II: 17

monopoly:

10 Monopoly is not a branch of economics; its relationship to industrial organization is similar to that of runaway inflation to monetary theory.
   'A Survey of Contemporary Economics' (1949), Sec.I.c: 95

11 Monopoly has become as popular a subject in economics as sin has been in religion. There is a characteristic difference: Economists are paid better to attack monopoly than the clergy are to wrestle with sin.
   Memoirs of an Unregulated Economist (1988), Ch.6: 95

Joseph Eugene Stiglitz (1942–)

capitalism:

1   Capitalism prospers best in an environment with a peculiar combination of self-interested behavior – enough to induce individuals to look for profitable activities – and non-self-interested behavior, where one's word is one's honor, where social rather than economic sanctions suffice to enforce contracts.
   Whither Socialism? (994), Ch.16: 271

Gustav Stolper (1888–1947)

capitalism:

1 The perfect order promised by capitalism is a society of free men and women acting under the impulse of their personal advantage to bring about the greatest common good for the greatest number. Since everyone gets his economically possible reward, there can be no conflict among classes. In a free society no one can use political power to withhold this proper reward from anyone else.
This Age of Fable (1942), Part I, Ch.III, Sec.2: 47

2 A 'free' capitalism with governmental responsibility for money and credit has lost its innocence. From that point on it is no longer a matter of principle but one of expediency how far one wishes or permits governmental interference to go. Money control is the supreme and most comprehensive of all governmental controls short of expropriation.
This Age of Fable (1942), Part I, Ch.III, Sec.8: 59

3 It is the fundamental wisdom of the capitalist system that it functions irrespective of the wisdom or the stupidity of the capitalists.
This Age of Fable (1942), Part I, Ch.VIII, Sec.10: 167

socialism:

4 We shall search in vain in the entire Socialist literature of all countries for guidance in the dark. The utmost we get is the elevation of some questionable or untried theory to the rank of a religious dogma without realization of how many question marks and theoretical and practical pitfalls this theory implies.
This Age of Fable (1942), Part I, Ch.VIII, Sec.10: 166

Sir John Richard Nicholas Stone
(1913–1991)

economics and economists:

1 For my own part, when I compare the knowledge available a hundred years ago and the knowledge available today, I am led to revise my habitual pessimism about modern times. The world may be going to the dogs, but economics certainly is not.
'Political Economy, Economics and Beyond' (1980), Sec.VI: 733

William Graham Sumner
(1840–1910)

concentration of wealth:

1 The concentration of wealth I understand to include the aggregation of wealth into large masses, and its concentration under the control of a few.
In this sense the concentration of wealth is indispensable to the successful execution of the tasks which devolve upon society in our time.
'Concentration of Wealth: Its Justification' (1902): 1036

economics and economists:

2 One may read, in scores of books and articles, that political economy is going through a transition stage. The inference appears to be that the period is a convenient one for any one who chooses to do so to contribute some crude notions to the prevailing confusion. It is certainly true that there is no body of economists engaged in carrying on the science of political economy by a consistent development of its older results according to such new light as can be brought to bear upon them. The science is exposed to the derision and flippant jests of those whose vested interest in old abuses is threatened by it, and it has forfeited its influence in the counsels of legislators and the cabinets of statesmen because those who call themselves economists are busy in turning economic science to scorn. Every science suffers more or less from men who meddle with it without mastering it, and from those who think carelessly, generalize rashly, or make concessions hastily; but a progressive science is always in the control, in the last resort, of a body of competent scholars who correct aberrations, and every such science possesses a body of criticism which is strong enough to repress presuming ignorance and charlatanism. Political economy is in no such position. A host of writers have been busy for the last twenty years introducing

conflicting and baseless notions which, for want of a competent criticism, have won standing in the science. Others have made a boast of turning their backs on scientific method, and of describing, by way of contributing to political economy, some portion of the surface appearance which is presented by the mass of economic phenomena in their sequence, variety, and complexity. That is as if a historian should boast of abandoning the attempt to trace social forces in history, and of returning to the description of royal marriages and diplomatic intrigues.
 'Wages' (1882): 241–242

industry:

3   Industry may be republican; it can never be democratic, so long as men differ in productive power and in industrial virtue.
 'Concentration of Wealth: Its Justification' (1902): 1037

poverty and poor relief:

4   Under the names of the poor and the weak, the negligent, shiftless, inefficient, silly, and imprudent are fastened upon the industrious and prudent as a responsibility and a duty.
 What Social Classes Owe to Each Other (1883), Ch.I: 20

5   [O]n the theories of the social philosophers ..., we should get a new maxim of judicious living: Poverty is the best policy. If you get wealth, you will have to support other people; if you do not get wealth, it will be the duty of other people to support you.
 What Social Classes Owe to Each Other (1883), Ch.I: 22

socialism:

6   The effort to realize the socialistic idea ... involves the destruction, first, of natural differences of ability by destroying all abilities above the lowest, and thus securing universal poverty; second, the destruction of love for wife and children, or the strongest passions of human nature; third, the removal of all differences of taste in the estimate of what brings happiness. In this form socialism passes over into communism, which cannot be defined satisfactorily because it is absurd and contradictory both to the facts of nature and to itself.
 'Socialism' (1878): 888

7   The projects of the socialists are based on the dogmas that man is born free and good, when he is, in fact, born helpless, and good or bad, as he works out his destiny; that the responsibility for vice and crime is on society, when, in truth, it is in the individual; that nature meets men at the outset with gratuitous bounty, which some appropriate to the exclusion of others, when, in fact, nature holds back every thing, and surrenders only to force and labor; that man is born endowed with 'natural rights,' when, in truth, nothing can be affirmed universally of the state of man by nature save that he is born to struggle for his own preservation, with nothing but the family to help him, and nothing but liberty, or the security of using his own energies for his own welfare, as a fair claim upon his fellow-men; that work is pleasant, or, under some circumstances, might be so, when, in truth, work is irksome; that men universally may be made, by some conventional agreement or sentimental impulse, to work for others to enjoy the product, or to save in order to give away; that they may be led universally to lay aside talents, health, and other advantages; that we can increase consumption and lessen production, yet have more; that all have an equal right to the product of some; that talents are the result of chance, which intelligence ought to correct, when, in truth, talents are the reward, from generation to generation, of industry, temperance, and prudence; that the passions need no control, and that self-denial is a vice. This is the socialistic creed, and from it it follows that a man has a 'natural right' to whatever he needs; that his wishes are the measure of his claims on his fellow-men; that, if he is in distress, somebody is bound to get him out; that somebody ought to decide what work every one should do, regardless of aptitude; to distribute the products equally, regardless of merit, and to determine consumption, regardless of taste or preference. As this 'some one' must be a pure despot, or, in fact, a god, all socialistic schemes annihilate liberty. Most of them are atheistic, and reject any other god than the master of society.
 'Socialism' (1878): 892–893

Paul Marlor Sweezy (1910–)

capitalism:

1 Marxists have always maintained that the productive forces generated by capitalism were powerful enough, if applied to the satisfaction of reasonable human needs, to eliminate poverty and create a society of abundance.
Four Lectures on Marxism (1981), Lecture 2: 44

economics and economists:

2 [E]conomic theorizing is primarily a process of constructing and interrelating concepts from which all specifically social context has been drained off. In actual application the social element may be (and usually is, since Robinson Crusoe is mostly serviceable and interesting in the preliminary stages of theorizing) introduced by way of *ad hoc* assumptions specifying the field of application.
The Theory of Capitalist Development (1942), Introduction: 5

socialism:

3 In the economics of a socialist society the theory of planning should hold the same basic position as the theory of value in the economics of a capitalist society. Value and planning are as much opposed, and for the same reasons, as capitalism and socialism.
The Theory of Capitalist Development (1942), Part One, Ch.III, Sec.4: 54

David Syme (1827–1908)

economics and economists:

1 Treated by the inductive method Political Economy is a science of the highest practical value; treated *à priori*, it is not a science at all, but only a scientific artifice, a mere theory of human action in one particular direction, and which has not even the merit of being approximately correct.
'On the Method of Political Economy' (1871): 97

2 The Political Economist observes phenomena with a foregone conclusion as to their cause. His method, in fact, is the method of the savage. The phenomena of nature, the thunder, the lightning, or the earthquake, strike the savage with awe and wonder; but he only looks within himself for an explanation of these phenomena. To him therefore the forces of nature are only the efforts of beings like himself, great and powerful no doubt, but with good and evil propensities, and subject to every human caprice. Like the Political Economist, he works within the vicious circle of his own feelings, and he cannot comprehend any more than the savage how he can discover the laws which regulate the phenomena which he sees around him. The savage would reduce the Divine mind to the dimensions of the human; the Political Economist would reduce the human mind to the dimensions of his ideal.
'On the Method of Political Economy' (1871): 100

T

William Howard Taft (1857–1930)
27th President of the United States; 10th Chief Justice, US Supreme Court

government:

1 [T]here is a line beyond which Government can not go with any good practical results in seeking to make men and society better. Efforts to do so will only result in failure and a waste of public effort and funds.
Popular Government (1913), Ch.II

regulation:

2 To say that a business is clothed with a public interest is not to determine what regulation may be permissible in view of the private rights of the owner. The extent to which an inn or a cab system may be regulated may differ widely from that allowable as to a railroad or other common carrier. It is not a matter of legislative discretion solely. It depends on the nature of the business, on the feature which touches the public, and on the abuses reasonably to be feared. To say that a business is clothed with a public interest is not to import that the public may take over its entire management and run it at the expense of the owner.
Charles Wolff Packing Co. v. Court of Industrial Relations of the State of Kansas, 262 U.S. 522, 539 (1923)

Frank William Taussig (1859–1940)

trade:

1 Unless we regard international trade as a game in which each party tries to overreach the other, we must put our relations with foreign countries on a basis which insures a benefit from the exchange to all parties.
'Reciprocity' (1892): 39

2 The essence of the doctrine of free trade is that *prima facie* international trade brings a gain, and that restrictions on it presumably bring a loss. Departure from this principle, though by no means impossible of justification, need to prove their case; and if made in view of the pressure of opposing principles, they are matter for regret. In this sense, the doctrine of free trade, however widely rejected in the world of politics, holds its own in the sphere of the intellect.
'The Present Position of the Doctrine of Free Trade' (1905): 65

Richard Henry Tawney (1880–1962)

capitalism:

1 [The philosophy of wealth] is the negation of any system of thought or morals which can, except by a metaphor, be described as Christian. Compromise is as impossible between the Church of Christ and the idolatry of wealth, which is the practical religion of capitalist societies, as it was between the Church and the State idolatry of the Roman Empire.
Religion and the Rise of Capitalism (1926), Ch.V: 286

economic organization:

2 The economic categories of modern society, such as property, freedom of contract and competition, are as much a part of its intellectual furniture as its political conceptions, and, together with religion, have probably been the most potent force in giving it its character.
Religion and the Rise of Capitalism (1926), Ch.I: 13

3 Both the existing economic order, and too many of the projects advanced for reconstructing it, break down through their neglect of the truism that, since even quite common men have souls, no increase in material wealth will compensate them for arrangements which insult their self-respect and impair their freedom. A reasonable estimate of economic organization must allow for the fact that, unless industry is to be paralyzed by recurrent revolts on the part of outraged human nature, it must satisfy criteria which are not purely economic.
Religion and the Rise of Capitalism (1926), Ch.V: 284

economics and economists:

4   The isolation of economic aims as a specialized object of concentrated and systematic effort, the erection of economic criteria into an independent and authoritative standard of social expediency, are phenomena which, though familiar enough in classical antiquity, appear, at least on a grand scale, only at a comparatively recent date in the history of later civilizations. The conflict between the economic outlook of East and West, which impresses the traveller today, finds a parallel in the contrast between medieval and modern economic ideas, which strikes the historian.
   Religion and the Rise of Capitalism (1926), Ch.V: 278

efficiency:

5   Economic efficiency is a necessary element in the life of any sane and vigorous society, and only the incorrigible sentimentalist will depreciate its significance. But to convert efficiency from an instrument into a primary object is to destroy efficiency itself. For the condition of effective action in a complex civilization is coöperation. And the condition of coöperation is agreement, both as to the ends to which effort should be applied, and the criteria by which its success is to be judged.
   Religion and the Rise of Capitalism (1926), Ch.V: 283

property:

6   [I]t is not private ownership, but private ownership divorced from work, which is corrupting to the principle of industry; and the idea of some socialists that private property in land or capital is necessarily mischievous is a piece of scholastic pedantry as absurd as that of those conservatives who would invest all property with some kind of mysterious sanctity.
   The Acquisitive Society (1920), Ch.VI: 86

7   Private property is a necessary institution, at least in a fallen world; men work more and dispute less when goods are private than when they are common. But it is to be tolerated as a concession to human frailty, not applauded as desirable in itself; the ideal – if only man's nature could rise to it – is communism.
   Religion and the Rise of Capitalism (1926), Ch.I, Sec.I: 32

socialism:

8   [H]owever varying in emphasis and in method, the general note of what may conveniently be called the Socialist criticism of property is what the word Socialism itself implies. Its essence is the statement that the economic evils of society are primarily due to the unregulated operation, under modern conditions of industrial organization, of the institution of private property.
   The Acquisitive Society (1920), Ch.V: 53

Overton H. Taylor (1897–1987)

economics and economists:

1   There is no reason why economists should think economic progress more important than it seems to other people, or be unsympathetic with popular, largely non-economic desires and values. Their business, simply as economists, is to study the conditions of attainment, at least cost, of whatever range and hierarchy of ends or satisfactions the public wishes to pursue. If the public is changing the balance in its scheme of ends, and if we as economists wish to serve it as fully as we can in our professional capacity, we must adapt the focus of our thinking to the somewhat altered problems set, in the sphere of means, by this new outlook in the sphere of ends.
   'Economic Theory and the Age We Live In' (1947): 107

2   [I]t seems to me that the 'economic' science and art of the pursuit of wealth and economic welfare by and for each human society and all its members needs development by each economist, never in complete isolation from the other branches of science, philosophy, and the whole group of the human-social-and-moral studies, but always with some – in each case, that particular economist's – fully explicit, broadly informed, and well-meditated, wider context of ideas or views about human-social life in its entirety, about history, and about the essentials and conditions of not just 'economic welfare' but complete human 'welfare.' The involvement of our special subject matter with

others 'in the real world,' seems to me to make this necessary; 'economic life' surely, in any reasonable view, is neither on the one hand the whole of real, complete human life, nor on the other hand a wholly distinct or separate part of it all, which can be studied with very valuable results in complete, conceptual isolation from the other aspects of entire-concrete societies and the entire-concrete lives of their members. 'Economic life' always is carried on within, and interacts with all other components of, complete, particular societies, cultures, polities, etc.; and these real contexts or *milieux* around it need some careful, though secondary, attention and study along with our efforts to study primarily the general processes and internal problems of 'economic life' itself. Economists need to be not only economists but also very broadly equipped, general scholars and social philosophers.
'Economic Science Only – Or Political Economy?' (1957), Introduction: 2–3

3 Diverse ideals and philosophies, which influence perspectives on and studies of reality and resulting contributions to economic science, may result in different, valuable insights as well as biases and blind spots; and we need to learn to appreciate impartially and combine the valid elements of all such contributions, and eliminate the illusions, exaggerations, distortions, etc. in them all – as only those whose own philosophies have been developed into broader, wiser, less narrow and intolerant ones than most men know, can readily do.
'Economic Science Only – Or Political Economy?' (1957), Sec.IV: 18

Peter Temin (1937–) and Geoffrey Peters

economics and economists:

1 The need for historical analysis to clarify the relation between theory and observation should be clear. The predictions of economic theory may fail to express historical reality for many reasons. And the historical record itself may be confused to the point where it is unclear which predictions have been fulfilled. Careful historical analysis can be avoided only at the economist's peril.
'Is History Stranger Than Theory? The Origin of Telephone Separations' (1985): 327

Thomas Perronet Thompson
(1783–1869)

economics and economists:

1 [T]here will no good come of Political Economy, till men apply to it with the same habits, the same accuracy, and the same *sang froid*, with which our philosophers of the last and preceding century investigated the motion of the moon or the theory of the tides. It takes a much greater quantity of what is vulgarly termed *elbow-grease* to make a political economist, than is commonly imagined. The pursuit is in fact a branch of mathematics of a high order; and till it is considered and treated as such, there will be no unanimity.
'Effects of Abolition and Commutation of Tithes' (1833): 180

2 Finally, it is recommended to all who follow after Political Economy and ensue it, to cultivate the habit of going *bride en main*, and not plunging hastily into conclusions of either truth or falsehood. If common truth be in a well, truth in Political Economy is at the centre of the earth; or at all events among the lowest strata to which human eyes have had access.
'Effects of Abolition and Commutation of Tithes' (1833): 180

William Thompson (1775–1833)
Irish socialist

competition:

1 Competition makes us regard from birth the interests of every one as opposed to and incompatible with the interest of every other person; because it really puts all interest in opposition to each other. In every happy face, we now see a successful rival. In life, at school, – competition, or as it is sometimes softened into the gentler term

emulation, is, where force is excluded, the leading spring of action. The pleasures of competition, founded on the inferiority of comforts, of intelligence, or of moral qualities of others, are fenced round with envies, jealousies, ill-will, suspicions, and dread of ill-offices from all around; and could never be approved as useful motives to human exertions, but as a manifest improvement on the former every-where existing system of compulsion, by open force, the dread of force, or force-supported fraud. But as the progress of improvement has already discarded these latter motives; so will a little further progress discard equally the motives to exertion arising from competition.
Labour Rewarded (1827), 'Of Insurance Schemes Against Various Casualties': 65

taxation:

2 [I]t would be a great blessing that all taxes not voluntary should be abolished, and that the currency should be fixed; because the evils arising from the necessarily unequal exchanges of Free Individual Competition are much less destructive to human happiness, and will much more naturally and quickly work out their own remedy, than the evils arising from open Force and from Force-supported Fraud.
Labour Rewarded (1827), 'Of a Fixed Metallic Currency. Taxes, Public Debts, &c.': 64

Johann Heinrich von Thünen (1783–1850)

taxation:

1 A state which raises taxes to the utmost limit will have nothing left to tax, and its coffers will ultimately be empty. A state which levies no taxes at all will attain its utmost possible expansion, but here too the treasury will be empty. There must be a point where taxation yields its maximum.
The Isolated State (1842; 2nd edn), Part I, Sec.3, 'Notes and Explanations on the Following Diagrams of the Isolated State': 220

Lester Carl Thurow (1938–)

economics and economists:

1 One of the peculiarities of economics is that it still rests on a behavioral assumption – rational utility maximization – that has long since been rejected by sociologists and psychologists who specialize in studying human behavior. Rational individual utility (income) maximization was the common assumption of all social science in the nineteenth century, but only economics continues to use it.
Dangerous Currents (1983), Ch.8: 216

Jan Tinbergen (1903–1994)

mathematics in economics:

1 [I]t is sometimes forgotten that arguments against the most general types of mathematics are just arguments against science in general, i.e., against the assumption that we can understand connections between phenomena – in this case economic phenomena – in some general way. If determinacy – in whatever loose form – is not accepted at all, there is no economics: no mathematical economics and no literary economics. Perhaps there would remain economic novels; personally I would prefer other novels then.
'The Functions of Mathematical Treatment' (1954): 368

James Tobin (1918–2002)

inflation:

1 [I]nflation is greatly exaggerated as a social evil. Even while prices are rising year after year, the economy is producing more and more of the goods, services, and jobs that meet people's needs. That, after all, is its real purpose.
The New Economics One Decade Older (1974), Concluding Remarks: 101

Count Leo Tolstoy (1828–1910)
Russian novelist

economics and economists:

1 It is astonishing that science – our vaunted free science – in its study of the economic

conditions of national life should fail to see the fact which is at the root of all economic conditions. One would suppose it to be the business of science to seek out the sources of its phenomena, and the general cause of a succession of phenomena; but Political Economy does exactly the contrary: it scrupulously conceals the sources of the phenomena it deals with, ignores their importance and carefully evades the most simple and pertinent questions. Like a lazy and capricious horse, it frisks up the hill when it has nothing to pull, but as soon as there is a load it turns back, pretending to have business at the bottom of the hill. Whenever science has before it a question of real moment, then forthwith begin scientific ratiocinations over matters which have nothing to do with the question, and which have but one aim: to turn attention from the question.

'Science and Money' (1903): 12

2 This science [of economics] has a very distinct aim which it achieves – the aim, namely, of maintaining superstition and deceit among men, and thereby of retarding humanity in its march toward the good and the true. The superstition which it seeks to perpetuate is one quite analogous to the superstitions of religion. It consists in maintaining that besides the obligations due to one's fellow men, there are still more weighty obligations due to an imaginary being. For religion this imaginary being is God, for political science it is the State. The imaginary being requires its victims – very often human lives – and to secure these all means are permissible – even violence. Men are to be subjected to a dreadful slavery, the worst that has ever existed, and to accomplish this science tries to make them believe that it is necessary, that it could not be otherwise.

'Science and Money' (1903): 13

money:

3 Money means nothing else than slavery. Its aim and its results are the same; the exempting of some from what a deep thinker of the people has justly called the primeval law, from what I call the natural law of life – the law of personal labor in payment for the satisfaction of personal needs. And the consequences of this slavery are: For the master, the engendering and fostering of artificial needs which are beyond satisfaction, impotent vanity and degeneracy; for the slave, his debasement from his station as man to that of an animal. Money, I repeat, is but a new and terrible form of slavery. Like the personal servitude of former days, it debases master and thrall, but it is much worse, for it does away with all mitigating human intercourse.

'Science and Money' (1903): 15

public goods:

4 The sole ground for the assertion that a thing is beneficial is where men adopt it of their free will. Ten laborers start a tannery to work in together, and in so doing they achieve something unquestionably beneficial to them. But one can hardly imagine that these laborers, if they force an eleventh to join them, could say that their common benefit was also that of this eleventh. The same would hold true of peasants who should decide to dig a pond. For those among them who regard that pond as a benefit worth the labor expended in digging it the possession of this pond would be the 'public good;' but for one among them who should consider that pond a benefit of less value than his work in the field with which he was getting behind, the digging of that pond could not be a good. The same is true of roads, churches, museums and all public works, social and governmental. These works cannot be good for any but such as judge them to be so, and especially to such only as undertake them of their own free will. As for works which men are obliged to do by constraint, by very virtue of that constraint such works cease to be for the common benefit.

'Science and Money' (1903): 13

Robert Torrens (1780–1864)

economics and economists:

1 The study of Political Economy, if it did not teach the way in which labour may obtain an adequate reward, might serve to gratify a merely speculative curiosity, but could scarcely conduce to any purposes of practical utility. It claims the peculiar attention of the benevolent and good, mainly

because it explains the causes, which depress and elevate wages, and thereby points out the means, by which we may mitigate the distress, and improve the condition, of the great majority of mankind. Political Economy is not, as has been erroneously stated, the appropriate science of the statesman and the legislator; it is peculiarly and emphatically, *the science of the people*.
On Wages and Combination (1834), Ch.I: 1–2

labor:

2 In the writings of political economists, we frequently meet with the phrases 'accumulated labour,' 'hoarded labour.' These forms of expression are incorrect. We may accumulate and hoard the articles which labour has produced; but the labour itself, the action of the human muscles, ceased to exist the instant it was performed, and became, in the nature of things, incapable of being either accumulated or hoarded. 'Accumulated labour,' and 'hoarded labour,' are, at the best, but figurative expressions, not of the happiest kind; and to introduce them into the precise and accurate discussions of Political Economy, is to substitute the diction of poetry for the nomenclature of science.

The term labour, then, when its meaning is unqualified by the epithet 'mental,' or 'intellectual,' signifies the action of the human muscles, directed to obtain the objects of desire; and it signifies *nothing more*.
On Wages and Combination (1834), Ch.I: 4

Hutches Trower (1777–1833)

economics and economists:

1 The Science of Political Economy owes its interest, and its importance, to its teaching us to trace to their true causes the *disorders*, which are constantly occurring in the course of human affairs, and thus enabling us to avoid the evils they occasion, by ascertaining the symptoms by which they are to be distinguished.
Letter to David Ricardo (29 September 1820)

George Tucker (1775–1861)

government:

1 For a nation to be at once safe, prosperous, and happy, it must have the advantage of good government and laws. Man will be neither industrious nor frugal, if a rapacious government is ready to seize on the fruits of his labor.
Political Economy for the People (1859), Ch.II: 30

2 [G]overnments sometimes err by a well-intended but vicious intermeddling; for in the body politic, too much regulation is as mischievous as too much medicine in the body natural.
Political Economy for the People (1859), Ch.II: 32

Rexford Guy Tugwell (1891–1979)

economics and economists:

1 Economics, instead of a dismal science, will be seen ultimately to be the science of enlightenment and progress, of the organization of man's experience in mastering nature. For if mankind is to lift itself by its bootstraps in the ways effort now is set, it will have to be the economists who provide the plans for its doing.
'Economics as the Science of Experience' (1928), Sec.VI: 40; cf. Thomas Carlyle 1; Ludwig von Mises 8; Robert Nathan 2

Gordon Tullock (1922–)

economics and economists:

1 From earliest times it has been noted that economists tend not to get along well with other people because the conclusions they draw are frequently thought to be unpleasant to whomever they are speaking. We are all brought up with a set of moral instructions, a set of things we would like to do, and the economist frequently tells us that we can't do all of them, that some of the moral propositions we have are in fact simply erroneous. This, needless to say, makes people unhappy.
'Does Mathematics Aid in the Progress of Economics?' (1994): 207

income distribution:

2 If I am correct, redistribution is a slogan behind which there is really very little rational thought. Most, albeit not all, people seem to be in favour of redistribution, but I am unable to find any significant agreement among them as to what they mean by the term or how much redistribution there should be.

'Reasons for Redistribution' (1986): 15

Anne-Robert-Jacques Turgot, Baron d'Aulne (1727–1781)

money:

1 We can take for a common measure of values only that which has a value, and which is received in Commerce in exchange for other values: and there is no pledge universally representative of a value save another equal value. A purely conventional money is therefore an impossibility.

Reflections on the Formation and the Distribution of Riches (1770), Sec.XL: 36

Charles Augustus Tuttle (1865–1935)

industrial democracy:

1 If trade-unionism and collective bargaining, profit sharing and industrial arbitration mean anything, they signify that the workman has quasi-property rights in the business in which he is employed. He may not own a dollar of the capital, he may not own a square foot of the land, he may not own even a minute fractional part of a machine; but the business is more than its capital, its land and its machines, and that the workman does have a quasi-property right in the business no one can deny. The productive process is social, and the traditional business owner, so strongly intrenched in our legal system as an industrial despot, is strangely out of harmony with the spirit of the age. In profit-sharing establishments, the workman is already tacitly recognized as a joint owner in the business. The realization of industrial arbitration would be a long step in the direction of industrial democracy and the recognition of the workman's quasi-property right in business.

'The Workman's Position in the Light of Economic Progress' (1902): 211–212

U

Abbott Payson Usher (1883–1965)

economic history:

1 Economic history must needs be more than an objective record of events. It involves a philosophy of life; and any given work, if it is to be fully appreciated, must be read with a conscious knowledge of the philosophy upon which it is based.
'The Application of the Quantitative Method to Economic History' (1932): 209

economics and economists:

2 The economist is primarily concerned with the study of the struggle for material existence. The use to be made of the individual life in spiritual and general intellectual interests is, after all, a separate subject of investigation.
'The Application of the Quantitative Method to Economic History' (1932): 191

laissez-faire:

3 The doctrine of laissez faire may best be regarded as a phase in the history of economic liberalism. Liberal thought emerges earlier, was never guilty of the extravagances that can legitimately be associated with laissez faire, and will persist long after the famous catchword has passed into history.
Round Table Conference: Economic History – The Decline of Laissez Faire (1931): 3

poverty:

4 The disposition to treat the problem of poverty as a problem of justice in distribution is unfortunate. It is not true that the material comfort of the wealthy and the middle classes is enjoyed at the expense of the poor; nor is it true that the misery of the poor is merited, a just judgment upon deficiency and inefficiency. It is naïve to suppose that difficulties and evils are all due to human wickedness, and that all of them can be overcome by mere honesty and competency in high places. Nothing is explained or accomplished by this disposition to apply opprobrious terms to either rich or poor, and it would seem that effective study of poverty and its alleviation would be most significantly furthered by abandoning this unfruitful discussion of justice.
'Justice and Poverty' (1921), Sec.IV: 701; cf. F.A. Walker 2

V

Rice Vaughan (?–1672?)

value:

1. *Use* and *Delight*, or the opinion of them, are the true causes why all things have a Value and Price set upon them, but the Proportion of that value and price is wholly governed by Rarity and Abundance. . . .
   A Discourse of Coin and Coinage (1675), Ch.IV: 19

Thorstein Bunde Veblen (1857–1929)

corporate structure:

1. Business enterprise may fairly be said to have shifted from the footing of free-swung competitive production to that of a conscientious withholding of efficiency, so soon and so far as corporation finance on a sufficiently large scale had come to be the controlling factor in industry. At the same time and in the same degree the discretionary control of industry, and of other business enterprise in great part, has passed into the hands of the corporation financier.
   'The Industrial System and the Captains of Industry' (1919): 554

economic action:

2. Economic action is teleological, in the sense that men always and everywhere seek to do something. What, in specific detail, they seek, is not to be answered except by a scrutiny of the details of their activity; but, so long as we have to do with their life as members of the economic community, there remains the generic fact that their life is an unfolding activity of a teleological kind.
   'Why Is Economics Not an Evolutionary Science?' (1898): 391

economics and economists:

3. In the days of the early classical writers economics had a vital interest for the laymen of the time, because it formulated the common sense metaphysics of the time in its application to a department of human life. But in the hands of the later classical writers the science lost much of its charm in this regard. It was no longer a definition and authentication of the deliverances of current common sense as to what ought to come to pass; and it, therefore, in large measure lost the support of the people out of doors, who were unable to take an interest in what did not concern them; and it was also out of touch with that realistic or evolutionary habit of mind which got under way about the middle of the century in the natural sciences. It was neither vitally metaphysical nor matter-of-fact, and it found comfort with very few outside of its own ranks. Only for those who by the fortunate accident of birth or education have been able to conserve the taxonomic animus has the science during the last third of a century continued to be of absorbing interest.
   'Why Is Economics Not an Evolutionary Science?' (1898): 385–386

4. Like other men, the economist is an individual with but one intelligence. He is a creature of habits and propensities given through the antecedents, hereditary and cultural, of which he is an outcome; and the habits of thought formed in any one line of experience affect his thinking in any other.
   'Why Is Economics Not an Evolutionary Science?' (1898): 395

5. The laws of the science, that which makes up the economist's theoretical knowledge, are laws of the normal case. The normal case does not occur in concrete fact. These laws are, therefore, in [John E.] Cairnes's terminology, 'hypothetical' truths; and the science is a 'hypothetical' science. They apply to concrete facts only as the facts are interpreted and abstracted from, in the light of the underlying postulates. The science is, therefore, a theory of the normal case, a discussion of the concrete facts of life in respect of their degree of approximation to the normal case. That is to say, it is a taxonomic science.
   'The Preconceptions of Economic Science' (1900), Part III: 254–255

Marxism:

6 Except as a whole and except in the light of its postulates and aims, the Marxian system is not only not tenable, but it is not even intelligible.
'The Socialist Economics of Karl Marx and His Followers: I' (1906): 575

private property:

7 Wherever the institution of private property is found, even in a slightly developed form, the economic process bears the character of a struggle between men for the possession of goods.
The Theory of the Leisure Class (1899), Ch.II: 24

William Spencer Vickrey
(1914–1996)

economics and economists:

1 Economic theory proper ... is nothing more than a system of logical relations between certain sets of assumptions and the conclusions derived from them. The propositions of economic theory are derived by logical reasoning from these basic assumptions in exactly the same way as the theorems of geometry are derived from the axioms upon which the system is built. The difference between economic theory and geometry is that while in geometry the axioms are intended to have some approximate relation to the real space of ordinary experience, in economic theory the axioms are intended to have some approximate relation to the properties of the real economic world. In addition, there is a marked difference in the care and rigor with which economists have typically stated their assumptions and deduced their conclusions, and the great complexity of the real economic world has called forth a relatively large number of different theoretical systems in an attempt to aid in the understanding of various aspects of reality. But this is essentially a matter of degree rather than of kind.
Microstatics (1964), Part I, Ch.I: 5

Marxism:

2 Marxist economics ... can be said to be the economics of capitalism rather than socialism: it has a great deal to say, rightly or wrongly, about the workings and especially the development of capitalist regimes, but is of little or no help and may actually be misleading in the running of a socialist economy.
Microstatics (1964), Part I, Ch.I: 11

Jacob Viner (1892–1970)

economics and economists:

1 The economist should not refrain from making his special contribution to decisions of public importance because of a doctrinaire adherence to an academic standard of scientific uninterestedness more appropriate – or less wasteful – in the physical laboratory than in the field of the social sciences.
Round Table Conference on the Relation Between Economics and Ethics (1922): 199

2 There are many economists; not quite so many good economists.
'The Tariff Question and the Economist' (1931), Part I: 593

3 [A] brilliant English economist discovered a few years ago that in the long run we will all be dead, and ever since economists have been somewhat apologetic and shamefaced about their ancient habit of taking the long view. It has been suggested, however, that the 'we' in this epigram is somewhat ambiguous, and that in its ambiguity resides all its force. It is the special function of the social scientist to attract attention to the policies necessary if assurance is to be had that there shall still be life, if not for us, then for our descendants, after the short-run is over. If the academic scholar tends to tilt the balance between the short and the long run somewhat unduly in favour of the distant and uncertain future, it is a providential counterpoise against the excessive predilection of the politician with the short life and the merry one – while it lasts!
'The Tariff Question and the Economist' (1931), Part I: 593

methodology:

4 I find it difficult to conceive what useful purposes the formal definition of the scope

of a discipline can serve, except the purposes of editors of encyclopedias and administrators of educational institutions, whose responsibility it may be to prevent overlapping, to obtain full coverage, and to arbitrate jurisdictional disputes. No damage is likely to be incurred by economics if serious consideration of these jurisdictional questions is confined to those for whom it is an unavoidable occupational responsibility.
Studies in the Theory of International Trade (1937), Appendix: 594

Daniel Rutledge Vining (1908–2000)

economics and economists:

1 To paraphrase a remark made about philosophy, one may say, I think, that political economy is not a doctrine or a theory but rather is an activity. A political economist, then, is one who participates in this activity.
. . .
'The Affluent Society: A Review Article' (1959), Sec.I: 112

W

Amasa Walker (1799–1875)

government:

1 If, then, the property of the citizen must be taken to meet the exigencies of government, it becomes highly important that those from whom it is taken should feel that it is equitably done. Nothing in relation to all the acts of government is more to be desired than that its mode of raising a revenue should be so wisely and economically arranged, so manifestly just and equal, and so well understood by all, that no opposition to its demands shall arise from a sense of oppression.
The Science of Wealth (1866; 2nd edn), Bk.IV, Ch.IX: 307

2 Political economy recognizes that humanity has other interests than wealth, and respects the claim of government to duties and services for the sake of a moral good. But such reasons should appear clearly. Nothing should be taken arbitrarily, or for contingent use. Man is the direct producer, and the product remains in his hands. If government, as indirectly engaged with him, enters with a claim to share the profits, it must show cause distinctly for whatever it takes. It is the part of the statesman, not of the economist, to judge of occasions like these.
The Science of Wealth (1866; 2nd edn), Bk.V, Ch.V: 403

taxation:

3 Every man knows, or should know, that when he creates any kind of wealth, a share of it belongs to government. He in fact, creates a fund out of which government is to be supported.
The Science of Wealth (1866; 2nd edn), Bk.IV, Ch.IX: 308

Francis Amasa Walker (1840–1897)

competition:

1 Competition, perfect competition, affords the ideal condition for the distribution of wealth.
Political Economy (1883), Para.466

government:

2 One cannot doubt that the line between those who have and those who have not, between those who have much and those who have little, is somewhat differently drawn from what it would be but for the laches or the positive acts of government. Government springs from injustice and must, in the nature of the case, perpetrate more or less of injustice. By the unwisdom of its laws, by the incompetence of its executive officers, or through decisions which sacrifice the individual to the supposed general good, some men are made richer and some poorer. It is of the very essence of tariffs, embargoes and wars to enrich the holders of certain kinds of property and correspondingly impoverish others. Delays and failures of criminal justice, the wrongful decisions of judges and juries, the incapacity of police and fire departments, the bungling over fraudulent bankruptcies, all these have to do with placing men higher or lower upon the scale of wealth.
'The Bases of Taxation' (1888): 4–5; cf. A.P. Usher 4

money:

3 Money does not serve as a store of value. When a commodity comes to serve as a store of value, it ceases to be money.
Money (1891), Ch.I, Sec.IV: 12; cf. Piero Sraffa 1

4 The reasons, if indeed they reason at all in the matter, which actuate individuals or the community in their preferences, may be mistaken, or the appetencies to which they yield may be such as the moral philosopher cannot approve. The economist has only to

do with the fact that, however it comes about, the willingness of the mass of the people to receive one article rather than others in payment for whatever they have to sell, furnishes the prime, the one essential, condition of a true money.
Money (1891), Ch.II: 25

5 [N]othing can perform the functions of money which is not money, for . . . an article is determined to be money solely by reason of its performance of certain functions. . . . *Money is that Money does*.
Money (1891), Ch.XVIII: 405

poverty:

6 Almost nothing can push the poor who are not of the pauper type across the line of self-support, and keep them there, so long as the spirit of independence exists in the community to which they belong. Beaten down by misfortune, no matter how sudden and terrible, they reassert their manhood and reappear on the side of those who owe, and will owe, no man anything.
'The Causes of Poverty' (1897): 210

7 Pauperism is, in truth, largely voluntary, to the full degree in which anything can be said to be voluntary in a world of causation – a matter, if not of definite and conscious choice, then of appetites and aptitudes indulged or submitted to from inherent baseness or cowardice or moral weakness. Those who are paupers are so far more from character than from condition. They have the pauper taint; they bear the pauper brand.
'The Causes of Poverty' (1897): 210–211

protection:

8 Were it admitted that a judicious system of protection, selecting always the right objects for governmental encouragement and support, and imposing only moderate and well-adjusted duties, would achieve all the benefits which the protectionist claims, it is certain that any actual system of protection will do much less than this; and it is always possible that a scheme of customs duties may do more harm than good, if the legislature enacting it be composed of men little conversant with the facts of industry and trade, strongly moved by personal, local, or sectional interests, and not altogether uninfluenced by popular clamor, parliamentary intrigue, or the addresses of a well-trained and unscrupulous lobby.
'Protection and Protectionists' (1890): 275

socialism:

9 I should apply the term socialistic to all efforts, under popular impulse, to enlarge the functions of government, to the diminution of individual initiative and enterprise, for a supposed public good.
'Socialism' (1887): 108

10 The socialistic talk of the day, in disparagement of competition, is either mere miserable cant, or else, if sincere, it is the expression of profound ignorance of the conditions which attend man's subjection of nature to his needs.
'What Shall We Tell the Working-Classes?' (1887): 622

taxation:

11 Economically considered, there cannot be a moment's question that the policy of laying the burdens of the state upon that portion of the product of industry which has escaped the maw of appetite, which is presumably reserved for useful employment, which is, in a sense, consecrated by worthy social ambitions, and which represents the courage, prudence and faith requisite to subordinate the present to the future, is thoroughly vicious.
'The Bases of Taxation' (1888): 4

Léon Marie Esprit Walras
(1834–1910)

economics and economists:

1 The primary concern of the economist is not to provide a plentiful revenue for the people or to supply the State with an adequate income, but to pursue and master purely scientific truths.
Elements of Pure Economics (1926, 'Definitive' edn), Part I, Lesson 1, §4: 52

2 Indeed, to say that the object of political economy is to provide a plentiful revenue

and to supply the State with an adequate income is like saying that the object of geometry is to build strong houses and that the aim of astronomy is to navigate the high seas in safety. This, in short, is to define a science in terms of its applications.

Elements of Pure Economics (1926, 'Definitive' edn), Part I, Lesson 1, §4: 53

mathematics in economics:

3   If the pure theory of economics or the theory of exchange and value in exchange, that is, the theory of social wealth considered by itself, is a physico-mathematical science like mechanics or hydrodynamics, then economists should not be afraid to use the methods and language of mathematics.

Elements of Pure Economics (1926, 'Definitive' edn), Part I, Lesson 3, §30: 71

4   Is it, or is it not worth while to demonstrate rigorously the fundamental laws of science? There are today heaven knows how many schools of political economy: the *deductive* school and the *historical* school, the school of *laisser-faire* and the school of *State intervention* or *Socialism of the Chair*, the *Socialist* school properly so-called, the *Catholic* school, the *Protestant* school, etc. For my part, I recognize only two: the school of those who do not demonstrate, and the school, which I hope to see founded, of those who do demonstrate their conclusions. By demonstrating rigorously first the elementary theorems of geometry and algebra, and then the resulting theorems of the calculus and mechanics, in order to apply them to experimental data, we have achieved the marvels of modern industry. Let us follow the same procedure in economics, and, without doubt, we shall eventually succeed in having the same control over the nature of things in the economic and social order as we already have in the physical and industrial order.

Elements of Pure Economics (1926, 'Definitive' edn), Appendix I, Part I, §4: 471

production:

5   Only useful things limited in quantity can be produced by industry and all things that industry produces are scarce. In fact we may be certain that industry does nothing but produce scarce things and that it endeavours to produce them all.

Elements of Pure Economics (1926, 'Definitive' edn), Part I, Lesson 4, §31: 73

Francis Wayland (1796–1865)
American clergyman, educator, philosopher

economics and economists:

1   The principles of Political Economy are so closely analogous to those of Moral Philosophy, that almost every question in the one, may be argued on grounds belonging to the other.

The Elements of Political Economy (1837), Preface: vi

2   Political Economy is *the Science of Wealth.* It is sometimes defined the Science of National Wealth. This definition seems not, however, sufficiently comprehensive; inasmuch as, the laws which govern the creation of wealth are essentially the same, whether they are considered in respect to man as an *individual*, or to man as a *society*.

By Science, as the word is here used, we mean a systematic arrangement of the laws which God has established, so far as they have been discovered, of any department of human knowledge. It is obvious, upon the slightest reflection, that the Creator has subjected the accumulation of the blessings of this life to some determinate laws. Every one, for instance, knows that no man can grow rich, without industry and frugality. Political Economy, therefore, is a systematic arrangement of the laws by which, under our present constitution, the relations of man, whether individual or social, to the objects of his desire, are governed.

The Elements of Political Economy (1837), Introduction: 3

government:

3   [A] surplus revenue is a public nuisance. It gives to the government a control over the monetary affairs of the country, at the best dangerous; and a control which is very liable to be exerted for the promotion of party purposes. It hence gives an additional, an unnecessary, and a dangerous power to a

majority, and gives them the means of perpetuating that power, indefinitely. It is taking productive capital from the hands of the owners, and vesting it in hands where there is every temptation to spend it uselessly, if not viciously. The world has never yet seen a government so pure, that it would not become corrupt, if a surplus revenue were permanently placed at its disposal.
The Elements of Political Economy (1837), Book Fourth, Chapter Third, Sec.I: 451

money:

4 Money is the instrument for facilitating exchanges. This, when considered as money, is its only office. By accomplishing this purpose in the least time, and at the least expense of labor, and transportation, and wear, it reduces the cost of every product, and thus adds immensely to the productiveness of human industry.
The Elements of Political Economy (1837), Book Second, Chapter Second, Sec.III: 221–222

5 A government has no right, *arbitrarily*, to alter the value of money; that is, to say that a dollar shall contain either more or less silver than it now contains. To do so, is, of necessity, to interfere with private contracts; and thus to expose one half of the community, a prey to the dishonesty of the other half.
The Elements of Political Economy (1837), Book Second, Chapter Second, Sec.IV: 246

poverty and the poor laws:

6 A common, where every one, at will, may pasture his cattle; and a forest, from which every inhabitant may procure his fuel; are severally encouragements to indolence, and serve to keep a community poor. Thus, also, funds left at large for the support of the poor, on which every one is supposed to have an equal right to draw, have generally been found to foster indolence. Poor laws, in so far as they are to be considered a fund for this purpose, have the same sort of injurious tendency.
The Elements of Political Economy (1837), Book First, Chapter Third, Sec.II: 113

7 [Poor Laws] are at variance with the fundamental law of government, that he who is able to labor, shall enjoy only that for which he has labored. If such be the law of God for us all, it is best for all, that all should be subjected to it. If labor be a curse, it is unjust that one part, and that, the industrious part, should suffer it all. If, as is the fact, it be a blessing, there is no reason why all should not equally enjoy its advantages.
The Elements of Political Economy (1837), Book First, Chapter Third, Sec.III: 125

8 With what spirit will a poor man labor, and retrench to the utmost his expenses, when he knows that he shall be taxed to support his next door neighbor, who is as able to work as himself; but who is relieved from the necessity of a portion of labor, merely by applying to the overseer of the poor for aid.
The Elements of Political Economy (1837), Book First, Chapter Third, Sec.III: 126

property:

9 [I]f he who labors be under obligation to support him that labors not; then the division of property and the right of property are at an end: for, he who labors has no better right to the result of his labor, than any one else.
The Elements of Political Economy (1837), Book First, Chapter Third, Sec.III: 126

taxation:

10 The more a people feel taxation, and the more jealously they watch over the public expenditure, the better it is for them and for their rulers.
The Elements of Political Economy (1837), Book Fourth, Chapter Third, Sec.I: 448

Sidney James Webb, Baron Passfield of Passfield Corner
(1859–1947)
British socialist

labor legislation:

1 The case [for establishing maximum labor hours] is not one of personal liberty in

self-regarding acts. No one wishes to prevent a man from working as long as he pleases; the community merely claims the right to prevent him from selling his excessive labour in such a way as to cause other workers to be compelled to work as long as he does. No one is to be coerced for his own supposed advantage, but only for the sake of others, in cases where his pursuit of that advantage operates so as to limit the industrial freedom of his fellows.
'The Limitation of the Hours of Labour' (1889): 869–870

laissez-faire:

2   The policy of '*Laisser faire*' is, necessarily, to a eugenist the worst of all policies, because it implies the definite abandonment of intelligently purposeful selection.
'Eugenics and the Poor Law: The Minority Report' (1910): 234

socialism:

3   Modern Socialism is ... not a faith in an artificial Utopia, but a rapidly-spreading conviction, as yet only partly conscious of itself that social health and consequently human happiness is something apart from and above the separate interests of individuals, requiring to be consciously pursued as an end in itself; that the lesson of evolution in social development is the substitution of consciously regulated co-ordination among the units of each organism for their internecine competition; that the production and distribution of wealth, like any other public function, cannot safely be intrusted to the unfettered freedom of individuals, but needs to be organized and controlled for the benefit of the whole community; that this can be imperfectly done by means of legislative restriction and taxation, but is eventually more advantageously accomplished through the collective enterprise of the appropriate administrative unit in each case; and that the best government is accordingly that which can safely and successfully administer most.
'The Difficulties of Individualism' (1891): 364

4   The progress of Socialism may be compared, indeed, to the approximation of the hyperbola to its asymptote: the time may never arrive when individual is entirely merged in collective ownership, but it is matter of common observation that every attempt to grapple with the 'difficulties' of our existing civilization brings us nearer to that goal.
'The Difficulties of Individualism' (1891): 381

Sidney James Webb, Baron Passfield of Passfield Corner (1859–1947) and (Martha) Beatrice [Potter] Webb (1858–1943)

capitalism:

1   The outstanding and entirely unexpected result of the capitalist organization of society is the widespread penury that it produces in the nation.
The Decay of Capitalist Civilization (1923), Ch.I: 3

2   The outrageous disparity in capitalist countries between one man and another, and between one class and another, independently of their merits, and often in the inverse ratio of their industry and social utility, is not produced by any defect in the working of capitalism, but is inherent in its very nature. It is not a transient phenomenon, but a permanent feature.
The Decay of Capitalist Civilization (1923), Ch.II: 17–18

eugenics:

3   To put the case more generally, we cannot afford to leave unchecked the influences that produce, not death alone, but even more widely slums and disease, physical starvation, mental perversion, demoralisation of character, and actual crime, however convinced we may be that the evil characters acquired in such an environment are not and will not be physically transmitted from parent to child. What does it profit us to be told that 'acquired characteristics are not inherited' if we permit the existence and therefore the social transmission of an environment which injures or corrupts each generation before it is born, and after it is born?
The Prevention of Destitution (1916), Ch.III: 49

4 The existing Poor Law operates almost exclusively as an anti-Eugenic influence; notably in the laxity of its provision for feeble-minded maternity, in the opportunities for undesirable acquaintanceship afforded by the General Mixed Workhouse, in its inability to search out defectives and wastrels who do not apply for relief, and in its failure to provide any practical alternative to the Outdoor Relief now afforded to tens of thousands of feeble-minded or physically defective parents.
The Prevention of Destitution (1916), Ch.III: 53

5 Such, indeed, are our present arrangements that the only necessitous persons who are effectively deterred from accepting public assistance at these crises are the very persons whom, as Eugenists, we should like to encourage to increase and multiply. Public subsidy without selection is bad enough, but here we have the Poor Law actually selecting, in practice, the inferior stocks for its subsidies.
The Prevention of Destitution (1916), Ch.III: 54

6 Whether we approach the problem from the standpoint of Christian humanitarianism concerned to prevent the continuance of unwitting prostitution and crime, or from the standpoint of Eugenics intent on eliminating the inherently bad stock, or from the standpoint merely of preventing (instead of relieving) this like other manifestations of destitution, we all converge on an identical line of reform. What we have to do is to search out and permanently segregate, under reasonably comfortable conditions and firm but kindly control, all the congenitally feeble-minded.
The Prevention of Destitution (1916), Ch.III: 56

morality:

7 However much we may better the material circumstances of a family, a class or a generation, if in so doing we have lessened the energy, lowered the intellectual standard or degraded the motives of those concerned, or of the community as a whole, we shall have achieved naught and less than naught. For as all experience tells us, and all philosophy teaches, we shall, in this 'debasing of the moral currency,' but have laid the foundation for more extended and more intense destitution and misery.
The Prevention of Destitution (1916), Ch.X: 293

self-interest:

8 There seems to be no limit to the willingness of fortunate men – even men of high ideals and great devotion – to accept excuses for the suffering of other people, so long as this suffering seems to be necessary to the maintenance of the position or the interests of their class or race.
The Decay of Capitalist Civilization (1923), Ch.I: 9

social insurance:

9 Those who desire to improve the present deplorable state of things have to accept popular obsessions and misunderstandings as part of the situation with which they have to deal. Hence, the philosophic onlooker will be prepared to accept both an unintelligent method of taxation and an equally unintelligent method of provision as a necessary preliminary to persuading the community to adopt a policy of preventing sickness and preventing unemployment.
The Prevention of Destitution (1916), Ch.VII: 213–214

Max Weber (1864–1920)

capitalism:

1 The impulse to acquisition, pursuit of gain, of money, of the greatest possible amount of money, has in itself nothing to do with capitalism. This impulse exists and has existed among waiters, physicians, coachmen, artists, prostitutes, dishonest officials, soldiers, nobles, crusaders, gamblers, and beggars. One may say that it has been common to all sorts and conditions of men at all times and in all countries of the earth, wherever the objective possibility of it is or has been given. It should be taught in the kindergarten of cultural history that this naïve idea of capitalism must be given up once and for all. Unlimited greed for gain is not in the least identical with capitalism, and

is still less its spirit. Capitalism *may* even be identical with the restraint, or at least a rational tempering, of this irrational impulse. But capitalism is identical with the pursuit of profit, and forever *renewed* profit, by means of continuous, rational, capitalistic enterprise. For it must be so: in a wholly capitalistic order of society, an individual capitalistic enterprise which did not take advantage of its opportunities for profit-making would be doomed to extinction.
The Protestant Ethic and the Spirit of Capitalism (1904–5), Introduction: 17

Daniel Webster (1782–1852)
American politician

money:

1 Every man of property or industry, every man who desires to preserve what he honestly possesses, or to obtain what he can honestly earn, has a direct interest in maintaining a safe circulating medium; such a medium as shall be a real and substantial representative of property, not liable to vibrate with opinions, not subject to be blown up or blown down by the breath of speculation, but made stable and secure by its immediate relation to that which the whole world regards as of a permanent value. A disordered currency is one of the greatest of political evils. It undermines the virtues necessary for the support of the social system, and encourages propensities destructive of its happiness. It wars against industry, frugality, and economy; and it fosters the evil spirits of extravagance and speculation. Of all the contrivances for cheating the laboring classes of mankind, none has been more effectual than that which deludes them with paper money. This is the most effectual of inventions to fertilize the rich man's field by the sweat of the poor man's brow. Ordinary tyranny, oppression, excessive taxation, these bear lightly on the happiness of the mass of the community, compared with a fraudulent currency, and the robberies committed by depreciated paper. Our own history has recorded for our instruction enough, and more than enough, of the demoralizing tendency, the injustice, and the intolerable oppression on the virtuous and well disposed, of a degraded paper currency, authorized by law, or in any way countenanced by government.
'Bank of the United States' (Speech before the US Senate, 25 May 1832): 394–395

2 He who tampers with the currency robs labor of its bread. He panders, indeed, to greedy capital, which is keen-sighted, and may shift for itself; but he beggars labor, which is honest, unsuspecting, and too busy with the present to calculate for the future. The prosperity of the working classes lives, moves, and has its being in established credit, and a steady medium of payment. All sudden changes destroy it. Honest industry never comes in for any part of the spoils in that scramble which takes place when the currency of a country is disordered. Did wild schemes and projects ever benefit the industrious? Did irredeemable bank paper ever enrich the laborious? Did violent fluctuations ever do good to him who depends on his daily labor for his daily bread? Certainly never. All these things may gratify greediness for sudden gain, or the rashness of daring speculation; but they can bring nothing but injury and distress to the homes of patient industry and honest labor.
'Reception at New York' (Speech at Niblo's Saloon, New York, 15 March 1837): 377

Richard Whately, Archbishop of Dublin (1787–1863)

economics and economists:

1 There are so many crude and mischievous theories afloat, which are dignified with the name of Political Economy, that the science is in no small danger of falling into disrepute with a large portion of the world. But this is not the only, or perhaps the greatest, evil to be apprehended. Not only may just views of Political Economy be neglected, but false ones may obtain currency; and if the cultivation of this branch of knowledge be left by the advocates of religion, and of social order, in the hands of those who are hostile to both, the result may easily be foreseen.
'Oxford Lectures on Political Economy' (1828): 170–171

2 I trust that, while due encouragement shall still be afforded to those more strictly *professional* studies which conduce to the professional advancement in life of each individual, Political-Economy will, ere long, be enrolled in the list of those branches of knowledge, which more peculiarly demand the attention of an endowed University; those, namely, which, while the cultivation of them is highly important to *the Public at large,* are not likely to be forwarded by the stimulus of private interest operating on individuals. The time is not, I trust, far distant, when it will be regarded as discreditable not to have regularly studied those subjects, respecting which, even now, every one is expected to feel an interest – most are ready to adopt opinions – and many are called on to form practical decisions.
Introductory Lectures on Political Economy (1831), Preface to first edition (published the following year): x

3 I wish for my own part there were no such thing as Political-Economy. I mean not now the mere *name* of the study: but I wish there had never been any necessity for directing our attention to the study itself. If men had always been secured in person and property, and left at full liberty to employ both as they saw fit; and had merely been precluded from unjust interference with each other – had the most perfect freedom of intercourse between all mankind been always allowed – had there never been any wars – nor (which in that case would have easily been avoided) any taxation – then, though every exchange that took place would have been one of the phenomena of which Political-Economy takes cognizance, all would have proceeded so smoothly, that probably no attention would ever have been called to the subject. The transactions of society would have been like the play of the lungs, the contractions of the muscles, and the circulation of the blood, in a healthy person; who scarcely knows that these functions exist. But as soon as they are impeded and disordered, our attention is immediately called to them. Indeed one of these functions did exist for several thousand years before it was even suspected. It is probable that (except among a small number of curious speculators) anatomy and physiology would never have been thought of, had they not been called for in aid of the art of medicine; and this, manifestly, would have had no existence, but for disease. In like manner it may be said to have been diseases, actual or apprehended – evils or imperfections, real or imaginary, that in the first instance directed the attention of men to the subjects about which Political-Economy is conversant: the attention, I mean, not only of those who use that term in a favourable sense, but of those no less who hold it in abhorrence, and of our ancestors who never heard it. Many, no doubt, of those evils have been produced or aggravated by the operation of erroneous views of Political-Economy; just as there are many cases in which erroneous medical treatment has brought on, or heightened diseases; but in these, no one will deny that it is from correct medical views we must hope for a cure.
Introductory Lectures on Political Economy (1832; 2nd edn), Lecture III: 84–86

4 Those therefore who, as writers or as readers, can take no interest in anything but brilliant description and impassioned declamation, should be exhorted to occupy themselves on some other subject, better adapted for the display of eloquence, and in which such a display is less likely to lead to mischievous results.
Introductory Lectures on Political Economy (1832; 2nd edn), Lecture IX: 255

wealth:

5 It is only when a rich man lays down in forest, like William the Conquerer, a quantity of fertile land, or in some such way diminishes human subsistence, that his wealth is detrimental to the community.
Introductory Lectures on Political Economy (1832; 2nd edn), Lecture VI: 152

Johan Gustav Knut Wicksell
(1851–1926)

economics and economists:

1 Of course, it is true that conflicts of opinion take place in other sciences [than economics], and indeed to some extent they constitute a real part of scientific life and research;

but there is this great difference, that in other fields of science these conflicts usually come to an end, the defenders of the false opinion are defeated and admit themselves beaten; or, as more frequently occurs perhaps, they withdraw from the struggle and no new defenders come forward to take their places.
'Ends and Means in Economics' (1904): 51

mathematics in economics:

2 [M]athematics has the same usefulness in economics as it has everywhere else – it helps us to think; that is, to the extent to which it can actually be applied, which unfortunately is not very far, on account of the lack of sufficient, or sufficiently exact, statistical data. It cannot replace actual thinking, of course – the occasional attempts which have been made in that direction have not turned out well – but it contributes a great deal to clarity and vigour of thought by *defining* inflexibly the assumptions and concepts upon which our reasoning is based, and which (otherwise) are only too liable to change their form, or even to become totally obscured, during the course of a long and complicated chain of reasoning, so that in the end there is no sure distinction between premiss and conclusion.
'Mathematical Economics' (1925): 204

3 That elegant lack of words which may be quite appropriate in purely mathematical papers, where the formulae may be left to speak for themselves without any doubt arising as to their meaning, is quite out of place when it is a matter of terms as vague and ill-defined as the basic concepts of economics; but sometimes it seems to be almost a matter of honour to allow the text to shrink to the same degree as the formulae are extended, instead of the other way about.
'Mathematical Economics' (1925): 208

Philip Henry Wicksteed (1844–1927)

economics and economists:

1 [U]nhappily the lay disciples of the economists have a tendency to adopt their conclusions and then discard their definitions.
The Alphabet of Economic Science (1888), Theory of Value – II: 84

2 If we engraft the current meaning of the word 'economy' (the avoiding of waste) upon its etymological meaning (the administration of a household), we shall arrive at 'the administration of the affairs and resources of a household in such a manner as to avoid waste and secure efficiency' as our conception of 'Economy.' 'Political' Economy would, by analogy, indicate the administration, in the like manner, of the affairs and resources of a State, regarded as an extended household or community, and regulated by a central authority; and the study of Political Economy would be the study of the principles on which the resources of a community should be so regulated and administered as to secure the communal ends without waste.
The Common Sense of Political Economy (1910), Book I, Ch.1

3 Let us suppose there were a recognised body of economic doctrine the truth and relevancy of which perpetually revealed itself to all who looked below the surface, which taught men what to expect and how to analyse their experience; which insisted at every turn on the illuminating relation between our conduct in life and our conduct in business; which drove the analysis of our daily administration of our individual resources deeper, and thereby dissipated the mist that hangs about our economic relations, and concentrated attention upon the uniting and all-penetrating principles of our study. Economics might even then be no more than a feeble barrier against passion, and might afford but a feeble light to guide honest enthusiasm, but it would exert a steady and a cumulative pressure, making for the truth. While the experts worked on severer methods than ever, populout appears would be found to drive homely illustrations and analogies into the general consciousness; and the roughly understood dicta bandied about in the name of Political Economy would at any rate stand in some relation to truth and to experience, instead of being, as they too often are at present, a mere armoury of consecrated paradoxes that cannot be understood because they are not true, that everyone uses as weapons while no one grasps them as principles.
'The Scope and Method of Political Economy in the Light of the "Marginal" Theory of Value and of Distribution' (1914), Sec.II: 22–23

Norbert Wiener (1894–1964)
American mathematician

mathematics in economics:

1   I have found mathematical sociology and mathematical economics or econometrics suffering under a misapprehension of what is the proper use of mathematics in the social sciences and of what is to be expected from mathematical techniques, and I have deliberately refrained from giving advice that, as I was convinced, would be bound to lead to a flood of superficial and ill-considered work.
    God and Golem, Inc. (1964), Ch.VII: 88

2   The success of mathematical physics led the social scientist to be jealous of its power without quite understanding the intellectual attitudes that had contributed to this power. The use of mathematical formulae had accompanied the development of the natural sciences and become the mode in the social sciences. Just as primitive people adopt the Western modes of denationalized clothing and of parliamentarism out of a vague feeling that these magic rites and vestments will at once put them abreast of modern culture and technique, so the economists have developed the habit of dressing up their rather imprecise ideas in the language of the infinitesimal calculus.
    God and Golem, Inc. (1964), Ch.VII: 89–90

3   [T]he economic game is a game where the rules are subject to important revisions, say, every ten years, and bears an uncomfortable resemblance to the Queen's croquet game in *Alice in Wonderland*. . . . Under the circumstances, it is hopeless to give too precise a measurement to the quantities occurring in it. To assign what purports to be precise values to such essentially vague quantities is neither useful nor honest, and any pretense of applying precise formulae to these loosely defined quantities is a sham and a waste of time.
    God and Golem, Inc. (1964), Ch.VII: 91

Friedrich, Freiherr von Wieser (1851–1926)

choice:

1   Choice is guided by the rules of morality, a sense of beauty, considerations of hygiene or good taste. In most cases there are added the admonitions of economic prudence. Not until these are applied is there economic consumption. Consumption becomes an economic act when it is accompanied and controlled by a consideration of the available means. To consume means to partake of. Where goods are free, one may partake of them without restraint. There is no need of economizing. But where they are available in limited amounts and the maximum total satisfaction is to be derived from their use, one is held by economic foresight to the rule of sparing enjoyment, to the curtailment of those present pleasures which desire would lead one to seek.
    Social Economics (1927), Bk.I, Sec.9: 45

mathematics in economics:

2   There can be no doubt that the mathematical method is properly applicable in economic theory; but the field of its usefulness is to be found in those portions of the material in which the most abstract, idealizing assumptions are admissible; namely, the theory of value and the theory of price, in so far as these doctrines are presented with the assumption of a static economy, showing neither progress nor retrogression. As regards an economy in process of development, even the doctrines of value and price can no longer be presented in strictly mathematical form. An investigation confining itself to this narrowest group of theoretical problems, a group open to extreme idealization, may resort to mathematical expression as the most exact instrument for formulating results. But an investigation passing by decreasing abstraction to the remaining problems of theory will find itself compelled to discard, in its further advance, the mathematical formula. None of the great truths of economic theory, none of their important moral and political applications, has been justified by mathematical means.

The justification could not have been thus established.
Social Economics (1927), Introduction, Sec.2: 13

methodology:

3 It is the problem of economic theory to exhaust scientifically the content of everyday economic experience and to interpret it.
Social Economics (1927), Introduction, Sec.1: 3

4 The method of economic theory is empirical. It is supported by observation and has but one aim, which is to describe actuality. Nevertheless, economic theory does not attempt to describe the actual in its entirety, as purely empirical sciences are wont to do. They strive to remain true to nature in every minute detail. But the economist is like an historian unfolding an individual historical course of events or a statistician summarizing a series of cases. He endeavors to place before us the typical phenomenon, the typical development, and to eliminate whatever may be subordinate, accidental or individual.
Social Economics (1927), Introduction, Sec.1: 5

5 True economic theory shuns speculation in a vacuum. From its very beginning it looks towards a union with the methods of purely empirical science for whose efforts it prepares the ground. It does not conflict with these methods; it remains in touch with them and complements their aims.
Social Economics (1927), Introduction, Sec.1: 7

private property:

6 That the institution of private property is most intimately interwoven with all the implications of the individual economy, may be demonstrated with the utmost brevity. Only such goods are made private property, as have entered into the economic quantitative relation. Who would ever dream of asserting rights of private property in goods abundantly free to everyone; goods from the enjoyment of which he could exclude no one, which no one could dispute to him? The rationale of private property is the rationale of all economy.
Social Economics (1927), Bk.II, Part IV, Sec.75: 390

socialism:

7 In the socialist theory of value pretty nearly everything is wrong. The origin of value, which lies in utility and not in labour, is mistaken. The relation of supply to demand – that fact which impels us to attribute utility to goods, and upon whose fluctuations depend, in the last resort, the fluctuations in amount of value – is overlooked. The objects to which value attaches are not all embraced, for among those must be included productive land and capital, both as elements in the calculation of costs, and also *per se*. And the service rendered by value in economic life is only half understood, inasmuch as the most essential part of it, the material control of economy, is neglected.
Natural Value (1893), Book II, Ch.VII: 66

taxation:

8 The state should never so use its prerogative of taxation as to eliminate existing inequalities of income and property; but in determining the contributions to be demanded of its citizens it should take into consideration the gradations of personal value that are the expression of inequalities of income and property. The plan of the state's management would offend economic principle were the private economies which are being assessed to be treated as units of equal wealth.
Social Economics (1927), Bk.III, Sec.80: 434

Edwin Bidwell Wilson (1879–1964)
American mathematician

mathematics in economics:

1 Everybody seems to agree that mathematics has to be used, is poorly understood by most economists, but should be better known to more. It is not so clear whether there is agreement about what science is or what theory is or even what economics or an economist is.
'Mathematics in Economics: Further Comment' (1955): 298

methodology:

2   [T]he methodology of the social studies depends first and foremost on whether the social studies are or are not sciences.
    'Methodology in the Natural and the Social Sciences' (1940): 659

3   The statement that the social sciences must develop their own methods can only mean that certain scientific methods which are necessary for the development of the social sciences have not as yet been developed either in them or in other sciences – and this statement may be equally true of any science and in respect to details must be true of all – but once those methods have been developed they become the general property of science and are available anywhere there is need for them. Only if it should prove true that some particular method useful in the social sciences had no applicability whatsoever elsewhere could it be affirmed a posteriori that it was in fact a strictly social science method, and so various are the social sciences that it may be doubted whether any method generally applicable in them would fail to find uses in some other branches of learning.
    'Methodology in the Natural and the Social Sciences' (1940): 664–665

Barbara Frances [Adam] Wootton, Baroness Wootton of Abinger
(1897–1988)

planning:

1   [P]lanning is possible without sacrifice of political freedom only if the limits of any plan which is to be exempt from continual disturbance fall within the boundaries of genuine agreement on the purposes which the plan is to achieve.
    Freedom Under Planning (1945), Ch.IX: 148

2   Effective long-term planning will be possible when, and only when, acceptance of certain peace-time objectives becomes as wholehearted, and is as fearlessly acknowledged, as is the necessity of military victory in war. . . .
    Freedom Under Planning (1945), Ch.IX: 148

Carroll Davidson Wright
(1840–1909)
American statistician

social science:

1   [The social scientist] is skeptical of all statements, whether resulting from personal observation or official inquiry, which bear upon the relations of men, and from which he hopes to deduce some law or establish beyond controversy the cause of some existing condition. If he be scientific in his methods of study, he cares not so much what the results of investigation show as to feel assured that the showing is an accurate one. He is ready at all times to recast his opinions, modify his reasoning, and even to turn his mind into new channels of thought, whenever the facts indicate that such changes should be made.
    'Contributions of the United States Government to Social Science' (1895): 241

2   The student of social science cannot be a partisan; he must accept conclusions which are proved. He may advocate reforms, he may insist upon changes in legislation, upon the adoption of new systems of finance or commerce, but he does all this because to his mind the ascertained facts lead to his conclusions, and until they are completely overturned he will adhere and must adhere to his position. . . .
    'Contributions of the United States Government to Social Science' (1895): 242

3   Care is taken [by the government] to secure only that information which has a positive bearing upon the current problems of the times, and the men engaged in the collection of the information are almost invariably so thoroughly interested in the ascertainment of the truth that their work is free from bias and may be accepted by the scientist as worthy of his use.
    'Contributions of the United States Government to Social Science' (1895): 275

wealth:

4   Progress would cease, industry stop, civilization itself be retarded, were it not for

the rich. There never was a time, moreover, when the rich did so much for society and for the poor as they are doing at the present time. God speed the day when the wealthy will fully comprehend that their wealth is held in trust; that they are but the means of helping the world, and that riches have been given them for this purpose. The world is recognizing this. Millionaires are understanding it more and more, and so those of low estate are securing the benefit.

'Are the Rich Growing Richer and the Poor Poorer?' (1897): 308

Y

Andrew Yarranton (1616–1684?)
English engineer and agriculturist

poor relief:

1 And now all you poor Men in *England*, that work or labour in Mechanick Arts, you are mine: I know now I shall have many questions asked me, and amongst the rest, What will you do with all these poor People which you say shall be yours? My answer is, I will make them all rich and happy, and their Families also.
   I will now begin to shew them the way; but when they are Reading my Project, as most will call it, I order them to act like Soldiers, and command Silence; Suffer not your Wives to use any Twit-twat, nor ask questions by the way; but Read it over and over again, and then lay all your Heads together, Wife, Children, and Servants, and it's possible the younger Fry may live to see it Crown'd with a beautiful Blazing-head, as the Monument near *London-Bridg* is with the Urn.
   England's Improvement by Sea and Land (1677): 170

Allyn Abbot Young (1876–1929)

economics and economists:

1 Every economic theorist ought to be something of an historian, and every student of the development of economic institutions ought to be something of a theorist.
   'Economics as a Field of Research' (1927), Sec.I: 10; cf. John Cairnes 1

Z

Frederik Ludvig Bang Zeuthen
(1888–1959)

mathematics in economics:

1 [I]t would be better wherever possible not to write in a more complicated way than necessary; and in some cases a translation ought to be given from the complicated mathematics in which a theory is originally constructed and discussed between specialists. Such translation would make the results accessible to a wider circle of people, and at the same time give more people occasion to criticize the realism of assumptions and consequences – criticism which is generally much more needed than is an opportunity of revising the calculations. On the other hand, all economists have to master some kind of mathematics: the logic of relations between quantities.

'Recent Developments in Economics' (1954), Sec.III: 179

References

Aaron, Henry J. (1989), 'Politics and the professors revisited,' *American Economic Review, Papers and Proceedings of the Hundred and first Annual Meeting of the American Economic Association*, vol. 79, no. 2 (May), pp. 1–15.

Adams, Henry Carter (1887), 'Relation of the state to industrial action,' *Publications of the American Economic Association*, vol. 1, no. 6 (January), pp. 7–85.

—— (1894), 'The social ministry of wealth,' *International Journal of Ethics*, vol. 4, no. 2 (January), pp. 173–88.

Akerlof, George A. (1984), *An Economic Theorist's Book of Tales*, Cambridge: Cambridge University Press.

Åkerman, Johan (1936), 'Annual survey of economic theory: the setting of the central problem,' *Econometrica*, vol. 4, no. 2 (April), pp. 97–122.

—— (1960), *Theory of Industrialism: Causal Analysis and Economic Plans*, Lund: G.W.K. Gleerup.

Alchian, Armen A. (1965), 'Some economics of property rights,' *Il Politico*, vol. 30, no. 4, pp. 816–29.

—— (1967), *Pricing and Society*, Institute of Economic Affairs occasional paper no. 17, London: Institute of Economic Affairs.

Allen, R.G.D. (1938), *Mathematical Analysis for Economists*, New York: St. Martin's Press.

—— (1949), 'The mathematical foundations of economic theory,' *Quarterly Journal of Economics*, vol. 63, no. 1 (February), pp. 111–27.

Aquinas, St. Thomas (1988), *St. Thomas Aquinas on Politics and Ethics*, translated and edited by Paul E. Sigmund, New York: W.W. Norton and Co.

Archibald, G.C. (1959), 'Welfare economics, ethics, and essentialism,' *Economica* (new series), vol. 26, no. 104 (November), pp. 316–27.

Aristotle (1988), *The Politics*, edited by Stephen Everson, translated by Jonathan Barnes, Cambridge: Cambridge University Press.

Arrow, Kenneth J. (1974), *The Limits of Organization*, New York: W.W. Norton.

Ashley, William J. (1907), 'The present position of political economy,' *Economic Journal*, vol. 17, no. 68 (December), pp. 467–89.

Atkinson, Edward (1890), 'A single tax upon land,' *The Century*, vol. XL, no. 3 (July), pp. 385–94.

Atwater, Lyman H. (1880), 'Political economy a science – of what?,' *Princeton Review*, (4th series), vol. 5, no. 3 (May), pp. 420–33.

Ayres, Clarence E. (1938), *The Problem of Economic Order*, New York: Farrar and Rinehart.

—— (1944), *The Theory of Economic Progress*, Chapel Hill, NC: University of North Carolina Press.

—— (1946), *The Divine Right of Capital*, Boston: Houghton Mifflin.

—— (1952), *The Industrial Economy: Its Technological Basis and Institutional Destiny*, New York: Houghton Mifflin.

Aytoun, W.E. (1847), 'Our currency, our trade, and our tariff,' *Blackwood's Edinburgh Magazine*, vol. LXII, no. 386 (December), pp. 744–67.

—— (1851), 'Latter days of the free-trade ministry,' *Blackwood's Edinburgh Magazine*, vol. LXIX, no. 426 (April), pp. 491–512.

Babbage, Charles (1835 [1989]), *The Economy of Machinery and Manufactures*, fourth edition, Volume 8 of *The Works of Charles Babbage*, edited by Martin Campbell-Kelly, New York: New York University Press.

Babson, Roger W. (1914), *The Future of Nations*, Boston: Babson Statistical Organization.

Bacon, Francis (1625), *The Essayes or Counsels, Civill and Morall, of Francis Lo. Verulam, Viscount St. Alban*, London: John Haviland for Hanna Barret.

Bagehot, Walter (1855), 'The first Edinburgh reviewers,' *National Review*, (October), as reprinted (1898), in *Literary Studies*, Vol. I, edited by Richard Holt Hutton, London: Longmans, Green and Co.

—— (1872 [1921]), *The English Constitution*, second edition, London: Kegan Paul, Trench, Trubner and Co.

—— (1873 [1962]), *Lombard Street: A Description of the Money Market*, Homewood, IL.: Richard D. Irwin.

—— (1876), 'The postulates of English political economy,' *Fortnightly Review*, vol. XIX (new series): Part I: no. CX (February 1), pp. 215–42; Part II: no. CXIII (May 1), pp. 720–41.

Bailey, Samuel (1852), 'On the science of political economy,' in Samuel Bailey (ed.), *Discourses on Various Subjects; Read Before Literary and Philosophical Societies*, London: Longmans, Brown, Green, and Longmans.

Balogh, Thomas (1949), *The Dollar Crisis: Causes and Cure. A Report to the Fabian Society*, Oxford: Basil Blackwell.

Baran, Paul A. (1958), 'On the nature of Marxism' ('Crisis of Marxism?,' Part II), *Monthly Review*, vol. 10, no. 7 (November), pp. 259–68.

Barbon, Nicholas (1690), *A Discourse of Trade*, London: Thomas Milbourn.

Barro, Robert J. (1996), *Getting It Right: Markets and Choices in a Free Society*, Cambridge, MA: MIT Press.

Basmann, R.L. (1972), 'Argument and evidence in the Brookings–S.S.R.C. philosophy of econometrics,' in Karl Brunner (ed.), *Problems and Issues in Current Econometric Practice*, Columbus, OH: College of Administrative Science, Ohio State University.

Bastable, Charles F. (1891), 'Taxation through monopoly,' *Economic Journal*, vol. 1, no. 2 (June), pp. 307–25.

Bastiat, Frédéric (1848 [1964]), 'Justice and fraternity,' in *Selected Essays on Political Economy*, Translated by Seymour Cain, edited by George B. de Huszar, Princeton: D. Van Nostrand Co. (originally published in the *Journal des économistes*, 15 June 1848).

—— (1848 [1964]), 'The state,' in *Selected Essays on Political Economy*, Translated by Seymour Cain, edited by George B. de Huszar, Princeton: D. Van Nostrand Co. (originally published in the *Journal des débats*, 25 September 1848).

—— (1850 [1964]), 'What is seen and what is not seen,' in *Selected Essays on Political Economy*, translated by Seymour Cain and edited by George B. de Huszar, Princeton: D. Van Nostrand Co.

—— (1850 [1964]), 'The law,' in *Selected Essays on Political Economy*, translated by Seymour Cain and edited by George B. de Huszar, Princeton: D. Van Nostrand Co.

Bauer, P.T. (1981), *Equality, the Third World, and Economic Delusion*, Cambridge, MA: Harvard University Press.

Bauer, P.T., and Alan A. Walters (1975), 'The state of economics,' *Journal of Law and Economics*, vol. XVIII, no. 1 (April), pp. 1–23.

Baumol, William J. (1958), 'Activity analysis in one lesson,' *American Economic Review*, vol. 48, no. 5 (December), pp. 837–73.

—— (1991), 'Toward a newer economics: the future lies ahead!,' *Economic Journal*, vol. 101, no. 404 (January), pp. 1–8.

Becker, Gary S. (1974), 'A theory of social interactions,' *Journal of Political Economy*, vol. 82, no. 6 (November–December), pp. 1063–93.

—— (1981), *A Treatise on the Family*, Cambridge, MA: Harvard University Press.

—— (1996), *Accounting for Tastes*, Cambridge, MA: Harvard University Press.

Bell, Daniel (1976), *The Cultural Contradictions of Capitalism*, New York: Basic Books.

Bentham, Jeremy (1781 [1988]), *The Principles of Morals and Legislation*, Amherst, NY: Prometheus Books.

—— (1787 [1952]), *Defence of Usury*, in William Stark (ed.), *Jeremy Bentham's Economic Writings*, vol. I, London: George Allen and Unwin for the Royal Economic Society.

—— (1793–75 [1952]), *Manual of Political Economy*, in William Stark (ed.), *Jeremy Bentham's Economic Writings*, vol. I, London: George Allen and Unwin for the Royal Economic Society.

—— (1801–4), *Institute of Political Economy*, in William Stark (ed.), *Jeremy Bentham's Economic Writings*, vol. III, London: George Allen and Unwin for the Royal Economic Society.

Berkeley, George (1721 [1948]), 'An essay towards preventing the ruin of Great Britain,' in A.A. Luce and T.E. Jessup (eds), *The Works of George Berkeley, Bishop of Cloyne*, Vol. Six, London: Thomas Nelson and Sons, Ltd.

Berle, Adolf A. (1963), *The American Economic Republic*, New York: Harcourt, Brace and World.

Berle, Adolf A., and Gardiner C. Means (1932), *The Modern Corporation and Private Property*, New York: Macmillan.

Bernstein, Eduard (1899 [1993]), *The Preconditions of Socialism*, edited and translated by Henry Tudor, Cambridge: Cambridge University Press.

Beveridge, William H. (1931), *Causes and Cures of Unemployment*, London: Longmans, Green and Co.

—— (1942), *Social Insurance and Allied Services*, New York: Macmillan.

—— (1945), *Full Employment in a Free Society*, New York: W.W. Norton.

Blaug, Mark (1976), 'Kuhn versus Lakatos *or* paradigms versus research programmes in the history of economics,' in Spiro Latsis (ed.), *Method and Appraisal in Economics*, Cambridge: Cambridge University Press.

— — (1986), 'Economic methodology in one easy lesson,' in Mark Blaug (ed.), *Economic History and the History of Economics*, New York: New York University Press.

Blinder, Alan S. (1987), *Hard Heads, Soft Hearts*, Reading, MA: Addison-Wesley.

Böhm-Bawerk, Eugen von (1894), 'The ultimate standard of value,' *Annals of the American Academy of Political and Social Science*, vol. 5 (September), translated by C.W. Macfarlane, pp. 1–60 [149–208].

Boland, Lawrence A. (1982), *The Foundations of Economic Method*, London: George Allen and Unwin.

Bonar, James (1898), 'Old lights and new in economic study,' *Economic Journal*, vol. 8, no. 32 (December), pp. 433–53.

Bork, Robert H. (1967), 'Antitrust and monopoly: the goals of antitrust policy,' *American Economic Review, Papers and Proceedings of the Seventy-ninth Annual Meeting of the American Economic Association*, vol. 57, no. 2 (May), pp. 242–53.

Boulding, Kenneth E. (1948), 'Samuelson's *Foundations*: the role of mathematics in economics,' *Journal of Political Economy*, vol. LVI, no. 3 (June), pp. 187–99.

— — (1950), 'Collective bargaining and fiscal policy,' *American Economic Review, Papers and Proceedings of the Sixty-Second Annual Meeting of the American Economic Association*, vol. 40, no. 2 (May), pp. 306–20.

— — (1967), 'The basis of value judgments in economics,' in Sidney Hook (ed.), *Human Values and Economic Policy: A Symposium*, New York: New York University Press.

— — (1969), 'Economics as a moral science,' *American Economic Review*, vol. 59, no. 1, pp. 1–12.

Bowen, Francis (1856), *The Principles of Political Economy Applied to the Condition, the Resources, and the Institutions of the American People*, Boston: Little, Brown, and Co.

Brandeis, Louis D. (1914), *Other People's Money, And How the Bankers Use It*, New York: Frederick A. Stokes.

Bronfenbrenner, Martin (1954), 'Changing fashions in philosopher-salesmen,' *Review of Economics and Statistics*, vol. 36, no. 3 (August), pp. 262–66.

— — (1972), 'Sensitivity analysis for econometricians,' *Nebraska Journal of Economics and Business*, (autumn), as reprinted in Martin Bronfenbrenner (ed.), *Keizaigaku Tokoro-Dokoro (Here and There in Economics)*, Aoyama Gakuin University, 1988.

Brougham, Henry (1803), 'Wheatley on currency and commerce,' *Edinburgh Review*, vol. III, no. 5 (October), pp. 231–52.

— — (1816), Article III: 'Defence of usury,' *Edinburgh Review*, vol. XXVII, no. 54 (December), pp. 338–60.

Brownson, Orestes A. (1840), *The Laboring Classes, An Article from the Boston Quarterly Review*, Boston: Benjamin H. Greene.

Brunner, Karl (1985), 'The poverty of nations,' *Business Economics*, vol. XX, no. 1 (January), pp. 5–11.

Bryan, William Jennings (1902), 'Concentration of wealth: a menace to government and civilization,' *The Independent*, vol. LIV, no. 2787 (May 1), pp. 1068–69.

Buchanan, James M. (1964), 'What should economists do?,' *Southern Economic Journal*, vol. XXX, no. 3 (January), pp. 213–22.

— — (1964), 'Confessions of a burden monger,' *Journal of Political Economy*, vol. 72, no. 5 (October), pp. 486–88.

— — (1975), 'A contractarian paradigm for applying economic theory,' *American Economic Review, Papers and Proceedings of the Eighty-seventh Annual Meeting of the American Economic Association*, vol. LXV, no. 2 (May), pp. 225–230.

— — (1979), *What Should Economists Do?*, Indianapolis, IN: Liberty Press.

Bukharin, N.I. (1930), *Imperialism and World Economy*, London: Martin Lawrence Ltd.

Burke, Edmund (1790), *Reflections on the Revolution in France, and on the Proceedings in Certain Societies in London Relative to that Event in a Letter Intended to Have Been Sent to a Gentleman in Paris*, London: printed for J. Dodsley in Pall-Mall, (as reprinted in J.C.D. Clark (ed.), *Edmund Burke: Reflections on the Revolution in France*, Stanford, CA: Stanford University Press, 2001.)

Burns, Arthur F. (1947), 'Keynesian economics once again,' *Review of Economic Statistics*, vol. 29, no. 4 (November), pp. 252–67.

Cairnes, John E. (1870), 'M. Comte and political economy,' *Fortnightly Review*, vol. VII (NS), no. XLI (May 1), pp. 579–602.

–– (1871), 'Political economy and laissez-faire,' *Fortnightly Review*, vol. X (NS), no. LV (July 1), pp. 80–97.

–– (1872), 'New theories in political economy,' *Fortnightly Review*, vol. XI (NS), no. LXI (January 1), pp. 71–6.

–– (1874), *Some Leading Principles of Political Economy Newly Expounded*, New York: Harper and Brothers.

–– (1888), *The Character and Logical Method of Political Economy*, second edn, London: Macmillan

Cannan, Edwin (1930), *Wealth: A Brief Explanation of the Causes of Economic Welfare*, third edn, London: P.S. King and Son.

Cantillon, Richard (1755 [2001]), *Essay on the Nature of Commerce in General*, translated by Henry Higgs in a reprint of the 1931 English-language edition of Cantillon's *Essai sur la Nature du Commerce en Général*, New Brunswick, NJ: Transaction.

Carey, Henry C. (1858), *Principles of Social Science*, Vol. I. Philadelphia: J.B. Lippincott and Co.

–– (1864), *Financial Crises: Their Causes and Effects*, Philadelphia: Henry Carey Baird.

–– (1872), *The Unity of Law; As Exhibited in the Relations of Physical, Social, Mental, and Moral Science*, Philadelphia: Henry Carey Baird.

Carlyle, Thomas (1839 [1899]), *Chartism*, in *Critical and Miscellaneous Essays*, vol. IV (vol. XXIX of *The Works of Thomas Carlyle*, centenary edition), New York: Charles Scribner's Sons.

–– (1849), 'Occasional discourse on the negro question,' *Fraser's Magazine for Town and Country*, vol. XL, no. CCXL (December), pp. 670–79.

Carnegie, Andrew (1891), 'The advantages of poverty,' *The Nineteenth Century*, vol. XXIX, no. 169 (March), pp. 367–85.

Carver, Thomas Nixon (1895), 'The ethical basis of distribution and its bearings on taxation,' *Publications of the American Economic Association*, vol. 10, no. 3, supplement in the handbook of the American Economic Association (March), pp. 96–101.

–– (1904), *The Distribution of Wealth*, New York: Macmillan.

–– (1904), 'The minimum sacrifice theory of taxation,' *Political Science Quarterly*, vol. 19, no. 1 (March), pp. 66–79.

–– (1915), *Essays in Social Justice*, Cambridge, MA: Harvard University Press.

–– (1918), 'The behavioristic man,' *Quarterly Journal of Economics*, vol. 33, no. 1 (November), pp. 195–200.

Cassel, Gustav (1903 [1957]), *The Nature and Necessity of Interest*, New York: Kelley and Millman.

–– (1923), *Money and Foreign Exchange After 1914*, New York: Macmillan.

–– (1928), 'The rate of interest, the bank rate, and the stabilization of prices,' *Quarterly Journal of Economics*, vol. 42, no. 4 (August), pp. 511–29.

Chadwick, Edwin (1836), 'Article X: the new poor law,' *Edinburgh Review*, vol. LXIII, no. 128 (July), pp. 487–537.

Chalmers, Thomas (1832), *On Political Economy, In Connexion with the Moral State and Moral Prospects of Society*, Glasgow: printed for William Collins.

Chamberlain, Joseph (1891), 'Favorable aspects of state socialism,' *North American Review*, vol. CLII, no. 414 (May), pp. 534–48.

Champernowne, D.G. (1954), 'On the use and misuse of mathematics in presenting economic theory,' *Review of Economic and Statistics*, vol. 36, no. 4 (November), pp. 369–72.

Child, Josiah (1694), *A Discourse of the Nature, Use and Advantages of Trade. Proposing some Considerations for the Promotion and Advancement thereof, By: A Registry of Lands. Preventing the Exportation of Coyn. Lowering the Interest of Money. Inviting Foreign Families into England*, London: printed and sold by Randal Taylor, near Stationers-Hall.

–– (1699), *A Method Concerning the Relief and Employment of the Poor: Humbly Offered to the Consideration of the KING and both Houses of PARLIAMENT. Taken out of Sir Josiah Child's Writings*, London: printed by the Advice of Some in Authority.

Christ, Carl F. (1991), 'Economics and public policy,' in Shripad Pendse (ed.), *Perspectives on an Economic Future: Forms, Reforms, and Evaluations*, New York: Greenwood Press.

Cicero (1913), *On Duties*, translated by Walter Miller, Cambridge, MA: Loeb Classical Library, Harvard University Press.

Clapham, J.H. (1922), 'Of Empty Economic Boxes,' *Economic Journal*, vol. 32, no. 127 (September), pp. 305–14.

Clark, Colin (1940), *The Conditions of Economic Progress*, London: Macmillan.

–– (1951), *The Conditions of Economic Progress*, second edn, London: Macmillan.

Clark, John Bates (1877), 'The new philosophy of wealth,' *The New Englander*, vol. XXXVI, no. CXXXVIII (January), pp. 170–87.
— — (1877), 'Unrecognized forces in political economy,' *The New Englander*, vol. XXXVI, no. CXLI (October), pp. 710–25.
— — (1878), 'How to deal with communism,' *The New Englander*, vol. XXXVII, no. CXLV (July), pp. 533–42.
— — (1879), 'Business ethics, past and present,' *The New Englander*, vol. XXXVIII, no. CXLIX (March), pp. 157–69.
— — (1879), 'The nature and progress of true socialism,' *The New Englander*, vol. XXXVIII, no. CLI (July), pp. 565–82.
— — (1881), 'The philosophy of value,' *The New Englander*, vol. XL, no. CXLI (July), pp. 457–70.
— — (1894), 'The modern appeal to legal forces in economic life,' *Publications of the American Economic Association*, vol. 9, no. 5/6 (October/November), pp. 9–30.
— — (1902), 'Concentration of wealth: a modified individualism,' *The Independent*, vol. LIV, no. 2787 (May 1), pp. 1066–68.
— — (1905), 'The Field of Economic Dynamics,' *Political Science Quarterly*, vol. 20, no. 2 (June), pp. 246–56.
— — (1910), 'Economics for Children,' *Journal of Political Economy*, vol. 18, no. 6 (June), pp. 432–34.
Clark, John Maurice (1916), 'The changing basis of economic responsibility,' *Journal of Political Economy*, vol. 24, no. 3 (March), pp. 209–29.
— — (1918), 'Economics and modern psychology,' *Journal of Political Economy*, part I: vol. 26, no. 1 (January), pp. 1–30; part II: vol. 26, no. 2 (February), pp. 136–66.
— — (1919), 'Economic theory in an era of social readjustment,' *American Economic Review, Papers and Proceedings of the Thirty-First Annual Meeting of the American Economic Association*, vol. 9, no. 1 (March), pp. 280–90.
— — (1936), *Preface to Social Economics: Essays on Economic Theory and Social Problems*, New York: Farrar and Rinehart, Inc.
— — (1948), *Alternative to Serfdom*, New York: Alfred A. Knopf.
— — (1949), *Guideposts in Time of Change: Some Essentials for a Sound American Economy*, New York: Harper and Brothers.
Clay, Henry (1832 [1904]), 'On the American system,' in Calvin Colton (ed.), *The Works of Henry Clay*, vol. 7: 'Speeches', part 2, New York: G.P. Putnam's Sons.
Clower, Robert W. (1964), 'Monetary history and positive economics,' *Journal of Economic History*, vol. XXIV, no. 3 (September), pp. 364–80.
— — (1989), 'How economists think,' *Business and Economic Review*, vol. 36, no. 1 (October–December), pp. 9–17.
— — (1994), 'Economics as an inductive science,' *Southern Economic Journal*, vol. 60, no. 4 (April), pp. 805–14.
Coase, Ronald H. (1974), 'Economists and public policy,' in J. Fred Weston (ed.), *Large Corporations in a Changing Society*, New York: NYU Press.
— — (1977), 'Economics and contiguous disciplines,' in Mark Perlman (ed.), *The Organization and Retrieval of Economic Knowledge*, London: Macmillan.
Coats, A.W. (1994), 'The past, present and future of economics,' in Cosimo Perrotta and Vitantonio Gioia (eds), *Where is Economics Going? Historical Viewpoints*, Università Degli Studi di Lecce: Congedo Editore.
Coke, Roger (1670), *A Discourse of Trade. In Two Parts. The first Treats of The Reason of the Decay of the Strength, Wealth, and Trade of England. The Latter, Of the Growth and Increase of the Dutch Trade above the English*, London: printed for H. Brome, at the Gun near the West-End of St. Paul's.
— — (1696), *A Treatise Concerning the Regulation of the Coyn of England, and How the East-India Trade may be Preserved and Encreased*, London: printed for Roger Clavel at the Peacock near St. Dunstan's Church in Fleetstreet.
Commons, John Rogers (1902), 'Concentration of wealth: its dangers,' *The Independent*, vol. LIV, no. 2787 (May 1), pp. 1040–44.
— — (1931), 'Institutional economics,' *American Economic Review*, vol. 21, no. 4 (December), pp. 648–57.
— — (1939), 'Twentieth century economics,' *Journal of Social Philosophy*, vol. 5 (October), pp. 29–41.
— — (1951), *The Economics of Collective Action*, New York: Macmillan.
Commons, John Rogers, and John B. Andrews (1916), *Principles of Labor Legislation*, second edn, New York: Harper and Brothers.
Croce, Benedetto (1914), *Historical Materialism and the Economics of Karl Marx*, translated by C.M. Meredith, London: George Allen and Unwin.

Crosland, C.A.R. (1956), *The Future of Socialism*, London: Jonathan Cape.
Cunningham, William (1878), 'Political economy as a moral science,' *Mind*, vol. 3, no. 11 (July), pp. 369–83.
— — (1892), 'The relativity of economic doctrine,' *Economic Journal*, vol. 2, no. 5 (March), pp. 1–16.
— — (1892), 'The perversion of economic history,' *Economic Journal*, vol. 2, no. 7 (September), pp. 491–506.
— — (1893), 'Political economy and practical life,' *International Journal of Ethics*, vol. 3, no. 2 (January), pp. 183–202.
— — (1894), 'A living wage,' *Contemporary Review*, vol. LXV, no. 1 (January), pp. 16–28.
— — (1914), *Christianity and Economic Science*, New York: Longmans, Green.
Cunynghame, Henry (1892), 'Some improvements in simple geometrical methods of treating exchange value, monopoly, and rent,' *Economic Journal*, vol. 2, no. 5 (March), pp. 35–52.
Davanzati, Bernardo (1588 [1696]), *A Discourse Upon Coins*, translated by John Toland, London: printed by J.D. for Awnsham and John Churchil, at the Black Swan in PaterNosterRow.
D'Avenant, Charles (1696), *An Essay on the East-India-Trade*, London.
— — (1698), *Discourses on the Publick Revenues, and on the Trade of England*, London: printed for James Knapton at the Crown in St. Paul's Church-yard.
Davenport, Herbert J. (1902), 'Proposed modifications in Austrian theory and terminology,' *Quarterly Journal of Economics*, vol. 16, no. 3 (May), pp. 355–84.
— — (1917), 'Scope, method, and psychology in economics', *Journal of Philosophy, Psychology, and Scientific Methods*, vol. XIV, no. 23 (November 8), pp. 617–26.
Deane, Phyllis (1983), 'The scope and method of economic science,' *Economic Journal*, vol. 93, no. 369 (March), pp. 1–12.
Debreu, Gerard (1991), 'The mathematization of economic theory,' *American Economic Review*, vol. 81, no. 1 (March), pp. 1–7.
De Leon, Daniel (1905), 'The Preamble of the IWW,' speech delivered in Minneapolis, Minnesota, 10 July, reprinted (1930) as *Socialist Reconstruction of Society*, New York: New York Labor News Company.
— — (1913), 'Industrial Unionism,' *The Daily People*, January 20, reprinted (1931) in *Industrial Unionism: Selected Editorials by Daniel De Leon*, New York: New York Labor News Company.
De Quincey, Thomas (1824 [1897]), 'Dialogues of three templars on political economy: chiefly in relation to the principles of Mr. Ricardo,' in David Masson (ed.), *The Collected Writings of Thomas De Quincey*, Vol. IX, London: A. and C. Black, originally published in *London Magazine*, March, April, May.
— — (1844 [1897]), The logic of political economy, in David Masson (ed.), *The Collected Writings of Thomas De Quincey*, Vol. IX. London: A. and C. Black.
Destutt Tracy, A. (1817 [1970]), *A Treatise on Political Economy, To Which is Prefixed a Supplement to a Preceding Work on the Understanding, or, Elements of Ideology*, translation edited by Thomas Jefferson, New York: Augustus M. Kelley.
Dew, Thomas R. (1829), *Lectures on the Restrictive System, Delivered to the Senior Political Class of William and Mary College*, Richmond, VA: Samuel Shepherd and Co.
Dobb, Maurice (1945), *Political Economy and Capitalism: Some Essays in Economic Tradition*, revised edition, New York: International Publishers.
— — (1960), *An Essay on Economic Growth and Planning*, London: Routledge and Kegan Paul.
Dorfman, Robert (1954), 'A catechism: mathematics in social science,' *Review of Economics and Statistics*, vol. 36, no. 4 (November), pp. 374–77.
Douglas, C.H. (1933), *Social Credit*, revised edition, New York: W.W. Norton.
Duesenberry, James S. (1954), 'The methodological basis of economic theory,' *Review of Economics and Statistics*, vol. 36, no. 4 (November), pp. 361–63.
— — (1974), 'Alternatives to monetary policy,' *American Economic Review, Papers and Proceedings of the Eighty-sixth Annual Meeting of the American Economic Association*, vol. 64, no. 2 (May), pp. 105–11.
Dunbar, Charles F. (1886), 'The reaction in political economy,' *Quarterly Journal of Economics*, vol. 1, no. 1 (October), pp. 1–27.
— — (1891), 'The academic study of political economy,' *Quarterly Journal of Economics*, vol. 5, no. 4 (July), pp. 397–416.
Dupuit, Jules (1844 [1952]), 'On the measurement of the utility of public works,' translated by R.H. Barback, *International Economic Papers*, no. 2. London: Macmillan.

Durbin, E.F.M. (1943), 'Economists and the future functions of the state,' *Political Quarterly*, vol. 14, no. 3, pp. 256–69.

Eatwell, John (1982), *Whatever Happened to Britain?: The Economics of Decline*, London: Duckworth and British Broadcasting Corporation.

Eden, Frederic Morton (1797 [1928]), *The State of the Poor: A History of the Labouring Classes in England, with Parochial Reports*, abridged and edited by A.G.L. Rogers, London: George Routledge and Sons, Ltd.

Edgeworth, Francis Y. (1881), *Mathematical Psychics*, London: C. Kegan Paul and Co.

—— (1889), 'Points at which mathematical reasoning is applicable to political economy,' *Nature*, vol. XL (September 19), pp. 496–509.

—— (1891), 'An introductory lecture on political economy,' *Economic Journal*, vol. 1, no. 4 (December), pp. 625–34.

—— (1898), 'Professor Graziani on the mathematical theory of monopoly,' *Economic Journal*, vol. 8, no. 30 (June), pp. 234–39.

—— (1923), 'Women's wages in relation to economic welfare,' *Economic Journal*, vol. 33, no. 132 (December), pp. 487–95.

Edmonds, Thomas Rowe (1833 [1969]), *Practical Moral and Political Economy or, the Government, Religion and Institutions Most Conducive to Individual Happiness and to National Power*, third edn, New York: Augustus M. Kelley, first edn (1828), London: Effingham Wilson, Royal Exchange.

Einstein, Albert (1949), 'Why socialism?,' *Monthly Review*, vol. 1, no. 1 (May), pp. 9–15.

Ellis, William (1850), 'Article VIII: relief measures,' *Westminster Review*, vol. LIII, no. 104 (April), pp. 77–87.

Elster, Jon (1986), 'Introduction', in Jon Elster (ed.), *Rational Choice*, Oxford: Basil Blackwell.

Ely, Richard Theodore (1886), 'Socialism in America,' *North American Review*, vol. CXLII, no. 355 (June), pp. 519–25.

—— (1887), 'Political economy in America,' *North American Review*, vol. CXLIV, no. 363 (February), pp. 113–19.

—— (1889), *An Introduction to Political Economy*, New York: Chautauqua Press.

—— (1898), 'Fraternalism vs. paternalism in government,' *The Century Magazine*, vol. LV, no. 5 (March), pp. 780–84.

—— (1931), *Hard Times – The Way In and the Way Out*, New York: Macmillan

Engels, Friedrich (1884), 'Marx and Rodbertus', preface to the first German edition of Karl Marx, *The Poverty of Philosophy*, in vol. 26 of *Karl Marx/Frederick Engels Collected Works*, New York: International Publishers.

—— (1888), 'Protection and Free Trade', preface to Karl Marx, *Speech on the Question of Free Trade*, in vol. 26 of *Karl Marx/Frederick Engels Collected Works*, New York: International Publishers.

—— (1901), *Socialism, Utopian and Scientific*, translated by Edward Aveling, New York: New York Labor News Company.

Erasmus, Desiderius (1516 [1986]), *The Education of a Christian Prince (Institutio principis christiani)*, translated by Neil M. Cheshire and Michael J. Heath, in A.H.T. Levy (ed.), *Collected Works of Erasmus*, vol. 27, Toronto: University of Toronto Press.

Eucken, Walter (1950), *The Foundations of Economics: History and Theory in the Analysis of Economic Reality*, translated by T.W. Hutchison, London: William Hodge and Co.

—— (1951), *This Unsuccessful Age, or the Pains of Economic Progress*, London: William Hodge and Co.

Everett, Alexander H. (1826), *New Ideas on Population: With Remarks on the Theories of Malthus and Godwin*, second edn, Boston: Cummings, Hilliard and Co.

Fawcett, Henry (1860), 'Article I: strikes: their tendencies and remedies,' *Westminster Review*, vol. LXXIV, no. 145 (July 1), pp. 1–23.

—— (1863), *Manual of Political Economy*, London: Macmillan and Co.

—— (1878), 'The recent development of socialism in Germany and the United States,' *Fortnightly Review*, vol. XXIV (NS), no. 143 (November 1), pp. 605–15.

Fawcett, Millicent Garrett (1892), 'Mr. Sidney Webb's article on women's wages,' *Economic Journal*, vol. 2, no. 5 (March), pp. 173–76.

Ferguson, Adam (1767 [1995]), *An Essay on the History of Civil Society*, edited by Fania Oz-Salzberger, Cambridge: Cambridge University Press.

Fetter, Frank A. (1904), *The Principles of Economics, with Applications to Practical Problems*, New York: The Century Co.

Fisher, Irving (1898), 'Cournot and mathematical economics,' *Quarterly Journal of Economics*, vol. 12, no. 2 (January), pp. 119–38.

—— (1912), *Elementary Principles of Economics*, third edn, New York: The Macmillan Co.

—— (1919), 'Economists in public service,' *American Economic Review, Papers and Proceedings of the Thirty-first Annual Meeting of the American Economic Association*, vol. IX, no. 1 (March), pp. 5–21.

—— (1920), *Stabilizing the Dollar: A Plan to Stabilize the General Price Level Without Fixing Individual Prices*, New York: The Macmillan Co.

—— (1930 [1954]), *The Theory of Interest, As Determined by Impatience to Spend Income and Opportunity to Invest It*, New York: Kelley and Millman.

—— (1932), *Booms and Depressions: Some First Principles*, New York: Adelphi.

Florence, P. Sargant (1929), *The Statistical Method in Economics and Political Science: A Treatise on the Quantitative and Institutional Approach to Social and Industrial Problems*, New York: Harcourt, Brace and Co.

Foxwell, Herbert Somerton (1899), 'Introduction', to Anton Menger, *The Right to the Whole Produce of Labour*, London: Macmillan.

Franklin, Benjamin (1729 [1907]), 'A modest enquiry into the nature and necessity of a paper-currency', in Albert Henry Smith (ed.), *The Writings of Benjamin Franklin*, volume II: 1722–1750, New York: Macmillan.

Friedman, Milton (1951), 'Comments on monetary policy,' *Review of Economics and Statistics*, vol. 33, no. 3 (August), pp. 186–91.

—— (1962), *Capitalism and Freedom*, Chicago: University of Chicago Press.

—— (1964), 'Post-war trends in monetary theory and policy,' *National Banking Review*, vol. 2, no. 1 (September), pp. 1–9.

—— (1966), 'What price guideposts?,' in George P. Shultz and Robert Z. Aliber (eds), *Guidelines, Informal Controls, and the Market Place: Policy Choices in a Full Employment Economy*, Chicago: University of Chicago Press.

—— (1967), 'First lecture', in Milton Friedman and Robert V. Roosa, *The Balance of Payments: Free Versus Fixed Exchange Rates*, Washington, DC: American Enterprise Institute.

—— (1967), 'Value judgments in economics,' in Sidney Hook (ed.), *Human Values and Economic Policy: A Symposium*, New York: New York University Press.

—— (1969), *The Optimum Quantity of Money, and Other Essays*, Chicago: Aldine Publishing Co.

—— (1970), *The Counter-revolution in Monetary Theory*, first Wincott Memorial Lecture, Institute of Economic Affairs occasional paper no. 33, London: Institute of Economic Affairs.

—— (1972), 'Have monetary policies failed?,' *American Economic Review, Papers and Proceedings of the Eighty-fourth Annual Meeting of the American Economic Association*, vol. LXII, no. 2 (May), pp. 11–18.

—— (1972), 'Is welfare a basic human right?,' *Newsweek*, vol. LXXX, no. 25 (December 18), p. 90.

—— (1973), interview in *Playboy*, vol. 20, no. 2 (February), pp. 51–74.

—— (1977), *From Galbraith to Economic Freedom*, Institute of Economic Affairs occasional paper no. 49. London: Institute of Economic Affairs.

—— (1985), 'Monetarism in rhetoric and in practice,' in Albert Ando, Hidekazu Eguchi, Roger Farmer, and Yoshio Suzuki (eds), *Monetary Policy in Our Times: Proceedings of the First International Conference Held by the Institute for Monetary and Economic Studies of the Bank of Japan*, Cambridge, MA: MIT Press.

—— (1994), *Money Mischief: Episodes in Monetary History*, New York: Harcourt Brace.

Frisch, Ragnar (1926 [1971]), 'On a problem in pure economics,' in J.S. Chipman, L. Hurwicz, M.K. Richter, and H.F. Sonnenschein (eds), *Preferences, Utility, and Demand: A Minnesota Symposium*, New York: Harcourt, Brace, Jovanovich, translation of 'Sur un problème d'économie pure' by John S. Chipman, reprinted in Olav Bjerkholt (ed.), *Foundations of Modern Econometrics: The Selected Essays of Ragnar Frisch*, vol. I, Aldershot: Edward Elgar.

—— (1970), 'From utopian theory to practical applications: the case of econometrics,' in *Reimpression de Les Prix Nobel en 1969*, Nobel Foundation, pp. 213–43, reprinted in Olav Bjerkholt (ed.), *Foundations of Modern Econometrics: The Selected Essays of Ragnar Frisch*, vol. II, Aldershot: Edward Elgar.

Galbraith, John Kenneth (1958), *The Affluent Society*, New York: Houghton Mifflin Company.

—— (1962), *Economic Development in Perspective*, Cambridge, MA: Harvard University Press.

— — (1962), 'The language of economics,' *Fortune*, vol. LXVI, no. 6 (December), pp. 128–30, 169, 171.

— — (1975), *Money: Whence It Came, Where It Went*, Boston: Houghton Mifflin.

Gauthier, David (1986), *Morals By Agreement*, Oxford: Oxford University Press.

George, Henry (1880 [1929]), *Progress and Poverty: An Inquiry Into the Cause of Industrial Depressions and of Increase of Want with Increase of Wealth*, fourth edn, New York: Modern Library.

— — (1883), *Social Problems*, volume II of *The Complete Works of Henry George*, New York: National Single Tax League.

— — (1890), 'A single tax on land values,' *The Century*, vol. XL, no. 3 (July), pp. 394–403.

— — (1894), 'How to help the unemployed,' *North American Review*, vol. CLVIII, no. 447 (February), pp. 175–84.

Georgescu-Roegen, Nicholas (1960), 'Mathematical proofs of the breakdown of capitalism,' *Econometrica*, vol. 28, no. 2 (April), pp. 225–43.

Goldberger, Arthur S. (1964), *Econometric Theory*, New York: John Wiley and Sons.

Goldman, Emma (1913), *Syndicalism: The Modern Menace to Capitalism*, New York: Mother Earth Publishing.

Goldsmith, James (1994), *The Trap*, New York: Carroll and Graf.

Goodrich, Carter (1960), 'Economic history: one field or two?,' *Journal of Economic History*, vol. 20, no. 4 (December), pp. 531–38.

Graham, Frank D. (1942), *Social Goals and Economic Institutions*, Princeton, NJ: Princeton University Press.

Greeley, Horace (1870), *Essays Designed to Elucidate the Science of Political Economy, While Serving to Explain and Defend the Policy of Protection to Home Industry, as a System of National Coöperation for the Elevation of Labor*, Boston: Fields, Osgood and Co.

Greenspan, Alan (1961), 'Antitrust,' in Ayn Rand, *Capitalism: The Unknown Ideal*, New York: Signet, 1967.

— — (1963), 'The assault on integrity,' *The Objectivist Newsletter*, vol. 2, no. 8 (August), pp. 31–2, reprinted in Ayn Rand (1967), *Capitalism: The Unknown Ideal*, New York: Signet.

— — (1966), 'Gold and economic freedom,' *The Objectivist*, vol. 5, no. 7 (July), pp. 11–16, reprinted in Ayn Rand (1967), *Capitalism: The Unknown Ideal*, New York: Signet.

Haberler, Gottfried (1966), 'Marxian economics in retrospect and prospect,' *Zeitschrift für Nationalökonomie*, vol. XXVI, no. 1 (January), pp. 69–82.

Hahn, Frank H. (1973), 'The winter of our discontent,' *Economica*, new series, vol. 40, no. 159 (August), pp. 322–30.

— — (1982), 'Reflections on the invisible hand,' *Lloyds Bank Review*, no. 144 (April), pp. 1–21.

— — (1984), 'Why I am not a monetarist,' in Frank Hahn (ed), *Equilibrium and Macroeconomics*, Cambridge, MA: MIT Press.

— — (1991), 'The next hundred years,' *Economic Journal*, vol. 101, no. 404 (January), pp. 47–50.

— — (1996). 'Rerum cognoscere causas,' *Economics and Philosophy*, vol. 12, no. 2 (October), pp. 183–95.

Hale, Matthew (1683), *A Discourse Touching Provision for the Poor*, London: printed for William Shrowsbery, at the Bible in Duke-Lane.

Hamilton, Robert (1830), *The Progress of Society*, London: John Murray.

Hansen, Alvin H. (1947), 'Dr. Burns on Keynesian economics,' *Review of Economic Statistics*, vol. 29, no. 4 (November), pp. 247–52.

Harrington, James (1656), *The Commonwealth of Oceana*, London: J. Streater, for Livewell Chapman.

Harrod, R.F. (1938), 'Scope and method of economics,' *Economic Journal*, vol. 48, no. 191 (September), pp. 383–412.

— — (1948), *Towards a Dynamic Economics: Some Recent Developments of Economic Theory and their Application to Policy*, London: Macmillan.

— — (1969), *Money*, London: Macmillan.

Hayek, Friedrich A von (1933), 'The trend of economic thinking,' *Economica*, (new series), vol. 0, no. 40 (May), pp. 121–37.

— — (1937), 'Economics and Knowledge,' *Economica*, (new series), vol. IV, no. 13 (February), pp. 33–54.

— — (1943), 'The facts of the social sciences,' *Ethics*, vol. 54, no. 1 (October), pp. 1–13.

— — (1944), *The Road to Serfdom*, Chicago: University of Chicago Press.

— — (1948), *Individualism and Economic Order*, Chicago: University of Chicago Press.

—— (1960), *The Constitution of Liberty*, Chicago: University of Chicago Press.

—— (1975), 'The pretence of knowledge,' *Swedish Journal of Economics*, vol. 77, no. 4, pp. 433–42.

—— (1976), *Choice in Currency: A Way to Stop Inflation*, Institute of Economic Affairs occasional paper no. 48, London: Institute of Economic Affairs.

—— (1976), *Law, Legislation, and Liberty*, volume II of *The Mirage of Social Justice*, Chicago: University of Chicago Press.

—— (1988), *The Fatal Conceit*, Chicago: University of Chicago Press.

Heckman, James J. (1997), 'The value of quantitative evidence on the effect of the past on the present,' *American Economic Review, Papers and Proceedings of the Hundred and fourth Annual Meeting of the American Economic Association*, vol. 87, no. 2 (May), pp. 404–8.

Hegel, G.W.F. (1821 [1996]), *Philosophy of Right*, translated by S.W. Dyde, Amherst, NY: Prometheus Books.

—— (1840 [1968]), *Hegel's Lectures on the History of Philosophy*, second 'amended' edition, vol. III, translated by E.S. Haldane and Frances H. Simson, London: Routledge and Kegan Paul.

Heilbroner, Robert L. (1956), *The Quest for Wealth: A Study of Acquisitive Man*, New York: Simon and Schuster.

—— (1965), *The Limits of American Capitalism*, New York: Harper and Row.

Hendry, David F. (1980), 'Econometrics – alchemy or science?,' *Economica*, vol. 47, no. 188 (November), pp. 387–406.

Hicks, John R. (1946), *Value and Capital: An Inquiry Into Some Fundamental Principles of Economic Theory*, second edn, Oxford: Clarendon Press.

—— (1960), 'Linear theory,' *Economic Journal*, vol. 70, no. 280 (December), pp. 671–709.

—— (1976), ' "Revolutions" in Economics,' in S.J. Latsis (ed), *Method and Appraisal in Economics*, Cambridge: Cambridge University Press.

Hilferding, Rudolf (1910 [1981]), *Finance Capital: A Study of the Latest Phase of Capitalist Development*, edited by Tom Bottomore from translations by Morris Watnick and Sam Gordon, London: Routledge and Kegan Paul.

Hobbes, Thomas (1651 [1985]), *Leviathan, or the Matter, Forme, and Power of a Commonwealth Ecclesiasticall and Civill*, edited with an introduction by C.B. Macpherson, Harmondsworth: Penguin.

Hobson, John A. (1893), 'The subjective and the objective view of distribution,' *Annals of the American Academy of Political and Social Science*, vol. IV (November), pp. 42–67 [378–403].

—— (1896), 'Is poverty diminishing?', *The Contemporary Review*, vol. LXIX (April), pp. 484–99.

—— (1917), *The Evolution of Modern Capitalism*, new edition, London: Walter Scott Publishing.

—— (1926), *Free-Thought in the Social Sciences*, New York: Macmillan.

—— (1929), *Economics and Ethics: A Study in Social Values*, New York: D.C. Heath and Co.

—— (1938), *Confessions of an Economic Heretic*, London: George Allen and Unwin.

Hodgskin, Thomas (1832), *The Natural and Artificial Right of Property Contrasted*, London: B. Steil.

Hodgson, Geoffrey M. (1999), *Economics and Utopia: Why the Learning Economy Is Not the End of History*, London: Routledge.

Hollander, Jacob H. (1916), 'Economic theorizing and scientific progress,' *American Economic Review, Papers and Proceedings of the Twenty-eighth Annual Meeting of the American Economic Association*, supplement, vol. VI, no. 1 (March), pp. 124–39.

—— (1922), 'The economist's spiral,' *American Economic Review*, vol. 12, no. 1 (March), pp. 1–20.

Hollis, Martin (1991), 'Penny pinching and backward induction,' *Journal of Philosophy*, vol. 88, no. 9 (September), pp. 473–88.

Holmes, Oliver Wendell, Jr. (1904), Lochner v. New York (dissenting opinion), in *Cases Argued and Decided in the Supreme Court of the United States, October Terms, 1903, 1904, in 195 196, 197, 198 U.S., Book 49, Lawyers' Edition*, Rochester, NY: Lawyers' Co-operative Publishing Company, 105.

—— (1922), Pennsylvania Coal Co. v. Mahon, in *Cases Argued and Decided in the Supreme Court of the United States, October Term 1922, in 260, 261, 262 U.S., Book 67, Lawyers' Edition*, Rochester, NY: Lawyers' Co-operative Publishing Company, 1924.

—— (1927), Compañia General de Tabacos v. Collector of Internal Revenue (dissenting opinon), in *Cases Argued and Decided in the Supreme Court of the United States, October Term, 1927, in 275, 276, 277 U.S., Book 72,*

Lawyers' Edition, Rochester, NY: Lawyers' Co-operative Publishing Company, 1929.

—— (1927), Panhandle Oil Company v. Mississippi ex rel. Knox, in *Cases Argued and Decided in the Supreme Court of the United States, October Term, 1927*, in 275, 276, 277 U.S., Book 72 *Lawyers' Edition*, Rochester, NY: Lawyers' Co-operative Publishing Company, 1929.

Horner, Francis (1803), 'Article XVI: M. Canard, *Principes d'Economie Politique*,' *Edinburgh Review*, vol. I, no. 2 (January), pp. 431–50.

Hoxie, Robert F. (1901), 'On the empirical method of economic instruction,' *Journal of Political Economy*, vol. IX, no. 4 (September), pp. 481–526.

—— (1917), *Trade Unionism in the United States*, New York: D. Appleton and Co.

Hume, David (1777 [1875]), *Essays, Moral, Political, and Literary*, edited by T.H. Green and T.H. Grose, London: Longmans, Green and Co.

Huskisson, W. (1810), *The Question Concerning the Depreciation of Our Currency Stated and Examined*, third edn, London, reprinted in J.R. McCulloch (ed.) (1857), *A Select Collection of Scarce and Valuable Tracts and Other Publications, on Paper Currency and Banking, from the Originals of Hume, Wallace, Thornton, Ricardo, Blake, Huskisson, and Others*, London.

Hutcheson, Francis (1725 [1971]), *An Inquiry Into the Origin of Our Ideas of Beauty and Virtue*, vol. I of *Collected Works of Francis Hutcheson*, Hildesheim, Germany: Georg Olms Verlagsbuchhandlung.

Hutchison, Terence W. (1938), *The Significance and Basic Postulates of Economic Theory*, London: Macmillan.

—— (1976), 'On the history and philosophy of science and economics,' in S.J. Latsis (ed.), *Method and Appraisal in Economics*, Cambridge: Cambridge University Press.

—— (1977), *Knowledge and Ignorance in Economics*, Chicago: University of Chicago Press.

Hutt, W.H. (1936), *Economists and the Public: A Study of Competition and Opinion*, London: Jonathan Cape.

Ingram, John K. (1915 [1967]), *A History of Political Economy*, revised edn, New York: Augustus M. Kelley, first edn (1888), Edinburgh: A. and C. Black.

Jaffé, William (1931), 'Round table conference: economic history — the decline of laissez faire', *American Economic Review*, supplement, *Papers and Proceedings of the Forty-third Annual Meeting of the American Economic Association*, vol. 21, no. 1 (March), pp. 3–5.

Jefferson, Thomas (1785), letter to James Madison, in Julian P. Boyd (ed.) (1953), *The Papers of Thomas Jefferson*, vol. 8: 25 February to 31 October 1785, Princeton: Princeton University Press.

—— (1813), letter to Isaac McPherson, in Albert Ellery Bergh (ed.) (1907), *The Writings of Thomas Jefferson*, definitive edn, vol. XIII, Washington, DC: The Thomas Jefferson Memorial Association.

—— (1816), letter to Benjamin Austin, in Albert Ellery Bergh (ed.) (1907), *The Writings of Thomas Jefferson*, definitive edn, vol. XIV, Washington, DC: The Thomas Jefferson Memorial Association.

—— (1816), letter to Governor Plumer, in Albert Ellery Bergh (ed.) (1907), *The Writings of Thomas Jefferson*, definitive edn, vol. XIV, Washington, DC: The Thomas Jefferson Memorial Association.

Jevons, W. Stanley (1876), 'The future of political economy,' *Fortnightly Review*, vol. XX, new series, no. 119 (1 November), pp. 617–31.

—— (1882 [1910]), *The State in Relation to Labour*, fourth edn, edited by Francis W. Hirst, London: Macmillan.

—— (1911), *The Theory of Political Economy*, fourth edn, edited by H. Stanley Jevons, London: Macmillan, first edn, 1871.

John XXIII (Pope) (1961), *Mater et Magistra – Encyclical of Pope John XXIII on Christianity and Social Progress* (15 May), as presented at the Vatican website: <http://www.vatican.va/holy_father/john_xxiii/encyclicals/documents/hf_j-xxiii_enc_15051961_mater_en.html>

Johnson, Harry G. (1974), 'The state of theory,' *American Economic Review, Papers and Proceedings of the Eighty-sixth Annual Meeting of the American Economic Association*, vol. 64, no. 2 (May), pp. 323–24.

Jones, Richard (1831), *An Essay on the Distribution of Wealth and on the Sources of Taxation*, London: John Murray.

Joplin, Thomas (1718), *An Essay on Money & Bullion. Wherein are considered, Value Intrinsick and Extrinsick. Money and Bullion compared. Mr. Locke's Considerations concerning Raising the Value of Coin. The*

Present State of our Coin. And a Scheme for Raising the Value of our Coin, as well as Gold and Silver, London: printed for B. Lintot.

Kaldor, Nicholas (1972), 'The irrelevance of equilibrium economics,' *Economic Journal*, vol. 82, no. 328 (December), pp. 1237–55.

Kalecki, Michal (1943), 'Political aspects of full employment,' *The Political Quarterly*, vol. 14, no. 4, pp. 322–31.

Kantorovich, Leonid V. (1965), *The Best Use of Economic Resources*, edited by G. Morton and translated by P.F. Knightsfield., Oxford: Pergamon Press.

Kautsky, Karl (1910), *The Class Struggle (Enfurt Program)*, translated by William E. Bohn from the eighth German edition (1907), Chicago: Charles H. Kerr and Co.

—— (1925), *The Labour Revolution*, translated by H.J. Stenning, London: George Allen and Unwin.

Keynes, John Maynard (1920), *The Economic Consequences of the Peace*, New York: Harcourt, Brace and Howe.

—— (1923), *A Tract on Monetary Reform*, London: Macmillan.

—— (1924), 'Alfred Marshall, 1842–1924,' *Economic Journal*, vol. 34, no. 135 (September), pp. 311–72.

—— (1926), 'Liberalism and labour,' *The Nation and the Athenæum*, vol. XXXVIII, no. 21 (February 20), pp. 707–8.

—— (1926), 'The end of laissez-faire,' *The New Republic*, part I: vol. XLVIII, no. 612 (August 25), pp. 13–15; part II: vol. XLVIII, no. 613 (September 1), pp. 37–41.

—— (1930), 'Economic possibilities for our grandchildren,' *The Nation and the Athenæum*, part I: vol. XLVIII, no. 2 (October 11), pp. 36–7; part II: vol. XLVIII, no. 3 (October 18), pp. 96–8.

—— (1932), 'The dilemma of modern socialism,' *Political Quarterly*, vol. 3 pp. 155–61.

—— (1934), 'Poverty in plenty: is the economic system self-adjusting?,' *The Listener* (21 November).

—— (1935), letter to R.B. Bryce (10 July), in Donald Moggridge (ed.), *The Collected Writings of John Maynard Keynes*, vol. XXIX: *The General Theory and After: A Supplement*, London and Cambridge: Macmillan and Cambridge University Press for the Royal Economic Society.

—— (1936), *The General Theory of Employment, Interest, and Money*, New York: Harcourt, Brace, Jovanovich.

Keynes, John Neville (1904), *The Scope and Method of Political Economy*, third edn, London: Macmillan.

Kirzner, Israel M. (1979), *Perception, Opportunity, and Profit: Studies in the Theory of Entrepreneurship*, Chicago: University of Chicago Press.

Klein, Lawrence R. (1954), 'The contributions of mathematics in economics,' *Review of Economics and Statistics*, vol. 36, no. 4 (November), pp. 359–61.

—— (1971), 'Whither econometrics?,' *Journal of the American Statistical Association*, vol. 66, no. 334 (June), pp. 415–21.

Knight, Frank H. (1921 [1964]), *Risk, Uncertainty, and Profit*, New York: Augustus M. Kelley.

—— (1922), 'Round table conference on the relation between economics and ethics', *American Economic Review, Papers and Proceedings of the Thirty-fourth Annual Meeting of the American Economic Association*, vol. XII, no. 1 (March), pp. 192–3.

—— (1922), 'Ethics and the economic interpretation,' *Quarterly Journal of Economics*, vol. 36, no. 3 (May), pp. 454–81.

—— (1923), 'The ethics of competition,' *Quarterly Journal of Economics*, vol. 37, no. 4 (August), pp. 579–624.

—— (1937), 'Unemployment: and Mr. Keynes's revolution in economic theory,' *Canadian Journal of Economics and Political Science*, vol. 3, no. 1 (February), pp. 100–23.

—— (1940), ' "What is truth" in economics?,' *Journal of Political Economy*, vol. XLVIII, no. 1 (February), pp. 1–32.

—— (1948), 'Free Society: Its Basic Nature and Problem,' *Philosophical Review*, vol. LVII, no. 1 (January), pp. 39–58.

—— (1951), 'The role of principles in economics and politics,' *American Economic Review*, vol. XLI, no. 1 (March), pp. 1–29.

—— (1951), *The Economic Organization*, New York: Augustus M. Kelley.

—— (1960), *Intelligence and Democratic Action*, Cambridge, MA: Harvard University Press.

Koopmans, Tjalling C. (1952), 'Toward partial redirection of econometrics: comment,' *Review of Economics and Statistics*, vol. 34, no. 3 (August), pp. 200–5.

—— (1957), *Three Essays on the State of Economic Science*, New York: McGraw-Hill.

Krugman, Paul R. (1993), 'The narrow and broad arguments for free trade,' *American Economic Review, Papers and Proceedings of the*

Hundred and fifth Annual Meeting of the American Economic Association, vol. 83, no. 2 (May), pp. 362–6.

Lancaster, Kelvin (1962), 'The scope of qualitative economics,' *Review of Economic Studies*, vol. 29, no. 2 (February), pp. 99–123.

Lange, Oskar (1936), 'On the economic theory of socialism, part I,' *Review of Economic Studies*, vol. 4, no. 1 (October), pp. 53–71.

— — (1937), 'On the economic theory of socialism, part II,' *Review of Economic Studies*, vol. 4, no. 2 (February), pp. 123–42.

— — (1962), 'Role of planning in socialist economy,' in Oskar Lange (ed.), *Problems of Political Economy of Socialism*, Warsaw: People's Publishing House.

Laughlin, J. Laurence (1896), 'Teaching of economics,' *The Atlantic Monthly*, vol. 77, no. 463 (May), pp. 682–88.

— — (1899), 'Economics and socialism,' *The Chautauquan*, vol. XXX, no. 3 (December), pp. 252–55.

— — (1912), *Industrial America*, the Berlin Lectures of 1906, New York: Charles Scribner's Sons.

Launhardt, Wilhelm (1885 [1993]), *Mathematical Principles of Economics*, translated by Hilda Schmidt and edited by John Creedy, Aldershot: Edward Elgar.

Laveleye, Emile de (1883), 'The progress of socialism,' *Contemporary Review*, vol. XLIII, no. 4 (April), pp. 561–82.

Law, John (1705), *Money and Trade Considered With a Proposal for Supplying the Nation with Money*, Edinburgh: Printed by the heirs and successors of Andrew Anderson, reprinted (1996) by Augustus M. Kelley, New York.

Lawson, Tony (1994), 'Critical realism and the analysis of choice, explanation, and change,' in Peter J. Boettke, Israel M. Kirzner, and Mario J. Rizzo (eds), *Advances in Austrian Economics*, vol. 1, Greenwich, CT: JAI Press.

Leamer, Edward E. (1983), 'Let's take the con out of econometrics,' *American Economic Review*, vol. 73, no. 1 (March), pp. 31–43.

Le Bon, Gustave (1899), *The Psychology of Socialism*, New York: Macmillan.

Lederer, Emil (1940), *State of the Masses: The Threat of the Classless Society*, New York: W.W. Norton and Co.

Leibenstein, Harvey (1978), *General X-Efficiency Theory and Economic Development*, New York: Oxford University Press.

Lenin, V.I. (1903 [1961]), 'To the rural poor: an explanation for the peasants of what the social-democrats want,' in *Lenin: Collected Works*, vol. 6: January 1902–August 1903, London: Lawrence and Wishart.

— — (1918 [1965]), 'The immediate tasks of the soviet government,' in *Lenin: Collected Works*, vol. 27: February–July 1918, London: Lawrence and Wishart.

— — (1918 [1965]), 'Session of the all-Russia C.E.C., April 29, part 2: reply to the debate on the report on the immediate tasks', in *Lenin: Collected Works*, vol. 27: February–July 1918, London: Lawrence and Wishart.

— — (1919 [1965]), 'Report on subbotniks, delivered to a Moscow city conference of the R.C.P. (B.), December 20', in *Lenin: Collected Works*, vol. 30: September 1919–April 1920, London: Lawrence and Wishart.

Leo XIII (Pope) (1878), *Quod Apostolici Muneris – Encyclical of Pope Leo XIII on Socialism* (28 December), as presented at the Vatican website: <http://www.vatican.va/holy_father/leo_xiii/encyclicals/documents/hf_l-xiii_enc_28121878_quod-apostolici-muneris_en.html>

— — (1891), *Rerum Novarum – Encyclical of Pope Leo XIII on Capital and Labor* (15 May), as presented at the Vatican website: <http://www.vatican.va/holy_father/leo_xiii/encyclicals/documents/hf_l-xiii_enc_15051891_rerum-novarum_en.html>

Leoni, Bruno (1961), *Freedom and the Law*, Princeton: D. Van Nostrand Co., Inc.

Leontief, Wassily (1954), 'Mathematics in economics,' *Bulletin of the American Mathematical Society*, vol. 60, no. 3 (May), pp. 215–33.

— — (1959), 'The problem of quality and quantity in economics,' *Daedalus*, vol. 88, no. 4 (Fall), pp. 622–32.

— — (1971), 'Theoretical assumptions and non-observed facts,' *American Economic Review*, vol. 61, no. 1 (March), pp. 1–7.

— — (1982), 'Academic economics,' *Science*, vol. 217, no. 4555 (July 9), pp. 104, 107.

Lerner, Abba P. (1961), *Everybody's Business*, Lansing, MI: Michigan State University Press.

Leslie, T.E. Cliffe (1879), 'Political economy and sociology,' *Fortnightly Review*, vol. XXV (NS), no. CXLV (January 1), pp. 25–46.

— — (1879), 'The known and the unknown in the economic world,' *Fortnightly Review*, vol. XXV (NS), no. 150 (June 1), pp. 934–49.

Lewis, W. Arthur (1966), *Development Planning: The Essentials of Economic Policy*, New York: Harper and Row.

—— (1965), 'A review of economic development,' *American Economic Review*, vol. 55, no. 1/2 (March), pp. 1–16.
Lindbeck, Assar (1971), *The Political Economy of the New Left: An Outsider's View*, New York: Harper and Row.
—— (1977), *The Political Economy of the New Left: An Outsider's View*, second edn, New York: Harper and Row.
Lindblom, Charles E. (1949), *Unions and Capitalism*, New Haven: Yale University Press.
List, Friedrich (1837 [1983]), *The Natural System of Political Economy*, translated and edited by W.O. Henderson, London: Frank Cass.
Little, I.M.D. (1957), *A Critique of Welfare Economics*, second edn, London: Oxford University Press.
Locke, John (1690), *Two Treatises of Government: In the former, The false Principles and Foundation of Sir Robert Filmer, And His Followers, are Detected and Overthrown. The Latter is an Essay Concerning the True Original, Extent, and End of Civil Government*, London: printed for Awnsham Churchill, at the Black Swan in Ave-Mary-Lane, by Amen-Corner.
—— (1692), *Some Considerations of the Consequences of the Lowering of Interest, and Raising the Value of Money*, London: printed for Awnsham and John Churchill, at the Black-Swan in Pater-Noster-Row.
Longfield, Mountifort (1834), *Lectures on Political Economy, Delivered in Trinity and Michaelmas Terms, 1833*, Dublin: Richard Milliken and Son.
Lucas, Robert E., Jr. (1987), *Models of Business Cycles*, Oxford: Basil Blackwell.
Luther, Martin (1524 [1962]), *Trade and Usury*, translated by Charles M. Jacobs and revised by Walther I. Brandt, in Walther I. Brandt (ed.), *Luther's Works*, vol. 45: *The Christian in Society II*, Philadephia: Muhlenberg Press.
—— (1525 [1967]), *Admonition to Peace: A Reply to the Twelve Articles of the Peasants in Swabia*, translated by Charles M. Jacobs and revised by Robert C. Schultz, in Robert C. Schultz (ed.), *Luther's Works*, vol. 46: *The Christian in Society III*, Philadephia: Fortress Press.
Luxemburg, Rosa (1913 [1951]), *The Accumulation of Capital*, translated by Agnes Schwarzchild, New Haven: Yale University Press.
—— (1918), *The Socialisation of Society*, vol. IV: *Gesammelte Werke*, Berlin: Dietz, and on line at Marxists.org.

—— (1968), *What Is Economics?*, originally writeen in 1916, Colombo, Ceylon: Young Socialist Publications.
Machlup, Fritz (1936), 'Why bother with methodology?,' *Economica* (New Series), vol. 3, no. 9 (February), pp. 39–45.
—— (1960), 'Micro- and macro-economics: contested boundaries and claims of superiority,' translated by Edith Penrose, in Fritz Machlup (ed.), *Essays in Economic Semantics*, New York: New York University Press, 1963.
—— (1974), 'Proxies and dummies,' *Journal of Political Economy*, vol. 82, no. 4 (July/August), p. 892.
Mackay, Thomas (1900), *A History of the English Poor Law*, vol. III: *From 1834 to the Present Time*, New York: G.P. Putnam's Sons.
—— (1901), *Public Relief of the Poor: Six Lectures*, London: John Murray.
Macleod, Henry Dunning (1875), 'What is political economy?,' *Contemporary Review*, vol. XXV, no. 6 (May), pp. 871–93.
Maitland, James, Earl of Lauderdale (1804), *An Inquiry Into the Nature and Origin of Public Wealth, and Into the Means and Causes of Its Increase*, Edinburgh: printed for Arch. Constable and Co.
Malinvaud, Edmond (1981), 'Econometrics Faced With the Needs of Macroeconomic Policy,' *Econometrica*, vol. 49, no. 6 (November), pp. 1363–75.
Malthus, Thomas Robert (1798), *An Essay on the Principle of Population as It Affects the Future Improvement of Society. With Remarks on the Speculations of Mr. Godwin, M. Condorcet, and Other Writers*, London: printed for J. Johnson, in St. Paul's Church-Yard.
—— (1827), *Definitions in Political Economy*, London: John Murray.
Mandeville, Bernard de (1732 [1924]), *The Fable of the Bees: Or, Private Vices, Publick Benefits*, edited by F.B. Kaye, Oxford: Clarendon Press.
Mao Tse-tung (1967), *Quotations from Chairman Mao Tse-tung*, edited by Stuart R. Schram, New York: Frederick A. Praeger.
Marshall, Alfred (1874), 'The province of political economy,' *The Bee-Hive*, no. 655 (May 2), pp. 3–4.
—— (1881), review of *Mathematical Psychics*, by F.Y. Edgeworth, *The Academy*, no. 476 (June 18), p. 457.
—— (1884), 'The housing of the London poor,' *The Contemporary Review*, vol. XLV, no. 266 (February), pp. 224–31.

—— (1885 [1925]), 'The present position of economics,' in A.C. Pigou (ed.), *Memorials of Alfred Marshall*, London: Macmillan.

—— (1889), 'Co-operation,' in A.C. Pigou (ed.), *Memorials of Alfred Marshall*, London: Macmillan.

—— (1890), *Principles of Economics*, London: Macmillan.

—— (1891), 'The post office and private enterprise', letter to the editor, *The Times*, no. 33,280 (Tuesday, March 24), p. 11.

—— (1892), 'The Poor Law in relation to state-aided pensions,' *Economic Journal*, vol. 2, no. 5 (March), pp. 186–91.

—— (1892), 'Poor-Law Reform,' *Economic Journal*, vol. 2, no. 6 (June), pp. 371–79.

—— (1894), letter to Benjamin Kidd (letter 450, June 6), in John K. Whitaker (ed.) (1996), *The Correspondence of Alfred Marshall, Economist*, vol. 2: *At the Summit*, Cambridge: Cambridge University Press.

—— (1899), letter to W.A.S. Hewins (letter 597, October 12), in John K. Whitaker (ed.) (1996), *The Correspondence of Alfred Marshall, Economist*, vol. 2: *At the Summit*, Cambridge: Cambridge University Press.

—— (1900), letter to Bishop Westcott (January 24), in A.C. Pigou (ed.), (1925), *Memorials of Alfred Marshall*, London: Macmillan.

—— (1901), letter to Arthur Bowley (letter 637, March 3), in John K. Whitaker (ed.) (1996), *The Correspondence of Alfred Marshall, Economist*, vol. 2: *At the Summit*, Cambridge: Cambridge University Press.

—— (1906), letter to Arthur Bowley (February 27), in A.C. Pigou (ed.) (1925), *Memorials of Alfred Marshall*, London: Macmillan.

—— (1907), 'The social possibilities of economic chivalry,' *Economic Journal*, vol. 17, no. 65 (March), pp. 7–29.

—— (1909), letter to Lord Reay (letter 949, November 12), in John K. Whitaker (ed.) (1996), *The Correspondence of Alfred Marshall, Economist*, vol. 3: *Towards the Close*, Cambridge: Cambridge University Press.

—— (1920), *Principles of Economics*, eighth edn, London: Macmillan.

Marshall, John (1918), McCulloch v. the State of Maryland et al., in *Cases Argued and Decided in the Supreme Court of the United States 1815–1819, 1, 2, 3, 4 Wheaton, Book 4, Lawyers' Edition*, Rochester, NY: Lawyers' Co-operative Publishing Company, 1901.

—— (1819), Trustees of Dartmouth College v. Woodward, in *Cases Argued and Decided in the Supreme Court of the United States 1815–1819, 1, 2, 3, 4 Wheaton, Book 4, Lawyers' Edition*, Rochester, NY: Lawyers' Co-operative Publishing Company, 1901.

Marx, Karl Heinrich (1843 [1975]), 'On the Jewish Question,' in *Karl Marx/Frederick Engels Collected Works*, vol. 3: *Marx and Engels: 1843–1844*, New York: International Publishers.

—— (1844 [1964]), *The Economic and Philosophic Manuscripts of 1844*, edited, with an introduction by Dirk J. Struik and translated by Martin Milligan, New York: International Publishers.

—— (1847 [1963]), *The Poverty of Philosophy*, translation of the French edition, New York: International Publishers.

—— (1848 [1988]), *The Communist Manifesto*, edited by Frederic L. Bender, New York: W.W. Norton.

—— (1859 [1970]), *A Contribution to the Critique of Political Economy*, edited, with an introduction by Maurice Dobb, New York: International Publishers.

—— (1887 [1996]), *Capital: A Critique of Political Economy*, first English edition translated from the third German edition by Samuel Moore and Edward Aveling, vol. 35 of *Karl Marx/Frederick Engels Collected Works*, New York: International Publishers.

Mayer, Thomas (1980), 'Economics as a hard science: realistic goal or wishful thinking?,' *Economic Inquiry*, vol. XVIII, no. 2 (April), pp. 165–78.

—— (1995), *Doing Economic Research: Essays on the Applied Methodology of Economics*, Aldershot: Edward Elgar.

McCloskey, Donald N. (1976), 'Does the past have useful economics?,' *Journal of Economic Literature*, vol. XIV, no. 2 (June), pp. 434–61.

—— (1990), 'Storytelling in economics,' in Don Lavoie (ed.), *Economics and Hermeneutics*, London: Routledge.

McCulloch, J.R. (1821), 'Article VI: effects of machinery and accumulation,' *Edinburgh Review*, vol. XXXV, no. 69 (March), pp. 102–23.

—— (1822), 'Article VIII: comparative productiveness of high and low taxes,' *Edinburgh Review*, vol. XXXVI, no. 72 (February), pp. 516–36.

—— (1828), 'Article III: progress of the national debt – best method of funding,' *Edinburgh*

Review, vol. XLVII, no. 93 (January), pp. 59–86.

— — (1828), 'Article II: Poor Laws,' *Edinburgh Review*, vol. XLVII, no. 94 (May), pp. 303–30.

— — (1849), *The Principles of Political Economy: With Some Inquiries Respecting Their Application, and a Sketch of the Rise and Progress of the Science*, fourth edn, Edinburgh: Adam and Charles Black.

— — (1854), *A Treatise on the Circumstances Which Determine the Rate of Wages and the Condition of the Labouring Classes Including an Inquiry Into the Influence of Combinations*, London: G. Routledge and Co.

— — (1863 [1975]), *A Treatise on the Principles and Practical Influence of Taxation and the Funding System*, third edn, edited by D.P. O'Brien., Edinburgh: Scottish Academic Press for the Scottish Economic Society.

McVickar, John (1825), *Outlines of Political Economy: Being a Republication of the Article Upon That Subject Contained in the Edinburgh Supplement to the Encyclopedia Britannica*, New York: Wilder and Campbell.

Meek, Ronald L. (1977), *Smith, Marx, and After: Ten Essays in the Development of Economic Thought*, London: Chapman and Hall.

Menger, Carl (1871 [1950]), *Principles of Economics*, translated by James Dingwall and Bert F. Hoselitz, Glencoe, IL: Free Press.

Merivale, Herman (1837), 'Article IV: definitions and systems of political economy; senior on political economy,' *Edinburgh Review*, vol. LXVI, no. 133 (October), pp. 73–102.

Mill, James (1808), *Commerce Defended. An Answer to the Arguments by which Mr. Spence, Mr. Corbett, and others, have attempted to prove that Commerce is not a Source of National Wealth*, second edn, London: printed for C. and R. Baldwin, reprinted in Donald Winch (ed.) (1966), *James Mill: Selected Economic Writings*, Edinburgh: Oliver and Boyd for the Scottish Economic Society.

— — (1808), 'Article III: Smith on money and exchange,' *Edinburgh Review*, vol. XIII, no. 25 (October), pp. 34–68.

— — (1813), 'Article IX: education of the poor,' *Edinburgh Review*, vol. XXI, no. 41 (February), pp. 207–19.

Mill, John Stuart (1848), *Principles of Political Economy, with Some of Their Applications to Social Philosophy*, two volumes, Boston: Charles C. Little and James Brown.

— — (1861), 'Utilitarianism,' *Fraser's Magazine*, vol. LXIV, no. 382 (October), pp. 391–406; vol. LXIV, no. 383 (November), pp. 525–34; vol. LXIV, no. 384 (December), pp. 659–73.

— — (1871 [1987]), *Principles of Political Economy, With Some of Their Applications to Social Philosophy*, seventh edn, edited by William Ashley, Fairfield, NJ: Augustus M. Kelley.

— — (1873), critical notice of *L'Avere et l'Imposta* by Costantino Baer, *Fortnightly Review*, vol. XIII (NS), no. 75 (March 1), pp. 396–98.

— — (1879), 'Chapters on socialism,' *Fortnightly Review*, vol. XXV (NS), no. 146 (February 1), pp. 217–37; no. 147 (March 1), pp. 373–82; no. 148 (April 1), pp. 513–30.

Mill, John Stuart, and William Ellis (1825), 'Article VI: M'Culloch's discourse on Political Economy,' *Westminster Review*, vol. IV (July), pp. 88–92.

Minsky, Hyman P. (1986), *Stabilizing an Unstable Economy*, New Haven: Yale University Press.

Mises, Ludwig von (1944), 'The treatment of "irrationality" in the social sciences,' *Philosophy and Phenomenological Research*, vol. 4, no. 4 (June), pp. 527–46.

— — (1949), *Human Action*, New Haven: Yale University Press.

— — (1953 [1981]), *The Theory of Money and Credit*, 'new' edn, translated by H.E. Batson, Indianapolis, IN: Liberty Classics.

— — (1956), *The Anti-Capitalistic Mentality*, Princeton: D. Van Nostrand.

— — (1957), *Theory and History: An Interpretation of Social and Economic Evolution*, New Haven: Yale University Press.

— — (1962), *The Ultimate Foundation of Economic Science: An Essay on Method*, Princeton: D. Van Nostrand.

— — (1981), *Socialism*, 'corrected' second English edition, Indianapolis, IN: Liberty Classics, first German edition, 1922.

Mitchell, Wesley Clair (1916), 'The rôle of money in economic theory,' *American Economic Review*, supplement, *Papers and Proceedings of the Twenty-eighth Annual Meeting of the American Economic Association*, vol. 6, no. 1 (March), pp. 140–61, reprinted (1937) in *The Backward Art of Spending Money*, New York: McGraw-Hill.

— — (1927), *Business Cycles: The Problem and Its Setting*, New York: National Bureau of Economic Research.

—— (1936), 'Intelligence and the guidance of economic evolution,' *Scientific Monthly*, vol. XLIII (November), pp. 450–65, reprinted (1937) in *The Backward Art of Spending Money*, New York: McGraw-Hill.

Molinari, Gustave de (1904), *The Society of Tomorrow: A Forecast of Its Political and Economic Organization*, translated by P.H. Lee Warner, New York: G.P. Putnam's Sons.

Moore, Henry L. (1908), 'The statistical complement of pure economics,' *Quarterly Journal of Economics*, vol. 23, no. 1 (November), pp. 1–33.

More, Thomas (1516 [1989]), *Utopia*, edited by George M. Logan and Robert M. Adams, Cambridge: Cambridge University Press.

Morgenstern, Oskar (1963), 'Limits to the uses of mathematics in economics,' in James C. Charlesworth (ed.), *Mathematics and the Social Sciences*, Philadelphia: American Academy of Political and Social Science.

Morrow, Glenn R. (1923), *The Ethical and Economic Theories of Adam Smith*, New York: Longmans Green and Co.

—— (1928), 'Adam Smith: moralist and philosopher,' in *Adam Smith, 1776–1926. Lectures to Commemorate the Sesquicentennial of the Publication of 'The Wealth of Nations,'* Chicago: University of Chicago Press.

Mosca, Gaetano (1939), *The Ruling Class (Elementi di Scienza Politica)*, translated by Hannah D. Kahn and edited by Arthur Livingston, New York: McGraw-Hill.

Mun, Thomas (1664), *England's Treasure by Forraign Trade. Or, the Ballance of our Forraign Trade is the Rule of our Treasure*, London: J.G. for Thomas Clark.

Musgrave, Richard A. (1959), *The Theory of Public Finance: A Study in Public Economy*, New York: McGraw-Hill.

Myrdal, Gunnar (1953), *The Political Element in the Development of Economic Theory*, translated by Paul Streeten, London: Routledge and Kegan Paul.

—— (1972), *Against the Stream: Critical Essays on Economics*, New York: Pantheon.

Nathan, Robert R. (1964), 'Economic analysis and public policy: the growing hiatus,' *American Economic Review, Papers and Proceedings of the Seventy-sixth Annual Meeting of the American Economic Association*, vol. 54, no. 3 (May), pp. 610–22.

Newcomb, Simon (1870), 'The let-alone principle,' *North American Review*, vol. CX, no. 226 (January), pp. 1–33.

—— (1880), 'Principles of taxation,' *North American Review*, vol. CXXXI, no. 285 (August), pp. 142–56.

—— (1886), *Principles of Political Economy*, New York: Harper and Brothers.

Nicholson, J. Shield (1893), address to the Economic Science and Statistics Section of the British Association, *Journal of Political Economy*, vol. 2, no. 1 (December), pp. 119–32.

—— (1897), inaugural address to the Scottish Society of Economists, November 9, *Economic Journal*, vol. 7, no. 28 (December), pp. 538–49.

North, Douglass C. (1965), 'The state of economic history,' *American Economic Review*, vol. 55, no. 1/2 (March), pp. 86–91.

North, Dudley (1691), *Discourses Upon Trade; Principally Directed to the Cases of the Interest, Coynage, Clipping, Increase of Money*, London: printed for Tho. Basset, at the George in Fleet-street.

Olson, Mancur (1965), *The Logic of Collective Action: Public Goods and the Theory of Groups*, Cambridge, MA: Harvard University Press.

Owen, Robert (1813–16 [1991]), 'A new view of society, or, essays on the principle of the formation of the human character, and the application of the principle to practice,' in Robert Owen, *A New View of Society and Other Writings*, edited by Gregory Claeys, Harmondsworth: Penguin.

—— (1817 [1991]), 'Address delivered at the City of London Tavern on Thursday, August 21st, 1817,' in Robert Owen, *A New View of Society and Other Writings*, edited by Gregory Claeys, Harmondsworth: Penguin.

—— (1840 [1991]), *Manifesto of Robert Owen* (fifth edition), in Robert Owen, *A New View of Society and Other Writings*, edited by Gregory Claeys, Harmondsworth: Penguin.

Palgrave, R.H. Inglis (1885), 'Taxes and taxation,' *Quarterly Review*, vol. 161, no. 322 (October), pp. 382–410.

Pantaleoni, Matteo (1898 [1957]), *Pure Economics*, translated by T. Boston Bruce, New York: Kelley and Millman.

Pareto, Vilfredo (1897), 'The new theories of economics,' *Journal of Political Economy*, vol. 5, no. 4 (September), pp. 485–502.

—— (1927 [1971]), *Manual of Political Economy*, translated from the French edition by Ann S. Schwier and edited by Ann S. Schwier and Alfred N. Page, New York: Augustus M. Kelley.

—— (1935), *The Mind and Society* [*Trattato di Sociologia generale*], translated by Andrew Bongiorno and Arthur Livingston and edited by Arthur Livingston, four volumes, New York: Harcourt, Brace and Co.

Patten, Simon N. (1891), 'The need of new economic terms,' *Quarterly Journal of Economics*, vol. 5, no. 3 (April), pp. 372–74.

—— (1892), 'The economic causes of moral progress,' *Annals of the American Academy of Political and Social Science*, vol. III (September), pp. 1–21.

—— (1909), 'The making of economic literature,' *American Economic Association Quarterly*, third series, vol. 10, no. 1: papers and discussions of the 21st annual meeting (April), pp. 1–14.

—— (1913), 'The background of economic theories,' *American Journal of Sociology*, vol. 18, no. 5 (March), pp. 689–93.

Peirce, Charles S. (1893), 'Evolutionary love,' *Monist*, vol. III, no. 2 (January), pp. 176–200.

—— (1893 [1933]), 'The logic of quantity,' in Charles Hartshorne and Paul Weiss (eds), *Collected Papers of Charles Sanders Peirce*, vol. IV: *The Simplest Mathematics*, Cambridge, MA: Harvard University Press.

Penrose, Edith (1952), 'Biological analogies in the theory of the firm,' *American Economic Review*, vol. 42, no. 5 (December), pp. 804–19.

Perlman, Mark (1981), editor's note, *Journal of Economic Literature*, vol. XIX, no. 1 (March), pp. 1–4.

—— (1990), 'The fabric of economics and the golden threads of G.L.S. Shackle,' in Stephen F. Frowen (ed.), *Unknowledge and Choice in Economics*, London: Macmillan.

—— (1997), 'Hayek, the purpose of the market, and American economic institutionalism,' in Stephen F. Frowen (ed.), *Hayek: Economist and Social Philosopher*, London: Macmillan.

Perlman, Selig (1923)., *A History of Trade Unionism in the United States*, New York: Macmillan.

Petty, William (1662 [1963]), *A Treatise of Taxes & Contributions, Shewing the Nature and Measures of Crown Lands, Assessments, Customs, Poll Moneys, Lotteries, Benevolence, Penalties, Monopolies, Offices, Tythes, Raising of Coins, Harth-Money, Excize, &c. With several intersperst Discourses and Digressions concerning Warres, The Church, Universities, Rents & Purchases, Usury & Exchange, Banks & Lombards, Registries for Conveyances, Beggars, Ensurance, Exportation of Money & Wool, Freeports, Coins, Housing, Liberty of Conscience, &c.*, in Charles H. Hull, (ed.), *The Economic Writings of Sir William Petty*, vol. I. New York: Augustus M. Kelley.

—— (1664 [1963]), *Verbum Sapienti*, in Charles H. Hull (ed), *The Economic Writings of Sir William Petty*, vol. I, New York: Augustus M. Kelley.

—— (1676 [1963]), *Political Arithmetick, Or a Discourse Concerning, The Extent and Value of Lands, People, Buildings; Husbandry, Manufacture, Commerce, Fishery, Artizans, Seamen, Soldiers; Publick Revenues, Interest, Taxes, Superlucration, Registries, Banks; Valuation of Men, Increasing of Seamen, of Militia's, Harbours, Situation, Shipping, Power at Sea, &c. As the same relates to every Country in general, but more particularly to the Territories of His Majesty of Great Britain, and his Neighbours of Holland, Zealand, and France*, in Charles H. Hull (ed.), *The Economic Writings of Sir William Petty*, vol. I. New York: Augustus M. Kelley.

Phelps, Edmund S. (1979), 'Justice in the theory of public finance,' *Journal of Philosophy*, vol. 76, no. 11 (November), pp. 677–92.

Phillips, Willard (1850), *Propositions Concerning Protection and Free Trade*, Boston: Charles C. Little and James Brown.

Pigou, Arthur Cecil (1920), *The Economics of Welfare*, London: Macmillan.

—— (1948), *Income: An Introduction to Economics*, London: Macmillan.

Pius XI (Pope) (1931), *Quadragesimo Anno – Encyclical of Pope Pius XI on Reconstruction of the Social Order to Our Venerable Brethren, the Patriarchs, Primates, Archbishops, Bishops, and Other Ordinaries in Peace and Communion with the Apostolic See, and Likewise to All the Faithful of the Catholic World* (15 May), as presented at the Vatican website: <http://www.vatican.va/holy_father/pius_xi/encyclicals/documents/hf_p-xi_enc_19310515_quadragesimo-anno_en.html>

Polanyi, Karl (1944), *The Great Transformation*, New York: Farrar and Rinehart.

Polanyi, Michael (1940), 'Collectivist planning,' in Michael Polanyi (ed.), *The Contempt of Freedom*, London: Watts and Co.

—— (1960), 'Towards a theory of conspicuous consumption,' *Soviet Survey*, no. 34 (October–December), pp. 90–9.

Posner, Richard A. (1987), 'The law and economics movement,' *American Economic Review, Papers and Proceedings*, vol. 77, no. 2 (May), pp. 1–15.

Price, Bonamy (1870), 'Free trade and reciprocity,' *Contemporary Review*, vol. XIII, no. 3 (March), pp. 321–45.

—— (1870), 'What is money? And has it any effect on the rate of discount?', *Contemporary Review*, vol. XIV, no. 2 (May), pp. 236–59.

—— (1870), 'Trade-unions,' *Blackwood's Edinburgh Magazine*, vol. CVII: Part I: no. 655 (May), pp. 554–69; part II: no. 656 (June), pp. 744–62.

Proudhon, Pierre-Joseph (1840 [1994]), *What is Property?*, translated and edited by Donald R. Kelley and Bonnie G. Smith, Cambridge: Cambridge University Press.

—— (1888), *System of Economical Contradictions: Or, the Philosophy of Misery*, translated by Benjamin R. Tucker.

Rae, John (1834), *Statement of Some New Principles on the Subject of Political Economy, Exposing the Fallacies of the System of Free Trade, and of Some Other Doctrines Maintained in the 'Wealth of Nations,'* Boston: Hilliard, Gray, and Co.

Rand, Ayn (1965), 'The new fascism: rule by consensus,' *The Objectivist Newsletter*, part I: vol. 4, no. 5 (May), pp. 19–20, 22; part II: vol. 4, no. 6 (June), pp. 23–6, reprinted (1967) in Ayn Rand, *Capitalism: The Unknown Ideal*, New York: Signet.

—— (1965), 'What is capitalism?,' *The Objectivist Newsletter*, part I: vol. 4, no. 11 (November), pp. 51–2; part II: vol. 4, no. 12 (December), reprinted (1967) in Ayn Rand, *Capitalism: The Unknown Ideal*, New York: Signet.

—— (1966), 'The roots of war,' *The Objectivist*, vol. 5, no. 6 (June), pp. 1–7, reprinted (1967) in Ayn Rand, *Capitalism: The Unknown Ideal*, New York: Signet.

—— (1967), 'Requiem for man,' *The Objectivist*, part I: vol. 6, no. 7 (July), pp. 1–7; part II: vol. 6, no. 8 (August), pp. 1–7; part III: vol. 6, no. 9 (September), pp. 1–7, reprinted (1967) in Ayn Rand, *Capitalism: The Unknown Ideal*, New York: Signet.

Rees, Albert (1986), 'The marketplace of economic ideas,' *American Economic Review, Papers and Proceedings of the Ninety-eighth Annual Meeting of the American Economic Association*, vol. 76, no. 2 (May), pp. 138–40.

Rescher, Nicholas (1980), *Unpopular Essays on Technological Progress*, Pittsburgh: University of Pittsburgh Press.

Ricardo, David (1818 [1952]), letter to Hutches Trower (letter 249, January 26), in vol. VII, *The Works and Correspondence of David Ricardo*, edited by Piero Sraffa with the collaboration of Maurice Dobb, Cambridge: Cambridge University Press for the Royal Economic Society.

—— (1819 [1952]), letter to Hutches Trower (letter 346, November 12), in vol. VIII, *The Works and Correspondence of David Ricardo*, edited by Piero Sraffa with the collaboration of Maurice Dobb, Cambridge: Cambridge University Press for the Royal Economic Society.

—— (1820 [1952]), letter to T.R. Malthus (letter 392, October 9), in vol. VIII, *The Works and Correspondence of David Ricardo*, edited by Piero Sraffa, with the collaboration of Maurice Dobb, Cambridge: Cambridge University Press for the Royal Economic Society.

—— (1821 [1951]), *On the Principles of Political Economy and Taxation*, third edn, vol. I of *The Works and Correspondence of David Ricardo*, edited by Piero Sraffa with the collaboration of Maurice Dobb, Cambridge: Cambridge University Press for the Royal Economic Society.

Robbins, Lionel (1930), 'The present position of economic science,' *Economica* (new series), vol. 0, no. 28 (March), pp. 14–24.

—— (1938), 'Live and dead issues in the methodology of economics,' *Economica* (new series), vol. 5, no. 19 (August), pp. 342–52.

—— (1939), *The Economic Basis of Class Conflict, and Other Essays in Political Economy*, London: Macmillan.

Robertson, D.H. (1955), 'The non-econometrician's lament,' from a poem prepared September 3, 1952, in Erik Lundberg (ed.), *The Business Cycle in the Post-War World: Proceedings of a Conference Held by the International Economic Association*, London: Macmillan.

Robinson, Joan (1951), 'Introduction,' to Rosa Luxemburg, *The Accumulation of Capital*, New Haven: Yale University Press.

—— (1953), *On Re-Reading Marx*, Cambridge: Students' Bookshops Ltd.

—— (1955 [1980]), *Marx, Marshall, and Keynes*, in Joan Robinson (ed.), *Collected Economic Papers*, vol. II, part I, Cambridge, MA: MIT Press.

— — (1960), *Exercises in Economic Analysis*, London: Macmillan.
— — (1962), *Economic Philosophy*, Chicago: Aldine.
— — (1968), 'Economic versus political economy,' *Indian Economic Review*, vol. III (NS), no. 1 (April), pp. 57–64.
— — (1970), *Freedom and Necessity: An Introduction to the Study of Society*, New York: Pantheon.
— — (1972), 'The second crisis of economic theory,' *American Economic Review*, vol. 62, no. 1/2 (June), pp. 1–10.
— — (1977), 'What are the questions?,' *Journal of Economic Literature*, vol. 15, no. 4 (December), pp. 1318–39.
— — (1980), 'Economics today,' in *Collected Economic Papers*, vol. IV, part I, ch. 13, Cambridge, MA: MIT Press.
Roemer, John E. (1994), *Egalitarian Perspectives: Essays in Philosophical Economics*, Cambridge: Cambridge University Press.
Rogers, J.E. Thorold (1885), 'Contemporary socialism,' *Contemporary Review*, vol. XLVII, no. 1 (January), pp. 51–64.
Roscher, Wilhelm (1878), *Principles of Political Economy*, in two volumes, translated by John J. Lalor from the 13th German edition of 1877, Chicago: Callaghan and Co.
Ross, Edward Alsworth (1899), 'The sociological frontier of economics,' *Quarterly Journal of Economics*, vol. 13, no. 4 (July), pp. 386–95.
Rostow, W.W. (1955), 'Marx was a city boy, or, why communism may fail,' *Harper's Magazine*, vol. 210, no. 1257 (February), pp. 25–30.
— — (1959), 'The stages of economic growth,' *Economic History Review*, second series, vol. XII, no. 1, pp. 1–16.
Rothbard, Murray N. (1960), 'The politics of political economists: comment,' *Quarterly Journal of Economics*, vol. 74, no. 4 (November), pp. 659–65.
— — (1961), 'Statistics: Achilles' heel of government,' *The Freeman*, vol. 11, no. 6 (June), pp. 40–4.
— — (1962), *Man, Economy, and State: A Treatise on Economic Principles*, two volumes, Princeton: D. Van Nostrand.
— — (1973), *For a New Liberty*, New York: Macmillan.
— — (1981), 'The myth of neutral taxation,' *Cato Journal*, vol. 1, no. 2 (Fall), pp. 519–64.
— — (1982), *The Ethics of Liberty*, Atlantic Highlands, NJ: Humanities Press.
Rousseau, Jean-Jacques (1755 [1973]), *A Discourse on the Origin of Inequality. (A Discourse on a Subject Proposed by the Academy of Dijon: What is the Origin of Inequality Among Men, and is it Authorized by Natural Law?)* in Jean-Jacques Rousseau, *The Social Contract and the Discourses*, translated by G.D.H. Cole, revised and augmented by J.H. Brumfitt and John C. Hall, New York: Everyman's Library (Alfred A. Knopf).
— — (1755 [1973]), *A Discourse on Political Economy*, in Jean-Jacques Rousseau, *The Social Contract and the Discourses*, translated by G.D.H. Cole, revised and augmented by J.H. Brumfitt and John C. Hall, New York: Everyman's Library (Alfred A. Knopf).
Ruskin, John (1860), 'Unto this last,' *Cornhill Magazine*, vol. II: part I: 'The roots of honour,' no. 8 (August), pp. 155–66; part II: 'The veins of wealth,' no. 9 (September), pp. 278–86; part III: 'Qui judicatis terram,' no. 10 (October), pp. 407–18; part IV: 'Ad valorem,' no. 11 (November), pp. 543–64.
— — (1862–3), 'Essays on political economy,' *Fraser's Magazine for Town and Country*, part I: vol. LXV, no. 390 (June 1862), pp. 784–92; part II: vol. LXVI, no. 393 (September), pp. 265–80; part III: vol. LXVI, no. 396 (December), pp. 742–56; part IV: vol. LXVII, no. 400 (April), pp. 441–60.
Samuelson, Paul A. (1947), *Foundations of Economic Analysis*, Cambridge, MA: Harvard University Press.
— — (1951), *Economics: An Introductory Analysis*, second edn, New York: McGraw-Hill.
— — (1952), 'Economic theory and mathematics – an appraisal,' *American Economic Review, Papers and Proceedings of the Sixty-fourth Annual Meeting of the American Economic Association*, vol. 42, no. 2 (May), pp. 56–66.
— — (1959), 'What economists know,' in Daniel Lerner (ed.), *The Human Meaning Of the Social Sciences*, New York: Meridian.
— — (1963), 'Modern economics realities and individualism,' *The Texas Quarterly*, vol. VI, no. 2 (Summer), pp. 128–39.
— — (1964), 'Personal freedoms and economic freedoms in the mixed economy,' in E.F. Cheit (ed.), *The Business Establishment*, New York: John Wiley, reprinted (1972) in Robert C. Merton (ed.), *The Collected Scientific Papers of Paul A. Samuelson*, vol. III, Cambridge, MA: MIT Press.

—— (1972), 'Economics in a golden age: a personal memoir,' in Gerald Holton (ed.), *The Twentieth-Century Sciences*, New York: W.W. Norton.

Sargent, Thomas J. (1985), ' "Reaganomics" and credibility,' in Albert Ando, Hidekazu Eguchi, Roger Farmer, and Yoshio Suzuki (eds), *Monetary Policy in Our Times: Proceedings of the First International Conference Held by the Institute for Monetary and Economic Studies of the Bank of Japan*, Cambridge, MA: MIT Press.

Say, Jean-Baptiste (1880), *A Treatise on Political Economy, or the Production, Distribution, and Consumption of Wealth*, new American edition, from the fourth French edition, translated by C.R. Prinsep, Philadelphia: Claxton, Remsen, and Haffelfinger, reprinted (1971), New York: Augustus M. Kelley.

Schmoller, Gustav (1894), 'The Idea of Justice in Political Economy,' *Annals of the American Academy of Political and Social Science*, vol. 4 (March), pp. 1–41.

Schultz, Henry (1927), 'Mathematical economics and the quantitative method,' *Journal of Political Economy*, vol. 35, no. 5 (October), pp. 702–6.

—— (1928), 'Rational economics,' *American Economic Review*, vol. 18, no. 4 (December), pp. 643–48.

Schultz, Theodore W. (1977), 'On economic history in extending economics,' in Manning Nash (ed.), *Essays in Economic Development and Cultural Change, in Honor of Bert F. Hoselitz*, supplement to vol. 25 of *Economic Development and Cultural Change*, pp. 245–53.

Schumacher, E.F. (1973), *Small Is Beautiful: Economics as if People Mattered*, New York: Harper and Row.

Schumpeter, Joseph A. (1927), 'The explanation of the business cycle,' *Economica*, vol. 0 (NS), no. 21 (December), pp. 286–311.

—— (1933), 'The common sense of econometrics,' *Econometrica*, vol. 1, no. 1 (January), pp. 5–12.

—— (1939), *Business Cycles: A Theoretical, Historical, and Statistical Analysis of the Capitalist Process*, two volumes, New York: McGraw-Hill.

—— (1950), *Capitalism, Socialism, and Democracy*, third edn, New York: Harper and Row.

Scitovsky, Tibor (1951), 'The state of welfare economics,' *American Economic Review*, vol. 41, no. 3 (June), pp. 303–15.

—— (1974), 'Are men rational or economists wrong?,' in Paul A. David and Melvin W. Reder (eds), *Nations and Households in Economic Growth: Essays in Honor of Moses Abramovitz*, New York: Academic Press.

—— (1980), 'Can capitalism survive? – an old question in a new setting,' *American Economic Review, Papers and Proceedings of the Ninety-second Annual Meeting of the American Economic Association*, vol. 70, no. 2 (May), pp. 1–9.

Scrope, G. Poulett (1831), 'Article I: the political economists,' *Quarterly Review*, vol. XLIV, no. 87 (January), pp. 1–52.

—— (1833), *Principles of Political Economy, Deduced From the Natural Laws of Social Welfare, and Applied to the Present State of Britain*, London: Longmans, Rees, Orme, Brown, Green, and Longmans.

Sedgwick, Theodore (1836), *Public and Private Economy*, part first, New York: Harper and Brothers.

—— (1838), *Public and Private Economy*, part second, New York: Harper and Brothers.

Seligman, E.R.A. (1903), 'Economics and social progress,' *Publications of the American Economic Association*, third series, vol. IV, no. 1 (February), pp. 52–70.

—— (1911), *The Income Tax: A Study of the History, Theory, and Practice of Income Taxation at Home and Abroad*, New York: Macmillan.

—— (1921), *A Debate on Capitalism vs. Socialism*, E.R.A. Seligman vs. Scott Nearing, New York: Fine Arts Guild, Inc.

—— (1921), *Principles of Economics, with Special Reference to American Conditions*, ninth edn, New York: Longmans, Green and Co.

Senior, Nassau W. (1836 [1965]), *An Outline of the Science of Political Economy*, Fairfield, NJ: Augustus M. Kelley.

—— (1841), 'Article I: Poor Law reform,' *Edinburgh Review*, vol. LXXIV, no. 149 (October), pp. 1–44.

—— (1843), 'Article I: free trade and retaliation,' *Edinburgh Review*, vol. LXXVIII, no. 157 (July), pp. 1–47.

Shackle, G.L.S. (1972), *Epistemics and Economics*, Cambridge: Cambridge University Press.

—— (1973), *An Economic Querist*, Cambridge: Cambridge University Press.

Shaw, George Bernard (1928), *The Intelligent Woman's Guide to Socialism and Capitalism*, New York: Brentano's Publishers.

Sichel, Werner (ed) (1989), *The State of Economic Science: Views of Six Nobel Laureates*, Kalamazoo, MI: W.E. Upjohn Institute for Employment Research.

Sidgwick, Henry (1879), 'Economic method,' *Fortnightly Review*, vol. XXV (NS), no. CXLVI (February 1), pp. 301–18.

— — (1901 [1924]), *The Principles of Political Economy*, third edn, London: Macmillan.

Simmel, Georg (1900 [1978]), *The Philosophy of Money*, translated by Tom Bottomore and David Frisby, London: Routledge and Kegan Paul.

Simon, Herbert A. (1957), *Models of Man, Social and Rational: Mathematical Essay on Rational Human Behavior in a Social Setting*, New York: John Wiley and Sons.

— — (1958), 'The role of expectations in an adaptive or behavioristic model,' in M.J. Bowman (ed), *Expectations, Uncertainty, and Business Behavior*, New York: Social Sciences Research Council, also in Herbert A. Simon (1982), *Models of Bounded Rationality*. vol. 2, Cambridge, MA: MIT Press.

— — (1976), 'From substantive to procedural rationality,' in S.J. Latsis (ed.), *Method and Appraisal in Economics*, Cambridge: Cambridge University Press, reprinted (1982) in Herbert A. Simon, *Models of Bounded Rationality*, vol. 2. Cambridge, MA: MIT Press.

Simon, Julian (1981), *The Ultimate Resource*, Princeton: Princeton University Press.

— — (1996), *The Ultimate Resource 2*, Princeton: Princeton University Press.

Simonde de Sismondi, J.C.L. (1815 [1966]), *Political Economy*, New York: Augustus M. Kelley.

— — (1827 [1991]), *New Principles of Political Economy, Of Wealth in Its Relation to Population*, second edn, translated and annotated by Richard Hyse, New Brunswick, NJ: Transaction.

Simons, Henry C. (1944), 'Some reflections on syndicalism,' *Journal of Political Economy*, vol. LII, no. 1 (March), pp. 1–25.

— — (1948), *Economic Policy for a Free Society*, Chicago: University of Chicago Press.

Sims, Christopher (1996), 'Macroeconomics and methodology,' *Journal of Economic Perspectives*, vol. 10, no. 1 (Winter), pp. 105–20.

Smart, William (1893), 'The place of industry in the social organism,' *International Journal of Ethics*, vol. 3, no. 4 (July), pp. 437–51.

Smith, Adam (1789 [1937]), *Wealth of Nations*, fifth edn (first edn, 1776), edited by Edwin Cannan, New York: Modern Library.

— — (1790 [1982]), *The Theory of Moral Sentiments*, sixth edn, (first edn, 1759) edited by D.D. Raphael and A.L. Macfie, Indianapolis, IN: Liberty Classics.

Smith, E. Peshine (1853), *A Manual of Political Economy*, New York: G.P. Putnam.

Smith, Vernon L. (1974), 'Economic theory and its discontents,' *American Economic Review, Papers and Proceedings of the Eighty-sixth Annual Meeting of the American Economic Association*, vol. 64, no. 2 (May), pp. 320–22.

Smith, W.H. (1848), 'Political economy, by J.S. Mill,' *Blackwood's Edinburgh Magazine*, vol. LXIV, no. 396 (October), pp. 407–28.

Solow, Robert M. (1954), 'The survival of mathematical economics,' *Review of Economics and Statistics*, vol. 36, no. 4 (November), pp. 372–4.

— — (1970), *Growth Theory: An Exposition*, New York: Oxford University Press.

— — (1997), 'It ain't the things you don't know that hurt you, it's the things you know that ain't so,' *American Economic Review, Papers and Proceedings of the Hundred and fourth Annual Meeting of the American Economic Association*, vol. 87, no. 2 (May), pp. 107–8.

Sombart, Werner (1929), 'Economic theory and economic history,' *Economic History Review*, vol. 2, no. 1 (January), pp. 1–19.

Southey, Robert (1816), 'Article VI: parliamentary reform,' *Quarterly Review*, vol. XVI, no. 31 (October), pp. 225–79.

— — (1831), 'Article VII: moral and political state of the British Empire,' *Quarterly Review*, vol. XLIV, no. 87 (January), pp. 261–317.

Sowell, Thomas (1980), *Knowledge and Decisions*, New York: Basic Books.

— — (1999), *The Quest for Cosmic Justice*, New York: Free Press.

Spencer, Herbert (1884), 'The coming slavery,' *The Contemporary Review*, vol. XLV, no. 268 (April), pp. 461–82.

— — (1884), 'The sins of legislators,' part II, *The Contemporary Review*, vol. XLV, no. CCLXX (June), pp. 761–75.

Sraffa, Piero (1932), 'Dr. Hayek on money and capital,' *Economic Journal*, vol. 42, no. 165 (March), pp. 42–53.

Stamp, Josiah C. (1938), *Christianity and Economics*, New York: Macmillan.

Stein, Herbert (1986), 'The Washington economics industry,' *American Economic Review,*

Papers and Proceedings of the Ninety-eighth Annual Meeting of the American Economic Association, vol. 76, no. 2 (May), pp. 1–9.

Steuart, James (1767 [1805]), *An Inquiry Into the Principles of Political Economy, Being an Essay on the Science of Domestic Policy in Free Nations. In Which are Particularly Considered Population, Agriculture, Trade, Industry, Money, Coin, Interest, Circulation, Banks, Exchange, Public Credit, and Taxes*, vols. 1–4 of *The Works, Political, Metaphysical, and Chronological, of the Late Sir James Steuart of Coltness, Bart*, six vols, edited by General Sir James Steuart, London: printed for T. Cadell and W. Davies.

Stevenson, William (1824–1825), 'The political economist,' *Blackwood's Edinburgh Magazine*, essay first: vol. XV, no. 88 (May), pp. 522–31; essay II, part I: vol. XV, no. 89 (June), pp. 643–55; essay II, part II: vol. XVI, no. 90 (July), pp. 34–45; essay III, part I: vol. XVI, no. 91 (August), pp. 202–14; essay III, part II: vol. XVII, no. 97 (February), pp. 207–20.

Stewart, Dugald (1855), *Lectures on Political Economy*, vol. I, Edinburgh: Thomas Constable and Co.

—— (1856), *Lectures on Political Economy*, vol. II, Edinburgh: Thomas Constable and Co.

Stigler, George J. (1949), 'A survey of contemporary economics,' *Journal of Political Economy*, vol. 57, no. 2 (April), pp. 93–105.

—— (1959), 'The politics of political economists,' *Quarterly Journal of Economics*, vol. 73, no. 4 (November), pp. 522–32.

—— (1982), *The Pleasures and Pains of Modern Capitalism*, Thirteenth Wincott Memorial Lecture, Institute of Economic Affairs occasional paper no. 64, London: Institute of Economic Affairs for the Wincott Foundation.

—— (1988), *Memoirs of an Unregulated Economist*, New York: Basic Books.

Stiglitz, Joseph E. (1994), *Whither Socialism?*, Cambridge, MA: MIT Press.

Stolper, Gustav (1942), *This Age of Fable: The Political and Economic World We Live In*, New York: Reynal and Hitchcock.

Stone, Richard (1980), 'Political economy, economics and beyond,' *Economic Journal*, vol. 90, no. 360 (December), pp. 719–36.

Sumner, William Graham (1878), 'Socialism,' *Scribner's Monthly*, vol. XVI, no. 6 (October), pp. 887–93.

—— (1882), 'Wages,' *Princeton Review*, vol. 10, no. 3 (November), pp. 241–62.

—— (1883 [1995]), *What Social Classes Owe to Each Other*, Caldwell, ID: Caxton Printers.

—— (1902), 'Concentration of wealth: its justification,' *The Independent*, vol. LIV, no. 2787 (May 1), pp. 1036–40.

Sweezy, Paul M. (1942), *The Theory of Capitalist Development: Principles of Marxian Political Economy*, New York: Oxford University Press.

—— (1981), *Four Lectures on Marxism*, New York: Monthly Review Press.

Syme, David (1871), 'On the method of political economy,' *Westminster Review*, vol. XCVI, no. 189 (July), pp. 94–100.

Taft, William Howard (1913), *Popular Government: Its Essence, Its Permanence and Its Perils*, New Haven: Yale University Press.

Taussig, F.W. (1892), 'Reciprocity,' *Quarterly Journal of Economics*, vol. 7, no. 1 (October), pp. 26–39.

—— (1905), 'The present position of the doctrine of free trade,' *Publications of the American Economic Association*, third series, vol. 6, no. 1, *Papers and Proceedings of the Seventeenth Annual Meeting*, part I (February), pp. 29–65.

Tawney, R.H. (1920), *The Acquisitive Society*, New York: Harcourt, Brace and Co.

—— (1926), *Religion and the Rise of Capitalism*, New York: Harcourt, Brace and Co.

Taylor, Overton H. (1947), 'Economic theory and the age we live in,' *Review of Economic Statistics*, vol. 29, no. 2 (May), pp. 102–7.

—— (1957), 'Economic science only – or political economy?,' *Quarterly Journal of Economics*, vol. 71, no. 1 (February), pp. 1–18.

Temin, Peter, and Geoffrey Peters (1985). 'Is history stranger than theory? The origin of telephone separations,' *American Economic Review, Papers and Proceedings of the Ninety-seventh Annual Meeting of the American Economic Association*, vol. 75, no. 2 (May), pp. 324–7.

Thompson, Thomas Perronet (1833), 'Article VII: Effects of abolition and commutation of tithes,' *Westminster Review*, vol. XVIII, no. 36 (April), pp. 178–80.

Thompson, William (1827 [1969]), *Labour Rewarded: The Claims of Labour and Capital Conciliated, or How to Secure to Labour the Whole Product of Its Exertion*, New York: Augustus M. Kelley.

Thünen, Johann von (1842 [1966]), *Von Thünen's Isolated State*, second edn, translated by Carla M. Wartenberg and edited by Peter Hall, Oxford: Pergamon Press.

Thurow, Lester C. (1983), *Dangerous Currents: The State of Economics*, New York: Random House.

Tinbergen, Jan (1954), 'The functions of mathematical treatment,' *Review of Economics and Statistics*, vol. 36, no. 4 (November), pp. 365–9.

Tobin, James (1974), *The New Economics One Decade Older*, Princeton: Princeton University Press.

Tolstoy, Leo (1903), 'Science and money,' *The Independent*, vol. LV, no. 2822 (January 1), pp. 12–15.

Torrens, Robert (1834), *On Wages and Combination*, London: Longman, Rees, Orme, Brown, Green, and Longman.

Trower, Hutches (1820 [1952]), letter to David Ricardo (letter 390, September 29), in vol. VIII, *The Works and Correspondence of David Ricardo*, edited by Piero Sraffa, with the collaboration of Maurice Dobb, Cambridge: Cambridge University Press for the Royal Economic Society.

Tucker, George (1859), *Political Economy for the People*, Philadelphia: C. Sherman and Son.

Tugwell, Rexford Guy (1928), 'Economics as the science of experience,' *Journal of Philosophy*, vol. 25, no. 2 (January 19), pp. 29–40.

Tullock, Gordon (1986), 'Reasons for redistribution,' in Gordon Tullock (ed.), *The Economics of Wealth and Poverty*, New York: New York University Press.

—— (1994), 'Does mathematics aid in the progress of economics?,' in Gordon L. Brady and Robert D. Tollison (eds), *On the Trail of Homo Economicus*, Fairfax, VA: George Mason University Press.

Turgot. A.R.J. (1770 [1963]), *Reflections on the Formation and the Distribution of Riches*, New York: Augustus M. Kelley.

Tuttle, Charles A. (1902), 'The workman's position in the light of economic progress,' *Publications of the American Economic Association*, third series, vol. 3, no. 1 (February), pp. 199–212.

Usher, Abbott P. (1921), 'Justice and poverty,' *American Journal of Sociology*, vol. 26, no. 6 (May), pp. 689–704.

—— (1931), 'Round table conference: economic history – the decline of laissez faire,' *American Economic Review*, Supplement, *Papers and Proceedings of the Forty-third Annual Meeting of the American Economic Association*, vol. 21, no. 1 (March), pp. 3–5.

—— (1932), 'The application of the quantitative method to economic history,' *Journal of Political Economy*, vol. 40, no. 2 (April), pp. 186–209.

Vaughan, Rice (1675), *A Discourse of Coin and Coinage: The first Invention, Use, Matter, Forms, Proportions and Differences, ancient & modern: with the Advantages and Disadvantages of the Rise and Fall thereof, in our own or Neighbouring Nations: and the Reasons. Together with a short Account of our Common Law therein*, London: printed by Th. Dawks, for Th. Basset, at the George, near Cliffords-Inn, in Fleet-street.

Veblen, Thorstein (1898), 'Why is economics not an evolutionary science?,' *Quarterly Journal of Economics*, vol. 12, no. 4 (July), pp. 373–97.

—— (1899), *The Theory of the Leisure Class*, New York: Macmillan.

—— (1900), 'The preconceptions of economic science III,' *Quarterly Journal of Economics*, vol. 14, no. 2 (February), pp. 240–69.

—— (1906), 'The socialist economics of Karl Marx and his followers: I,' *Quarterly Journal of Economics*, vol. 20, no. 4 (August), pp. 575–95.

—— (1919), 'The industrial system and the captains of industry,' *The Dial*, vol. LXVI, no. 791 (May 31), pp. 552–7.

Vickrey, William S. (1964), *Microstatics*, New York: Harcourt, Brace and World.

Viner, Jacob (1922), round table conference on the relation between economics and ethics, *American Economic Review, Papers and Proceedings of the Thirty-fourth Annual Meeting of the American Economic Association*, vol. XII, no. 1 (March), pp. 198–200.

—— (1931), 'The tariff question and the economist,' *The Nation and Athenæum*, vol. XLVIII: part I: no. 19 (February 7), pp. 592–4; part II: no. 20 (February 14), pp. 626–8.

—— (1937), *Studies in the Theory of International Trade*, New York: Harper and Brothers.

Vining, Rutledge (1959), 'The affluent society: a review article,' *American Economic Review*, vol. 49, no. 1 (March), pp. 112–19.

Walker, Amasa (1866), *The Science of Wealth: A Manual of Political Economy. Embracing the Laws of Trade, Currency, and Finance*, second edn, Boston: Little, Brown.

Walker, Francis Amasa (1883), *Political Economy*, New York: Henry Holt and Co.

—— (1887), 'Socialism,' *Scribner's Magazine*, vol. I, no. 1 (January), pp. 107–19.

—— (1887), 'What shall we tell the working-classes,' *Scribner's Magazine*, vol. II, no. 5 (November), pp. 619–27.

—— (1888), 'The bases of taxation,' *Political Science Quarterly*, vol. III, no. 1 (March), pp. 1–16.

—— (1890)., 'Protection and protectionists,' *Quarterly Journal of Economics*, vol. 4, no. 3 (April), pp. 245–75.

—— (1891), *Money*, New York: Henry Holt and Co.

—— (1897), 'The causes of poverty,' *The Century Magazine*, vol. LV, no. 2 (December), pp. 210–16.

Walras, Léon (1926 [1954]), *Elements of Pure Economics, or the Theory of Social Wealth*, 'definitive' edition, translated by William Jaffé, Homewood, IL: Published for the American Economic Association and the Royal Economic Society by Richard D. Irwin.

Wayland, Francis (1837), *The Elements of Political Economy*, New York: Leavitt, Lord and Co.

Webb, Sidney (1889), 'The limitation of the hours of labour,' *Contemporary Review*, vol. LVI, no. 6 (December), pp. 859–83.

—— (1891), 'The difficulties of individualism,' *Economic Journal*, vol. 1, no. 2 (June), pp. 360–81.

—— (1910), 'Eugenics and the Poor Law: the minority report,' *Eugenics Review*, vol. II, no. 3 (November), pp. 233–41.

Webb, Sidney, and Beatrice Webb (1916), *The Prevention of Destitution*, London: Longmans, Green and Co.

—— (1923), *The Decay of Capitalist Civilization*, New York: Harcourt, Brace and Co.

Weber, Max, (1904–5 [1930]), *The Protestant Ethic and the Spirit of Capitalism*, translated by Talcott Parsons, New York: Charles Scribner's Sons.

Webster, Daniel (1832 [1851]), 'Bank of the United States,' in *The Works of Daniel Webster*, vol. III, Boston: Charles C. Little and James Brown.

—— (1837 [1851]), 'Reception at New York,' in *The Works of Daniel Webster*, vol. I. Boston: Charles C. Little and James Brown

Whately, Richard (1828), 'Article VII: Oxford lectures on political economy,' *Edinburgh Review*, vol. XLVIII, no. 95 (September), pp. 170–84.

—— (1832), *Introductory Lectures on Political Economy*, second edn, London: B. Fellowes, reprinted (1966), New York: Augustus M. Kelley.

Wicksell, Knut (1904 [1958]), 'Ends and means in economics,' in Erik Lindahl (ed.), *Knut Wicksell: Selected Papers on Economic Theory*, Cambridge, MA: Harvard University Press, originally published in Swedish in *Ekonomisk Tidskrift*.

—— (1925 [1958]), 'Mathematical economics,' in Erik Lindahl (ed.), *Knut Wicksell: Selected Papers on Economic Theory*, Cambridge, MA: Harvard University Press, originally published in Swedish in *Ekonomisk Tidskrift*.

Wicksteed, Philip H. (1888), *The Alphabet of Economic Science: Elements of the Theory of Value or Worth*, London: Macmillan.

—— (1910), *The Common Sense of Political Economy*, London: Macmillan.

—— (1914), 'The scope and method of political economy in the light of the "Marginal" theory of value and of distribution,' *Economic Journal*, vol. 24, no. 93 (March), pp. 1–23.

Wiener, Norbert (1964), *God and Golem, Inc. A Comment on Certain Points Where Cybernetics Impinges on Religion*, Cambridge, MA: MIT Press.

Wieser, Friedrich von (1893), *Natural Value*, translated by Christian A. Malloch and edited by William Smart, London: Macmillan and Co.

—— (1927), *Social Economics*, translated by A. Ford Hinrichs, New York: Greenberg.

Wilson, E.B. (1940), 'Methodology in the natural and the social sciences,' *American Journal of Sociology*, vol. 45, no. 5 (March), pp. 655–68.

—— (1955), 'Mathematics in economics: further comment,' *Review of Economics and Statistics*, vol. 37, no. 3 (August), pp. 297–300.

Wootton, Barbara (1945), *Freedom Under Planning*, Chapel Hill: University of North Carolina Press.

Wright, Carroll D. (1895), 'Contributions of the United States government to social science,' *American Journal of Sociology*, vol. 1, no. 3 (November), pp. 241–75.

—— (1897), 'Are the rich growing richer and the poor poorer?,' *Atlantic Monthly*, vol. LXXX, no. 479 (September), pp. 300–9.

Yarranton, Andrew (1677), *England's Improvement by Sea and Land. To Out-do the* Dutch *Without Fighting, To Pay Debts without Moneys, To Set at Work all the Poor of*

England *with the Growth of our own Lands. To prevent unnecessary Suits in Law; With the Benefit of a Voluntary Register. Directions where vast quantities of Timber are to be had for the Building of Ships; With the Advantage of making the Great Rivers of* England *Navigable. Rules to prevent Fires in* London, *and Other Great Cities; With Directions how the several Companies of Handicraftsmen in* London *may always have cheap Bread and Drink*, London: printed by R. Everingham for the author.

Young, Allyn A. (1927), 'Economics as a field of research,' *Quarterly Journal of Economics*, vol. 42, no. 1 (November), pp. 1–25.

Zeuthen, Frederik (1954), 'Recent developments in economics,' *Quarterly Journal of Economics*, vol. 68, no. 2 (May), pp. 159–80.

Index

a priori: Jones 2; J.M. Keynes 3; Syme 1
   propositions: Hicks 1
ability:
   socialism destroys all above lowest: Sumner 6
abortions: Carlyle 1
absolutes:
   key institutions must be accepted as: Friedman 20
abstinence:
abstraction: Ashley 2; Bagehot 6, 8; Baumol 2; Boulding 5; Bowen 7; Croce 2; Dobb 3; Eatwell 2; Frisch 1; Pareto 6; Roscher 4; Veblen 5; Wieser 2
   language of, is passion of economist: M. Perlman 1
   tends to make expression of thought terse: M. Perlman 2
   to make hold in actuality means to destroy actuality: Hegel 1
abundance: Vaughan 1
   Marxists maintain capitalism can produce society of: Sweezy 1
academic scholar: Viner 3
academic scribblers: J.M. Keynes 8
accounting:
   economics should dominate and coordinate activities of: C. Clark 2
accumulation: Bowen 3; Robinson 5; Rousseau 1; Say 3; Torrens 2
   law of capitalist: Marx 6
   nature of, and exploitation: Marx 6
   not aim of socialism: Luxemburg 3
   political economy science of laws which regulate: McCulloch 1
   taxes lessen: Ricardo 9
acquisition:
   impulse to: Weber 1
act(s): Shackle 4
   every voluntary, preceded by decision of the mind: Malthus 11
   only individuals can: Mayer 4
   self-regarding: Webb 1
action: Knight 1; Leslie 2; Schumpeter 7
   competition leading spring of: W. Thompson 1
   cravings, love, desire urge men to: Malthus 11
   freedom of: Scrope 5
   pretended motive for: Hodgskin 1
   rational: Mises 24
   theories have limited effect in determination of: Pareto 1
   ultimate end of is satisfaction of desires: Mises 24
actuality:
   to make abstractions hold in, means to destroy: Hegel 1
administration: Senior 3; Spencer 2
   errors of: A. Smith 20

   just principles of: Stewart 2
   of territory: Erasmus 2
advantage: Bagehot 6; Bentham 9; Petty 4; Ricardo 1; A. Smith 2; Sumner 7; Wayland 7
   and exchange: Ruskin 6
   exchange gives: Shackle 4
   mutual: Gauthier 1, 2
   of consumers: Simonde de Sismondi 3
   of employer of labor: Simonde de Sismondi 2
   political economy not selfish study for individual: Fetter 3
   private: J.M. Keynes 27
   pursuit of individual, connected with universal good: Ricardo 2
adventure: Shaw 1
Æsthetics:
   special science of human nature: Bowen 2
affection: Joplin 3
   economic man freed from voluntary: Gauthier 2
   family: George 5
affirmations:
   socialism powerful in region of: Le Bon 1
affluent society: Galbraith 1
agency: Knight 15
aggregates: Sidgwick 2
aggregation: Shackle 3
agreement: Sumner 7
agricultural science:
   economics should dominate and coordinate activities of: C. Clark 2
agriculture: Rousseau 1; Southey 2
   use of land in must be of necessity exclusive: J.S. Mill 10
agriculturists: Bailey 1
aid: Wayland 8
   reliance on, mischievous: J.S. Mill 7
airplane:
   socialism as: Lange 5
ale-house: Malthus 8
algebra: Leontief 4; Roscher 4; Walras 4
   application to political economy: Stevenson 3
   economic: Goodrich 1
   most perfect instrument yet invented by man: Horner 1
   peculiar language of: Horner 1
   political economy does not require: Horner 1
Alice in Wonderland: Wiener 3
Alice's Wonderland: Greenspan 1
alienation: Marx 1
allocation: Lindbeck 2
   socialism has Pigouvian problem of: meek 1
alms:
   crucifies feeling of personal independence: George 3
   house: Everett 1
   makes the most industrious a tramp: George 3

alms (*cont.*):
    unnatural that should be asked for those able to work: George 2
altruism: Rand 2; Rogers 1
    and family: Leslie 1
    less common in market transactions than families: Becker 1
    reliance on, objection to socialism: J.M. Clark 8
    socialism seeks to engage: J.M. Keynes 24
ambition: Bowen 1; Hodgskin 1
    condition of human progress: A. Marshall 1
    social: F.A. Walker 11
America: Barro 1; J.S. Mill 13; S. Perlman 1; Ricardo 2
American Economic Association:
    least efficient monopoly in America: Barro 1
American Revolution: Morrow 2
analogy: Wicksteed 3
    biological: Penrose 1
    political economy borrows from mathematics: Horner 1
anarchism: Commons 5; Hilferding 1
    and market: Lindbeck 3
    syndicalism economic expression of: Goldman 1
anarchist(s): Patten 5
    consistent liberal not an: Friedman 9
anatomy: Whately 3
angels: Boulding 5
    could not form socialistic community: Mises 30
anger: Hoxie 3
animal kingdom: Malthus 14
annuities: Petty 1
anthropologist: Mitchell 3
anthropology: Akerlof 1
anthropomorphism:
    and social justice: Hayek 25
antitrust:
    reminiscent of Alice's Wonderland: Greenspan 1
antitrust law:
    economics of: Bork 1
anxiety:
    destroyed by security: Bowen 1
apes: Robinson 1
apologists:
    market needs no: Mises 4
appetite: Petty 5; F.A. Walker 11
appropriation: Marx 9
    of land, question of general expediency: J.S. Mill 12
aptitude: Sumner 7
Arabian desert: De Quincey 1
arbitration: Hobson 2; Tuttle 1
argument: Petty 5
aristocracy: Schumpeter 11
aristocratic instinct: Galbraith 2
Aristotle: Edgeworth 2; Jevons 4; Nicholson 3
arithmetic:
    economic: Goodrich 1
armaments: Cunningham 5
armed force:
    basis of regulation: Greenspan 3

army: Schumpeter 11; Shackle 5
    supported by taxes: Harrington 3
art(s): Mun 4; Rousseau 1; Ruskin 4; Schumpeter 11; Simonde de Sismondi 3; A.Smith 6
    economics like: Hicks 3
    political economy can have none attached to: Hobson 6
Art of Living: J.S. Mill 4
arteries: Joplin 2
artificer: Barbon 1
artificial:
    economics science of: H. Simon 3
artisans: J.S. Mill 13
artists: Weber 1
as-if: Hahn 3
asceticism: Schumpeter 11
    imposition of: Hayek 21
association:
    desire of, with fellow men: Carey 5
assumptions: Sweezy 2; Vickrey 1; Wicksell 2; Zeuthen 1
    arbitrary: Leslie 5; Leontief 5
    convenient: Eatwell 3
    realistic: Eatwell 3
astrologers: Petty 4
astrology: Ruskin 3; Samuelson 6
astronomers: T.W. Schultz 1; Senior 3
    economists in position of: Boulding 5
astronomy: Pareto 3; Roscher 3; Ruskin 3; Spencer 3
    economics is social: Clower 5
asylum:
    workhouse is, for able-bodied poor: McCulloch 3
asymptote: Webb 4
atheism: Schumpeter 11
    and socialists: Sumner 7
atomic theory: Bernstein 2
atoms: Lindbeck 1
austerity:
    politic to summon rich to: Erasmus 3
Austria: Ross 2
authority: More 1
    reckless pursuit of: J.M. Keynes 20
automata: Robinson 15
autonomy: Sowell 1
avarice: Carey 5; Mises 20; Ruskin 2
average: Shackle 5
axioms:
    of geometry: Vickrey 1

bad: Sumner 7
baker: Ruskin 10; A. Smith 2
balloon:
    capitalism as: Lange 5
bank balance:
    rather a man should tyrannize over, than fellow citizens: J.M. Keynes 20
bankers: Mosca 1
banking: Bagehot 1
    private: Sedgwick 1

bankruptcy: F.A. Walker 2
　greatest and most humiliating calamity:
　　A. Smith 1
　of government: J.M. Keynes 13
banks: Shaw 2
barbarism: Kautsky 2; A. Marshall 29; Newcomb 9
bargaining: Mises 6
　of market: A. Smith 24
barter: A. Smith 7
　propensity to, apocryphal: K. Polanyi 1
baseness: F.A. Walker 7
bastard science: Ruskin 3
Batman: Boulding 3
beauty: Bernstein 2; Schumacher 1
　choice guided by: Wieser 1
beggars: McCulloch 3; Weber 1
behavior: Robinson 17
　individual: Hayek 10
　prediction of: Little 3
belief: Ely 3
　knowledge is: Leamer 3
beneficence:
　and money: Cicero 1
benefit: Bentham 9; Locke 6; Simonde de Sismondi 7
　common: Tolstoy 4
　duty of state to secure: Spencer 2
benevolence: Malthus 7, 12; Owen 4; Senior 4;
　　A. Smith 2, 3; Torrens 1
　economic man and: Boulding 4
bequests:
　taxes on, unjust: George 9
betrayal:
　money regarded as cause of: Mises 20
bias: Wright 3
billiards: Petty 5
biological analogies:
　in social science: Penrose 1
biologist: Mitchell 3
biology: Ely 3; Mises 27
birds: Leamer 1
Black Emancipation: Carlyle 1
blame: Croce 1
blood: Joplin 2; Senior 3; Whately 3
blue: Cannan 2; Jevons 6
board of directors:
　similar to communist committee of commissars:
　　Berle and Means 1
body natural: Tucker 2
body politic: McCulloch 13; Tucker 2
body social: Roscher 2
Bolsheviks: Seligman 6
Bolshevism: S. Perlman 1
bonus: Bastiat 8
books: Rees 1
boots: Schumpeter 2
borrowing: Bacon 5; Barbon 2; Locke 3
　charge of: Locke 1
bounty: Sumner 7
bourgeois: Engels 2; Hahn 6; Seligman 6
　family: Marx 12
　property: Marx 21

bourgeoisie: J.M. Keynes 12; Schumpeter 4
　absurdities of, regarding socialism: Lenin 2
　foundation of family: Marx 12
　natural institution: Marx 10
bowles: Petty 5
bread: Shaw 2
　not brought in the abstract: Carver 5
　one buys concrete: Carver 5
brewer: A. Smith 2
bribery:
　money blamed for: Mises 20
bridges: H. Simon 3; Simonde de Sismondi 3; Stamp 1
British Association for the Advancement of Science:
　Bonar 1
Buddhist monk: Mises 13
buildings: Luther 2; A. Smith 26
bullion: Joplin 1
　exportation of: Joplin 2
　preserves life of trade: Joplin 2
Bunyan: George 4
burden: Simonde de Sismondi 4
bureaucrats: Greenspan 2; Rothbard 2
　statistics only form of economic knowledge:
　　Rothbard 1
bureaucracy: Goldsmith 1
business: Ely 2; A. Smith 23
　academic economics conflicts with ordinary usage
　　of: Fisher 5
　and capitalism synonymous: Heilbroner 2
　and credit: Bagehot 2
　becomes unprofitable in depression: Fisher 4
　class: S. Perlman 1
　clothed with public interest: Taft 2
　common word for daily operation of capitalism:
　　Heilbroner 2
　dynamo of capitalist system: Heilbroner 3
　economic historians exalted rationality to be
　　sovereign rule of: Dobb 1
　failure, consequence of depression: Fisher 4
　firm: H. Simon 7
　forecasting, discredited: Cassel 1
　government interference in: Mises 12
　history of capitalism and: Heilbroner 3
　interests the whole mind: Bagehot 2
　joint-stock: Hobson 2
　laissez-faire served interest of: Robinson 16
　men playing game of: Knight 3
　more agreeable than pleasure: Bagehot 2
　owner of is industrial despot: Tuttle 1
　people: J. Simon 2
　people understand own, better than does
　　government: J.S. Mill 2
　practitioners of: Hobson 8
　shifted from competitive production to withholding
　　of efficiency: Veblen 1
　transmission of management of, passes not without
　　injury: Carnegie 3
business cycles: Leontief 3; Solow 2
　as tangle of coincidence and contradiction: Fisher 1
　like beat of heart, of the essence of organism:
　　Schumpeter 1

business cycles (*cont.*):
  mean neither more nor less than analyzing economic process of capitalist era: Schumpeter 1
  not, like tonsils, separable things: Schumpeter 1
businessmen: Mosca 1; Schumpeter 10
busybody:
  more dreaded than tyrant: Bowen 5
butcher: A. Smith 2

Cairnes, John E.: Veblen 5
cake: Ruskin 10
calculation: Boulding 2, 6; Hoxie 3
calculus: Leontief 4; Peirce 2; Walras 4; Wiener 2
  application to political economy: Stevenson 3
  economic: Goodrich 1
Calcutta: Luther 3
can openers: Hendry 3
canals: Simonde de Sismondi 3, 7; Southey 2
Canary Islands: Bacon 2
cannonball: J.B. Clark 4
capital: McCulloch 2; Morrow 2; Moore 1; Patten 1; Price 3; Proudhon 5; Ricardo 2, 13; Scrope 5; Seligman 3; Shaw 1; Simonde de Sismondi 2; A. Smith 10, 16; Tuttle 1; Wieser 7
  accumulation: Ayres 1; J.M. Keynes 2; Marx 5
  all taxes fall on: Ricardo 9
  and rate of wages: Marx 5
  and stationary state: J.S. Mill 4
  bourgeois family will vanish with vanishing of: Marx 12
  collective product: Marx 2
  constant, embodiment of labor power: Robinson 10
  contest between capitalist and wage laborer dates to origin of: Marx 3
  dictatorship of finance: Bukharin 2
  family based on: Marx 12
  freedom of, presupposes complete freedom of labor: Bagehot 3
  he who tampers with currency, panders to greedy: Webster 1
  in support of domestic industry: A. Smith 21
  labor produces for self-expansion of: Marx 4
  man most versatile form of: Fisher 2
  material embodiment of: Marx 3
  object only ours when it exists as: Marx 21
  social power: Marx 2
  socialism does not seek to abolish: Ely 7
  socialism movement of class antagonism against owners of: Carver 7
  taxes on: Ricardo 10, 13
  taxes take from, its just reward: George 11
  tempted from trade to trade by prospect of high profits: Bagehot 4
  transformation of labor into: Marx 5
  where men unite in owning of, form of socialism: J.B. Clark 8
  wise employment of: Ely 1
capital theory:
  and Cicero: Phelps 1

capitalism: Ayres 1, 2; Dobb 1; Engels 4; Kalecki 1; Kantorovich 1; Mises 14; Schumpeter 1, 2; Sweezy 3
  allows social universe to unfold as if beyond human interference: Heilbroner 5
  anarchic character of: Heilbroner 4
  and business synonymous: Heilbroner 2
  and family: Marx 13
  and full employment: Kalecki 2
  and government: Shaw 1
  based on self-interest and self-esteem: Greenspan 2
  best way to destroy, debauch currency: J.M. Keynes 12
  breakdown of: Heilbroner 4
  breaks through every barrier: Shaw 2
  business is dynamo of: Heilbroner 3
  by nature, a form or method of economic change: Schumpeter 3
  can be made more efficient than any alternative: J.M. Keynes 1
  cannot function under socialist government: Lange 2
  Communist Manifesto enthusiastic eulogy of: Lange 1
  communists out to destroy: Simons 7
  compared to balloon: Lange 5
  contradictions of, will cause it to explode: Bukharin 1
  convulsions of, are expression of contradictions: Bukharin 1
  credit system antithesis of: Hilferding 1
  cultural and moral justification of: Bell 1
  cultural contradiction of: Bell 1
  defects in: Webb and Webb 2
  difference between socialism and: Kautsky 4
  disparities in: Webb and Webb 2
  evolution of into socialism: Shaw 7
  first mode of economy with weapon of propaganda: Luxemburg 1
  flexibility of: Scitovsky 1
  form of life: Georgescu-Roegen 1
  free, has lost innocence: Stolper 2
  freedom in socialist society would require men be free to advocate: Friedman 1
  fundamental wisdom of: Stolper 3
  handles everybody according to contribution to well-being of fellow-men: Mises 5
  has been carrier of greatest economic progress: Lange 1
  historian's term: Heilbroner 2
  history of, continuing struggle between business and nonbusiness: Heilbroner 3
  identical with pursuit of profit: Weber 1
  improved standard of living: Mises 4
  impulse to acquisition has nothing to do with: Weber 1
  in many ways extremely objectionable: J.M. Keynes 1
  integrity and trustworthiness cardinal virtues of: Greenspan 2
  laissez-faire served interest of: Robinson 16
  managerial: Robinson 1

capitalism (cont.):
  Marxist economics is economics of: Vickrey 2
  Marxists maintain productive forces of powerful enough to eliminate poverty: Sweezy 1
  meaning of: Shaw 1
  merits of: Scitovsky 1
  must break down: Luxemburg 1
  never can be stationary: Schumpeter 3
  no social system more beneficial than: Mises 4
  not attractive form of social organization: Scitovsky 1
  obsolete as classically understood: Berle 1
  only social system based on recognition of individual rights: Rand 1
  only system fundamentally opposed to war: Rand 1
  opposed to socialism: Shaw 6
  order promised by: Stolper 1
  pacifism and international morality products of: Schumpeter 4
  prepares the ranks of its own grave-diggers: Bukharin 2
  produces widespread penury: Webb and Webb 1
  product of historical forces: Heilbroner 1
  progress of, retarded: Ayres 2
  prospers in environment of self-interest and non-self-interest: Stiglitz 1
  rationalistic and anti-heroic: Schumpeter 4
  religion of: Tawney 1
  so-called failure of, a failure of political state: Simons 1
  social arrangement: Heilbroner 1
  socialism and: Lange 7
  socialism needs to learn lesson of: Lenin 3
  socialism not alternative to: Mises 27
  sternness of: Mises 5
  strives to become universal: Luxemburg 1
  structure of: Bukharin 3
  tendency towards among well-to-do peasants: Mao 1
  tends to engulf entire globe: Luxemburg 1
  term belongs in museum of 19th century thought and culture: Berle 1
  unable to exist by itself: Luxemburg 1
  unrestricted, as completely antiquated as saurians: J.B. Clark 2
capitalist(s): Ayres 1; Bernstein 1; Hayek 20; Lewis 1
  always living on product of past labor: Fisher 3
  as human vehicle of capital accumulation: Ayres 1
  contest between wage laborer and: Marx 3
  convulsions of, are expression of contradictions: Bukharin 1
  farmers would join, in defense of private property: S. Perlman 1
  necessarily takes into consideration all advantages one occupation possesses over another: Ricardo 1
  requires social status in production: Marx 2
  socialism seeks to abolish: Ely 7
  wisdom or stupidity of: Stolper 3
capitalist enterprise:
  evolution of: Hobson 2
capitalist ethic: Kalecki 1

capitalist production: Kantorovich 1
  law of: Marx 4
  necessity for: Marx 11
  production of surplus value: Marx 4
capitalistic relation:
  reproduction of: Marx 6
caprice: Syme 2
Carlyle, Thomas: A. Marshall 23; Pigou 3
cartels:
  result from aid of state: Jaffé 1
casuists: Steuart-Denham 3
catallactics: Merivale 1; Mises 11
  economics larger than: Ingram 1
  Political Economy called: Bowen 3
Catholic:
  no one can be good, and be true socialist: Pius XI 1
  school of political economy: Walras 4
Catholicism: Pius XI 1
cattle: Wayland 6
causation: F.A. Walker 7
cause and effect: A. Marshall 21
cauterizations: Hale 1
celestial bodies: T.W. Schultz 1
cellars: Sedgwick 5
Central Africa: Lenin 3
Central Asia: Ross 2
central bank: Meek 1
centralization:
  idea of, appalls most people: Hayek 5
ceteris paribus: J.S. Mill 20
chance: Sumner 7
chaos: Clower 5
character:
  demoralization of: Webb and Webb 3
  economic activity agency for formation of: Knight 3
charisma: Mises 28
charity: Friedman 9; Laveleye 3; A. Marshall 27; Mises 22; Ricardo 7; Senior 4
  men ought not to be left to: Hobbes 1
  no true, except that which will help others help themselves: Carnegie 1
  support of: J.S. Mill 8
charlatanism: Sumner 2
chemical phenomena: Seligman 5
chemists: Marx 25; Menger 1
chemistry: Menger 1; Mises 27; Roscher 3; Seligman 5; Spencer 3
chess:
  disputes about method of are useless: Pareto 8
  economics like: H. Simon 7
chicanery: McCulloch 9
child, saw king who had no clothes: Duesenberry 1
children: J.B. Clark 7; Hale 1; Jefferson 3; J.M. Keynes 15; Malthus 7; Marx 13; Senior 4; Yarranton 1
  and poor laws: Ricardo 5
  mortality in: Aristotle 2
chivalry: Samuelson 4; Webb and Webb 3
  age of, is gone: Burke 1
choice: Ross 1; F.A. Walker 7
  act of a particular person: Shackle 4
  algebra of: Dobb 2

choice (cont.):
  by taxation, government interferes with free: Fetter 5
  etherealized objects of: Dobb 4
  exchange is: Shackle 4
  guided by morality, beauty, hygiene, good taste: Wieser 1
  illusory: Lawson 1
  law of: Knight 1
  necessity and power of: Hayek 28
chrematistics: Merivale 1
Christian humanitarianism: Webb and Webb 6
Christianity:
  plea of, is justice: Knight 2
  socialism irreconcilable with: Pius XI 1
church: Morrow 2; Shaw 7; Tolstoy 4
  holds right of property and ownership inviolate: Leo XIII 1
  recognizes inequality among men: Leo XIII 1
Church of Christ: Tawney 1
Church of England: Shaw 7
church wardens: Malthus 5
chrysology: Merivale 1
Cicero: Phelps 1
cities:
  socialism brings about disappearance of: Seligman 7
civil society: Shaw 1
  property true foundation of: Rousseau 3
  real founder of: Rousseau 2
civil war: S. Perlman 1
civilization: Knight 3; A. Marshall 33; Mises 1; Tawney 4; Webb 4
  dare not trust terms of exchange to tribal custom in: J.M. Clark 1
  destinies of, safer when entrusted to common sense of people: Carver 4
  growth of, rests on individuals making use of accidents encountered: Hayek 24
  progress arrested by private monopoly: Bryan 2
  progress of: George 1
  socialism and: Rogers 1
  socialism brings about disappearance of: Seligman 7
  would be retarded if not for rich: Wright 4
class: Webb and Webb 8
  business: S. Perlman 1
  socialism abolishes: Lenin 2
class antagonism: Fisher 13; Marx 22
class consciousness:
  socialism fails when fails to include majority: Carver 7
  socialism succeeds when becomes strong enough: Carver 7
class war:
  socialism red flag of: Fisher 13
classroom: Kaldor 2
cleanliness: Ricardo 1
clergy: Stigler 11
cloth: Schumpeter 2
clothes: Luther 2
coachmen: Weber 1
coal mines: J.M. Keynes 10

coercion: Lenin 1; Rand 3; Rothbard 10, 11, 12
  government and: Mises 17
coin:
  gold and silver, done away with: Bowen 7
  value of: Joplin 2
collective action: Atkinson 1
  control, liberation, and expansion of individual action: Commons 6
  restrictions in law upon, inconsistent with collective bargaining: Commons and Andrews 4
collective bargaining: Tuttle 1
  bargaining at point of a gun: Mises 6
  dictate forced upon employer: Mises 6
  in interest of public that labor be free to: Commons and Andrews 3
  not a market transaction: Mises 6
  produces institutional unemployment: Mises 6
  pseudo: Commons and Andrews 3
  restrictions in law upon collective action inconsistent with: Commons and Andrews 4
collectivism:
  extreme form of governmental centralization: Simons 3
  when intellectuals reject: Friedman 21
college professors:
  political economy cannot be safely left to: George 1
college students: Rees 1
combinations: Spencer 1
comfort: J.S. Mill 21; Peirce 1; Scrope 3; W.H. Smith 2; Spencer 3
  arises from labor of poor: Mandeville 4
  in virtuous world, no one would derive larger share of: A. Marshall 2
  of wealthy and middle class: Usher 4
  original condition of: Mackay 4
commerce: Berkeley 3; Hume 1; Jevons 5; Joplin 1; Ricardo 2; Rousseau 1; Simonde de Sismondi 3; W.H. Smith 2; Turgot 1; Wright 2
  money hypothetical or abstract medium of exchange in all larger transactions of: Bowen 7
  money not subject of: Hume 4
  regulation of: A. Smith 19
  success in requires stamina: Schumpeter 4
  vicissitudes of: Senior 5
  when government protect, acts with precipitation: Simonde de Sismondi 3
commissars:
  committee of, similar to corporate board of directors: Berle and Means 1
commodities: Bowen 6; Carey 4; Joplin 1; More 1; D. North 2; A. Smith 25
  adulterate: Petty 2
  and money: Marx 17
  exchangeable value of: Ricardo 12
  labor as positive and negative: Pantaleoni 2
  labor converted into: Marx 18
  money embased to purchase more: Petty 1
  money expresses magnitude of value in other: Marx 19
  money instrument to facilitate exchange of: Hume 4
  money is universal: Locke 3

money representation of: Hume 5
move not by themselves but by men: Boulding 5
required by exchange: Boulding 5
smuggled: McCulloch 9
common carriers: Taft 2
common man: Mises 18
common sense: Clower 2; Edgeworth 5; W.H. Smith 1; Veblen 3
half-baked economists studied just enough to lose: Carver 4
commons: Locke 6
commonwealth: Harrington 2
every man owes his defense to: Hobbes 2
men ought to be provided for by laws of: Hobbes 1
communal action: Hayek 2
communal ends: Wicksteed 2
communication: Simonde de Sismondi 3
cheapening of, alters action of forces tending to localize industries: A. Marshall 32
communism: Bowen 1; Berle and Means 1; Commons 5; J.N. Keynes 3; Laveleye 2; Rostow 2; Seligman 6; Tawney 7
associations durable and prosperous: J.S. Mill 19
deprives no man of power to appropriate products of society: Marx 9
disease of the body social: Roscher 2
distinguishing feature of, abolition of bourgeois property: Marx 22
exploitation of strong by weak: Proudhon 2
inconvenience of: Proudhon 1
is inequality: Proudhon 2
is oppression and slavery: Proudhon 2
legislative: Mackay 1
makes mediocrity of talent and achievement equal to excellence: Proudhon 2
morally sound: Hobson 3
necessary pattern of immediate future: Marx 8
need for money reduced by: Shaw 3
negation of negation: Marx 8
not goal of human development: Marx 8
not inconsistent exaggeration of principle of equality: Roscher 1
obsolete as classically understood: Berle 1
opposed to free exercise of faculties: Proudhon 2
plea of, is justice: Knight 2
positive transcendence of private property: Marx 7
practicable: Hobson 3
principle 'From each according to his ability, to each according to his needs': Hobson 4
principles and schemes of turn upon human nature: Hobson 13
proposes to reform society by methods of violence: J.B. Clark 1
requires high standard of moral and intellectual education: J.S. Mill 18
return of man to himself: Marx 7
riddle of history solved: Marx 7
socialism passes into: Sumner 6
system under which people form habit of performing social duties: Lenin 1
term belongs in museum of 19th century thought and culture: Berle 1
theory of national, and religion: Phillips 1
when intellectuals reject: Friedman 21
communist(s):
little reason needed to confute: Bowen 1
out to destroy capitalism: Simons 7
thinks of community in terms of state: Berle and Means 1
unaware opulence and poverty are stimuli: Bowen 1
unionists like: Simons 7
Communist Manifesto (Marx): Lange 1
community: Frisch 2; J.M. Keynes 26; Mises 22; Newcomb 8; Senior 5; W.H. Smith 2; F.A. Walker 4; Wayland 5, 6; Webb 3; Webb and Webb 7, 9
academic economists apt to be carried off by bias of: Fisher 7
adds to wealth by creating wealth: Rae 2
claims right to prevent workers from selling excessive labor: Webb 1
communist thinks of, in terms of state: Berle and Means 1
desire of members: Rae 4
detrimental effect of wealth on: Whately 5
good of: Hobson 3
happiness of: Bentham 9
if individuals behave as members of, individual interests given large scope: J.M. Clark 7
income of: J.M. Keynes 10
of goods: Aquinas 1; Leo XIII 1
of land: Locke 2
over-taxation capable of ruining most industrious: J.S. Mill 23
people poverty-stricken when income falls behind that of: Galbraith 7
poverty injurious to: Hobson 10
profit for: Kautsky 4
socialists propose using state to fashion: H. Fawcett 5
state is extended: Wicksteed 2
supremacy of: J.M. Clark 7
welfare of: J.M. Clark 7
worlds is one: Phillips 1
community of goods: Aquinas 1
contrary to natural right: Leo XIII 5
main tenet of socialism: Leo XIII 5
must be rejected: Leo XIII 5
companies:
joint-stock: Hobson 2
compass: H. Schultz 3
Sperry gyroscopic: H. Schultz 4
compensation: Simonde de Sismondi 2
competition: Bowen 3; J.B. Clark 8; Friedman 9; A. Smith 16; Tawney 2
affords ideal condition for distribution of wealth: F.A. Walker 1
and business enterprise: Veblen 1
and cooperation: A. Marshall 1, 2
and interests of persons: W. Thompson 1
and socialism: Lange 6

competition (*cont.*):
   arguments in favor of: Hayek 3
   cut-throat: Greenspan 1
   desirable under socialism: J.S. Mill 15
   equity of: Newcomb 1
   even best forms of, are relatively evil: A. Marshall 2
   every extension of, is good: J.S. Mill 13
   every restriction of, an evil: J.S. Mill 13
   exists because of the state: Jaffé 1
   for benefit of laborers: J.S. Mill 13
   free, because controlled by justice and law: J.B. Clark 5
   free individual: W. Thompson 2
   great equalizer: Lerner 2
   ideal of political economy, not unrestricted: J.B. Clark 5
   implies selfish motives: J.B. Clark 2
   interest of dealers to narrow: A. Smith 19
   internecine: Webb 3
   leading spring of action: W. Thompson 1
   main safeguard against exploitation: J.M. Clark 1
   mechanism is one of fooling entrepreneurs: Lange 3
   necessary stimulus: J.S. Mill 13
   of labor and *for* labor: J.S. Mill 13
   out of place in virtuous world: A. Marshall 2
   peculiar system: Lange 3
   perfect: *see* perfect competition
   pleasures of: W. Thompson 1
   principle of, and political economy: J.S. Mill 1
   requires pursuit of maximum profit: Lange 3
   socialism disparages: F.A .Walker 10
   socialism opens way for: Lenin 2
   socialists charge upon all economical evils: J.S. Mill 13
   source of high wages: J.S. Mill 13
   tends to reduce to a minimum the equivalent men charge for services: Newcomb 1
   to be protected against, is to be protected in idleness: J.S. Mill 13
   to destroy would be to kill society: Proudhon 3
   unregulated, forces economic life to level of worst: Ely 2
   vital force which animates collective being: Proudhon 3
   wages should be left to: Ricardo 6
   when free, tendency is to equalize prices: J.S. Mill 15
   wherever is not, monopoly is: J.S. Mill 13
   works simple miracle: J.M. Clark 1
competitive model:
   mode of thinking underlying: Leibenstein 1
compilations:
   of economic historians, cannot be recommended: Sombart 1
complexity: Sumner 2
compulsion: Spencer 2; W. Thompson 1
   government and: Mises 17
computation: H. Simon 7
conclusions: Vickrey 1
   non-testable: Archibald 1

conduct: Bowen 4; Malthus 11; Mises 3
   intelligence in service of greed ensures most enlightened: Peirce 1
   political economy and: A. Marshall 4
   private: Hobson 5
confidence:
   firms compete for: Hodgson 1
confiscation: Holmes 6; Rothbard 10
   by government of wealth through inflation: J.M. Keynes 12
   effected by taxation: Greenspan 6
conflict:
   between man and nature: Marx 7
   resolution of: Marx 7
confusion: J.S. Mill 26
congestion: Krugman 2
conscience: Mises 3; Proudhon 2
consciousness: Jones 2
   wealth as state of: Florence 2
   welfare includes states of: Pigou 1
consequences: Hoxie 3
conservation:
   of society: Ingram 2
conservatism: Ely 6
conservatives:
   and sanctity of property: Tawney 6
constable:
   needed to enforce contracts: Samuelson 4
   needed to protect property rights: Samuelson 4
constant returns:
   must always remain a mathematical point: Clapham 1
constitutions: Holmes 1, 4
   not intended to embody particular economic theory: Holmes 2
consumer:
   greed of businessman protector of: Greenspan 4
consumer protection: Greenspan 3
consumers: Destutt Tracy 1; Mises 17, 32; A. Smith 4
   advantage of: Simonde de Sismondi 3
   welfare of, goal of antitrust law: Bork 1
consumption: Babbage 1; Barbon 8; Cantillon 2; Hobbes 2; Lerner 4; A. Marshall 2, 33; Marx 1; Molinari 1; Patten 1; Robertson 1; Ross 1; Roscher 4; A. Smith 18; Sumner 7; Wieser 1
   and population and income: J. Simon 1
   best taxes levied on: Hume 8
   cause of: Barbon 7
   diminished by amount of tax: Ricardo 9
   effect of taxation on: Say 5
   fundamental psychological law of: J.M.Keynes 3
   lower-class: Knight 7
   political economy as science of: Macleod 1
   political economy science of laws which regulate: McCulloch 1
   sole end and purpose of production: A. Smith 4
   taxes on, expensive in levying: Hume 8
   taxes on, produce sobriety and frugality: Hume 8
   unproductive: Ricardo 9

contract: Edgeworth 1; Hayek 18; Law 1; Malthus 10;
    Newcomb 9; Rousseau 3; Shaw 1; Stiglitz 1;
    Wayland 5
  and expectation: Steuart-Denham 1
  constable needed to enforce: Samuelson 4
  enforcement: Friedman 9
  freedom of: Tawney 2
  freedom of, opposed to state control: Cairnes 3
  intelligence in service of greed ensures fairest:
    Peirce 1
  liberty to: Holmes 1
  provides rationale for voluntary social relationships:
    Gauthier 1
contractarian:
  economic man as radical: Gauthier 1
contributions:
  no modern state able to support itself through
    voluntary: Olson 1
control: J.M. Keynes 27; Rand 3
controversy: J.N. Keynes 2; Wright 1
convenience: Hume 2; A. Smith 26
  trade and: Coke 4
conventions: Sraffa 1
cooperation: Gauthier 2; Mises 21, 27; Tawney 5
  actions which bring about: Mises 31
  aim of, to remove selfishness: A. Marshall 1
  under division of labor: Mises 33
cooperative movement: Mao 1
coordination: Lindbeck 2
  spontaneous: Buchanan 3
corn: Ricardo 2
corporations: J.B. Clark 8; Robinson 1; Simons 2
  as artificial being: J. Marshall 1
  board of directors, similar to communist committee
    of commissars: Berle and Means 1
  exists only in contemplation of law: J. Marshall 1
  finance: Veblen 1
corruption:
  causes of: Rousseau 1
  government: Wayland 3
  taxation begets: George 11
cost: Hobson 6
  commercial condition: Ruskin 14
  quantity of labor required to produce something:
    Ruskin 14
cost of production:
  value governed by: A. Marshall 34
cotton: Schumpeter 2
Council of Economic Advisors: McCloskey 1
counterfeiting:
  inflation as legal: Fisher 9
countryside: Rostow 1
coup d'état: S. Perlman 1
courage: F.A. Walker 11
courts: Mises 6
covetousness: Locke 6
  a vice prejudicial both to man and to trade: Barbon 6
cowardice: F.A. Walker 7
craft unions: *see* unions
crafts: Rousseau 1
craps: Mayer 2

cravings: Malthus 11
Creator: John XXIII 1
credit: Bagehot 1; D. North 2
  comes many times unfought for: D'Avenant 1
  depends on hope and fear: D'Avenant 1
  government responsibility for: Stolper 2
  hangs upon opinion: D'Avenant 1
  interest-free: Bastiat 8
  is a value raised by opinion: Barbon 5
  nothing more fantastical than: D'Avenant 1
  often goes away without reason: D'Avenant 1
  prosperity of working classes has being in
    established: Webster 2
  reasonable expectation that others make good:
    Steuart-Denham 1
  useful to public as it promotes industry: Berkeley 2
  when lost, hard to recover: D'Avenant 1
  without producing labor and industry, is gaming:
    Berkeley 2
credit system:
  adapted to capitalist society: Hilferding 1
  antithesis of capitalism: Hilferding 1
  fraudulent kind of socialism: Hilferding 1
  has source in socialism: Hilferding 1
crime: McCulloch 4; Rousseau 2; Sumner 7; Webb and
    Webb 3, 6
  and poverty: Aristotle 2
criminals: Laughlin 8; Rothbard 13
  must bear brunt of defects: Chamberlain 1
criticism: J.M. Keynes 21; Robinson 16
crusaders: Weber 1
Crusoe, Robinson: Marx 14; Mises 13; Sweezy 2
culinary art:
  disputes about method of are useless: Pareto 8
cultural history: Weber 1
culture: J.M. Clark 1; Ruskin 4; Taylor 2
  socialism brings about disappearance of: Seligman 7
cupboard: Ruskin 10
currency: Sedgwick 1
  best way to destroy capitalism is to debauch: J.M.
    Keynes 12
  disordered, one of greatest of all political evils:
    Webster 1
  he who tampers with, robs labor of its bread:
    Webster 2
  taxation by depreciation of: J.M. Keynes 13
  under inflation, real value of fluctuates:
    J.M. Keynes 12
current: Schumpeter 9
custom: J.S. Mill 13; A. Smith 8; Steuart-Denham 2
  social, may be discarded: J.M. Keynes 2
  tribal, terms of exchange of, not trusted in
    sophisticated civilization: J.M. Clark 1
customer satisfaction: Hodgson 1
cycle: Robertson 1
Czar: Ross 2

dainties: Sedgwick 5
data: Shackle 5; Sims 1
  analysis: Leamer 1
  blade of scissors: H. Simon 5

data (*cont.*):
  large public bank: Klein 1
  quantitative numerical: Klein 2
data mining: Bronfenbrenner 1
David: A. Marshall 4
dealers:
  interest of to widen market and narrow competition: A. Smith 19
death: J.S. Mill 8; Webb and Webb 3
debt: Hobbes 2; Locke 3; Sedgwick 1; Simonde de Sismondi 4
  money standard of: Sraffa 1
decathlon: McCloskey 1
deceit:
  economics has aim of maintaining: Tolstoy 2
decency: Sowell 1
deception: A. Smith 19
  money regarded as cause of: Mises 20
decision making:
  collective: Buchanan 6
decision theorists: Rescher 1
decision theory:
  an empty principle: Boulding 1
  large mathematical apparatus: Boulding 1
deduction: Hutchison 1; Leslie 3, 4, 5; H. Simon 2
Deductive school of political economy: Walras 4
defectives: Webb and Webb 4
defense: Scrope 9; Shaw 1
definitions: Myrdal 1; Samuelson 3; W.H. Smith 3; Viner 4; Walras 2
  conditions to satisfy: Sidgwick 1
  economic laws of socialism consist of: Meek 2
  in economics: Patten 2; Wicksell 3; Wicksteed 1
  in political economy: Atwater 1; Bagehot 9; Southey 1
  science unable at beginning to provide: Eucken 1
  study of, uninteresting: Longfield 3
deflation: Boulding 8
deformation: Marx 1
degeneracy: Tolstoy 3
degradation:
  of lower classes: Say 3
delight:
  true cause of value and price: Vaughan 1
demand: Solow 5; Wieser 7
  and value: law 2
  cuts in government expenditure reduce: Eatwell 4
  distribution of wealth regulates nature and extent of: Maitland 4
  effectual: A. Smith 25
  elasticity of: Clapham 1
demand curve: Solow 3
democracy:
  extends sphere of freedom: Tocqueville 1
  monopoly is enemy of: Simons 2
  planning as pillar of: Frisch 2
dentists:
  economists on level with: J.M. Keynes 5
depopulation: Ricardo 13
depression:
  business failures and widespread unemployment consequences of: Fisher 4
  called Private Profits disease: Fisher 4
  condition in which business becomes unprofitable: Fisher 4
  form of universal poverty: Fisher 4
desert: Berkeley 4; J.M. Keynes 12
design:
  establishments not result of human: Ferguson 2
desire: George 3; Malthus 11; Robinson 15
  non-economic: Taylor 1
  objects of: Torrens 2
despair: McCulloch 10, 11
desperation:
  too little money causes: Mandeville 3
despoilers:
  shut out of heaven: Leo XIII 1
despotism:
  taxation that is variable, shifting, dependent on personal whim is: Fetter 6
destiny: Sumner 7
destitution: J.S. Mill 6; Owen 4; Webb and Webb 6, 7
  must be relieved: Ellis 1
  unrelieved, is intolerable: Ellis 1
determinacy:
  without, there is no economics: Tinbergen 1
devastation: Coke 3
developing countries: *see* Third World
devil incarnate: Friedman 12
devotion: Laveleye 3
dexterity: A. Smith 5
diamonds: Marx 25
  value of: Law 2
  value of, not due to labor: J.B. Clark 12
difference equations: M. Perlman 2
digestion:
  and positive economics: Pareto 3
dignity: Hutcheson 1; John XXIII 2
diligence: Senior 5
dinner: A. Smith 2
discernment:
  socialists suppose men not endowed with: Bastiat 10
discipline: Hale 1; Schumpeter 11
discovery: Ayres 2; Bowen 7; Roscher 3; Simonde de Sismondi 3
  result of spontaneous activities of citizens: Spencer 3
  state not responsible for: Spencer 3
discrimination: Mises 25
discussion:
  freedom of: Simons 2
disease: Roscher 2; A. Smith 20; Webb and Webb 3; Whately 3
dishonesty: George 6
dismal science: Carlyle 1; Mises 8; Nathan 2
dispiritedness:
  too little money causes: Mandeville 3
distress: Eden 1
  poor laws designed to remedy: Malthus 5
  state and relief of: A. Marshall 27
distribution: Nicholson 3; Sedgwick 5; W.H. Smith 2
  and growth: Lewis 1

function of money system to furnish information necessary to direct: Douglas 1
justice in: Carver 8
money part of capital required for: Brougham 1
of necessaries of life: A. Smith 13
political economy as science of: Macleod 1
political economy science of laws which regulate: McCulloch 1
distribution of income: *see* income distribution
distribution of wealth: *see* wealth distribution
divines: Steuart-Denham 3
division of labor: Jevons 2; Maitland 1; Mises 17; Morrow 2; K. Polanyi 1; Ross 1; A. Smith 5, 6, 8
  market is man-made mode of acting under: Mises 1
  not effect of human wisdom: A. Smith 7
  society is: Mises 31
  ultimate and sole source of man's success in struggle for survival: Mises 33
doctrine: Senior 3
dogma: Rescher 1
  projects of socialists based on: Sumner 7
  socialism as religious: Stolper 4
  universal part of political economy has no: A. Marshall 5
dogmatism:
  model user must avoid: Malinvaud 1
dogs: Stone 1
dollar:
  silver content of: Wayland 5
dominion: Harrington 1
Don Quixote: Samuelson 4
double-talk: Ayres 7
double-vision: Ayres 7
dreamers: A. Marshall 2
dreams:
  socialism powerful in region of: Le Bon 1
dress: A. Smith 26
drink: Luther 2; Sedgwick 5
drunkards:
  must bear brunt of defects: Chamberlain 1
dummy: Machlup 1
duties: F.A. Walker 8
  customs and excises: A. Smith 18
  import: Erasmus 5
  reduction of on smuggled commodities reduces smuggling: McCulloch 9
duty: J.S. Mill 18; Newcomb 8; Robinson 5; A. Smith 11; Sumner 4
  and political economy: A. Marshall 4
  in virtuous world, men think only of: A. Marshall 2
  law of: Proudhon 2
  of every man, to relieve fellow creatures in distress: Eden 1
  political economy cannot set forth positive rules of: Cunningham 5

earth:
  common to all: Locke 4
  fruits of: Rousseau 2
  products of, are effects of labor: Locke 2
earthquake: Syme 2

ease: Ricardo 1
eating:
  as beneficial as trade: Bentham 4
  no politician ever thought of giving bounties upon: Bentham 4
econometricians:
  bound to be frustrated: Koopmans 1
  economists are by instinct: Schumpeter 10
  not primarily engaged in measuring heights of economists: Hendry 1
  pitifully short of information: Klein 2
  positive help to economics: Hendry 3
  public data bank for: Klein 1
  recommendations of, determined by philosophic attitudes: Basmann 1
  tend to look where light is: Hendry 3
  uncertain of conclusions: Malinvaud 1
  use proxy for risk and dummy for sex: Machlup 1
econometrics: Hendry 1; Mayer 1, 2
  aims of: Frisch 1
  and economics: Frisch 1
  economic theory will only progress to the extent it can transform itself into: Harrod 1
  forecasting main criterion of success: Koopmans 1
  fundamental problem of: Leamer 2
  main purpose of model construction: Koopmans 2
  models: Hahn 3; Solow 1
  prestige of: Bauer and Walters 1
  sole beneficiary from government manipulation of economy: Hendry 2
  specialized needs of: Klein 1
economic:
  economic things can best be described as: Cannan 2
  useful word in everyday conversation: Cannan 1
economic action:
  teleological: Veblen 2
economic activity:
  agency for want- and character-formation: Knight 3
  competitive sport: Knight 3
  economics deals with social organization of: Knight 10
  field of creative self-expression: Knight 3
  free enterprise predominant method of social organization of: Knight 10
  means of want-satisfaction: Knight 3
  price system predominant method of social organization of: Knight 10
  subject matter of economics: Carver 2
economic advisers: Bronfenbrenner 2
economic aims: Tawney 4
economic assumptions: Carey 1
economic behavior: T.W. Schultz 1; H. Simon 1
  more complex than our thoughts about it: T.W. Schultz 3
economic botany: Ross 1
economic change:
  capitalism is by nature form or method of: Schumpeter 3
economic controversy:
  thankless task: Edgeworth 3
economic criteria: Tawney 3

economic data:
　strengths and weaknesses of: McCloskey 1
economic development: Lange 4; Lewis 1; Wieser 2
　and socialism: Kautsky 2
economic ethic: Boulding 6
economic facts:
　words can be applied to, expressing approval or disapproval: Croce 1
economic freedom:
　and socialists: Hayek 28
　cannot be freedom from economic care: Hayek 28
　prerequisite of other freedoms: Hayek 28
economic growth: Koopmans 2; Rostow 1
　and distribution: Lewis 1
　and poverty: Robinson 2
　and profits: Lewis 1
　necessity of relief evidence of stunted: Mackay 3
　purpose of nationalization to achieve: Schumacher 2
economic historians:
　exalted rationality to be sovereign rule of business life: Dobb 1
　have extra gene: T.W. Schultz 2
　inadequate equipment of, responsible for valueless compilations: Sombart 1
　rely heavily on economic arithmetic: Goodrich 1
　will learn to use economic algebra and economic calculus: Goodrich 1
economic history: Mises 19
　and economic theory: Heckman 1
　as high-quality research: D.C. North 1
　contribution to knowledge of: Heckman 1
　crude collection and interpretation of facts part of: A. Marshall 9
　importance and necessity of: T.W. Schultz 1
　involves philosophy of life: Usher 1
　must be more than objective record of events: Usher 1
　perversion of: Cunningham 6
economic ideas:
　medieval: Tawney 4
　modern: Tawney 4
economic interests: Cannan 1
economic journals:
　filled with mathematical formulas: Leontief 5
economic knowledge:
　imagined as tapestry: M. Perlman 3
economic language:
　more comprehensive than standard economic theory: T.W. Schultz 3
economic laws: Lange 4; Mosca 1, 2
　depend on voluntary actions: J.B. Clark 3
　inflation engages hidden forces of: J.M. Keynes 12
　of socialism, consist either of definitions or platitudes: Meek 2
　reduce to a few trifling generalities: Proudhon 4
economic life: Taylor 2
　arbitrary and widespread control over: Friedman 6
　processes of: Mises 20
economic man: H. Simon 2
　carries liberalism to extreme: Gauthier 1
　count every cost and ask for every reward: Boulding 4
　economists suspicious of: Boulding 3
　freed from voluntary affection: Gauthier 2
　has no Freudian complexes: Boulding 3
　never afflicted with mad generosity or uncalculating love: Boulding 4
　new kind, constructed by behavioristic school: Carver 1
　no one in his senses would want his daughter to marry: Boulding 4
　radical contractarian: Gauthier 1
　result of over-emphasis of non-pecuniary motive: Carver 1
　result of under-emphasis of pecuniary motive: Carver 1
　society made up of, would be fantastic monstrosity and physical impossibility: Knight 4
　thinks of future as place to realize pleasure: Patten 1
economic method:
　no philosopher's stone in: Baumol 2
economic models: Akerlof 1
　cautious economist, has little scope beyond discussion of: Champernowne 1
economic motives: Bonar 2
economic nonsense: Carver 3
economic order: Tawney 3; Walras 4
economic organon: A. Marshall 6
economic phenomena: Robbins 1; Sumner 2
　interdependence of: Pareto 3
　not similar to physical phenomena: Cunningham 4
　not uniform, regular, or unchanging: Cunningham 4
　possess observable quantitative dimensions: Leontief 4
　stated in shape of mathematical formulae: Pareto 4
economic planning:
　as pillar of living democracy: Frisch 2
economic point of view: Cannan 1
economic policy: Aaron 1; Bacon 1; Friedman 6; Koopmans 2; Malinvaud 1
　acceptable: Little 1
　economists needed to say something about alternatives: Buchanan 2
　implication of new ideas: Krugman 1
　Murphy's Law of: Blinder 1
　simple truths in, are commonly ignored: Coase 1
economic principle(s): J.B. Clark 7; Wicksteed 3
　non-mechanical nature of: Croce 1
economic problem:
　legitimate to appeal to mathematics for solution of: Pareto 5
economic process: Klein 2
　struggle between men for possession of goods: Veblen 7
economic progress: Taylor 1
economic questions: Cannan 1
　concerns wealth and its enjoyment: Newcomb 3
economic reality: Eucken 1, 2
economic reform: Schmoller 1
economic relations: Wicksteed 3
　expressible by means of mathematical functions: Allen 1

economic rent: *see* rent, economic
economic sense: Carver 3
economic society: Dobb 4
economic student:
  education of: Laughlin 2
  intellectual ferment of: Laughlin 5
economic systems: Fisher 1
economic teaching: Ashley 1
  disesteem of economics due to inadequate: Hoxie 1
economic theorem:
  may be expressed in form of conclusion of syllogism: Pantaleoni 1
economic theorists: *see* economists
economic theory: *see* economics
economic tricks: Hendry 1
economic truths: J.N. Keynes 1
Economical Century: Peirce 1
economics: Aaron 1; Åkerman 1, 2; Alchian 2; Allen 1, 2; Ashley 1, 2; Ayres 1, 3, 4, 5, 6, 9; Boulding 2, 3, 4, 6, 7, 9, 10; Bowen 2, 3, 4; Frisch 1; Hobson 7; Mises 14; Pareto 2; M. Perlman 1; Rees 1; Robbins 1; Stigler 3; Walras 4; Wicksteed 3; Wieser 3; Wilson 1
  AEA failure at restricting entry into profession: Barro 1
  ability to judge relevance of, rarely associated with ability to understand advanced mathematics: Champernowne 2
  abstains from value judgments: Mises 9
  academic, conflicts with ordinary usage of business: Fisher 5
  advises politicians and businessmen: Schumpeter 10
  aim is discovery and verification of body of principles: Laughlin 1
  ambition of nearly every teacher of to put name to new formulation: C. Clark 1
  and economic history: Heckman 1
  and economizing man: Menger 1
  and mathematics: Hayek 9; A. Marshall 20; T. Thompson 1
  and new discoveries: H. Schultz 1
  and Occam's razor: Rothbard 4
  and policy: Krugman 1
  and social policy: Heckman 1
  and socialism: Le Bon 1
  any branch worth preserving if it contributes to useful knowledge: Heckman 2
  appears to be nonplused: Cunningham 9
  arguments in devoted to supporting doctrines: Robinson 7
  art founded on maxims of several sciences: Merivale 1
  as abstract science: Bagehot 6, 8
  as common sense: Samuelson 3
  as dismal science: Carlyle 1
  as empirical science, cannot yet offer indubitable conclusions: Leoni 1
  as metaphysics: Archibald 1
  as preserve of higher mathematicians: Boulding 10
  as science: Bailey 1; Basmann 1; Bowen 3, 4; Kaldor 1
  assumes men produce in order to consume: Knight 7
  at best in analyzing phenomena of past and present: Cunningham 9
  at home in craft unionism: De Leon 2
  attraction of writers on: A. Marshall 3
  basic problems of, simple: Johnson 1
  basis of social progress: Seligman 4
  bearing of on well-being has been overlooked: A. Marshall 12
  becomes applied mathematics or engineering: Buchanan 3
  becoming more formal: Hayek 9
  behavioristic school of: Carver 1
  bitter attacks on, by Carlyle and Ruskin: A. Marshall 23
  bludgeons reality: Shackle 2
  both creature and creator: Seligman 4
  branch of pure logic: Hayek 9
  branch of theology: Robinson 8
  branch of theory of human action: Mises 13
  calculus: Jevons 3
  can throw little light on socialist society of the future: Einstein 1
  cannot forecast future sufficiently to provide guidance: Cunningham 9
  casual observation in, created flabby science: Stigler 2
  central principle not economizing process: Buchanan 3
  central principle not maximization: Buchanan 3
  central weakness of modern, reluctant to produce unambiguously refutable theories: Blaug 1
  classical: Veblen 3
  clear thinking in regard to: Knight 9
  compared to meteorology: Bowen 4
  concerns itself with best means of satisfying given ends: Samuelson 2
  conflicts in: Wicksell 1
  confronted with theonomics: Boulding 6
  confused state of: Bauer 1
  consists of laws of wealth systematically deduced: Pantaleoni 1
  consists of number of different problems thrown together: Myrdal 1
  contemptuously dubbed mere utilitarian science: Hayek 8
  contributions to: Taylor 3
  criticism of recent tendencies in: Hayek 9
  critics urge abandonment of by economists: V. Smith 1
  deals with actions of real men: Mises 11
  deals with *homo agens*: Mises 7
  deals with problems of mankind: Commons 3
  deals with quantities: Jevons 6
  deals with psychological, physiological, and physical phenomena: Laughlin 1
  deals with social organization of economic activity: Knight 10
  definitions can have no place in, at outset: Eucken 1
  definitions in: Patten 2; Wicksell 3; Wicksteed 1
  department of social philosophy: Commons 2

economics (*cont.*):
- did not pursue knowledge for own sake: Hayek 8
- difficult to prove originality in: Fisher 8
- disciples have tendency to adopt conclusions and discard definitions: Wicksteed 1
- disesteem of, due to inadequate economic teaching: Hoxie 1
- dismal science: Carlyle 1; Mises 8; Nathan 2
- distinction between and other social sciences: Nicholson 1
- does not attempt to describe the actual in entirety: Wieser 4
- does not contend that man strives only after material wealth: Mises 7
- does not contribute to formal study of human learning: Boulding 7
- does not deal with imaginary *homo oeconomicus*: Mises 7
- does not direct legislation: Merivale 1
- does not have predestined mission to dispel mysteries of market: Posner 2
- driven to submit to demands of mathematics: Debreu 1
- easy subject at which few excel: J.M. Keynes 4
- econometrics aims to turn into science: Frisch 1
- economic activities subject matter of: Carver 2
- economic effects of: Robinson 5
- economists have no choice but to agree about: Durbin 1
- economists suppose students have background in: Clower 2
- engine for discovery of concrete truth: A. Marshall 5
- equilibrium: Kaldor 1
- expanding boundaries: Coase 2
- explanatory power of: Lawson 1
- exposure to political influences and intellectual fashion: Bauer 1
- facts in, capable of appraisement: Croce 1
- fails to see fact at root of all economic conditions: Tolstoy 1
- few men of intelligence recognize importance of: Hoxie 1
- field of, quite definite: Laughlin 1
- finds secret of universe in supply and demand: Carlyle 1
- first lesson, things often not what they seem: Samuelson 1
- first principle of, every agent actuated by self interest: Edgeworth 1
- function of, to advance knowledge: Florence 1
- fundamental ideas of, have come to afflict practitioners: Bauer and Walters 2
- further progress in, awaits psychologists: Davenport 1
- game where rules are subject to revision: Wiener 3
- generalizations lie in realm of useful things: J.M. Clark 5
- goal of, in complex system: Frisch 2
- good mathematical theorem dealing with economic hypotheses unlikely to be good: A. Marshall 22
- great antinomy is: Eucken 4
- happy science, not dismal science: Nathan 2
- has aim of maintaining superstition and deceit: Tolstoy 1
- has been conceded some of dignity and prestige of physical sciences: Hayek 11
- has become less informative because of mathematics: Bauer 5
- has become stagnant: Jevons 4
- has effect on law making: J.B. Clark 6
- has wealth for subject matter: A. Marshall 12
- hedonic premise of: Pantaleoni 1
- heterodoxy must be driven out of discussion: Ely 3
- higher function of, to hold out against nonsense: Solow 4
- historians of, rummage through writings of Marx: Haberler 1
- historical school darkened by mass of anecdotes: Croce 2
- history of, suggests we shall never reach perfectly definitive conclusions: Hansen 1
- hypotheses in, what we lack the least: H. Simon 4
- if choice all that it postulated, cannot provide more than algebra of choice: Dobb 2
- if determinacy not accepted, there is no: Tinbergen 1
- if science, one whose powers of prediction and control are limited: Deane 1
- if student of untrained in power to trace cause and effect, is not an economist: Laughlin 3
- ignores social context: Sweezy 2
- in concrete, does not command interest or respect: Hoxie 1
- indistinguishable from 'cargo-cult' science: Clower 6
- institutional: Commons 4, 5
- is social astronomy: Clower 5
- lack of statistical data in: Wicksell 2
- larger than catallactics: Ingram 1
- last word in, will be said after last work done in philosophy or psychology: Davenport 3
- laws: Leslie 5, 6; Veblen 5
- laws of, compared with laws of tides: A. Marshall 13
- like chess: H. Simon 7
- limps along with one foot in untested hypotheses and other in untestable slogans: Robinson 6
- literary: Klein 3; H. Schultz 4; Tinbergen 1
- literary writers on, interested in administrative problems: Knight 8
- little effort made to state assumptions of: Knight 8
- little regarded by practical men: Cunningham 10
- logic in, corrupted by opinions: Robinson 8
- long run in: Viner 3
- main function of: Solow 4
- makes for truth: Wicksteed 3
- many noneconomists do: Posner 1
- Marxian: Haberler 1
- Marxist is economics of capitalism: Vickrey 2
- mathematical: Allen 1, 2; Boulding 9, 10; Dorfman 1; Klein 3; Leontief 3, 4, 5; Morgenstern 1; Pareto 3; T.W. Schultz 3; Tinbergen 1

mathematical, acquired attitudes of empirical sciences: Leontief 2
mathematical, cannot be deciphered by economists without proper key: Debreu 2
mathematical laws of gravitation have no application to: Ayres 4
mathematical methods in, nearly always waste of time: A. Marshall 21
mathematical, suffers misapprehension of proper use of mathematics: Wiener 1
mathematicians have revived dignity in, of abstract analysis: Croce 2
mathematics cannot be worse than prose in: Samuelson 9
mathematics gin in martini of: Solow 5
mathematics has not purged of irrelevance: Mayer 5
mathematics in: A. Marshall 22; Morgenstern 2; Samuelson 8; Wicksell 2, 3; Wieser 2; Zeuthen 1
mathematics in, should not be condemned: Launhardt 1
mathematics neither necessary nor sufficient condition for career in: Samuelson 10
may be disintegrating into departments: Coats 1
may lose humanistic and empirical quality: Boulding 10
methodology embodied in neoclassical: Boland 1
methodology of: Wieser 4
methods to maintain intellectual discipline in, similar to Marines: Leontief 1
mistakenly believed to have no concern for any but selfish motives: A. Marshall 23
money center around which clusters: A. Marshall 23
money root of: Mitchell 1
monopoly has become popular subject in: Stigler 11
monopoly not a branch of: Stigler 10
more like art or philosophy than science: Hicks 3
most professors of, have nebulous idea of subject matter: Luxemburg 2
most quantitative of all sciences: Schumpeter 9
moving into other disciplines: Coase 2
much misunderstanding as to scope of: A. Marshall 7
must be mathematical: Jevons 6
must do as in other scientific investigations: Newcomb 2
must keep abreast of modern thought: Davenport 2
must maintain independence from other sciences: Eucken 4
must proceed from individual and historical nature of subject: Eucken 6
must take place in hierarchy of arts and sciences: C. Clark 2
must understand distinction between facts and judgment: Knight 6
natural science: Knight 11
nature of: J.M. Keynes 17
needless misunderstandings introduced into: Patten 2
neither astrology nor theology: Samuelson 6
neoclassical, will be dethroned: Elster 1
next line of advance in, may be psychological: Davenport 1

no more self-contained than the economy: Hollis 1
no position which cannot be reached by competent use of respectable: Stigler 4
no reason for pride in mental power of general body of thinkers in: Laughlin 4
no such thing as measurement in: Mises 19
no value judgments in: Friedman 5
Nobel Memorial Prize in: Hayek 11
non-mathematical contributions to, tend to be fat, sloppy, vague: Klein 3
not branch of history: Mises 10
not dismal science: Mises 8
not going to dogs: Stone 1
not jurisprudence or political science or ethics: Ross 1
not physics: Sims 1
not science of choosing ends: Mises 9
object of, to understand reality: Robbins 3
of antitrust law: Bork 1
of socialism: Robinson 12
offshoot of interventionism: Mises 12
opinions, not reason, appealed to: Jevons 4
organic whole: A. Marshall 9
original idea in: Nicholson 3
orthodoxy must be driven out of discussion: Ely 3
outgrowth of economic conditions: Seligman 1
over-optimistic: Lerner 1
peculiarities of: Thurow 1
phenomena seeks to explain, are subject to change: Deane 1
philosophy of, takes subject too seriously: Hahn 2
physico-mathematical science: Walras 3
political economy inconvenient title for: Merivale 1
political force: Eucken 5
positive: Pareto 2
prediction does not belong to: Cassel 1
predictions of: Temin and Peters 1
prejudice of mathematics introduced into: Croce 2
present state of theoretical is distressing: Robinson 8
preserve of higher mathematics: Boulding 10
principle it should convey is spontaneous coordination: Buchanan 3
price: Knight 5
probably no science has so great a need of additional terms: Patten 2
problem of, to maximize pleasure: Jevons 3
produces rabbits out of a hat: Hicks 1
product of social unrest: Seligman 1
profession, takes pride in intellectual diversity: Debreu 2
prolonged commitment to mathematical exercises in, damaging: Galbraith 5
prop of ethical upbuilding: Seligman 4
propositions of derived from logical reasoning: Vickrey 1
public image of, and econometricians: Hendry 3
pure: Frisch 1
pure, is not applied: Pareto 3
pure, makes use of abstractions: Pareto 6
pure mathematical theory of: H. Schultz 4
pure, problem of: Pareto 5

economics (*cont.*):
    pure theory only small part of: H. Schultz 2
    purpose of studying, to avoid being deceived by economists: Robinson 4
    purpose of, to treat nature of wealth and wants: Fisher 6
    qualitative: Lancaster 1
    quantification of, not mechanical task: Goldberger 1
    quantitative work: Schumpeter 10
    quantitative worker needs theory: H. Schultz 3
    raison d'etre of as separate science: A. Marshall 14
    realization of perfection of science, to which Greek thought aspired: Edgeworth 2
    realm bordered by other realms: Ross 1
    recent contributions to: Åkerman 1
    regards man in abstract: Merivale 1
    relation of theory to life: Seligman 5
    reluctance of to relinquish classical model of economic man: H. Simon 2
    restatements of theory only occasionally needed: C. Clark 1
    right way to do: Mayer 4
    science and art of pursuit of wealth: Taylor 2
    science best confined to analysis and shunning the normative: Bork 2
    science of: List 1
    science of householdry: Boulding 3
    science of human behavior: J.M. Clark 3; Florence 2
    science of human nature: Bowen 2, 3
    science of price: Ayres 6
    science of the artificial: H. Simon 3
    science which treats of laws which govern relations of exchangeable quantities: Macleod 2
    scope and limit of: Hahn 5; Knight 10
    seeks to break down the whole congeries of social organization: Ayres 9
    serious theory in: Clower 6
    shall hunt in vain to find exposition of socialism that approaches consistency of: Foxwell 1
    should come back into conversation of mankind: McCloskey 2
    should dominate and coordinate activities of sciences: C. Clark 2
    should not be burdened with sins of practitioners: Clower 3
    should not exist as serious intellectual pursuit if successful prediction sole criterion of merit: Clower 1
    shuns speculation in vacuum: Wieser 5
    similar to mechanics: A. Marshall 5
    social: Cassel 4
    social enthusiasm beginning of: Pigou 3
    social science: Hicks 2
    sociology is Central Asia of: Ross 2
    somewhat peculiar: Laughlin 1
    sort of the press would like is wrong or misapprehended: Robbins 2
    specialized terminology of: Leontief 4
    spread of mathematical, helped by esoteric character: Debreu 2
    standard theory more comprehensive than mathematical economics: T.W. Schultz 3
    strayed from principle: H. Simon 5
    studies individual and social action connected with attainment of well-being: A. Marshall 11
    study of activities in which men engage in getting a living: Ayres 3
    study of, an excellent thing: Mosca 3
    study of, does not require specialized gifts: J.M. Keynes 4
    study of man earning a living: Fetter 1
    study of man's actions in ordinary business of life: A. Marshall 8
    study of mankind in ordinary business of life: A. Marshall 11; Pigou 2
    study of property rights: Alchian 2
    subjective element in positive: Lindbeck 1
    system of free enterprise principal topic of: Knight 10
    system of logical relations between assumptions and conclusions: Vickrey 1
    systematized common sense: Clower 2
    taxonomic science: Veblen 5
    teaches how men act under given circumstances: J.B. Clark 3
    teachers of, resent adverse appraisals: Nathan 1
    temptation to choose assumptions that are convenient: Eatwell 3
    textbooks: Robinson 14
    theorems of are neutral with regard to judgments of value: Mises 7
    theoretical science: Mises 9
    theory and practice divorced from one another: List 1
    theory of all human action: Mises 10
    theory should be based on realistic, comprehensive, unbiased foundation: J.M. Clark 4
    theory should be relevant to issues of the time: J.M. Clark 4
    thought and feeling embodied in: Hobson 8
    to be of real service, must deal with important phenomena: Seligman 2
    to furnish principles of progress requires extension of: J.B. Clark 6
    too large a proportion of mathematical, are mere concoctions: J.M. Keynes 17
    transfer of methods from other sciences inapposite and misleading: Eucken 4
    turned imprecision into science: Shackle 3
    turned to scorn: Sumner 2
    universal part of, has not dogma: A. Marshall 5
    very easy subject, compared to philosophy or science: J.M. Keynes 4
    weakness of, that social ideas have been neglected: Patten 6
    welfare: Knight 5
    wert-frei is an ideal: Friedman 5
    what is seen is built upon what is thought: Shackle 1
    will only progress to the extent it can transform itself into econometrics: Harrod 1

without theory of information, incentives, allocation, coordination, not like Hamlet: Lindbeck 2
writing of: J.M. Keynes 7
economists: Aaron 1; Akerlof 1; Ashley 2; Ayres 1, 8; Aytoun 1; Boulding 2; Bukharin 3; J.N. Keynes 1; Lange 6; Lawson 1; Marx 6; Nathan 1; Robinson 3, 5; Ruskin 2, 11; H. Simon 6; A. Walker 2; F.A. Walker 4
abstraction is language of: M. Perlman 1
abstraction-minded: Baumol 2
academic, always nagging away at Marx's system: Robinson 11
academic, apt to be carried off by bias of community: Fisher 7
academic, claim to produce knowledge that society wants: Mayer 3
acquire by lifelong familiarity a vision of necessities: Schumpeter 6
age of, has succeeded: Burke 1
agreement among is not news: Rees 2
and development problem: Lewis 3
and economic history: D.C. North 1
and ethical standards: Knight 5
and government: Lewis 3
and long run: J.M. Keynes 16; Stigler 1
and methodology: Hutchison 3
and mystery of evil: A. Marshall 10
and new discoveries: H. Schultz 1
and noneconomists do economics: Posner 1
and political action: Dunbar 1
and policy alternatives: Buchanan 2
and right way to do economics: Mayer 4
and scientific vantage: Hollander 2
and theorizing: Hollander 2
and theory: Burns 1
and theory of demand: M. Perlman 4
annoyingly unsympathetic: Ashley 1
antipathy to methodology among: Machlup 3
any 10 interpret contents of boxes 11 ways: Hendry 3
apologetic and shamefaced of taking long view: Viner 3
appears out of tune with his time: Hayek 7
are human: Scitovsky 2
are schizophrenic: Friedman 8
as advisers, failed to teach legislators: Minsky 1
as ascribers of rationality to others: Arrow 1
as calculators: Boulding 4
as defenders of capitalists: Ayres 1
as deploring the character of the capitalists: Ayres 1
as free-traders: Krugman 2
as French chefs: Akerlof 1
as guardians of rationality: Arrow 1
as organizers and systematizers of the ideas of the community: Ayres 8
as prescribers of rationality to the social world: Arrow 1
as scientists: Ayres 4; Hutchison 5; Knight 14
as social engineers: Buchanan 2
as teacher: Hollander 1
as textbook writer: Hollander 1

ashamed to admit place of logic: Hayek 10
assumptions and conclusions of: Vickrey 1
attempt to ignore psychology: J.M. Clark 3
aware that men behave: Boulding 5
bad, confines himself to visible effect: Bastiat 3
believe myth that scientific inference is objective: Leamer 3
business of, to study hierarchy of ends: Taylor 1
busy turning economic science to scorn: Sumner 2
by education and tradition are revolutionists: Patten 5
called on to halt accelerating inflation brought on by their policies: Hayek 11
came to paint great canvas but found themselves in studio of miniaturist: Hahn 1
can examine facts and propose lines of action: Cassel 1
can never grasp full meaning of social experience: Morrow 1
can prove demand curve negatively inclined: Samuelson 11
can reduce objections to rational mathematics: Boulding 6
cannot achieve expected standards of performance: Friedman 6
cannot alter their nature by denying their name: Jevons 6
cannot decipher mathematical economics without proper key: Debreu 2
cannot ignore human nature: J.M. Clark 3
cannot stand aloof from issues: Dobb 3
cautious, has little scope beyond discussion of economic models: Champernowne 1
classical: Ayres 4
classical, found theories on relations of man to action: Commons 5
come up with projects for making world better: Lerner 1
competent, rarest of birds: J.M. Keynes 4
conceal valuations underlying analytical structures: Myrdal 4
concerned with study of struggle for material existence: Usher 2
conclusions of, do not authorize advice: Senior 1
condemn practical men: List 1
consider it more easy to discover uniformity in human action than elsewhere: Bonar 2
considers every action individual: Morrow 1
continue to bend before strong wind: Stigler 5
could get gods from poetry or history of philosophy: McCloskey 2
counts on personal interest individually pursued: Laveleye 1
critics urge abandonment of economics by: V. Smith 1
damage in physicists playing role of: Leoni 2
deductive: Leslie 4, 5
despise methodologists: Little 2
difference between bad and good: Bastiat 3
difficult to predict colleagues' views: Hutchison 4
discipline leads them to favor markets: Friedman 8

economists (*cont.*):
- disputes among: Robbins 1
- do bad job of communicating principles of agreement: Rees 1
- do good job of teaching theory to college students: Rees 1
- do not differ so much: Schumpeter 5
- do not grow bitter gracefully: Hahn 1
- do not take history seriously: Cunningham 6
- dress up imprecise ideas in language of calculus: Wiener 2
- duty of, to denounce specious pleas: Durbin 2
- econometricians by instinct: Schumpeter 10
- econometricians not primarily engaged in measuring heights of: Hendry 1
- education of: Coats 1
- esoteric: Baumol 2
- establishment, have retained welfare theory of neoclassicals: Myrdal 2
- exalted rationality to be sovereign rule of business life: Dobb 1
- expert in field of economic legislation: Mises 12
- exposed to romantic and heroic criticism: Boulding 4
- failure to furnish principles for guidance of progress bring discredit to: J.B. Clark 6
- fashionable to abuse: Stigler 6
- few discuss methodology: Boland 1
- few know meaning of 'welfare': Little 4
- few members of public not prepared to question validity of teachings of: Hutt 1
- few neoclassical practice what they preach: Boland 1
- first task of, grasp economic reality: Eucken 2
- function of: Musgrave 1
- gives unpractical advice: Hayek 7
- glaringly mistaken: Ashley 1
- good, takes into account both the effect that can be seen and those that must be foreseen: Bastiat 3
- half-baked, studied just enough to lose common sense: Carver 4
- hanker to do what physicists do: T.W. Schultz 1
- has narrow perspective on present: McCloskey 1
- has to be careful in providing judgments on practical problems: A. Marshall 7
- has to see events as part of individual-historical situation: Eucken 2
- has to see events as presenting general-theoretical problems: Eucken 2
- have brought art of double-vision and double-talk to high degree of perfection: Ayres 7
- have been so often in the wrong: Ashley 1
- have certain inner satisfaction: Buchanan 2
- have done harm by claiming more than can be delivered: Friedman 7
- have duty to be ahead of their time: Myrdal 3
- have encouraged politicians to make extravagant promises: Friedman 7
- have made a mess of things: Hayek 11
- have natural desire to delineate boundary between those who belong and those who do not: Galbraith 2
- have not concerned themselves with illusions: Mosca 3
- have proved that value and property derive from labor: Laveleye 2
- have rarely been profound students of history: Cairnes 1
- have singular method of procedure: Marx 10
- have sneaking suspicions of empiricism: Boulding 3
- have sometimes missed useful lessons: Sidgwick 1
- have their favorite remedies for theoretical illness: Blaug 2
- have to be content with not being able to reach perfectly definite conclusions: Hansen 1
- have to bear the sins of our predecessors: Ashley 1
- have to master some kind of mathematics: Zeuthen 1
- heartless, pitiless man, a dry philosopher, an individualist, a bourgeois: Bastiat 1
- hedonic, found theories on relation of man to nature: Commons 5
- heterodox: Ely 4
- historians have rarely been: Cairnes 1
- historical analysis avoided at peril: Temin and Peters 1
- humanity will derive answers from work of: J.M. Clark 2
- ideas of, clash with popular perceptions of free trade: Krugman 2
- ideas of, follow events: Eatwell 1
- ideas of, more powerful than commonly understood: J.M. Keynes 8
- if successful, will never be important again: J.M. Keynes 6
- if untrained in power to trace operation of cause and effect, student of economics is not: Laughlin 3
- imagination of: Smart 1
- in the position of astronomer: Boulding 5
- in role of physicists: Leoni 1
- inclined to cast economics in mathematical form: Cunningham 10
- individual with but one intelligence: Veblen 4
- insecurity of, induced by mathematics: Bauer and Walters 3
- Institutional, concerned with relation of man to man: Commons 5
- intellectual hired guns of special interests: Eatwell 2
- intellectual sanitation workers: Solow 4
- is optimist: Laveleye 1
- join hands with anarchists, socialists, other advocates of violent change: Patten 5
- judgment as to best solution of practical problems: A. Marshall 7
- know how to produce shortages and surpluses: Friedman 4
- like historian: Wieser 4
- like mathematicians, have no choice but to agree about economic theory: Durbin 1
- like pedants: Samuelson 5
- like to think we have price and value: Stein 1
- little agreement among: Rescher 1
- look upon everything as subordinate to statistical curves: Cassel 1

looking for fields in which they can have some
   success: Coase 2
macroeconomic predictions of mathematical, not as
   successful as hunches: Boulding 9
main contribution is description of what is learned:
   Boulding 7
master, must possess rare combination of gifts:
   J.M. Keynes 4
mathematical: Bauer and Walters 3; Baumol 2;
   Boulding 9
mathematical, accused of forming exclusive guild:
   Fisher 11
mathematical, cope with toughest problems the
   science offers: Dorfman 1
mathematical, have commonly been mathematicians
   first: Knight 8
mathematical methods place them at mercy of
   intellectual fashion: Bauer and Walters 3
mathematics poorly understood by: Wilson 1
mathematics provides language and method for:
   Debreu 1
may hope to contribute to better society: Musgrave 1
members of a highly skilled profession: Ayres 7
merits of orthodox: Nicholson 1
mindset of, determined by mode of analysis:
   Leibenstein 1
money affords main subject-matter of: A. Marshall
   23
money needs protection from, and their quack
   remedies: Hayek 15
most born with urge to sell wares to policymakers:
   T.W. Schultz 2
most incompetent group of scientists: J.M. Keynes 6
must be aloof and incorruptible: J.M. Keynes 4
must be prepared to accept any conclusion to which
   facts lead: Bonar 1
must be purposeful and disinterested: J.M. Keynes 4
must convince themselves they are not groping in
   the dark: Clower 4
must descend from cloister: Dobb 3
must discover sources of national wealth and
   universal prosperity: McVickar 2
must make choice: Scitovsky 2
must proceed without fear or favor: Seligman 3
must study present in light of past for purposes of
   future: J.M. Keynes 4
need to be general scholars and social philosophers:
   Taylor 2
needs caution and reserve in advocacy:
   A. Marshall 16
needs imagination to develop ideals: A. Marshall 16
needs perception, imagination, reason:
   A. Marshall 15
neoclassical: Myrdal 2
no one is, until has said to himself 'I wish I were an
   editor': Patten 4
none engaged in carrying on science of political
   economy: Sumner 2
not a phase of social life not within his province:
   Ely 5
not concerned merely with material life of man: Ely 5

not to frame systems for increasing wealth of
   particular classes: McVickar 2
not trained in principles, like a traveler in dark:
   Laughlin 2
not very different from poets and novelists:
   McCloskey 2
nothing produces jobs for, like government controls:
   Friedman 8
number of scientific has always been small:
   A. Marshall 12
objectivity of: Scitovsky 2
of the English or American school: Bastiat 1
of repute: Nicholson 2
on level with dentists: J.M. Keynes 5
ordinary, assumes free competition: Cunningham 6
orthodox: Balogh 1; Ely 4
ought not to be recluses: Fisher 11
ought to be something of an historian: Young 1
paid remembrancers of public conscience: Durbin 2
paid to attack monopoly: Stigler 11
partly to blame for misunderstanding of political
   economy: Cunningham 7
philosophers of science should be suspicious of
   claims made by: Hutchison 6
policies of: Hayek 11
position of, in intellectual life: Hayek 7
pourers of cold water: Stigler 6
practical men usually slaves of some defunct:
   J.M. Keynes 8
practice of, sufficiently uniform: Cannan 1
practice physics-worship: McCloskey 2
prediction primary task of: Hutchison 2
primary concern of, to pursue and master scientific
   truths: Walras 1
proclaim skepticism regarding efficiency of
   government: Aaron 1
profess interest in history: Cunningham 6
profession of: Mises 12
professional, have little influence on convictions of
   great body of people: Laughlin 5
professional is specialist instrumental in designing
   measures of government interference: Mises 12
professional prophets: Durbin 2
projects deemed impracticable: Lerner 1
proper business of, to advance own understanding of
   economy: Clower 4
public interests ought always to form exclusive
   objects of: McVickar 2
purpose of studying economics is to avoid being
   deceived by: Robinson 4
recommendations of, determined by philosophic
   attitudes: Basmann 1
regarded as doctrinaire by practical men: List 1
remember how appearance of easy remedies has
   proven deceptive: Edgeworth 4
resembles a traveler: Eucken 3
role of, in public policy: Friedman 3
room for only two or three theorists in each
   generation: C. Clark 1
sad state of affairs when anyone can assume the
   title: Barro 1

economists (*cont.*):
  schools of: Hansen 2
  scientific: W.H. Smith 1
  scratch libertarian, find Don Quixote: Samuelson 4
  seem willing to give advice on questions about which they know little: Coase 1
  self-interest leads them to favor intervention: Friedman 8
  sell themselves short if all they see in market is venue for exchange: M. Perlman 5
  set themselves too easy, too useless a task: J.M. Keynes 16
  shall not be contributing to wind: Stigler 5
  should attend to changing efficiency of scientific machinery: Moore 1
  should face their basic responsibility: Buchanan 1
  should know what micro- and macro-theory mean: Machlup 2
  should not refrain from making special contribution to decisions of public importance: Viner 1
  should not refuse to accept obvious conclusions: Buchanan 5
  should not retreat into technical and terminological obscurity: Buchanan 5
  should seek journalistic experience: Patten 4
  should treat mathematics as part of scaffolding: Edgeworth 6
  should try to know their subject matter: Buchanan 1
  sign of moral depravity if finds anything in economics to marvel at: Hayek 8
  skill depends on ability to abstract: Boulding 5
  socialists make merry at differences of opinion among: Foxwell 1
  some of most eminent, and quantitative standards: Sidgwick 2
  some think care only about money: Christ 1
  someone who would sell grandmother to highest bidder: Christ 1
  sophisticated, sometimes errs: Solow 3
  Soviet: Meek 2
  special knowledge of: Hayek 7
  start with knowledge of ultimate causes: Cairnes 5
  subject to coercion of ruling ideologies: Stigler 3
  sufficient to establish sound principles: Merivale 1
  suppose students have background in economics: Clower 2
  supposed to be dry as dust: Samuelson 4
  symbols necessary for: Edgeworth 6
  take aims for granted: Stamp 1
  take methodology for granted: Boland 1
  take Wall Street point of view: Fisher 7
  tend not to get along with other people: Tullock 1
  testimony to Congress by: Stigler 7
  there are many, not quite so many good: Viner 2
  too easy to convert good literary into mediocre mathematical: Samuelson 10
  transgress frontiers of economics: Hutchison 1
  true, a guide: Ely 4
  unconfused by values and valuations: Stamp 1
  understand microeconomics but not macroeconomics: Solow 2
  unfair to impose on mathematical, problems of literary lucidity: Dorfman 1
  use complicated jargon: Samuelson 3
  use words not to elucidate but to distort their meaning: Balogh 1
  used to regard perfect competition as ideal: Samuelson 7
  value judgments of, influence subjects and conclusions: Friedman 5
  value methodology that boosts prestige: Hutchison 5
  when disregard political or social question, there is room for reprobation: Dunbar 1
  wish to reduce power of state to minimum: Laveleye 1
  would not sell grandmother to highest bidder, unless bid was high enough: Christ 1
economizing man: Menger 1
economizing process: Eucken 1; Wieser 1
  not central principle of economics: Buchanan 3
economy: Wieser 7
  capitalism first mode of, unable to exist by itself: Luxemburg 1
  capitalism first mode of, with weapon of propaganda: Luxemburg 1
  disordered currency wars against: Webster 1
  first and most important of republican virtues: Jefferson 4
  meaning of: Wicksteed 2
  not an isolable realm of social life: Hollis 1
  planless: Dobb 1
  socialism harmonious and universal system of: Luxemburg 3
econo-mystics: Hendry 1
Eddy, Mary Baker: Shaw 7
editor:
  economists as: Patten 4
education: Bagehot 6; Bastiat 8, 9; Cassel 4; Hayek 24; Hegel 3; Jones 2; A. Marshall 28; Roscher 4; Scrope 3; Simonde de Sismondi 7; Veblen 3
  moral and intellectual: J.S. Mill 18
  public: J. Mill 5
  state: Bastiat 9
educational institutions: Viner 4
efficiency: Hobson 9; J.M. Keynes 21; Rostow 1
  and business enterprise: Veblen 1
  and capitalism: J.M. Keynes 1
  economic: Tawney 5
  pecuniary: Knight 5
  purpose of nationalization to achieve: Schumacher 2
  social: Knight 5
egalitarianism:
  policies ignore poor: Bauer 4
ego, egoism: Proudhon 2; Robinson 1
Egypt: Cassel 4
elasticity of demand: Clapham 1
elbow-grease: T. Thompson 1
elections: Rostow 2
electricity:
  riches are power like: Ruskin 11
emancipation: Marx 8
embargo: F.A. Walker 2

emigration: Aytoun 2
emotion: Hoxie 3; Mises 7
empire: Harrington 1
   no people, over-charged with Tribute, is fit for: Bacon 4
empirical sciences: Wieser 5
   economics acquired attitudes of: Leontief 2
empiricism: W.H. Smith 1
employers:
   advantage of, nothing but plunder: Simonde de Sismondi 2
   should be allowed to combine: Commons and Andrews 3
employment: J.S. Mill 13; Ricardo 1
   abolition of private property may be needed for: Beveridge 1
   capitalism and full: Kalecki 2
   full, attainable under private enterprise: Beveridge 1
   of disposable population: Chalmers 1
   of poor, and foreign trade: Mun 4
   ostentatious expenditure by state, enemy to good: A. Marshall 19
   right to: Bastiat 8
   socialization of investment, only means of securing full: J.M. Keynes 26
   unproductive channels of: Scrope 9
   useful: F.A. Walker 11
empty box: Clapham 1; Hendry 3
emulation:
   destroyed by security: Bowen 1
encyclopedias: Viner 4
endowment: Hegel 5
   differences in, and division of labor: K. Polanyi 1
ends: Samuelson 2
   hierarchy of: Hayek 26; Taylor 1
Engels, Friedrich: Mises 16
engineering:
   economics should dominate and coordinate activities of: C. Clark 2
   society built on, imposes human will on universe: Heilbroner 5
engineers: Bailey 1; A. Marshall 7; Robinson 15; Stamp 1
   economists needed instrument to allow them to play: Buchanan 2
England: Malthus 5, 6, 8; McCulloch 3; Ricardo 2; A. Smith 9; W.H. Smith 4; Yarranton 1
English lace: Barbon 7
enjoyment(s): Newcomb 3; Scrope 3; W.H. Smith 2
   diminish as taxation proceeds: Ricardo 10
   no circumstances under which taxation does not abridge: Ricardo 14
ennui: W.H. Smith 3
   men devoured by, when made secure: Bowen 1
enterprise: Gauthier 2; Proudhon 5; Simonde de Sismondi 2; Veblen 1; F.A. Walker 8; Weber 1
   collective: Webb 3
   evolution of: Hobson 2
   free: *see* free enterprise
   freedom of: Simons 2
   inhibited by pursuit of equality: Bauer 5
   private: *see* private enterprise
   public: Lewis 1
   socialists have no desire to penalize: Crosland 1
   socialists desire to restore rewards to: Crosland 1
   steeply graduated income tax discourages: Pigou 6
   vast field of, for economist to consider: Cunningham 6
   without hope there is no: A. Marshall 33
enthusiasm: J.M. Keynes 21
entrepreneur: Mises 17; Rothbard 1; Stigler 2
   competition mechanism of fooling: Lange 3
   has no assurance investment will continue: Dobb 1
   incentive of: Kirzner 1
entrepreneurship: Bacon 2
entry:
   restrictions on: Barro 1
envelopes: Robinson 3
environmentally-friendly policies: Hodgson 1
envy: W. Thompson 1
   and social justice: Sowell 1
   created by poverty and ignorance: Owen 6
epistemology: Mayer 6
epithets: Sidgwick 1
equalitarianism: Schumpeter 11
equality: More 1; Roemer 1; Tocqueville 1
   and sacrifices required by government: J.S. Mill 21
   augments power of state: Hume 2
   communism not inconsistent exaggeration of principle of: Roscher 1
   complete, unsuitable to human nature: Hamilton 3
   diminishes less the happiness of rich than adds to that of poor: Hume 2
   human nature most suitable to: Hume 2
   imposed by state: Bastiat 9
   in taxation: J.S. Mill 20
   inborn: Leo XIII 1
   laws necessary to enable working classes to maintain: Brownson 1
   makes extraordinary taxes paid with cheerfulness: Hume 2
   of income: Shaw 6
   of results: Laughlin 7
   of reward: Laughlin 7
   of sacrifice: J.S. Mill 20
   principle of, demands all taxes be imposed directly: E.P. Smith 3
   pursuit of, inhibits enterprise: Bauer 5
   pursuit of, obstructs social and economic mobility: Bauer 5
   pursuit of, politicizes life: Bauer 5
   relief of poverty has nothing to do with: Bauer 4
   taxation must be done with, to avoid hate of people: Mun 2
   without, can be no permanent virtue or stability in society: Owen 2
equilibrium: Kaldor 2
   analysis: Hayek 9
   economics: Kaldor 1
equitability:
   of government: A. Walker 1

equity: John XXIII 2; Ruskin 10
  of free competition: Newcomb 1
  unless property set upon basis of, riches may be injurious: Hobson 10
error: Maitland 2
essence: Marx 7, 17
estates:
  covetous man's: Barbon 6
  men should contribute to public charge according to: Petty 10
estrangement: Marx 7, 17
ethical data: Laughlin 1
ethics: Dunbar 2; H. Fawcett 2; Hobson 6, 7; Hoxie 2; J.N. Keynes 2; Mises 21; Nicholson 1; Ross 1; Samuelson 2; Schumpeter 11
  government is testing ground of: Musgrave 1
  in business: Hodgson 1; Knight 5
  may give ideal for human society: Cunningham 5
  political economy subservient to: Cunningham 5
  principle of free market: Friedman 2
  science of: A. Marshall 4
  sister of political economy: A. Marshall 4
  special science of human nature: Bowen 2
Euclid: Senior 3
eudemonism: Schumpeter 11
eugenics: Webb 2; Webb and Webb 3, 4, 5, 6
Europe: J.M. Keynes 15; Morrow 2; A. Smith 18
  glory of, extinguished for ever: Burke 1
evil: Bentham 9; Brandeis 1; Hutcheson 1; Longfield 1; Malthus 9, 12; Mises 20; D. North 3; Owen 4, 7; Ricardo 5, 7; Rogers 1; Roscher 2; Ruskin 10; Schumpeter 7; Senior 3; Simonde de Sismondi 2, 5; Simons 3, 4; E.P. Smith 4; Stevenson 3; Syme 2; W. Thompson 2; Trower 1; Webb and Webb 3
  and political economy: Whately 3
  disordered currency one of greatest political: Webster 1
  duty of state to deal with: Spencer 2
  economic: Tawney 8
  every restriction of competition is: J.S. Mill 13
  government as panacea for: Molinari 2
  government useful in warding off: Dew 2
  greatest, when there are poor to be defended and rich to be restrained: Rousseau 1
  inflation greatly exaggerated as social: Tobin 1
  money not root of: Mitchell 1
  mystery of: A. Marshall 10
  not all due to wickedness: Usher 4
  of taxes: Ricardo 11, 12
  ordeal of virtue to resist all temptation to: Malthus 14
  poor laws spread: Malthus 5
  property is power to do: Sedgwick 3
  selfishness as: A. Marshall 1
  socialists charge upon competition all economical: J.S. Mill 13
  taxation in every form is: McCulloch 8
  taxation is choice of: Newcomb 7
evils of mankind:
  governments make out they can cure: Bagehot 10
evolution: Mises 16; Peirce 1; Veblen 3; Webb 3
  mathematics too rigid and simple to handle: Georgescu-Roegen 1
  of capitalism into socialism: Shaw 7
  of capitalist enterprise: Hobson 2
  of society: Ingram 2
evolutionary process:
  market is product of: Mises 1
excellence: Proudhon 2
exchange: Aristotle 1, 5; Bowen 3; C. Clark 2; Law 1; A. Smith 7; Taussig 1; Turgot 1
  and advantage: Ruskin 6
  double: J.S. Mill 26
  general law of: Ruskin 6
  involves preference and sacrifice: Shackle 4
  is choice: Shackle 4
  is deliberate: Shackle 4
  money instrument to facilitate: Hume 4; Wayland 4
  money is crystal formed of necessity in course of: Marx 18
  money medium of: Sraffa 1
  political economy as science of: Macleod 1
  propensity to, apocryphal: K. Polanyi 1
  requires people and commodities: Boulding 5
  secrecy, invisibility, and silence of: Simmel 4
  takes only one person: Shackle 4
  theory of: Walras 3
  unequal: W. Thompson 2
  value expresses circumstance of: Jevons 8
  value in: Walras 3
exchange rate: Solow 2
exchange value:
  no chemist ever discovered: Marx 25
exchangeable value: Bagehot 11; McCulloch 1
  question from which all political economy moves: De Quincey 2
excise tax: Petty 9
excogitation: M. Perlman 3
exertion: W. Thompson 1
  excessive weight of taxation destroys: McCulloch 11
Exeter Hall philanthropy: Carlyle 1
existence: Marx 7
  economists concerned with struggle for: Usher 2
expectation: Dobb 1; J.M. Keynes 12; Pigou 5; Robertson 1
  and contracts: Steuart-Denham 1
  rational: Hahn 3
expediency:
  appropriation of land, question of general: J.S. Mill 12
expenditure: Simonde de Sismondi 6
  government alive to injurious consequences of extravagant and wasteful: McVickar 3
  ostentatious, by state, enemy to good employment: A. Marshall 19
  to increases taxes for, not recommended as cure for pessimism of investors: Robbins 6
experience: Jones 2; J.M. Keynes 3; Knight 1; Leontief 2; W.H .Smith 1; Stevenson 1; Veblen 4; Vickrey 1; Wicksteed 3; Wieser 3
experiment: T.W. Schultz 1
  political economy science of: McVickar 1

experts: Hutchison 5
exploitation: Marx 22
   competition main safeguard against: J.M. Clark 1
   nature of accumulation and: Marx 6
   of labor: Marx 6
exportation:
   of bullion: Joplin 2
expropriation: Bukharin 2
   by government: Stolper 2
extravagance: Owen 4
   disordered currency fosters evil spirit of: Webster 1
eyeglasses: Stigler 9

fabric: Schumpeter 2; Spencer 3
factory: Aytoun 2; Hobson 2; Marx 11
facts: H. Simon 5; Stevenson 1; Wright 2
   and theory: Sombart 1
   by indicating origin and consequences of, statistics becomes political economy: Say 1
   concrete: Veblen 5
   like beads: Sombart 1
   political economy science of: McVickar 1
   theory must be made to fit: Seligman 5
   vs. judgment: Knight 6
fairness: J.S. Mill 22
faith: F.A. Walker 11
fallacies: Robinson 11
fallibility: H. Simon 5
family, families: Ely 6; Hegel 3; Locke 6; Malthus 6, 7; McCulloch 10; Robinson 5; Sumner 7; Webb and Webb 7; Yarranton 1
   affections, provide for those who could not provide for themselves: George 5
   altruism more common than in market transactions: Becker 1
   altruism more efficient in than market: Becker 1
   and altruism: Leslie 1
   and capitalism: Marx 13
   based on capital: Marx 12
   bourgeois will vanish with vanishing of capital: Marx 12
   dissolution of: Marx 13
   in difficult circumstances: Berkeley 1
   income and consumption: Becker 2
   motivation of members: Becker 2
   selfishness of members: Becker 2
   state should encourage voluntary action for individuals to provide more than minimum for: Beveridge 2
   welfare of: Becker 2
   without, work of world would come to standstill: Leslie 1
famine: Ricardo 13; Sedgwick 1
farm: D. North 7
farmers: Malthus 8; S. Perlman 1
fashion: Sedgwick 2
fatalists:
   and planning: Hayek 4
fathers: Senior 4
fear: Greenspan 2; Hoxie 3
   taxation brings into field: McCulloch 11

feeble-minded: Webb and Webb 4, 6
fees: Petty 1
felicity: Bentham 8
feudalism: Marx 15
   artificial institution: Marx 10
Feuerbach, Ludwig: Shaw 7
Feynman, Richard: Clower 6
finance: Bukharin 2; Palgrave 1; Wright 2
   corporation: Commons 4; Veblen 1
   principles of: Cassel 4
financier: Bastable 1
finery: Sedgwick 2, 5
fire departments: F.A. Walker 2
firms:
   compete for confidence and trust, not profit: Hodgson 1
   have to abandon profit maximization: Hodgson 1
   mission: Hodgson 1
   theory of: Bork 1
   unsophisticated theory by which gain monopoly: Bork 1
fiscal theory:
   and Cicero: Phelps 1
fishermen: Marx 14
fishes: Lindbeck 1
fluctuations: McCulloch 2
   violent, do harm to labor: Webster 2
folly: A. Smith 10
food: Luther 2; Malthus 14; McCulloch 13; Peirce 1; A. Smith 26
   poor laws increase population without increasing: Malthus 6
fools:
   must bear brunt of defects: Chamberlain 1
football team:
   example of system for which *laissez-faire* not good idea: Sargent 1
force: W. Thompson 1, 2
   and morality: Sowell 1
forced labor camp:
   planned economy like: M. Polanyi 1
forecast:
   economics cannot give: Cunningham 9
forecasting: Koopmans 1
   becomes discredited: Cassel 1
   political economy gives best means of: Cunningham 8
foreign aid:
   central to economic relations of West and Third World: Bauer 2
foreign commodities, prohibition of: Barbon 7
foreign trade: *see* free trade; trade
foresight: M. Polanyi 1; Robinson 5; Wieser 1
   and planning: Hayek 4
forest: Wayland 6; Whately 5
fortune: McCulloch 11; J.S. Mill 22; Mosca 1; A. Smith 22, 23
   attempt to imitate others of superior, may come to ruin: Mandeville 1
   function of government to prevent extreme inequality of: Rousseau 1

fortune (*cont.*):
  inequality of, principal impediment to increase of public wealth: Maitland 3
fortune-teller: Petty 4
fortunes: Berkeley 4; Bonar 2
Foundations of Economic Analysis (Samuelson): Samuelson 9
fountains: Simonde de Sismondi 7
Fourier, Joseph: J.S. Mill 16
Fourteenth Amendment: Holmes 1
franc-tireurs: Foxwell 1
France: Ricardo 2
fraternity:
  and free trade argument: Phillips 1
fraud: Bastiat 4; W. Thompson 2
  taxation begets: George 11
free enterprise:
  failure of, a failure of political state: Simons 1
  predominant method of social organization of economic activity: Knight 10
  system of, principal topic of economics: Knight 10
free trade: Ashley 2; Aytoun 2, 3; Morrow 2; Scrope 2; W.H. Smith 4
  assumes whole world is one community: Phillips 1
  brings gain: Taussig 2
  call for, as cry of spoiled child: Clay 1
  doctrine of: Taussig 2
  economists committed to: Krugman 2
  game in which each party tries to overreach: Taussig 1
  gives more wealth and profit: Price 3
  never existed: Clay 1
  place where ideas of economists clash with popular perceptions: Krugman 2
  reduces people to pauperism: Aytoun 2
  we have tried, and it has failed: Aytoun 3
  wisdom or unwisdom of not capable of conclusive proof: Ashley 2
free traders:
  assure people they favor tariffs: Greeley 1
free will: Penrose 1; Tolstoy 4
freedom: J.B.Clark 5; Menger 1; Roscher 2; Tawney 3; Webb 3; Whately 3
  and market: Mises 2
  democracy extends: Tocqueville 1
  economic: *see* economic freedom
  increased by increased taxation: Ely 10
  increases willingness and power for work: A. Marshall 33
  industrial: Webb 1
  of discussion: Simons 2
  of enterprise: Simons 2
  planning is wholesale destruction of: M. Polanyi 1
  private property most important guarantee of: Hayek 19
  security blanket is not worth surrender of: Friedman 21
  security always involves constraints on: A. Marshall 33
  security of person and property condition of: A. Marshall 33
  socialism restricts: Tocqueville 1
freemen:
  for slave to have virtues of, must first be free: George 4
French chefs: Akerlof 1
French cooking: Akerlof 1
Freudian complexes, economic man has no: Boulding 3
friendly society: McCulloch 5
'From each according to his ability, to each according to his needs': Hobson 4
frugality: Wayland 2
  disordered currency wars against: Webster 1
  placed at disadvantage by over-taxation: J.S. Mill 24
  taxes on consumption produce: Hume 8
fuel: Wayland 6
Führer: Mises 28
fundamental psychological law: J.M. Keynes 3
furniture: A. Smith 26
future: Viner 3; F.A. Walker 11
  every step of multitude, made with equal blindness of: Ferguson 2
  influenced by coming events: Cassel 1
  not determined by analysis of statistical curves: Cassel 1
  prediction of, does not belong to economic science: Cassel 1

gain: Croce 1; Leslie 1; More 1
  pursuit of: Weber 1
gallows: A. Smith 1
gamblers: Weber 1
gambles: J.M. Keynes 12
gang instinct: Galbraith 2
gay science: Carlyle 1
general equilibrium: Leontief 3
General Theory of Employment, Interest, and Money (Keynes): Knight 12
general will: Rousseau 1
generalizations: C. Clark 1; Dew 1; Peirce 1
genius: Pareto 3; A. Smith 8
geography: Pareto 3
  differences in, and division of labor: K. Polanyi 1
geologists: J.B. Clark 2
geometry: Hayek 9; Hobson 6; Pareto 7; Walras 2, 4
  axioms of: Vickrey 1
  theorems of: Vickrey 1
Germany: Ely 1; J.M. Keynes 15; Ross 2; Roscher 3
germs of existence: Malthus 14
gesticulation: J.M. Keynes 25
gewgaws: Sedgwick 5
gibbets: Hale 1
Gibbs, Willard: Samuelson 9
gin: Solow 5
gloves: Barbon 7
God: Dew 1; Ely 6; Erasmus 1; Marx 10; Shaw 7; Solow 1; Tolstoy 2; Wayland 7; Wright 4
  author and defender of right: Leo XIII 1
  but for Grace of: Bronfenbrenner 1
  gave earth for use and enjoyment of human race: Leo XIII 3
  gave world to men in common: Locke 6

has given all things richly: Locke 5
law established by: Wayland 2
made all things for the use of man: Coke 1
nothing made by, for man to destroy: Locke 5
regulates things by general laws: Bowen 5
responsibility of man towards: Carey 5
socialists reject: Sumner 7
stealing and robbery forbidden by: Leo XIII 1
gold: Bowen 7; Huskisson 1; Jevons 8; Mandeville 4; Sedgwick 1
Golden Age: A. Marshall 2
   original condition of comfort in: Mackay 4
good: Bentham 9; Longfield 1; A. Marshall 2; Simonde de Sismondi 5; Sumner 7; Syme 2; Torrens 1; A. Walker 2
   common: Stolper 1
   concentrated power as force for: Friedman 21
   every extension of competition is: J.S. Mill 13
   general: F.A. Walker 2
   government cannot procure positive: Dew 2
   material: Florence 2
   of all: Rae 4
   of community: Hobson 3
   property is power to do: Sedgwick 3
   pursuit of individual advantage connected with universal: Ricardo 2
   quantity of: Hutcheson 1
   socialism forces individual to surrender liberty and property for general: Newcomb 5
   truth able to conserve: Ely 11
   when men consult for public, usually esteem own interest to be common measure of good and evil: D. North 3
goods: Tobin 1
   community of: Aquinas 1; Leo XIII 1
   division of: Bowen 1
   have value from use: Law 2
   possession of: Veblen 7
   valued by measure of money: Law 1
   well-being ultimate standard for value of: Böhm-Bawerk 1
government: Aaron 1; Babson 1; Bagehot 10, 13; Harrington 3; Jones 2; J. Marshall 1; Mises 6; Rogers 1; Tucker 1; F.A. Walker 8
   abolition of taxation, blow to: Ely 9
   action by to limit competition, called criminal: Greenspan 1
   advantages negative, not positive: Dew 2
   agencies of: Spencer 1
   alive to injurious consequences of extravagant and wasteful expenditure: McVickar 3
   all require taxes: E.P. Smith 2
   almost any is beneficial: Olson 1
   and capitalism: Shaw 1
   and claim to share profits: A. Walker 2
   and coercion: Mises 17
   and compulsion: Mises 17
   and development: Lewis 1
   and economists: Lewis 3
   and monetary affairs: Wayland 3
   and money: Joplin 1

   and planning: Mises 17
   and private enterprise: Lewis 1
   and private sector: Lewis 2
   and public sector: Lewis 2
   and public utilities: Southey 2
   anticapitalist: Mises 15
   arbitrary mandate of: J.S. Mill 24
   as expenditure of increases, enjoyment of people diminishes: Ricardo 10
   as master: Molinari 1
   bankruptcy of: J.M. Keynes 13
   benefits and costs considered: Say 2
   bent on introducing socialism is threat to private enterprise: Lange 2
   best is that which can safely and successfully administer most: Webb 3
   by taxation, interferes with free choice and impersonal economic forces: fetter 5
   can help poor by getting out of the way: Rothbard 8
   can live a long time by printing paper money: J.M. Keynes 14
   can play tricks with value of money: Shaw 4
   cannot be ranked amongst consumers of industrious class: Destutt Tracy 1
   capitalism cannot function under socialist: Lange 2
   collectivism extreme form of centralization: Simons 3
   coming of socialist, must cause financial panic and economic collapse: Lange 7
   compels payment from individuals without exchange in utility: Florence 3
   condemnation of intervention of: J.S. Mill 2
   conduct of: Musgrave 1
   consumes produce of labor of others: McVickar 3
   constitutional: Ely 9
   contribution of persons to expenses of: J.S.Mill 20
   controls and intervention produce jobs for economists: Friedman 8
   corruption: Wayland 3
   could print good edition of Shakespeare, but not get it written: A. Marshall 18
   countenance of degraded paper money by: Webster 1
   creates scarcely anything: A. Marshall 17
   debases money while denying doing it: Friedman 12
   does wrong to release person from obligation: Newcomb 9
   drains money from pockets of people: A. Smith 12
   duties and services for sake of moral good: A. Walker 2
   duty of: Shaw 1
   duty of, keep value of money steady: Shaw 4
   econometrics sole beneficiary from manipulation of economy: Hendry 2
   efficiency of: Aaron 1
   end of, to make governed and governors happy: Owen 1
   errs by intermeddling: Tucker 2
   euphemisms of: Greenspan 3
   exigencies of: A. Walker 1

government (*cont.*):
- expends money in different ways from individual: Fetter 5
- expensive, is curse: J. Mill 2
- extravagance of: A. Smith 20
- few inventions made by: A. Marshall 17
- first act of, limitation of itself: Brownson 1
- first duty of, to maintain equality of income: Shaw 6
- first duty of, to secure means of subsistence: Scrope 7
- first necessity of, to secure working of great law of property: Ruskin 10
- fiscal and financial measures: Southey 1
- freedom and: Friedman 21
- function of, to prevent extreme inequality of fortunes: Rousseau 1
- good (efficient) tax allows to grow: Barro 2
- good, wants only own excellence and people sufficiently instructed: J. Mill 3
- great object of: Dew 2
- has important functions to perform: Friedman 9
- has no right to alter value of money: Wayland 5
- inferior in intelligence and knowledge of people as a nation: J.S. Mill 3
- injustice turns into machine by which unscrupulous rob neighbors: George 6
- integrity in doing justice most necessary in: Rousseau 1
- interests of: Stewart 2
- interference: Bagehot 10; Bentham 3
- interference in business: Mises 12
- intervention: Rothbard 1, 2
- intervention of, worsens things: J.S. Mill 2
- intrusion into business is danger to social progress: A. Marshall 17
- inventions and discoveries not brought about by: Spencer 3
- is best which produces greatest happiness of greatest number: Owen 1
- issuing money: Hayek 18
- jeopardized by private monopoly: Bryan 2
- legal tender ultimate reserve of: J.M. Keynes 13
- line beyond which cannot go with good results: Taft 1
- maintenance of, involves costs and outgoings: Rousseau 3
- make out that they can cure the evils of mankind: Bagehot 10
- makes posterity debtor: Simonde de Sismondi 4
- may propose, but economy disposes: Minsky 1
- mischief of, not sole reason for unstable money: Harrod 4
- money supreme and most comprehensive of all controls of: Stolper 2
- necessary: Brownson 1
- never does good to trade: Simonde de Sismondi 3
- nothing remains from labor it pays: Destutt Tracy 1
- obtains income by coercion and violence: Rothbard 10
- organized expression of wants and wishes of nation: Chamberlain 1
- ought to set example: J.S. Mill 21
- over-taxation by, great evil: J.S. Mill 24
- paternal: Cairnes 3; Ely 6
- philosophy of: Shackle 5
- policies have been responsible for demeaning citizens: Friedman 23
- policies urged on by economists: Hayek 11
- policy of, is statistical: Shackle 5
- political economy only useful as it directs to right measures in taxation: Ricardo 3
- poor laws at variance with fundamental law of: Wayland 7
- positive acts of: F.A. Walker 2
- prerogatives of: Bastiat 2
- private monopoly due to perversion of: Bryan 2
- profusion of, retarded progress: A. Smith 9
- proper, would not permit trade in luxuries: Luther 3
- provision for expense of, purpose of taxation: Fetter 4
- purpose of, to make people more truly happy: Babson 1
- rapacious: Tucker 1
- regulation: Greenspan 3
- regulation does not build quality into goods: Greenspan 3
- requires sacrifices of comfort or indulgence: J.S. Mill 21
- responsibility for money and credit: Stolper 2
- role of in private enterprise: Rand 3
- seeks all acts of civil life which afford opportunity of asking money: Simonde de Sismondi 6
- services rendered by: Scrope 9
- share of wealth belongs to: A. Walker 3
- should do things which are not done at all: J.M. Keynes 9
- should not lay taxes on capital: Ricardo 10
- should rise to true conception of duties: Chamberlain 1
- skill of: Say 2
- socialism confuses with society: Bastiat 9
- socialism enlarges functions of: F.A. Walker 9
- socialist, must carry out program at one stroke or abandon it: Lange 7
- spend as much as people will allow: J. Mill 2
- spending beyond that necessary diminishes happiness of people: J. Mill 2
- springs from injustice: F.A. Walker 2
- tax assessor agent of popular: Fetter 7
- tax is portion of taken and disposed of by government: McCulloch 12
- taxation best and most powerful engine of: Edmonds 2
- taxation instrumentality of, where common people obtain liberties: Ely 9
- taxation, power of to take private property: Commons and Andrews 1
- taxes should be levied to promote general purposes of: E.P. Smith 4
- testing ground of social ethics and civilized living: Musgrave 1
- too much: Brownson 1

uses inflation as means of confiscation of wealth: J.M. Keynes 12
when protecting commerce, acts with precipitation: Simonde de Sismondi 3
where mortgaged revenues, sinks into state of languor, inactivity, impotence: Hume 6
wrong kind: Brownson 1
government spending: Eatwell 4
  abolish superfluous: Erasmus 2
graduate students: Solow 1
grandmother:
  economist not someone who would sell to highest bidder, unless bid high enough: Christ 1
  economist someone who would sell to highest bidder: Christ 1
graphs: Samuelson 3
gratification:
  from labor: Newcomb 3
  of desires: Fetter 1
gratuities: Petty 1
gravitation: Ayres 4; Ricardo 8; Senior 3
  laws of: A. Marshall 13
Great Depression: Friedman 16
greatest good of the greatest number: Stolper 1
  as criterion of justice: Carver 8
greatest happiness for the greatest numbers: Hutcheson 1; Owen 1
greatest happiness of masses: Chamberlain 1
greed: George 6; Weber 1
  beneficial effects of: Peirce 1
  brings injury and distress to industrious and honest: Webster 2
  intelligence in service of ensures justest prices: Peirce 1
  of businessman, protector of consumer: Greenspan 4
  socialists dislike bourgeois: Hahn 6
groceries: Sedgwick 5
guidance:
  socialism rejects, from superior classes: Ely 8
guild:
  mathematical economists accused of forming exclusive: Fisher 11
guild instinct: Galbraith 2
guinea: Ruskin 11

habit(s): McCulloch 11; H. Simon 6; A. Smith 8; Sraffa 1; Steuart-Denham 2; Stevenson 3; Viner 3
  evolutionary: Veblen 3
  of thought: Kaldor 1; Veblen 4
Hamlet: Lindbeck 2
handicrafts: Marx 11
happiness: Ayres 10; Babson 1; Bentham 9; Hume 1; Hutcheson 1; Simonde de Sismondi 7; A. Smith 22; Sumner 6; W. Thompson 2; Tucker 1; Tullock 1; Webb 3; Yarranton 1
  and political economy: Hobson 6
  disordered currency destructive of: Webster 1
  equality diminishes less of rich than adds to poor: Hume 2
  government spending beyond that necessary diminishes: J. Mill 2

greatest, of masses: Chamberlain 1
increase of, ought to be leading object: Hamilton 1
influence of system of finance on: Palgrave 1
material relief does not bring: A. Marshall 26
misleading to take individual, as unit from which good of mankind can be built: Cunningham 9
of a people, depends on many things: Hayek 26
of society: A. Smith 17
poor laws weaken incentive to: Malthus 8
stimulus of poverty necessary to promote: Malthus 7
wealth form of: Florence 2
would have been greater if poor laws never existed: Malthus 9
hardware: Ricardo 2
harmony: Schumacher 1
hate: Hoxie 3; Mun 2
  causes of: Rousseau 1
health: Mandeville 5; Schumacher 1; A. Smith 20; Sumner 7
heart: Joplin 2
  business cycles like beat of: Schumpeter 1
hedonism:
  cultural justification of capitalism: Bell 1
Hegel, Georg Wilhelm Friedrich: Shaw 7
Hegelian:
  dialectic: Shaw 7
  stuff and nonsense: Robinson 10
helplessness: Sumner 7
heresy: Robinson 11
heroic:
  demand for Boulding 3
  excesses of: Boulding 3
Hertz: Pigou 1
higgling:
  of market: A. Smith 24
historian(s): Bukharin 3; J.M. Keynes 4; T.W. Schultz 2; Sumner 2; Tawney 4
  economists like: Wieser 4
  economists ought to be: Young 1
  have rarely be economists: Cairnes 1
  knowledge of Political Economy part of equipment of: Cairnes 1
historical development:
  communism not goal of: Marx 8
Historical school of political economy: Walras 4:
  economics darkened by mass of anecdotes of: Croce 2
history: Marx 15; Robinson 14; Taylor 2
  economist professes to be interested in: Cunningham 6
  economists do not take seriously: Cunningham 6
  economists have rarely been profound students of: Cairnes 1
  influence of Marxian socialism on: J.M. Keynes 23
  materialist conception of: Engels 4
  riddle: Marx 7
  training in, and utopias, panaceas, and revolutions: Hobson 12
hoards: D. North 1; Torrens 2
Holmes, Oliver Wendell, Jr.: Bork 1
Holy Ghost: Shaw 7

homme moyen: Mises 11
homo agens:
  economics deals with: Mises 7
  often weak, stupid, inconsiderate, and badly instructed: Mises 7
homo economicus: Mises 11; Pareto 6, 7
  economics does not deal with: Mises 7
homo ethicus: Pareto 7
homo religiosus: Pareto 7
honesty: Newcomb 9; Sowell 1
honor: Laveleye 3
  sense of: J.M. Clark 1
hope: George 3; McCulloch 11
  condition of human progress: A. Marshall 1
  increases willingness and power for work: A. Marshall 33
  without, there is no enterprise: A. Marshall 33
horse: Ruskin 12
hospitals: Rousseau 1
household:
  head of, motivated to maximize family opportunities: Becker 2
  management: Aristotle 1
  state is extended: Wicksteed 2
householdry:
  economics is science of: Boulding 3
human action: Mises 11; Syme 1
  course of: A. Marshall 13
  economics branch of theory of: Mises 13
  economics is theory of all: Mises 10
  establishments result of, not of human design: Ferguson 2
  motives of: J.B. Clark 3
  necessarily always rational: Mises 24
  political economy cannot give limits to: Cunningham 5
  praxeology science of: Mises 8
  tendencies of: A. Marshall 13
human body: McCulloch 13
human frailty: Tawney 7
human nature: Jevons 1; Marx 15; Mises 22; Owen 2; A. Smith 7; Tawney 3
  any concept of, matter of psychology: J.M. Clark 3
  cause of poverty not in: George 6
  complete equality unsuitable to: Hamilton 3
  equality most suitable to: Hume 2
  general science of: Bowen 2
  impossible for economist to ignore: J.M. Clark 3
  moral or mental laws of: Bailey 1
  political economists exhibit peculiarities of: Laughlin 4
  political economy treated as moral science, considering resources of: Cunningham 2
  social affections accidental and disturbing elements in: Ruskin 2
  socialism and communism turn upon nature of: Hobson 13
  tendency of, to make private property disappear: Holmes 3
  utopias wrecked upon rocks of: Hobson 13

human progress:
  hope and ambition conditions of: A. Marshall 1
human race: Ruskin 1
  all world's good primarily for support of: John XXIII 1
  elevation of: Peirce 1
  future progression of: J.S. Mill and Ellis 1
  God gave earth for use and enjoyment of: Leo XIII 3
human will: Menger 1; Pareto 3
humanism: Marx 7
humanitarianism:
  Christian: Webb and Webb 6
humanity: Owen 5; A. Smith 2
  has other interests than wealth: A. Walker 2
humility:
  fundamental attitude of individualism: Hayek 13
hunger: Malthus 11; Shaw 2
  character building value of: Galbraith 1
hunter: Marx 14
husbandry: Bailey 1; Locke 2
husbands: Senior 4
hydrodynamics: Clower 6; Walras 3
hygiene:
  choice guided by: Wieser 1
hyperbola: Webb 4
hypotheses: Kaldor 1; Little 2; Newcomb 2; Robbins 5, 6; Robinson 7
  in economics, what we lack the least: H. Simon 4

icon-ometrics: Hendry 1
ideas: Moore 1; Patten 6; Stigler 2; Taylor 2
  germ of, in early writers: Fisher 8
  implications of, for economic policy: Krugman 1
  nothing so powerful as, whose time has come: Eatwell 1
  origin of: Eatwell 2
  should freely spread: Jefferson 3
ideals: Taylor 3
ideology: Robinson 6, 16; Schumpeter 4
idleness: Senior 4
  effects of prevention of: Hale 1
  to be protected against competition is to be protected in: J.S. Mill 13
idlers:
  must bear brunt of defects: Chamberlain 1
idolatry: Tawney 1
ignorance: Lerner 1; Owen 4, 5; Sumner 2; F.A. Walker 10
  creates envy, jealousy, and desire to possess: Owen 6
  exists amidst wealth and privilege: Owen 6
  justified by high cost of search or learning: Kirzner 2
  of leading principles of political economy: J. Mill 1
  optimal: Kirzner 2
illiterate: Maitland 2
imagination: List 1; Malthus 12; Patten 1
  economist needs: A. Marshall 15, 16
  mankind arrives at ends which could not anticipate: Ferguson 1

imitation:
    can lead to ruin: Mandeville 1
impartiality, scientific: J.M. Clark 4
imperialism:
    how Marxists must approach: Bukharin 3
imports: Sedgwick 5
impoverishment: F.A. Walker 2
    and depression: Fisher 4
    and taxation: Say 4
imprisonment: Rothbard 10
improvidence: Senior 4
imprudence: Sumner 4
impulse: Sumner 7
incentives: Bastiat 8; Lindbeck 2; Rostow 2
inclinations: Leslie 2
income: J.M. Keynes 3; Samuelson 2; Simonde de Sismondi 7; Walras 1
    ascertainment of individual, extremely difficult: Seligman 9
    concept: Hayek 30
    consumption greater due to increase in: J. Simon 2
    equality of: Shaw 6; Wieser 8
    equality of, and socialism: Kautsky 3
    minimum: Galbraith 1
    of community: J.M. Keynes 10
    tax on: Scrope 10
    taxes paid from: Ricardo 10
    whoever can subsist and lives above, is a fool: Mandeville 1
income distribution: Boulding 8
    and socialism: A. Marshall 29
    ethical principle of: Friedman 2
    liberals find it hard to see justification for graduated taxation for: Friedman 22
    never avowed purpose of social security: Hayek 22
    see also: redistribution
independence: J.M. Keynes 21; Ricardo 7; F.A. Walker 6
India: Luther 3
indigent, indigence:
    disappearance of, caused by growth of wealth: Carey 5
    protection against, object of usury laws: Brougham 2
    removal proper object of poor laws: Chadwick 1
    support of: Chalmers 1
individual(s): Adams 1; Alchian 1; Atkinson 1; J.M. Keynes 27
    acting separately, are too ignorant or weak to attain ends: J.M. Keynes 11
    and cooperation: Mises 31
    duty of: Carver 9
    happiness of: Bentham 9
    profit for: Kautsky 4
    social animals, not self-seeking monsters or machines: J.M. Clark 7
    socialism is intellectual's way of solving problem of saving: Lederer 1
    state should encourage voluntary action, to allow provision for self and family: Beveridge 2

individual development:
    as remedy for poverty: Atkinson 1
individualism: Bastiat 1; Marx 14, 15; Rostow 2
    chief concern of writers: Hayek 12
    humility fundamental attitude of: Hayek 13
    not antithetical to socialism: Graham 2
    safe for community to give interests large scope: J.M. Clark 7
individuality:
    growth of wealth, restrains development of: Carey 5
indolence: Bowen 1; Wayland 6
    socialists overlook natural: J.S. Mill 13
induction: Syme 1
indulgence: J.S. Mill 21; Robinson 5
industrial arts: J.S. Mill 4
industrial chemistry:
    economics should dominate and coordinate activities of: C. Clark 2
industrial democracy: Tuttle 1
industrial despot: Tuttle 1
industrial legislation: Cairnes 2
industrial organization: Stigler 10; Tawney 8
industrial reform: Cairnes 3
industrial society:
    science of: Adams 1
industriousness: Locke 6; McCulloch 10, 11; J.S. Mill 8, 23; Owen 4; Ricardo 7; Simonde de Sismondi 3; A. Smith 11; Sumner 4, 7; Tucker 1; Wayland 2, 4, 7; Webb and Webb 2
    monopoly is taxation of: J.S. Mill 13
    of people, each increase in public burden increases proportionately: Hume 7
    poor laws weaken incentive to: Malthus 8
    proper to do nothing to weaken spirit of: McCulloch 4
    schemes and projects do not benefit: Webster 2
industry: Coke 1; Marx 13; McCulloch 2; Pigou 4; Ricardo 2; Senior 5; Simonde de Sismondi 2; A. Smith 16, 21, 23; F.A. Walker 8; Walras 4
    and the state: J.N. Keynes 3
    discretionary control of: Veblen 1
    disordered currency wars against: Webster 1
    divorce of private ownership from work, corrupting to: Tawney 6
    does nothing but produce scarce things: Walras 5
    easy to contrive projects for encouragement of: Berkeley 5
    evolution of: Hobson 2
    is republican, can never be democratic: Sumner 3
    localization of: A. Marshall 32
    man sagacious enough to see what branches most profitable: Bowen 3
    paralyzed by heavy taxation: McCulloch 11
    placed at disadvantage by over-taxation: J.S. Mill 24
    products of: F.A. Walker 11
    protection cripples: Price 3
    riches motive to: Berkeley 3
    socialism would reduce produce of: Sidgwick 3
    socialized: Fisher 13
    spontaneous direction of: Scrope 5
    success in requires stamina: Schumpeter 4

industry (*cont.*):
    tax on: J.S. Mill 22
    taxation on, restrains production: George 6
    taxes commonly converted into punishment on: Hume 9
    violent fluctuations do harm to: Webster 2
inefficiency: Sumner 4
inequality: Aquinas 2; Carlyle 2; Jefferson 3; Laveleye 1
    and virtue, justice, and knowledge: Owen 3
    church recognizes: Leo XIII 1
    concern for: Galbraith 3
    function of government to prevent extreme: Rousseau 1
    of fortune, impoverishes lower orders: Maitland 3
    of fortune, principal impediment to increase of public wealth: Maitland 3
    of income and property: Wieser 8
    of skill: Hegel 5
    of taxes: Hume 9
    of wealth: Hegel 5
    of wealth, justly established, benefits nation: Ruskin 5
    of wealth, unjustly established, injures nation: Ruskin 5
    reduction of, requires eliminating causes of: Lerner 2
    state should never use taxation to eliminate: Wieser 8
    world cannot be supported without: Owen 3
inference: H. Simon 1
inflation: Cassel 4; Solow 2; Stigler 10
    always and everywhere a monetary phenomenon: Friedman 10, 12
    attributed to other devils incarnate: Friedman 12
    caused by monopoly unions: Lindblom 1
    classical medicine cannot halt: Friedman 6
    economists called on to halt accelerating: Hayek 11
    greatest difficulty in curtailing, people would rather have sickness than cure: Friedman 11
    greatly exaggerated as social evil: Tobin 1
    legal counterfeiting: Fisher 9
    lubricates trade: Galbraith 4
    means of confiscation of wealth by government: J.M. Keynes 12
    monetary policy has not stopped without recession: Friedman 17
    only way to stop is to restrain rate of growth of money supply: Friedman 10
    rescues traders from errors: Galbraith 4
    secular: Boulding 8
    true opium of the people: Mises 15
inflationism: J.M. Keynes 12
information: Kirzner 2; Lindbeck 2; Wright 3
    econometricians pitifully short of: Klein 2
    function of money system, to direct to production and distribution: Douglas 1
    transmission of: Hayek 1
ingenuity: McCulloch 11; Ricardo 2
inheritance:
    dead hand of: Crosland 1

land is original: J.S. Mill 12
    taxes on, unjust: George 9
iniquity: Ruskin 10
initiative: F.A. Walker 9
    and general good: A. Marshall 2
    socialists have no desire to penalize: Crosland 1
    socialist suppose man devoid of: Bastiat 10
injustice: Laughlin 6; J.S. Mill 10; A. Smith 11
    and income tax: Seligman 8
    as cause of poverty: George 6
    government springs from: F.A. Walker 2
    ignores true rights of property: George 6
    of degraded paper: Webster 1
    socialism does not depend on: Carver 7
    taxes are, by nature: George 9
innocence: Stolper 2
innovation(s): Malthus 3; Mises 16
    are the births of time: Bacon 3
insolence:
    too much money causes: Mandeville 3
inspection: Hobson 2
inspiration: Locke 5
institutional economics:
    derives methodology from corporation finance: Commons 4
    is assets and liabilities of concerns: Commons 4
Institutionalism:
    relation of man to man: Commons 5
institutions: Ayres 9; Babson 1; Brunner 1; Edgeworth 4; Holmes 1; J.M. Keynes 4; J. Marshall 2; Shaw 2; H. Simon 1, 3; A. Smith 11; Young 1
    artificial and natural: Marx 10
    as basic category of social analysis: Ayres 9
    collective action in control, liberation, and expansion of individual action: Commons 6
    key, must be accepted as absolutes: Friedman 20
    private property as: Knight 15
    set of, by which man could be induced to contribute to needs of all: Hayek 12
    social: Dobb 4
    social insurance as: Mises 26
integrity: Seligman 9
    cardinal virtue of capitalism: Greenspan 2
    in doing justice, most necessary in government: Rousseau 1
intellect: A. Marshall 3
intellectual autonomy: Hollander 1
intellectual discipline:
    in economics departments: Leontief 1
intellectual diversity: Debreu 2
intellectual faculties: E.P. Smith 1
intellectual furniture: Tawney 2
intellectual goods: Mayer 4
intellectual interests: Usher 2
intellectual standards: Webb and Webb 7
intellectuals: Lederer 1
    some believe in concentrated power as force for good: Friedman 21
intelligence: Sumner 7; W. Thompson 1
    of individuals and nation: J.S. Mill 3
intemperance: Owen 4

interest: D. North 7; Petty 11
  and usury: Newcomb 9
  applied to breeding of money: Aristotle 5
  birth of money from money: Aristotle 5
  commonly reckoned for money: Barbon 2
  high rate of will bring money out of hoards:
    D. North 1
  horrible formulas for explaining phenomena of:
    Cassel 2
  impossible to make law against: Locke 1
  index of amount of good that money is doing:
    Newcomb 4
  justice of: Aquinas 2
  legal: D. North 2; Steuart-Denham 3
  most unnatural mode of getting wealth: Aristotle 5
  no part of economics has suffered more than theory
    of: Cassel 2
  nothing esteemed more certain sign of flourishing
    nation than lowness of: Hume 3
  paid for stock: Barbon 2
  rule that the merchant trades by: Barbon 1
  when laws restrain, trade is lopt off: D. North 2
interference: Stolper 2
international relations: Schumpeter 4
international trade: *see* free trade; trade
internationalism: Schumpeter 11
interlocking directorates:
  root of many evils: Brandeis 1
intervention:
  economics offshoot of: Mises 12
  economists' self-interest leads them to favor:
    Friedman 8
intrigue: Sumner 2
intuition: J.M. Keynes 7
  atrophy of: Galbraith 5
invention: Adams 2; Bacon 2; Bowen 7; McCulloch
    11; Rae 2
  cannot be subject of property: Jefferson 2
  few of importance made by government:
    A. Marshall 17
  only power on earth that can be said to create:
    Rae 3
  result of spontaneous activities of citizens:
    Spencer 3
  state not responsible for: Spencer 3
inventiveness:
  and general good: A. Marshall 2
inventories: H. Simon 7
inventors: J. Simon 2
inverted cone: Boulding 1
investment: Lerner 4
  capitalism and: Shaw 2
  money and: Newcomb 4
  socialization of, only means of securing full
    employment: J.M. Keynes 26
invisibility:
  of exchange: Simmel 4
invisible hand: Hahn 3; A. Smith 13, 21
involuntary servitude:
  taxation form of: Rothbard 11
iron: Jevons 8

iron works: A. Marshall 19
irrationality: Dobb 1; Mises 8, 13; Owen 4
  inappropriate and meaningless: Mises 24
ivory tower: Johnson 1

jails: Hale 1
Japanese garden: Friedman 15
jargon: Proudhon 4; Samuelson 3
jealousy: Proudhon 2; W. Thompson 1
  created by poverty and ignorance: Owen 6
Jesus Christ: Shaw 7
jobs: Tobin 1
joint-stock companies: Hobson 2
journals: Krugman 1; Stigler 2
judges: F.A. Walker 2
judgment: Bacon 2; Robinson 8; Seligman 3;
    A. Smith 5
  atrophy of: Galbraith 5
  vs. facts: Knight 6
juries: F.A. Walker 2
jurisdictional disputes: Viner 4
jurisprudence: Hayek 10; Ross 1
jurists: Nicholson 1
justice: H. Fawcett 2; John XXIII 2; J.M. Keynes 15;
    Laughlin 6; J.S. Mill 22; Owen 3; Schmoller 1;
    Schumacher 1; A. Smith 16; Usher 4
  administration of: Scrope 9; Simonde de Sismondi
    3; A. Smith 11
  and income tax: Seligman 8
  and private property and inequality: Owen 3
  and state, in respect of taxes: Carver 9
  and taxation: Steuart-Denham 5
  criminal: F.A. Walker 2
  difference between material and formal:
    Schmoller 2
  equal, and equal imposition of taxes: Hobbes 2
  for socialism, informed by law: Laveleye 1
  free competition controlled by: J.B. Clark 5
  ideal of: Hayek 6
  in distribution: Carver 8
  in taxation: Scrope 10
  integrity in, most necessary in government:
    Rousseau 1
  object of socialism to secure distribution of wealth
    founded on: J.B. Clark 8
  of distribution of produce of labor, no criterion
    provided by theory of value: Bernstein 2
  of taxes, comparative: J.S. Mill 25
  plea of communism and Christianity: Knight 2
  principles of: Laveleye 2
  socialism does not depend on: Carver 7
  standards of: Schmoller 2
  tax on land values has element of: George 9
  usury contrary to: Aquinas 2

Kaiser: Ely 1
Kalecki, Michal: Robinson 12
Kapital (Marx): Shaw 7
Keynes, John Maynard: Knight 12; Meek 1
Keynesianism: Hayek 17; Meek 1
kitchens: Sedgwick 5

knowledge: Carey 3; C. Clark 1; Friedman 6; Hayek 24; Heckman 2; Jevons 2; J.M. Keynes 3, 21; Kirzner 2; A. Marshall 6, 12; Owen 3; Rothbard 1, 2; T.W. Schultz 1; A. Smith 11; W.H. Smith 1; Wayland 2
  academic economists claim to produce: Mayer 3
  and private property and inequality: Owen 3
  availability of: Stone 1
  contribution to, of economic history: Heckman 1
  division of: Hayek 1
  economics did not pursue for own sake: Hayek 8
  genetics of: Boulding 7
  is belief: Leamer 3
  is opinion: Leamer 3
  objective, realistic, precise: Florence 1
  of individuals and nation: J.S. Mill 3
  political economy systematized body of: Fetter 2
  special, of economist: Hayek 7
  stock of useful: J. Simon 1

labels:
  misleading: Hansen 2
labor, laborer: Marx 21; Morrow 2; Proudhon 2; Ricardo 2, 8; Ross 1; Ruskin 6, 14; Scrope 2, 5; Simonde de Sismondi 4; A. Smith 16, 21, 23; Tolstoy 3, 4; Tucker 1; Wayland 4; Wieser 7
  abstract: Marx 23
  accumulated: Torrens 2
  advantage of employer, nothing but plunder: Simonde de Sismondi 2
  alone is productive: Marx 4
  and commons: Locke 6
  and industrial arts: J.S. Mill 4
  and pain: Adams 2
  and property: Locke 5
  and taxation: Edmonds 2
  aversion from: Leslie 2
  capitalist always living on product of past: Fisher 3
  class of: Malthus 12
  competition benefits: J.S. Mill 13
  competition *of* and competition *for*: J.S. Mill 13
  condition of: Newcomb 6
  contribution of, to production: Leo XIII 3
  converted into commodities: Marx 18
  curse of: Wayland 7
  demand for: Carver 6
  distribution of produce, not justified by theory of value: Bernstein 2
  elevated by consciousness that he has not neglected opportunities: McCulloch 5
  excessive: Webb 1
  exploitation of: Marx 6
  forced: Rothbard 11
  form which produces wealth: Cantillon 3
  freedom of, presupposed by freedom of capital: Bagehot 3
  giver of all value: George 2
  gratification from: Newcomb 3
  he who tampers with currency, robs of its bread: Webster 2
  hoarded: Torrens 2
  if supply excessive, socialism cannot prevent remuneration from being low: J.S. Mill 13
  in interest of public, should be free to bargain collectively: Commons and Andrews 3
  is an evil: Pantaleoni 2
  is negative commodity: Pantaleoni 2
  machinery and: Marx 3
  machinery increase number of slaves of: Marx 11
  maintenance of: Ricardo 10
  man's inclination to, controlled by his desire: Bowen 3
  means of relief procured from: Ellis 2
  mixed with nature, becomes property: Locke 4
  money embased to purchase more: Petty 1
  money representation of: Hume 5
  nothing on common with paupers: McCulloch 5
  no such thing as abstract: Carver 5
  not true, functional social group: Hoxie 2
  of others, direct or instrumental commodity: Pantaleoni 2
  of others, positive commodity: Pantaleoni 2
  of poor: Wayland 8
  of poor, from which arise comforts of life: Mandeville 4
  once spent, has no influence on future value: Jevons 5
  paid and unpaid: Marx 5
  persons ought to receive fruits of: Hume 2
  political economy teaches way to achieve adequate reward for: Torrens 1
  produces for capital: Marx 4
  productive powers of: A. Smith 5
  products of earth are effects of: Locke 2
  products of, equated to one another: Marx 18
  property of laborer: Locke 4
  property of, should overbalance community of land: Locke 2
  quantity used in production, measure of value: Cantillon 2
  right to results of: Wayland 9
  self-interest great incentive to: Laveleye 3
  socialism seeks reconstruction of society so that product of accrues to: Ely 7
  subjugation of: Marx 9
  supply of: Carver 6
  tax is portion of taken and disposed of by government: McCulloch 12
  taxation affects amount employed on luxuries and production of wealth: Edmonds 1
  taxes take from, its just reward: George 11
  the more powerful, the less powerful the laborer: Marx 1
  transformation into capital: Marx 5
  unnatural that should not be exchangeable for equivalent in food, shelter, clothing: George 2
  value and: Marx 17
  value and property derive from: Laveleye 2
  various kinds, in the concrete: Carver 5
  violent fluctuations do harm to: Webster 2
  wise employment of: Ely 1

labor hours:
  maximum: Webb 1
labor market:
  overstocking of: J.S. Mill 13
labor movement:
  impact on flexibility of price structure: Boulding 8
  questioning virtues of like attacking religion: Simons 5
  slight embarrassment: Boulding 8
labor power:
  constant capital, embodiment of: Robinson 10
labor problem:
  he who increases demand for or supply of has right to speak on: Carver 6
labor unions: *see* unions
laboratory: Viner 1
laissez-faire: Cunningham 6
  and liberalism: Hayek 14
  Constitution not intended to embody: Holmes 2
  defined: Bowen 5
  destitute of all scientific authority: Cairnes 2
  football team example of system for which is not good idea: Sargent 1
  has no scientific basis: Cairnes 2
  market system plus anarchism: Lindbeck 3
  meaning of: Mises 17, 18
  mere handy tool of practice: Cairnes 2
  monopoly comes into existence because of: Jaffé 1
  must not stand in way of social or industrial reform: Cairnes 3
  only social system based on recognition of individual rights: Rand 1
  only system fundamentally opposed to war: Rand 1
  opposed to state control: Cairnes 3
  phase in history of economic liberalism: Usher 3
  policy of, worst of all: Webb 2
  practical rule, not doctrine of science: Cairnes 3
  proof of impossibility no reason for preventing people from doing what they want to do: Cairnes 3
  school of political economy: Walras 4
  served interest of capitalist business: Robinson 16
  socialism departs from: J.M. Keynes 24
  tyranny of: Adams 1
land: Barbon 6; Morrow 2; Mun 5; D. North 7; Scrope 5; Shaw 1; A. Smith 16, 23; Whately 5; Wieser 7
  appropriation of, question of general expediency: J.S. Mill 12
  community: Locke 2
  fertility of: Cantillon 2
  left to nature, is waste: Locke 7
  no man made: J.S. Mill 12
  of crown: A. Smith 18
  original inheritance of whole species: J.S. Mill 12
  private property in: J.S. Mill 12
  production of: Leo XIII 3
  productive power of, and exclusiveness: J.S. Mill 10
  proprietor of, should not be mere sinecurist: J.S. Mill 11
  quantity used in production, measure of value: Cantillon 2

  source or matter of wealth: Cantillon 3
  tax: Petty 9
  tenure: H. Fawcett 2
  use of in agriculture must be of necessity exclusive: J.S. Mill 10
language: Price 1; Samuelson 9
  common use of: Sidgwick 1
lash: Spencer 4
law(s): Aquinas 3; Bentham 8; Friedman 9; George 11; Greenspan 1; Heilbroner 1; J.S. Mill 8; Mises 20, 25; Newcomb 8; Ricardo 8; Rothbard 6; Ruskin 10; Senior 4; Simonde de Sismondi 3; A. Smith 19; Tucker 1; Wayland 2
  administration of, ought to proceed upon supposition of universal fraternity: Phillips 1
  courts of: McCulloch 9
  curse to every part of society: Owen 7
  determining profit, prices, production: Leslie 5
  economics has effect on making: J.B. Clark 6
  enact such as necessary to enable laborers to maintain equality: Brownson 1
  every man owes conformity to: Child 2
  evil of greatest magnitude: Owen 7
  free competition controlled by: J.B. Clark 5
  fundamental: Harrington 1
  general, of the universe: Bowen 5
  of economic world: Leslie 6
  of physical world: Leslie 6
  opinions of majority embodies in: Holmes 1
  ought to pay attention to what is most easily taken away: Rousseau 3
  prerequisite of all civilized economic activity: Olson 1
  preventive: Greenspan 2
  primeval: Tolstoy 3
  regulate price of money: Locke 1
  repeal all which bear against laboring classes: Brownson 1
  respect for: Rousseau 1
  restraining interest on money: D. North 2
  social: Jefferson 2; Ruskin 10
  special privileges always supported by: Commons 1
  Sunday: Holmes 1
  traders cannot evade: D. North 2
  unwisdom of: F.A. Walker 2
  usury: Holmes 1
law of nature: Malthus 12, 13, 14; Marx 6
  causes humans to suffer from want: Malthus 15
lawyer:
  nobody will do anything for: Mandeville 5
laymen: Bauer and Walters 2
laziness: Lerner 1; More 1
  too much money causes: Mandeville 3
leadership:
socialism rejects, from superior classes: Ely 8
learning: Boulding 7
  high cost of, and ignorance: Kirzner 2
legal penalties: Aquinas 3
legal tender:
  creation of, government's ultimate reserve: J.M. Keynes 13

legislation: Carlyle 2; Senior 3; Webb 3; Wright 2
  economics does not direct: Merivale 1
  economist specialist in: Mises 12
  guidance in directing or limiting competitive action: Adams 1
  interference: Senior 5
  just and wise: J.S. Mill 22
  maximum price: Cassel 4
  ought to proceed upon supposition of universal fraternity: Phillips 1
legislative interference: Hobson 2
legislator(s): Jefferson 3; Stewart 1; Sumner 2; Torrens 1
  attempt of to control industry, productive of harm: Bowen 5
  never ought to interfere: Rae 1
  should direct energy of community toward furtherance of power of invention: Rae 2
legislature: McCulloch 2; Rogers 1; W.H. Smith 2; F.A. Walker 8
  effort needed by to regulate numbers of poor: Ricardo 7
  interference of: Ricardo 6
lending: Aquinas 2; Bacon 5
Lenin, V.I.: J.M. Keynes 12
'Let alone': Phillips 1
liberal:
  consistent, is not an anarchist: Friedman 9
  finds it hard to justify graduated taxation to redistribute income: Friedman 22
liberal ethos: Bell 1
liberalism:
  and *laissez-faire*: Hayek 14; Usher 3
  socialism corrupted by: Simons 4
liberality:
  and money: Cicero 1
libertarianism: Rothbard 8; Samuelson 4
libertarians:
  and socialists: Simons 4
liberty: Adams 2; J.M. Keynes 21; Rousseau 3; Sumner 7; Whately 3
  aim must be to amend: M. Polanyi 1
  and market: Mises 2
  democracy seeks equality in: Tocqueville 1
  every encroachment of, prepares acceptance of socialism: H. Fawcett 6
  natural: A. Smith 11, 16
  no system of socialism possible without abridgment of: Newcomb 6
  of citizen: Holmes 1
  personal: Webb 1
  poor sacrifice blessing of: Malthus 10
  sacrificed to join socialistic community: H. Fawcett 5
  socialism proposes that society shall force individual to surrender: Newcomb 5
  socialism takes away from man's natural: J.M. Keynes 24
  socialist would deprive worker of: Leo XIII 4
  socialistic schemes annihilate: Sumner 7
  taxation instrument of government whereby common people obtain: Ely 9
  to contract: Holmes 1
  true and false: J.B. Clark 5
license: J.B. Clark 5
licensing:
  AEA dismal failure at establishing: Barro 1
life: Solow 1
  business of: J.S. Mill 2
  conveniences of: Locke 6
  pace of: Simmel 5
  preservation of: Rousseau 3
lightning: Syme 2
linguistics: Hayek 10
literae humaniores: Edgeworth 2
literary lucidity:
  unfair to impose problems of, on mathematical economists: Dorfman 1
lobby: F.A. Walker 8
logic: Dupuit 2; Samuelson 9
  bad: Samuelson 11
  economics as branch of pure: Hayek 9
  science of apodictic certainty: Atwater 1
logical methods: Edgeworth 2
logical reasoning:
  propositions of economics derived from: Vickrey 1
logical relations:
  economics a system of: Vickrey 1
London: A. Marshall 24
London Bridge: Yarranton 1
long-run: Leslie 4; J. Simon 1
  we are all dead: J.M. Keynes 16; Stigler 1; Viner 3
  we are all out of office: Hayek 17
loss: Barbon 1; Croce 1; Rothbard 1
lottery: J.M. Keynes 12
  as tax: Petty 4
  prohibition of: Holmes 1
love: Boulding 4; Hoxie 3; Joplin 3; Malthus 11
  socialism destroys: Sumner 6
lovers: Boulding 6
loyalty: Robinson 1
lungs: Whately 3
Luther, Martin: Shaw 7
luxury; luxuries: Hobbes 2; Luther 2; Mandeville 1; Ricardo 9; Rousseau 1; Ruskin 10; Scrope 3
  best taxes levied on: Hume 8
  in virtuous world, no one would derive larger share of: A. Marshall 2
  proper government would not permit trade in: Luther 3
  taxation diminishes labor employed on: Edmonds 1
  must be made cheap to those who consume it: Babbage 1
  where riches instrument to, enervate and dispirit: Berkeley 3

machinery:
  increases number of slaves of labor: Marx 11
  introduction of, and labor: Marx 3
  political economists of standing on: Marx 11
machines: Lenin 3; Tuttle 1
  for making cloth: Bailey 1
macroeconomics: Boulding 9; Solow 2
  models: Buchanan 4

need not have been born at all: Buchanan 4
receives attention in newspapers: Lucas 1
macro-theory: Machlup 2
magic: M. Polanyi 1; Wiener 2
magistracy: Shaw 1
magistrates: More 1
Mahomet: Shaw 7
majority:
    opinions of, embodied in law: Holmes 1
    power of: Wayland 3
malevolence: Graham 1
    economic man and: Boulding 4
man: Schumpeter 7
    amelioration of condition of, ought to be leading object: Hamilton 1
    appetites of, main spur to trade: D. North 4
    arrives at ends which imagination could not anticipate: Ferguson 1
    as completely social as a termite: Knight 17
    as social animal: Mises 31
    behaves economically well or ill: Croce 1
    behavior of: Little 3
    by nature a social animal: George 5
    cannot equalize conditions of: Chamberlain 1
    conversation: McCloskey 2
    depravity of: Malthus 12
    directed by circumstances in which he is placed: Ferguson 2
    does not live by bread alone: Mosca 3
    economic condition of: J.S. Mill 17
    economics deals with problems of: Commons 3
    God made all things for use of: Coke 1
    governed by products of own brain: Marx 6
    has property in own person: Locke 4
    imperfection of: Aquinas 3
    inadequate conceptions of: J.B. Clark 4
    individualization of: Marx 16
    influence of system of finance on happiness and habits of: Palgrave 1
    material life of, not sole concern of economist: Ely 5
    most versatile of all forms of capital: Fisher 2
    nature of: J.B. Clark 3
    none lives out of society: Coke 2
    not influenced solely by hope, but also fear: McCulloch 11
    perfectability of: Malthus 3
    practical actions of: Fetter 2
    progress of: Aristotle 3
    social activities of, cannot be adequately determined: J.B. Clark 4
    social animal: Marx 16
    socialists suppose a form of vegetation: Bastiat 10
    socialist suppose devoid of initiative: Bastiat 10
    zoon politikon: Marx 16
management: Ely 1; Taft 2
    communistic less favorable than private: J.S. Mill 17
    monopoly great enemy to good: A. Smith 15
mankind, evils of:
    governments make out they can cure: Bagehot 10
manners: Steuart-Denham 2
manufacturers: Bailey 1; Engels 1; Marx 11; Simonde de Sismondi 3; Southey 2; Spencer 3

Marconi: Pigou 1
mariner: H. Schultz 4
Marines: Leontief 1
market: Eatwell 2; Hahn 5; Mises 3, 12; Rostow 2
    all is harmony: Rothbard 5
    altruism less common in than families: Becker 1
    altruism less efficient in than families: Becker 1
    and anarchism: Lindbeck 3
    becomes chaotic muddle if private property is eliminated: Mises 3
    brings about freedom and liberty: Mises 2
    defects of, lead to usury: Cassel 4
    economics does not have predestined mission to dispel mysteries of: Posner 2
    ethical principle of free: Friedman 2
    exemplifies ideal of interaction: Gauthier 2
    free: Friedman 2, 8, 21
    higgling and bargaining of: A. Smith 24
    if taxes grow beyond moderate limit, turn into devices for destruction of: Mises 34
    imperfections of: Friedman 8; Lewis 3
    interest of dealers to widen: A. Smith 19
    is the best judge of value: Barbon 1
    man-made mode of acting under division of labor: Mises 1
    monetarism most bizarre form of devotion to: Eatwell 4
    needs no apologists and propagandists: Mises 4
    product of evolutionary process: Mises 1
    serves variety of functions: M. Perlman 5
    socialism tendency to transcend self-regulating: K. Polanyi 2
    socialism violent abolition of: Rothbard 9
    spontaneous coordination of: Buchanan 3; Hayek 25
    wages should be left to fair and free competition of: Ricardo 6
market place:
    Victorian: Samuelson 4
marriage: Edgeworth 4; Malthus 6, 7; Ricardo 7; Sumner 2
Mars: Stigler 3
martini: Solow 5
Marx, Karl: Engels 4; Haberler 1; Meek 1; Mises 29; Robinson 10, 11, 12; Rostow 2; Shaw 7
    method of: Bukharin 3
Marxism: Seligman 6
    always an intellectual attitude: Baran 1
    cannot teach much about cunning central bank: Meek 1
    close of: Haberler 1
    equivalent to communism: Berle 1
    fundamental principle of: Baran 1
    how must approach analysis of imperialism: Bukharin 3
    illogical and dull: J.M. Keynes 23
    influence on history: J.M. Keynes 23
    is economics of capitalism: Vickrey 2
    is not and never was intended to be a positive science: Baran 1
    is opium of Marxists: Robinson 9
    is religion: Schumpeter 7
    not tenable or intelligible: Veblen 6

Marxism (*cont.*):
   promises paradise: Schumpeter 7
Marxists: Samuelson 6
   maintain productive forces of capitalism powerful
      enough to eliminate poverty: Sweezy 1
   Marxism is opium of: Robinson 9
   opponents of, in sin: Schumpeter 8
mass: Schumpeter 9
masses:
   condition of, satisfactory in proportion to
      millionaires: Carnegie 5
materialism: Mises 20
   philosophy of: Schumacher 1
maternity: Webb and Webb 4
mathematical computation: J.B. Clark 4
mathematical formulae: Pareto 4
mathematical laws:
   operate in hypothetical vacuum: Roscher 4
mathematical method: Fisher 10; Pareto 8
   in economics, nearly always waste of time:
      A. Marshall 21
mathematical physics: Edgeworth 2
mathematical proof: J.M. Keynes 7
mathematical reasoning:
   and economics: A. Marshall 20
mathematically unwashed: Boulding 9
mathematicians: Boulding 10; J.M. Keynes 4;
      Morgenstern 2
   economists have commonly been first: Knight 8
   economists like: Durbin 1
   good ones avoid fudging: Robinson 13
   have feeling for scientific procedure: Croce 2
   revived dignity in economics: Croce 2
   who make false calculation: Dupuit 2
mathematics: Allen 1, 2; Ayres 4; Baumol 1, 2;
      Boulding 1, 6, 9, 10; Cassel 1; J.B. Clark 7;
      Cunningham 10; Edgeworth 5; Frisch 1; Horner
      1; Hutt 1; Jevons 6; Klein 3; J.M. Keynes 17;
      A. Marshall 9; McCloskey 2; Morgenstern 1, 2;
      Pareto 5; Roscher 3; Senior 3; Stevenson 3;
      Zeuthen 1
   ability to understand advanced, rarely associated
      with relevance of economic theory:
      Champernowne 2
   analogy of, to political economy: De Quincey 1
   and economics: Hayek 9; A. Marshall 20
   arguments against, are arguments against science:
      Tinbergen 1
   asks for weak assumptions, strong conclusions,
      greater generality: Debreu 1
   can be useful: Robinson 13
   cannot be worse than prose in economic theory:
      Samuelson 9
   cannot explain all aspects of economic problems:
      Launhardt 1
   constructions should be treated as scaffolding:
      Edgeworth 6
   contributes to clarity of thought: Wicksell 2
   criticisms of, childish: Duesenberry 1
   economics analogous to: Roscher 4
   economics and: T. Thompson 1
   gin in martini of economics: Solow 5
   good theorem, unlikely to be good economics:
      A. Marshall 22
   has not purged economics of irrelevance: Mayer 5
   in economics: Leontief 2, 3, 4, 5; Samuelson 8;
      Wicksell 2; Wieser 2
   in social science: Wiener 1, 2
   inappropriate employment of, in economics: Bauer 3
   is a language: Samuelson 9
   is language: Samuelson 9
   knowledge of, neither necessary nor sufficient
      condition for career in economics: Samuelson 10
   limited application in social sciences: Cairnes 4
   methods and language of: Walras 3
   must be used in social sciences: Carey 3
   once used, should be burned: A. Marshall 22
   political economy approaches strict science of:
      Malthus 2
   political economy in realm of: Dupuit 2
   poorly understood by most economists: Wilson 1
   prejudice of, introduced into economics: Croce 2
   prestige of methods: Bauer and Walters 3
   prolonged commitment to in economics is
      damaging: Galbraith 5
   provides economist with language and method:
      Debreu 1
   scaffolding or steel framework of economic theory:
      Allen 2
   should not condemn application of: Launhardt 1
   too rigid and simple to handle evolution:
      Georgescu-Roegen 1
   uncritical enthusiasm for, conceals ephemeral
      substantive content: Leontief 4
   use of: Wiener 2
   used as shorthand: A. Marshall 22
   veil rather than reveal reality: Dobb 4
   when carried too far: Cairnes 4
   when used for reasoning, regarded with distrust:
      Cairnes 4
maximization:
   individual: Buchanan 2
   not central principle of economics: Buchanan 3
   social: Buchanan 2
measurability: M. Perlman 4
measure: Petty 5
measurement: Schumpeter 9; Shackle 2; Wiener 3
   money one obvious instrument of: Pigou 1
   no such thing as in economics: Mises 19
   of motives: A. Marshall 14
   without theory: Goldberger 1
meat: Ruskin 12
mechanic arts: Yarranton 1
mechanics: Croce 1; Pareto 5, 6; Walras 3, 4
   economics similar to: A. Marshall 5
medical profession:
   should not be burdened with sins of quacks:
      Clower 3
medicine: Friedman 17; Ruskin 3; Tucker 2; Whately 3
mediocrity: Proudhon 2
mendacity:
   may be extirpated: Chadwick 1

mendicancy: Scrope 6
Mensheviks: Seligman 6
mental gymnastics: Hobson 6; Samuelson 8
merchants: Mun 4, 5; Ruskin 6; A. Smith 21; Spencer 3
metaphor: H. Schultz 4; H. Simon 5
metaphysics: Archibald 1; J.S. Mill 6; Myrdal 1; Veblen 3
meteorologist: Mitchell 3
meteorology: Newcomb 2
   Political Economy no more art than: Bowen 4
method: Petty 5; Wieser 5
   deductive: Pareto 8
   good and bad: Pareto 8
   historical: Pareto 8
   inductive: Pareto 8
   mathematical: *see* mathematical method
   of political economy: Pareto 8; Syme 2
   pseudo-mathematical: J.M. Keynes 17
   rigorous: Knight 8
   scientific: Hollander 1
   transfer of from other sciences to economics inapposite and misleading: Eucken 4
methodologists:
   as final interpreter of past and dictator of future efforts: Harrod 2
   cannot take refuge behind cloak of modesty: Harrod 2
   despised by economists: Little 2
   exposed as a bore: Harrod 2
   should model themselves on peace corps worker: Mayer 6
methodology: Åkerman 2; Allen 1; Baumol 2; H. Fawcett 3; Hahn 4; Hutchison 3, 5, 6; Koopmans 3
   antipathy to among economists: Machlup 3
   crude questions of, directly relevant: Machlup 4
   economists have their favorite: Blaug 2
   economists take for granted: Boland 1
   economists trapped in maximization paradigm: Buchanan 3
   few economists discuss: Boland 1
   is like medicine: Blaug 2
   mainstream embodied in neoclassical economics: Boland 1
   of economics: Wieser 4
   of social studies: Wilson 2
   profound philosophy not essential to: Machlup 4
   so forbidding, likely to drive away reader: Machlup 4
   social sciences must develop: Wilson 3
microeconomics: Solow 2
micro-theory: Machlup 2
Middle Ages: Morrow 2; Schumpeter 4
middle class: J.S. Mill 21; Rothbard 8
   comfort of: Usher 4
   equally powerless against treasures of rich and penury of poor: Rousseau 1
military: Southey 2
   men: Boulding 6
   victory: Wootton 2

Mill, John Stuart: Jevons 4
millennium: Phillips 1
millionaires: Wright 4
   condition of masses satisfactory in proportion to: Carnegie 5
   looking after wealth on behalf of rest of us: Lerner 4
   when donate grounds or pictures, wealth diminished: Hobson 14
Milton, John: Edgeworth 4
mineralogy: Ely 3
minimum wage: Pigou 4; Price 2
   generates unemployment: Rothbard 6
   law that makes it illegal to hire employees with limited skills: Friedman 13
miracles: Hahn 3
mischief: Bentham 9
miser: Leslie 2
misery: Coke 3; Hutcheson 1; McCulloch 10; Owen 5; Ricardo 13; A. Smith 17; Webb and Webb 7
   and money: Simmel 1
   increasing population produces: Malthus 4
   necessary consequence of law of nature: Malthus 14
   of lower classes: Say 3
   of poor: Usher 4
   poor laws change wealth and power into: Ricardo 8
   poor relief necessary for removal of: A. Marshall 26
   to prevent recurrence of, beyond power of man: Malthus 10
misfortune: Senior 4; F.A. Walker 6
   poor laws alleviated: Malthus 5
mission statements: Hodgson 1
missionaries: Mayer 6
misspecification: Bronfenbrenner 1
mobility:
   social and economic obstructed by pursuit of equality: Bauer 5
models: Solow 1, 4
   choice of: Malinvaud 1
modeling:
   macroeconometric: Buchanan 4
Molière: M. Perlman 1
monarchy: A. Smith 18
monastery:
   planned economy like: M. Polanyi 1
monetarism:
   dislike term: Friedman 18
   most bizarre form of devotion to market: Eatwell 4
   sensational in conclusions: Hahn 5
   triumph of artifact over plain thinking: Hahn 5
monetarists: Samuelson 6
monetary phenomena: Mises 20
monetary policy: Hayek 15, 16, 17, 18
   had been tried perversely: Friedman 16
   had not been tried: Friedman 16
   has not produced nirvana: Friedman 17
   has not stopped inflation without recession: Friedman 17
   in one sense, clearly failed: Friedman 17
   more we use, less satisfactory it seems: Duesenberry 2

monetary system:
  could not work more effectively to frustrate men's efforts: Graham 1
  stability of, important for promoting trade and welfare: Cassel 3
monetary theory: Stigler 10
  has respectable ancient name: Friedman 18
  like Japanese garden: Friedman 15
money: Aquinas 2; Aristotle 5; Ayres 10; Bacon; Bagehot 6, 7, 11, 12, 13; Barbon 6; Bentham 7; Bowen 4, 6, 7; Horner 1; Luther 2; Morrow 1; Mun 5; Ruskin 14; Simonde de Sismondi 6, 7; A. Smith 18; Southey 2; Webster 1, 2
  absolute means and purpose for most people: Simmel 3
  and investments: Newcomb 4
  and trade and usury: Mun 5
  and usury: Newcomb 9
  anonymity and colorlessness of: Simmel 4
  arbitrary scale of equal parts: Steuart-Denham 4
  as exchangeable value: Bagehot 11
  as universal form or garb: Bowen 6
  borrowing: Locke 1
  breeding of: Aristotle 5
  cannot make money just with: Luther 1
  center around which economic science clusters: A. Marshall 23
  cheap: Hayek 16
  circulation of: Joplin 2
  coinage of: Erasmus 1
  common measure: Huskisson 1
  condition of true: F.A. Walker 4
  considered all powerful: Schumacher 1
  control of, supreme and most comprehensive of government controls: Stolper 2
  convenient means of measuring human motive on large scale: A. Marshall 23
  conventional is impossible: Turgot 1
  credit system socializes other people's: Hilferding 1
  crystal formed of necessity in course of exchange: Marx 18
  curse attached to: Kautsky 1
  debasement of: Friedman 12
  debases master and thrall: Tolstoy 3
  degrades gods of man: Marx 17
  depends upon what people think it is or ought to be: Harrod 3
  distribution of, in society: Malthus 6
  documentary claim to wealth: Ruskin 7
  does away with all human intercourse: Tolstoy 3
  duty of government to keep value steady: Shaw 4
  easier to live without, than without poor: Mandeville 2
  economic life based upon conception of: Cassel 2
  economist though to care only about: Christ 1
  embasement of, is tax: Petty 1, 2
  essence of: Simmel 3
  estranged essence of man's work and existence: Marx 17
  every exaction of, is discouragement: Holmes 5
  everybody can understand: Ruskin 8
  excellent invention: Davanzati 1
  expresses magnitude of value in other commodities: Marx 19
  expression of right: Ruskin 7
  formlessness and abstractness of: Simmel 4
  foundation of system of prices: Mitchell 1
  government and: Joplin 1
  government can live a long time by printing: J.M. Keynes 14
  government can play tricks with value of: Shaw 4
  government drains from pockets of people: A. Smith 12
  government has no right to alter value of: Wayland 5
  government issuance of: Hayek 18
  government responsibility for: Stolper 2
  has no certificate of origin: Simmel 4
  high interest will bring out of hoards: D. North 1
  highest interest of trading country to make plentiful: Franklin 1
  importance of, flows from being link between present and future: J.M. Keynes 19
  inconvertible paper: Sedgwick 1
  index of amount of good to fellow men: Newcomb 4
  inflation accompanied by rise in quantity of: Friedman 10
  instrument of doing good: Davanzati 1
  instrument to facilitate exchange: Hume 4; Wayland 4
  intended to be used in exchange: Aristotle 5
  interest commonly reckoned for: Barbon 2
  interest on: D. North 2; Steuart-Denham 3
  invented for measuring respective value: Steuart-Denham 4
  is a value made by a law: Barbon 4
  is but fat of body politic: Petty 6
  is like Muck: Bacon 1
  is power: Ayres 10
  is that money does: F.A. Walker 5
  least liable to change in value: Law 1
  lending of: Petty 11
  love of: J.M. Keynes 2; Mises 20
  machinery for doing quickly and commodiously what would be done without it: J.S. Mill 5
  makes possible secrecy, invisibility, and silence of exchange: Simmel 4
  makes the mare go: Ayres 10
  man is poorer for having estate all in: D. North 7
  market, always in perfect health implies infallible wisdom: Carey 2
  means slavery: Tolstoy 3
  measure by which goods are valued: Law 1
  measure of means and foreign commerce: Mun 1
  measure of value: Simmel 2
  measured by goods against which it is exchanged: Simmel 2
  medium of exchange and store of value: Sraffa 1
  mischief of government not sole reason for unstable value: Harrod 4
  misery and: Simmel 1

molds objective behavior: Mitchell 1
moralist declaims: Mises 20
most secure value: Law 1
must perform certain functions: F.A. Walker 5
necessary to trade: Locke 3
need for reduced by communism: Shaw 3
needs protection from economists and quack remedies: Hayek 15
needs protection from politics: Hayek 17
never second-hand: Bagehot 12
no intrinsic worth in: Mandeville 4
no man borrows out of pleasure: Locke 1
normative idea: Simmel 2
not a pledge: Law 1
not a special kind of wealth: Hegel 2
not intended to increase at interest: Aristotle 5
not one of subjects of commerce: Hume 4
not root of evil: Mitchell 1
not store of value: F.A. Walker 3
nothing but representation of labor and commodities: Hume 5
nothing can perform functions of which is not: F.A. Walker 5
nothing more honorable and noble than to be indifferent to: Cicero 1
objective of science of, to yield practical maxims: Harrod 4
obviates and takes away difficulties: Mandeville 5
obvious instrument of measurement in social life: Pigou 1
oil which renders motion of wheels smooth and easy: Hume 4
one sum distinguished from another by amount: Marx 20
only a hypothetical or abstract means of exchange: Bowen 7
only important for what it will procure: J.M. Keynes 18
only thing that can render laboring man industrious: Mandeville 3
paid for by money: Simmel 2
paper, invention to fertilize rich man's fields by sweat of poor man's brow: Webster 1
part of capital of every nation: Brougham 1
price of, cannot be regulated by law: Locke 1
proper function of system, to furnish information: Douglas 1
pursuit of: Weber 1
quantity of: Hayek 16
quantity theory of: Friedman 18
raising by taxes: Steuart-Denham 6
rates at which can be exchanged: Hayek 18
rationalizes economic life: Mitchell 1
realization of what is common to economic objects: Simmel 1
regarded as cause of theft and murder: Mises 20
representation of wealth: Leslie 7
restraint in growth of, only way to stop inflation: Friedman 10
robbed world of value: Marx 17
root of economic science: Mitchell 1
serves to get valuable things away from other people: Knight 13
shortage of: Simmel 1
social phenomenon: Harrod 3
socialism called on to remove degrading effects of: Kautsky 1
some maintain an ill invention: Davanzati 1
stable value: Harrod 4
symbol in which regulators of practical life are frozen: Simmel 3
tendency of, to converge and accumulate: Simmel 5
universal commodity: Locke 3
universal element in all wealth: Hegel 2
universal form which all items constituting wealth assume: Bowen 6
universal self-established value of all things: Marx 17
useful to public as it promotes industry: Berkeley 2
vague and confused ideas on: J. Mill 4
value by which goods are exchanged: Law 1
value in which contracts are payable: Law 1
when bad, people want it better: Galbraith 6
when good, people think of other things: Galbraith 6
when government sees much, it should take some: Bagehot 13
where shifted hand to hand, leads to abandoned luxury and wantonness or extreme madness and despair: Berkeley 4
without producing labor and industry, is gaming: Berkeley 2
money-making:
  motive of: J.M. Keynes 20
  opportunities for: J.M. Keynes 20
money-motive: J.M. Keynes 2
money supply:
  growth of: Eatwell 4
money trust:
  we must break, or it will break us: Brandeis 2
moneyless society:
  idea of, harmful to theory of interest: Cassel 2
monogamy: Simons 5
monopolist(s):
  duty of economists to denounce pleas of: Durbin 2
  man cannot long be, and believe in republic: Bryan 1
monopoly: Erasmus 5; Friedman 8, 9; Hobson 1; J.S. Mill 13; Petty 9
  AEA is least efficient in America: Barro 1
  autocracy of man over himself: Proudhon 5
  enemy of democracy: Simons 2
  existence of, due to *laissez-faire*: Jaffé 1
  great enemy to good management: A. Smith 15
  ignores inalienable rights: Bryan 1
  implies absence of alternatives: Friedman 19
  inhibits freedom of exchange: Friedman 19
  is, wherever competition is not: J.S. Mill 13
  not a branch of economics: Stigler 10
  popular subject in economics: Stigler 11
  price of: A. Smith 14
  private, due to perversion of government: Bryan 2
  private, jeopardizes government: Bryan 2

monopoly (cont.):
  rests upon arbitrary power: Bryan 1
  sole selling power: Petty 7
  taxation of industrious for support of indolence:
    J.S. Mill 13
  unions as: Lindblom 1
  unsophisticated theory of means by which firms
    gain: Bork 1
monstrosities: Carlyle 1
moon: T. Thompson 1
mooncalves: Carlyle 1
moral currency: Webb and Webb 7
moral depravity:
  and the economist: Hayek 8
moral faculties: E.P. Smith 1
moral induction: Horner 1
moral philosophy: Merivale 1; Myrdal 2
  principles of, analogous to those of political
    economy: Wayland 1
moral science: Bagehot 9; Schumpeter 9
  one of great obstacles to progress of is tendency of
    doctrines to reappear: Senior 3
  political economy as: Cunningham 2
moral weakness: F.A. Walker 7
moralists: Eden 1; Nicholson 1
  declaim money: Mises 20
morality; morals: Cairnes 1; Hayek 25; Hutcheson 1;
    J.M. Keynes 15; McCulloch 3; J.S. Mill 18, 19;
    Mises 21; Rand 2; Schmoller 2; Schumpeter 4;
    Scrope 3; Shaw 2; W. Thompson 1; Tullock 1;
    A. Walker 2
  and force: Sowell 1
  and wealth accumulation: J.M. Keynes 2
  choice guided by: Wieser 1
  Christian: Tawney 1
  foundation of: J.S. Mill 6
  input into social process: Sowell 1
  political economy approaches science of:
    Malthus 2
mortality: Aristotle 2
mortgage: A. Smith 18
motherhood: Simons 5
motivation:
  socialists suppose men not endowed with:
    Bastiat 10
motives: Leslie 2; Mises 7; W. Thompson 1
  economics mistakenly believed to have no concern
    for any but selfish: A. Marshall 23
  measurement of: A. Marshall 14
  money convenient way of measuring on grand scale:
    A. Marshall 23
  non-pecuniary: Carver 1
  pecuniary: Carver 1
  product of capitalism: Schumpeter 4
motorcars: Schumpeter 2
murder: Rousseau 2
  money regarded as cause of: Mises 20
Murphy's Law of Economic Policy: Blinder 1
muscles: Whately 3
museums: Tolstoy 4
Myrdal, Gunnar: Rostow 2

Nathan: A. Marshall 4
nation(s):
  a parched piece of land: Bastiat 11
  desires of: Cunningham 5
  economical conditions of: Bailey 1
nationalism: Schumpeter 11
nationalization: Schumacher 2
nationhood:
  tariffs protect: List 3
Natural History:
  Political Economy more allied with Philosophy of
    Mind than: Bowen 3
natural law: Aquinas 1; Bowen 8; Malthus 13;
    Tolstoy 3
  of social growth, not cause of poverty: George 6
natural liberty: J.M. Keynes 11
natural price:
  every new tax raises: Ricardo 13
natural rights: Ingram 1; Jefferson 2; Newcomb 9;
    Sumner 7
  community of goods, contrary to: Leo XIII 5
  poverty denies to man: George 6
natural science: Laughlin 2; Shackle 1; Veblen 3
  economics as: Knight 11
  mathematics in: Wiener 2
natural selection: Solow 5
naturalism: Marx 7
nature: Jefferson 2; Locke 2; Petty 5; Ricardo 2;
    Schumacher 1; A. Smith 8; Sumner 7; Syme 2
  gift of: J.S. Mill 10
  labor mixed with: Locke 4
  land left wholly to, is waste: Locke 7
  law of: see law of nature
  scattered seeds of life abroad: Malthus 14
  subjection of: F.A.Walker 10
navy: Southey 2
necessaries: Ricardo 9; Scrope 3
  distribution of: A. Smith 13
  not to be taxed: Rousseau 4
necessitarianism: Peirce 1
need(s): Hobson 9; More 1
  artificial: Tolstoy 3
  personal: Tolstoy 3
negligence: Sumner 4
neighborhood effects: Friedman 9
neoclassical economics: Akerlof 1
New Deal: Friedman 21
newspapers: Peirce 2; Rees 1
  macroeconomics receives attention in: Lucas 1
Newton, Isaac: Ayres 4
nirvana: Friedman 17
Nobel Memorial Prize in Economics Science: Hayek
    11
nobles: Weber 1
nomenclature: Torrens 2
non-testable conclusions: Archibald 1
normality:
  fiction of economic textbooks: Robinson 14
norms:
  money obeys: Simmel 2
novelists: McCloskey 2

novels:
  economic: Tinbergen 1
  number: Petty 5

oaths: McCulloch 9
objectification: Marx 7
obligation: Sraffa 1; Tolstoy 2
  government does wrong to release person from: Newcomb 9
  of support: Wayland 9
  principle of: Carver 9
observation: Jones 2; Mitchell 3; Robbins 5; H. Simon 2; Stigler 2; Wieser 4; Wright 1
  and theory: Temin and Peters 1
obstinacy: Lerner 1
Occam's razor: Rothbard 4
occupation: Ricardo 1
officials: Weber 1
omniscience:
  human beings do not have: Hicks 2
one-man-one-vote: Rostow 2
ontology:
  political economy resembles: Proudhon 4
operations research: H. Simon 7
opinion: Hayek 7; Hobson 8; Jones 1; Leamer 2; Maitland 1; Malthus 1; Nicholson 3; Petty 5; Robinson 8; Senior 3; Sraffa 1; Stevenson 2; Whately 2; Wright 1
  and circulating medium: Webster 1
  conflicts of, in science: Wicksell 1
  knowledge is: Leamer 3
  value independent of: Ruskin 13
opium:
  inflation is: Mises 15
  Marxism is, of Marxists: Robinson 9
opportunity: J.M. Keynes 21; J.S. Mill 22; J. Simon 2
  desire for social justice eliminates: Hayek 24
  equality of, aim of socialists: Crosland 1
  equality of, only possible through concessions to social entity: Graham 2
oppression: Hayek 6; A. Smith 11, 19; A. Walker 1
  and fraudulent currency: Webster 1
  communism is: Proudhon 2
optimism: Ingram 1
opulence: Hume 1; Maitland 1; Senior 5; A. Smith 6, 7, 20
  causes of: Rousseau 1
  stimulus which keeps up energy and activity of human race: Bowen 1
oratory: J.M. Keynes 25
order: Roscher 2
oriental rug: M. Perlman 3
organization: J.M. Keynes 27
originality:
  difficult to prove in economics: Fisher 8
ornaments: A. Smith 26
Owen, Robert: J.S. Mill 16
ownership:
  church holds right of inviolate: Leo XIII 1
  collective: Webb 4
  stable, gift of social law: Jefferson 2

pacifism:
  product of capitalism: Schumpeter 4
pain: Bentham 9; Bukharin 1; Commons 4; Hobson 11; Jevons 3; A. Marshall 33; Spencer 4
  bound with labor: Adams 2
  governs us in all we do: Bentham 8
  sovereign master: Bentham 8
panacea:
  easy for uneducated people to accept: Hobson 12
Panama Canal: A. Marshall 7
pantries: Sedgwick 5
Paraclete: Shaw 7
paradise: Patten 1
  Marxist socialism promises: Schumpeter 7
paradoxes: Jones 1
parasitic caste: Rothbard 3
parents: J.M. Keynes 15; Webb and Webb 3
Pareto principle: Rescher 1
parish assistance: Malthus 6
parish laws:
  contributed to impoverishment: Malthus 8
  raise price of provisions: Malthus 8
parliamentarism: Wiener 2
parliamentary intrigue: F.A. Walker 8
Parris Island: Leontief 1
partial differentials: J.M. Keynes 17
passion:
  between sexes is necessary: Malthus 13
  serves in determination of actions: Pareto 1
pasturage: Locke 7; Wayland 6
paternalism: A. Marshall 28
  Constitution not intended to embody: Holmes 2
  of government: Ely 6
  socialism has too little respect for: Ely 8
patriotism: Olson 1; Rousseau 1
pauperism: Carnegie 5
  free trade reduces people to: Aytoun 2
  largely voluntary: F.A. Walker 7
  unfair to hold socialists responsible for failure to make an honorable condition: Mackay 1
paupers: McCulloch 3; F.A. Walker 6
  class of: Hegel 4
  have nothing in common with laborers: McCulloch 5
peace: Scrope 6; Simons 3
  must endeavor to reform society by methods of: J.B. Clark 1
Peace Corps: Mayer 6
pearls: Marx 25
peasants: Luther 2; Rostow 1
  tendency towards capitalism among well-to-do: Mao 1
pecuniary gain: Leslie 2
pedagogy: Samuelson 9
pedantry: Horner 1
pedants:
  economists like: Samuelson 5
penalty: Spencer 4
pensioners: Scrope 9
pensions: Petty 1

penury: Simonde de Sismondi 2
    produced by capitalism: Webb and Webb 1
perception:
    economist needs: A. Marshall 15
perfect competition: Knight 8
    all the world is exception to: Samuelson 7
perfection:
    no reason to assume production of, by changing
        government and industrial production: Laughlin 8
perjury: McCulloch 9
personality:
    poverty injurious to: Hobson 10
personification:
    and social justice: Hayek 25
perversion: Webb and Webb 3
pessimism: Stone 1
    increased taxes not recommended as cure for:
        Robbins 6
philanthropists: H. Fawcett 3; Stigler 6
    believe in necessity for capitalist production:
        Marx 11
philanthropy: Carlyle 1
philippics: Dew 1
philosopher's stone:
    none in economic method: Baumol 2
philosophers: J.M. Keynes 4; Rogers 1; Senior 3;
        A. Smith 8; F.A. Walker 4
    economic advisers as: Bronfenbrenner 2
    social: Taylor 2
philosophers of science:
    should be suspicious of claims made by economists:
        Hutchison 6
philosophy: Laveleye 3; J. Mill 5; McCloskey 2;
        Pigou 3; Taylor 2, 3; Usher 1; Vining 1
    and national affairs: Southey 1
    bad: Samuelson 11
    economics easy, compared to: J.M. Keynes 4
    economics like: Hicks 3
    last word in economics awaits last word in:
        Davenport 3
    of wealth: Tawney 1
Philosophy of Mind: Bowen 3
physical phenomena: J.N. Keynes 4
physical sciences:
    and myth that scientific inference is objective:
        Leamer 3
    laws of: Scrope 4
    Political Economy more allied with Philosophy of
        Mind than: Bowen 3
physicians: Weber 1
    can purchase nothing of a man whose family is in
        perfect health: Mandeville 5
physicists: Cairnes 5; Lindbeck 1; Pareto 4
    damage from, playing role of economists:
        Leoni 2
    economists in role of: Leoni 1; T.W. Schultz 1
    symbols an elegance to: Edgeworth 6
physics: Peirce 1; Roscher 3; T.W. Schultz 1;
        Spencer 3
    economics not: Sims 1
    economists misunderstand: McCloskey 2

success of mathematical: Wiener 2
    worship: McCloskey 2
physiologists: A. Marshall 33; Senior 3
physiology: Dunbar 1; Ross 1; Whately 3
pictures: M. Perlman 2
Pigou, Arthur Cecil: Meek 1
planets: Boulding 5
planning: Kantorovich 1; M. Polanyi 2
    and fatalism: Hayek 4
    cultural, end of all inspired enquiry: M. Polanyi 1
    effective long term: Wootton 2
    every political act is act of: Hayek 4
    fallacy of reformers, that will be carried out by
        people who think as they do: J.M. Clark 6
    meaning of: Mises 17
    means of subjecting economic laws and economic
        development to direction of human will: Lange 4
    opposed to value: Sweezy 3
    popularity of: Hayek 4
    possibility of: Wootton 1
    purpose of nationalization to achieve:
        Schumacher 2
    security of distribution of wealth requires: Hayek 6
    theory of: Sweezy 3
    wholesale destruction of freedom: M. Polanyi 1
planting: Locke 7
plate: D. North 1
    man is poorer for having estate all in: D. North 7
platitudes: Nicholson 1
    economic laws of socialism consist of: Meek 2
Plato: Mises 29; Nicholson 3; Rogers 1
pleasure: Barbon 10; Commons 4; Jevons 3; Malthus 3;
        A. Marshall 33; A. Smith 22; Wieser 1
    governs us in all we do: Bentham 8
    primitive man associates with present: Patten 1
    sovereign master: Bentham 8
plebiscite: Mises 32
plenty: Barbon 1
    a dead stock: Barbon 6
    must resist all remedies for poverty which get rid of:
        J.M. Keynes 22
    trade acquires domination with pleasant aspect of:
        Coke 3
Plumbtrees:
    mere tax, is but pulling of: Harrington 3
plunder: J.S. Mill 13; Scrope 6, 9
    advantage of employer of labor nothing but:
        Simonde de Sismondi 2
    socialism as legal: Bastiat 8
poetry: McCloskey 2; Torrens 2
poets: A. Marshall 2; McCloskey 2
Poland: Ricardo 2
police: Scrope 6; Shaw 1; F.A. Walker 2
police power: Holmes 3; Mises 6
police state: Rostow 1
police truncheon: Ruskin 10
policemen: Rostow 1
policy: Senior 3
    no close relation to theory: Friedman 14
policy makers:
    differ from academics: Friedman 14

most economists born with urge to sell wares to: T.W. Schultz 2
political action:
and the economist: Dunbar 1
political arithmetic: Petty 5
political conduct: Cairnes 1
political economists: Aytoun 1, 2; Torrens 2
attached too much importance to putting bounds on science: Roscher 3
business of: J.S. Mill 1
business of, neither to recommend nor dissuade: Senior 1
business of, to watch over concerns of all: Stewart 1
cannot see symptoms of social condition: W.H. Smith 4
cast into dismay: Aytoun 1
concerned only with investigating motives or principles of human nature: Bailey 1
differences of opinion among: Malthus 1
differences of opinion taken as argument against economics: Longfield 2
exhibit peculiarities of human nature: Laughlin 4
have lost bearings: Cunningham 9
have wasted time: W.H. Smith 3
heart as hard as the machinery he drives: Aytoun 2
men thank God they are no: Dew 1
method of the savage: Syme 2
no English gentleman ever sorry for the death of: Bagehot 5
not too apt to follow in each other's track: Longfield 2
objective treatment of: Hobson 6
observes phenomena with conclusion as to cause: Syme 2
of standing, on machinery: Marx 11
one who participates in activity: Vining 1
philosophy of: Southey 1
practical rules of policy laid down by: J.S. Mill 14
preparatory labors of: Roscher 4
quarrel with: W.H. Smith 2
reasoning of, loses touch with actuality: Cunningham 9
takes elbow-grease to make: T. Thompson 1
unprofitable discussions on definition of terms: W.H. Smith 3
use terms differently: Malthus 1
political economy: Bagehot 6, 7, 8, 9; Mosca 2; Torrens 2; *see also* economics
abstract or hypothetical science: J.S. Mill 1
accuracy of conclusions of, depend on assumptions: J.B. Clark 3
accused of not taking morality into account: Pareto 7
allows analysis of conduct: A. Marshall 4
analogous to mathematical sciences: De Quincey 1; Roscher 4
anarchy is predominant in: De Quincey 1
and analogies borrowed from mathematical learning: Horner 1
and duty: A. Marshall 4
and ethics: Dunbar 2, Hobson 6
and happiness: Hobson 6

and mathematical demonstrations: Scrope 4
and mathematical reasoning: Peirce 2
and politics: Dunbar 2, Hobson 6
and principle of competition: J.S. Mill 1
and statistics: Say 1
and theory of value: J.S. Mill 26
and wealth: H. Fawcett 2
application of algebra or calculus to reasoning in: Stevenson 3
applied to practical questions: H. Fawcett 1
approaches more nearly sciences of morals and politics: Malthus 2
approaches strict science of mathematics: Malthus 2
art of: Steuart-Denham 2
as abstract science: Bagehot 6, 8
as branch of mental gymnastics: Hobson 6
as branch of sociology: Hobson 6
as department of political philosophy: J.B. Clark 5
as science: J.S. Mill 1; Southey 1; Stevenson 1
as subject of university teaching: Whately 2
assumes that every man who buys, buys with his whole heart: Bagehot 6
assumes that every man who makes anything, makes it for money: Bagehot 6
at once science and art: Bentham 1, 2
best tradition of: Dobb 3
borrows language from common life: Price 1
business of: H. Fawcett 2
called catallactics: Bowen 3
can have no art attached to: Hobson 6
can never be any, till issues of psychology are settled: Davenport 3
cannot agree on definitions: Southey 1
cannot be safely left to college professors: George 1
cannot give limits to human action and responsibility: Cunningham 5
cannot lay down universal laws: Cunningham 4
cannot set forth positive rules of duty: Cunningham 5
cannot yield general principles: Jones 1
capable of throwing light on evolutions of history: Cairnes 1
Catholic school: Walras 4
class of transactions about which conversant: J. Mill 4
closely allied with Philosophy of Mind: Bowen 3
clothed in algebraic formula: Roscher 4
comprehends a large body of truths: Bailey 2
conceals sources of phenomena it deals with: Tolstoy 1
concerned with activity of human beings: J.N. Keynes 4
concerned with quantities susceptible of more or less: Dupuit 1
conclusions of: Newcomb 2; T. Thompson 2
confusion of boundaries of: Dunbar 2
considerations outside sphere of: J.N. Keynes 3
controversial: J.N. Keynes 2
crude and mischievous theories of: Whately 1
deals with general tendencies: Senior 2
deductive school: Walras 4

political economy (*cont.*):
  definitions in: Atwater 1; Bagehot 9
  demand for instruction in: J.S. Mill and Ellis 1
  determines whether human interests are naturally harmonious or antagonistic: Bastiat 2
  development of: Sumner 2
  difficulty with which salutary doctrines are propagated: J. Mill 1
  dismal science: Carlyle 1
  displays of eloquence in, likely to lead to mischievous results: Whately 4
  distrusted: Jones 1
  does not advance: De Quincey 1
  does not approve or condemn: Cunningham 8
  does not require algebra: Horner 1
  enquiry into laws which determine division of produce of industry among classes: Ricardo 4
  errors of: J.S. Mill 14; Whately 3
  extending definition of, we can describe economic questions: Dunbar 2
  finds secret of universe in supply and demand: Carlyle 1
  first principles of, may be considered universally true: Jevons 1
  followers of deductive, have never grasped own premises or conclusions: Leslie 3
  formula of redemption: Peirce 1
  founded on false assumptions: Scrope 2
  frequently only investigates and affirms tendencies: H. Fawcett 1
  furnishes scientific basis for socialism: Laveleye 2
  gives best means of forecasting: Cunningham 8
  going through transition stage: Sumner 2
  has been science of mechanism: Cunningham 2
  has been science of things: Cunningham 2
  has vast literature: Nicholson 2
  historical: Jevons 1
  Historical school: Walras 4
  ideal of, not unrestricted competition: J.B. Clark 5
  ideal of, should be science arriving at statement of laws: Fetter 2
  if kept within proper limits, does not provide code of social ethics: H. Fawcett 2
  ignorance prevails in leading principles of: J. Mill 1
  in danger of falling into disrepute: Whately 1
  in no sense the highest study of mind: Bagehot 7
  in realm of mathematics: Dupuit 2
  inconvenient title: Merivale 1
  influence of in directing rules to just principles of administration: Stewart 2
  knowledge of, is necessary part of equipment of historian: Cairnes 1
  labor unions appeal to: Price 5
  laissez-faire school: Walras 4
  laws of: Jevons 1; Roscher 4
  laws of, express estrangement of worker: Marx 1
  laws of, not principles for practical guidance: Cunningham 7
  logical methods exemplified in: Edgeworth 2
  makes it impossible for failures to be adopted: Friedman 6
  may be exhibited mathematically: Cairnes 4
  meaning of: Wicksteed 2
  men in, exhibit peculiarities of human nature: Laughlin 4
  misunderstanding of, common enough: Cunningham 7
  moral science: Cunningham 2
  must be on guard against rash conclusions: Stevenson 2
  must be studied to teach nations: Longfield 1
  must have foundation in facts and experience: Stevenson 1
  must necessarily have erred in the past: Bailey 2
  need for accuracy in investigations: T. Thompson 1
  neither art nor science: Ruskin 4
  no one axiom valid for all times and circumstances: Jefferson 1
  no way of establishing true doctrines of except by reasonings about limits: Peirce 2
  not art, but science: Bowen 4
  not art of money-making: Bowen 4
  not doctrine or theory, but activity: Vining 1
  not possible to treat as indivisible science: Jevons 2
  not science of speculation, but of fact and experiment: McVickar 1
  not science of statesman and legislator: Torrens 1
  not selfish study for individual advantage: Fetter 3
  object of: Bailey 1; E.P. Smith 1; Walras 2
  only useful as it directs government to right measures in taxation: Ricardo 3
  owes importance to teaching causes of disorders: Trower 1
  political or social questions treated as problem of: Dunbar 1
  principles of: Scrope 4
  principles of, analogous to those of moral philosophy: Wayland 1
  progress of: W.H. Smith 1
  Protestant school: Walras 4
  provides socialists with formidable weapons: Laveleye 2
  public disappointed because it failed to come to expectations: Cunningham 3
  purpose of, to unfold natural laws of wealth: Cairnes 1
  real science distinguished from bastard science: Ruskin 3
  real science of, teaches nations to desire and labor for things that lead to life: Ruskin 3
  recent works on: Scrope 1
  recognizes humanity has other interests than wealth: A. Walker 2
  regarded by public as rules of conduct: J.N. Keynes 1
  relation to truth and experience: Wicksteed 3
  relative to ethical aims: Cunningham 5
  resembles ontology: Proudhon 4
  revels in hideous theory: Marx 11
  school of state intervention: Walras 4
  schools of: Walras 4
  science of: De Quincey 1; Hobson 6

science of laws which regulate production, accumulation, distribution, and consumption: McCulloch 1
science of production, distribution, consumption, and wealth, or exchange: Macleod 1
science of tendencies: Leslie 4
science of the people: Torrens 1
science of wealth: Wayland 2
scientific character of: Peirce 1
scientific principles applied to: Dupuit 1
search for truth: Fetter 2
should not have been necessary to direct attention to study of: Whately 3
sister of ethics: A. Marshall 4
so-called laws of, are hypothetical principles: Cunningham 7
social study for social ends: Fetter 3
socialism starts from bourgeois: Engels 2
Socialist school: Walras 4
sociological elements and: Pareto 2
soi-disant science of: Ruskin 1
special science of human nature: Bowen 2
statements of, either untrue or badly expressed: Cunningham 1
studies individual and social action connected with attainment of well-being: A. Marshall 11
studies laws or tendencies that govern production and distribution of wealth: Mosca 1
study of, and rewards of labor: Torrens 1
study of definitions in: Longfield 3
study of man earning a living: Fetter 1
study of man's actions in ordinary business of life: A. Marshall 8
study of mankind in ordinary business of life: A. Marshall 11
subjectivication of: Hobson 6
subservient to ethics and religion: Cunningham 5
suffered from fact that public formed undue estimate of: Cunningham 3
supposes man disposed to accumulate wealth beyond need for immediate gratification: Bowen 3
system of conduct and legislature: Ruskin 4
systematic arrangement of laws which govern relations of man: Wayland 2
systematized body of knowledge: Fetter 2
takes priority over political science: Bastiat 2
teaches art of managing resources of society: Scrope 3
theoretical: Frisch 1
theoretically, to make good progress: J.N. Keynes 2
theory of: Pareto 2
treated *a priori*, is not science: Syme 1
treated by inductive method, is a science: Syme 1
truth of: T. Thompson 2
value is question from which all moves: De Quincey 2
verbal difficulties of: Bagehot 9
well-being object of: Simonde de Sismondi 1
writers on, have indistinct notion of nature and limits of subject: Scrope 2
young science: Macleod 1
political fashions: Eatwell 1
political interests:
  economists intellectual hired guns of: Eatwell 1
political opinion: Cairnes 1
political order: Simons 3
political phenomena: J.N. Keynes 4
political philosophers:
  ideas of, more powerful than commonly understood: J.M. Keynes 8
political philosophy: Merivale 1
  distinction between freedom and licence needs to be preserved in: J.B. Clark 5
  political economy as department of: J.B. Clark 5
political privilege: Adams 1
political problem: J.M. Keynes 21
political science: Mosca 2; Ross 1
  and the state: Tolstoy 2
  function of, to advance knowledge: Florence 1
  political economy takes priority over: Bastiat 2
political scientists:
  maintain economist's projects are impracticable: Lerner 1
politicians: Aaron 1; Eden 1; H. Fawcett 3; Hayek 17; J.M. Keynes 4; Nicholson 1; Rothbard 2; Schumpeter 10; Viner 3
  goodwill of: Aaron 1
  have been encouraged by economists to make extravagant promises: Friedman 7
  maintain economist's projects are impracticable: Lerner 1
  none ever thought of giving bounties upon eating: Bentham 4
  politics cannot be safely left to: George 1
politics: Dunbar 2; Friedman 3; Heilbroner 1; Hobson 6, 7; Taussig 2
  cannot be safely left to politicians: George 1
  equality of taxation as maxim of: J.S. Mill 20
  maxim of: J. Mill 5
  money needs to be protected from: Hayek 17
  political economy approaches science of: Malthus 2
  special science of human nature: Bowen 2
pollution: Krugman 2
pomp of life: Barbon 10
poor: Barbon 6; Brougham 2; Carlyle 2; Eden 1; Everett 1; Hegel 3; Hobbes 2; Laveleye 1; Luther 2; Rothbard 2; Ruskin 11; Smart 1; A. Smith 17, 25; Stigler 8; Sumner 4; Usher 4; F.A. Walker 6; Yarranton 1
  and indirect taxes: Lenin 4
  and original condition of comfort: Mackay 4
  become degraded if they get help when unneeded: A. Marshall 25
  comforts of life arise from labor of: Mandeville 4
  condition of: Ricardo 6
  created by poor laws: Malthus 6
  cruel and risky to reduce to hunger and servitude: Erasmus 3
  easier to live without money than without: Mandeville 2

poor (cont.):
  either keep in ignorance or form into rational beings: Owen 5
  employment of, and foreign trade: Mun 4
  general condition of, depressed by poor laws: Malthus 6
  giving, for employment and education of: Child 1
  government can help by getting out of the way: Rothbard 8
  have no right to property of rich: Ruskin 9
  interested in inviolability of property: Say 3
  irresponsible paper money one of greatest scourges of: Sedgwick 1
  labor of: Wayland 8
  live from hand to mouth: Malthus 8
  millions collected annually for: Malthus 5
  misery of: Usher 4
  need for system to care for: Pigou 4
  needed to do work: Mandeville 2
  no need to abase rich to raise: Chamberlain 1
  passion for finery and fashion makes: Sedgwick 2
  penury of: Rousseau 1
  placed under care of state: Carnegie 4
  policies of egalitarianism ignore: Bauer 4
  relief of: McCulloch 4
  sacrifice blessing of liberty: Malthus 10
  schemes for enabling to live better: A. Marshall 24
  seldom save: Malthus 8
  seldom think of future: Malthus 8
  self-respect of: A. Marshall 24
  rate: Chalmers 1
  support for: Wayland 6
  tax on: Wayland 8
  taxes always fall on: George 11
  well-being of, cannot be secured without regulation of numbers: Ricardo 7
  when riches in hands of few, rich conspire against poor: Hume 2
  workhouse asylum for able-bodied: McCulloch 3
Poor Laws: A. Marshall 27; Wayland 6; Webb and Webb 5
  alleviated misfortune: Malthus 5
  announcement that whoever will not work ought not to live: Carlyle 2
  anti-eugenic influence: Webb and Webb 4
  at variance with fundamental laws of government: Wayland 8
  change is needed, to restore to original intention: Ricardo 5
  change wealth and power into misery and weakness: Ricardo 8
  created poor: Malthus 6
  designed to remedy distress of common people: Malthus 5
  deteriorate condition of rich and poor: Ricardo 6
  diminish power and will to save: Malthus 8
  humanity compels provision for actual wants: Carnegie 4
  if never existed, happiness would be greater: Malthus 9
  increase population without increasing food: Malthus 6
  legislation, has greater permanence than any other: Mackay 2
  principle of, maintenance of peace and security of society: Scrope 6
  publicly proclaim encouragement to idleness, ignorance, extravagance, intemperance: Owen 4
  removal of indigence object of: Chadwick 1
  socialistic experiment: Mackay 1
  sphere of: Ricardo 7
  spread evil over larger surface: Malthus 5
  tend to depress general condition of poor: Malthus 6
  tendency of, in direct opposition to principle of noninterference: Ricardo 6
  weaken incentive to sobriety, industry, and happiness: Malthus 8
poor rate: Senior 4
poor relief: see relief
population: Aristotle 2; J. Simon 1
  and means of subsistence: Malthus 4
  and stationary state: J.S. Mill 4
  cannot be checked: Malthus 4
  consumption greater due to increases in: J. Simon 2
  increase of: Malthus 4
  increasing, produces misery and vice: Malthus 4
  maintenance of disposable: Chalmers 1
  natural law of: Marx 5
  poor laws increase, without increasing food: Malthus 6
porters: A. Smith 8
Portugal: Ricardo 2
positive law: Aquinas 1
positivists: Myrdal 4
possession: W.H. Smith 2
  limits of private, fixed by man's industry: Leo XIII 3
  right of man: Leo XIII 2
post-Keynesians: Samuelson 6
post office: Holmes 1
postal services: Lenin 3
potassium cyanide: Mises 27
potatoes: M. Perlman 4; M. Polanyi 2
poverty: Aristotle 2; Atkinson 1; Bacon 2; Bowen 1, 8; Coke 3; Harrod 5; Hegel 3; Mises 13; D. North 7; Owen 5; M. Polanyi 1; Ricardo 8
  alleviation of: A. Marshall 28; Usher 4
  alleviation of, identical with promotion of equality: Bauer 5
  and depression: Fisher 4
  and economic growth: Robinson 2
  attempts at extirpating can have no effects but bad ones: Chadwick 1
  banish, you banish wealth: Chadwick 1
  begets waste: Fisher 12
  cause of, in injustice: George 6
  cause of, not in human nature: George 6
  causes of: Rousseau 1
  causes men to lose advantages of society: Hegel 3
  community regards those in as indecent: Galbraith 7

creates envy, jealousy, and desire to possess: Owen 6
denies natural rights to man: George 6
depression form of universal: Fisher 4
effects of prevention of: Hale 1
exists amidst wealth and privilege: Owen 6
extreme, cannot hold balance of commonwealth: Harrington 2
injurious to human personality and community: Hobson 10
is best policy: Sumner 5
lives of, are advantageous: Carnegie 2
Marxists maintain productive forces of capitalism powerful enough to eliminate: Sweezy 1
may be extinguished by wisdom of society: J.S. Mill 9
must reject all remedies for which get rid of plenty: J.M. Keynes 22
natural, primitive, general, unchangeable state of man: Chadwick 1
no reason in nature for: George 5
not result of natural laws: George 6
occurs when income falls behind that of community: Galbraith 7
ought to be held disgraceful: Malthus 7
parent of revolution and crime: Aristotle 2
parish laws contribute to: Malthus 8
poor relief subsidization of: Rothbard 7
problem of: Mackay 4; Usher 4
relief of, has nothing to do with pursuit of equality: Bauer 4
remedy for: Atkinson 1
riches of rich not cause of: Mises 23
right of property has not made: McCulloch 6
serves to rationalize egalitarianism: Bauer 5
slough of despond: George 4
social organization determines whether nation persists in: Brunner 1
socialism secures universal: Sumner 6
socialists argue, should not be peaceably endured: Leo XIII 1
state contributes to sustained: Brunner 1
state produces more than it cures: Bastiat 4
stimulus of, promotes happiness: Malthus 7
stimulus which keeps up energy and activity of human race: Bowen 1
subjective condition: Hobson 9
tends to generate poverty: Bowen 8
transient and permanent: Fisher 4
victims of, driven to despair: McCulloch 4
waste begets: Fisher 12
power: Hoxie 3
concentration of: Simons 2, 3
poor laws change into misery and weakness: Ricardo 8
reckless pursuit of: J.M. Keynes 20
practical men:
condemned by economists: List 1
regard economists as doctrinaire: List 1
practice:
vs. science: Knight 8

praise: Croce 1
praxeology: Mises 11
science of human action: Mises 8
preachers: Boulding 6
predation: Rothbard 3
predictability: Menger 1
prediction: Bowen 4; Kaldor 1; Knight 14; Little 3
can never make, independent of our own actions: Cassel 1
does not belong to economic science: Cassel 1
essence of science: Penrose 1
if sole criterion of merit of science, economics should not exist as serious intellectual pursuit: Clower 1
in economics: Temin and Peters 1
of economists, not as successful as hunches: Boulding 9
powers of, limited in economics: Deane 1
primary task of economists: Hutchison 2
preference functions: Boulding 7
preferences: Boulding 7; Sumner 7; F.A. Walker 4
exchange involves: Shackle 4
press: Robbins 2
prestige: Hoxie 3
price(s): Barbon 1; Bowen 3, 5; J.S. Mill 1; J. Simon 2; Stein 1
commercial condition: Ruskin 14
determination of: Alchian 2
intelligence in service of greed ensures justest: Peirce 1
laws of: Leslie 5
maximum: Cassel 4
natural formation of: Cassel 4
prohibition of rising: Cassel 4
tendency in competition is to equalize: J.S. Mill 15
use and delight true causes of: Vaughan 1
price control: Simons 2
price system: Krugman 2
as information transmitter: Hayek 1
predominant method of social organization of economic activity: Knight 10
price theory: Ayres 5, 6; Wieser 2
all things to all men: Ayres 5
pride: George 3
private advantage: J.M. Keynes 27
private enterprise: J.M. Keynes 10
and government: Lewis 1
consistent with full employment: Beveridge 1
requires security of private property: Lange 2
role of government in: Rand 3
socialist government must guarantee immunity of: Lange 7
private initiative:
and public authority: J.M. Keynes 26
private interest:
does not coincide with social: J.M. Keynes 11
private ownership: Kantorovich 1
divorced from work: Tawney 6
social function inherent in: John XXIII 1
Private Profits disease: Fisher 4

private property: Alchian 1; Aquinas 1; Aristotle 3;
    Berle and Means 1; Beveridge 1; Rostow 2;
    Shaw 1; Tawney 8
  abolition of: Kautsky 1
  and virtue, justice, and knowledge: Owen 3
  barrier to capitalist production: Hilferding 1
  bourgeois: Marx 22
  can be changed or abolished at will: Knight 15
  communism is transcendence of: Marx 7
  crown lands become: A. Smith 18
  farmers would join capitalists in defense of:
    S. Perlman 1
  if eliminated, market becomes chaotic muddle:
    Mises 3
  in capital: Tawney 6
  in land: Tawney 6
  institution of: Veblen 7; Wieser 6
  inviolability of: Leo XIII 5
  life of: Marx 21
  made us stupid: Marx 21
  most important guarantee of freedom: Hayek 19
  necessary institution: Tawney 7
  necessary to alleviation of masses: Leo XIII 5
  no sound theory of ever contemplated that
    proprietor of land should be mere sinecurist:
    J.S. Mill 11
  out of place in virtuous world: A. Marshall 2
  rationale of: Wieser 6
  reformers disparage as selfishness: Mises 3
  right of: Shaw 6; Wieser 6
  security of, necessary to private enterprise: Lange 2
  social institution: Knight 15
  socialist government must guarantee immunity of:
    Lange 7
  unionism has had moderating effect upon society in
    diffusion of: S. Perlman 2
  world cannot be supported without: Owen 3
privation: Galbraith 3
  character building value of: Galbraith 1
privilege: Leo XIII 1; Robbins 4
  always supported by law: Commons 1
  improvement not promoted by prolonging:
    J.S. Mill 13
  poverty and ignorance exist amidst: Owen 6
  taxes take from individuals in proportion of special:
    George 9
prodigality:
  a vice prejudicial to man but not to trade: Barbon 6
producers: A. Smith 4
production: Bailey 1; C. Clark 2; A. Marshall 2; Marx
    1, 6, 13; J.S. Mill 26; Nicholson 3; Roscher 4;
    Sedgwick 5; A. Smith 6; Sumner 7; Walras 5
  agents of: Scrope 5
  and business enterprise: Veblen 1
  capitalist mode of: Marx 3, 11
  consumption sole end and purpose of: A. Smith 4
  control of means of: Hayek 19, 20
  discouraged by taxation: Bentham 6
  employment of all factors of in socialism directed by
    one agency: Mises 28
  every new tax becomes new charge on: Ricardo 13

  function of money system to furnish information
    necessary to direct: Douglas 1
  instruments of under socialism common property:
    J.S. Mill 16
  laws of: Leslie 5
  machinery of: De Leon 1
  means of: Marx 3; Mises 32
  modern man has built system of: Schumacher 1
  no such thing as: Roscher 4
  ostentatious spending by state does not create
    sources of: A. Marshall 19
  ownership of instruments of, not important for state
    to assume: J.M. Keynes 26
  painful efforts of: Hobson 11
  political economy as science of: Macleod 1
  political economy science of laws which regulate:
    McCulloch 1
  process of, is social: Tuttle 1
  regulation of: K. Polanyi 2
  relations of: Bukharin 3
  restrained by taxation on industry and thrift:
    George 6
  right to tools of: Bastiat 8
  socialist: Kautsky 3
  tax anything of, there will be less of it: George 10
  taxation can encroach on future: McCulloch 14
  to be capitalist requires social status in: Marx 2
production functions: Boulding 7
professionalism: Myrdal 9
profit(s): Babbage 1; Bagehot 4; Barbon 1; Bowen 3;
    J.S. Mill 1; D .North 3; Price 3; Proudhon 5;
    Rostow 2; Rothbard 1; Scrope 2; Senior 4;
    Simonde de Sismondi 2; A. Smith 23;
    A. Walker 2
  above natural level, an absurd tax: A. Smith 19
  and growth: Lewis 1
  capitalism identical with pursuit of: Weber 1
  competition requires pursuit of maximum: Lange 3
  difference between socialist and capitalist:
    Kautsky 4
  disdain of, due to ignorance: Hayek 21
  firms do not compete for: Hodgson 1
  laws of: Leslie 5
  restrictions on: Hayek 21
  right to: Bastiat 8
  substitution of welfare for does not create
    satisfactory social order: Mises 3
profit-making: Weber 1
profit-maximization:
  firms have to abandon: Hodgson 1
profit-seeking:
  of businessman, protector of consumer: Greenspan 4
profit-sharing: Tuttle 1
profiteers: J.M. Keynes 12
programming:
  economic content of: Baumol 1
progress: Ayres 2; Ruskin 2
  industrial: George 7
  laws of: J.B. Clark 6
  natural: A. Smith 20
  profusion of government retarded: A. Smith 9

wealth mainspring of: Leslie 7
would cease if not for the rich: Wright 4
prohibitions:
   productive of uncertainty and fluctuations: McCulloch 2
projector: Bowen 5
   when people are weary of one tax, propounds another: Petty 9
proletariat: Marx 12; Schumpeter 11
   dictatorship of: Shaw 7
   dictatorship of revolutionary: Bukharin 2
promises:
   socialism powerful in region of: Le Bon 1
propaganda:
   capitalism first mode of economy with weapon of: Luxemburg 1
propagandists:
   market needs no: Mises 4
propensities: Veblen 4
   semi-criminal, semi-pathological: J.M. Keynes 2
property: Bukharin 2; Fetter 7; Harrington 1; J. Marshall 1, 2; Ross 1; Rousseau 5; Simonde de Sismondi 3; Tawney 2; Whately 3
   abolition of bourgeois: Marx 22
   abolition of private, may be needed for full employment: Beveridge 1
   and labor: Locke 5
   and natural law: Aquinas 1
   cause of happiness: Sedgwick 4
   church holds right of inviolate: Leo XIII 1
   common ownership of: Aristotle 3, 4
   common use of: Aristotle 3, 4
   constable needed to protect right of: Samuelson 4
   contributed to make wealth: McCulloch 6
   derives from labor: Laveleye 2
   descent of: Jefferson 3
   distribution of: Aquinas 1
   division of: Wayland 9
   equal division of, impracticable: Jefferson 3
   exploitation of weak by strong: Proudhon 2
   fair distribution of: Sedgwick 5
   great law of: Ruskin 10
   inequality of condition in is result of force: Proudhon 2
   inventions cannot be subject of: Jefferson 2
   is theft: Proudhon 6
   kinds of: F.A. Walker 2
   labor becomes, when mixed with nature: Locke 4
   legislators cannot invent too many devices for subdividing: Jefferson 3
   levy upon, for support of indigent: Chalmers 1
   limit to equalization of: Hamilton 3
   man has, in own person: Locke 4
   may be regulated: Holmes 3
   power to do good or evil: Sedgwick 3
   private: *see* private property
   protection of right of: Holmes 3
   restrictions on: Rousseau 3
   right of, has not made poverty: McCulloch 6
   right of, most sacred of all rights of citizenship: Rousseau 3
   rights: Alchian 1, 2; Friedman 9; Rand 3; Ruskin 9; Wayland 9
   rights of workers in business: Tuttle 1
   sanctity of: Tawney 6
   security of, condition of hopefulness and freedom: A. Marshall 33
   security of individual: Hobson 1; Mandeville 2; McCulloch 4
   socialism does not abolish right of: J.B. Clark 8
   socialism forces individual to surrender: Newcomb 5
   socialism not dependent on concentration of: Bernstein 1
   socialist criticism of: Tawney 8
   socialists would destroy right of: Leo XIII 1
   stolen: Alchian 1
   taking of must be equitable: A. Walker 1
   tax is portion of taken and disposed of by government: McCulloch 12
   that God gave earth for use and enjoyment of human race, no bar to: Leo XIII 3
   true foundation of civil society: Rousseau 3
   unequal distribution of, forces taxes on: Crosland 1
   unless set upon basis of equity, riches may be injurious: Hobson 10
prophets: Boulding 6
propositions: Hutchison 1
   a priori: Hicks 1
   self-evident: Hayek 9
proprietors:
   class of: Malthus 12
prosperity: Babson 1; Ely 1; Tucker 1
   economist must discover sources of universal: McVickar 2
   national, measured by riches: Berkeley 3
   not dependent on protection: H. Fawcett 4
   political economy gives best means of forecasting result of change in effects on: Cunningham 8
prostitutes: Weber 1
prostitution: Marx 12; Webb and Webb 6
   money blamed for: Mises 20
protection: Bastiat 8; Harrington 1; List 2; Phillips 1; A. Smith 11
   and free traders: Greeley 1
   cripples industry: Price 3
   loss entailed by must not be measured by difference of price of article protected: Price 3
   plan for artificially manufacturing manufacturers: Engels 1
   plan for artificially manufacturing wage-laborers: Engels 1
   prosperity not dependent upon: H. Fawcett 4
   system of: F.A. Walker 8
Protestant school of political economy: Walras 4
provision:
   method of: Webb and Webb 9
prudence, prudent: Ricardo 7; Sumner 4, 7; F.A. Walker 11
   always first in race: Chamberlain 1
   choice guided by: Wieser 1
pseudo-mathematical methods: J.M. Keynes 17
pseudo-moral principles: J.M. Keynes 2

psychic data: Laughlin 1
psychological phenomena: J.N. Keynes 4
psychologists: Thurow 1
    further progress in economics awaits: Davenport 1
psychology: Akerlof 1; Hayek 10; Pareto 3; Roscher 4
    any concept of human nature is matter of:
        J.M. Clark 3
    bad: Samuelson 11
    economists attempts to ignore: J.M. Clark 3
Psychology (field):
    and satisficing: Elster 1
    can be no political economy till issues of are settled: Davenport 3
    last word in economics awaits last word in: Davenport 3
    special science of human nature: Bowen 2
public assistance: Webb and Webb 5
public authority:
    and private initiative: J.M. Keynes 26
public condition:
    desire to improve: Holmes 4
public debt:
    greatest of dangers to be feared: Jefferson 4
public economy:
    subject of discussion: Maitland 2
public finance: Musgrave 1; Wayland 10
public good: J.M. Keynes 27; J.S. Mill 22; A. Smith 21; Tolstoy 4; F.A. Walker 9
    not cognizable by human faculties: Hodgskin 1
    recalcitrant to precise definition: Hayek 27
    when men consult for, usually esteem own interest to be common measure of good and evil: D. North 3
public housing: Stigler 9
public interest:
    business clothed in: Taft 2
    causes of: Rousseau 1
    promotion of: A. Smith 21
public revenue: *see* revenue, public
public spirit:
    required to make system run properly: J.M. Clark 8
public utility: Southey 2
public work:
    under communism, unpaid becomes general phenomenon: Lenin 1
public works: A. Smith 11; Tolstoy 4
punishment: Newcomb 9; Senior 4

quality: Hodgson 1
    government regulation does not build into goods: Greenspan 3
quantification:
    meaningless without going behind the figures: Bauer and Walters 1
quantitative standard: Sidgwick 2
Queen Elizabeth: Schumpeter 2

race: Webb and Webb 8
railroads: Fisher 4; Taft 2
rarity: Vaughan 1

rate of substitution:
    infinite: Boulding 2
rational choice: Boulding 6; H. Simon 6
rational man:
    weighs utilities against disutilities: Hoxie
rationality: Becker 4; Dobb 1; Hayek 4; Hicks 2; Hoxie 3; Locke 6; Malthus 11; Mises 8, 13; Owen 5; Rescher 1; H. Simon 7; Tullock 2
    economist as guardian of: Arrow 1
    if one has perfect economic, he does not behave rationally as human being: Knight 16
    inappropriate and meaningless: Mises 24
    instrumental: Elster 1
reaction patterns: Knight 14
reality: Baran 1; Hegel 2
    interpretation of: Knight 7
reason: Aquinas 1; Baran 1; Bentham 8; Hume 7; Joplin 3; Malthus 14; Mises 30
    economist needs: A. Marshall 15
    predominant element in humans: Leo XIII 2
    socialism not propagated by: Le Bon 1
    voice of: Locke 5
reasoning: Åkerman 2; Wright 1
    systematic and organized methods of: A. Marshall 6
rebellion: Newcomb 6
recession:
    monetary policy has not stopped inflation without: Friedman 17
Rechtsstaat: Mises 25
redistribution:
    most people in favor of: Tullock 2
    slogan of little rational thought: Tullock 2
reform: Atkinson 1; Kalecki 2; Webb and Webb 6; Wright 2
reformer(s): Bowen 5; Rothbard 2; Stigler 6
    fallacy of, that plans will be carried out by people who think as they do: J.M. Clark 6
    thinks of preservation of sound members among poor: Carnegie 4
regression: McCloskey 1
regularities: Stigler 2
regulation(s): Bowen 5; Hamilton 3; Holmes 6; Malthus 10; McCulloch 2; Rand 3; Rousseau 3; Taft 2; Tucker 2
    armed force basis of: Greenspan 3
    at bottom of, lies a gun: Greenspan 3
    constitutions as: Holmes 1
    does not build quality into goods: Greenspan 3
    if goes too far, is a taking: Holmes 3
    of production: K. Polanyi 2
    spread of: Spencer 2
rehabilitation: Pigou 4
relief: A. Marshall 24, 25, 27, 28; McCulloch 4; J.S. Mill 6; Webb and Webb 6
    condition for receipt of: J.S. Mill 8
    condition necessary for removal of misery: A. Marshall 26
    does not bring happiness: A. Marshall 26
    means of, are procured from labor and self-denial of others: Ellis 2

necessity of, evidence of stunted growth or social
    disorder: Mackay 3
  outdoor: Webb and Webb 4
  right to: Bastiat 8
  subsidization of poverty: Rothbard 7
religion: Cairnes 1; Hegel 3; Jones 2; J.M. Keynes 15;
    Laveleye 3; Marx 6, 8, 10; Nicholson 1;
    Schumpeter 11; Scrope 3; Shaw 2; Simons 5;
    Steuart-Denham 3; Tawney 2
  and political economy: Whately 1
  and socialism: Rogers 1
  Marxism is: Schumpeter 7
  may give ideal for human society: Cunningham 5
  monopoly as popular in economics as sin in:
    Stigler 11
  of capitalist societies: Tawney 1
  political economy subservient to: Cunningham 5
  private monopoly materializes: Bryan 2
  socialism as: Le Bon 1; Phillips 1; Stolper 4
  state: Bastiat 9
  superstitions of: Tolstoy 2
rent: J.S. Mill 1; Petty 1; Ross 1; Scrope 2;
    A. Smith 23
  economic: Brunner 1
  no such thing as: Roscher 4
reproduction: Ricardo 11
  of capitalistic relation: Marx 6
reputation: Senior 3
research: Myrdal 1; D.C. North 1
resources:
  allocating scarce: Meek 1
responsibility: Hayek 28; Sumner 4
  necessary to production of wealth: Laveleye 3
  political economy cannot give limits to:
    Cunningham 5
  socialism takes off man and puts on state:
    A. Marshall 31
restraint: Spencer 2; Weber 1
  socialism seeks equality in: Tocqueville 1
restrictions:
  productive of uncertainty and fluctuations:
    McCulloch 2
retail trade: Aristotle 1
retribution:
  primitive man associates with future: Patten 1
revenge: Hoxie 3
revenue: Simonde de Sismondi 6; A. Smith 18;
    Walras 1, 2
  accumulation of: Ricardo 14
  all taxes fall on: Ricardo 9
  and tariffs: Greeley 1
  and taxes: E.P. Smith 3
  granted conditionally: Ely 9
  monarchs obliged to ask for: Ely 9
  most welcome way of increasing: Erasmus 2
  natural and only original object of taxation:
    Bentham 5
  of society: A. Smith 21
  public: Burke 2
  raising of: A. Walker 1
  state acquires by coercion: Rothbard 12

  surplus is public nuisance: Wayland 3
  tax on highest earner's last dollar of earnings affords
    no gain of: Phelps 2
  taxes and: A. Smith 23
  where government mortgages, sinks into state of
    languor, inactivity, impotence: Hume 6
revolution: Bastiat 4; Bronfenbrenner 2; J.S. Mill 19;
    Patten 5; S. Perlman 1
  and poverty: Aristotle 2
  easy for uneducated people to accept: Hobson 12
reward: J.M. Keynes 26; Stolper 1
  equality of, with equality of results, would make
    desert of rich and populous land: Laughlin 7
  to men of unequal powers: Laughlin 6
Ricardo, David: Marx 14, 15
rich: Hayek 20; Hobbes 2; Laveleye 1; Mun 5;
    Rothbard 8; Usher 4; Wayland 2; Yarranton 1
  and indirect taxes: Lenin 4
  have no right to property of poor: Ruskin 9
  interested in inviolability of property: Say 3
  no need to abase to raise poor: Chamberlain 1
  politic to summon to austerity: Erasmus 3
  poor laws make poor: Ricardo 6
  progress would cease if not for: Wright 4
  riches of, not cause of poverty: Mises 23
  treasures of: Rousseau 1
riches: Bacon 2; Hume 1; Joplin 2; J.S. Mill 21;
    W.H. Smith 2
  are power like electricity: Ruskin 11
  exorbitant, can overthrow balance of
    commonwealth: Harrington 2
  inflation leads to arbitrary rearrangement of:
    J.M. Keynes 12
  love of, characteristic of narrowness and littleness of
    soul: Cicero 1
  measure of national prosperity: Berkeley 3
  men should contribute to public charge according to:
    Petty 10
  men speak and write as if absolute: Ruskin 11
  of rich, not cause of poverty: Mises 23
  require industry or merit: Berkeley 4
  when dispersed among multitudes, burden is
    lightened: Hume 2
  when engrossed by a few, contribute to supplying of
    public necessities: Hume 2
  when in hands of few, rich conspire against poor:
    Hume 2
  when in hands of few, they enjoy power: Hume 2
  where instrument to luxury, enervate and dispirit
    bravest: Berkeley 3
  where motive to industry and virtue, of great
    advantage: Berkeley 3
  where promote commerce, of great advantage:
    Berkeley 3
right: Mises 25
  God author and defender of: Leo XIII 1
  money expression of: Ruskin 7
  principles of: Laveleye 2
  sense of: Hegel 4
rights: Sumner 7
  inalienable, ignored by monopoly: Bryan 1

rights (*cont.*):
   of property, most sacred: Rousseau 3
risk: Hayek 3, 28; J.S. Mill 17; Proudhon 5
roadmaking: Bailey 1
roads: Simonde de Sismondi 3, 7; Southey 2; Tolstoy 4
robbery: Everett 1
   forbidden by God: Leo XIII 1
   usury as: Cassel 5
Robbins, Lionel: Rostow 2
Robin Hood:
   state as myopic: Stigler 8
Rockefeller, John D.: Ely 1
rocking chair: Fisher 1
rocks:
   chemical properties of: Dunbar 1
Roman Church: Schumpeter 4
Roman Empire: Kautsky 2; Morrow 2; Tawney 1
Rome: J.M. Keynes 13
Rotten Kid Theorem: Becker 2, 3
routine: List 1
rubbish: J.M. Keynes 10
rules: Mises 3, 25
Ruskin, John: A.Marshall 23

sacrifice: Mises 21
   and taxation: J.S. Mill 20
   equality of: J.S. Mill 20
   exchange involves: Shackle 4
   imposed by taxation: McCulloch 11
   of saving: Hobson 11
safety: Tucker 1
sailor: H. Schultz 3
Saint Augustine: Shaw 7
Saint Dominic: Shaw 7
Saint Paul, injunction of: Ely 7
St. Paul's Cathedral: Mises 4
salesmen:
   economic advisers as: Bronfenbrenner 2
salvation: Schumpeter 7; Shaw 7
sanitation workers:
   economists are intellectual: Solow 4
satisfaction: Mises 24; Pantaleoni 1; Tolstoy 3
   hierarchy of: Taylor 1
   objects of: Hobson 9
   welfare of community more than aggregate of individual: Cunningham 9
satisfaction function: Knight 14
satisficing:
   and psychology: Elster 1
saurians:
   unrestricted capitalism as completely antiquated as: J.B. Clark 2
savagery: Mises 1
savings: Lerner 4; Leslie 1; J.S. Mill 22; Ricardo 13; Sedgwick 5
   and taxes: Ricardo 9
   expectation of direct tax lessens inducement to: Pigou 5
   sacrifice of: Hobson 11
   socialists have no desire to penalize: Crosland 1
   taxation and: McCulloch 14

savings bank: McCulloch 5
scaffolding (economic structure): Allen 2; Edgeworth 6
scaling: Koopmans 3
scarcity: Alchian 2; Boulding 3; Meek 1; Mises 8; J. Simon 2; Walras 5
science: Cairnes 3; Carey 3; Clower 1, 2, 5, 6; Croce 2; Dupuit 2; Edgeworth 2, 5, 6; Eucken 4; Frisch 1; Hayek 7; Horner 1; A. Marshall 7; Moore 1; Morgenstern 1; Myrdal 1; Price 1; Robinson 6; Rothbard 4; Ruskin 4; Samuelson 2; Senior 3; Shackle 3; H. Simon 5; Stevenson 3; Taylor 2; Torrens 2; Walras 2; Wilson 1, 3
   all whose main object is production and exchange, economics should dominate and coordinate activities of: C. Clark 2
   arguments against mathematics are arguments against: Tinbergen 1
   body of theorems based on assumptions empirically derived: Kaldor 2
   business of, to seek out sources of phenomena: Tolstoy 1
   'cargo-cult': Clower 6
   committed to collective destiny: Heilbroner 5
   conflicts of opinion in: Wicksell 1
   definitions in: Atwater 1
   develops from within, never from without: Carey 1
   distinction between, and application: Dunbar 1
   economics easy, compared to: J.M. Keynes 4
   economics more like art or philosophy than: Hicks 3
   economics most quantitative of: Schumpeter 9
   economics must maintain independence from others: Eucken 4
   economics physico-mathematical: Walras 3
   goal of, to know uniformities of phenomena: Pareto 8
   honesty best policy in: Bonar 1
   hypothetical: Veblen 5
   incapable at beginning to provide definitions: Eucken 1
   inductive: Clower 5
   laws of: Walras 4
   never tells a man how he should act: Mises 9
   of numbers: A. Marshall 9
   political economy as: Syme 1
   possesses body of criticism: Sumner 2
   prediction is essence of: Penrose 1
   progressive always in control: Sumner 2
   should ever keep its glance directed to the future: Ely 3
   systematic arrangement of laws which God established: Wayland 2
   theorems of pure: J.N. Keynes 1
   tree of, grows from roots upward: Carey 1
   vs. practice: Knight 8
   without honesty, there is no: Bonar 1
science fiction: Robinson 12
scientific inference:
   myth of objectivity of: Leamer 3
   whimsical character of: Leamer 2
scientific laws:
   Pareto 8

scientific method: Hollander 1; Little 2; Sumner 2; Wilson 3; Wright 1
scientific vantage: Hollander 2
scientists: Little 2; Mayer 4; Robbins 5; Robinson 15, 16; Wright 3
   classical economists endeavored to be: Ayres 4
   economists as: Hutchison 5; Knight 14
scissors:
   and value: A. Marshall 34
   theory and data two blades of: H. Simon 5
scrimshankers: Harrod 5
sculpture: Bernstein 2
sea craft: Fisher 1
search:
   high cost of, and ignorance: Kirzner 2
secrecy:
   of exchange: Simmel 4
security: Bowen 1; Hume 1; Ricardo 1; Scrope 6; Simonde de Sismondi 7; A. Smith 21; Sumner 7
   always involves restraints on freedom: A. Marshall 33
   of person and property, conditions of hopefulness and freedom: A. Marshall 33
   of property: Mandeville 2
security blanket:
   not worth surrender of freedom: Friedman 21
selection:
   socialism destroys constructive force of: A. Marshall 30
self-aggrandizement:
   reckless pursuit of: J.M. Keynes 20
self-confirmation: Marx 7
self-consciousness:
   and socialism: Marx 8
self-denial: Sumner 7
self-discipline: Robinson 5
self-employment: Hayek 30
self-esteem:
   capitalism based on: Greenspan 2
self-evident truth: Rescher 1
self-expression:
   economic activity field of creative: Knight 3
self-government: J.S. Mill 8
self-indulgence: Robinson 5
self-interest: Gauthier 2; Hodgskin 1; Laveleye 1; Robinson 1; Shaw 1; A. Smith 2, 16, 21
   and capitalism: Stiglitz 1
   as basis for progress: Aristotle 3
   capitalism based on: Greenspan 2
   compels people to produce less to sell for more: J.M. Clark 1
   economist counts on: Laveleye 1
   first principle of economics, by which every agent actuated: Edgeworth 1
   great incentive to labor and economy: Laveleye 3
   necessary to production of wealth: Laveleye 3
   not always enlightened: J.M. Keynes 11
   of economists, leads to intervention: Friedman 8
   reliable force: J.M. Clark 8
   serves in determination of actions: Pareto 1
   unregulated: Adams 1

self-love: A. Smith 2
   mainspring of great machine: Malthus 12
self-ordering processes: Hayek 25
self-preservation: Sumner 7
self-reliance:
   nations reduce by converting citizens into dependants: Goldsmith 1
self-respect: Tawney 3
   of poor: A. Marshall 24
self-restraint: Hobson 11
self-sacrifice:
   socialism needs human beings full of: Luxemburg 4
self-seeking monsters: J.M. Clark 7
self-support: F.A. Walker 6
selfish persons:
   socialists cannot assure no bad activity of: Laughlin 8
selfishness: Hayek 21; A. Marshall 13, 23; A. Smith 22
   an evil: A. Marshall 1
   and human welfare: Hobson 5
   fowl and apes imperfect picture of result of in man: J.B. Clark 2
   laws of wealth cannot be inferred from postulate of: Ingram 2
   political economy not study for individual advantage: Fetter 3
   private property disparaged as: Mises 3
   social order must be result of free play allowed to individual: Laveleye 1
   socialist industry would find ways of utilizing: J.M. Clark 8
sellers:
   miss opportunity in selling produce: Cantillon 1
   too obstinate in keeping up prices in market: Cantillon 1
semi-autonomous bodies: J.M. Keynes 27
senate: A. Smith 10
sentiment(s): Nicholson 1; Peirce 1
sentimentalism: Tawney 5
servants: Yarranton 1
services: Tobin 1
servitude: J.M. Keynes 15
   cruel and risky to reduce poor to: Erasmus 3
   socialism seeks equality in: Tocqueville 1
   taxation form of involuntary: Rothbard 11
sex:
   differences in, and division of labor: K. Polanyi 1
Shakespeare: De Quincey 1
   government could print good edition of, but not get it written: A. Marshall 18
shiftlessness: Sumner 4
shoe-making: A. Marshall 27
short run: Viner 3
shortages: J. Simon 2
   economists know how to produce: Friedman 4
sickness:
   prevention of: Webb and Webb 9
silence:
   of exchange: Simmel 4
silk: Barbon 7
silliness: Sumner 4

silver: Bowen 7; Huskisson 1; Mandeville 4; Morrow 2; Sedgwick 1
    content of dollar: Wayland 5
sin(s): Aquinas 3
    in religion, as popular as monopoly in economics: Stigler 11
    of our predecessors: Ashley 1
    opponents of Marxism in: Schumpeter 8
sinecurists: Scrope 9
sinusoidal curve: Robertson 1
skill: Hegel 3; A. Smith 5
    depends on capital: Hegel 5
    inequalities of: Hegel 5
    limited: Friedman 13
    placed at disadvantage by over-taxation: J.S. Mill 24
    wealth based partly on: Hegel 5
skyscraper: Rand 2
slave(s):
    machinery increases number of: Marx 11
    to have virtues of freemen, must first be free: George 4
slavery: Molinari 1; Tolstoy 2, 3
    communism is: Proudhon 2
    essence of, is forced work: Rothbard 11
    socialism abolishes: Lenin 2
    socialism involves: Spencer 5
slogans: Robinson 6
slums: Webb and Webb 3
Smith, Adam: Ayres 1; Friedman 8; Jevons 4; Malthus 2; Marx 14, 15; Scrope 1
Smith, Joseph: Shaw 7
smuggling:
    prevent by reducing duties on smuggled commodities: McCulloch 9
    to put down, render it unprofitable: McCulloch 9
sneakers: Solow 1
sobriety:
    poor laws weaken incentive to: Malthus 8
    taxes on consumption produce: Hume 8
social activity: Webb and Webb 2
social affections:
    accidental and disturbing elements in human nature: Ruskin 2
social animal:
    man is by nature: George 5
social benefit: Simonde de Sismondi 7
social cancer: Carnegie 4
social choice: Rescher 1
social classes: Jevons 7
social compact: J.M. Keynes 11
social control: Hayek 3; Hobson 1
social development: Webb 3
social disorder:
    necessity of relief evidence of: Mackay 3
social duties:
    communism and: Lenin 1
social expediency: Tawney 4
social health: Webb 3
social industrial organism: Hobson 1
social insurance:
    creates illness and inability to work: Mises 26

institution which tends to encourage disease: Mises 26
social interest:
    does not coincide with private: J.M. Keynes 11
social justice: J.M. Keynes 21
    aim of socialists: Crosland 1
    and envy: Sowell 2
    based on desire to eliminate effects of accident: Hayek 24
    consequence of anthropomorphism: Hayek 25
    desire for, eliminates opportunity: Hayek 24
social lepers: Carnegie 4
social mischief: Rogers 1
social norms: Elster 1
social order: Simons 3; Walras 4
    and political economy: Whately 1
social philosophers:
    theories of: Sumner 5
social philosophy:
    economics department of: Commons 2
social policy:
    economics and: Heckman 1
social problems: Nicholson 1
social process: Sowell 1
social progress:
    economics is basis of: Seligman 4
social reform: Cairnes 3; Schmoller 1
    taxation most flexible and effective but dangerous instrument of: Myrdal 5
social relations:
    material: Hilferding 1
social sciences: Åkerman 2; Hayek 10; Mosca 2; Pigou 2; Robinson 16, 17; Schumpeter 9; Thurow 1; Viner 1
    and development: Lewis 3
    and natural science: Lindbeck 1
    biological analogies in: Penrose 1
    distinction between economics and: Nicholson 1
    economics is: Hicks 2
    every method in, has shortcomings: Baumol 2
    limited application of mathematics in: Cairnes 4
    mathematics in: Wiener 1, 2
    mathematics must be used in: Carey 3
    must develop own methods: Wilson 3
    not business of to say what is good and bad: Mitchell 2
    student of, cannot be partisan: Wright 2
social scientists: Robinson 15, 17
    conceal valuations underlying analytical structures: Myrdal 4
    function of, to attract attention to policies: Viner 3
    skepticism of: Wright 1
social security:
    income distribution never avowed purpose of: Hayek 22
    increased benefits under may bring scrimshankers: Harrod 5
    may be achieved by state-individual cooperation: Beveridge 2
Social Statics (Spencer): Holmes 1
social studies: Taylor 2

social unrest:
  economics product of: Seligman 1
social wealth:
  sources and causes of: Stevenson 1
social welfare: Buchanan 2; Hobson 1; Krugman 2
socialism: Alchian 1; Kantorovich 1; J.N. Keynes 3;
    Mises 14; Sweezy 3; Vickrey 2; Wieser 7
  abolishes class and slavery: Lenin 2
  aim of, satisfaction of toiling humanity's wants:
    Luxemburg 3
  aims not to abolish capital but capitalists: Ely 7
  anarchistic: Seligman 6
  and distribution of income: A. Marshall 29
  and economics: Le Bon 1
  and equality of incomes: Kautsky 3
  and free competition: Lange 6
  and religious movements: Rogers 1
  as legal plunder: Bastiat 8
  as movement, development of class antagonism
    against owners of capital: Carver 7
  as movement, development of class spirit among
    propertyless workers: Carver 7
  as religion: Le Bon 1; Stolper 4
  based on theory of society peculiar to itself:
    Pius XI 1
  bourgeoisie spread absurdities about: Lenin 2
  brings about disappearance of culture, cities,
    civilization: Seligman 7
  brings about universal starvation: Seligman 7
  called on to remove degrading effects of money:
    Kautsky 1
  cannot calculate value: Mises 30
  cannot prevent remuneration of labor from being
    low if supply excessive: J.S. Mill 13
  capitalism cannot function under: Lange 2
  capitalism opposed to: Shaw 6
  chief danger of, sterilizing influence on mental
    activity: A. Marshall 29
  Christian: Pius XI 1
  claims for efficiency-generating properties of,
    collapse: Buchanan 6
  communistic: Seligman 6
  compared to airplane: Lange 5
  competition desirable under: J.S. Mill 15
  confuses government with society: Bastiat 9
  contains some truth: Pius XI 1
  corrupted by liberalism: Simons 4
  credit system has source in: Hilferding 1
  criticism of property: Tawney 8
  crude and imperfect: J.B. Clark 11
  cultural indeterminateness of: Schumpeter 11
  demise of Soviet Union setback for: Roemer 1
  denies private right of property: Shaw 6
  departs from *laissez-faire*: J.M. Keynes 24
  destroys all abilities above lowest: Sumner 6
  destroys love: Sumner 6
  difference between capitalism and: Kautsky 4
  difficulty of defining: Seligman 6
  discoveries making a science: Engels 4
  disease of the body social: Roscher 2
  dislikes Bourgeois greed: Hahn 6

  disparages competition: F.A. Walker 10
  distinction between former and current:
    H. Fawcett 5
  distinctive feature of: J.S. Mill 16
  doctrinaire, misses significance of what is
    happening: J.M. Keynes 24
  does not depend on justice or injustice: Carver 7
  does things which are economically sound and
    unsound: J.M. Keynes 25
  duty of writers to give light to: Le Bon 3
  economic laws of, consist either of elementary
    platitudes or definitions: Meek 2
  enlarges functions of government: F.A. Walker 9
  error of, overlooked difference between material and
    formal justice: Schmoller 2
  essence of, new mode of making power of society
    felt: J.B. Clark 11
  essential mark of, that *one will* acts alone: Mises 28
  essentially tendency to transcend self-regulating
    market: K. Polanyi 2
  every encroachment on liberty, prepares acceptance
    of: H. Fawcett 6
  evolution of capitalism into: Shaw 7
  exist where men unite in owning of capital: J.B.
    Clark 8
  experiment of: Le Bon 3
  factors of production in, directed by one agency:
    Mises 28
  fails when class consciousness fails to include
    majority: Carver 7
  first and last commandment of: Shaw 5
  forces individual to surrender property for general
    good: Newcomb 5
  fraternal: Ely 8
  freedom in capitalist society means men free to
    advocate: Friedman 1
  guild: Seligman 6
  harmonious and universal system of economy:
    Luxemburg 3
  has no definite objective: Foxwell 1
  has no slumps: Meek 1
  has outlived many superstitions: Bernstein 1
  has Pigouvian problem of allocation: Meek 1
  has two heads and two hearts: J.M. Keynes 25
  high tax rates are: Lerner 3
  illusion that it will make masses richer: Mises 29
  illusions of: Le Bon 3
  impracticability of, result of intellectual incapacity:
    Mises 30
  industrial unionism is, in the making: DeLeon 3
  industry under, would find ways to utilize
    selfishness: J.M. Clark 8
  influence of: Le Bon 1
  insists that first duty of government is to maintain
    equality of income: Shaw 6
  instruments of production under, common property:
    J.S. Mill 16
  intellectual's way of solving problem of how to save
    the individual: Lederer 1
  invocation of state power essential characteristic of:
    Cairnes 6

socialism (*cont.*):
  involves slavery: Spencer 5
  irreconcilable with Christianity: Pius XI 1
  little better than dusty survival of a plan: J.M. Keynes 24
  main tenet of, community of goods: Leo XIII 5
  man's positive self-consciousness: Marx 8
  Marx did not have much to say about economics of: Robinson 12
  Marxian, illogical and dull: J.M. Keynes 23
  Marxist: Seligman 6
  Marxist belongs to subgroup which promises paradise: Schumpeter 7
  mental state, not doctrine: Le Bon 2
  monopolization of productive sphere of state: Rothbard 9
  most intelligent socialist will be zealous opponent of what is termed: J.B. Clark 9
  motley group of theorists: Fisher 13
  movement for taking responsibility off man and putting it on state: A. Marshall 31
  needs human beings full of passion and enthusiasm: Luxemburg 4
  needs to learns lessons of capitalism: Lenin 3
  no obvious case for, beyond socialization of investment: J.M. Keynes 26
  no system of is possible without abridgment of liberty: Newcomb 6
  not a doctrine, but a practical movement: J.B. Clark 8
  not alternative to capitalism: Mises 27
  not an economic policy for the timid: Lange 7
  not antithetical to socialism: Graham 2
  not propagated by reason: Le Bon 1
  object to secure distribution of wealth founded on justice: J.B. Clark 9
  objection to, relies on altruism: J.M. Clark 8
  objection to, would reduce produce of industry: Sidgwick 3
  only a theory: Seligman 6
  opens way for competition on mass scale: Lenin 2
  passes into communism: Sumner 6
  paternal: Ely 8
  political economy furnishes scientific basis for: Laveleye 2
  possesses importance incalculably greater than earlier communistic schemes: H. Fawcett 5
  powerful in region of dreams, affirmations, promises: Le Bon 1
  practicability of not in dispute: J.S. Mill 16
  practical, would be put back 100 years if theoretical inaugurated: J.B. Clark 9
  preached as new church: Shaw 7
  pretends society is compelled to guarantee life and well-being of individual: Molinari 1
  principles and schemes of turn upon human nature: Hobson 13
  production in: Kautsky 3
  progress of: Webb 4
  proposes that society shall force individual to surrender liberty: Newcomb 5
  prospects of, depend on increase of social wealth: Bernstein 1
  purpose of, to overcome and advance human development: Einstein 1
  rapidly-spreading conviction: Webb 3
  red flag of class war: Fisher 13
  rejects leadership and guidance from superior classes: Ely 8
  religious: Pius XI 1
  removes all differences of taste: Sumner 6
  restricts freedom: Tocqueville 1
  scientific: Seligman 6
  secures universal poverty: Sumner 6
  seeks equality in restraint and servitude: Tocqueville 1
  seeks reconstruction of society such that product of labor accrues to labor: Ely 7
  seeks to engage altruistic impulses: J.M. Keynes 24
  sentimental: Seligman 6
  shall hunt in vain to find exposition of, that approaches consistency of economics: Foxwell 1
  stands on justice informed by law: Laveleye 1
  starts from bourgeois political economy: Engels 2
  state: J.M. Keynes 24, 26; Seligman 6
  succeeds when class consciousness becomes strong enough: Carver 7
  takes from man's natural liberty to make a million: J.M. Keynes 24
  takes up Ricardian theory of value: Engels 2
  tends not to abolish private property, but vests ownership in social organizations: J.B. Clark 8
  theoretical, if put in practice, would put practical back 100 years: J.B. Clark 9
  to make science of, has first to be placed on real basis: Engels 3
  true danger of, lies in tendency to destroy variation and selection: A. Marshall 30
  truth in: George 7
  two kinds: Ely 8
  violent abolition of market: Rothbard 9
  ways plan of, might come to completion: J.B. Clark 10
  we are all, nowadays: Fisher 13
  when intellectuals reject: Friedman 21
  without postal and telegraph services, or machines, emptiest of phrases: Lenin 3
  word is ambiguous: Rogers 1
  would begin everywhere at once: J.B. Clark 10
socialist(s): Ayres 1; Nicholson 3; Patten 5; Seligman 3
  accept economic conclusions without reserve: Laveleye 2
  and economic freedom: Hayek 28
  and libertarians: Simons 4
  argue property should not be peaceably endured: Leo XIII 1
  cannot assure no bad activity: Laughlin 8
  charge upon competition all economical evils: J.S. Mill 13
  common error of, to overlook natural indolence: J.S. Mill 13

confused and erroneous notions of working of society: J.S. Mill 13
desire to lighten load of taxation of income from work: Crosland 1
desire to restore rewards to enterprise: Crosland 1
dislike Bourgeois greed: Hahn 6
do not deny that capitalism has been carrier of greatest economic progress: Lange 1
equality of opportunity aim of: Crosland 1
feasibility of schemes: Cairnes 6
great error of: Laveleye 3
have no desire to penalize small savings or enterprise and initiative: Crosland 1
have the advantage of *franc-tireurs*: Foxwell 1
is pessimist: Laveleye 1
make merry at differences of opinion among economists: Foxwell 1
most intelligent, zealous opponents of what terms itself socialism: J.B. Clark 9
no desire of, to advance through expansion of poor law: Mackay 1
no one can be good Catholic and true: Pius XI 1
not responsible for failure to make pauperism honorable: Mackay 1
of the chair: Walras 4
projects of, based on dogma: Sumner 7
propose to use state to fashion community: H. Fawcett 5
provided with powerful weapons by political economy: Laveleye 2
reject God: Sumner 7
schemes of, annihilate liberty: Sumner 7
schemes of early: H. Fawcett 5
scholastic pedantry of: Tawney 6
so many, so many social philosophies: Foxwell 1
social justice aim of: Crosland 1
strike at interests of wage earners: Leo XIII 4
supposes men endowed with neither motivation nor discernment: Bastiat 10
would destroy right of property: Leo XIII 1
socialist commonwealth:
  and economic development: Kautsky 2
  may be more statues in of Pigou than Keynes or Marx: Meek 1
socialist community:
  angels could not form: Mises 30
socialist economy:
  Marxist economics of little help in running of: Vickrey 2
socialist ownership: Kantorovich 1
Socialist school of political economy: Walras 4
socialist society: Schumpeter 11
socialization program: Lange 7
society: Shackle 5; A. Smith 6, 16, 23; W.H. Smith 2; Spencer 2; Sumner 1, 7; Taylor 2
  civilized based on principle that people be allowed to do what they like: Cairnes 3
  communism proposes to reform, by methods of violence: J.B. Clark 1
  concerted action: Mises 31
  conservation of: Ingram 2
  contractual order of: Mises 25
  division of labor and combination of labor: Mises 31
  economic categories of modern: Tawney 2
  effort of government to make better: Taft 1
  ends of: Robinson 17
  evolution of: Ingram 2
  general interests of: Malthus 11
  interests of: A. Smith 21
  makes discoveries: Ayres 2
  makes mistakes: Ayres 2
  no man lives out of: Coke 2
  none can flourish when greater part of members are poor: A. Smith 17
  of free men: Stolper 1
  offers individual best living it can: Newcomb 6
  only by united action of all, can capital be set in motion: Marx 2
  outcome of conscious and purposeful behavior: Mises 31
  poor law principle for maintenance of: Scrope 6
  poverty causes men to lose advantages of: Hegel 3
  prescribes conditions for living: Newcomb 6
  sane and vigorous: Tawney 5
  socialism confuses government with: Bastiat 9
  state of: Newcomb 8
  to destroy competition would be to kill: Proudhon 3
  transactions of: Whately 3
  under socialism, forces individual to surrender liberty and property: Newcomb 5
  wants of: Steuart-Denham 2
  will and convenience of: Jefferson 2
sociologists: Thurow 1
  maintain economist's projects are impracticable: Lerner 1
sociology: Akerlof 1; Elster 1; Hobson 7; Nicholson 1
  and political economy: Hobson 6
  Central Asia of economics: Ross 2
  mathematical, suffers misapprehension of proper use of mathematics: Wiener 1
soldiers: Shackle 5; Weber 1; Yarranton 1
souls: Tawney 3
  narrowness and littleness of: Cicero 1
South America: Patten 5
sovereign: A. Smith 11, 23
sovereignty:
  tariffs protect: List 3
Soviet Union: Roemer 1
specialization: Nicholson 1
specie: Bowen 5
speculation: H. Simon 5
  and tampering with currency: Webster 2
  disordered currency fosters evil spirit of: Webster 1
  economics shuns: Wieser 5
  political economy not science of: McVickar 1
speech, freedom of: Frisch 2
Spencer, Herbert: Holmes 1; Rogers 1
spending:
  public, always a substitute for private: Bastiat 12
spirit: Steuart-Denham 2
spiritual interests: Usher 2
spoliation: Say 3

spontaneous order: Buchanan 3; Hayek 25
squaring the circle: Böhm-Bawerk 1
stability: Hayek 16, 17
    only quality demanded of monetary system: Cassel 3
    without equality of condition, can be no: Owen 2
stairs of sand: De Quincey 1
stamina:
    success in industry and commerce requires:
        Schumpeter 4
standard of living: Rothbard 8
    capitalism improved: Mises 4
    when people sink below essential, pauper class
        arises: Hegel 4
Standard Oil Company: Ely 1
starvation: Carnegie 4; Webb and Webb 3
    socialism brings about progression of: Seligman 7
state: Bacon 1; Berkeley 4; Goldsmith 1; Malthus 12;
        Ricardo 13; Rothbard 7, 13; Walras 1, 2
    a mysterious personage: Bastiat 5
    action: Friedman 2
    and inequality: Wieser 8
    and maintenance of poor: Pigou 4
    and political science: Tolstoy 2
    and property rights: Alchian 1
    and relief of distress: A. Marshall 27
    and taxes: Say 4; Thünen 1
    arbiter, master, of all destinies: Bastiat 7
    burdens of: F.A. Walker 11
    can take from workers only what is strictly
        indispensable: Bastiat 4
    cannot remedy all that is unsatisfactory:
        H. Fawcett 4
    cartels result from aid of: Jaffé 1
    centralized, regularized organization of theft:
        Rothbard 12
    communist thinks of community in terms of: Berle
        and Means 1
    contributes to sustained poverty: Brunner 1
    control: Cairnes 3
    cultivation of grain by: Bastiat 9
    does not let alone: Jaffé 1
    duty of, in respect of taxes: Carver 9
    duty of, to deal with evil and secure benefits:
        Spencer 2
    economist wishes to reduce power of: Laveleye 1
    education: Bastiat 9
    efficient and beneficent: Aaron 1
    equality augments power of: Hume 2
    equality imposed by: Bastiat 9
    every encroachment on liberty by, prepares
        acceptance of socialism: H. Fawcett 6
    expenses of, for administration of justice:
        Scrope 9
    extended household or community: Wicksteed 2
    failure of capitalism is failure of: Simons 1
    function of, to distribute wealth to everybody:
        Bastiat 4
    great fictitious entity by which everyone seeks to
        live at expense of everyone else: Bastiat 6
    greatness of: Hume 1
    hegemonic: Mises 25
    how much ought to do in justice: Carver 9
    in establishing national minimum, should encourage
        voluntary action: Beveridge 2
    in organizing security, should not stifle incentive:
        Beveridge 2
    interference: Hobson 1
    invoked by socialists for wealth distribution:
        Cairnes 6
    maintenance of, involves costs and outgoings:
        Rousseau 3
    maladministration of funds of: Rousseau 1
    multiplies taxes and produces more poverty than it
        cures: Bastiat 4
    myopic Robin Hood: Stigler 8
    no modern able to support itself through voluntary
        dues and contributions: Olson 1
    not a producer or wealth: Brunner 1
    not important to assume ownership of instruments of
        production: J.M. Keynes 26
    not responsible for inventions or discoveries:
        Spencer 3
    obstructs wealth creation: Brunner 1
    only legal institution that acquires revenue by
        coercion: Rothbard 12
    ostentatious expenditure by, enemy to good
        employment: A. Marshall 19
    poor placed under care of: Carnegie 4
    power of taxation inherent in: J.M. Keynes 13
    provides channel for predation on property of
        producers: Rothbard 3
    relations with trade and industry: J.N. Keynes 3
    religion: Bastiat 9
    represents institutions which impede expanding
        welfare: Brunner 1
    restrictions: Robbins 4
    semi-autonomous bodies in: J.M. Keynes 27
    shapes conditions which encourage wealth:
        Brunner 1
    should offer security for service and contribution:
        Beveridge 2
    socialism: J.M. Keynes 24, 26
    socialism is compulsory monopolization of
        productive sphere of: Rothbard 9
    socialism takes responsibility off man and puts it on:
        A. Marshall 31
    socialists propose to use, to fashion community:
        H. Fawcett 5
    too great disproportion among citizens weakens:
        Hume 2
    trusts result from aid of: Jaffé 1
    under socialism, assumes control of industries:
        J.B. Clark 10
    understands the use of role public entrusts to it:
        Bastiat 7
    wealth of: Maitland 2
    What is it? Where is it? What does it do? What
        should it do?: Bastiat 5
    will end by acquiring overwhelming proportions:
        Bastiat 7
State Intervention school of political economy:
    Walras 4

statesmen: J.M. Keynes 4; Newcomb 8; Senior 1, 3; A. Smith 10; Sumner 2; Torrens 1; A. Walker 2
statics:
  comparative: Lancaster 1
stationary state: J.S. Mill 4
statistical series: Klein 1
statistics: Cassel 1; Frisch 1; Mitchell 3; Samuelson 3
  and political economy: Say 1
  bureaucrat's only form of economic knowledge: Rothbard 1
  eyes and ears of interventionists: Rothbard 2
  function of, to make sure knowledge is objective, realistic, precise: Florence 1
  study of, can never be productive of advantage: Say 1
statistician(s): H. Simon 6; Wieser 4
  look upon everything as subordinate to statistical curves: Cassel 1
  without economic training: Cassel 1
stealing:
  forbidden by God: Leo XIII 1
sterility: Aristotle 2
stochastic: Robertson 1
stock: D. North 2, 7
  cultivates land: A. Smith 23
  employs labor: A. Smith 23
  proprietor of: A. Smith 23
stockholders: Berle and Means 1
  in depression, are compelled to live on reserves: Fisher 4
stockings: Schumpeter 2
stores: Sedgwick 5
strong:
  always first in race: Chamberlain 1
struggle:
  lives of, are advantageous: Carnegie 2
stylized models: Akerlof 1
subjugation:
  of labor of others: Marx 9
submen: Schumpeter 11
subsidies: Bastiat 8
subsistence: Aristotle 4; J.S. Mill 7; Pigou 4; Ricardo 8; Senior 5; Steuart-Denham 2; Whately 5
  first duty of government, to secure means of: Scrope 7
  population and: Malthus 4
subversion:
  of government: J. Mill 3
success: Ayres 10
suffering: Spencer 4; Webb and Webb 8
  diminishing of: A. Marshall 30
Sugar Man: Bacon 2
suicide:
  totalitarian society only allows freedom to commit: Mises 2
summum bonum:
  intelligence in service of greed leads to: Peirce 1
superfluities: D. North 6; Owen 6
  and taxes: Rousseau 5
  may be taxed: Rousseau 4
Superman: Boulding 3

supermen: Schumpeter 11
superstition: Adams 2
  economics has aim of maintaining: Tolstoy 2
  of religion: Tolstoy 2
supply: Solow 5; Wieser 7
supply and demand:
  law of, not to be conned: Greenspan 5
  laws of: Jevons 6
supply curve: Solow 3
surplus: Ricardo 13
  economists know how to produce: Friedman 4
  law of distribution of objective: Hobson 6
  revenue is public nuisance: Wayland 3
surplus value: Engels 4
  production of: Marx 4
  socialism not dependent on absorption of by capitalist behemoths: Bernstein 1
survival:
  struggle for: Mises 33
sustenance:
  of one class transferred to another: Chalmers 1
  right to: Mises 22
sword: Ruskin 12
syllogism: Pantaleoni 1
symbols: J.M. Keynes 17; Samuelson 3
  an elegance to physicists: Edgeworth 6
  necessary for economists: Edgeworth 6
sympathy: J.S. Mill 18; Senior 4
  social, provides for those who could not provide for themselves: George 5
  socialism needs human beings full of: Luxemburg 4
syndicalism: Robbins 4
  economic expression of anarchism: Goldman 1

t-values: Leamer 1
taking:
  and regulation: Holmes 3
talent: Proudhon 2; A. Smith 8; Sumner 7
tannery: Tolstoy 4
tapestry: M. Perlman 3
tariffs: Bastiat 8; Peirce 2; F.A. Walker 2
  and free traders: Greeley 1
  great nuisance, but lesser of two evils: List 3
  protect sovereignty and nationhood: List 3
taste: Sumner 7
  choice guided by: Wieser 1
  socialism removes all differences of: Sumner 6
tax(es): H. Fawcett 2; Mun 2; Simonde de Sismondi 3, 6, 7; A. Smith 19
  a life-giving rain: Bastiat 11
  all governments require: E.P. Smith 2
  all must fall on capital or revenue: Ricardo 9
  all not voluntary should be abolished: W. Thompson 2
  always fall on poor: George 11
  and state: Thünen 1
  and support of army: Harrington 3
  anything of human production, there will be less of it: George 10
  as little as possible on necessities: Erasmus 5
  as voluntary contributions: Carver 9

tax(es) (*cont.*):
  authority: Galbraith 8
  best are levied on consumption, especially luxury: Hume 8
  burden of: Erasmus 5; Hume 9; Steuart-Denham 6
  cannot be collected fairly: George 9
  collection: Atkinson 2; Galbraith 8; George 11
  commonly converted into punishments on industry: Hume 9
  compulsory are needed: Olson 1
  confiscatory, cannot be tolerated: Luther 2
  discourages trade: Bentham 6
  draws moisture from soil and dries it up: Bastiat 11
  dries up every source of revenue: A. Smith 23
  embasement of money is: Petty 1
  equal imposition of: Hobbes 2
  equality demands all be imposed directly: E.P. Smith 3
  equality makes extraordinary, paid with cheerfulness: Hume 2
  equitable levy: Rousseau 5
  evasion: Babbage 2; George 11
  every new, becomes new charge on production: Ricardo 13
  every new, creates new liability in subject: Hume 7
  evil of: Ricardo 12
  excise: Petty 9
  expectation of direct, tends to lessen inducement to work and save: Pigou 5
  expectation of indirect, tends to divert resources to less productive channels: Pigou 5
  failure to pay: Newcomb 8
  forced payments: Carver 9
  graduated: Hayek 29
  he who possesses only necessaries, should pay nothing: Rousseau 4
  he who possesses superfluities may be taxed on everything over and above necessaries: Rousseau 4
  high rates are socialism: Lerner 3
  how much state should take: Carver 9
  if grow beyond moderate limits, turn into devices for destruction of market: Mises 34
  imposing of, does not create power to bear: Palgrave 3
  in difficult circumstances, should have been felt less: Berkeley 1
  income: Bastiat 8; Hayek 29; Rothbard 11; Scrope 10
  income, may be graduated: Hayek 29
  income, most difficult to assess with justice and accuracy: Seligman 8
  income, most equitable: Newcomb 8
  income, most unfair and demoralizing: Newcomb 8
  indirect, place heavy burden on small incomes: Hayek 29
  individual, may be graduated: Hayek 29
  inequality of, unavoidable: Hume 9
  injurious to working classes: Chalmers 2
  justice of, comparative: J.S. Mill 25
  land: Petty 9
  levied by consent or imposition: Bacon 4
  lottery is properly: Petty 4
  mere, is but pulling of Plumbtrees: Harrington 3
  most pernicious are arbitrary: Hume 9
  none is absolutely just: J.S. Mill 25
  none which have not a tendency to lessen power to accumulate: Ricardo 9
  not an unconstitutional regulation: Holmes 6
  not voluntary contributions: Carver 9
  on bequests and inheritances, unjust: George 9
  on capital or income, paid from income: Ricardo 10
  on consumption, expensive in levying: Hume 8
  on consumption, produce sobriety and frugality: Hume 8
  on earnings of industry, beget fraud, corruption, evasion: George 11
  on highest earner's last dollar of earnings, a spiteful penalty: Phelps 2
  on income, unjust: George 9
  on land, discourage cultivation: Ricardo 12
  on land values, has element of justice: George 9
  on larger incomes: J.S. Mill 22
  on poor: Wayland 8
  on products of labor, beget fraud, corruption, evasion: George 11
  on savings, beget fraud, corruption, evasion: George 11
  operates as prohibition: Bentham 6
  oppressiveness of: Chalmers 2
  payment of cannot be objected to: McCulloch 13
  poll: Petty 9
  poor rates: Ricardo 8
  portion of property or labor of individuals taken and disposed of by government: McCulloch 12
  power to, is power to destroy: J. Marshall 2
  power to, not power to destroy: Holmes 6
  problem with a good (efficient): Barro 2
  produce of, is to body politic what food is to human body: McCulloch 13
  progressive: Hayek 29; Rostow 2
  raising money by: Steuart-Denham 6
  right ones to choose: Robbins 6
  should be levied to promote general purposes of government: E.P. Smith 4
  state multiplies: Bastiat 4
  statesmen too often consider public wealth a fund to draw: Hamilton 2
  steeply graduated income, hits successful and unsuccessful adventurers and discourages enterprise: Pigou 6
  takes from individual in proportion of special privileges: George 9
  takes from labor and capital their just reward: George 11
  that which angers men most: Petty 8
  to increase expenditure by increasing, not recommended as cure for pessimism of investors: Robbins 6
  unfair: Newcomb 8
  unjust and unequal: George 11
  usefulness must be proven: Bastiat 12

voluntary payment of, would be matter of individual conscience: Carver 9
what we pay for civilized society: Holmes 5
when need for has passed, should be lifted and people reimbursed: Erasmus 4
when people are weary of one, projector propounds another: Petty 9
will not stay where they are put: Atkinson 3
tax assessor:
  despot: fetter 7
tax collector: Newcomb 8; Schumpeter 4
taxation: Atkinson 2, 3; J.N. Keynes 3; Simonde de Sismondi 3; Webb 3; Whately 3
  abolition, of, blow to popular government: Ely 9
  acts on expenditures: Ricardo 11
  always object of repugnance: Simonde de Sismondi 5
  and capital: Ricardo 13
  and Cicero: Phelps 1
  and fraudulent currency: Webster 1
  and justice: Steuart-Denham 5
  and sacrifice: J.S. Mill 20
  and work not synonymous: George 8
  and work synonymous: Atkinson 2
  best and most powerful engine of government: Edmonds 2
  blessing, not an evil: Ely 9
  brings fear into field: McCulloch 11
  by currency depreciation: J.M. Keynes 13
  by, government interferes with free choice and impersonal economic forces: Fetter 5
  can only be paid in the products of work: George 8
  cannot be dispensed with: McCulloch 7
  choice of evils: Newcomb 7; Ricardo 11
  coerced levy: Rothbard 10
  compulsory seizure of property: Rothbard 13
  confiscation effected by: Greenspan 6
  curse to every part of society: Owen 7
  diminution of, enables individuals to preserve place with less industry and economy: McCulloch 10
  direct, readiest method of raising revenue: Palgrave 2
  equality in: J.S. Mill 20
  essential condition of, that governments compel payment: Florence 3
  every form of objectionable: Newcomb 7
  evil of greatest magnitude: Owen 7
  evil of in general amount of effects taken collectively: Ricardo 9
  excess, productive of despair and misery: McCulloch 10
  excessive ruinous to a country: Nicholson 4
  excessive weight of destroys exertion: McCulloch 11
  freedom increased by: Ely 10
  graduated: Friedman 22
  has become nearly intolerable burden: Simonde de Sismondi 5
  heavy, paralyzes industry: McCulloch 11
  if necessary, least hardship should fall on poor: Erasmus 3
  in every form is an evil: McCulloch 8
  increase of, has same effect on nation as increase of family on individual: McCulloch 10, 11
  increase of, superadds fear of being cast down to lower station: McCulloch 11
  indirect, most unfair form: Lenin 4
  indirect, tax on poor: Lenin 4
  injustice and impolicy of: Scrope 9
  injustice in, produced by sudden changes: Cunynghame 1
  instrument of government, whereby common people obtain liberties: Ely 9
  is taking: Say 5
  is theft: Rothbard 13
  justice in: Carver 8; Scrope 10
  liberals find it hard to justify graduated, to redistribute income: Friedman 22
  limit beyond which no institution and no property can bear: J. Marshall 2
  lower the better: McCulloch 7
  maximum: Thünen 1
  method of: Webb and Webb 9
  monopoly is, of industrious: J.S. Mill 13
  most flexible and effective but dangerous instrument of social reform: Myrdal 5
  must affect distribution: Carver 8
  must be done with equality to avoid hate of people: Mun 2
  necessity for future: E.P. Smith 4
  negative income: Friedman 23
  net produce of earth fund liable to: Steuart-Denham 5
  no *a priori* system of: Bastable 1
  no circumstances under which does not abridge enjoyments: Ricardo 14
  nothing advantageous to productive classes: McCulloch 7
  nothing more difficult than fixing true incidence of, when secondary effects considered: Cunynghame 1
  nothing productive in: McCulloch 7
  of earnings: Hayek 30
  on industry and thrift, restrains production: George 6
  on productive, cannot be escaped: Ricardo 11
  one of most severest scourges to which people can be subjected: McCulloch 14
  only limit to, is patience of people: Scrope 8
  over-, by government great evil: J.S. Mill 24
  over-, capable of ruining industrious community: J.S. Mill 23
  place of, in proportion to influence: Palgrave 1
  political economy only useful as it directs government to right measures in: Ricardo 3
  power of, authorizes government taking of private property: Commons and Andrews 1
  power of, inherent in state: J.M. Keynes 13
  primitive notion of: Bagehot 13
  printing of money is form of, hardest to evade and weakest to enforce: J.M. Keynes 14
  proper object of, to increase national power: Edmonds 1

taxation (*cont.*):
    proper system of: Newcomb 8
    purpose of, provision for expense of government: Fetter 4
    pushed to extreme, impoverishes individual: Say 4
    revenue natural and only original object of: Bentham 5
    should never be carried to such extent as to incapacitate: McCulloch 11
    socialists desire to lighten load on income from work: Crosland 1
    state should never use to eliminate inequality: Wieser 8
    system of, a form of involuntary servitude: Rothbard 11
    temporary and occasional: Burke 2
    that is variable, shifting, dependent on personal whim, is despotism: Fetter 6
    the more people feel, the better for them and rulers: Wayland 10
    to carry to excess would banish confidence: J. Marshall 3
    unequal distribution of property forces: Crosland 1
    wealth increased through increase of: McCulloch 11
    when sums taken by, not fully compensated, future production encroached upon: McCulloch 14
    without representation: Friedman 12
taxonomy: Veblen 3
taxpayer: Seligman 9; Simonde de Sismondi 7
teaching: Myrdal 1
technics: Hicks 2
technological progress: Mises 16
technology: Boulding 7; Heilbroner 1; Ross 1
tedium: Shackle 2
telegraph services: Lenin 3
teleology: Ingram 1
    economic action and: Veblen 2
telephone: Spencer 3
television: Rees 1
temperance: Sumner 7
temperate:
    always first in race: Chamberlain 1
temptation:
    to evil: Malthus 14
tendencies: H. Fawcett 3; Mosca 1; Senior 2
    of human action: A. Marshall 13
    political economy frequently only investigates and affirms: H. Fawcett 1
    political economy science of: Leslie 4
tennis: Petty 5
termite:
    man as completely social as: Knight 17
textbooks: Hollander 1; Kaldor 2; Robinson 14
theater: McCulloch 9
theft: Rothbard 12, 13
    money regarded as cause of: Mises 20
theologians: Marx 10
theology: Robinson 7, 8; Samuelson 6
theonomics: Boulding 6
theorems: Schumpeter 6
    of geometry: Vickrey 1

theorists: Dew 1; Senior 3; Young 1
    find few readers: Patten 3
theory: Ashley 2; Boulding 2; Johnson 1; Kaldor 2; Leslie 4; Maitland 1; H. Simon 5, 7; W.H. Smith 1; Solow 4, 6; Wilson 1
    and observation: Temin and Peters 1
    blade of scissors: H. Simon 5
    conformity with facts: Burns 1
    facts and: Sombart 1
    good one, has powerful antibodies: Hahn 7
    limited effect in determination of actions: Pareto 1
    modern economics reluctant to produce unambiguously refutable: Blaug 1
    nothing harder to construct than true: Seligman 5
    pure, will become less enjoyable and less possible: Hahn 8
    quantitative worker needs: H. Schultz 3
    testing: Burns 1
    true, must fit every fact: Seligman 5
therapeutics: Dunbar 1
thermometer:
    indispensable but limited instrument: Beveridge 3
thieves:
    shut out of heaven: Leo XIII 1
Third International: Shaw 7
Third World:
    foreign aid central to relations to West: Bauer 2
    without foreign aid there is no: Bauer 2
thrift:
    taxation on, restrains production: George 6
thunder: Syme 2
tides: T. Thompson 1
    laws of, compared to laws of economics: A. Marshall 13
tillage: Locke 7
tithes: Ricardo 12
toil:
    excessive: Adams 2
tolerance: J.M. Keynes 21
tonsils:
    business cycles not like: Schumpeter 1
totalitarianism:
    even communist cannot afford enough policemen to follow peasant in daily round: Rostow 1
    only allows freedom to commit suicide: Mises 2
trade: Barbon 6, 7, 8; Bowen 5; Hume 1; Locke 3; D. North 1, 7; Simonde de Sismondi 4; F.A. Walker 8
    acquires domination with pleasant aspect of wealth and plenty: Coke 3
    advantage of: Barbon 8
    all laws to give it rules, seldom advantageous to public: D'Avenant 2
    and money and usury: Mun 5
    and the state: J.N. Keynes 3
    art of getting, preparing, and exchanging things commodious: Coke 4
    becomes the Lady: Coke 3
    bullion preserves life of: Joplin 2
    cause of: Barbon 7
    discouraged by taxation: Bentham 6

eating as beneficial as: Bentham 4
finds own channel: D'Avenant 2
foreign, ordinary means to increase wealth and treasure: Mun 3
free: *see* free trade
government never does good to: Simonde de Sismondi 3
inflation lubricates: Galbraith 4
live and let live, honest and usual saying in: Child 2
main spur to is exorbitant appetites of men: D. North 4
naturally free: D'Avenant 2
not unprofitable to public: D. North 5
nothing but commutation of superfluities: D. North 6
of luxuries, would not be permitted by proper government: Luther 3
stability of monetary system important for promoting: Cassel 3
suppression of: Barbon 8
true form and worth of foreign: Mun 4
trade unions: *see* unions
trades: Hobbes 2
tradesmen: Malthus 8
Trafalgar: Southey 2
traffic: Spencer 3
training: Pigou 4
   rational and useful: Owen 5
transactions: M. Perlman 4; Ruskin 6; Solow 3; Spencer 3
transformation:
   of labor into capital: Marx 5
transportation: Barbon 8; Ross 1; Wayland 4
trash: Sedgwick 5
tread wheels: Spencer 4
treasure: Mun 4
   foreign trade ordinary means to increase: Mun 3
treasury: J.M. Keynes 10; Thünen 1
   largesse of: Stigler 9
tribal instinct: Galbraith 2
tribute: Bacon 4; Rothbard 12
trifles: Sedgwick 5
truck: A. Smith 7
   propensity to, apocryphal: K. Polanyi 1
trust: Hilferding 1
   firms compete for: Hodgson 1
trusts:
   result from aid of state: Jaffé 1
trustworthiness:
   cardinal virtue of capitalism: Greenspan 2
truth: Dobb 3; Ely 3; Malthus 11; Nicholson 2; Pantaleoni 1; Seligman 3; Scrope 1; Senior 3; Stevenson 2; Wicksteed 3; Wright 3
   able to conserve the good: Ely 11
   economics engine for discovery of: A. Marshall 5
   hypothetical: Veblen 5
   inevitable and imperishable: De Quincey 1
   of political economy: T. Thompson 2
   political economy a search for: Fetter 2
   self-evident: Rescher 1
turmoil: More 1

tweedledee: Lancaster 1
tweedledum: Lancaster 1
twit-twat: Yarranton 1
tyranny: Adams 1
   and fraudulent currency: Webster 1
tyrants: Bowen 5

ugliness: Bernstein 2
uncertainty: A. Marshall 3; McCulloch 2; J.S. Mill 26
uncharitableness: Hobbes 1
unemployment: J.M. Keynes 10; Petty 3; M. Polanyi 1; Solow 2
   causes by monopoly unions: Lindblom 1
   collective bargaining produces institutional: Mises 6
   consequence of depression: Fisher 4
   cure for, bound to produce more: Hayek 17
   cuts in government expenditure worsen: Eatwell 4
   like headache: Beveridge 3
   minimum wage generates: Rothbard 6
   prevention of: Webb and Webb 9
unemployment insurance:
   compulsory, likely to aggravate evil meant to cure: Hayek 23
union(s): Jevons 7; Price 2, 4; Simons 2
   and arbitration: Tuttle 1
   and collective bargaining: Tuttle 1
   and profit-sharing: Tuttle 1
   appeal to political economy: Price 5
   as likely to abuse power as manufacturers: Commons and Andrews 2
   instinct: Galbraith 2
   monopoly, destroys price system: Lindblom 1
   organization necessarily tyrannical: George 12
unionism:
   capitalist at home in: De Leon 2
   conservative social force: S. Perlman 2
   has had moderating effect upon society: S. Perlman 2
   industrial, is socialist republic in the making: De Leon 3
   mission, of, to organize for final victory: De Leon 1
unionists:
   all classes are, at heart: Jevons 7
   duty of economists to denounce pleas of: Durbin 2
   like communists: Simons 7
   utopia of: Simons 7
United States: Sedgwick 2
United States Congress:
   testimony to, from economists: Stigler 7
United States Constitution: Holmes 5
United States Supreme Court: Holmes 6
universe, laws of: Bowen 5
universities: Fisher 7
   political economy taught in: Whately 2
unselfishness: J.M. Keynes 21; A. Marshall 1, 2
urban areas: Rostow 1
use: Leo XIII 2, 3
   goods have value from: Law 2
   true cause of value and price: Vaughan 1
   where none, there is no value: Bentham 10

usefulness: McCulloch 1
 of thing, depends on number of people who can and will use it: Ruskin 12
usury: Aquinas 2, 3; Aristotle 5; Bacon 1, 5; D. North 1
 allowed by law to avoid interference with useful activities: Aquinas 3
 and law: Aquinas 3
 and money and trade: Mun 5
 as increases, trade decreases: Mun 5
 compensation for time: Petty 11
 is a *Concessum propter Duritiem Cordis*: Bacon 5
 law of, relic of barbarism: Newcomb 9
 laws against: Holmes 1
 most hated sort of wealth-getting: Aristotle 5
 must be permitted, as men will not lend freely: Bacon 5
 no man should be hindered from making bargain: Bentham 7
 one variety of robbery: Cassel 5
 protection against indigence object of: Brougham 2
 unconscionable: Child 2
 unjust: Aquinas 2
 unnatural mode of getting wealth: Aristotle: 5
utilitarianism: Rostow 2; Schumpeter 4
 economics as mere: Hayek 8
utility: Boulding 6; Hobson 6; Hoxie 3; Jefferson 2; Jevons 5; Knight 1; Samuelson 11; Schmoller 1; A. Smith 7; Torrens 1
 defined: Bentham 9
 depends on relative human capacity: Ruskin 12
 government compels from individuals without exchange in: Florence 3
 maximization: Little 3; Thurow 1
 nothing can have value without being object of: Marx 24
 pain and pleasure foundations of: Bentham 8
 principle of: Bentham 8
 value founded on: Bentham 10
 value governed by: A. Marshall 34
 value quantitative measure of: J.B. Clark 13
utility functions: Boulding 2
utopia: Mises 29; Webb 3
 easy for uneducated people to accept: Hobson 12
 of unionists: Simons 7
 wrecked upon rocks of human nature: Hobson 13
utopianism: Laveleye 2

vacuum: Pareto 4; Roscher 4; Wieser 5
vagabonds:
 supported by alms of wealthy, a source of moral infection: Carnegie 4
vagrancy: Scrope 6
value(s): Barbon 6; Boulding 7; Marx 1; J.S. Mill 21; Scrope 2; Stamp 1; Stein 1
 adjusted by higgling and bargaining of market: A. Smith 24
 advocates of separate theory of: Cassel 2
 affection of the mind: Joplin 3
 and demand: Law 2
 common measure of: Turgot 1

comparative: Bowen 6
comprehensive scale of: Hayek 26
credit is a, raised by opinion: Barbon 5
derives from labor: Laveleye 2
does not provide theory for justice or injustice of distribution: Bernstein 2
exchange: J.B. Clark 13
expresses circumstance of exchange: Jevons 8
fluctuations of: Wieser 7
founded on utility: Bentham 10
goods have, from use: Law 2
governed by utility or cost of production: A. Marshall 34
human well-being ultimate standard of: Böhm-Bawerk 1
in exchange: Walras 3
in market, depends on humors and fancies of men: Cantillon 2
independent of opinion: Ruskin 13
intrinsic: Cantillon 2
labor and: Marx 24
labor giver of all: George 2
life-giving power of anything: Ruskin 14
market the best judge of: Barbon 3
measure of quantity of land and labor entering into production: Cantillon 2
measure of resistance to be overcome obtaining commodities required for our purposes: Carey 4
money as form of: Simmel 4
money expresses magnitude of, in other commodities: Marx 19
money invented for measuring: Steuart-Denham 4
money is a, made by a law: Barbon 4
money is, by which goods are exchanged: Law 1
money least liable to change in: Law 1
money measure of: Law 1; Simmel 2
money most secure: Law 1
money not store of: F.A. Walker 3
money robbed world of specific: Marx 17
money store of: Sraffa 1
money universal measure of comparative: Bowen 6
money universal self-established: Marx 17
non-economic: Taylor 1
non-material: Schumacher 1
nothing can have without being object of utility: Marx 24
nothing in laws of which remain to clear up: J.S. Mill 26
of all wares arises from their use: Barbon 9
of diamonds, due to mental calculation, not labor expended: J.B. Clark 12
of money: Shaw 4; Simmel 5; Wayland 5; Webster 1
of useful articles: Marx 23
once spent, labor has no influence on: Jevons 5
opposed to planning: Sweezy 3
quantitative measure of utility: J.B. Clark 13
question of, is fundamental: J.S. Mill 26
Ricardian theory of, taken up by socialism: Engels 2
socialist theory of: Wieser 7
stable, of money: Harrod 4

subjective theory of: Dobb 4
theory of: Sweezy 3; Wieser 2
use: J.B. Clark 13; Marx 23
use and delight true causes of: Vaughan 1
value judgments: Musgrave 1; Robinson 8, 17
no society can be stable unless there is basic core of: Friedman 20
none, in economics: Friedman 5
of economists, influence subjects and conclusions: Friedman 5
theorems of economics are neutral with regard to: Mises 7
vanity: J.S. Mill 21; Tolstoy 3
variation:
socialism destroys constructive force of: A. Marshall 30
variety: Hegel 5; J.M. Keynes 21; Simmel 5; Sumner 2
vegetable kingdom: Malthus 14
veins: Joplin 2
velocity: Schumpeter 9
Venice: Barbon 7
verification: Kaldor 1
Verstehen: Mises 19
vice: Greenspan 2; Hegel 3; Hutcheson 1; Owen 4; Sumner 7
consequence of law of nature: Malthus 14
increasing population produces: Malthus 4
victory: Schumpeter 4
vigor: A. Marshall 30; A. Smith 20
village idiot: Robbins 5
violence: Bastiat 4; Rothbard 10, 12; A. Smith 11; Tolstoy 2
communism proposes to reform society by methods of: J.B. Clark 1
virtue: George 4; Greenspan 2; J.M. Keynes 2; A. Marshall 2; Owen 3, 4; Ricardo 7; Rousseau 1
and private property and inequality: Owen 3
disordered currency undermines: Webster 1
economy first and most important of republican: Jefferson 4
in proportion to number of persons to whom happiness extends: Hutcheson 1
industrial: Sumner 3
is as quantity of happiness: Hutcheson 1
moral sense of: Hutcheson 1
ordeal of, to resist all temptation to evil: Malthus 14
riches motive to: Berkeley 3
without equality of condition, can be no: Owen 2
vision: Seligman 3
vulgar: Maitland 2

wage-labor: Engels 1
contest between capitalist and: Marx 3
wages: Bowen 3; Hobbes 2; Lewis 1; A. Marshall 28; J.S. Mill 1; Price 2; Proudhon 2; Scrope 2; Sedgwick 5; A. Smith 23
and capital: Marx 5
competition source of high: J.S. Mill 13
like other contracts, should be left to fair and free competition of market: Ricardo 6
minimum: *see* minimum wage

political economy and cause of depression or elevation of: Torrens 1
rate of: Marx 5
right to: Bastiat 8
same, for same work: M. Fawcett 1
socialists would deprive worker of liberty of disposing of: Leo XIII 4
waiters: Weber 1
Wall Street:
point of view: Fisher 7
want: Eden 1; Malthus 10
humans suffer from, through laws of nature: Malthus 15
to make people industrious, they must be removed from: George 4
want-formation:
economic activity agency for: Knight 3
wants: Bowen 1; Mises 21; Mun 4; Pantaleoni 1; Ross 1
increase with wishes: Barbon 10
of society: Steuart-Denham 2
of the mind are infinite: Barbon 10
political economy treated as moral science, considering satisfaction of: Cunningham 2
purpose of economics to treat nature of human: Fisher 6
satisfaction of, aim of socialism: Luxemburg 3
want satisfaction:
economic activity means of: Knight 3
war: Bukharin 3; Coke 3; Edgeworth 1; Erasmus 2; Mises 16; Mun 4; Rousseau 2; F.A. Walker 2; Whately 3; Wootton 2
laissez-faire capitalism only system opposed to: Rand 1
waste: Owen 6; Wicksteed 2
begets poverty: Fisher 12
caused by monopoly unions: Lindblom 1
poverty begets: Fisher 12
wastefulness: Bowen 1
wastrels: Webb and Webb 4
water:
value of: Law 2
Waterloo: Mises 19; Southey 2
weakness: Sumner 4
poor laws change wealth and power into: Ricardo 8
wealth: Aristotle 1, 5; Bagehot 7; Bowen 6, 8; Cassel 4; Edgeworth 4; Hobson 6; John XXIII 2; Leslie 1; Marx 6; Newcomb 3; Price 3; Ricardo 4; Rousseau 1; Schumacher 1; Scrope 3, 9; Senior 5; Simmel 4; Smart 1; A. Smith 9, 16; W.H. Smith 2; Taylor 2; Wieser 8; Wright 4
accumulates in hands of a few: Hegel 4
accumulation and dissipation of: Fisher 6
accumulation of: Bowen 3; J.M. Keynes 2; Ruskin 2
and industrial arts: J.S. Mill 4
and morality: J.M. Keynes 2
as aim of human effort: A. Marshall 23
as state of consciousness: Florence 2
banish poverty, you banish: Chadwick 1
based on skill and capital: Hegel 5
belongs to society: Lerner 4

wealth (*cont.*):
   community adds to by creating: Rae 2
   concentration of: Bacon 1; Sumner 1
   creation of: Longfield 1; Rae 4
   danger of concentration of, is danger of perpetuation through law of special privileges: Commons 1
   desire for: A. Marshall 23
   desire of, destroys power of prediction: Leslie 7
   desire of, mainspring of industrial and commercial activity: Leslie 7
   diminished when millionaire donates grounds or pictures: Hobson 14
   economics does not contend that man strives only after material: Mises 7
   economics is abstract science of national: Merivale 1
   economist must discover sources of: McVickar 2
   every restraint is hindrance to acquiring: Rae 1
   exchange of: H. Fawcett 2
   favors growth of wealth: Bowen 8
   foreign trade ordinary means to increase: Mun 3
   form of happiness or welfare: Florence 2
   government uses inflation as means of confiscation of: J.M. Keynes 12
   growth of, restrains development of individuality: Carey 5
   grows with growth of power of man to satisfy first and greatest want: Carey 5
   humanity has other interests than: A. Walker 2
   idolatry of: Tawney 1
   if people do not get help, they are unable to contribute to: A. Marshall 25
   increased taxation causes greater production of: McCulloch 10
   increased through increase of taxation: McCulloch 11
   inequalities of: Hegel 5
   inequalities of, justly established, benefit nation: Ruskin 5
   inequalities of, unjustly established, injure nation: Ruskin 5
   labor form which produces: Cantillon 3
   land source or matter of: Cantillon 3
   law of, must be inferred from fact of: Ingram 2
   laws governing creation of: Wayland 2
   left to young men, is disadvantageous: Carnegie 2
   man competes with fellows to gain: Bowen 3
   material: Tawney 3
   may be detrimental: Whately 5
   money documentary claim to: Ruskin 7
   money not a special kind of: Hegel 2
   money universal element in all: Hegel 2
   national, consists of aggregate of individual: Cunningham 9
   natural laws of: Cairnes 1
   nothing but maintenance, convenience, and superfluity of life: Cantillon 3
   object of socialism to secure distribution of, founded on justice: J.B. Clark 8
   obscene to regard as anonymous, tribal product: Rand 4
   of community: Bailey 1
   only when possesses special privileges is concentration dangerous: Commons 1
   opportunities for: J.M. Keynes 20
   ownership of: Fisher 6
   philosophy of: Tawney 1
   political economy and: H. Fawcett 2
   political economy as science of: Macleod 1; Wayland 2
   poor laws change into misery and weakness: Ricardo 8
   poverty and ignorance exist amidst: Owen 6
   power of individual to produce: Newcomb 8
   principles of exchange: Fisher 6
   production and distribution of: Mosca 1, 2; Webb 3
   public economy professes to teach means of increasing: Maitland 2
   purpose of economics to treat nature of: Fisher 6
   scale of: F.A. Walker 2
   self-interest and responsibility necessary to production of: Laveleye 3
   share of belongs to government: A. Walker 3
   social organization determines whether nation accumulates: Brunner 1
   socially created: Kautsky 1
   state not a producer of: Brunner 1
   state obstructs creation of: Brunner 1
   state shapes conditions which encourage: Brunner 1
   statesmen too often consider public, as fund to draw taxes: Hamilton 2
   study of, scarcely mentions human beings: Florence 2
   subject matter of economics: A. Marshall 12
   taxation adds to labor engaged in production of: Edmonds 1
   trade acquires domination with pleasant aspect of: Coke 3
   transmission of, without merit or qualifications, may pass one to another without injury: Carnegie 3
   true ministry not performed until distributed: Adams 2
   welfare state mechanism to confiscate: Greenspan 6
wealth distribution: Adams 2; Bailey 1; Bastiat 4; Cairnes 6; H. Fawcett 2; John XXIII 2; J.M. Keynes 2; Longfield 1; Mosca 1, 2; Webb 3
   competition affords ideal condition for: F.A. Walker 1
   imperiously regulates nature and extent of demand: Maitland 4
   obscenity: Rand 4
   requires economic planning: Hayek 6
wealth-getting: Aristotle 1, 5
Wealth of Nations (Smith): Morrow 2
wealth production: Bailey 1; H. Fawcett 2
wealthy:
   comfort of: Usher 4
   weapons: Mises 16
   weather: Bowen 4
   weight: Petty 5
   welfare: Florence 1; Little 4; Price 4; Rostow 2; Rothbard 8; Scrope 7, 9; Senior 1; Sumner 7; Taylor 2

can be brought under category of greater or less: Pigou 1
cannot be measured on scale of more or less: Hayek 26
common, recalcitrant to precise definition: Hayek 27
consumer, goal of antitrust law: Bork 1
economic: Edgeworth 4
includes states of consciousness only: Pigou 1
of a people, depends on many things: Hayek 26
of community: J.M. Clark 7
of community, more than aggregate of individual satisfaction: Cunningham 9
promotion of: Pigou 1
public: Child 2
selfishness and: Hobson 5
small business, goal of antitrust law: Bork 1
stability of monetary system important for promoting: Cassel 3
state represents institution which impedes expansion of: Brunner 1
substitution of for profit does not create satisfactory social order: Mises 3
wealth form of: Florence 2
welfare economics: Archibald 1
   foundation of: Myrdal 2
welfare state: Greenspan 2; Rothbard 8
   nothing more than mechanism to confiscate wealth: Greenspan 6
well-being: Laveleye 1; A. Marshall 3; Mises 33; W.H. Smith 2
   bearing of economics on has been overlooked: A. Marshall 12
   capitalism handles everybody according to contribution to: Mises 5
   object of political economy: Simonde de Sismondi 1
   of consumers: Simonde de Sismondi 3
   socialism pretends society is compelled to guarantee: Molinari 1
   study of economics connected with attainment of: A. Marshall 11
   ultimate standard of value: Böhm-Bawerk 1
whipping posts: Hale 1
wickedness:
   not all evils due to: Usher 4
wife: Senior 4; Yarranton 1
will-o'-the-wisp: T.W. Schultz 1
William the Conqueror: Whately 5
wills: Rousseau 3
windfalls: J.M. Keynes 12
wine: Ricardo 2
wisdom: Carey 2; Owen 4; A. Smith 7, 11
   of society, may extinguish poverty: J.S. Mill 9

wise:
   always first in race: Chamberlain 1
witchcraft: Ruskin 3
Wohlfahrtsstaat: Mises 25
women: Malthus 11; Marx 13
   equality of wages with men, not always advisable: M. Fawcett 1
Wordsworth: Boulding 6
work: Hobson 6; Sedgwick 5; Sumner 7
   and taxation not synonymous: George 8
   and taxation synonymous: Atkinson 2
   dislike of: Hegel 3
   divorce of ownership from: Tawney 6
   expectation of direct tax lessens inducement to: Pigou 5
   freedom and hope increase willingness and power for: A. Marshall 33
   man willing, but unable to find, saddest sight Fortune's inequality exhibits: Carlyle 2
   one hires individual men to do specific kinds of: Carver 5
   poor needed to do: Mandeville 2
   right to seek: Newcomb 6
   social security creates inability to: Mises 26
   synonymous with taxation: Atkinson 2
   taxation can only be paid in the products of: George 8
workers:
   estrangement of: Marx 1
   have quasi-property rights in business: Tuttle 1
   joint owners of business: Tuttle 1
   organization of: Simons 6
   see also: labor
workhouse: Aytoun 2; Carnegie 4; Malthus 6; Webb and Webb 4
   asylum for able-bodied poor: McCulloch 3
   in England, have been too comfortable: McCulloch 3
   not to be made into respectable inns: McCulloch 3
working class: Ashley 1
   no faith in systems of elevating: Brownson 1
   public spending adds nothing to the lot of: Bastiat 12
   taxes injurious to condition of: Chalmers 2
Wren, Christopher: Mises 4
wrong: Hegel 3

Yale University: Samuelson 9

zoologists: Lindbeck 1
zoology: Ross 1
zoon politikon: Marx 16